Commerce, Complexity, and Evolution

Commerce, Complexity, and Evolution is a significant contribution to the new paradigm straddling economics, finance, marketing, and management, which acknowledges that commercial systems are evolutionary systems and must therefore be analysed with evolutionary tools. Evolutionary systems display complicated behaviours that are to a significant degree generated endogenously, rather than being solely the product of exogenous shocks; hence the conjunction of complexity with evolution. The papers in this volume consider a wide range of systems, from the entire economy at one extreme to the behaviour of single markets at the other. The papers are united by methodologies that, at their core, are evolutionary, although the techniques cover a wide range, from philosophical discourse to differential equations, genetic algorithms, multiagent simulations, and cellular automata. Issues considered include the dynamics of debt deflation, stock management in a complex environment, interactions among consumers and their effect on market behavior, and nonlinear methods to profit from financial market volatility.

William A. Barnett is Professor of Economics at Washington University in St. Louis, Missouri, editor of the series *International Symposia in Economic Theory and Econometrics*, and founding editor of the journal *Macroeconomic Dynamics*, both published by Cambridge University Press. *The Theory of Monetary Aggregation*, a collection of Professor Barnett's published papers on that subject with unifying discussion, was recently published in the North-Holland series *Contributions to Economic Analysis*, coedited by Dale Jorgenson, Jean-Jacques Laffont, and Torsten Persson. The volume is coedited by William Barnett and Apostolos Serletis and contains a preface written by W. Erwin Diewert.

Carl Chiarella is Professor and former head of the School of Finance and Economics of the University of Technology, Sydney. He has also taught at the University of New South Wales and has served as a visiting scholar at leading universities in North America, Europe, and Japan. Professor Chiarella is an associate editor of the journals *Financial Engineering* and *Japanese Markets, Macroeconomic Dynamics, and Computational Economics.* His research interests cover all aspects of quantitative finance and computational economics.

Steve Keen is Senior Lecturer in Economics and Finance at the University of Western Sydney Macarthur. He has published articles in such journals as the *Journal of Post Keynesian Economics, Journal of the History of Economic Thought, Nonlinear Dynamics, Review of Political Economy*, and *Economies et Societes.* Professor Keen's research interests are in debt inflation, macrodynamic modeling, and the history of economic thought.

Robert Marks is Head of the Economics Group at the Australian Graduate School of Management. He has also taught at the University of California, Berkeley, and MIT and holds a research affiliation with the Santa Fe Institute. Professor Marks has published over 50 papers in publications such as the *Journal of Economic Dynamics & Control, Management Science, Economic Letters, Journal of Evolutionary Economics*, and the *Australian Journal of Management*, of which he is currently General Editor. His research interests include evolutionary techniques in economics and game theory.

Hermann Schnabl is Professor of Microeconomics at the University of Stuttgart and has served there as Director of the Department of Microeconomics, Institute for Social Research. He is the author, editor, or coeditor of 12 books and approximately 65 papers in journals and book chapters. Professor Schnabl's research interests include input–output analysis, chaos theory with an emphasis on empirical testing in financial time series, neural networks and genetic algorithms, and innovation theory.

International Symposia in Economic Theory and Econometrics

Editor
William A. Barnett, *Washington University in St. Louis*

Other edited works in the series

William A. Barnett and A. Ronald Gallant
New approaches to modeling, specification selection, and econometric inference

William A. Barnett and Kenneth J. Singleton
New approaches to monetary economics

William A. Barnett, Ernst R. Berndt, and Halbert White
Dynamic econometric modeling

William A. Barnett, John Geweke, and Karl Shell
Economic complexity

William A. Barnett, James Powell, and George E. Tauchen
Nonparametric and semiparametric methods in econometrics and statistics

William A. Barnett, Bernard Cornet, Claude D'Aspremont, Jean J. Gabszewicz, and Andreu Mas-Colell
Equilibrium theory and applications

William A. Barnett, Melvin J. Hinich, and Norman J. Schofield
Political economy: Institutions, competition and representation

William A. Barnett, Hervé Moulin, Maurice Salles, and Norman J. Schofield
Social choice, welfare, and ethics

William A. Barnett, Giancarlo Gandolfo, and Claude Hillinger
Dynamic disequilibrium modeling

William A. Barnett, Alan P. Kirman, and Mark Salmon
Nonlinear dynamics and economics

William A. Barnett, David F. Hendry, Svend Hylleberg, Timo Teräsvirta, Dag Tjøstheim, and Allan Würtz
Nonlinear econometric modeling in time series analysis

Commerce, Complexity, and Evolution

Topics in Economics, Finance, Marketing, and Management: Proceedings of the Twelfth International Symposium in Economic Theory and Econometrics

Edited by

WILLIAM A. BARNETT
Washington University in St. Louis

CARL CHIARELLA
University of Technology, Sydney

STEVE KEEN
University of Western Sydney Macarthur

ROBERT MARKS
Australian Graduate School of Management

HERMANN SCHNABL
University of Stuttgart

CAMBRIDGE
UNIVERSITY PRESS

CAMBRIDGE UNIVERSITY PRESS
Cambridge, New York, Melbourne, Madrid, Cape Town, Singapore, São Paulo, Delhi

Cambridge University Press
The Edinburgh Building, Cambridge CB2 8RU, UK

Published in the United States of America by Cambridge University Press, New York

www.cambridge.org
Information on this title: www.cambridge.org/9780521620307

First published 2000
This digitally printed version 2008

A catalogue record for this publication is available from the British Library

Library of Congress Cataloguing in Publication data

International Symposium in Economic Theory and Econometrics (12th : 1996 :
University of New South Wales)

Commerce, complexity, and evolution : topics in economics, finance, marketing, and management : proceedings of the Twelfth International Symposium in Economic Theory and Econometrics / William A. Barnett . . . [et al.].

p. cm. – (International symposia in economic theory and econometrics)

Includes bibliographical references.

ISBN 0-521-62030-9

1. Econometrics–Congresses. 2. Evolutionary economics–Congresses. 3. Institutional economics–Congresses. 4. Economics–Methodology–Congresses. I. Barnett, William A. II. Title. III. Series.

HB139.I566 1996
330′.01′5 – dc21

99-047721

ISBN 978-0-521-62030-7 hardback
ISBN 978-0-521-08821-3paperback

Contents

Series editor's preface

This volume is the twelfth in a series, called *International Symposia in Economic Theory and Econometrics*. The proceedings series is under the general editorship of William Barnett. Individual volumes in the series generally have coeditors, who differ for each volume, as the topics of the conferences change each year. The co-organizers of the twelfth symposium, which produced the current proceedings volume, were Carl Chiarella, Steve Keen, Bob Marks, and Hermann Schnabl. The coeditors of this proceedings volume are William Barnett, Carl Chiarella, Steve Keen, Bob Marks, and Hermann Schnabl.

The topic of the conference and focus of this book is "Commerce, Complexity, and Evolution: Complexity and Evolutionary Analysis in Economics, Finance, Marketing, and Management." The volume showcases the many facets of the new evolutionary approach to analyzing and modeling commercial systems. The collection is distinguished by the wide range of methodologies presented, ranging from philosophical discourse at one extreme to multiagent modeling at the other. The volume is a significant contribution to the new paradigm acknowledging that commercial systems are evolutionary systems and must therefore be analyzed by use of evolutionary tools. This new paradigm straddles economics, finance, marketing, and management.

The conference that produced this volume was held at the University of New South Wales in Sydney, Australia, in 1996, and attracted participants from Australia, Japan, Europe, and the United States. The conference was sponsored by the Faculty of Commerce at the University of New South Wales. Many of the prior volumes in this series were sponsored by the IC2 Institute at the University of Texas at Austin, and some have been cosponsored by the RGK Foundation.

The first conference in this Cambridge series was co-organized by William Barnett and Ronald Gallant, who also coedited the proceedings volume. That volume has appeared as the Vol. 30, October/November 1985, edition of the *Journal of Econometrics* and has been reprinted as a volume in this Cambridge

University Press monograph series. The topic was "New Approaches to Modeling, Specification Selection, and Econometric Inference."

Beginning with the second symposium in the series, the proceedings of the symposia appear exclusively as volumes in this Cambridge University Press monograph series. The co-organizers of the second symposium and coeditors of its proceedings volume were William Barnett and Kenneth Singleton. The topic was "New Approaches to Monetary Economics." The co-organizers of the third symposium, which was on "Dynamic Econometric Modeling," were William Barnett and Ernst Berndt; and the coeditors of that proceedings volume were William Barnett, Ernst Berndt, and Halbert White. The co-organizers of the fourth symposium and coeditors of its proceedings volume, which was on "Economic Complexity: Chaos, Sunspots, Bubbles, and Nonlinearity," were William Barnett, John Geweke, and Karl Shell. The co-organizers of the fifth symposium and coeditors of its proceedings volume, which was on "Nonparametric and Semiparametric Methods in Econometrics and Statistics," were William Barnett, James Powell, and George Tauchen. The co-organizers and proceedings coeditors of the sixth symposium, which was on "Equilibrium Theory and Applications," were William Barnett, Bernard Cornet, Claude d'Aspremont, Jean Gabszewicz, and Andreu Mas-Colell. The co-organizers of the seventh symposium, which was on "Political Economy," were William Barnett, Melvin Hinich, Douglass North, Howard Rosenthal, and Norman Schofield. The coeditors of that proceedings volume were William Barnett, Melvin Hinich, and Norman Schofield.

The eighth symposium was part of a large-scale conference on "Social Choice, Welfare, and Ethics." That conference was held in Caen, France, on June 9–12, 1993. The organizers of the conference were Maurice Salles and Herve Moulin. The coeditors of that proceedings volume were William Barnett, Herve Moulin, Maurice Salles, and Norman Schofield. The ninth volume in the series was on "Dynamic Disequilibrium Modeling: Theory and Applications," and was organized by Claude Hillinger at the University of Munich, Giancarlo Gandolfo at the University of Rome "La Sapienza," A. R. Bergstrom at the University of Essex, and P. C. B. Phillips at Yale University. The coeditors of the proceedings volume were William Barnett, Claude Hillinger, and Giancarlo Gandolfo.

Much of the contents of the tenth volume in the series comprises the proceedings of the conference "Nonlinear Dynamics and Economics," held at the European University Institute in Florence, Italy, on July 6–17, 1992. But the volume also includes the related, invited papers presented at the annual meetings of the American Statistical Association held in San Francisco on August 8–12, 1993. The organizers of the Florence conference, which produced part of the tenth volume, were Mark Salmon and Alan Kirman at the European University Institute in Florence, and David Rand and Robert MacKay from the Mathematics Department at Warwick University in England, and the organizer of the invited American Statistical Association sessions, which produced the other papers in the volume, was William Barnett, who was Program Chair in Economic and Business Statistics of the American Statistical Association during that year.

The eleventh volume was the proceedings of a conference held at the University of Aarhus, Denmark, on December 14–16, 1995. In addition to being the eleventh in this series, that volume was the proceedings of the Sixth Meeting of the European Conference Series in Quantitative Economics and Econometrics (EC)2. The organizer of the Aarhus conference was Svend Hylleberg at the University of Aarhus. The editors of the proceedings volume were William A. Barnett, David F. Hendry, Svend Hylleberg, Timo Teräsvirta, Dag Tjøstheim, and Allan Würtz. The topic of the conference and focus of that book was "Nonlinear Econometric Modeling," with an emphasis on nonlinear time series.

The intention of the volumes in this proceedings series is to provide refereed journal-quality collections of research papers of unusual importance in areas of currently highly visible activity within the economics profession. Because of the refereeing requirements associated with the editing of the proceedings, the volumes in the series do not necessarily contain all of the papers presented at the corresponding symposia.

William A. Barnett
Washington University in St. Louis

Volume editors' preface

Commerce, Complexity, and Evolution is a significant contribution to the new paradigm straddling economics, finance, marketing, and management, which acknowledges that commercial systems are evolutionary systems and must therefore be analyzed with evolutionary tools. Evolutionary systems also display complicated behaviors that are, to a significant degree, generated endogenously, rather than being solely the product of exogenous shocks, hence the conjunction of complexity with evolution. The papers in this volume consider a wide range of systems, from the entire economy at one extreme to the behavior of single markets at the other. The authors consider commerce from a variety of perspectives, ranging from marketing to macroeconomics. The papers are united by methodologies that, at their core, are evolutionary, although the techniques cover a wide range, from philosophical discourse to differential equations, genetic algorithms, multiagent simulations, and cellular automata. Some of the many issues considered include the dynamics of debt deflation, stock management in a complex environment, interactions among consumers and their effect on market behavior, and nonlinear methods to profit from financial market volatility. Because intellectual analysis is itself an evolutionary process, several of the papers critically analyze this newly emerging approach to understanding humankind's most complex invention, its social system.

The papers are a refereed, revised, and updated subset of those first presented to the twelfth conference in the series *International Symposia in Economic Theory and Econometrics*. The conference was held at the University of New South Wales in Sydney, Australia, in 1996, and attracted participants from Australia, Japan, Europe, and the United States.

This volume, edited by William A. Barnett, Carl Chiarella, Steve Keen, Robert Marks and Hermann Schnabl, consists of four parts: Part I considers the philosophical and methodological implications of the evolutionary approach to economic and social analysis; Part II presents several nonlinear models of macroeconomic dynamics and presents nonlinear techniques for analyzing financial data; Part III presents a range of applied evolutionary techniques to single markets, including nonlinear cobweb models, genetic algorithms, neural networks, complex systems simulations and cellular automata; and Part IV present complex system approaches to analyzing marketing and interdependent behaviors.

The Papers: An Introduction

Martens ("Toward a generalized Coase theorem: a theory of the emergence of social and institutional structures under imperfect information") applies concepts from systems theory, evolution, and psychology to consider the treatment of innovation in economic theory. He argues that, in contrast to neoclassical new growth theory and nonneoclassical Schumpeterian analysis, innovation cannot be properly treated without considering uncertainty, information-processing constraints, and the endogenous development of consumer preferences. This line of analysis leads to a vision of the market economy as a third tier of evolution above Darwinian survival and Lamarckian learned adaptation, in which the trading system enables the inexpensive exchange of critical information, thus enhancing overall survival. As Coase (1960) argued, however, trading introduces transaction costs, which can themselves prevent exchange if they are too high. Martens argues that this hypothesis can be extended to cover public goods, and this leads to a perspective on innovation and the evolution of institutions as uncertainty-reducing adaptations.

Nightingale ("Universal Darwinism and social research: the case of economics") casts a critical eye over the potentially faddist use of the term evolutionary to describe "any notion of alternative states of an economic system." He proposes a definition for a genuinely evolutionary approach to economics and asks whether it is possible for the evolutionary paradigm to be any more than a poor analogy, with economists "digging around the mullock heaps of the more developed sciences, searching for scraps of sustenance." Although his answer is a tentative "yes" in terms of present-day contributions to evolutionary economics, he argues that the concepts of evolution has as much inherent validity in the economic sphere as it does in biology.

Juniper ("Uncertainty, risk, and chaos") considers Keynes' discussions of investment behavior under uncertainty, expectations formation, and the concept of the "state of confidence" as a weight that is placed on forecasts in a world with an uncertain future. His survey of recent literature criticizes the attempt to use so-called evolutionary notions to argue for the reduction of uncertainty to risk and situates the modern concept of chaos theory within Keynes' rubric.

Standish ("The role of innovation in economics") concludes these philosophical papers and provides a bridge to the analytic, modeling, and simulation papers that follow. Arguing that there are strong parallels between ecology and economics, Standish notes that the two disciplines have followed a similar path of development, from statics through dynamics, to now arrive at evolutionary computation. He introduces an evolutionary program, *Ecolab*, which analyzes the development of an open-dimensional generalized Lotka–Volterra system of species interaction. The interaction matrix expands as new species are produced by means of mutation and crossover, and the interactions drive some species to extinction. The system displays self-organizing criticality as the dominant eigenvalue of the system tends toward zero. This ecological model is extended to include the economy by considering products as species and innovation as the analogy of mutation. Equilibrating price dynamics are introduced, not in the belief that prices achieve equilibrium in a dynamic setting but in the spirit of an ansatz whose dynamics can then be explored.

Keen ("The nonlinear economics of debt deflation") gives an excellent account of Fisher's appreciation of the dynamics underlying great depressions and Minsky's financial instability hypothesis. He constructs a nonlinear model, which incorporates insights of Fisher and Minsky and can generate the debt-induced depressions they foresaw. His model is locally stable but globally unstable. Keen goes on to model Minsky's insight that a government sector can stabilize the market. The model then becomes locally unstable but globally stable. His concluding comments on the current debt crises in Asia (which has subsequently spread to other parts of the world economy) underlines the significance and relevance of his modeling framework for economists wishing to develop prescriptions for the unfolding world economic order.

Chiarella and Flaschel ("The emergence of complex dynamics in a 'naturally' nonlinear integrated Keynesian model of monetary growth") develop a general six-dimensional Keynesian model of economic growth and cycles, because to date the literature has relied on partial models of Keynesian dynamics. Their results therefore provide a more considered yardstick by which to judge the alleged achievements of later non-Keynesian models. In contrast to the model in Keen, which has relatively simple production and distribution relations but uses nonlinear behavioral functions, the model in this chapter has quite a detailed model incorporating stocks, savings behavior, capacity utilization, and price dynamics in the context of simple linear behavioral relations. The nonlinearities that emerge in this model and determine its behavior are thus a natural product of the sectoral interactions in an economic system, without the additional consideration of nonlinear behavioral relations. The model demonstrates that a fully specified Keynesian model with no extrinsic nonlinearities is able to demonstrate complex dynamic behavior, which has not hitherto been appreciated in the macroeconomic literature. Results that wage flexibility destabilizes the system whereas price flexibility stabilizes it are also novel with respect to mainstream economic analysis (although consistent with results from Keen).

Barnett and Xu ("Stochastic volatility in interest rates and complex dynamics in velocity") demonstrate that money velocity is nonlinear even within a general-equilibrium model, to support the contention that money velocity may be unstable within the actual economic system. This theoretical result is offered as an explanation of the otherwise inexplicable behavior of money velocity since the late 1970s, as money velocity is traditionally regarded as a stable function of relatively few determinants. Barnett and Xu show that an infinite-horizon representative-agent model can generate a money velocity equation that follows a nonlinear dynamic process whose stability depends on model parameters and that can, under plausible conditions, demonstrate logistic map chaos. The introduction of exogenous uncertainty results in money velocity's being stochastically nonlinear. Data from 1960 till 1992 confirm the prediction of the chapter that high-risk aversion will reduce the stability of money velocity.

Colin's chapter ("A genetic-programming-based approach to the generation of foreign-exchange trading models") brings to mind the experience of one of the editors' Master's students, who recently went looking for successful applications of genetic algorithms (GAs) in finance. He found few examples, probably not because there are no applications of GAs in finance (see Debroeck's 1994 anthology for some early examples), but because there were some very successful examples – so successful, in fact, that their programmers were in no rush to make them publicly available (see Drake and Marks, 1998, for the survey). Given this dearth of published papers, we are pleased to have Colin's chapter on using GAs to assist in foreign-exchange trading. Colin argues that genetic programming (not specifically GAs) is appropriate for the generation of trading systems, which can aid in enhancing portfolio returns. The genetic-programming approach allows for greater complexity than GAs because it can incorporate data structures that can grow or shrink according to the requirements of the fitness function. Thus trading models can be developed without any prior assumptions being made about the complexity of the market. His results suggest that, when used in conjunction with disciplined money management techniques, these models may be useful in enhancing portfolio returns.

Lajbcygier et al. ("Hybrid option pricing with an optimal weighted implied standard deviation") show that a hybrid model – consisting of the Black–Scholes model augmented by an artificial neural network – is significantly more accurate at pricing options than the modified Black–Scholes model. The model was applied to the All Ordinaries Share Price Index (AO SPI) on the Sydney Futures Exchange. The research indicates that the deviations of actual data from the modified Black–Scholes model are of the order of 2% and are not noise but systematic deviations.

Schnabl ("Evolutionary patterns of multisectoral growth dynamics") outlines a technique that can identify the main interlinkages in an economy from input–output data. He also discusses evolutionary patterns displayed by an application of this analysis across time, which enables the death of certain industries and the birth of others to be detected. Policy makers could use this analysis to determine whether an economy's investment in product-innovation strategies is too low.

Foster and Wild ("The detection of evolutionary change in nonlinear economic processes: a new statistical methodology") extend spectral analysis, a technique that has been available in econometrics packages since at least the early 1970s, when the National Bureau of Economic Research used TROLL (for Time-Shared Reactive Library, developed at MIT and running on IBM 370 mainframes and compatibles) by means of the Tymshare remote network for research. Foster and Wild note that, nonetheless, the interest in evolutionary economics has not yet been matched by the development of econometric tests designed to investigate processes of change in an evolutionary economic system. Evolutionary economic processes, they argue, can be characterized in terms of time irreversibility, structural change, and true uncertainty. They propose a new methodology that can detect the time irreversibility, nonequilibrium, and unstable characteristics of evolutionary change in an economic system, the method of time-varying spectral analysis by using sliding windows over the data. They present an econometric approach to evolutionary processes that uses spectral methods to decompose the residual variances of econometric models of diffusion processes with logistic trajectories in order to establish, first, whether or not time irreversibility exists, second, whether the process can be viewed as a nonequilibrium process in nature (which provides evidence of structural change), and, third, whether the process is unstable in the saturation phase of logistic diffusion (which provides evidence of true uncertainty in the structural change). Fourier decompositions of the data generated by a logistic diffusion process will display dominant low-frequency components in the early growth stage, middle-frequency components in the inflexion stage, and a dominance by high-frequency components during the saturation stage. Together with other quoted work of the authors, this study can be seen as starting to lay the foundations of an econometrics of evolutionary economic processes.

Matsumoto ("Ergodic chaos in a piecewise linear cobweb model") extends the literature on nonlinear cobweb models with a model in which a linear supply function has upper and lower bounds. This model has the advantage of restricting system outputs to meaningful values (nonnegative prices and quantities), in contrast to earlier models with only upper bounds. Using an effective combination of analysis and numerical simulations, he shows that the range of dynamic behavior can range from stable periodic cycles to ergodic chaos.

Gaffney et al. ("The cobweb model and a modified genetic algorithm") extend the work of Arifovic, which itself was motivated by the contrast between the instability of cobweb models and the comparative stability of experimental markets. They translate the underlying genetic ideas into more meaningful equivalent economic concepts and model the mutation and crossover rules in a more economically meaningful way. Inspired by Carlson's demonstration that the model converges if agents base their price forecasts on the average of previous prices, Gaffney et al. use a real-number representation of the GA and averaging, instead of the standard binary GA representation and the crossover operator. They also add an "election" operator to simulate suppliers choosing between old and new forecasts on the basis of predicted profitability. Their modified GA always converges to the equilibrium and does so more smoothly than Arifovic's binary GA.

Pearce ("The convergence of genetic learning algorithms, with particular reference to recent cobweb models") discusses convergence and nonconvergence of GAs. In particular he shows that some of the basic results concerning nonconvergence of GAs hold in a much more general setting than previous mathematical analyses would suggest. His results also give greater insight into the convergence obtained by Gaffney et al. in their simulation study of the cobweb model.

Johnston and Betts ("A complex-systems simulation approach to evaluating plan-based and reactive trading strategies") evaluate the relative effectiveness of just-in-time reactive pull inventory management techniques and material requirements planning push methods by using a multiagent simulation. The environment of the simulation is affected by the actions of the agents, thus allowing the possibility of a wildly varying environment over time, with complex consequences for the nature and the stability of evolved strategies. For reasons of parsimony and focus, the model consists of a number of agents trading and maintaining their stock of a generic nonproduced good, in which some agents plan ahead whereas others commit to orders only one period in advance and trade to immediate demand. Simulations indicate that the prevalence of planners over reactions is a positive function of individual stocks and that the niche for reactor agents increases as the future becomes less predictable and peaks close to the complete breakdown of order.

Yao and Darwen ("Genetic algorithms and evolutionary games") generalize the iterated prisoners' dilemma beyond its standard 2-person bounds to consider populations as high as 16. The issues of interest are whether cooperation can emerge from an initial population of random strategies, how group size affects the evolution of cooperation, and how stable evolved strategies are. Yao and Darwen use a GA representation in which information on the number of cooperators in each previous round is stored, rather than the actual actions of each agent; this method is both more compact and more realistic. They find that cooperation can still evolve in larger groups, but it is harder to achieve as group size rises and is a positive function of the memory length. Cooperative strategies are in general not evolutionarily stable, but in a result that has interesting applications to predator–prey modeling, coevolution with the addition of extra noncooperative strategies gives more general strategies that do cooperate well with each other, but are still not exploited by noncooperative strategies.

Marks ("Evolved perception and the validation of simulation models") has undertaken a research program that evaluates the performance of market simulation experiments against real historical data for a specific oligopolistic market, that for instant coffee. The real and the simulated agents in this strategic game deal with the "curse of dimensionality" by partitioning the external reaction space, mapping from this external state to a more compact internal perceived state, and reacting to a rival's action only if it changes this perceived state. This raises the issue of the manner in which partitioning and mapping occur, and Marks discusses three possible measures for determining the optimal partition in this context of bounded rationality.

Oda et al. ("The application of cellular-automata and agent models to network externalities in consumers' theory: a generalization-of-life game") criticize the conventional treatment of demand in the presence of interactions among consumers, as it removes feedback between purchasing decisions and decision formation by presuming that no purchases occur until all buyers have made their purchasing decisions. They develop a simple but richer model of interactive demand functions in which there is no dichotomy between decision formation and economic activity. This model indicates that equilibrium values cannot be determined a priori and that there is no tendency for a convergence to equilibrium, with limit cycles and other dynamic phenomena being equally likely outcomes from a given set of initial conditions. They conclude with observations on the veracity of equilibrium analysis of consumer behavior and observe that the diffusion of a network-influenced product may follow a stable logistic process with heterogeneous consumers but may not if consumers are homogeneous.

Gans ("Engendering change") considers the possibility of coordination failure in circumstances in which multiple equilibria can occur, in which case the economy can be trapped in a low-efficiency equilibrium when such an equilibrium is locally stable but globally unstable. The example considered is racial discrimination in the labor market, and the policy issue investigated is whether the best strategy to escape from the low-efficiency equilibrium (of discrimination against individuals on the grounds of a perceived difference between groups) involves individually targeted or broad-effect policies. The situation of racial discrimination is characterized as one in which imperfect information on individuals results in the wage received by a worker, reflecting in part his or her marginal product and also information concerning the productivity of other members of the same group. The author finds that inflexible employer beliefs are best tackled with broad-effect policies, whereas flexible employer beliefs are best altered by policies targeted at the behavior of individual workers.

REFERENCES

Coase, R. H. (1960). The problem of social cost. In *The Legacy of Ronald Coase in Economic Analysis*, Vol. 2, ed. S. G. Medema, Ashgate, Brookfield, VT.

Debroeck, G. J., ed. (1994). *Trading at the Edge: Neural, Genetic, and Fuzzy Systems for Chaotic Financial Markets*, Wiley, New York.

Drake, A. E., and Marks, R. E. (1998). *Genetic Algorithms in Economics and Foreign Exchange – A Review*, AGSM Working Paper 98-004, Australian Graduate School of Management, Sydney.

Editors

William A. Barnett

William A. Barnett is Professor of Economics at Washington University in St. Louis, St. Louis, Missouri, and has previously been Stuart Professor of Economics at the University of Texas at Austin. Before his career in economics, Professor Barnett worked on rocket engine development for the Boeing Company. He has made research contributions in a substantial number of fields of economics, including the properties of the joint maximum likelihood estimator for systems of nonlinear seemingly unrelated regression equations, system modeling by use of microeconomic theory, the development of ideal indices for monetary aggregates, and the validity of tests for chaos in economic data. He is the series editor for the Cambridge University Press monograph series *International Symposia in Economic Theory and Econometrics*, of which this is volume 12, as well as editor of the Cambridge University Press journal *Macroeconomic Dynamics*. He has a B.S. in mechanical engineering from the Massachusetts Institute of Technology, an M.B.A. in finance and economics from University of California at Berkeley, an M.A. in economics, and a Ph.D. in statistics from Carnegie Mellon University.

Carl Chiarella

Carl Chiarella holds a Ph.D. in applied mathematics (University of New South Wales, 1970) and a Ph.D. in economics (University of New South Wales, 1988). He has taught applied mathematics at the University of Technology, Sydney, and finance and economics at the University of New South Wales and the University of Technology, Sydney. He has been a visiting scholar at the University of California, Berkeley, l'Université Catholique de Louvain, Tokyo Metropolitan University, l'Universite du Quebecà Montreal, and the University of Bielefeld. He has publications in a number of the leading international journals in finance, economics, and applied mathematics including *Applied Mathematical Finance, The Journal of Financial Engineering, Financial Engineering and the Japanese Markets, European Journal of Finance, Macroeconomic Dynamics, Journal of Economic Behavior and Organization, European Journal of Political Economy, Annals of Operations Research, International Economic Review, Economic Modeling, Chaos, Solitons and Fractals*, and *Mathematics of Computation*. He has two books forthcoming on his research in economic dynamics, one with Cambridge University Press and the other with Springer-Verlag. His research interests cover all aspects of quantitative finance and economic dynamics. He regularly presents his research work at international conferences such as Society of Computational Economics, Society for Nonlinear Dynamics and Econometrics, Asia Pacific Finance Association, and the Society for Economic Dynamics and Control. Professor Chiarella is a member of the Committee of the Asia Pacific Finance Association and of the Council of the Society for Computational Economics. He is an Associate Editor of *Financial Engineering and the Japanese Markets, Macroeconomic Dynamics*, and *Computational Economics*. He is on the International Advisory Board of the journal *Discrete Dynamics in Nature and Society*. He served as Head of School of Finance and Economics at the University of Technology, Sydney, from 1990 to 1996 at a time when Australian universities were undergoing great change.

Steve Keen

Steve Keen is Senior Lecturer in Economics and Finance at the University of Western Sydney Macarthur. His research interests are in debt deflation, macrodynamic modeling, and the history of economic thought, and he has published in a range of journals including the *Journal of Post Keynesian Economics*, the *Journal of the History of Economic Thought, Nonlinear Dynamics, Psychology and Life Sciences*, the *Review of Political Economy*, and *Économies et Sociétés*. Before his academic career, Steve worked in the fields of secondary education, overseas aid, international journalism, conference organization, and computer software development and evaluation. He has a B.A. and an LL.B. from Sydney University, a Dip. Ed. from Sydney Teachers College, a Master of Commerce Honors, and a Ph.D. from the University of New South Wales.

Robert Marks

Robert Marks is head of the economics group at the Australian Graduate School of Management, where he has taught since his graduation from Stanford University. He has also taught at the University of California, Berkeley, and MIT, and has a research affiliation with the Santa Fe Institute. In 1987 a program of his won the Second MIT Competitive Strategy Tournament, and in 1988 he became the first economist to publicly present economic simulation results of using the genetic algorithm. Bob has published over 50 papers in such journals as the *Journal of Economic Dynamics and Control, Management Science, Economics Letters*, the *Journal of Evolutionary Economics*, the *Energy Journal*, and the *Australian Journal of Management*, of which he is currently General Editor. His research interests have included evolutionary techniques in economics and game theory, as well as energy policy, drugs policy, and labor economics. He has recently been simulating and analyzing historical oligopolistic behavior.

Hermann Schnabl

Professor Dr. Hermann Schnabl was born 1940 in Munich and studied economics at the University of Munich. His Ph.D. was on intrabrain information handling at the University of Nuremberg. His 1987 Habilitation on a simulation model of consumer behavior was taken at the University of Munich. Since 1979 he has been Professor of Microeconomics at the University of Stuttgart, Director of the Department of Microeconomics, Institute for Social Research, University of Stuttgart. His research areas include input–output analysis, especially structure analysis or so-called qualitative input–output analysis, chaos theory with emphasis on empirical testing for chaos in financial time series, neural networks and genetic algorithms, innovation theory, and higher education. He is the author, coauthor, or editor of 12 books, and approximately 65 papers in journals or books, across all topics in economics.

List of contributors

Yasunori Baba
Research into Artifacts Centre for Engineering
University of Tokyo
4-6-1 Komaba, Meguro-ku
Tokyo 153, Japan
oda@cc.kyoto-su.ac.jp

William Barnett
Department of Economics
Washington University in St. Louis
One Brookings Drive
St. Louis, MO 63130-4899 USA
barnett@wuecon.wustl.edu

John Betts
School of Business Systems
Monash University
Clayton VIC 3168, Australia
John.Betts@fcit.monash.edu.au

Carl Chiarella
School of Finance and Economics
University of Technology Sydney
PO Box 123 Broadway
Sydney NSW 2007, Australia
carl.chiarella@uts.edu.au

Andrew Colin
Zurich Australia Funds Management
Level 3, 5 Blue Street
North Sydney NSW 2060, Australia
acolin@zurich.com.au

Paul Darwen
Department of Computer Science
Brandeis University
Waltham, MA 02254-9110 USA
darwen@cs.brandeis.edu

Peter Flaschel
Faculty of Economics
University of Bielefeld
PO Box 10 01 31
Bielefeld 33501, Germany
p.flaschel@wiwi.uni-bielefeld.de

Andrew Flitman
Department of Business Systems
Monash University
Clayton VIC 3168, Australia
aflitman@fcit-m1.fcit.monash.edu.au

John Foster
Department of Economics
University of Queensland
Brisbane QLD 4072, Australia
foster@commerce.uq.edu.au

Janice Gaffney
Department of Applied Mathematics
University of Adelaide
Adelaide SA 5005, Australia
jgaffney@maths.adelaide.edu.au

Joshua Gans
Melbourne Business School
University of Melbourne
200 Leicester Street
Carlton VIC 3053, Australia
J.Gans@mbs.unimelb.edu.au

Robert Johnson
School of Business Systems
Monash University
FCIT Building 63
Wellington Road
Clayton VIC 3168, Australia
johno@fcit-m1.fcit.monash.edu.au

James Juniper
Department of Economics
University of South Australia
Adelaide SA 5000, Australia
James.Juniper@unisa.edu.au

Steve Keen
Department of Economics and Finance
University of Western Sydney Macarthur
PO Box 555
Campbelltown NSW 2560
Australia
s.keen@uws.edu.au

Paul Lajbcygier
Department of Business Systems
Monash University
Clayton VIC 3168, Australia
plajbcyg@fcit-m1.fcit.monash.edu.au

Robert Marks
Australian Graduate School of Management
University of New South Wales
Sydney NSW 2052, Australia
r.marks@unsw.edu.au

Bertin Martens
European Commission
External Relations – Eastern Europe
200, rue de la Loi
Brussels B-1049, Belgium
Bertin.martens@ping.be

Akio Matsumoto
Department of Economics
Chuo University
742-1, Higashi-Nakano
Hachioji, Tokyo 192-0393, Japan
akiom@tamacc.chuo-u.ac.jp

Ken Miura
c/o Y. P. Gunji, Graduate School of Science and Technology
Kobe University
1-1 Rokkodai-cho, Nada-ku
Kobe 657, Japan
miuraken@mbox.kyoto-inet.or.jp

John Nightingale
School of Economics, Faculty of Commerce and Administration
Griffith University
Nathan QLD 4111, Australia
J.nightingale@cad.gu.edu.au

Sobei Oda
Faculty of Economics
Kyoto Sangyo University
Motoyama, Kamigamo,
Kita-ku
Kyoto 603, Japan
oda@cc.kyoto-su.ac.jp

Marimuthu Palaniswami
Department of Electronic and Electrical Engineering
University of Melbourne
Parkville VIC 3052, Australia
m.palaniswami@ee.mu.oz.au

Krystyna Parrott
Department of Applied Mathematics
University of Adelaide
Adelaide SA 5005, Australia
kparrott@maths.adelaide.edu.au

Charles Pearce
Department of Applied Mathematics
University of Adelaide
Adelaide SA 5005, Australia
cpearce@maths.adelaide.edu.au

Franz Salzborn
Department of Applied Mathematics
University of Adelaide
Adelaide SA 5005, Australia
fsalzbor@maths.adelaide.edu.au

Hermann Schnabl
Department of Microeconomics, Institute for Social Research
University of Stuttgart
Keplerstrasse 17
Stuttgart D-70174, Germany
schnabl@sofo.uni-stuttgart.de

Russell Standish
High Performance Computing Support Unit
University of New South Wales
Sydney NSW 2052, Australia
r.standish@unsw.edu.au

Kanji Ueda
Faculty of Engineering
Kobe University
1-1 Rokkodai-cho, Nada-ku
Kobe 657-8501, Japan
ueda@mech.kobe-u.ac.jp

Phillip Wild
School of Economics
University of Manchester
Dover Street
Manchester M13 9PL, UK
MSRASPW@fs1.ec.man.ac.uk

Haiyang Xu
Department of Economics
Washington University in St. Louis
One Brookings Drive
St. Louis, MO 63130 USA
xu@wueconc.wustl.edu

Xin Yao
Professor of Computer Science
Department of Computer Science
The University of Birmingham
Edgbaston, Birmingham B15 2TT
xin@cs.bham.ac.uk

PART I

Philosophical and methodological implications of complexity and evolution in economic systems

CHAPTER 1

Toward a generalized Coase theorem: a theory of the emergence of social and institutional structures under imperfect information

Bertin Martens

Present-day mainstream neoclassical economic theory is built on the perfect competition paradigm. It can be shown that, when the paradigm and its underlying assumptions are satisfied, an economy ends up in general equilibrium that represents the highest possible state of welfare. To reach this state, three assumptions must be satisfied. First, perfectly competitive markets must exist, including perfect information for all agents operating on these markets. Second, there must be two exogenous sets of fixed parameters, consumer preferences and production technology. Third, all agents must adopt utility maximization as their behavioral motive. Equilibrium is reached when all pairs of marginal costs and benefit ratios are equalized. At that point entropy is maximized and economic activity – agents making choices – must necessarily cease because no agent can further improve his or her position. At best, economic activity goes on in the reproductive mode, whereby agents eternally exchange the same mix of goods and services at the same prices. In the absence of external impulses, the economic system dies an entropy death.

From a systems theory point of view, the neoclassical perfect competition paradigm is incomplete because it has no entropy-decreasing mechanism and is not self-sustainable. In the case of economic systems, a competition-reducing force is required to keep it going. That is precisely the role of innovation. In terms of the neoclassical model, innovation can be introduced only through modification of exogenous behavioral parameters, consumer preferences, and production technology. In ordinary language, this is called inventions and the introduction of new consumer ideas.

To make innovation a regular feature of the economic model, these exogenous parameter modifications need to be endogenized in the system. This was attempted in the 1980s by two major schools of thought: endogenous growth theory (Romer 1986, Lucas 1988) and the neo-Schumpeterians (Nelson and Winter 1982). The endogenous growth school, by and large, remained within the confines of the neoclassical perfect competition paradigm. However, Romer (1990a, 1994) has shown that innovation-based endogenous growth theory basically conflicts with the neoclassical model because it violates the convexity requirement that is needed to reach equilibrium. The neo-Schumpeterian school has never tried to remain within the neoclassical paradigm.

Whichever of the two schools of thought one prefers to follow, mainstream economic theory clearly needs to switch to a new model and indeed a new paradigm that covers not only competitive optimizing behavior but also innovation as a means to escape from competition and entropy death. An attempt is made here to develop an outline of such a model. Although it maintains competition and optimizing behavior as key features, it constitutes a departure from the neoclassical model to the extent that it assumes that individual behavior is based on imperfect or incomplete information. The model is not driven by individual utility or profit maximization but by making optimal use of limited individual information-processing capacity. It is shown how this results, at the level of individual agents, in the emergence of rule-based rather than permanent optimizing behavior and, at the level of social interaction, in the emergence of norms, rules, and institutions. The proposed approach not only endogenizes innovation but also institutional developments. In fact, the two cannot be separated. It makes extensive use of Coase's (1937, 1960) ideas on the role of transaction costs in the emergence of firms and the settlement of externalities. For this reason, the model in this paper could be considered as a generalized version of the well-known Coase theorem.

First Romer's argument on the conflict between neoclassical production theory and innovative producer behavior is retraced. The same arguments are transplanted to consumer behavior, a domain neglected both by endogenous growth theory and the neo-Schumpeterian innovation school. The (narrative) outlines of a new model that focuses on uncertainty reduction as a behavioral motive are presented in Section 3. It is shown how this approach is not only consistent with findings in evolutionary biology but also explains the emergence of trade itself, as well as social rules of behavior and institutions. Finally, it is demonstrated how this cognitive model can be derived from a generalized formulation of the Coase theorem.

1 Innovative producer behavior

Since the early 1950s, mainstream economics' treatment of production and economic growth has been almost entirely based on the neoclassical Solow model (Solow 1956). The production process is a technological black box that transforms factor inputs (capital goods and labor) into outputs (production). Transformation ratios between factor inputs and outputs (factor productivity) are considered exogenous to the economic process. Empirical estimation of these transformation ratios, by Solow (1957) himself and others, showed, however, that its capacity to explain output growth was limited. An important growth residual that could not be explained in terms of changes in factor inputs remained: the so-called Solow residual. It can be explained only in terms of productivity growth or technological progress inside the production black box, which the neoclassical model considers to be exogenous to the economic system.

In the 1980s, two different gateways were explored to endogenize technological progress in the economic system. The first started from the microeconomic evolutionary approach of Nelson and Winter (1982) to economic change that builds the foundations for most of the recent wave of neo-Schumpeterian entrepreneurial innovation models. The second gateway was situated at a more macroeconomic level, in which Romer (1986, 1987, 1990b) and Lucas (1988) transformed Arrow's (1962) learning-by-doing model into an endogenous growth model.

Nelson and Winter and the neo-Schumpeterian school have sought inspiration in genetic adaptation models in biology to explain innovative producer behavior.[1] Production processes are described as algorithms. As with genes in biology, they consist of a set of behavioral instructions to be performed on a set of inputs in order to arrive at a specific (set of) output(s). Competitiveness is treated as an evolutionary problem: Producers must adapt or perish. Adaptation means changes in production algorithms. The market position or relative monopoly power and profit margin of individual firms continually changes because of innovations by competitors. Successful innovators become price setters rather than price takers in markets.

In line with Darwinian evolutionary theory, neo-Schumpeterian models basically treat changes in production algorithms as random processes. Investments in research and development yield innovations through a stochastic mechanism.[2] These innovations are then linked to a standard firm-level production model in which they improve the quality of output and/or increase productivity in the production process. Quality improvements are reflected in price increases as consumers are willing to pay a higher price for "better" products. Productivity improvements result in production cost savings. Both improvements are coupled to time patterns of diffusion of innovation and to the

[1] The exclusive focus on the firm as the locus of innovation allows us to classify the neo-Schumpeterians as evolutionary supply siders. Their own models explain how this supply-side bias has been caused by historical path dependency (David 1993) on Schumpeter's (1934) initial firm- and entrepreneur-focused approach.

[2] A good overview with recent examples is presented in the September 1994 issue of the *Journal of Evolutionary Economics*, including articles by Dosi and Nelson (1994), Ulph and Owen (1994), etc. Aghion and Howitt (1993) have developed a micro–macro model in which economic growth, including business cycles, is driven by innovation and creative destruction.

evolution of relative monopoly power in the market. Although the replication of ideas can normally be done at virtually zero marginal cost, the diffusion of ideas is protected in practice by legal patents, secrecy, and time-consuming learning processes to acquire the ideas.

Endogenous growth models are more conservative in their approach. They attempt to explain the Solow productivity residual at a macroeconomic level by building in explanatory mechanisms for productivity growth. Clearly learning plays an essential role here. Learning or knowledge has to be embodied, either in goods or in persons, before it can be used. Arrow (1962) embodies new knowledge, accumulated through learning by doing in production processes, in a new generation of capital good outputs. Human capital models embody learning in labor or in a new production factor, knowledge (Becker and Murphy 1992, Tamura 1991). A core issue here concerns the nature of knowledge. In the neoclassical tradition, knowledge, like any other information, is a pure (nonrival and nonexcludable) public good, freely available to everybody. This excludes monopolistic market situations caused by innovation. However, more realistic approaches assume that knowledge is a nonrival but at least partially excludable good, thereby permitting the emergence of monopolistic product and factor markets. In the latter interpretation, all innovation-based models, including the neo-Schumpeterian, violate fundamental neoclassical principles.

First, they introduce imperfect competition in product markets as the driving force for innovation. Innovation allows producers to increase product prices above prevailing market prices for standard (noninnovative) products and indeed above the marginal cost. General competitive equilibrium analysis does not hold anymore.[3] In neo-Schumpeterian models, for example, prices are typically determined through markup procedures, completed by market share allocation mechanisms among producers, without taking into account changes in consumer demand.

Second, they result in imperfect competition in factor markets. Contrary to ordinary goods, ideas are nonrival goods. They can be used by many users at the same time without loss of benefits or additional costs for any of them, despite the fact that the material carrier of the idea (paper, diskettes, video, any communication media) is a rival good. Romer (1990a) has demonstrated that nonrival goods result in production functions that have a degree of homogeneity higher than 1. Consequently, Euler's theorem on the allocation of factor income according to marginal productivity is not valid anymore and factors are not remunerated according to their marginal productivity. Classic production functions, for instance those of the Cobb–Douglas type, can, in principle, not be used anymore because they become meaningless for the allocation of factor

[3] Dixit and Stiglitz (1977) have presented a new approach to imperfect product markets that may still result, in some situations, in a Pareto-optimal equilibrium.

income. Some models try to solve this problem by splitting the economy into two sectors, one that produces nonrival innovation and a second that produces ordinary rival goods (with bought innovation inputs) that remains subject to the classical production functions (see, for example, Aghion and Howitt 1993). But this does not solve the problem of the first sector's incompatibility with neoclassical welfare optimization.

Because of the very nature of knowledge, innovation-driven models violate neoclassical principles. The neo-Schumpeterians have never claimed to be, or wanting to be, consistent with the neoclassical paradigm. On the contrary, they thrive on imperfect competition, which they claim – rather successfully – to be closer to reality. Indeed, the objective of business managers is not to operate on a perfect level playing field with their competitors but rather to differentiate their products through price and nonprice strategies. But it is a far cry from neoclassical general equilibrium theory.

2 Innovative consumer behavior

A fundamental problem with the introduction of innovation in production processes is that new goods are likely to appear that were previously unknown to the consumer. When the number of produced goods changes from n to $n + 1$, the number of arguments in a consumer's utility function should also increase from n to $n + 1$ and may upset all existing utility preferences. Somehow, a method has to be found to account for the emergence *ex nihilo* of preference arguments for such new goods. Lancaster (1966b) has already noted that this is one of the toughest nuts to crack in a neoclassical consumer framework. Both endogenous growth theory and the neo-Schumpeterian approach to innovation have neglected the consumer side of the innovation story.

Clearly, preferences must be at least partially endogenized to make an innovation-based model work. Very few authors seem to be aware of this problem. Among them, Ulph and Owen (1994) augment consumer preferences by the amount of quality improvement as reflected in product price increases. This merely shifts the problem from exogenous preferences to exogenous quality parameters.

By far the strongest statement in defense of the neoclassical assumption of exogenous consumer preferences has been made by Becker and Stigler (1976), although Becker (1991) seems to have somewhat softened his views. Pollak (1976a, 1976b, 1977, 1978) has weakened the neoclassical stance and allowed for various sources of endogenous influences on consumer preferences: habit formation or own past preference, social influences or preferences of other consumers, and price-dependent preferences. Since Pollak's seminal work on this issue, an endless series of variations on this theme has been developed. Bikchandani et al. (1992) introduce a theory of fads, fashion, and customs, based on "information cascades": Consumers can save on information costs by simply copying consumer behavior from others. Ditmar (1994) erodes consumer sovereignty to the bone. Empirical socioeconomic investigations lead to the conclusion that consumer behavior is largely dependent on norms and values within peer groups. A substantial body of psychoeconomic literature has developed around the theme of socialization of consumers from early childhood onward (see, for instance, Lea 1990). In short, the sovereign neoclassical consumer, who maximizes utility solely in the function of personal ex ante exogenous preferences, does not exist anymore in present-day economic theory (if this consumer had ever existed in reality, then the vast amounts spend on marketing campaigns would never have made sense).

Lancaster (1966a) replaces the traditional approach to consumer demand, whereby goods are the direct objects of utility, with the view that utility is derived from specific properties or characteristics of goods. For example, different color characteristics of a car result in different preferences: The utility derived from a red car is not the same as that from a gray car. Similarly, different design characteristics of clothing: This season's fashion design yields higher utility than that of last seasons. He assumes that characteristics are nonnegative quantities, "universally recognizable" and "objectively measurable." Whereas in the neoclassical approach a one-to-one link is assumed among a good, its characteristics, and consumer preferences for it, Lancaster's approach allows for consumer preferences for an entire set of characteristics that are reflected in a set of goods.

This enables him to define a new good – an innovation – as the addition of one or more choices to a bundle of goods within a given set of characteristics. When we know the new good's characteristics, through its "objective" and "universal" characteristics matrix, we can situate it in the bundle of available goods for a particular set of preferred characteristics. A new or innovative good will be preferred if its total characteristics vector yields a higher level of consumer satisfaction for the same budget outlay. If a consumer would get less of all preferred characteristics for the same budget outlay, then the new good is unlikely to succeed in the market.

Innovative goods are thus treated as substitutes for existing one. They are new only to the extent that they provide an original (re)combination of preferred characteristics. They are not totally new in the sense that they embody characteristics that were previously totally unknown. There is no demand for unknown characteristics, and such goods would simply fail in the market. Innovation thus builds on existing preferences for characteristics and provides only an original or enhanced (re)combination of a bundle of characteristics.

Lancaster's model might tempt us to conclude that innovation can be taken into account without endogenizing consumer preferences. This would be true if all sources of variation in utility would stem from variations in objectively measurable characteristics of goods. However, some may stem from new information received by the consumer, through the appearance of new goods or through publicity campaigns. An advertisement for a fast car can be interpreted as conveying objective information ("these cars are indeed fast") that may or may not fit in with your existing preference for that characteristic. Alternatively, it may convey the message that a fast car is something you should really have, thereby enhancing your preference for that characteristic. The first interpretation is compatible with exogenous consumer preferences; the second is not. With exogenous preferences, consumers get only what they want; with endogenous preferences, they may also want what they get.

Endogenous preferences create a fundamental problem. All neoclassical economic models assume that consumers maximize utility, subject to a given set of preferences and a budget constraint. If both the budget constraint and preferences are endogenized, there is no longer an objective function for maximizing behavior. Economic models become steerless in that case. This question cannot be solved within existing economic frameworks. As in every detective story, we need a motive for behavior. The search for a new motive – beyond consumer preference – is the subject of Section 3. We leave economics for a while, and start roaming around in information and evolution theories, biology, and psychology.

3 Uncertainty-reducing behavior as a response to imperfect information

The neoclassical world view starts from the assumption that economic agents are, at any moment, rational optimizers and that they possess all the necessary information to do so, at zero opportunity cost. Exogenously given consumer preferences and production technology parameters are but a consequence of this perfect information assumption. Perfectly informed agents can be expected to know precisely what they want (preferences) and how to get it (technology). Clearly, these assumptions are unrealistic.

A more realistic set of assumptions, revolving around imperfect information and uncertainty, could be formulated as follows. First, the amount of information available in the universe is, for all practical purposes, virtually infinite. Second, the information-processing capacity of any agent operating in the universe, human or nonhuman, and whatever the agent's intelligence, is necessarily limited. Third, evolutionary selection mechanisms will favor survival of agents who are best at giving appropriate responses to the widest possible range of events in their universe. Consequently, any agent's implicit objective function could be formulated as minimizing uncertainty, subject to an information-processing capacity constraint.

Decision making under uncertainty means choosing the option that is most likely to give an appropriate outcome. To do so, predicting outcomes becomes an important issue. Prediction requires analysis of regularities in incoming information flows. The more and the better an agent can analyze these, the better the agent's chances of survival. Enhancing the chances of survival becomes a question of making more efficient use of limited information-processing capacities. As will be shown in subsequent pages, the fundamental building blocks of the economic universe can be derived from the answers to this optimization question.

It is in response to imperfect information and uncertainty that complex adaptive systems have developed in nature, and recently in laboratories. Gell-Mann (1995) calls them information gathering and utilizing systems (IGUSs). IGUSs sift through the limited amount of available information to identify regularities in an uncertain universe. Regularities separate randomness and uncertainty from order and predictability. Although they are only an imperfect approximation of reality, they enable IGUSs to reduce uncertainty in their environment and consequently to improve their survival probability. Rather than passively awaiting the course of external events and hoping that none of these will be harmful or even lethal, IGUSs can try to predict the course of events and actively devise strategies or algorithms to reduce harm and increase benefits. Agents equipped with IGUSs capacity have a competitive advantage in nature's evolutionary selection process, compared with agents who do not have it. Identifying regularities and devising behavioral algorithms[4] in response to them is called learning. The capacity to store learned algorithms in memory, rather then reconstructing them every time, further enhances the survival probability[5] of IGUSs.

Agents may well have explicit behavioral motives other than uncertainty reduction. However, if they do not minimize uncertainty, they are subject to higher risks and have lower survival chances. Evolutionary selection will work against them. The advantage of the implicit approach is that there is no need to identify teleological behavioral motives such as utility or profit maximization, cooperative behavior, love, paternal or maternal instincts, etc. All these implied motives may well exist in peoples' minds, but they are all behavioral guidelines derived from, and subordinate to, uncertainty reduction. To the extent that they contradict the latter, they constitute a handicap, which may have an evolutionary rationale too (Zahavi 1975, Grafen 1990a) but is not discussed here.

[4] In this paper, the words algorithm, (behavioral) rule, and (behavioral) norms are used interchangeably. They are all defined as a (possibly multidimensional) set of behavioral instructions.

[5] Survival probability maximization should not necessarily be interpreted strictly in the life-or-death sense but should be considered in a context of mostly marginal behavioral adaptations that facilitate life.

4 Making more efficient use of limited information-processing capacities

Order-creating IGUSs exist at various levels of complexity, from simple biological structures to complex entities with cognitive capacities, like humans. Three stages can be identified in evolution, corresponding to ever more efficient ways of dealing with the uncertainty problem.

First, simple biological structures react mechanically to external events. Their behavioral algorithms are preprogrammed in such a way as to permit them to collect the necessary material and energy inputs that prevent the internal entropy-increasing process from reaching the limits as which the structure disintegrates. If unforeseen (unprogrammed) events have an impact on the structure, it may disintegrate. In more complex biological structures, algorithms are genetically encoded, which allows programming of far more diversified but still fixed or innate reaction patterns. Genetically preprogrammed behavioral algorithms cannot adapt to unforeseen incoming information. However, in evolution, random mutations in genetic structures may result in better adapted species with increased survival chances. The word random is essential here: The behavior of the biological structure itself does not influence these mutations. The Lamarckian evolutionary model is not applicable at this stage of development.

In a second stage, the evolution toward cognitive capacity and the emergence of brains marks the gradual shift from purely Darwinian selection, with random mutations in preprogrammed genetic algorithms, to Lamarckian selection with adaptive programming through learning or information gathering processes that are not random but purposeful (Hodgson 1993): They lower information entropy. The development of cognition means that organisms acquire the capacity to create a second layer of behavioral algorithms on top of their genetic structure that can be learned and memorized and even repeatedly reprogrammed in the course of the organism's lifetime. This has considerably enhanced uncertainty reduction and flexibility of behavior in a more varied range of environments and circumstances. The effective internal complexity[6] (Gell-Mann 1995, p. 56) of IGUSs behavior has thus increased because it is able to identify and memorize more concise descriptions of regularities in its environment and react accordingly.

In a third stage, limited cognitive capacity can be used more efficiently within a group of agents through specialization and exchange of goods. This occurs when a division of labor emerges in a social setting. What are the evolutionary advantages of the division of labor and cognitive specialization? The short answer is that, given limited individual cognitive capacity, a group of specialized

[6] The internal effective complexity of a system is defined by Gell-Mann (1995, p. 56) as "the length of a concise description" of the regularities in the system's environment as identified by the system.

agents can accumulate more uncertainty-reducing behavioral algorithms – knowledge – than a group of identical (nonspecialized) agents. But this short answer is rather trivial. It merely says that the union of a number of differentiated knowledge sets contains more knowledge elements than the union of the same number of undifferentiated (or identical) knowledge sets. Showing how the actual mechanics of the division of labor work in reality is a more complicated matter that requires a longer answer.

To do this, a major disadvantage of specialization is first pointed out: Specialization increases risks for individuals within a population. They become dependent on a narrow set of knowledge, which may be advantageous in particular circumstances but disadvantageous in others, thereby endangering their survival. A corollary to this risk is increasing interdependence among individuals. Specialization or division of labor is apparently advantageous for the group but is not in the interest of the individual as it increases his or her risk exposure. To find an insurance system that protects individuals against the risks of specialization and fosters collaboration among specialized individuals to their mutual benefit, we must analyze the way in which individual knowledge can be put at the disposal of other individuals.

Limits to individual cognitive capacity make straightforward copying of specialist knowledge to interested individuals an uninteresting proposition: Copying the entire set does not generate any savings in scarce information-processing time. Potential recipients would have no (economic) interest in acquiring these copies. Hayek (1949) and Von Weiszacker (1991) pointed out that flows of knowledge in a society characterized by a division of labor are not meant to provide full information to all its members. In fact, individuals are not interested in full information but only in what they consider to be relevant information for their decision-making situations. Computer buyers, for instance, decide on hardware and software purchases on the basis of the relevant problem-solving algorithms that are embodied in these goods; they are not interested in the details of chips and hard disk manufacturing (unless they are computer freaks). Relevant information is a very elusive and subjective concept. Although manufacturing details may not be relevant to buyer *A*, they may be very relevant in the decisions of buyer *B*. When the machine breaks down, however, even buyer *A* may start wondering about certain manufacturing details. Clearly, the neoclassical hypothesis of perfect symmetric information on all relevant aspects of a market is not a workable concept anymore. Trading parties have different ideas on what they consider relevant aspects. Hayek (1949) summarizes this very well:

> "We make constant use of formulas, symbols, and rules whose meaning we do not understand and through the use of which we avail ourselves of the assistance of knowledge which individually we do not possess."

Here lies the clue to understanding the evolutionary advantages of specialization. Although we do not individually master all the details of all domains of knowledge accumulated by others, we are able to use these domains because they have been embodied in transferable carriers that, with a minimal input of knowledge and activities from our side, produce an output that is relevant to us. Take the example of clothing. Buyers usually do not bother about the textile production processes (i.e., that consumers don't in general worry about the process of production). They know how to put them on and keep them clean (user inputs). This way, clothing produces the relevant outputs, that is, protection against body health losses and social recognition.

Evidently the benefits of the division of labor can be realized only if the products of each agent's specialized knowledge can be traded. Because they permit communication of truncated or relevant parts only of knowledge sets, trading systems provide agents in a group with effective access to a far larger stock of potential problem-solving and uncertainty-reducing knowledge than they could ever hope to accumulate on their own. Societies that allow specialization and trading systems to emerge thus have an evolutionary advantage over those that do not. They widen an individual citizen's access to problem-solving and uncertainty-reducing knowledge.

Economic systems are more efficient survival machines than biological or genetic reproduction mechanisms. Although genetic reproduction involves copying an individual's entire set of algorithms into every new generation, communication and trading systems require only the reproduction of a small subset of a "parent's" behavioral algorithms into a material carrier that transfers this to any other recipient. This is far more "economical" than genetic reproduction of entire bodies.

5 The emergence of transaction costs

The division of labor is thus a more efficient way of using limited information processing or cognitive capacities. At the same time, however, the emergence of the division of labor, and trade that goes along with it, creates new types of opportunity costs called transaction costs.

Coase (1937, 1960) was the first to introduce this concept in economics. His definition (1960) points to the existence of imperfect information:

> "In order to carry out a market transaction it is necessary to discover who it is that one wishes to deal with, to inform people that one wishes to deal and on what terms, to conduct negotiations leading up to a bargain, to draw up the contract, to undertake the inspection needed to make sure that the terms of the contract are being observed, and so on."

In this view, transaction costs represent resource losses that are due to lack of information and to uncertainty. They are induced by cognitive differentiation or specialization between individuals. As such, transaction costs are a subset of information costs. The latter refer to the opportunity cost of any type of information; the former refer only to the information input required for achieving a transaction between two individuals with different knowledge sets. Whereas information costs are costs incurred to reduce general uncertainty, transaction costs are incurred to reduce uncertainties concerning interindividual transactions.

This definition excludes costs that are due to geographical differentiation, such as transport costs, which are sometimes used a substitutes for transaction costs (Yang and Borland 1991). It firmly roots the transaction costs concept in a world of imperfect information in which no individual has perfect information on the good or service he or she wishes to acquire, and no two individuals have identical knowledge sets. Cognitive differentiation is both the source of comparative advantage, and thus of exchange, and of transaction costs.

Transaction costs are inherent in an economy with a division of labor and specialization. This can easily be understood in light of the preceding description of the requirements of information exchange between individuals. Because exchange of complete knowledge packages would not be efficient, truncated packages are exchanged, embodied in goods. However, these truncated packages have to be understandable to the receiver, who needs to share a minimum amount of common knowledge with the producer so as to be able to use the good. According to Polanyi (1958), making truncated messages understandable is achieved through codification and the presence of tacit knowledge among interacting agents.

Transaction costs may run up so high that they prevent a transaction from taking place. When uncertainty prevails and the cost of acquiring all the necessary information to make the outcome of a transaction more predictable exceeds the potential value of a transaction, then it will not take place. In general, transaction costs prevent agents from reducing uncertainty in their environment and in their dealings with other agents. They have to be overcome in order to satisfy an agent's implicit behavioral motive of uncertainty reduction, subject to the agent's information capacity constraint. How this can be done is the subject of Section 6.

6 Toward a generalized Coase theorem

The transaction cost debate was initiated by Coase (1937, 1960) and revived by Williamson and the New Institutional School in the 1980s (Williamson 1995). Coase (1937) opened the debate from a supply-side angle: Why do firms exist? Why can't individual producers trade parts of production processes among each other to arrive at the same final product? Alternatively, why can't all firms be absorbed into one huge company? Coase's answer was that firms are a means to circumvent transaction costs inherent in market-based exchanges: the cost of acquiring information on supply and demand, the cost of negotiating a separate deal for each transaction, the cost of uncertainty. Firms are more cost effective than a network of individual producers working through open-market transactions because they work on the basis of contracts that fix quantities, qualities, and prices, rather than passing every time through an open-market transaction. Fixed and repeatable contractual arrangements save transaction costs. On the other hand, all firms cannot be amalgamated into a single company because the amount of information required for supervising the whole company would be overwhelming (and very costly). It could not possibly be processed by a single agent and would thus require decentralized decision making anyway, thereby eroding the benefits of integration.

Coase saw the firm as a set of contracts between individual producers who economize on transaction costs by bypassing the market. Coase shows that, contrary to the neoclassical view that competitive markets represent the highest degree of efficiency in an economy, it is indeed possible to outwit the allocative function of the market, precisely because of the presence of imperfect information. The neoclassical economic universe appears to be just a special and unrealistic case of the Coasian Universe, with transaction (and information) costs set to zero.

Grossman and Hart (1986) show that transaction costs can never be reduced to zero. That would amount to fixing all possibilities in contractual rules and leave no space for unforeseen events. But even the most elaborate contract is necessarily incomplete as rules have been identified in a boundedly rational environment. Because of this inherent uncertainty, transaction costs are always positive. In his 1960 article on "the problem of social cost," Coase demonstrated how positive transaction costs can impinge on property rights and prevent a solution of the problem of externalities. Because property rights are necessarily incompletely defined, events can occur that require further negotiations on property rights issues. The cost of dealing with all parties concerned, however, may run up so high that it is not worth seeking a settlement of the issue. This led Coase to the conclusion that externalities can always be settled or internalized again through interindividual bargaining, subject to a transaction cost. Stigler (1966) later on coined the label Coase theorem for Coase's 1960 analysis and summarized it as follows: In an efficient economy, the difference between private and social costs can never exceed the level of transaction costs.

Dixit and Olson (1997), in line with a long series of arguments concerning the nonexcludable nature of public goods started by Samuelson (1954), argue that the Coase theorem is not applicable to public goods and therefore is not a theorem in the sense of a statement of general validity. Public goods are, by definition, nonexcludable and their benefits are entirely dispersed through externalities. No amount of bargaining and investment in transaction costs will ever be able to internalize these externalities. Free riding on public goods is rational from an individual point of view and can be contained only through government intervention that overrules individual rationality.

The argument of Dixit and Olson (1997) is correct when considered in the context of a single transaction. However, Ullman-Margalit (1977), Axelrod (1984), and Skaperdas (1991, 1992) demonstrate how free riding and externalities can be contained in a game-theoretic setting of the Prisoner's Dilemma type. Repeated games lead to the emergence of norms of behavior that rein in free riding and settle into a long-run stable strategy with an equitable distribution of costs and benefits, at least with respect to the initial resource distribution. The norms or rules of behavior constitute a decision on the appropriation of costs and benefits, without free riding. Credible commitment devices, such as tit-for-tat strategies in repeated Prisoner Dilemma games, ensure that free riding does not occur. Ultimately, the emergence of norms serves as a transaction-cost-reducing and uncertainty-reducing device. Uncertainty about the mind-set of the other players results in initial very high transaction costs that prevent players in the game from moving to a better situation for all of them: If one takes the initiative to move, the others may free ride on the benefits he or she generates and make him or her even worse off. Gradually awareness of this situation grows and players communicate, directly or indirectly, and build up mutual confidence that allows them to move jointly to a better situation. Uncertainty reduction, or transactions costs, is at the root of a solution to Prisoner's Dilemma games, in both a theoretical setting and in social reality.

If we take the norms and rules of behavior that emerge out of Prisoner's Dilemma-type situations as the sources of decision making on public goods, then the Coase theorem is indeed a theorem of general validity whose applicability extends to public goods and even to situations in which no ex ante defined and enforceable property rights exist.

More in general, the 1960 Coase theorem can be combined with Coase's 1937 article on the role of transaction costs in the emergence of firms and generalized into a theorem on the role of norms, rules of behavior, and public laws, etc., as uncertainty-reducing devices in society. They give rise to islands of reduced transaction costs, groups of agents who adhere to a specific set of rules of behavior, thereby enhancing the prospects for more efficient transactions and stimulating economic growth.

7 Conclusions

It has been demonstrated that the neoclassical paradigm of perfect competition, based on perfect information and exogenously fixed consumer preferences and production technology, is an unsuitable starting point from which to introduce innovation into economic models. Attempts to do so by so-called endogenous growth theory and by the neo-Schumpeterian School have ended up in models that are basically inconsistent with the neoclassical paradigm. The introduction of innovation into consumer behavior and the endogenization of consumer preferences has been largely neglected in the literature, except for Lancaster's contribution.

Another route has been presented toward endogenization of innovation by the introduction of the concept of IGUSs, derived from evolutionary science and information theories. IGUSs are uncertainty-reducing – and therefore survival-probability-enhancing – devices that come in two kinds, preprogrammed and reprogrammable. The latter are classified as cognitive carriers because they have the ability to learn and store learned behavioral algorithms in memory. It has also been shown that the introduction of specialization and the division of labor represents a further step toward uncertainty reduction, as it makes more efficient use of limited cognitive capacities. However, it also creates new risks, uncertainties, and transaction costs, as the mind-sets of interacting agents differentiate. Transaction costs and uncertainties can be reduced through normative behavior, the introduction of laws, and institutions.

Coase introduced both the concept of transaction costs and the so-called Coase theorem in the literature. Here it is shown how the two can be combined in a single, more general theorem that explains the emergence of rule-based behavior and institutions, both private (companies, clubs, households) and public (government), as an attempt to overcome transaction costs and uncertainty. This generalized Coase theorem is nothing but a continuation of the evolutionary search for more adaptive and flexible complex survival systems.

REFERENCES

Aghion, P., and Howitt, P. (1993). A model of growth through creative destruction. In *Technology and the Wealth of Nations*, eds. D. Foray and C. Freeman, OECD, London.

Arrow, K. J. (1962). The economic implications of learning by doing. *Rev. Econ. Stud.*, **29**, 385–406.

Axelrod, R. (1984). *The Evolution of Cooperation*, Basic Books, New York.

Becker, G. S. (1991). A note on restaurant pricing and other examples of social influences on price. *J. Polit. Econ.*, **99**, 1109–16.

Becker, G. S., and Murphy, K. M. (1992). The division of labor, coordination costs, and knowledge. *Q. J. Econ.*, **107**, 1137–60.

Becker, G. S., and Stigler, J. (1976). De gustibus non est disputandum. *Am. Econ. Rev.*, **67** (2), 76–90.

Bikhchandani, S., Hirschleifer, D., and Welch, I. (1992). A theory of fads, fashion, custom and cultural change as informational cascades. *J. Polit. Econ.*, **100**, 992–1026.

Coase, R. (1937). The nature of the firm. *Economica*, **4**, 386–405.

(1960). The problem of social cost. *J. Law Econ.*, **3**, 1–44.

David, P. A. (1993). Path dependence and predictability in dynamic systems: a paradigm for historical economics. In *Technology and the Wealth of Nations*, eds. D. Foray, and C. Freeman, OECD, London.

Dietrich, M. (1994). *Transaction Cost Economics and Beyond*, Routledge, London.
Ditmar, H. (1994). Material possessions as stereotypes: material images of different socioeconomic groups. *J. Econ. Psychol.*, **15**, 561.
Dixit, A., and Olson, M. (1997). The Coase theorem is false: Coase's insight is nonetheless mainly right, Working Paper. University of Maryland at College Park, College Park, MD.
Dixit, A., and Stiglitz, J. (1977). Monopolistic competition and optimum product diversity. *Am. Econ. Rev.*, **67**(3), 297–308.
Dosi, G., and Nelson, R. (1994). An introduction to evolutionary theories in economics. *J. Evol. Econ.*, **4**, 153–72.
Gell-Mann, M. (1995). *The Quark and the Jaguar*, Freeman, New York.
Grafen, A. (1990a). Biological signals and handicaps. *J. Theor. Biol.*, **144**, 517–46.
(1990b). Sexual selection unhandicapped by the Fisher process. *J. Theor. Biol.*, **144**, 473–516.
Grossman, S., and Hart, O. (1986). The costs and benefits of ownership. *J. Polit. Econ.*, **94**, 691–719.
Hayek, F. A. (1949). *Individualism and Economic Order*, Routledge and Kegan Paul, London.
Hodgson, G. (1993). The nature of selection in biology and economics. In *Rationality, Institutions and Economic Methodology*, eds. U. Maki, B. Gustafsson, C. Knudsen, Routledge, London.
Lancaster, K. (1966a). A new approach to consumer theory. *J. Polit. Econ.*, **74**, 132–57.
(1966b). Change and innovation in the technology of consumption. *Am. Econ. Rev.*, **56**, 14–23.
Lea, S. (1990). On socialization. Special issue of the *Journal of Economic Psychology*.
Lucas R. E. (1988). On the mechanics of economic development. *J. Monet. Econ.* **22**, 3–42.
Nelson, R., and Winter, S. (1982). *An Evolutionary Theory of Economic Change*, Harvard University Press, Cambridge, MA.
North, D. C. (1993). What do we mean by rationality. *Public Choice*, **77**, 159–62.
(1994). Economic performance through time. *Am. Econ. Rev.*, **84**, 359–68.
Polanyi, M. (1958). *Personal Knowledge: Towards a Post-Critical Philosophy*, Routledge and Kegan Paul, London.
Pollak, R. (1970). Habit formation and dynamic demand functions. *J. Polit. Econ.*, **78**, 745–63.
(1976a). Interdependent preferences. *Am. Econ. Rev.*, **66**, 309–20.
(1976b). Habit formation and long-run utility functions. *J. Econ. Theory*, **13**, 272–97.
(1977). Price dependent preference. *Am. Econ. Rev.*, **67**, 64–75.
(1978). Endogenous tastes in demand and welfare analysis. *Am. Econ. Rev.*, **68**, 374–79.
Romer, P. (1986). Increasing returns and long-run growth. *J. Polit. Econ.*, **94**, 1002–37.
(1987). Growth based on increasing returns due to specialization. *Am. Econ. Rev.*, **77**, 56–62.
(1990a). Are non-convexities important for understanding growth? *Am. Econ. Rev.*, **80**, 97–103.
(1990b). Endogenous technological change. *J. Polit. Econ.*, **98**, 71–102.
(1994). The origins of endogenous growth. *J. Econ. Perspect.*, **8**, 3–22.
Samuelson, P. (1954). The pure theory of public expenditures. *Rev. Econ. Stat.*, **36**, 387–89.

Schumpter, J. (1934). *The Theory of Economic Development*, Oxford University Press, Oxford, England.
Skaperdas, S. (1991). Conflict and attitudes toward risk. *Am. Econ. Rev.*, **81**, 116–20.
(1992). Cooperation, conflict and power in the absence of property rights. *Am. Econ. Rev.*, **82**, 720–39.
Solow, R. (1956). A contribution to the theory of economic growth. *Q. J. Econ.*, **70**, 65–94.
(1957). Technical change and the aggregate production function. *Rev. Econ. Stat.*, **39**, 312–20.
Stigler, G. (1966). *The Theory of Price*, Macmillan, New York.
(1992). Law or economics. *J. Law Econ.*, **35**, 455–68.
Tamura, R. (1991). Income convergence in an endogenous growth model. *J. Polit. Econ.*, **99**, 522–40.
Ullmann-Margalit, E. (1977). *The Emergence of Norms*, Clarendon, Oxford, England.
Ulph, D., and Owen, R. (1994). Racing in two dimensions. *J. Evol. Econ.*, **4**, 185–206.
Von Weizsacker, C. Chr. (1991). Antitrust and the division of labor. *J. Inst. Theor. Econ.*, **147**, 99–113.
Williamson, O. (1995). The institutions and governance of economic development and reform. In *Proceedings of the World Bank Annual Conference on Development Economics*, World Bank, Washington, D.C.
Yang, X., and Borland, J. (1991). A microeconomic mechanism for economic growth. *J. Polit. Econ.*, **99**, 460.
Zahavi, A. (1975). Mate selection, a selection for handicap. *J. Theor. Biol.*, **53**, 205–214.

CHAPTER 2

Universal Darwinism and social research: the case of economics

John Nightingale

The revival of interest in evolutionary theory by economists among other social scientists is one of the most interesting developments in social science of the past 20 or more years. Hodgson's book (1993a) shows just how deep this form of theorizing is in the history of economics. He points to the current developments, but does not presume to constrain the potential directions of future development or make any explicit suggestions about theory himself.

Any reading of the literature that identifies itself as belonging to the class of theories dealing with irreversible economic change, diversity, and emergent structures indicates the vitality of the program. That there are so many inventive and pregnant ideas indicates the evolutionary nature of scientific endeavor. Examples may be cited of analytical models that yield deterministic, if path-dependent and nonergodic, predictions. Models relying on nonlinear dynamics, such as chaos models that Day (1994) or Goodwin (1990) have developed are of this kind. There are explicitly evolutionary analytical models (Metcalfe 1989, Iwai 1981) as well as the more commonly seen numerical models (Nelson and Winter 1982). Some theories are explicitly gradualist, directly following those of Darwin himself. Marshall's gradualist motto (*natura non facit saltum*) could also be that of Nelson and Winter. Others have developed theories of revolutionary or punctuated evolutionary change. Schumpeter's "creative destruction" is the paradigm case of the latter. Gersick (1991) explicitly seeks out examples of punctuated equilibrium. Gowdy (1992) focuses on the hierarchical structure of evolutionary theories. But there are also a growing number of theorists and theories that are appropriating the term evolution as a means of characterizing any notion of alternative states of an economic system, whether because they think evolution has a fashionable ring to it, or there are evolutionary journals out there to be colonized, or from a genuine misunderstanding of the meaning of evolution within scientific communities (Borland and Yang 1995). The evolutionary research program is clearly in a "preparadigmatic stage," to use Kuhn's terminology. Despite this lack of any generally accepted structure, there are a number of ways in which evolutionary theory can be characterized, ways that are at least consistent with those of other disciplines that use the term.

One of these is set out in Nightingale (1994), in which I use Lakatos' methodology of scientific research programs to define four essential elements for any evolutionary theory:

(1) Time passes, forward, never backward.
(2) Social organisms have a substantial fixed body of practices and structures that condition their behavior.
(3) Organisms differ in their possession of such characteristics.
(4) The environment within which these exist favors some over others, leading to increasing shares of system resources by some at the expense of others, as time passes.

In this proposal I was following a number of others, most explicitly Hodgson (1993a), but also Metcalfe (1989, p. 56).[1] Evolutionary theories in economics are very different from those of neoclassical orthodoxy, not simply for being different in scope and emphasis, but more fundamentally for being a different class of theory. Hodgson begins his book with a review of some aspects of methodology. In this he distinguishes the Cartesian basis of mechanical mathematical modernist economics of the neoclassical school from the "realism, pragmatism and organicism" that he sees at the center of the project with which he is concerned. The *as-if* instrumentalism of orthodoxy dismisses concern that the world is not really like the theoretical categories and their arrangement into predictive models. This he almost explicitly accuses of being an idealist, à la Cartesian, belief in the power and efficacy of reason, notably mathematical reason, to discover truth deductively and inductively (the latter in the sense of inducing the correct mathematical models, which can then be used deductively). This is closely associated with the mechanical analogy now so deeply embedded in economics that it required the sandblasting of Mirowski (1989) to reveal the analogical framework to even part of the profession. The alternative evolutionary economics project he depicts by contrast as realistic, and, moreover, as naturalistic, "[a] realist cannot support the proposition that either human society or human ideas are completely separable from their foundation in nature" (Hodgson 1993, p. 11).

A recent paper (Jackson 1995) points to the differing implications that naturalism and antinaturalism, and revisions of simple naturalism such as that he calls "critical naturalism," have for scientific inquiry in the social sciences. Positivistic naturalism has problems coping with subjectivity and consciousness; antinaturalism falls into relativism and an inability to order observations by any theoretical criteria. Jackson's suggested "critical naturalism" attempts to avoid

[1] Metcalfe proposes a principle of variation, a principle of heredity, and a principle of selection.

this problem by distinguishing reality from perceptions of reality and taking the scientific project as theorizing about those perceptions most effectively argued to be near to the "transcendental reality," which is imperfectly apprehended. The descent into relativism is prevented by appeal to that external reality, while the nature of that reality is subject to argument.

My interest in this question is sparked by the use of analogy, or metaphor, by evolutionary economists, many of whom argue that they are theorizing about social phenomena as if they were biological. Marshall is the most famous of these theorists. His famous phrase, "The Mecca of the economist is economic biology rather than economic dynamics" (Marshall 1920, p. xii), encapsulates the notion that this social science should imitate the natural science, drawing on the latter to generate insights for the former. But social science is about phenomena remote from the phenomena of biology, in the same way that social science is remote from physics. A nice example of this reasoning is Gowdy's paper (1991). His task here was to illustrate from the controversies in modern biology some of the issues that economics might face: gradualism versus punctuated equilibrium, general sorting mechanisms rather than what he sees as a narrower "natural selection" mechanism, and hierarchy as against reductionism. Looked at in this way, the social scientist can be pictured as a scavenger digging around the mullock heaps of the more developed sciences, searching for scraps of sustenance. This is not an attractive analogy in itself and is perhaps much too pejorative for serious consideration. However, it does emphasize a danger for the social science project: its failure to consider carefully the implications of naturalism for scientific endeavor. Can such metaphorical models be more than heuristic devices whose implications are merely indications of directions in which to look for the appropriate theory that will fulfill the criteria for a realistic critical naturalist theory?

Is it possible that an evolutionary social science, including economics, is not disjointed from evolutionary theories used in life sciences generally? Can evolutionary social theory be anything but metaphor or analogy in the sense with which we are familiar?

I would not wish to say that the following suggestion is the only possible answer to that question, but I am going to argue that the answer is yes. In doing so I suggest that much current evolutionary theorizing, being either explicitly or implicitly in the nature of metaphor, is attempting too much too soon. My caution is that the broader implications of the ideas being appropriated are not being appreciated. Given the increasing flow of quite technically demanding and ambitious work being attempted and published, it seems important to me that general methodological criteria be better understood. This in itself may not lead to any single definitive theory, nor should it for some little time, if ever. But it may discipline authors, editors, and referees in judging the worth of contributions to the debates in quest of scientific progress.

1 Evolutionary epistemology: a naturalistic methodology of scientific progress in the understanding of living systems

Plotkin's work, *The Nature of Knowledge* (Plotkin 1994), is extraordinarily ambitious. In this book he attempts to unify under the one simple theory the whole of human understanding of life, its origin, development, and diversity. His project is no less than explaining the existence and structures of all living systems, whether biological, social, or cultural, under the rubric of what Dawkins first called *universal Darwinism* (UD).[2] This he calls "evolutionary epistemology as science" as distinct from its treatment as philosophy (Plotkin 1994, p. 248).[3] Plotkin's use of the phrase universal Darwinism indicates the universal applicability of Darwinism to life processes both within and between organisms, along with his understanding of the distinction between Darwinian and Lamarckian processes. This distinction is of some importance as it will lead us to include in the UD classification much that is often loosely described as Lamarckian by social science. I will return to this following my summary of Plotkin's project.

His methodology can be placed within that of Jackson's "critical naturalism" and that of Lawson's preferred ontological theory of "transcendental realism" (Lawson 1995, p. 13).[4] My argument here is that Plotkin is attempting to understand phenomena by reference to an underlying real structure. He is not merely proposing an inductive theory nor is he positing axioms that yield predictions about observed behavior. He puts forward a theory about the structure of living systems that applies in an hierarchical way at every level from the microbiological to the global socioeconomic–political–ecological. His is thus a "grand conceit," but one that not only bears examination, but provides a criterion by reference to which evolutionary social theories may be evaluated.

[2] Albeit, in the rather different context of arguing that if life existed elsewhere in the universe, it would follow the Darwinist rules.

[3] The term evolutionary epistemology (EE) has many meanings when examined closely. Plotkin sees EE as a mechanism underlying the world of living things (note the title of the paperback edition of his book: *Darwin Machines and the Nature of Knowledge*). Callebaut (1993) brings together a range of philosophers, mainly philosophers of science, whose uses of, or agreement with, EE range from seeing biological evolution as a useful analogy in explaining how we come to justify beliefs (EE as theory), to those who, as Plotkin does, see evolution underlying behavior in which selection processes are not always biological, to those who insist that blind variation and selective retention are the only mechanisms that can be considered within the canon of UD, and that that mechanism explains everything. Campbell (see below) is accused of having held that position, at least at some time (Callebaut 1993, pp. 288–293).

[4] Both these economists are followers of the realist philosopher R. Bhaskar. See their papers for reference.

Plotkin's argument is, very roughly, as follows:

(1) UD can be characterized in a number of ways.[5] All of these characterizations apply directly to the biota at levels other than the human social and cultural, and most clearly at the levels below those in which learning is an important aspect of an organism's behavior.
(2) Adaptations and behavior are related in a very distinct way. Adaptations he defines as a "feature or attribute of an organism that helps it to survive and reproduce" (Plotkin 1994, p. 246). Behavior is defined as an "adaptive action or doing." This definition of behavior is narrower than that of general usage, excluding "having" completely, and excluding doing or acting that is not goal directed or adaptive. This definition comes from Piaget. Although this means that behavior is adaptation, by definition, the reverse is not true. Genetically created adaptations are behaviors only in the limited sense that they allow behaviors (e.g., the use of particular senses in different species).
(3) Different types of organism have different forms of adaptations, from the genetically selected attributes of all organisms to cultural and social behaviors of, most importantly, humanity. Language is the most spectacular example of cultural and social adaptation. Language has allowed an enormous range of cultural and social behaviors to develop. Between the genetic inheritance and its mutations, however they may arise, and the adaptations of culturally active humanity, there are the various forms of learning. These are adaptations seen in organisms as simple as flatworms, which can learn, by operant conditioning, to follow a wire to a food source.
(4) The different forms of adaptation or behavior suit different types of organism. Those for which the environment changes more rapidly than a lifespan of the organism benefit from learning. For such, generally the mobile organisms of the animal kingdom, it is not much use adapting genetically to changes that happen to apply at the time the parents succeed in procreating. The more rapid the environmental change, the less adaptive are genetic mutations, the more adaptive are forms of change that can be undertaken by an individual during its lifetime. Learning is the meta-adaptation that provides a powerful tool for survival. But learning is not the only such adaptive behavior. Humans are

[5] UD processes have been suggested in general forms by biologists: for example, Lewontin's three principles of phenotypic variation, differential fitness, and fitness heritability; Richard Dawkins' Replicator, Interactor, Lineage model, and Donald Campbell's blind variation, selective retention model, which Plotkin and Odling-Smee (Plotkin 1994, p. 139) transform into the generate, test, regenerate schema. These are the examples expounded in some depth by Plotkin (Plotkin 1994, Chap. 3).

skilled at changing their environments to suit themselves: This is social and cultural change. The creation of environmental characteristics by humans, the transmission of knowledge about how to maintain and improve these creations and the ability to keep creating constitutes the third great means of adaptation. We use a mixture of learning and created change in attempting to survive and reproduce.

(5) Now for the biggest leap: The repositories of adaptations, be they genetic codes, stored memories of learned responses, stored cultural values in brains, books, magnetic media, organizational routines etc., are defined as knowledge. Moreover, all knowledge is stored coding of adaptations.

Thus Plotkin makes a sustained argument based squarely on naturalistic realism for what has previously been merely an audacious claim that the theory of UD can be used to structure our understanding of the whole biota.[6] The various formulations of UD (phenotypic variation / differential fitness / heritable states, replicator / interactor / lineage, generate / test / regenerate) can be used as appropriate to explain structures, conduct, and performance at any level. The only requirement is that the basic principles are being applied.

This evolutionary epistemology bears a striking resemblance to Popper's analysis of the growth of knowledge as an evolutionary process having all the characteristics of UD (Popper 1972, especially Chap. 7). Popper, somewhat controversially, characterizes Darwinism as a metaphysical research program (Popper 1974, Chap. 37). Popper's argument is that the program is both untestable, and thus metaphysical, and pregnant with enormous power, not of direct explanation but of suggestion. It is this power that has led to the extraordinary predominance of Darwinism and of UD as a framework for scientific research. This resemblance is noted by Plotkin (Plotkin 1994, p. 69), who particularly quotes Popper's insistence that knowledge growth is a Darwinian process in no metaphorical sense, but as much Darwinian as anything biological. Popper does go on to differentiate the growth of human knowledge from that of nonhuman biological knowledge. His argument is that "pure knowledge . . . is dominated by a tendency towards increasing integration towards unified theories" (Popper 1972, p. 262). This is in contrast to the increasing differentiation of life forms and human culture into diverse and specialized forms suited to environmental niches. This is explained as the distinction among practical problems that are solved by creative invention, the Darwinian paradigm, and problems of explanation. The latter is solved conditionally by conjecturing theories that survive in the face of critique of their ability to be seen to be consistent with

[6] Dennett's (1995) *Darwin's Dangerous Idea* is another work with a similar argument, a work that, however, lacks Plotkin's focus on developing a scientific concept of knowledge. Plotkin's EE allows him the logic of his argument on which others may not be willing to venture.

facts and compatible with other knowledge (Popper 1972, p. 263). This trajectory of criticism is one of integration of theories into ever more powerful ones, in which power is measured by the breadth of phenomena to which it applies. The process belongs to that of UD, of the generation of variety, of theories, their test against alternatives, and the regeneration of the successful.[7] Plotkin's suggestion takes Popper's theory further, in that Plotkin explicitly identifies human knowledge within the broader spectrum of biological phenomena, putting the need to rely on as-if metaphorical reasoning further beyond the pale.

A further link can be made with Kelly's *Psychology of Personal Constructs* (1955), a theory of personality that has close links with Popperian ideas; despite the lack of any entry for Popper in his bibliography or index,[8] Kelly proposes a set of ideas he calls "constructive alternativism." Like Popper, he suggests that "all thinking is based, in part, on prior convictions" (Kelly 1955, p. 5). The living creature[9] is able to represent the environment in which it lives. The universe is real to that creature, but it is not inexorable. The creature is able, with its creative capacity, to construct its theory of that universe, to act on that theory, and to change that theory if it finds the theory wanting. As a psychotherapist, Kelly was interested in how and under what circumstances a theory would change. He recognized that people held onto their own constructions by various means, filtering out information that was adverse to their theory and seeking information supporting it. However, it was predominantly a theory of creation of insights, selection of particular theories that suited the environment, and the re-creation in the light of experience of the environment. His theory may be characterized as "the individual as scientist" (Kelly 1955, pp. 4–5, 9). Constructs are grounds for prediction, as "the universe is essentially a course of events, the testing of a construct is a testing against subsequent events" (Kelly 1955, p. 9). Constructs are therefore interim and subject to revision and replacement. This he emphasizes in recognizing "the essentially active nature of our universe. The world is not an abandoned monument. It is an event of tremendous proportions, the conclusion of which is not yet apparent" (Kelly 1955, p. 14). This theory is clearly a member of the UD class of theories,[10] emphasizing creativity and selection as the psychological basis of human action.

[7] I argue below that it is not appropriate to label modification by learning "Lamarckian," a common claim made by social scientists.

[8] Nor (much less surprisingly) does Kelly appear in Popper 1972 or 1974.

[9] It is not clear from the context whether Kelly was referring to humans or to all living creatures. It would be sympathetic with Plotkin's argument, were the latter to be the referent. However, the theory held by a single-cell animal about its environment can change only genetically. It extends the concept theory or construction rather further than one might like to go.

[10] In fact, it is arguably a member of the class to which Plotkin's belongs, wherein variation and selection are no mere biological analogies but real phenomena with their own mechanism for generating variation and selecting between them.

The relationship among the ideas of Kelly, Plotkin, and Popper (in alphabetical order) can be summarized as follows: Plotkin suggests that knowledge is held in adaptations made by living creatures, under a UD mechanism of evolutionary change. Kelly attempts to explain human personality by using a UD mechanism, being a subset of Plotkin's. Kelly's theories at the broadest level of generality fit exactly into the space allowed by Plotkin's discussion of human learning and culture. Kelly, moreover, has had many of the same insights about theory construction that Popper developed, especially those in which explicit Darwinian exposition is used. In particular, Popper's concern that observation requires prior theory is one of the fundamentals of Kelly's theory. The development and the organization of knowledge, over time, have thus been examined from at least these perspectives with the conclusion that knowledge is a phenomenon explicable under a UD framework.

2 Darwin or Lamarck?

It is now necessary to give some further explanation of the reason why Plotkin chooses to place learning and social and cultural knowledge under the rubric UD when it appears on the surface to include the inheritance of acquired characteristics, that is, a Lamarckian process.

Plotkin examines Lamarck's theories (Plotkin 1994, pp. 24–28) in some detail: These theories begin with the popularly believed observation, now generally dismissed as erroneous, that all organisms are "wonderfully well adapted at all times and in all places" (Plotkin 1994, p. 26). But environments change over time; therefore organisms must change over time. This occurs by the organisms' responding with modifications of bodily structures, specifically that more intensively used elements would develop at the expense of less intensively used parts. These are passed on to offspring, another commonplace but erroneous belief. Governing these processes is the principle of change "from simplicity and imperfection to complexity and perfection of form" (Plotkin 1994, p. 27). Thus an ascent of life forms from the primeval slimes to man can be traced. Lamarck was thus conveniently consistent with natural theology and harmonious creation (Plotkin 1994, pp. 32–33).

Lamarck's theory relies on some substrate that can respond to instruction from the environment to put forth appropriate adaptations. They are immanent, preexistent, rather than emergent creations. When the instruction is given, the preexisting substrate responds with the appropriate adaptation from the repertoire of available adaptations. There is no need for selection, as only the appropriate emerges from obscurity. The fit of an organism to environment is optimal; there is no room for chance or uncertainty.

Lamarck's theory also implies the existence of very many trees of life, in contrast to Darwin's single tree of life. Human beings are the product of the oldest, or most potentially complex, tree: The primeval slime from which humanity evolved contained the necessary ingredients for the characteristics we have developed. By contrast, what remains as slime, bacteria, worms, and trees, became stuck (for lack of inherent qualities) at stages we have long eclipsed (Sober 1993, p. 8). Lamark's theory is of evolution that has been substantially finished. God's handiwork may be admired as a completed perfection.

Biological evolution has clearly been shown not to be well represented by this instructionist theory. But the various forms of learning and problem solving in human society would seem on the surface to be good candidates for explanation by Lamarckian theory. In those cases, the environment does call forth the behavior. Conscious adaptation in the case of human society represents attempts to fit itself perfectly to the demands of the environment. Innovations are created precisely to overcome the difficulties of a changing environment. In the case of learning, of whatever kind, the solution to the problem is sought from that which already exists.

The contrast with Darwinian evolution is striking: Darwin saw the generation of variety as independent of environment, a natural process of excessive creativity pouring potential variation of organisms and of speciation into an environment that was simply there. That environment selected those varieties that were adaptive, rejected those that were maladaptive, and ignored the remainder, the behaviorally irrelevant features of nature that defy adaptive explanation such as the profusion of morphological peculiarities of butterfly species of neighboring valleys: no suggestion of perfection at any point in time, no attempts by organisms to adapt to an environment by conscious or unconscious choice, certainly no passing on of acquired characteristics to future generations.

On this reading (Plotkin 1994, pp. 32–33), Lamarck and Darwin discovered the two great alternative principles of evolution. Consider the essential differences between Lamarck and Darwin: Darwin was selectionist, Lamarck instructionist. Darwin's genetical variants appear randomly and are selected over by an environment that happens to favor survival of individuals with that variant characteristic. It is blind or undirected. Lamarck's variations are produced to order: The environment requires feathers for flying out of trouble on the ground, so feathers grow. Darwin's variations were original and emerged out of existing materials and codes by a process of creation. Lamarck's variations all exist, albeit in small or insignificant occurrence until they have to be called forth. Creation on the Lamarckian theory has been long time past taken care of in some mysterious way, ready for all eventualities. Only those characteristics required for the current environment will come forth, and those characteristics will ensure the fitness of each species. Species are always beautifully adapted to be their best in this best of all possible worlds. There is no need for selection, as only the appropriate will come forth.

How can it be argued that UD is a paradigm that subsumes all types of knowledge, of behavior, of organized information, and the cultural inheritance of humanity? The argument rests on an hierarchical structure of *g–t–r* heuristics that explain evolution. Plotkin calls the genetic and developmental level the primary heuristic (Plotkin 1994, p. 250). At this level, the standard biological level with which Darwin's natural selection is usually understood, mutation generates variety randomly. Those very few that turn out to be adaptive are selected by the environment for propagation. This is a powerful mechanism of organization in which the environment changes slowly relative to the generations of organisms. Successive generations are winnowed by the same environment; therefore success in many generations predicts well for success in many further generations. Autotrophs seemingly cope with knowledge, in Plotkin's terminology (Plotkin 1994, pp. 116–125), limited to this level. Each individual is planted into the ground in a single location. Typically their descendants share that location. There is no hint of Lamarck here. This also works well for members of the animal kingdom, the better, the more predictable the environments within which the animal lives. Individual intelligence is not an important requirement for worms, or even birds. However, the ability to take advantage of operant conditioning, to name probably the simplest type of learning, is a form of genetically inherited knowledge that allows many animals to supplement their instinctual behaviors with variations imposed by an environment predictable within a generation, but easily modified for the next; again, no room for Lamarckian interpretation.

The secondary heuristic defined by Plotkin is that of certain systems within the organism, the immune system and the central nervous system and brain. The immune system generates variety in response to damage to the physical body of the organism: Each event, such as invasion by bacteria, is met by hordes of agents in an immune response. Only those effective against the particular invader are propagated in that particular event. When the invader is beaten, the propagation of these agents ceases. This has clearly been shown to be a UD mechanism in that there is neither preselection by the environment (within the organism's body) nor a catalog of available varieties ready to be pressed into service, but a generalized rush of random varieties, most of which are ephemeral because of lack of nutritious invaders. But the other partition of Plotkin's secondary heuristic is the ability to learn. The primary heuristic provides the substrate for learning, the nervous system and brain; the learning itself is part of the secondary. But is it Darwinian or Lamarckian? And does it matter?

The "processes of discovery and invention making up the adaptations . . . concerned with tracking the spatial and temporal relationships of events and objects in the world are what I am collectively referring to as intelligence" (Plotkin 1994, pp. 153–154). This learning and memory comprise the other part of the secondary heuristic. The various modi operandi of intelligence, from the modest attribute of a flatworm to the heights of human achievements, are still mysterious at many levels but the common feature remains the creation of behaviors followed by selection of a limited set for repetition. Operant conditioning provides the clearest picture: The organism satisfies a drive, to eat for example, only by some of a large number of behaviors. Those few are replicated. At higher levels of intelligence many other forms of learning are seen. But to constrain these to a Lamarckian framework would be extremely limiting. There is no menu of given possibilities that are available for use. Intelligent behavior by individuals and groups is creative, contingent on environment or circumstance, very subject to error, and may be characterized in the way that Kelly has done explicitly for individual human behavior, and as Popper did to understand scientific progress, as a selection process. Pure instruction, as implied by Lamarck's theory, would make the diversity of human culture difficult to explain. The general absence of a uniquely optimal solution to such problems would also suggest that an instructionist view is far too limiting. This is not to deny the conscious goal orientation of much behavior in populations other than human, let alone human. It is, however, to assert that experiment, chance, creativity in excess of need, play, and rational indeterminacy are important. The conclusion is that to label intelligent and intentional behavior as Lamarckian instruction following is an oversimplification that would prevent explanation of emergent change in populations exhibiting such behavior.

The secondary heuristic is one of the generation of varieties of possible behaviors,[11] the testing of those possibilities by experimentation, and the propagation of that select set that proves at least viable, contingent on the environment at every point in time. Plotkin presents an argument based on the investigation of brain development (Plotkin 1994, pp. 166–173) that supports the above argument, but perhaps the most telling argument is that of D. T. Campbell (cited in Plotkin 1994, p. 172) that selectional processes are required for any new knowledge: Lamarckian instruction can at the most support mere deduction. Moreover, even explicit instruction is contaminated to a greater or a lesser degree by emergent creativity. Arguments for instructionism must demonstrate the worth of increasing the complexity of the fundamental UD explanation with auxiliary hypotheses that have a Lamarckian flavor.

A similar argument applies at the level of the tertiary heuristic, the world of social and cultural behavior. At that level creativity is even more critical than at the level of the individual organism's resolving the problem of tonight's dinner. Two contrasts might be made here with seemingly Lamarckian economic theory. The first is with a process neoclassical economic theory in which an

[11] Even, and perhaps predominantly in many cases, from memories of past behaviors as recorded in the brain or libraries, taught by schools and other institutions devoted to learning in human society. Studies of animal behavior also record teaching and learning, including alternative parenting styles (Aldehoven and Carruthers 1992) and family traditions (lyrebirds' and butchbirds' songs) that have adaptive significance.

entity (firm, household, etc.) is assumed to have full knowledge of both an objective function and all the constraints on its optimization. Even relaxing the assumption of full knowledge of constraints to asymmetrical knowledge relative to other agents, the theory deduces the behavior from the available information and optimization algorithms. There is no creativity. This is truly Lamarckian. The second is with neo-Schumpeterian evolutionary economics, as represented by Nelson and Winter (1982). Here, behavior is problem solving, but imperfectly. An entity will continue to act routinely until the routine fails to deliver a satisfactory outcome. Then the entity searches past behaviors to rediscover previous solutions (the garbage-can model of organizational behavior), or searches for new behaviors, innovates, to find a feasible solution (Cyert and March 1963). This search is not random but directed. Nor are the two types of search clearly distinguishable within organizational search routines. Can this behavior be called Lamarckian, following so many authors, such as Nelson and Winter (1982) and Metcalfe (1989)? If the search is confined to existing routines, albeit unused, if the prior evaluations of rediscovered routines are always accurate, if only appropriate solutions are enacted, and if the organization's environment has only an ex ante role in evaluation of the success of the adaptation, then Lamarck's instructionist evolution may be adduced to explain it. There is no selection in this setting. It should be clear that my argument is opposed to allowing that neo-Schumpeterian theory could be called Lamarckian. The satisficing search processes that Nelson and Winter, following Cyert and March, discuss cannot exclude ex post mistakes, outcomes that do not fulfill the most optimistic expectations. At worst the outcome will be considered just feasible, that is, satisfying ex ante minimum conditions for adoption. At best it may be ex post optimal, but purely by chance. Their argument is a selectionist one, and explicitly so (Nelson and Winter 1982, Chaps. 6, 10, 11). They do not even expect or predict that there will be any optimality properties to a selection equilibrium (Nelson and Winter 1982, Chap. 11).

Thus, even those who claim some Lamarckism in their theories hold that selection processes are fundamental in shaping the social and cultural world within which their studies are set. This seems to me to show that the *g–t–r* paradigm copes with all levels of behavior, under a nested hierarchy of selection environments. The primary heuristic conditions the possibilities of the secondary, which in turn conditions the possibilities of the tertiary.

For economic behavior, in the realm of the secondary and the tertiary heuristics, a UD mode of analysis translates into a population-thinking set of models in which variety is generated by economic entities or organisms making choices, creating solutions that are tested for feasibility within or beyond the organism. The secondary heuristic (within entities) can be seen in feasibility studies, ex ante benefit cost calculations, or a parent's forbidding some childish fancy. The tertiary heuristic is seen in the process of market competition, or in the constraints of a legal system, or in the rules of an international body such as the World Trade Organization. Selection or testing of varieties is seen in the growth or decline of individual economic entities over time. Regeneration is seen in the attempts at minor and major transformations made by these entities, usually an endogenous process flowing from the testing process. Discovering new knowledge is the goal of firms, households, and all the other institutions of the modern economy, in their efforts to avoid the worst consequences of their testing by the economic environment.

3 The end of analogy

Two aspects of this seem to me to be very important. The first is that we can put aside the notion of analogy or metaphor: There is no need for economists to argue as if they were using biology. It makes as much sense to claim that, for example, economic models use biological analogy as biological models use economic analogy, or sociological analogy, etc. We have a hierarchy of UD theory that is not arguing as if at any level. From the clonal selection of antibody receptors on lymphocytes to the foreign exchange markets to the cycles of fashion in popular culture, identical structures underlie living processes. This is not to say that metaphors and analogies are not important ways of illustrating arguments and deriving critical insights. These are tools of critical analysis and the development of science. At the deepest level it can be argued that language about reality is simply metaphor. However, no discipline is privileged over another in this regard.

The second is that this single underlying structure suggests a criterion by which a theory can claim to be evolutionary in character. This may not seem to be important, but consider two common assertions. The first is the misuse of the term evolution by writers who mean merely the logical consequence of an equilibrium solution to an optimization problem, as mentioned above. There is no Darwinian process here. Lamarckist instruction may be seen at its most logically simple in that the instruction of optimization and perfect knowledge together yield the perfect outcome. The second concerns the many statements of social scientists[12] that some or other evolutionary theory embodies Lamarckian principles. Such a statement usually means that the definition of Lamarckian is restricted in some way. Nelson and Winter (1982), for example, profess to be unabashedly Lamarckian in that their theory "contemplates both the 'inheritance' of acquired characteristics and the timely appearance of variation under the stimulus of adversity" (Nelson and Winter 1982, p. 11). However, it can be seen from a more complete understanding of Lamarck's theory that neither inheritance of culturally created characteristics nor imperfectly (or boundedly

[12] Including myself, I might add.

rational) goal-seeking behavior implies Lamarckism as an alternative theory of evolution. When cultural innovation is looked at from a Darwinian point of view, the act of creation happens often, yielding diverse possibilities. These are then selected by whatever selection or sorting mechanism is appropriate to the situation. Merely adaptive learning implies that creativity is irrelevant and Lamarck's instruction model significant, whereas it is argued here that the distinction between learning and creation is impossible to draw.[13] The splendid fecundity of the human mind in creating ideas is seen under Plotkin's grand theory as a UD machine for creating divers adaptations. But try to bind the human mind into a Lamarckian framework: although the garbage can of past solutions to past problems is a resource for solving present problems, as March and Simon pointed out (1958), Lamarck's instructionism offers no further resource, no creativity, no elements of chance or uncertainty.

What many, including Nelson and Winter (1982), have called, and may continue to call, Lamarckian is directed, as opposed to random, adaptation. Human adaptations are virtually entirely directed. But the direction is from the fertile and experimental creativity of the human mind's imagining new possibilities. The mind itself knows all too imperfectly whatever deposit is available from the past; the ability to calculate is similarly bounded; the environment it attempts to comprehend is uncertain. Human adaptations and the processes that lead to them are thus an element of the Darwin machine, that for creating variation. The processes that lead to these creations and sort them into those that persist over time and those that do not, into those which achieve acceptance in a larger or a smaller niche within human society, are a study of the social sciences.

4 Conclusion

My argument is that a naturalistic and realistic evolutionary economics and more generally social theory are possible under the rubric of UD, as defined by Plotkin (1994). The theory is hierarchical, relying on no as-if statements for application. The fundamental mechanisms of the theory, those being selectionist, remain unchanged at all levels of the hierarchy. Application of the theory requires discretion and argument about precisely how the fundamental mechanisms are to be interpreted, but Lamarckian instructionism is not required. Whether this UD paradigm proves to be as powerful as Plotkin believes remains to be shown by scientific endeavor. I think it is worth the effort to find out. One hope is that a UD interpretation of work done with no intention to be Darwinian will provide a source of simplification and reconciliation in the spirit of Occam's

[13] Cambell's argument is central. I might mention an earlier evolutionary economist, Jack Downie, who made an argument against distinguishing between imitation and innovation (Downie 1958, p. 91).

Razor. The more this turns out to be the case, the more powerful will the UD program appear. The response of those skeptical of the program, that it is merely reinterpretation of other theories, can be met by this appeal to Occam's Razor: Why use a special theory when UD can be applied to x phenomena as well as to $(a \cdots w, y, z)$ phenomena?

In doing this it may also provide a means of disciplining the enthusiastic excesses of the converts to evolutionary and related theories amongst social scientists and users of technically advanced tools subject to the old garbage in–garbage out syndrome. Understanding of the general principles of UD is diffusing among us more slowly than we like to think. I certainly do not regard my own as particularly profound or complete.

REFERENCES

Aldenhoven, J., and Carruthers, G. (1992). *Faces in the Mob*, Video documentary, National Geographic Society, Washington, D.C., Australian Broadcasting Commission, Sydney.

Borland, J., and Yang, X. (1995). Specialization, product development, evolution of the institution of the firm, and economic growth. *J. Evol. Econ.*, **5**, 19–42.

Callebaut, W. (1993). *Taking the Naturalistic Turn, or How Real Philosophy of Science is Done*, University of Chicago Press, Chicago.

Cyert, R. M., and March, S. G. (1963). A behavioural theory of the firm. Prentice-Hall, Englewood Cliffs, New Jersey.

Day, R. H. (1994). *Complex Economic Dynamics*, MIT Press, Cambridge, MA.

Dennett, D. C. (1995). *Darwin's Dangerous Idea*, Simon & Schuster, New York.

Downie, J. (1958). *The Competitive Process*, Duckworth, London.

Gersick, C. (1991). Revolutionary change theories: a multilevel exploration of the punctuated equilibrium paradigm. *Acad. Manage. Rev.*, **16**, 10–36.

Goodwin, R. M. (1990). *Chaotic Economic Dynamics*, Clarendon, Oxford, England.

Gowdy, J. (1991). New controversies in evolutionary biology: lessons for economists? *Methodus*, **3**, 86–9.

(1992). Higher selection processes in evolutionary economic change. *J. Evol. Econ.*, **2**, 1–16.

Hodgson, G. M. (1993). The mecca of Alfred Marshall. *Econ. J.*, **103**, 406–415.

(1993a). *Economics and Evolution*, Polity Press, Cambridge, England.

Iwai, K. (1981). Schumpeterian dynamics, parts I and II. *J. Econ. Behav. Organ.*, **5**, 159–90; 321–51.

Jackson, W. A. (1995). Naturalism in economics. *J. Econ. Iss.*, **29**, 761–80.

Kelly, G. A. (1955). *The Psychology of Personal Constructs*, Norton, New York.

Lawson, T. (1995). A realist perspective on contemporary economic theory. *J. Econ. Iss.*, **29**, 1–32.

March, J. G., and Simon, H. A. (1958). *Organizations*, Wiley, New York.

Marshall, A. (1920). *Principles of Economics*, 8th ed., Macmillan, London.

Metcalfe, J. S. (1989). Evolution and Economic Change. In *Technology and Economic Progress*, ed. A. Silbertson, Macmillan, London, pp. 54–85.

Mirowski, P. (1989). *More Heat than Light*, Cambridge University Press, Cambridge, England.

Nelson, R. R., and Winter, S. (1982). *An Evolutionary Theory of Economic Change*, Belknap, Cambridge, MA.

Nightingale, J. (1994). Situational determinism revisited. *J. Econ. Method.*, **1**, 233–52.

(1997). Anticipating Nelson & Winter: Jack Downie's theory of evolutionary economic change. *J. Evol. Econ.*, **7**, 147–68.

Plotkin, H. (1994). *The Nature of Knowledge*, Penguin, London.

Popper, K. (1972). *Objective Knowledge, An Evolutionary Approach*, Clarendon, Oxford, England.

(1974). *Unended Quest, an Intellectual Biography*, Fontana/Collins, Glasgow.

Sober, E. (1993). *Philosophy of Biology*, Oxford University Press, Oxford, England.

CHAPTER 3

Uncertainty, risk, and chaos

James Juniper

I clarify the distinction between economic uncertainty and risk and consider the implications that both risk and uncertainty have for decision making and behavior. To this end, I review recent assessments of Keynes' views about the influence of probability over human conduct. Bill Gerrard, for example, has argued that the traditional "Keynes-as-philosopher" research has largely neglected probability theory. However, he goes on to criticize those Keynesian fundamentalists who assert that Keynes rejected the "probability calculus" out of hand as means of understanding economic behavior under uncertainty. Gerrard complains that this fundamentalist viewpoint offers a negative critique only and does not put forward a constructive alternative in its place. He demonstrates that new Keynesian scholarship has remedied this defect and proceeds to show how Keynes' early philosophical writings can be gainfully used to illuminate key arguments in later economic works like the *General Theory*.

I provide an outline of Gerrard's own framework to clarify the important difference among risk, uncertainty associated with chaotic systems, and the fundamental uncertainty associated with liquidity preference and the irreversibility of investment decisions. I suggest that this conceptual divergence must also, of necessity, be reflected in significant differences in analysis, econometric methodology, and also policy prescription.

In a related vein, Bayesian theorists have questioned the relevance of Frank Knight's original distinction between risk and uncertainty by interpreting the latter as a form of subjective risk.[1] These pernicious attempts to tame the untamable

[1] In private discussions, T. K. Rhymes has suggested to me that Frank Knight's original notion of uncertainty differs from that advanced by Keynes in the *Treatise*. Knight's notion was closer to the concept of uninsurable risk rather than the level of credence that agents have in their estimates of probability distributions. In this case, Knight's distinction probably has more affinities with the new Keynesian arguments about the significance of missing markets for contingent goods because of adverse selection, adverse incentive, moral hazard, and transactions costs, than with post-Keynesian arguments about fundamental uncertainty and the role of nominal contracts, conventions, rule-guided behavior, sentiments, and the irreversibility of investment.

have been competently criticized by Joachem Runde, who has demonstrated that liquidity preference is incompatible with Savage's canonical version of the Bayesian model. I show that Runde's critique illuminates the way in which the phenomenon of liquidity preference operates to prevent any gradual movement from a position of uncertainty to one of risk as subjective probabilities based on incomplete knowledge become more and more objective through some sort of evolutionary selection or learning process.

I go on to examine other forms of uncertainty associated with investment and technological change to question further the relevance of any risk-based probability calculus in this field. Finally, these applications are compared with recent attempts to use chaos theory as an alternative justification for government macroeconomic intervention. I raise a number of concerns about the fashionable and seductive attractions of chaos theory for the theorist and the policy maker, and then go on to consider some methodological and econometric issues raised by the existence of both uncertainty and chaos in economic systems.

1 Keynes on uncertainty – laying the foundations

For reasons of brevity I will not enter into all the subtleties and nuances of the debate that Keynes articulated in the *Treatise*, particularly in the celebrated Chap. 26. Other writers have provided admirable overviews to which the reader is referred (Gerrard 1994, Davidson 1991, Runde 1994). Keynes argued that the imperative to act rationally provides a justification for the determination of rational degrees of belief. An individual's preference for a more probable belief over alternative beliefs is always made with reference to action or conduct, implying that it is practical, not speculative, reason that operates in the application of probability to human affairs. Nevertheless, in many cases, because the goodness or worth of a particular action may not be numerically measurable or additive, the determination of the mathematical expectation of an outcome or event may not be possible or meaningful.[2]

Even when probabilities and worth are measurable, if only in an ordinal sense, any assessment must include both the weight of argument and the associated risk. The weight comprises both the amount of relevant evidence and the completeness of evidence. In other words, evidence determines the extent of our relative knowledge about the situation compared with the relative degree of our ignorance. Additional evidence may only confirm the extent of our relative ignorance about relevant processes and relationships rather than increase our

[2] In his 1911 paper, "The principal averages and the law of errors which lead to them," Keynes applied what has come to be known as the maximum likelihood method to argue that the mathematical expectation was not necessarily the most probable forecast but depended on the form of error associated with a particular probability distribution (Gerrard 1994).

level of confidence.[3] Furthermore, Keynes contended that any assessment of evidence must account for risk in the sense of the mathematical expectation of the loss attached to a particular action.

2 Keynes' discussion of short-run and long-run expectations

Gerrard demonstrates that Keynes' later economic writings display a strong sense of continuity in the presence of change – although practical empiricism replaces speculative reason, expectations still provide the link between earlier philosophical analysis and later economic research. In a manner analogous to the distinction made in the *Treatise* between mathematical expectation and weight, in the *General Theory* expectations depended not just on the most probable forecast but also on the state of confidence.

Keynes consistently distinguished between short-run and long-run expectations in the *General Theory*. The former were assumed to apply to pricing and output decisions, e.g., to the expected amount of proceeds that determine the position of the aggregate supply and aggregate demand curves. Keynes contended that the vagueness of probability distributions prevented the exact calculation of mathematical expectations and that awareness of vagueness changed the behavior of agents. Accordingly, for Keynes short-run expectations were subject to constant, gradual revisions and recently realized results were presumed to exercise the most influence over expectation formation simply because of the imperative to act. Keynes asserted that agents would assume that the future would be like the recent past unless reasons existed for thinking otherwise. Keynes believed that fluctuations in, or disappointments over, short-term expectations were only a source of frictional unemployment and argued that the relative frequency approach was often a reasonable presumption if sufficient stability in market conditions obtained.

Keynes argued that long-term expectations were influenced by two components – the most probable forecast and the state of confidence. Here, the latter was viewed as depending on both the size of the change and uncertainty about the precise form that changes would take. In other words, confidence was related to the concept of weight, not probability. In a manner similar to the determination of short-term expectation, Keynes believed that long-term expectations were also affected disproportionately by the recent past because of the conventional practice of projecting the existing situation into the future. Nevertheless, he asserted that the investment decision at any particular moment

[3] Keynes criticized Moore's position expounded in the *Principia Ethica* that growing ignorance was a justification for discounting future consequences relative to the present. Keynes argued that Moore was too attached to the relative frequencies view of probability, thereby ignoring the effect of uncertainty about the future on the weight of evidence (Gerrard 1994).

in time was a unique choice for which no relevant frequency distribution existed, not least because market conditions changed systematically over time. However, Keynes conceded that in stable conditions, comparability of probabilities might be reasonable for hypotheses of a similar type related to a similar choice system.

In this context Gerrard has convincingly argued the Keynesian notion of "animal spirits" as the spontaneous urge to action rather than inaction is most appropriately viewed as determined by the state of confidence rather than by some sort of nonrational motivation.

Gerrard summarizes Keynes' views on uncertainty by distinguishing among uncertainty, fundamental uncertainty, and risk based on two dimensions: the completeness or incompleteness of knowledge and the structural determinacy or indeterminacy of the choice situation. Perfect certainty, for example, implies complete knowledge of a structurally determinate choice situation. Uncertainty implies either limited knowledge of a structurally determinate situation or more or less knowledge of a structurally indeterminate situation. Chance uncertainty implies complete knowledge of long-run relative frequencies and is equivalent to what conventional economists define as risk.

According to Gerrard, Keynes argued that the propensity to act on expectations depends on credence. For instance, certainty implies complete credence and probabilities equal either zero or one, whereas risk implies complete credence (otherwise known as absolute degrees of belief) and probabilities (referred to as relative degrees of belief) that are long-run relative frequencies. In conditions of ambiguity there is less than complete credence, and, correspondingly, degrees of belief must reside somewhere between zero and one.

Here, Paul Davidson's use of the distinction between ergodic and nonergodic reality may be useful[4] (Davidson 1994). In ergodic environments agents either know the future in the sense of actuarial certainty equivalents, or, alternatively, their knowledge is incomplete in the short run because of bounded rationality. But in the latter case, it is presumed that subjective probabilities would ultimately converge to objective probabilities in the long run either because of the operation of certain learning processes or some form of Darwinian selection. However, in a nonergodic environment, knowledge is

[4] Paul Davidson argues that if a stochastic process is ergodic, then for an infinite realization, time and space averages will coincide; here, space averages are calculated from cross-sectional data at fixed points in time, whereas time averages are calculated from time-series data at a fixed realization. For finite realizations, the space and the time averages will gradually converge. The ergodic axiom is that space or time averages calculated from past data provide reliable estimates of the space averages that will exist at a future date. For a stationary process, the estimates of time averages do not vary with the historical calendar period under consideration. Nonstationarity is a sufficient but not a necessary condition for nonergodicity (Davidson 1994, p. 90).

Table 3.1. *Knightian/Keynesian uncertainty (Gerrard and Davidson)*

	Incomplete knowledge	Complete knowledge
Structurally determinant	Uncertainty (e.g., chaos)	Perfect certainty
Structurally indeterminant	Fundamental uncertainty (Type 2 or 3)	Risk (Type 1)

Immutable ergodic reality:

- Type 1: Agents know the future in the sense of actuarial certainty equivalents
- Type 2: Agents' knowledge of ergodic reality is incomplete in the short run because of bounded rationality
  - Subjective probabilities converge to objective probabilities through learning or Darwinian selection by the market of more rational techniques

Transmutable nonergodic reality:

- Type 3: Agents believe sufficient information does not exist to predict the future by means of frequency distribution
  - Relevant to decisions involving investment, finance, and the accumulation of wealth

intrinsically incomplete.[5] Davidson argues that nonergodic reality is a feature associated with all long-term decisions about investment and wealth creation, which:

"[i]mplies the possibility that there is a permanent and positive role for government in designing policies and institutions to provide results preferable to those that would be generated by competitive markets in a non-ergodic environment" (Davidson 1994).

To clarify these arguments, Table 3.1 merges Gerrard's exposition with that of Davidson.

The top right-hand quadrant of Table 3.1 represents an environment of perfect foresight, the most straightforward and simple assumption that can be made in economic analysis. Most orthodox theories presume an environment of

[5] This argument raises a series of issues that concern the relationship between cognition and reality. From a critical realist perspective the cognitive capabilities of agents come to operate as a part of the very mechanisms and structures that the human sciences are seeking to explain. Therefore, in addition to changes in sentiments or the breakdown of conventions and other institutional arrangements, fundamental uncertainty about events, in and of itself, can give rise to structural breaks and unpredictable changes in the relationships determining these same events. As such, variations in subjective cognition and attitudes can give rise to variations in objective processes and conditions, but causality also flows in the opposite direction. Keynes argued that for both reasons, economic processes were too changeable for aleatory notions of probability (based on the determination of relative frequencies) to apply with any degree of confidence to the world of human conduct. In this chapter it is henceforth assumed that uncertainty reflects structural changes both to subjective judgments and also to objective processes.

risk – represented by the bottom right-hand quadrant – in which economic agents can determine the optimal trade-off between variance and return for any transaction or group of transactions. In this quadrant, agents have complete knowledge of the future in the sense that outcomes can be described in terms of actuarially certain equivalents.

From the diagram, it is obvious that chaos theory occupies the top left-hand quadrant of the table – incomplete knowledge of a structurally determinant system. In the case of chaos, knowledge is incomplete because of the sensitivity of the system to initial conditions.

Grandmont has argued that the existence of nonlinear chaotic macroeconomic systems justifies a permanent and positive role for government (Grandmont 1985, 1987). In this context, the role of policy is to nudge the economy onto more preferable, but still attainable, trajectories or to manipulate key parameters to prevent any transition from systems with well-behaved and stable dynamics to ones subject to complex, chaotic dynamics.[6] Nevertheless, there are a number of grounds for caution about this justificatory resort to chaos theory that are examined in Section 6.

The bottom left-hand quadrant of Table 3.1 represents an environment in which agents have incomplete knowledge of a structurally indeterminant system. Many orthodox models allow for the existence of uncertainty in this sense but are predicated on the notion that knowledge that is initially incomplete can gradually become complete. It is this foundational principle of much neoclassical analysis that I now wish to interrogate.

3 Barriers to evolution from uncertainty to risk – the Bayesian conquest

A familiar version of the narrative that has knowledge evolving from incompleteness to completeness or actuarial certainty is grounded in the Bayesian notion that agents initially form subjective probabilities about uncertain economic events. Over time, these subjective probabilities are tested and improved on until they asymptotically approach the true objective probabilities associated with the relevant events.

A recent paper by Joachem Runde presents a rigorous critique of Bayesian attempts to tame uncertainty in this manner by placing it at one end of a

[6] More formally, intergenerational fiscal and monetary transfers flatten the intertemporal offer curve that obtains in the space spanned by real balances today and real balances tomorrow. These interventions have the potential to convert a system subject to chaotic cycles into a well-behaved one that monotonically converges onto a golden-rule steady state without cycles (see Rosser 1990). Of course, "... this requires not only that the government knows what it is doing, but that economic agents believe that the government knows what it is doing, a tall order indeed" (Rosser 1990, p. 279).

Table 3.2. *Runde's critique of Bayesian approach*

Degree of belief in h determined by agent's indifference between

- Certainty of b
- Two-way gamble between a if h, d if not h

$$u(b) = p(h)u(a) + [1 - p(h)]u(d)$$

- i.e.,

$$\text{hence } p(h) = \frac{u(b) - u(d)}{u(a) - u(d)}$$

Table 3.3. *Savage's canonical version of Bayesian model*

States	S_1	S_2	...	S_m
Acts	Outcomes			
a_1	c_{11}	c_{12}		c_{1m}
a_2	c_{21}	c_{22}		c_{2m}
...				
a_m	c_{n1}	c_{n2}		c_{nm}

continuum with subjective probabilities or "hunches" at one end and objective probabilities at the other. Ramsey, for example, represents the rational Bayesian agent's utility by a real-valued utility function (unique up to order and scale) defined over the set of possible consequences. If the agent is indifferent between the certainty of b on one hand and a two-way gamble between a if h obtains and d if not-h obtains, then his or her degree of belief in h $[p(h)]$ is equal to $[u(b) - u(d)]/[u(a) - u(d)]$. In other words, the probability of an event h is defined implicitly by the equivalence relation: $u(b) = p(h)u(a) + [1 - p(h)]u(d)$.

However, the agent is presumed to be perfectly definite in his or her valuations of the consequences and their associated probabilities, i.e., the calculated mathematical expectations. Runde contends that whereas Bayesians emphasize the agent's disposition to act (see Table 3.2), Keynes instead emphasizes inaction or the potential reversibility of actions (i.e., asset markets provide a means by which investors are saved from having to make irrevocable investment decisions). Whereas a bet promises a fixed net gain or loss when it is taken, assets can usually be liquidated when expectations are disappointed. Hence their attractiveness may depend on the way they function as a mechanism for transferring purchasing power through time onto other potentially lucrative, but yet to be determined, assets.

In Savage's canonical version of the Bayesian model, illustrated in Table 3.3, agents are assumed to choose from a set of acts $(a_1, a_2, \ldots, a_n)$, taking into

Table 3.4. *Runde continued*

Savage's canonical version of Bayesian model:

- Preference relations defined for any pair of acts
- Any assignment of consequences to states constitutes an act of liquidity preference
- Inaction as opposed to action
- Potential reversibility of actions
- Return on specific asset depends on characteristics of act
- Liquidity depends on counterexpected events
  - each state – other acts
  - each act – other states

i.e., formally, for any act a_i, the utility of any c_{ik} reflects a liquidity premium that is a function of

- a_js (j not equal to i)
- s_js (j not equal to k)

account the consequences (c_{ij}) of each act for each possible state of the world ($s_1, s_2, \ldots, s_m$). Preference relations are then defined for any pair of acts defined in this way. Any assignment of consequences to states constitutes an act but these consequences may not include a reference to features of any particular act, state, or choice problem.

However, liquidity considerations lead to violations of this "rectangular field" assumption. The return on a specific asset, for example, will depend on the particular characteristics of that asset (e.g., liquidity of houses and tractors versus bonds or equities). As shown in Table 3.4, Runde asserts that for each act liquidity will depend on counterexpected events, i.e., on how the situation would look if other states had obtained and what might have been for each state if a different act had been chosen.[7]

"More formally, for any act a_i the utility of every c_{ik} will reflect a liquidity premium that is a function of the s_j's ($j \neq k$) and the a_j's ($i \neq j$).... Liquidity and Keynes's notion of liquidity premium make it impossible to separate consequences from acts, states and particular choice problems in the way that the Bayesian model requires."

It should be noted that liquidity preference implies incomplete markets for contingent commodities, because of the impossibility of insuring against the capital loss arising from a potential collapse in asset prices, particularly for durable goods (Runde 1994). Hence it is impossible for optimizing agents to determine the appropriate trade-off between risk and return. It is frequently argued that the government should act as a second-best insurer where equity or

[7] On an equally fundamental level, Paul Davidson (1991) has questioned whether the full range of relevant states of nature can actually be determined by economic agents, let alone assigned an appropriate set of probabilities.

insurance markets operate inefficiently (e.g., the venture capital market) either because of problems of moral hazard and adverse selection or because firms face collateral constraints on their borrowing and suffer from a lack of reputation. This uncertainty perspective provides a compelling alternative to the traditional neoclassical market-failure justification for government intervention in capital markets.[8]

In conclusion, Runde argues that liquidity preference is less concerned with the choice between certain acts, each of which elicits varying outcomes depending on which randomly distributed states of nature come to pass, than with the choice of inaction over action or the potential irreversibility of actions.[9] Moreover, while the returns on assets depend on the specific characteristics of the act, he suggests that the magnitude of liquidity premia on various assets depends on uncertainty about the likely occurrence of counterexpected events:

> "In the Bayesian approach to choice under uncertainty an agent's degree of belief is a causal property of it, reflected in the extent that he or she is prepared to act on it. In the *General Theory*, in contrast, the emphasis is on uncertainty leading to investor inaction and on liquid assets making it possible to suspend judgment altogether, or at least to go for assets the consequences of which are not fixed and irrevocable. On the Keynesian view, then, the behavior of agents under uncertainty reflects their inability to form subjective point probabilities rather than something in which such probabilities are implicit."[10]

4 Additional arguments against convergence

In a paper on uncertainty that appears in the same publication as that of Runde, Davidson makes a distinction between what he calls the Keynes "productive efficiency gain," which is ensured through maintenance of effective demand, and what he calls the Schumpeter "creative destruction" efficiency gain, which arises because of the pressure exerted by sustained full employment on incentives for employers to search for more innovative means to raise productivity

[8] Foss has convincingly argued that similar notions of uncertainty inform Oliver Williamson's transactions cost theory and serve to distinguish Williamson's work from that of the more formal principal-agent and property-rights theorists (Foss 1994).

[9] The analysis of economic uncertainty and related fluctuations in liquidity preference underlie the post-Keynesian contention there can be no guarantee that the level of investment in a capitalist, monetary production economy will be sufficient to fully absorb growth in labor force, irrespective of the level attained by real wages (see Lavoie 1992 for an overview of this literature; also Rogers 1989 and Wray 1990, 1991, 1992).

[10] In a microeconomic study of industry types, Salais and Storper examine the modus operandi of firms producing with standardized technology for uncertain markets. They suggest that such firms are driven to contract out capacity to minimize the problems associated with the irreversibility of investment decisions and self-consciously point to analogies with the more general Keynesian notion of liquidity preference (Salais and Storper 1992).

and performance. This simple distinction serves to link post-Keynesian and Schumpeterian notions of uncertainty together in a policy context.[11]

In an environment subject to rapid technological change, long-run convergence of investors' subjective probabilities to objective probabilities (a gradual movement from a situation of uncertainty to one of risk) is precluded by the open-ended, unpredictable nature of innovation. Nevertheless, there can still be a strong guiding role for policy here though, because even if we cannot predict the emergence of novelty in products and processes, we can understand and strategically influence the cumulative processes of selection and generation of variety that are at play (Metcalfe 1995). This view of uncertainty is a common feature of work in the field of evolutionary economics (see Freeman 1995 for a comprehensive survey of this rapidly growing literature).

Another argument against the presumption that subjective probabilities will gradually converge onto objective probabilities is implicit in Scott's idiosyncratic interpretation of the new growth theory. Scott argues that investment activity both creates and reveals unpredictable opportunities for further investment. Hence agents cannot coordinate their activity or prepare to exploit these opportunities in advance. The marginal returns of latecomers will tend to fall below those of first movers who were fortunate enough to be in the right place at the right time. In this context, uncertainty not only precludes the possibility of any Coasian internalization of externalities but also acts as an obstacle to neoclassical stochastic optimization[12] (Scott 1989, 1992).

5 The family of real business-cycle models

Economic decisions generally take place within a noisy and turbulent environment. In one class of model, these turbulent and erratic processes have been viewed as arising within an otherwise deterministic system, which is subject to shocks from a series of random exogenous variables.

As Diebold and Rudebusch (1996, p. 68) argue, vector autoregressive analysis of comovement among typical business-cycle variables usually requires more degrees of freedom than are available in macroeoconomic samples. Factor or index-structure models allow for a reduction in the dimensionality of vector autoregressive representations of the cycle through a presumption that "... the co-movement of contemporaneous economic variables may be due to the fact that they are driven in part by common shocks."

[11] Alice Amsden has refined and applied Schumpeterian notions of uncertainty that are associated with technological change in her detailed historical analysis of South Korean development (Amsden 1989, 1990, 1994).

[12] Analogous arguments about inappropriable externalities have come to the fore in recent debates about coordination failure in the context of industrialization – the so-called "big-push" argument for intervention in development (Rodrik 1995, Matsuyama 1991, Murphy et al. 1989, Rosenstein-Rodan 1943).

Table 3.5. *Stock and Watson's dynamic factor model*

$$x_t = \beta + \lambda f_t + u_t$$

$$N \times 1 N \times 1 N \times 1 1 \times 1 N \times 1,$$

$$D(L)u_t = \varepsilon_t,$$

$$\phi(L)(f_t - \delta) = \eta_t$$

For example, Stock and Watson's (1991) dynamic factor model was developed for computing a composite index of coincident indicators (Diebold and Rudebusch 1996). In their model (Table 3.5), movements in the N macroeconomic variables of interest, x_t, are determined by changes in a one-dimensional unobserved common factor f_t and by the N-dimensional idiosyncratic component u_t.

Here, all idiosyncratic dynamics are driven by ε_t, whereas all common stochastic dynamics, which are embodied in the common factor, are driven by η.

Common factor structures arise in a variety of models, but are mostly associated with the linear-quadratic equilibrium models of the sort favored by real business-cycle theorists. Typically, in these models the stochastic component of the cycle is driven by a common Weiner process that gives rise to productivity and preference shocks that are linear transformations of the original process. The productivity shocks feed into a linear technology that yields a composite output of both consumption and investment goods. Shocks to preferences directly affect the functional relationships that determine intertemporal choices among work, leisure, savings, and consumption.

In another closely related class of optimizing models of the business cycle – so-called liquidity-effect models – money has effects on real asset prices and economic activity deriving from a temporary segmentation between goods and asset markets. Adjustments to the portfolio choices of households cannot be made instantaneously following innovations in monetary policy or shocks (see Grilli and Roubini 1996 for a recent overview). Liquidity-effect models generally assume that while goods prices adjust instantaneously, asset prices adjust gradually, whereas the opposite is assumed by sticky-price models.

Although this chapter cannot provide a comprehensive survey and assessment of these models, a recent paper by King and Watson (1996) represents a major contribution in the evaluation of competing business-cycle models. The authors compare three benchmark rational expectations models: a real business-cycle model with endogenous money, a sticky-price model with slow adjustment in commodity markets, and a liquidity-effect model with slow adjustment in portfolios, to determine how well they explain the observed relationship between money prices and interest rates.

Each model is built around a common core that features first a representative household choosing a plan for consumption and leisure that maximizes expected lifetime utility; second, a representative firm that chooses a plan for production, labor demand, and investment to maximize the expected present value of its real profits; and third, an economywide constraint equating income to the sum of consumption and investment (the models ignore fiscal interventions and international trade).

The real business-cycle model incorporates shocks to a money demand function and the Fisherian theory of real interest rate determination. The sticky-price model introduces monopolistic competition and lagged price adjustment. Derived labor demand is positively influenced by output and negatively by capital and productivity shocks. Finally, in the liquidity-effect model, at time t households, subject to a cash constraint (expenditure at time t must equal the sum of wage income and cash), select a portfolio of money to spend without knowing the date t values of relevant technology or money supply shocks.

After the shocks have occurred, households adjust their portfolios by balancing the value of having an additional unit of money to spend against the time costs of portfolio adjustment. Firms make investment and labor demand decisions, recognizing that households are constrained in spending the profits derived from their ownership of firms. Equilibrium is established through the joint actions of households, financial intermediaries, and firms (see King and Watson 1996, p. 42).

For simulation purposes, the driving process for each of the three models must be governed by as many innovations as there are endogenous variables (otherwise with forward-looking expectations the spectral density matrix is singular). This process is modeled as a vector autoregression (VAR) ($x = Q\delta$, where $\delta = \rho\delta_{-1} + h\xi$) with white-noise zero-mean residuals (ξ). Q varies with each model chosen such that the autocovariances of the driving variables match those of their relevant empirical counterparts. In addition, the VAR process is specified by use of a mixture of levels and differences to capture the integration characteristics of the data. Despite these efforts to ensure that the driving process faithfully captures the essential properties of real-world relationships and observations, overall, the authors conclude,

> "... that all prominent macroeconomic models – those which stress a single set of economic mechanisms – have substantial difficulties matching the core features of nominal and real interactions. Most strikingly, all of the models do a poor job at matching the interaction of real and nominal interest rates with real activity" (King and Watson 1996, p. 52).

For this reason, alternative models of the business cycle have attracted increasing interest from macroeconomic researchers. One candidate in this intensely competitive field is the set of endogenous business-cycle models that incorporate self-fulfilling expectations.

6 Chaos theory and models of endogenous expectations

In 1979, Benhabib and Nishimura's paper on optimal economic growth introduced chaos theory as an alternative framework, one that models the apparently random behavior as generated by endogenous competitive processes.

Endogenous business-cycle models have played an important part in the new Keynesian critique of both real business-cycle theory and its conservative conclusions about the ineffectiveness of systematic stabilization policy and the inefficiency of unsystematic stabilization policy (see Azariadis 1981, Cass and Shell 1983, and Rosser 1990 for useful surveys of recent issues in chaos theory).

In these models expectations are self-fulfilling in the sense that the beliefs of economic agents are viewed as determining which equilibrium will be selected from a multitude of possible equilibria. It is presumed that agents' beliefs are driven by an exogenous random factor labeled extrinsic uncertainty to distinguish it from the intrinsic uncertainty associated with unpredictable shocks to preferences, the money supply, endowments, or technology that is responsible for cyclical behavior in real business-cycle models. It should be emphasized that both of these notions of uncertainty are equivalent to what has been identified as risk in this chapter.

Azariadis (1981) and Cass and Shell (1983) have argued that the existence of either a contingent market on the source of extrinsic uncertainty or complete markets through all time, respectively, could eliminate self-fulfilling or "sunspot" equilibria. Nevertheless, in the real world of individuals with finite lives, imperfect bequests, and incomplete options markets, they have argued that this mechanism for the dissolution of chaos is highly improbable.

In the self-fulfilling expectations approach, equilibrium dynamics are determined by a process in which one steady-state outcome is selected from a multiplicity of *potential* equilibria by means of the intrinsic expectations mechanism. In a recent paper by Brock and Hommes, the selection mechanism common to members of the class of adaptively rational equilibrium dynamic (ARED) models is, apparently, less arbitrary.[13] Under the ARED, agents adapt their beliefs over time by choosing an optimal predictor function (rational or naive) from a set of different predictor functions in accordance with a publicly available performance or fitness measure that is based on observations of past performance. When prices are close to their steady-state values, the net information cost of the rational predictor is higher than that of the naive, short-memory or adaptive predictor. However, at prices far from the steady state, net information costs are reversed and the net benefits of using the rational predictor exceed those of the native predictor:

[13] I am grateful to an anonymous referee for drawing this paper to my attention.

"There is thus one 'centripetal force' of 'far-from-equilibrium' negative feedback when most agents use the sophisticated predictor and another 'centrifugal force' of 'near-equilibrium' positive feedback when all agents use the simple predictor. The interaction between these two opposing forces can lead to very complicated Adaptive Rational Equilibrium Dynamics when the intensity of choice to switch beliefs is high. In an unstable market with information costs for sophisticated predictors, local instability and irregular dynamics may thus be a feature of a fully rational notion of equilibrium" (Brock and Hommes 1997, p. 1060).

The mechanism described in this chapter, like related research by Chiarella (1992), Lux (1995), and Sethi (1996) (all cited in Brock and Hommes 1997), seems to have been inspired by the early catastrophe-theoretic analysis of instability in stock prices conducted by Zeeman and others in the 1980s. In Zeeman's work, switching of membership occurs between the camp of extrapolative "chartists" and that of the rational expectations "fundamentalists" in response to a widening or narrowing of the gap between market valuations and fundamental valuations of stock prices. Stock price trajectories move along a catastrophic manifold, alternatively collapsing and ballooning out after periods of relatively stable upward and downward adjustment. Nevertheless, the recent generation of ARED models elicits a far more complex array of dynamic equilibrium time paths than their catastrophe-theory-based predecessors.

As Brock and Hommes indicate (1997, p. 1061), their approach also has affinities with the Sante Fe Institute's research into "artificial economic life" – a set of experimental models built around large-scale parallel-processing simulation models – in which (nonhomogenous) agents are assumed to choose from a range of predictors in determining their financial positions: Each agent's choice of the optimal predictor is made through the application of a genetic algorithm (Arthur 1992, Arthur et al. 1996). Unsurprisingly, in this type of simulation model the more frequently financial positions are recalculated, the more likely it is that asset prices will exhibit turbulent or chaotic dynamics.

The Institute's approach to artificial intelligence has recently been critically evaluated by Sent (1996, 1997), who focuses on the characteristics that distinguish it from the satisficing, sequential, symbolic logic approach of researchers like Hal Simon. Sent argues that the latter's approach is more congruent with what is revealed about the characteristics of human cognitive processes in psychological research.

A similar notion of asset-price instability appears in the literature on noise trading (Shliefer and Vishny 1990). In noise-trading models, because rational arbitrageurs are constrained by short-term investment horizons they cannot hold long-duration assets over a time period that is sufficient for prices to return to their fundamental values. Because of institutionally imposed investor myopia, rational arbitrage is not complete, and the prices of long-duration assets, or those with relatively uncertain returns, are buffeted by alternating waves of optimistic and pessimistic sentiment. However, these models are to be distinguished from their ARED counterparts, insofar as it is the behavior of irrational noise traders that is responsible for the deviation of asset prices away from their fundamental values and not net information costs.

The objective in this chapter, however, is to once again clarify the distinction between these neoclassical or new Keynesian approaches (rational or irrational) and the heterodox approach of theorists like Davidson (1988, 1991), who emphasize the role played by either numerically indeterminate and noncomparable probability relations on nonergodic stochastic processes. Just because operational calculations may be impossible or meaningless in this context, this does not lead to the inevitable conclusion that indeterminacy, noncomparability, and nonergodicity must be denied on the basis of what must be ontologically presupposed to justify any rigorous scientific investigation of economic events. On the contrary, it behooves us, as economists, to comprehend fully and rigorously the implications of uncertainty, in the post-Keynesian or Knightian sense, for economic decision making and behavior.

7 Econometric estimation of endogenous business-cycle models

In econometric terms, endogenous business-cycle models are members of a broader class of regime-switching models in which cycles are characterized by a systematic switching between a finite number of better or worse states. Regime switching can also arise in macroeconomic models that incorporate either game-theoretic strategic complementarities and spillovers or externalities associated with learning-by-doing and search behavior (see Diebold and Rudebusch 1996, p. 71, for a brief survey).

To provide some insight into the nature of these regime-switching models, it is worthwhile considering a recent paper by Garcia and Perron, who present estimates of a three-state model for the U.S. real interest rate over the period from 1961 to 1986 that utilizes an autoregressive specification of the order of 2 (Garcia and Perron 1996):

$$y_t - \mu(S_t) = \phi_1[y_{t-1} - \mu(S_{t-1})] + \phi_2[y_{t-2} - \mu(S_{t-2})] + \sigma(S_t)\varepsilon_t,$$

where the mean μ and the standard deviation σ of the process depend on the regime that operates at time t, indexed by S_t, a discrete-valued variable, and ε_t is a sequence of independent identically distributed $N(0, 1)$ random variables. Following Hamilton (1988, 1989, 1990), S_t is modeled as the outcome of an unobserved discrete-time, discrete-three-state Markov process, where S_t can take the values of 0, 1, or 2 in accordance with the following transition probability matrix:

$$P = \begin{bmatrix} P_{00} & P_{01} & P_{02} \\ P_{10} & P_{11} & P_{12} \\ P_{20} & P_{21} & P_{22} \end{bmatrix},$$

where $P_{ij} = \Pr[S_t = j \mid S_{t-1}]$ with $\sum_{j=0}^{2} P_{ij} = 1$ for all i.

A linear specification is used for the state-dependent means and variances:

$$\mu(S_t) = a_0 + a_1 S_{1t} + a_2 S_{2t},$$
$$\sigma(S_t) = \omega_0 + \omega_1 S_{1t} + \omega_2 S_{2t},$$

where S_{it} takes value 1 when S_t is equal to i and 0 otherwise. This allows the first equation to be rewritten as

$$y_t = a_0 + a_1 S_{1t} + a_2 S_{2t} + z_t,$$
$$z_t = \phi_1 z_{t-1} + \phi_2 z_{t-2} + (\omega_0 + \omega_1 S_{1t} + \omega_2 S_{2t})\varepsilon_t.$$

The authors apply Hamilton's nonlinear filter, which operates recursively much like the more familiar Kalman filter, to yield the likelihood function for the y_t, the so-called filter probabilities of being in state 0, 1, or 2 at time t, given the information available at time t, and also the more accurate smoothed probabilities that use information available at time $t + 1$, $t + 2$, etc., up to the end of the sample.

Garcia and Perron (1996, pp. 118–123) perform various misspecification tests to determine the appropriate number of states, judge whether different autoregressive structures arise within different regimes, investigate the presence of any remaining heteroskedasticity in the residuals, and confirm the existence of structural changes in the relevant series over all possible break points. They conclude that the ex post real interest rate is essentially random with means and variances that are different for the periods 1961–1973, 1973–1980, and 1980–1986. However, within each period the interest rate is reasonably constant, supporting traditional arguments for mean reversion.[14]

Nevertheless, in practice empirical investigations of regime switching rarely apply any underlying causal or structural mechanisms beyond the Markov process. In the absence of universally accepted equations of motion, these econometric studies amount to a sophisticated form of empiricism. Although different regimes can be identified, there is no guarantee that the same Markov process will continue to govern switching between regimes or that the same state-dependent autoregressive processes will continue to determine the realization of key endogenous variables, or for that matter, that the linear relationship between state-dependent means and variances will be preserved over time. This

[14] In an effort to bridge the two camps of real business-cycle and endogenous business-cycle theory, Diebold and Rudebusch's paper, discussed above, proposes an integration of common factor and regime-switching models of economic processes. To this end, they analyze the U.S. Commerce Department's modified Composite Coincident Index and its individual indicators reasoning that their dynamics are well approximated by a two-regime Markov switching model. Their results infer that one regime is significantly negative whereas the other is significantly positive, within state dynamics display substantial persistence, expansion durations are longer than contraction durations, and that the timing of contractionary states accords well with the professional consensus on business-cycle history (1996, pp. 73–76).

controversial position has to be justified in more detail. In particular, the chaos-theoretic foundations of self-fulfilling expectations models of regime switching must be exposed to further interrogation.

8 Chaos-theoretic models – an epistemological critique

In reference to the burgeoning economic research into qualitative dynamics, Bausor has cautioned that

> "[m]uch of this literature seeks to demonstrate the possibility of deterministic chaos in overlapping generations models of competitive processes, referring to Li and Yorke (1975) to argue the generality of chaotic motion. Since much of it refers to 'toy' examples such as the logistic (Day 1982, Baumol and Quandt 1985) or the Lorentz equations (Benhabib and Day 1981), however, they serve more to illustrate hypothetical possibilities than to compel scientific acceptance. Deep *economic* motivation for the particular equations of motion have not been readily forthcoming" (Bausor 1994).

Bausor contends, for example, that there is nothing in economic theory that is strictly analogous to the fundamental role played by the Navier–Stokes equations in hydrodynamics. The absence of generally accepted equations of motion detracts from the value of efforts to analyze the highly complex and chaotic behavior of trajectories around degenerate points in the manifold that surrounds bifurcations. In addition, he suggests that economists are generally unwilling to relinquish the security afforded by their assumption that global stability conditions (e.g., associated with the Liapunov function) usually obtain (e.g., see Arrow et al. 1959, cited in Bausor 1994). Moreover, unlike researchers into fluid dynamics, economists are also denied the luxury of access to laboratory experimentation. For these reasons Bausor concludes that

> "[w]ithout confidence that particular differential equations adequately model the true motion of competitive processes, no great scientific compulsion to trust much to its particular bifurcation structure emerges. The logistic and the Lorenz equations may be mathematically intriguing, but that alone is insufficient for them to become vital to economics."

Bausor suggests that the indeterminacy of such analysis has resulted in a considerable flurry of empirical work designed to distinguish deterministic chaos from random stochastic variation in time series (Brock 1987, Brock and Dechert 1988, Barnett and Chen 1988). From his review of these empirical studies Bausor argues that the inconclusiveness of results arising from the application of techniques such as the Grassberger–Procaccia tests is inevitable because

> "... these techniques cannot isolate bifurcations, since they presume all the data arise from the same side of a structural instability. Since they test for motion on a strange

attractor, they necessarily cannot adjudicate whether or not the dynamic system has undergone a bifurcation during the time span covered by the data, thereby perhaps creating or destroying such a hypothetical attractor. Empirical methods presuming one qualitative type of motion cannot be used identify transitions between qualitatively distinct phases. . . . The parameter rigidity required for these empirical tests cannot cope with bifurcations of the flow. Moreover, these methods cannot identify the underlying equations of motion, which is necessary for the scientific pursuit of qualitative economic dynamics."

These criticisms notwithstanding, the theoretical arguments about uncertainty outlined above suggest further and more fundamental grounds for pessimism about the move toward chaos theory. I have argued above that Grandmont's justifications for government intervention are based on the adverse effects of a form of uncertainty associated with incomplete knowledge of structurally determinant, chaotic systems. In such cases, completeness of knowledge is precluded because of the extreme sensitivity of the system to initial conditions. However, if most longer-term economic decisions are actually made in the context of fundamental uncertainty rather than chaotic uncertainty, a range of different approaches may be required for successful theoretical development and empirical investigation.

9 Methodological approaches to situations of fundamental uncertainty

One possible contender in the methodological race to develop techniques for studying nonequilibrium dynamics has been proposed by Foster and Wild in a series of recent papers (Foster 1992, 1993; Foster and Wild 1995a, 1995b). Foster and Wild argue that evolutionary models of endogenous growth and self-organization deal with cumulative and nonequilibrium processes (1995a). Such systems are best viewed as hierarchical, but interlinked through flows of energy, information, or money. Each subsystem within the hierarchy faces a boundary constraint that influences its development trajectory and may act as a source of nonlinear discontinuity.

For the analysis of such systems, Foster and Wild favor the adoption of a modified logistic equation whose trajectory can be influenced by two sets of parameters (1995a). One set influences the net rate of growth of the variable under investigation in a simple additive fashion at all points on the trajectory, whereas another set influences the capacity limit or asymptote of the diffusion process. Lagged dependent variables can also be included in the regression equation to allow for partial hysteresis effects (i.e., positive feedback oscillations).

Unlike the cointegration and error correction modeling approach, there is no prior assumption that the diffusion process can simply be separated into a long-run equilibrium and a short-run disequilibrium component. In contrast, as the diffusion process nears the relevant capacity constraint dissipative forces may be released associated with uncertainty, structural change and breakdown. To identify the existence and influence of such dissipative forces Foster and Wild (1995b) propose the use of time-varying spectral methods of analysis (e.g., Tukey and Parzen windows that move along the time series) that measure changes in the total variance or power of the process or identify regions of nonstationarity or shifts in the spectral decomposition.

Nevertheless, there is a more basic issue at stake here. If Keynes' analysis of the closed economy in the *General Theory* is essentially correct, a long-period, involuntary unemployment equilibrium could eventuate, conditioned by the psychological propensity to consume, the psychological attitude to liquidity, the psychological expectation of the yield on capital, and the policy stance of the monetary authority. Such an equilibrium, represented by the intersection of the aggregate demand and aggregate supply curves at the point of effective demand, would be stable in the sense that both short- and long-run expectations would be satisfied and not liable to adjustment (see Rogers 1989, Chap. 10).

In the *General Theory*, Keynes postulated that increasing uncertainty would be reflected in a higher level of liquidity preference. As a result, the demand or spot price of capital goods could fall below their future or supply price, leading to a collapse in investment. By means of the multiplier, the contraction in investment would lower aggregate demand, shifting the point of effective demand inward. It could take some time for expectations of proceeds to adjust to their new long-run position. In contrast to chaotic models of sunspot equilibria it is not so much a question of self-fulfilling expectations, but more a question of heightened uncertainty leading to fears of capital loss that become validated as agents reduce their demand for illiquid and more durable assets. In other words, uncertainty that is due to concerns about future, possibly adverse, movements in asset prices becomes self-validating.

At first sight, it would appear that the identification and the modeling of such an equilibrium could be achieved with traditional econometric techniques based on short-run adjustment to a long-run steady state without the need to resort to spectral methods. The latter would then have more limited applicability either to conditions of high uncertainty and instability of expectations or to a more localized microeconomic analysis of unpredictable technological change and market growth.

However, recent efforts to integrate post-Keynesian monetary theory with both dynamic models of financial instability and Kaleckian models in which the growth process is driven by fluctuations in income distribution (see Sarantis 1993) are grounded in a conviction that periods of stability may be self-destructive (see Lavoie 1995 and Palley 1995, Chap. 12). These theoretical developments favor the development and the application of more sophisticated econometric techniques that can accommodate regime switching from periods of relative stability – not precluding the operation of various short-run adjustment processes – to periods of rising uncertainty and perhaps chaotic, if not catastrophic, financial instability.

On the one hand, the techniques proposed by Foster, despite their somewhat ad hoc methodological underpinnings, could be used to identify structural breaks and periods of dissipative breakdown, whereas, on the other hand, standard time-series techniques, including cointegration methods, could be successfully applied, but only to processes operating during periods of relative stability.[15]

10 Conclusion

Periods of increasing uncertainty would reflect both a lowering of confidence in the subjective probability distributions that agents assign to economic events and structural changes in objective processes. In response, agents would more often choose inaction or act in a more cautious manner to minimize the less predictable adverse consequences of the irreversibility of their actions.

Keynesian notions of liquidity preference that view it as a response to fundamental uncertainty rather than risk have the implication that regime switching is not adequately captured by stable Markov processes that govern the state-dependent moments of endogenous variables. This is because regime switching is perceived to be driven by a complex array of conditioning variables that include changes in institutional arrangements, fluctuations in investor, saver, and financier sentiment, and transmutations in economic conventions. As a result, a continuum of liquidity preference states may arise that will have unpredictable and differential effects over investment, savings, and financial behavior.

The wide range of dynamic mechanisms operating at both the microeconomic and macroeconomic level can be only theoretically captured by models that, at times, allow for convergence onto a stable equilibrium (albeit, perhaps to one of a multitude of possible equilibria), and at other times, reveal forces that give rise to dissipative forces combining convergent, divergent, chaotic, catastrophic, and limit cycle trajectories. At times, agents' expectations may be elastic and at other times, inelastic or even self-fulfilling.

In this context, policy interventions must be viewed as not only influencing structural variables but also as directly influencing uncertainty and hence the assumed and actual pattern of risk in the economy. Accordingly, econometric tests for structural breaks will uncover changes that are occurring to both the

[15] For example Watts and Mitchell (1990 and 1991) apply cointegrating regression techniques, presuming the operation of post-Keynesian mechanisms in labor markets, whereas Sarantis (1993) uses instrumental variable techniques to estimate a Kaleckian open-economy model of accumulation including a variable to account for additional capacity-related constraints on employment.

underlying economic mechanisms, the associated subjective probabilities of agents, and also the objective probabilities embodied in economic phenomena. No one econometric approach can hope to represent this complex and ever-changing reality. More sophisticated techniques of econometric *bricollage* must be developed in conjunction with ever more complex theoretical models that do not impose unnecessary constraints on either the stochastic nature of economic phenomena or agents' expectations.[16]

REFERENCES

Amsden, A. (1994). Why isn't the whole world experimenting with the East–Asian model to develop: review of *The East Asian Miracle*. *World Dev.*, **22**, 627–33.

Amsden, A. E. (1989). *Asia's Next Giant: South Korea and Late Industrialization*, Oxford University Press, London.

(1990). Third World industrialization: 'Global Fordism' or a new model? *New Left Rev.*, No. 182, July–August, 5–31.

Arrow, K. J., Block, H. D., and Hurwicz, L. (1959). On the stability of the competitive equilibrium II. *Econometrics*, **27**, 82–109.

Arthur, B. (1992). On learning and adaptation in the economy. Sante Fe Institute Paper 92-07-038, Santa Fe Institute, Santa Fe, NM.

Arthur, B., Holland, J., LeBaron, B., Palmer, R., and Tayler, P. (1996). Asset pricing under endogenous expectations in an artificial stock market. Sante Fe Institute Working Paper 96-12-093, Santa Fe Institute, Santa Fe, NM.

Azariadis, C. (1981). Self-fulfilling prophecies. *J. Econ. Theor.*, **25**, 380–96.

Barnett, W., and Chen, P. (1988). The aggregation-theoretic monetary aggregates are chaotic and have strange attractors. In *Dynamic Econometric Modeling*, Proceedings of the Third International Symposium in Economic Theory and Econometrics, eds. W. Barnett, E. Berndt, and H. White, Cambridge University Press, New York.

Baumol, W. J., and Quandt, R. E. (1985). Chaos models and the implications for forecasting. *East. Econ. J.*, **11**, 3–15.

Bausor, R. (1994). Qualitative dynamics in economics and fluid dynamics: a comparison of recent applications. In *Natural Images in Economic Thought: Markets Read in Tooth and Claw*, ed. P. Mirowski, Cambridge University Press, Cambridge, England, pp. 109–27.

Benhabib, J., and Day, R. H. (1981). Rational choice and erratic behavior. *Rev. Econ. Stud.*, **48**, 459–71.

Benhabib, J., and Nishimura, K. (1979). The Hopf bifurcation and the existence and stability of closed orbits in multisectoral models of optimal economic growth. *J. Econ. Theor.*, **21**, 421–44.

[16] In an interesting and original paper, Ferderer (1993) has utilized deviations in forecasters' point predictions to calculate a synthetic measure of uncertainty that he incorporates into two otherwise traditional regression equations explaining fluctuations in investment activity. Essentially, this interesting attempt to capture uncertainty assumes that only subjective and not objective probability distributions are influenced by variations in uncertainty. Unfortunately, no tests of structural change are reported. The results "suggest that uncertainty about future interest rates are a more powerful determinant of investment spending than is the level of interest rates" (Ferderer, 1993, p. 31).

Brock, W. A. (1987). Distinguishing random and deterministic systems: abridged version. In *Nonlinear Economic Dynamics*, ed. J. M. Grandmont, Academic, New York [originally published in *Journal of Economic Theory* **40** (1986)].

Brock, W. A., and Dechert, W. D. (1988). Theorems on distinguishing deterministic from random systems. In *Dynamic Econometric Modeling*, Proceedings of the Third International Symposium in Economic Theory and Econometrics, eds. W. Barnett, E. Berndt, and H. White, Cambridge University Press, Cambridge, England.

Brock, W. A., and Hommes, C. H. (1997). A rational route to randomness, *Econometrica*, **65**, 1059–95.

Cass, D., and Shell, K. (1983). Do sunspots matter? *J. Polit. Econ.*, **91**, 193–227.

Chiarella, C. (1992). The dynamics of speculative behavior. *Ann. Oper. Res.*, **37**, 101–23.

Davidson, P. (1994). Uncertainty in economics. In *Keynes, Knowledge and Uncertainty*, eds. S. Dow and J. Hillier, Elgar, Aldershot, England.

(1991). Is probability theory relevant for uncertainty: a post-Keynesian perspective. *J. Econ. Perspect.*, **5**, 129–43.

(1988). A technical definition of uncertainty and the long-run non-neutrality of money. *Cambridge J. Econ.*, **12**, 329–37.

Day, R. H. (1982). Irregular growth cycles. *Am. Econ. Rev.*, **72**, 406–14.

Diebold, F. X., and Rudebusch, G. D. (1996). Measuring business cycles: a modern perspective. *Rev. Econ. Stat.*, **78**(1), 67–77.

Ferderer, J. P. (1993). Does uncertainty affect investment spending? *J. Post-Keynesian Econ.*, **16**.

Foss, N. J. (1994). The two Coasian traditions. *Rev. Polit. Econ.*, **6**, 37–61.

Foster, J. (1992). The determination of Sterling M3, 1963–88: an evolutionary macroeconomic approach. *Econ. J.*, **102**, 481–96.

(1993). Economics and the self-organization approach: Alfred Marshall revisited? *Econ. J.*, **103**, 975–91.

Foster, J., and Wild, P. (1995a). The logistic diffusion approach to econometric modeling in the presence of evolutionary change. Department of Economics, Discussion Papers, No. 181, September, The University of Queensland, Queensland, Australia.

(1995b). The application of time-varying spectra to detect evolutionary change in economic processes. Department of Economics, Discussion Papers, No. 182, September, The University of Queensland, Queensland, Australia.

Freeman, C. (1994). The "National System of Innovation" in historical perspective. *Cambridge J. Econ.*, **18**, 463–514.

(1995). Critical survey: the economics of technical change. *Cambridge J. Econ.*, **18**, 5–24.

Garcia, R., and Perron, P. (1996). An analysis of the real interest rate under regime shifts. *Rev. Econ. Stat.*, **78**(1), 111–25.

Gerrard, W. (1994). Probability, uncertainty and behavior: a Keynesian perspective. In *Keynes, Knowledge and Uncertainty*, eds. S. Dow and J. Hillier, Elgar, Aldershot, England.

Grandmont, J. M. (1985). On endogenous competitive business cycles. *Econometrica*, **53**, 995–1096.

(1987). Stabilizing competitive business cycles. In *Nonlinear Economic Dynamics*, ed. J. M. Grandmont, Academic, New York.

Grilli, V., and Roubini, N. (1996). Liquidity models in open economies: theory and empirical evidence. *Eur. Econ. Rev.*, **40**, 847–59.

Hamilton, J. D. (1988). Rational expectations econometric analysis of changes in regimes: an investigation of the term structure of interest rates. *J. Econ. Dyn. Control*, **12**, 385–423.

(1989). A new approach to the economic analysis of non-stationary time-series and the business cycle. *Econometrica*, **57**, 357–84.

(1990). Analysis of time-series subject to changes in regime. *J. Economet.*, **45**, 39–70.

Juniper, J. (1993). The production systems debate, work organization and management practices. Faculty of Business and Management, Working Paper Series, No. 10, June, University of South Australia, Adelaide.

King, R. G., and Watson, M. W. (1996). Money, prices, interest rates and the business cycle. *Rev. Econ. Stat.*, **78**(1), 35–53.

Lavoie, M. (1992). *Foundations of Post-Keynesian Economic Analysis*, Elgar, Aldershot, England.

(1995). Interest rates in post-Keynesian models of growth and distribution. Department of Economics, Seminar Papers, No. 4/95, Monash University, Melbourne, Australia.

Li, T. Y., and Yorke, J. A. (1975). Period three implies chaos. *Am. Math. Mon.*, **82**, 895–992.

Lux, T. (1995). Herd behavior, bubbles and crashes. *Econ. J.*, **105**, 881–96.

Matsuyama, K. (1991). Increasing returns, industrialization and indeterminacy of equilibrium. *Q. J. Econ.*, **106**, 617–50.

Metcalfe, J. S. (1995). Technology systems and technology policy in an evolutionary framework. *Cambridge J. Econ.*, **19**, 25–46.

Murphy, K., Schliefer, A., and Vishny, R. (1989). Industrialization and the big-push. *J. Polit. Econ.*, **97**, 1003–26.

Palley, T. (1995). *Post-Keynesian Macroeconomics*, Elgar, Aldershot, England.

Rodrik, D. (1995). Getting interventions right: how South Korea and Taiwan grew rich. *Econ. Policy*, **21**, 55–107.

Rogers, C. (1989). *Money, Interest and Capital: A Study in the Foundations of Monetary Theory*, Cambridge University Press, Cambridge, England.

Rosenstein-Rodan, P. (1943). Problems of industrialization of Eastern and South- Eastern Europe. *Econ. J.*, **53**, 202–211.

Rosser, J. B. Jr. (1990). Chaos theory and the new Keynesian economics. *The Manchester School*, **48**, 265–91.

Runde, J. (1994). Risk, uncertainty and Bayesian decision theory: a Keynesian view. In *Keynes, Knowledge and Uncertainty*, eds. S. Dow and J. Hillard, Elgar, Aldershot, England.

Salais, R., and Storper, M. (1992). The four 'worlds' of contemporary industry. *Cambridge J. Econ.*, **16**, 169–93.

Sarantis, N. (1993). Distribution, aggregate demand and unemployment in OECD countries. *Econ. J.*, **103**, 459–67.

Scott, M. F. G. (1989). *A New View of Economic Growth*, Clarendon, Oxford, England.

(1992). A new theory of endogenous growth. *Oxford Rev. Econ. Policy*, **8**(4), 29–42.

Sent, E. M. (1996). Convenience: the mother of all rationality in Sargent. *J. Post-Keynesian Econ.*, **19**, 3–34.

(1997). Sargent versus Simon: bounded rationality unbound. *Cambridge J. Econ.*, **17**, 323–38.

Shliefer, A., and Vishny, R. W. (1990). Equilibrium short horizons of investors and firms. *AEA Papers and Proceedings*, **80**(2), 148–65.

Stock, J. H., and Watson, M. W. (1991). A probability model of the coincident economic indicators. In *Leading Economic Indicators: New Approaches and Forecasting Records*, eds. K. Lahiri and H. Geoffrey, Cambridge University Press, New York, pp. 63–90.

Watts, M., and Mitchell, W. (1990). Australian wage inflation: real wage resistance, hysteresis and incomes policy: 1968(3)–1988(3). *The Manchester School*, **58**, 142–64.

(1991). Alleged instability of the Okun's Law relationship in Australia: an empirical analysis. *Appl. Econ.*, **23**, 1829–38.

Wray, L. R. (1990). *Money and Credit in Capitalist Economies: The Endogenous Money Approach*, Elgar, Aldershot, England.

(1991). Boulding's balloons: a contribution to monetary theory. *J. Econ. Iss.*, **25**, 1–20.

(1992). Alternative theories of the rate of interest. *Cambridge J. Econ.*, **16**, 69–89.

CHAPTER 4

The role of innovation in economics

Russell K. Standish

Comparative statics is a special case of dynamics in which a unique stable equilibrium is assumed to exist, and two equilibria – determined by different parameter values – are compared. Similarly, dynamics is a special case of an evolutionary process, in which the degrees of freedom of the system are held constant. Marshall, whose *Principles* played a large role in setting economics on the comparative statics course, was nonetheless aware of the primacy of the evolutionary paradigm when he wrote that

"the Mecca of the economist lies in economic biology rather than in economic dynamics. But biological conceptions are more complex than those of dynamics; a volume on Foundations must therefore give a relatively large place to mechanical analogies; and frequent use of the term 'equilibrium,' which suggest something of a statical analogy. . . . The modern mathematician is familiar with the notion that dynamics includes statics. If he can solve a problem dynamically, he seldom cares to solve it statically also. . . . But the statical solution has claims of its own. It is simpler than the dynamical; it may afford useful preparation and training for the more difficult dynamical solution; and it may be the first step towards a provisional and partial solution in problems so complex that a complete dynamical solution is beyond our attainment" (Marshall 1920, p. xiv).

At the time Marshall penned these words, Darwin's theory of evolution had captured the scientific and public imagination. It defined state-of-the-art biology at the time, but although it had enormous explanatory power, the theory had little predictive power. By contrast, the dynamics of the time (nowadays called classical dynamics) had been refined over the previous two centuries, culminating in the work of Laplace and Poincarè. This theory had enormous predictive value, so much so that the prevalent view was that if the initial states were known precisely, the behavior of the system could be predetermined for all time.

One century later, intellectual progress has enabled us to contemplate the construction of evolutionary models of processes that could once be modeled only statically. It is not surprising that Marshall, faced with the problem of understanding the world of human affairs and having two such starkly different world views available, would claim that economics is better understood as a biological (meaning evolutionary) system. Now, a century later, a bridge is being built between these two world views. This leads to the possibility of a predictive economics that is cognizant of its evolutionary heredity.

Progress in the understanding of ecology illustrates this point. Until the 1970s, ecology was studied statically, and early ecological theories followed a path of development similar to that of economic theory. Interactions between organisms were studied in order to determine the population densities that kept the ecology in equilibrium, and the only form of dynamics considered was instantaneous movement from one equilibrium to another. It was always assumed that an ecology was always near a stable equilibrium, in spite of counterexamples such as the stable limit cycles in the Lotka–Volterra predator–prey system (Maynard-Smith 1974).

In the 1960s, interest in dynamical systems was reawakened, and the study of chaos was born. These techniques were applied to ecology in the 1970s, and it was realized that the situation was vastly more complicated, with not only limit cycles being possible, but also entities called strange attractors. Over the years, appreciation has grown that the stable equilibrium is more of an exception than the norm.

In the mid-1980s, Raup and Sepkowski (1986) noticed certain statistical regularities with the pattern of speciation and extinction in the fossil record. These were later shown to be in the form of a power law (Bascompte and Sole 1996, Newman 1996), i.e., the pattern of extinctions was such that the frequency of an extinction event of size x is proportional to x^{-a}, where a is a small positive constant. Power laws crop up in many different areas (Schroeder 1991).

Bak (Bak et al. 1988) studied a model of a sandpile that had a continuous stream of sand added to the top. Bak's process goes by the name of self-organized criticality, and he, along with Kauffman (Kauffman 1993), promotes this as an explanation for Raup's data. It now seems likely that evolution is an endogenously self-organized critical process[1] that obeys a power-law spectrum.

In my work, which I introduce later, I have demonstrated the existence of self-organized criticality in a model evolutionary ecology. The criticality is quite a robust feature over a wide range of input parameters. This indicates that that evolutionary systems are typically endogenously critical.

[1] Alternatively, perhaps exogenous influences (such as volcanos, meteorites, climatic fluctuations, supernovae, etc.) obey a power-law spectrum. It is quite possible that both endogenous and exogenous effects contribute to the statistical properties of biological evolution and that a future research program will look at untangling the two effects. To this effect, Newman (1997) provides an interesting perspective.

In summary, we have a hierarchy of approaches, from the static to the dynamic to the evolutionary:

$$\text{statics} \subset \text{dynamics} \subset \text{evolution}.$$

The state of ecological thought has followed this chain from left to right, as computational techniques have improved to embrace the computationally more difficult dynamical models, and then the even more computationally difficult evolutionary models. It is to be hoped that the same path will be followed by economic modeling. It is perhaps a truism that economics and ecology must have something in common. After all, ecology is all about the distribution of resources – energy, material, territory etc. – just as economics deals with much the same problems in the human sphere, albeit with the added complications of money and prices. In biology, the fundamental theoretical plank is the theory of evolution,[2] as initiated by Darwin, and developed considerably throughout this century. Evolutionary theory is built on the twin strands of mutation and ecology. Mutation provides the natural variation on which natural selection, the outcome of ecological interactions, acts. Just as ecology is a central component of biological evolution, so is economics an equally important component of technological and economic evolution.

There is a clear parallel between the development of ecological thought and that of economic thought. Dynamics was introduced to economics and championed by Kaldor and Goodwin et al. in the 1950s and 1960s, and boosted by the developments in nonlinear analysis in the 1980s through the work of people like Blatt (Blatt 1983). This volume testifies to a growing industry of dynamical economic modeling. However, perhaps now is the time to embark on the next rung up the ladder and approach economics from an evolutionary point of view. Then perhaps we might be catching a glimpse of the Mecca that Marshall referred to a hundred years ago.

This paper first considers a general dynamical system undergoing evolution of the determining equation, then outlines *Ecolab*, a model of species interaction undergoing evolution, finally introducing a possible economics model based on the von Neumann model with evolution of the interaction coefficients.

1 Linearization of a dynamical system

Our launchpad for a theory of evolutionary systems is dynamical systems theory (Hirsch and Smale 1974). Typically this will be manifested in a first-order nonlinear differential equation of the form

$$\dot{\mathbf{x}} = \mathbf{f}(\mathbf{x}),$$

[2] Evolution of species is a fact, as testified by the fossil record. However, there are also theories of evolution, which attempt to explain that fact.

where $\mathbf{x} \in \Re^n$ and $\mathbf{f} : \Re \to \Re$. The dot refers to the derivative with respect to time.

Dynamical systems theory starts by considering the equilibria of the system, i.e., the points $\hat{\mathbf{x}}$ such that $\mathbf{f}(\hat{\mathbf{x}}) = 0$. Then in the neighborhood of $\hat{\mathbf{x}}$, the behavior of the system is determined by the linear approximation

$$\dot{\mathbf{x}} = \mathbf{Df}|_{\hat{\mathbf{x}}} \cdot (\mathbf{x} - \hat{\mathbf{x}}).$$

The stability of $\hat{\mathbf{x}}$ is determined by the negative definiteness of $\mathbf{Df}|_{\hat{\mathbf{x}}}$.[3] This condition imposes n inequalities on the system constraining the form of $\mathbf{f}$. There may additionally be further n inequalities for $\hat{\mathbf{x}}$ to be a meaningful solution; for example if the components of $\hat{\mathbf{x}}$ are production values, every component of $\hat{\mathbf{x}}$ must be nonnegative.

General equilibrium economics has attempted to find the conditions under which a unique, stable equilibrium will exist. This need not be the case, and interesting (i.e., bounded) behavior can take place around unstable equilibria in the form of limit cycles or even the strange attractors beloved of chaos theorists. A favorite model of the latter researchers is the logistic equation, which first arose in a biological context (May 1976), but has been applied to economics (Thompson 1992), among other things.

That limit cycles and chaotic behavior can be observed in economics is a view that should have by now been accepted (Blatt 1983). However, the question remains as to whether this behavior is pathological, i.e., whether linear neoclassical theory is applicable in most cases, and the only remaining difficulty is determining whether linear theory applies to a specific economy (the econometric problem) or whether chaotic behavior is indeed the norm.

2 Limits of linear economic theory

Returning to the question of stability, the fact that $2n$ inequalities must be satisfied would imply that a randomly chosen n-dimensional economics model would have a probability of 4^{-n} of a given equilibrium's being stable. The situation does look bleak, but economics is not generated randomly in the real world; rather, it is the result of an evolutionary process. We need to examine the process of cultural evolution to answer this question.

The analog of mutation in biology would be innovation in economics, as a new process or technique introduced into production, or as a new form of marketing, or a new company with a somewhat unusual approach to doing business. The effect of innovation is to add new degrees of freedom to the dynamical system, which usually will destabilize the system. The system will

[3] $\mathbf{Df}|_{\hat{\mathbf{x}}}$ is negative definite if $\mathbf{x} \cdot \mathbf{Df}|_{\hat{\mathbf{x}}} \cdot \mathbf{x} < 0$ for all $\mathbf{x}$. This also implies that all eigenvalues of Df have a negative real part.

then tend to evolve so as to lose some of the degrees of freedom, by, for example, old production techniques being abandoned or companies going bankrupt. This is analogous to species becoming extinct in the natural world.

Let us consider what happens to the largest eigenvalue of $\mathbf{Df}|_{\hat{\mathbf{x}}}$. Suppose that initially the system has a stable equilibrium, in which case all the eigenvalues have negative real part. As innovations are added to the system, the largest eigenvalue will increase toward zero. As it passes zero, the system destabilizes, and the system will start to exhibit limit cycles or chaotic behavior. As further innovations are added to the system, a property called permanence[4] is no longer satisfied, and some event such as a bankruptcy will occur to remove active processes from the system. This will restore permanency to the system and possibly even stability. Such a process is called self-organized criticality (Bak et al. 1988), which gives rise to a power-law spectrum of the booms and busts, successful innovations, and bankruptcies.[5]

3 Ecolab and the dynamics of evolution

This section outlines a model of an evolving ecology (Standish 1994, 1996) that is analogous to an economic system with input–output relations of production and product innovation. The ecology is described by a generalized Lotka–Volterra equation, which is perhaps the simplest ecological model to use:

$$\dot{n}_i = r_i n_i + \sum_{j=1}^{n_{sp}} \beta_{ij} n_i n_j. \tag{4.1}$$

Here $\mathbf{r}$ is the difference between the birth rate and the death rate for each species, in the absence of competition or symbiosis. β is the interaction term between species, with the diagonal terms referring to the species' self-limitation, which is related in a simple way to the carrying capacity K_i for that species in the environment by $K_i = -r_i\beta_{ii}$. In the literature (e.g., Strobeck 1973, Case 1991) the interaction terms are expressed in a normalized form, $a_{ij} = -K_i/r_i\beta_{ij}$, and $a_{ii} = 1$ by definition. $\mathbf{n}$ is the species density.

These equations are simulated on a simulator called Ecolab. The vectors $\mathbf{n}$ and $\mathbf{r}$ are stored as dynamic arrays, the size of which (i.e., the system dimension) can change in time. The interaction array is stored in row/column sparse form, consisting of the four arrays: diag, val, row, and col. Equation (4.1) can be

[4] A property in which there is a set of points $\mathbf{x}_0$ whose trajectories $\mathbf{x}(t)$ always remain away from the boundary, i.e., $\mathbf{x}_i(t) > \delta\, \exists \delta > 0$.

[5] This really implies that conclusions derived from comparative static economic analysis are almost never valid, except perhaps on sufficiently small time scales while the maximum eigenvalue of $\mathbf{Df}|_{\hat{\mathbf{x}}}$ is negative.

written as

$$\text{tmp[row]} = \text{beta.val} * n[\text{beta.col}]; \quad n \mathrel{+}= (r + \text{beta.diag} + \text{tmp}) * n;$$

this code makes up the *generate* operator in the Ecolab system. Other operators include *compact*, which removes species that have become extinct from the system (to optimize computational performance) and *mutate*, which adds a certain number of new species to the system, according to a specific algorithm to be discussed later. The operators can be called from a scripting language called Tcl (Ousterhout 1994), which allows different types of experiments to be performed without recompiling the code.

Before we discuss the mutation algorithm in more detail, Eq. (4.1) must be analyzed to determine the conditions that β must satisfy for the system to be real and also to determine the different regimes of dynamics from the linear (stable equilibrium) case to limit cycles and chaos to the actual breakdown of the ecosystem.

Linear analysis

Linear analysis starts with the fixed point of Eq. (4.1):

$$\hat{\mathbf{n}} = -\beta^{-1}\mathbf{r}, \tag{4.2}$$

where $\dot{\mathbf{n}} = 0$. There is precisely one fixed point in the interior of the space of population densities (i.e., $\mathbf{n}$ such that $n_i > 0$), provided that all components of $\hat{\mathbf{n}}$ are positive, giving rise to the following inequalities:

$$\hat{n}_i = (\beta^{-1}\mathbf{r})_i > 0, \quad \forall i. \tag{4.3}$$

This interior space is denoted as $\Re_+^{n_{\mathrm{sp}}}$ mathematically.

There may also be fixed points on the boundary of $\Re_+^{n_{\mathrm{sp}}}$ where one or more components of $\mathbf{n}$ is zero (corresponding to an extinct species). This is because the subecology with the living species only (i.e., with the extinct species removed) is equivalent to the full system.

The stability of this point is related to the negative definiteness of derivative of $\dot{\mathbf{n}}$ at $\hat{\mathbf{n}}$. The components of the derivative are given by

$$\frac{\partial \dot{n}_i}{\partial n_j} = \delta_{ij}\left(r_i + \sum_k \beta_{ik} n_k\right) + \beta_{ij} n_i. \tag{4.4}$$

Substituting Eq. (4.2) into Eq. (4.4) gives

$$\left.\frac{\partial \dot{n}_i}{\partial n_j}\right|_{\hat{\mathbf{n}}} = -\beta_{ij}(\beta^{-1}\mathbf{r})_i. \tag{4.5}$$

Stability of the fixed point requires that this matrix be negative definite. Because the $(\beta^{-1}\mathbf{r})_i$ are all negative by virtue of inequalities (4.3), this is equivalent to β's being negative definite, or equivalently, that its $n_{\rm sp}$ eigenvalues all have negative real parts. Taken together with inequalities (4.3), this implies that $2n_{\rm sp}$ inequalities must be satisfied for the fixed point to be stable. This point was made by Strobeck (1973) in a slightly different form. (Note that Strobeck implicitly assumes that $\sum_i r_i\hat{n}_i/K_i > 0$ and so comes to the conclusion that $2n_{\rm sp} - 1$ conditions are required.) If one were to pick coefficients randomly for a Lotka–Volterra system, then it has a probability of 4^{-n} of being stable, i.e., one expects ecosystems to become more unstable as the number of species increases (May 1974).

Permanence

Although stability is a nice mathematical property, it has rather less relevance when it comes to real ecologies. For example the traditional predator–prey system studied by Lotka and Volterra has a limit cycle. The fixed point is decidedly unstable, yet the ecology is permanent in the sense that both species' densities are larger than some threshold value for all time. Hofbauer et al. (1987) and Law and Blackford (1992) discuss the concept of permanence in Lotka–Volterra systems, which is the property that there is a compact absorbing set $\mathbf{M} \subset \Re_+^{n_{\rm sp}}$, i.e., once a trajectory of the system has entered $\mathbf{M}$, it remains in $\mathbf{M}$. They derive a sufficient condition for permanence, which is due to Jansen (1987), of the form

$$\sum_i p_i \mathbf{f}_i(\hat{\mathbf{n}}_B) = \sum_i p_i \left(r_i - \sum_j \beta_{ij}\hat{\mathbf{n}}_{Bj} \right) > 0, \quad \exists p_i > 0 \tag{4.6}$$

for every $\hat{\mathbf{n}}_B$ equilibrium points lying on the boundary ($\hat{\mathbf{n}}_{Bi} = 0\ \exists_i$), provided the system is bounded (or equivalently dissipative). This condition is more general than stability of the equilibrium – the latter condition implies that a local neighborhood of the equilibrium is an absorbing set. Also, the averaging property of Lotka–Volterra systems implies that the equilibrium must lie in the positive cone $\Re_+^{n_{\rm sp}}$. So inequalities (4.3) must still hold for permanence.

Consider the boundary points $\hat{\mathbf{n}}_B$ that are missing a single species i. Then Jansen's condition for these boundary points is

$$r_i - \sum_j \beta_{ij}\hat{n}_{Bj} > 0. \tag{4.7}$$

This set of conditions is linearly independent. Let the number of such boundary points be denoted by $n_B \leq n_{\rm sp}$. Then the set of conditions (4.6) will have rank $n_B \leq \nu \leq n_{\rm sp}$ (the number of linearly independent conditions), so the system has at most probability $2^{-n_{sp}-\nu}$ of satisfying Jansen's permanence condition if the coefficients are chosen uniformly at random. As stability is also sufficient for permanence, the probability lies between $4^{-n_{sp}}$ and $2^{-n_{sp}-\nu}$.

Another rather important property is resistance to invasion (Case 1991). Consider a boundary equilibrium $\hat{\mathbf{n}}_B$. If it is proof against invasion from the missing species, then the full system cannot be permanent. For the boundary points that miss a single species, this implies that condition (4.7) is necessarily satisfied for permanence, along with inequalities (4.3). The probability of permanence is then bounded above by $2^{-n_{sp}-n_B}$.

Thus although a randomly selected ecology is more likely to be permanent than to have a stable equilibrium, the likelihood decreases exponentially with an increase in species number.

Boundedness

It is necessary that the ecology be bounded, i.e., that $\sum n_i < N\ \exists N,\ \forall t > 0$. This requires that

$$\sum_i \dot{n}_i = \mathbf{r}\cdot\mathbf{n} + \mathbf{n}\cdot\beta\mathbf{n} < 0,\ \ \forall\mathbf{n} : \sum_i n_i > N\ \exists N. \tag{4.8}$$

As $\mathbf{n}$ becomes large in any direction, this functional is dominated by the quadratic term, so this implies that

$$\mathbf{n}\cdot\beta\mathbf{n} \leq 0,\ \ \forall\mathbf{n} : n_i > 0. \tag{4.9}$$

If strict equality holds, then $\mathbf{r}\cdot\mathbf{n} < 0$. Negative definiteness of β is sufficient, but not necessary for this condition. Another sufficient condition is to require that $\forall i, j, \beta_{ii} < 0$ and $\beta_{ij} + \beta_{ji} \leq 0$, which is used in the current study. This condition is satisfied by the predator–prey equations and so does allow multitrophic systems to be built, but does not allow the possibility of symbiosis. Its main advantage is its simplicity of implementation, along with the range of interesting (i.e., nonlimit point) behavior it encompasses.

Mutation

Adding mutation involves adding an additional operator to Eq. (4.1):

$$\dot{\mathbf{n}} = \mathbf{r} * \mathbf{n} + \mathbf{n} * \beta\mathbf{n} + \text{mutate}(\mu, \mathbf{r}, \mathbf{n}), \tag{4.10}$$

where $*$ refers to elementwise multiplication.

The mutation operator must generate new degrees of freedom $i > n_{sp}$ (where n_{sp} is the number of species currently in the ecology), somehow defining the new ecological coefficients $\{r_i \mid i > n_{sp}\}$, $\{\beta_{ij} \mid i > n_{sp}$ or $j > n_{sp}\}$

from the previous state of the system. In reality, there is another layer [hidden in Eq. (4.1)] called the genotypic layer, in which each organism has a definite genotype. There is a specific map from the genotypic layer to the space of ecological coefficients (hereafter called the phenotypic layer) called the embryology. Then the mutation operator is a convolution of the genetic algorithm operations operating at the genotypic layer, with the embryology. A few studies, including Ray's *Tierra* world, do this with an explicit mapping from the genotype to some particular organism property (e.g., interpreted as machine language instructions or as weight in a neural net). These organisms then interact with one another to determine the population dynamics. In this model, however, we are doing away with the organismal layer, and so an explicit embryology is impossible. The only possibility left is to use a statistical model of embryology. The mapping between genotype space and the population parameters r and β is expected to look like a rugged landscape; however, if two genotypes are close together (in a Hamming sense) then one might expect that the phenotypes are likely to be similar, as would the population parameters. This I call random embryology with locality. Here we tend to idealize genotypes as bit strings, although strings over an arbitrary alphabet (e.g., the four DNA bases, adenine, cytosine, guanine, and thymine) can equally be considered.[6] In the simple case of point mutations, the probability $p(x)$ of any child lying distance x in genotype space from its parent follows a Poisson distribution, as this is the distribution of the number of bit flips or deletions that might occur with a point mutation. Random embryology with locality implies that the phenotypic parameters are distributed randomly about the parent species, with a standard deviation that depends monotonically on the genotypic displacement. The simplest such model is to distribute the phenotypic parameters in a Gaussian fashion about the parent's values, with standard deviation proportional to the genotypic displacement. This constant of proportionality can be conflated with the species' intrinsic mutation rate to give rise another phenotypic parameter μ. It is assumed that the probability of a mutation's generating a previously existing species is negligible and can be ignored. We also need another arbitrary parameter ρ, "species radius," which can be understood as the minimum genotypic distance separating species, conflated with the same constant of proportionality as μ.

We may represent the Ecolab embryology as a probability distribution,

$$f(p, g) = \sqrt{\frac{2}{\pi}} \frac{\mu e^{-(\frac{\mu p}{2g})^2}}{g},$$

[6] The Hamming distance is the number of bits (bases) that differ between the two strings. For example, if a single bit has been removed from one string, the Hamming distance is one.

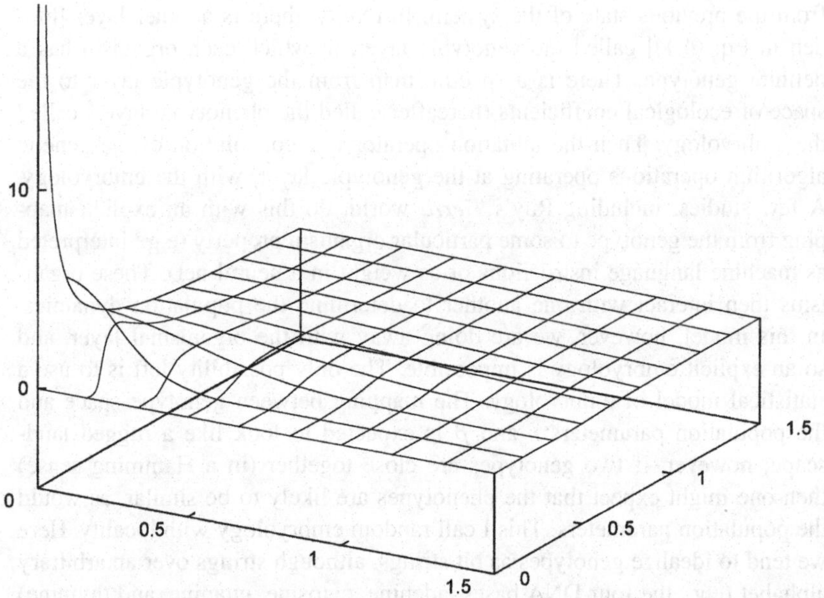

Figure 4.1. Probability distribution of the relation between genotype difference and the corresponding phenotype difference.

where $p = |r_i - r_j|/|r_i|$ or $p = |\beta_{ik} - \beta_{jk}|/|\beta_{ik}|$ is the distance between two species' phenotypic parameters, and g is the difference between the two genotypes. Figure 4.1 shows the general form of this probability distribution.

Figure 4.2 shows the probability distribution of a mutant phenotypical coefficient about that of its parent's value. This is given by

$$\int_0^\infty \sqrt{\frac{2}{\pi}} \frac{e^{-g/\mu-(\frac{\mu p}{2g})^2}\mu}{g} \mathrm{d}g. \tag{4.11}$$

In summary, the mutation algorithm is as follows:

(1) The number of mutant species arising from species i within a time step is $\mu_i r_i n_i/\rho$. This number is rounded stochastically to the nearest integer, e.g., 0.25 is rounded up to 1 25% of the time and down to 0 75% of the time.

(2) Roll a random number from a Poisson distribution $e^{-x/\mu+\rho}$ to determine the standard deviation σ of phenotypic variation.

(3) Vary **r** according to a Gaussian distribution about the parent's values, with σr_0 as the standard deviation, where r_0 is the range of values that **r** is initialized to, e.g., $r_0 = \max_i r_i|_{t=0} - \min_i r_i|_{t=0}$.

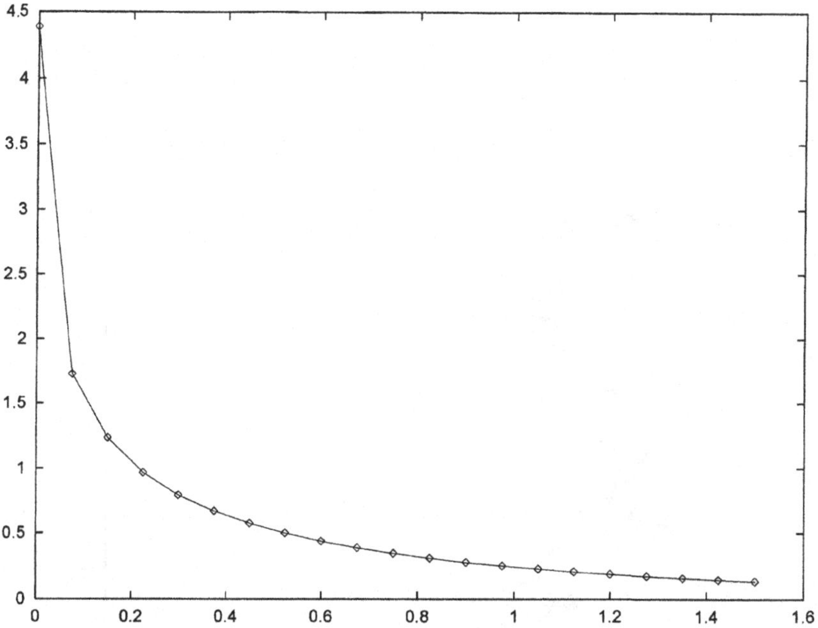

Figure 4.2. The probability distribution of a mutant phenotypical coefficient about that of its parent's value. This has been calculated by numerical integration from formula (4.11). Note that the curve actually diverges at 0.

(4) The diagonal part of β must be negative, so vary β according to a log-normal distribution. This means that if the old value is β, the new value becomes $\beta' = -\exp[-\ln(\beta) + \sigma]$. These values cannot arbitrarily approach 0, however, as this would imply that some species make arbitrarily small demands on the environment and will become infinite in number. In Ecolab, the diagonal interactions terms are prevented from becoming larger than $-r/(0.1 * INT\_MAX)$, where r is the corresponding growth rate for the new species.

(5) The off-diagonal components of β are varied in a similar fashion to those of $\mathbf{r}$. However, new connections are added or old ones removed according to $\lfloor 1/p \rfloor$, where $p \in (-2, 2)$ is chosen from a uniform distribution. The values on the new connections are chosen from the same initial distribution that the off-diagonal values were originally set with, i.e., the range $\min_{i \neq j} \beta_{ij}|_{t=0}$ to $\max_{i \neq j} \beta_{ij}|_{t=0}$. Because condition (4.9) is computationally expensive, we use a slightly stronger criterion that is sufficient, computationally tractable yet still allows interesting nondefinite matrix behavior, namely, that the sum $\beta_{ij} + \beta_{ji}$ should be nonpositive.

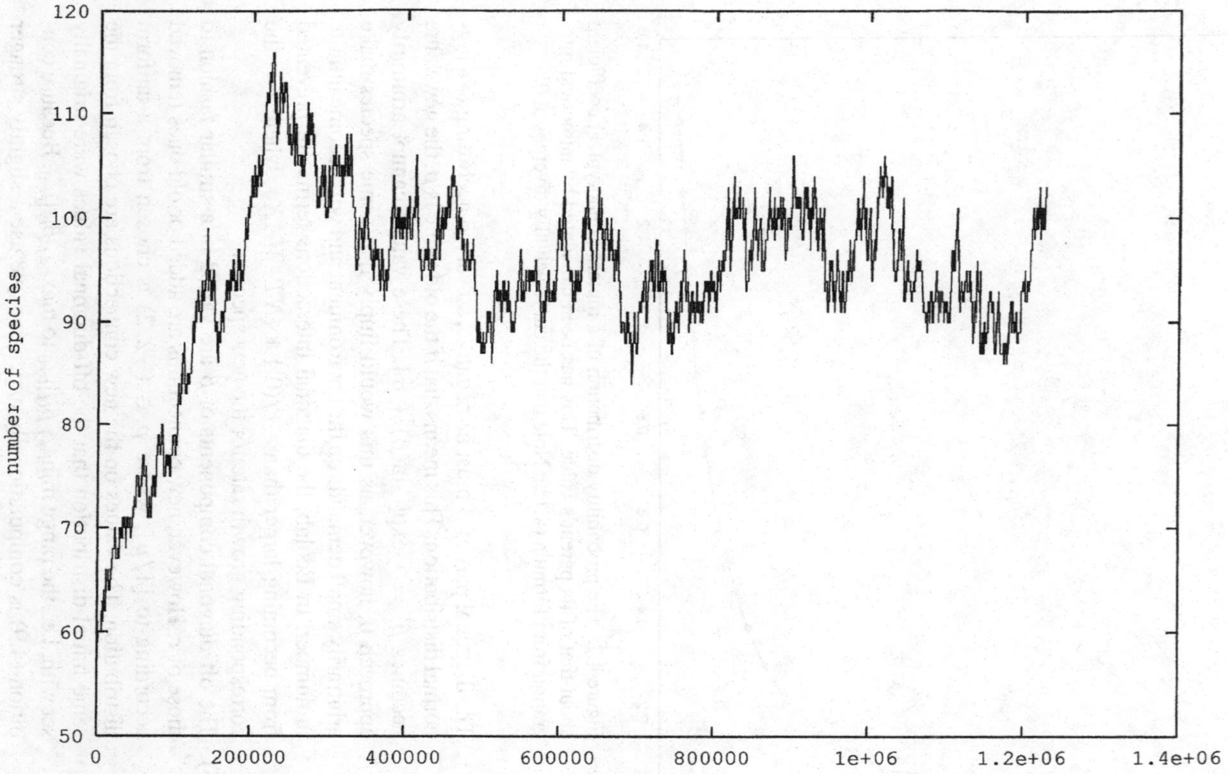

Figure 4.3. n_{sp} as a function of time step.

(6) μ must be positive and so should evolve according to the log-normal distribution like the diagonal components of β. Similar to β, it is a catastrophe to allow μ to become arbitrarily large. In the real world, mutation normally exists at some fixed background rate – species can reduce the level of mutation by improving their genetic repair algorithms. In Ecolab, this ceiling on μ is given by the mutation (random, maxval) variable.

Typical results

Figure 4.3 shows the time behavior for the number of species in the ecosystem for a typical run. The phenotypic parameters were seeded randomly in the ranges $-0.005 \leq \mathbf{r} \leq 0.01$, $-5 \times 10^{-5} \leq \beta_{\text{diag}} \leq -1 \times 10^{-4}$, $-0.001 \leq \beta_{\text{offdiag}} \leq 0.001$, and $0 \leq \mu \leq 0.09$. The $\mathbf{r}$ and β values were chosen so that several hundred individuals will be supported in the case of a single-species system, and the off-diagonal terms were large enough to permit interesting interactions between species, but not so large that the system collapsed to zero immediately. ρ was set at 10^4, which was chosen by examination of the histogram of differences among all the species. If ρ was too small, then a species' mutant offspring would be too similar to its parent to be really a new species. This shows up as a peak at small separation values of the histogram, which should not be there according to the law of competitive exclusion.

The system rapidly evolves to one of the fixed points (by a massive extinction event!) with a negative definite β. Over time, mutations build up in the system, decreasing the stability of the system. What then follows are periods of episodic extinctions and system growth through speciation. This is an example of self-organized criticality (Bak et al. 1988) and gives rise to power-law behavior.

Do we see the same power-law behavior observed by others (Bak and Sneppen 1993, Adami and Brown 1994)? The answer is emphatically yes. If speciation and extinction events occurred uniformly throughout history, as one might naively expect, one would expect a Poisson distribution for species lifetimes. On a log-linear plot, this would be a straight line. Alternatively, if a power-law spectrum was evident, the log–log plot would be straight. The two plots are shown in Figs. 4.4 and 4.5.

Effectively, these two plots tell us that not only is there not a stable ecological equilibrium, there is not even a steady state whereby extinctions are balanced by speciation (a common ecological assumption).

This model then is a concrete example of the self-organized criticality predicted in these types of systems in Section 2. Section 4 examines a possible economic model that is analogous to Ecolab and could even be implemented with the same simulation software. It would be surprising if the dynamics were not critically self-organized.

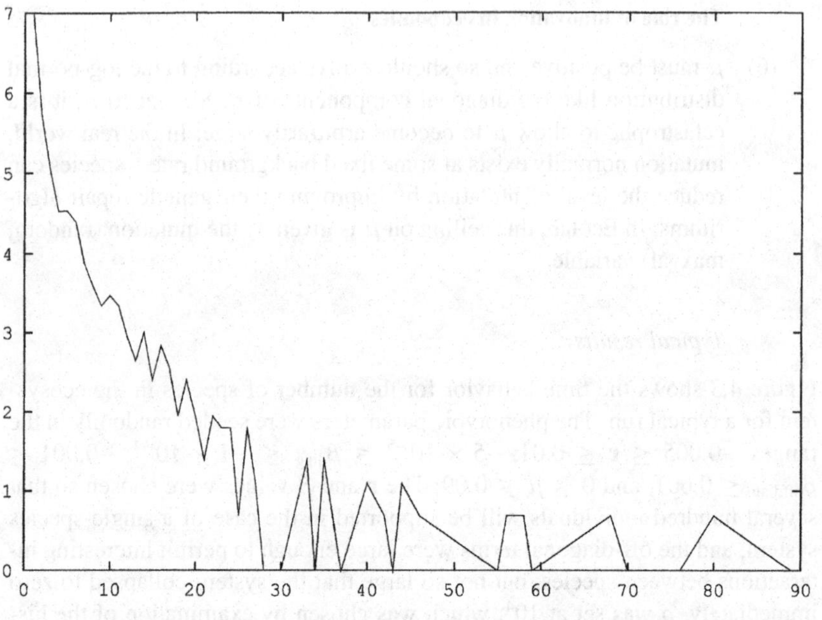

Figure 4.4. Distribution of species lifetimes on a log-linear plot. Distribution is unnormalized. Horizontal scale is the natural logarithm of species lifetime in time steps.

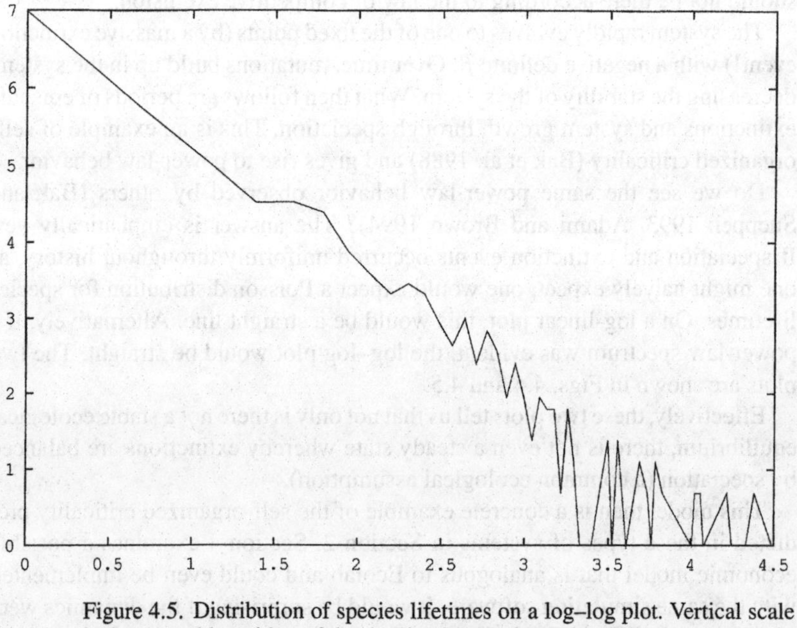

Figure 4.5. Distribution of species lifetimes on a log–log plot. Vertical scale is the natural logarithm of that in Fig. 4.4. Horizontal scale is the same.

4 Building an economic dynamics

Many inferential similarities can be drawn between the biological evolutionary model of Ecolab and the processes of a capitalist economy. The obvious analogy for a biological species is a product and for Darwinian evolution the process of technological change. I consider a model economics (*Econolab*) based on the insights of von Neumann, one of the founders of complexity theory, who introduced von Neumann technology in the late 1930s (von Neumann 1945). In this model economy, there is a set of commodities labeled $i \in \mathbf{N} = \{1 \cdots N\}$ and a set of technologies or processes labeled $m \in \mathbf{M} = \{1 \cdots M\}$. Each process has an activity z_m, input coefficients a_{mi}, and output coefficients b_{mi}, such that in one time step, $a_{mi} z_m$ of commodity i (among others) is consumed to produce $b_{mj} z_j$ of commodity j (among others). The coefficients a_{mi} and b_{mi} may be zero for some values of m and i, corresponding respectively to processes that do not require a particular input or do not produce a particular output. This differs from von Neumann's original approach and is more in line with that of Kemeny, Morgenstern, and Thompson (Kemeny et al. 1956). Blatt (Blatt 1983) gives a good introduction to this model, discussing its flexibility in dealing with a range of economic processes. In the words of Blatt (1983, p. 67),

> "The von Neumann work is a great achievement of mathematical model building in dynamic economics. It is the best available theory of capital and of rate of return."

That said, there are many issues of significance in capitalism that are not captured in the von Neumann method and that cannot be modeled in an initial rendition of Econolab. These include effective demand (Chiarella and Flaschel 1998), income distribution, variable capacity and utilization, and credit and debt (Keen 2000; Andresen 1999).

To relate von Neumann's work back to the Ecolab ecological model, the input–output coefficients a_{mi}/b_{mi} are fixed like the r_i/β_{ij}, of Eq. (4.1), and z_m is a free variable like n_i. In von Neumann's work, the dynamics is imposed in the form of an exponential growth condition:

$$z_m(t+1) = a z_m(t) \ \forall m \in \mathbf{M}. \tag{4.12}$$

However, rather than assuming a particular form for the dynamics, we should be looking for a first-order differential equation (or its difference equation equivalent) that describes the dynamics. Consider the monetary value of capital K_m associated with process m. The rate of change of this capital may be written as

$$\dot{K}_m = z_m \left(\sum_{i=1}^{N} b_{mi} p_i - \sum_{i=1}^{N} a_{mi} p_i \right), \tag{4.13}$$

where p_i is the price of commodity i. This has introduced two new sets of free variables, K_m and p_i, for which we need to find closure relations. Clearly activity is limited by the availability of capital (we do not allow the possibility of credit here):

$$\sum_{i=1}^{N} a_{mi} p_i z_m \leq K_m. \tag{4.14}$$

For simplicity, let us assume that each process invests a fixed proportion of its capital into production, i.e.,

$$\sum_{i=1}^{N} a_{mi} p_i z_m = \kappa_m K_m, \ \exists \kappa_m : 0 < \kappa_m \leq 1. \tag{4.15}$$

Substituting Eq. (4.13) into relation (4.15) gives

$$\dot{z}_m = \kappa_m \left(\frac{\sum_{i=1}^{N} b_{mi} p_i}{\sum_{i=1}^{N} a_{mi} p_i} - 1 \right) z_m. \tag{4.16}$$

This then is a model dynamics analogous to the Lotka–Volterra equation (4.1). If price is a fixed quantity (as assumed in von Neumann theory) then Eq. (4.16) is equivalent to the ansatz equation (4.12). This is the equilibrium situation, rather like assuming that $\mathbf{n} = \hat{n}$.

In reality, prices are not fixed and must have their own dynamics. The simplest way to do this is to look for a closure relation that relates prices to activities. The neoclassical and Austrian traditions propose that price dynamics should act as a negative feedback on the activity dynamics [Eq. (4.16)], whereas the post-Keynesian tradition does not see price as an equilibrating mechanism (Sraffa 1926). In this work, however, an ansatz is proposed in the form of the negative feedback, in a similar fashion to the ansatz used by Nosè and Hoover (Hoover 1985) to describe the thermostat that regulates the temperature of a nonequilibrium steady-state system in a heat bath:

$$\dot{p}_i = \pi_i \left(\frac{\text{demand}}{\text{supply}} - 1 \right) p_i = \pi_i \left(\frac{\sum_{m=1}^{M} a_{mi} z_m}{\sum_{m=1}^{M} b_{mi} z_m} - 1 \right) p_i. \tag{4.17}$$

This differs from von Neumann, who assumes that demand never exceeds supply, and if supply exceeds demand (i.e., a surplus), then the commodity is free ($p_i = 0$). This would imply $\dot{p}_i = 0$, freezing prices. In effect this makes the system very stiff – Eq. (4.17) softens the dynamics with π_i controlling the stiffness.

5 Adding evolution

Now that we have an economic dynamics established, we need to consider how to develop an analogy between ecological and economic evolution. By direct analogy with Ecolab, it is clear that when a process exhausts its capital ($K_m = 0$), it forever remains that way, so this is equivalent to extinction in ecosystems. Adding new processes and commodities is conceptually easy. Blatt is again cited (Blatt 1983, pp. 57–58):

> "What about technological progress? This can be included by assuming that the list of activities $m = 1, 2, \ldots, M$ is not final, but new activities may be invented and hence become available for use, as time goes on. This makes the total number of processes a function of time: $M = M(t)$.... Von Neumann himself developed his theory on the basis of an unchanged technology (all input coefficients, output coefficients and the number of processes M are constant in time), and his successors have done the same. The inclusion of technological progress appears to us to be a highly interesting avenue for further exploration."

The difficulty is deciding how to choose new coefficients a_{mi}, b_{mi}, κ_i, and π_i when a new process is added. There is no genotype of a process – the closest thing to it is Dawkins's meme, and there is no genetic algorithm theory of the meme. Clearly new processes arise evolutionarily, with the new processes modeled on the old. The new coefficients will be varied randomly about the old values according to some kind of central distribution.

Recent results from Ecolab indicate that the emergent dynamics of the system is rather insensitive to the specific type of mutation algorithm chosen. Work is currently under way to classify exactly what effects different assumptions make.

In 1962, Arrow (Arrow 1962) pointed out that the cost per unit for production of an artifact falls as an inverse power of the number of units produced: cost/unit $\propto N^{-a}$.

This power law is most likely a consequence of the dynamics of technological innovation, relating to the statistical properties of the underlying fitness landscape, as can be seen in Kauffman's NK model (Kauffman 1993). Presumably an evolutionary algorithm that searches process (and commodity) space according to the same power law would be optimally matched to generating change; however, another search algorithm would probably generate the same distribution of successful innovations, albeit on a different temporal scale. It should also be pointed out that large changes of process are likely to cost proportionally more than smaller changes. As any research budget is finite, the distribution of process improvements must therefore be finitely integrable (have a finite area underneath the curve), which the power-law distribution is not, but the normal (Gaussian) distribution is.

6 Conclusion

Economics is clearly a dynamic process, which, given its complexity, will be poorly described by a linear approximation about a stable equilibrium. Rather the properties of the equilibrium will be determined by cultural evolution that operates over a longer time scale than economics. It is likely that cultural evolution will produce a self-organized critical system, and this would be one of the first questions to study. Other questions that might be looked at include looking for evidence for the Arrow law and looking for analogs to various biological laws, such as the species-area law[7] and dependence of biodiversity with latitude.

Perhaps the most important point I would like to make is that rather than studying a finite-dimensional dynamical system, we should be studying what might be called open-dimensional dynamical systems, in which the number of degrees of freedom is finite but not fixed at any point in time. These systems must lie between finite-dimensional spaces and infinite-dimensional functional-analysis-type spaces. Only then might we achieve Marshall's economic biology and have an understanding of why economic systems have evolved to be the way they are.

REFERENCES

Adami, C., and Brown, C. T. (1994). Evolutionary learning in the 2d artificial life system 'avida.' In *Artificial Life IV*, eds. R. Brooks and P. Maes, MIT Press, Cambridge, MA.

Andresen, T. (1999). The dynamics of long-range financial accumulation and crisis. *Nonlinear Dyn. Psychol. Life Sci.*, **3**(2), 161–96.

Arrow, K. (1962). The economic implications of learning by doing. *Rev. Econ. Stud.*, **29**, 166.

Bak, P., and Sneppen, K. (1993). Punctuated equilibrium and criticality in a simple model of evolution. *Phys. Rev. Lett.*, **71**, 4083.

Bak, P., Tang, C., and Wiesenfeld, K. (1988). Self-organized criticality. *Phys. Rev. A*, **38**, 364–74.

Bascompte, J., and Sole, R. V. (1996). Habitat fragmentation and extinction thresholds in spatially explicit models. *J. Animal Ecol.*, **65**(4), 465–73.

Blatt, J. M. (1983). *Dynamic Economic Systems: A Post-Keynesian Approach*, Sharpe, New York.

Case, T. J. (1991). Invasion resistance, species build-up and community collapse in metapopulation models with interspecies competition. *Bio. J. Linnean Soc.*, **42**, 239–66.

Chiarella, C., and Flaschel, P. (1998). Dynamics of natural rates of growth and employment. *Macroecon. Dyn.*, **2**(3), 345–68.

Hirsch, M. W., and Smale, S. (1974). *Differential Equations, Dynamical Systems, and Linear Algebra*, Academic, New York.

[7] The number of species on an island is related by a power law to the area of the island.

Hofbauer, J., Hutson, V., and Jansen, W. (1987). Coexistence for systems governed by difference equations of Lotka-Volterra type. *J. Math. Biol.*, **25**, 553–70.

Hoover, W. G. (1985). Canonical dynamics: Equilibrium phase-space distributions. *Phys. Rev. A*, **31**, 1695.

Jansen, W. (1987). A permanence theorem for replicator and Lotka-Volterra systems. *J. Math. Biol.*, **25**, 411–22.

Kauffman, S. A. (1993). *The Origins of Order: Self Organization and Selection in Evolution*, Oxford University Press, New York.

Keen, S. (2000). The nonlinear economics of debt deflation. Chapter 5 of this volume.

Kemeny, J. G., Morgenstern, O., and Thompson, G. L. (1956). A generalization of the von Neumann model of an expanding economy. *Econometrica*, **24**, 115–35.

Law, R., and Blackford, J. C. (1992). Self-assembling food webs: a global viewpoint of coexistence of species in Lotka-Volterra communities. *Ecology*, **73**, 567–78.

Marshall, A. (1920). *Principles of Economics*, 8th ed., Macmillan, London.

May, R. (1974). *Stability and Complexity in Model Ecosystems*, Princeton University Press, Princeton, NJ.

(1976). Simple mathematical model with very complicated dynamics. *Nature (London)*, **26**, 457.

Maynard-Smith, J. (1974). *Models in Ecology*, Cambridge University Press, London.

Newman, M. E. J. (1996). Self-organized criticality, evolution, and the fossil extinction record. *Proc. of the Royal Society of London*, B ser., **263**, 1605–10.

(1997). A model of mass extinction. *J. Theor. Biol.*, **189**, 235–52.

Ousterhout, J. K. (1974). *Tcl and the Tk Toolkit*, Addison-Wesley, Reading, MA.

Raup, D. M., and Sepkowski, J. J. Jr. (1986). Periodic extinctions of families and genera. *Science*, **231**, 833–36.

Schroeder, M. (1991). *Fractals, Chaos, Power Laws*, Freeman, New York.

Sraffa, P. (1926). The law of returns under competitive conditions. *Econ. J.*, **36**, 538–50.

Standish, R. K. (1994). Population models with random embryologies as a paradigm for evolution. In *Complex Systems: Mechanism of Adaptation*, IOS, Amsterdam; also *Complexity International*, **2**, http://www.csu.edu.au/ci.

(1996). Ecolab: Where to now? In *Complex Systems: From Local Interaction to Global Phenomena*, eds. R. Stocker, H. Jelinek, B. Durnota, and T. Bossomeier, IOS, Amsterdam, pp. 263–71; also *Complexity International*, **3**, http://www.csu.edu.au/ci.

Ecolab documentation. Available at http://parallel.acsu.unsw.edu.au/rks/ecolab.html.

Strobeck, C. (1973). *n* species competition. *Ecology*, **54**, 650–54.

Thompson, C . J. (1992). Chaos in economics and management. In *Nonlinear Dynamics and Chaos*, eds. R. L. Dewar and B. I. Henry, World Scientific, Singapore, pp. 213–29.

von Neumann, J. (1945). A model of general economic equilibrium. *Rev. Econ. Stud.*, **13**, 1–9.

PART II

Finance and the macroeconomy

CHAPTER 5

The nonlinear economics of debt deflation

Steve Keen

1933 was a pivotal year for economics. Practically, it marked the perigee of the Great Depression – although no end was yet in sight to capitalism's greatest slump. Academically, it saw a bifurcation in economic theory, with two leading economists presenting diametrically opposed interpretations of the cyclical nature of capitalism. In one view, cycles – even, it seems, great depressions – were caused by exogenous shocks to an otherwise stable economic system. In the other, cycles were endemic to capitalism – and indeed, capitalism harbored a tendency toward complete collapse.

The former view was put forth by Frisch in his celebrated and well-known paper "Propagation problems and impulse problems in economics" (Frisch 1933); the latter was put forth by Fisher in his much less well-known paper "Debt deflation theory of great depressions" (Fisher 1933a).[1] The former paper is credited with playing a key role in the development of the then fledgling subdiscipline of econometrics; the latter remained largely ignored[2] until its revival, among the underworld of economics, in the form of Minsky's "Financial instability hypothesis" (Minsky 1977). In this chapter I argue – with the benefit of nonlinear hindsight – that the majority of the profession took the wrong fork back in 1933.

1 Frisch's linear premise

Frisch's initial premise was that "the majority of the economic oscillations which we encounter seem to be . . . produced by the fact that certain exterior

[1] Fisher's views were more fully elaborated in *Booms And Depressions Some First Principles* (Fisher 1933). However, the paper in *Econometrica*, (Fisher 1933a), the journal that Frisch established, is more widely available.

[2] Although Frisch did refer to Fisher's argument concerning the impact of debt (Frisch 1933, pp. 180–81), he did not use it in his modeling.

impulses hit the economic mechanism and thereby initiate more or less regular oscillations" (Frisch 1933, p. 171). This premise was not the product of empirical research into the actual nature of economic cycles, but the byproduct of a linear interpretation of sustained oscillations in a dynamic system: Mathematically stable linear models can generate only irregular cycles if the model is subjected to external shocks. This characteristic of mathematical models of cycles was thus extended by analogy to be seen as a characteristic of the complex real-world system the mathematical model purported to portray.

Today it is well known that Frisch's presumption was incorrect, as nonlinear systems can produce aperiodic cyclical behavior.[3] However, at the time Frisch's argument was convincing, and the profession chose to model the trade cycle by using damped linear models. Although Frisch himself provided a quite elaborate model of the trade cycle, the archetypal specimen of this approach was the Hansen–Samuelson multiplier–accelerator second-order difference equation. The linear weaknesses of this model (before the introduction of ceilings and floors) are well known; before moving on to consider Fisher's more perceptive analysis, I will point out a more crucial weakness: Hansen–Samuelson multiplier–accelerator models are economically invalid.

2 Invalidity of multiplier–accelerator models

Multiplier–accelerator models were purportedly derived by combining the multiplier, which relates consumption to income, with the accelerator, which relates investment to changes in income. When Samuelson's formulation is used (in the absence of a government sector), the derivation starts with the identity that total output is the sum of consumption and investment output:

$$Y_t \equiv C_t + I_t. \tag{5.1}$$

Consumption was defined as a lagged function of income:

$$C_t = \alpha Y_{t-1}. \tag{5.2}$$

Investment was defined as a lagged function of the change in consumption:

$$I_t = \beta(C_t - C_{t-1}). \tag{5.3}$$

[3] Curiously, the final analogy that Frisch used to link the "stable system subject to exogenous shocks" interpretation of the trade cycle with Schumpeter's concept of an innovation-driven cycle – a forced pendulum driven by a continuously replenished water reservoir and a rotating nozzle – describes a forced oscillator that is very similar to the forced dual pendulum and whose behavior may therefore be chaotic (Frisch 1933, pp. 203–205). Had Frisch attempted to model this system, he may well have introduced nonlinear analysis into economics.

Substituting Eqs. (5.2) and (5.3) into Eq. (5.1) yielded the second-order equation:

$$Y_t = \alpha(1+\beta)Y_{t-1} - [\alpha\beta(Y_{t-2})]. \tag{5.4}$$

(Samuelson 1939, p. 76).

The economic fallacy in this model arises from the definition of investment. Equation (5.3) clearly refers to intended investment, yet this was substituted into Eq. (5.1), which is an identity for only actual values of output, consumption, and investment. Actual investment in period t is the increment to capital:

$$I_t \equiv K_t - K_{t-1}. \tag{5.5}$$

This can be related to output by means of the accelerator:

$$I_t = \nu(Y_t - Y_{t-1}). \tag{5.6}$$

When this is substituted into Eq. (5.1), what results is a first-order equation:

$$Y_t = \nu Y_t - (\nu - \alpha)Y_{t-1}. \tag{5.7}$$

This first-order relation generates exponential growth with positive savings, which can easily be seen if α is replaced with $(1-s)$, where s is the propensity to save:

$$Y_t = \nu Y_t - [\nu - (1-s)]Y_{t-1},$$

or

$$\frac{Y_t - Y_{t-1}}{Y_{t-1}} = \frac{s}{\nu - 1}. \tag{5.8}$$

Hansen–Samuelson multiplier–accelerator models were therefore not simply limited by their linearity: They were also badly specified. They effectively equated actual savings to desired investment, two magnitudes that neither pre- nor post-Keynesian economics claim are equal at all times. Because multiplier–accelerator models related both variables to income, the only level of income that guaranteed their equality was zero, and the trade cycles these models generated were simply iterations en route to this trivial solution.

Nevertheless, although linear models in general should be abandoned, it is useful to show that an interesting model of cyclical growth can be derived from a properly specified linear model.

3 A linear model of divergent growth

We start with the Hansen–Samuelson presumption that desired investment is a lagged linear function of changes in consumption (c is therefore a behavioral constant, representing the desired change in capital stock for a given change in consumption[4]):

$$\begin{aligned} I_{d_t} &= c(C_{t-1} - C_{t-2}), \\ C_t &= (1-s)Y_t, \\ I_{d_t} &= c(1-s)(Y_{t-1} - Y_{t-2}). \end{aligned} \tag{5.9}$$

Desired investment then becomes actual investment, so that this amount is added to the capital stock:

$$\begin{aligned} I_t &= I_{d_t}, \\ K_t &= K_{t-1} + I_{t-1}. \end{aligned} \tag{5.10}$$

The new level of capital stock then determines output by means of the accelerator, thus closing the model:

$$\begin{aligned} Y_t &= \frac{1}{\nu} K_t \\ &= \frac{1}{\nu}(K_{t-1} + I_{t-1}) \\ &= \frac{1}{\nu}[\nu \times Y_{t-1} + c(1-s)(Y_{t-2} - Y_{t-3})] \\ &= Y_{t-1} + \frac{c(1-s)}{\nu}(Y_{t-2} - Y_{t-3}). \end{aligned} \tag{5.11}$$

It is obvious by inspection that this model produces both interdependent growth and cycles. Its eigenvalues are 1, $\{[c(1-s)]/\mathrm{v}\}^{1/2}$, and $(-\{[c(1-s)]/\mathrm{v}\}^{1/2})$ in the general case in which $c(1-s) \neq \mathrm{v}$, and (1,1,−1) in the special case that $c(1-s) = \nu$. These indicate that any sustained level of output is a marginally unstable equilibrium[5]: If the model is perturbed, it will generate sustained exponential growth and cycles for $c(1-s) > \nu$, sustained linear cycles for $c(1-s) = \nu$, and diminishing cycles toward a new equilibrium for $c(1-s) < \nu$. The fact that the growth and the cyclical eigenvalues are identical in magnitude means that the cycles generated are always proportional to the level of output, thus making this model the exception to Blatt's rule that linear cyclical models with unstable equilibria are invalid (Blatt 1983, p. 150). The reduced form for the general case of $c(1-s) \neq \nu$ can be decomposed into an

[4] Consumption is unlagged in this model, as the time span for consumption is significantly shorter than that for investment. Consumption was lagged in the Hansen–Samuelson models, not because this made economic sense, but because unlagged consumption gave rise to a first-order difference equation, which of course did not generate the desired cycles. The two-period lag for investment here is because a lag must be presumed between changes in consumption and investment plans based on changes in consumption.

[5] In the vernacular of econometrics, the system has a unit root.

equilibrium term [which is positive when $\nu > c(1-s)$ and negative otherwise], a growth term, and a cycle term:

$$
\begin{aligned}
Y_t = {} & \frac{\nu Y_2 - c(1-s)Y_0}{\nu - c(1-s)} \\
& + \frac{1}{2}\left[\frac{\sqrt{\nu c(1-s)}(Y_1 - Y_0) + \nu(Y_2 - Y_1)}{c(1-s) - \sqrt{\nu c(1-s)}}\right]\left[\sqrt{\frac{c(1-s)}{\nu}}\right]^t \\
& - \frac{1}{2}\left[\frac{\sqrt{\nu c(1-s)}(Y_1 - Y_0) - \nu(Y_2 - Y_1)}{c(1-s) + \sqrt{\nu c(1-s)}}\right]\left[-\sqrt{\frac{c(1-s)}{\nu}}\right]^t.
\end{aligned}
\tag{5.12}
$$

The ratio of the constant in the growth expression to the constant in the cycle expression is

$$
\frac{\sqrt{\nu c(1-s)}(Y_1 - Y_0) + \nu(Y_2 - Y_1)}{\sqrt{\nu c(1-s)}(Y_1 - Y_0) - \nu(Y_2 - Y_1)} \frac{c(1-s) + \sqrt{\nu c(1-s)}}{c(1-s) - \sqrt{\nu c(1-s)}}, \tag{5.13}
$$

which ensures that the magnitude of cycles will always be smaller than, but in proportion to, the level of output.

The model can also be shown to generate large divergences in growth rates for small differences in c, the desired incremental capital-to-output ratio (ICOR). In the case of two economies that differ only in their ICORs, the ratio of their long-term growth rates is

$$
\frac{\sqrt{c_1 c_2 (1-s)^2} + \sqrt{c_1(1-s)\nu} - \sqrt{c_2(1-s)\nu} - \nu}{c_2(1-s) - \nu}, \tag{5.14}
$$

which is a quasi-linear but very steep function of the ratio of the preferred ICORs. Figure 5.1 plots this function with $\nu = 3$ and $c(1-s)$ values for the two countries ranging between 3 and 3.3. At one extreme of the function, a 1% difference in ICORs results in a 10% difference in rates of growth for values of the base $c(1-s)$ and ν of 3.3 and 3, respectively. As Fig. 5.1 indicates, the ratio of relative growth rates is more extreme the closer $c(1-s)$ is to ν in the denominator country. For $\nu = 3$, $c(1-s) = 3.1$, a 1% difference between $c(1-s)$ values results in a 30% difference in growth rates. At the other extreme, when $c(1-s)$ is 3.01 for country 2 and 3.3 for country 1, the growth rate of country 1 is 32 times that of country 2.

Finally, this model provides a dynamic equivalent of the "Paradox of Thrift": An increase in the savings rate will cause a decrease in the rate of growth.

All these results – interdependent cycles and growth, divergent growth rates for countries with differing investment propensities, and a dynamic paradox of thrift – stand in strong contrast to the characteristics of multiplier–accelerator

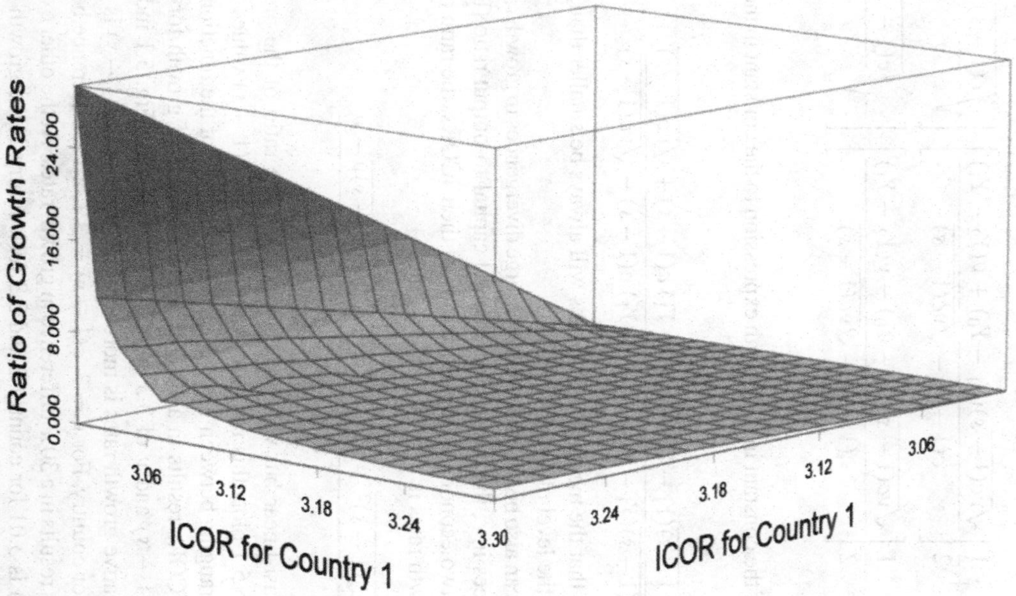

Figure 5.1. Ratio of growth rates for countries with differing ICORs.

models and of neoclassical growth theory. Yet the model is fundamentally the product of a correct specification of the Hansen–Samuelson proposition that investment is a lagged function of changes in consumption. One can only speculate as to how trade and growth theory might have developed had this model been derived at the birth of linear trade-cycle modeling, rather than at its death. Instead, it was Fisher's more enlightened vision that was stillborn.

4 Fisher's vision: the Great Depression as catastrophe

Fisher's appreciation of the dynamics underlying the Great Depression was still constrained by his knowledge of linear models of cycles, and as a result tantalizingly modern perceptions were frequently reduced to embellishments on a linear perspective. However, the gems of nonlinearity in Fisher's thinking stand out strongly against the linear backdrop. Thus, although he concedes that "we may tentatively assume that, ordinarily and within wide limits, all, or almost all, economic variables tend, in a general way, towards a stable equilibrium," the qualifications overwhelm the rule: although equilibrium is stable, it is "so delicately poised that, after departure from it beyond certain limits, instability ensues"; although every variable has an ideal equilibrium, disturbances are so myriad that "any variable is almost always above or below the ideal equilibrium" (Fisher 1933a, p. 339).

These fluctuations can explain mild economic cycles, of course, but Fisher's interest is not in these but in the truly deep declines. Here his thinking strongly departs from the equilibrium norm as he considers the self-reinforcing dynamics that can turn a downturn into a deflation. The process begins with overconfidence, which, although it is crucial to the initiation of a great depression, "seldom does great harm except when, as, and if, it beguiles its victims into debt." The two key factors in the development of a great depression are "*over-indebtedness* to start with and *deflation* following soon after" (Fisher 1933, p. 341). The former results in an exponential growth in the level of nominal debt, as interest on outstanding debts exceeds the repayment ability of some businesses. The latter amplifies this initial disturbance by increasing the real value of debt even as firms attempt to reduce its nominal value: As Fisher evocatively puts it in what can be called Fisher's Paradox, "*the more debtors pay, the more they owe*. The more the economic boat tips, the more it tends to tip. It is not tending to right itself, but is capsizing" (Fisher 1933a, p. 344).

To this point, Fisher's model explains a catastrophe (in the popular sense). To explain cycles, he argues that if one of the two causal factors – overindebtedness and deflation – is absent, then the initial disturbance will correct itself. Thus if a deflation occurs in the absence of overindebtedness or if overindebtedness is not followed by deflation, the situation "is then more analogous to stable equilibrium: the more the boat rocks the more it will tend to right itself. In that case, we have a truer example of a cycle" (Fisher 1933a, pp. 344–45). This analysis leads Fisher to support government reflationary measures as a means to avoid the occurrence of great depressions (Fisher 1933, pp. 346–47). These themes have been elaborated on and combined with a nonstandard interpretation of Keynes by Minsky, resulting in the "Financial Instability Hypothesis" (see Minsky 1977, Keen 1995).

5 The Financial Instability Hypothesis

Fisher's contribution consists of the insights that, in the real world, economic variables will always deviate from equilibrium values and that, in the case of investment behavior, overconfidence can lead to a runaway process of debt accumulation and price deflation. Minsky built on the theories of Fisher (and Keynes) to provide a historicoanalytic explanation for this process.

Minsky's analysis begins at a time when the economy is growing relatively stably, but when firms and banks evaluate investment projects conservatively, because of the memory of a recent economic crisis. The combination of a relatively tranquil economy with conservatively evaluated investment projects means that most projects succeed. Two things gradually become evident to managers and bankers: "Existing debts are easily validated and units that were heavily in debt prospered: it pays to lever" (Minsky 1977, 1982, p. 65). As a result, both managers and bankers come to regard the previously accepted risk premium as excessive. Investment projects are evaluated with less conservative estimates of prospective cash flows, so that with these rising expectations go rising investment and asset prices. The general decline in risk aversion thus sets off the growth in debt-financed investment, which is the foundation both of the boom and its eventual collapse.

The economy enters a phase that Minsky describes as "the euphoric economy" (Minsky 1970, 1982, pp. 120–24), in which both lenders and borrowers believe that the future is ensured and that therefore most investments will succeed. Asset prices are revalued upward as previous valuations are perceived to be based on mistakenly conservative grounds. Highly liquid, low-yielding financial instruments are devalued, leading to a rise in the interest rates offered by them as their purveyors fight to retain market share. Financial institutions now accept liability structures both for themselves and their customers "that, in a more sober expectational climate, they would have rejected" (Minsky 1970, 1982, p. 123.).

Asset price inflation in the euphoric economy phase makes it possible to profit by trading assets on a rising market, giving rise to a class of speculators Minsky calls "Ponzi financiers," after the American real estate and bank swindler of the 1920s. These capitalists are willing to incur debts whose servicing costs exceed the cash flows of the assets they buy, because they expect to be able to on-sell these assets at a profit. However, the rising interest rates that also occur in this period eventually force some nonspeculative investors to sell capital assets to meet their debt commitments, and the entry of these new sellers into the asset market pricks the exponential rise in prices on which Ponzi financiers depend. The leading Ponzis go bankrupt, bringing the euphoric economy to an abrupt end and ushering in another debt-induced systemic crisis.

In Minsky's model, the commodity inflation conditions at the time of the crisis determine whether the economy experiences a depression. If commodity price inflation is high, then, although real economic activity collapses, inflation eventually brings corporate cash flows into line with the debts that were accumulated during the boom; the economy limps along with low growth and high inflation, but a true calamity is avoided. If commodity price inflation is low, however, then the level of corporate debt remains beyond that which can be financed out of the depressed cash flows of a recession, and debt continues to accumulate, setting off a chain reaction of bankruptcies – Fisher's Paradox strikes.

Minsky argues that the one means by which a market economy can avoid Fisher's Paradox is by means of the institution of government. With a developed social security system, the collapse in cash flows that occurs when a boom becomes a panic will be at least partly ameliorated by a fall in tax revenues and a rise in government spending – the classic "automatic stabilizers," although this time seen in a more monetary light. Similarly, progressive taxation rates can restrain the ability of capitalists to indulge in speculative investment during the boom phase of the cycle. By proposing that the main purpose of economic policy was not to avoid cycles, but to prevent a debt deflation, Minsky thus puts a Fisherian slant on the Keynesian practice of countercyclical economic policy.

6 Modeling debt deflation

There are elements in Fisher's analysis that are consonant with modern nonlinear analysis, although these are interspersed between comments that are consonant with the generally linear understanding of cycles of the time. However, Fisher had only his creed[6] to offer in competition with Frisch's detailed linear research project, and it had little influence on the development of economics until Minsky.

[6] Fisher set out his analysis as a creed in the sense of an analysis "expressed dogmatically and without proof" (Fisher 1933a, p. 337).

In this section I show that the catastrophic[7] aspect of Fisher's and Minsky's analysis can be modeled by using an extended version of Goodwin's predator–prey model of cyclical growth. The basic Goodwin model reduces to the coupled equations

$$\frac{d\omega}{dt} = \omega[w(\lambda) - \alpha],$$
$$\frac{d\lambda}{dt} = \lambda\left(\frac{1-\omega}{\nu} - \alpha - \beta\right), \tag{5.15}$$

where λ is the rate of employment, ω is the wages share of output, $w(\lambda)$ is a Phillips curve, α is the output-to-labor ratio, and β is the rate of population growth.

The first step in extending this model is to replace the linear assumption that capitalists invest all their profits [$1-\omega$ in the previous model is the profit to output ratio $\pi = (\Pi/Y)$] with the more realistic assumption that investment is a nonlinear function $k()$ of the rate of profit [$(\Pi_n/K) = (\pi_n/\nu)$], where π_n is the profit share net of interest payments.[8] This does not disturb the underlying nature of the model, which still results in a stable limit cycle, but it sets the scene for the introduction of a finance sector.

We introduce finance into the model by assuming the existence of a banking sector that exists solely to finance capitalist investment. The rate of change of debt in this system is thus simply interest on outstanding debt, plus new investment, minus gross profits:

$$\frac{dD}{dt} = rD + I_g - \Pi, \tag{5.16}$$

where $I_g = k(\pi_n/\nu)Y$ represents gross investment (in what follows, depreciation is introduced at the constant rate of γ per annum). This produces the following three-dimensional system:

$$\frac{d\omega}{dt} = \omega[w(\lambda) - \alpha],$$
$$\frac{d\lambda}{dt} = \lambda\left\{\left[\frac{k(\pi_n/\nu)}{\nu} - \gamma\right] - \alpha - \beta\right\},$$
$$\frac{dd}{dt} = d\left\{r - \left[\frac{k(\pi_n/\nu)}{\nu} - \gamma\right]\right\} + k\left(\frac{\pi_n}{\nu}\right) - \pi, \tag{5.17}$$

[7] This is not a catastrophe in the sense of catastrophe theory, but an "inverse tangent" (Pomeau and Manneville 1980) chaotic process.

[8] The term Π will be retained for gross profit or output minus wages throughout. The term Π_n will signify gross profit minus all other outgoings, which in this model means interest on outstanding debt. In the next section, Π_n will signify gross profit minus interest payments and taxation minus subsidies.

where d is the debt-to-output ratio D/Y and π_n is the profit share of output:

$$\pi_n = 1 - \omega - rd. \tag{5.18}$$

As is well known, a three-dimensional system introduces the possibility of chaotic behavior, and this particular model follows the inverse tangent route to chaos first identified by Pomeau and Manneville (1980). Even at this basic level, the model contains some important insights into the role of debt in a market economy and the impact of the rate of interest in a model in which, in contrast to the standard IS-LM model, debt is explicitly accounted for.

Perturbation analysis

As is easily shown, with the functional form chosen for the Phillips curve, the equilibrium value of employment is[9]

$$\lambda_e = \frac{\ln(\alpha - C) - A}{B} = 97.12\%. \tag{5.19}$$

There is an equilibrium value for profit share:

$$\pi_e = \frac{\ln[\nu(\gamma + \alpha + \beta) - G] - E}{F} = 16.18\%, \tag{5.20}$$

which corresponds to a rate of profit of approximately 5.4% and, given the investment function, an investment share of output of 16.5%. The equilibrium value for the debt-to-output ratio is

$$d_e = \frac{k\left(\frac{\pi_n}{\nu}\right) - \pi_n}{\frac{k\left(\frac{\pi_n}{\nu}\right)}{\nu} - \gamma} = 7.02\%. \tag{5.21}$$

Because the net profit share is a linear combination of ω and d [Eq. (5.18)], this gives the curious result that, at the equilibrium, workers' share of output and bankers' share are in direct opposition to each other, whereas capitalists' share is constant. This is, unremarkably, significantly different from standard economic models of income distribution, which argue that remuneration reflects relative factor productivity and that are not equipped to deal with a return to accumulated debt. It is also, however, significantly different from the unconventional Sraffian school of economics, which sees a linear trade-off between capitalist and worker shares in the economic surplus.

This equilibrium vector is locally stable but globally unstable, a significant echo of Fisher's intuition in 1933 that the market system has an equilibrium that "though stable, is so delicately poised that, after departure from it beyond certain limits, instability ensues" (Fisher 1933, p. 339).

[9] With the parameter values used in the following simulations, which were derived by a nonlinear regression of Phillip's original data against the rate of unemployment.

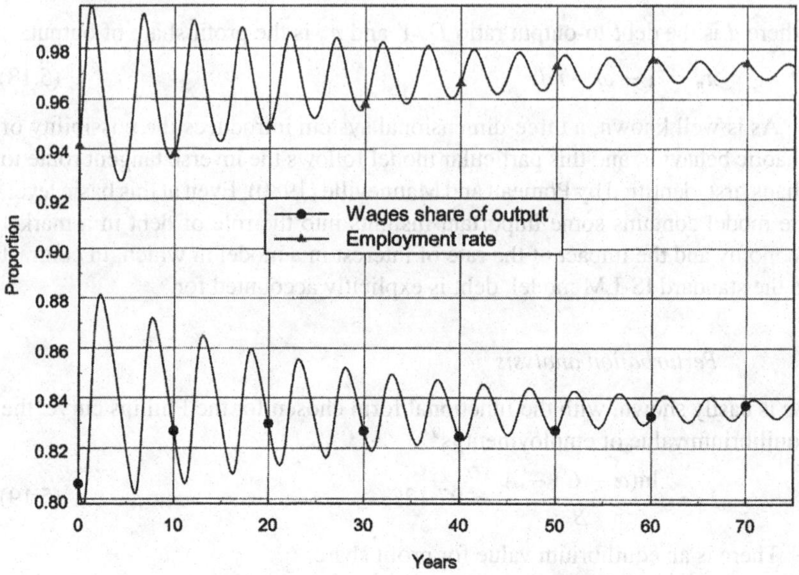

Figure 5.2. Wages share and employment near equilibrium.

Conventional IS-LM analysis argues that an increase in the interest rate will reduce investment (which is portrayed as a monotonically decreasing function of the interest rate, in contrast to this model's argument that the rate of profit determines the level of investment) and thus growth; however, any impact on the accumulation of debt is ignored. The final equation of system (5.17) indicates that, when debt is explicitly accounted for, it is possible for debt to overwhelm the system.

When the initial conditions of the model are in the vicinity of the equilibrium point, the system converges to the equilibrium with cycles of approximately 5 years, a similar period to those of the basic two-dimensional Goodwin model (see Fig. 5.2).

Figure 5.3 shows the time path of the debt-to-output ratio, which rises in a cyclical fashion initially, but then also tapers toward its equilibrium value.

The phase diagram in Fig. 5.4 and the period interactions shown in Fig. 5.5 give a clear picture of the near-equilibrium dynamics of this three-dimensional system. The initial conditions of slightly higher-than-equilibrium debt, workers' share of output, and employment lead to a downturn, as investment stagnates because of the resulting low rate of profit. The excess of profit over investment leads to debt being reduced, but the downturn eventually leads to falling wage demands, and this leads to a boost in investment well before debt is fully repaid. Debt then rises with rising employment as investment boosts output, only to lead eventually to rising wage demands that cut into profits and once again cut

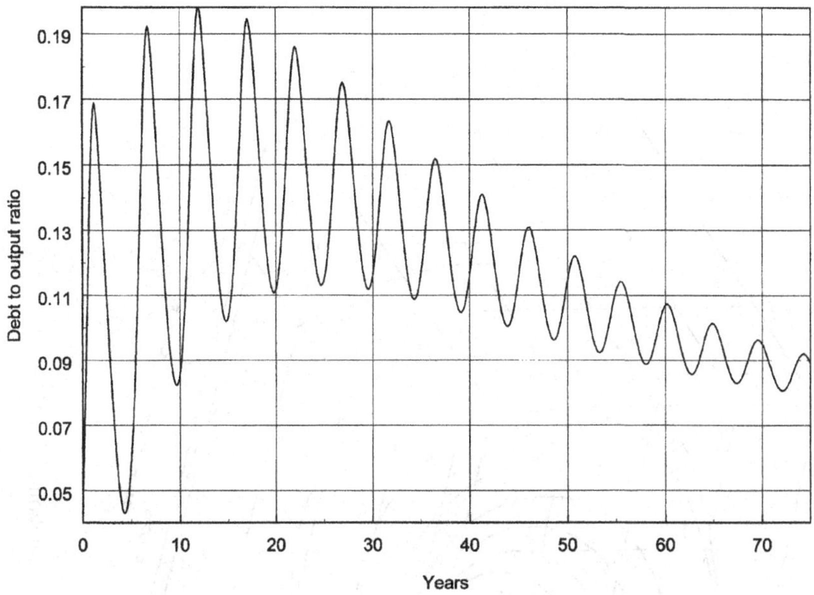

Figure 5.3. Debt-to-output ratio near equilibrium.

off investment. The cycle then continues, with the system tapering toward a stable-equilibrium debt-to-equity ratio, wages share, and rate of employment.

Figure 5.5 shows the interactions among employment, wages share, and debt at the level of a single cycle. During the boom phase, rising investment causes both rising employment and rising debt, as firms borrow to finance investment at above the level of retained earnings. In the early stage of this process, wages share continues to fall because employment, although rising, is still below the level that triggers the demand for wage rises at above the level of productivity growth. However, after roughly half the boom, wage demands lead to a rising wages share that cuts into profit share, adding to the negative effect of the increase in debt repayments. The incentive to invest thus evaporates, growth ceases, profits are devoted to repaying debt, unemployment rises, and eventually wages fall, leading to a renewal of the cycle.

Conversely, as Figs. 5.6–5.8 indicate, at a more extreme distance from the equilibrium vector, the system is unstable, as the nonlinearity of the system results in centripetal forces that drive it toward a debt-induced breakdown. The breakdown can take several forms, given the nature of the initial conditions – the one shown in Figs. 5.6–5.8 is precipitated by an extreme blowout in wages share during a boom, with initial conditions of wages share 0.11 below equilibrium, employment 0.05 below equilibrium, and debt at its equilibrium value.

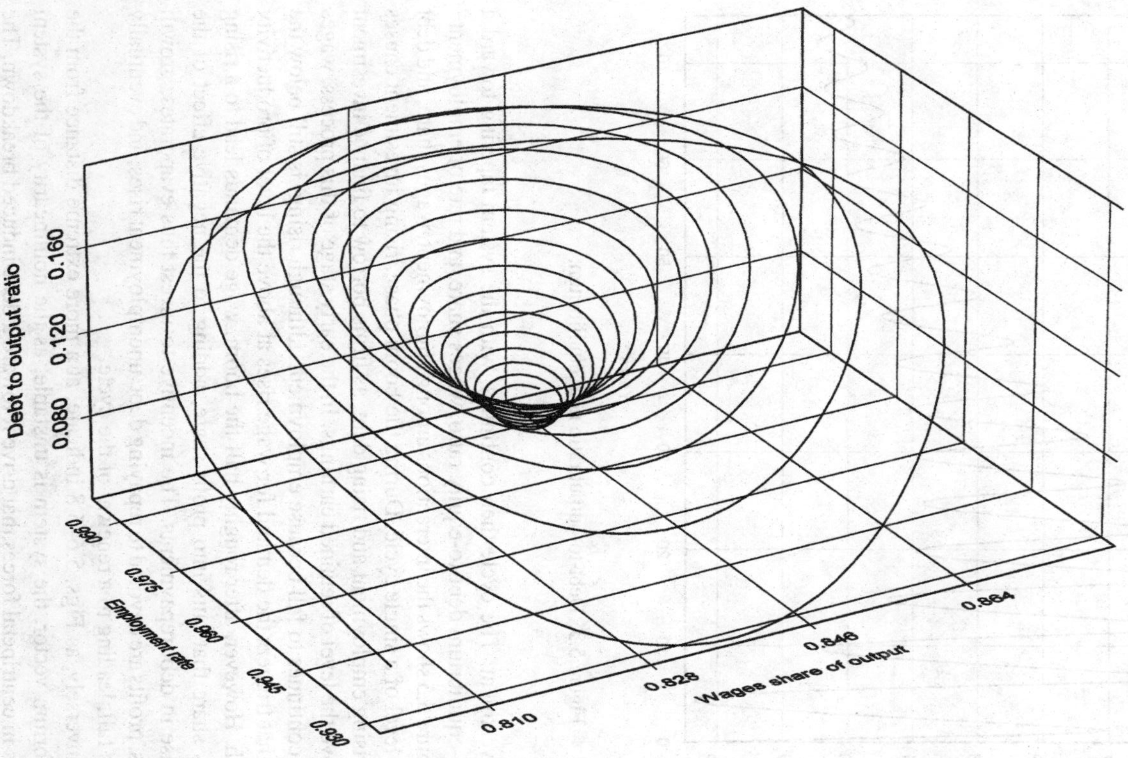

Figure 5.4. Wages share, employment, and debt interactions near equilibrium.

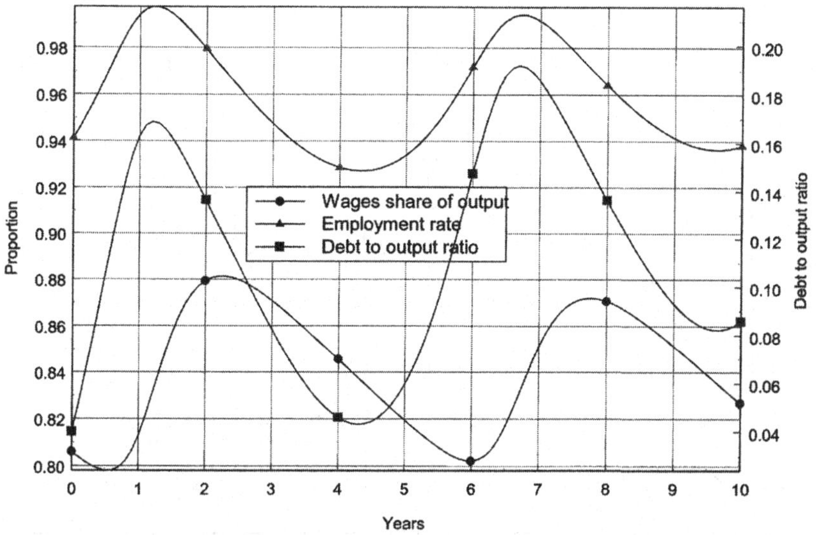

Figure 5.5. Period interactions of wages share, employment, and debt near equilibrium.

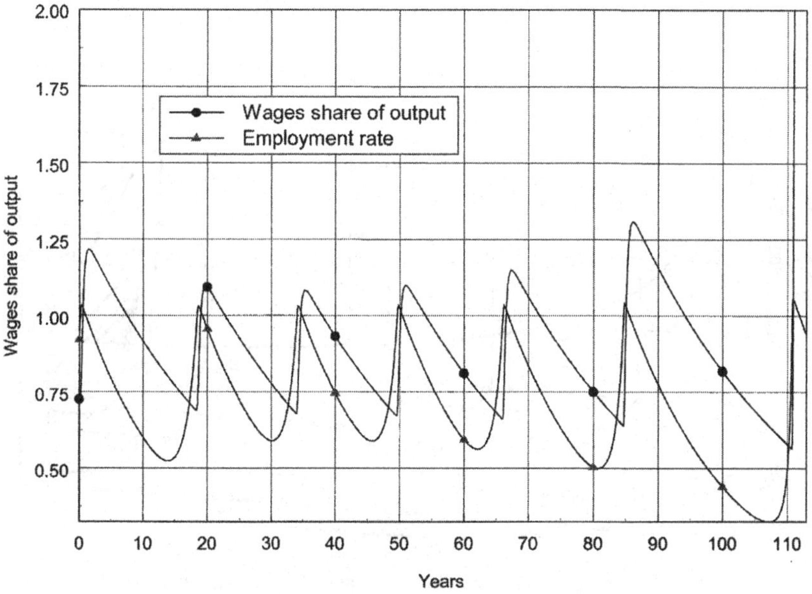

Figure 5.6. Wages share and employment far from equilibrium.

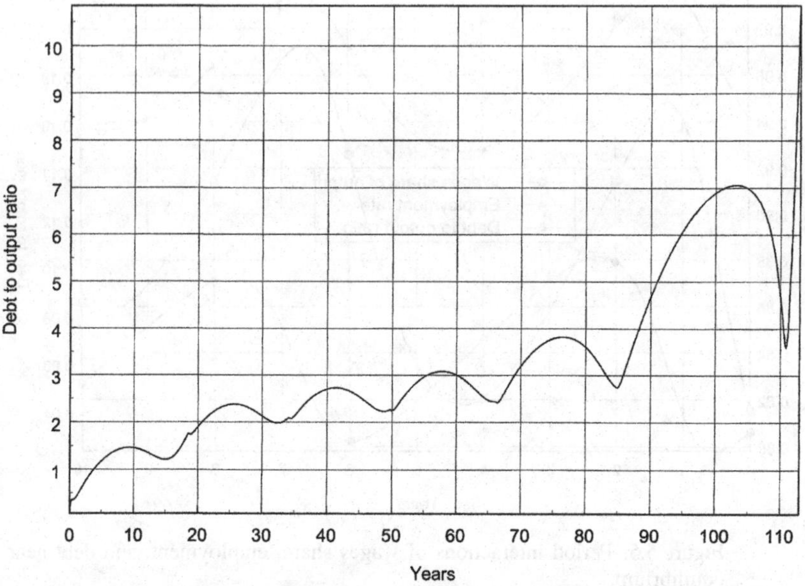

Figure 5.7. Debt-to-output ratio far from equilibrium.

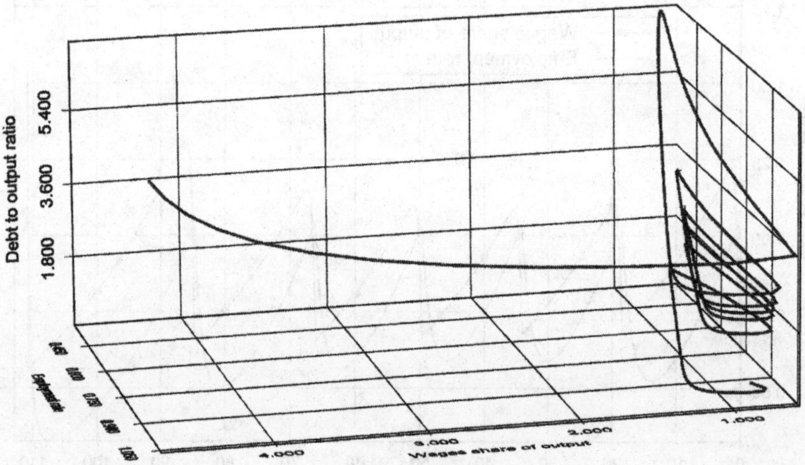

Figure 5.8. Wages share, employment, and debt interactions far from equilibrium.

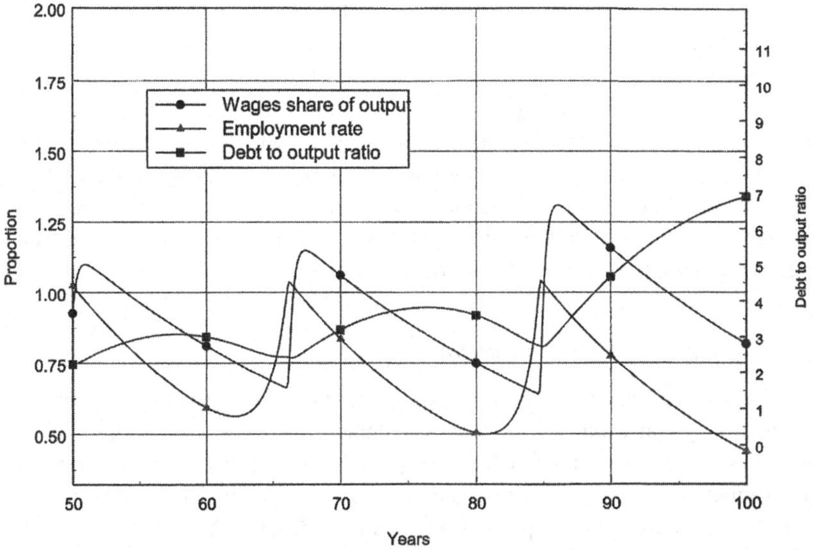

Figure 5.9. Period interactions of wages share, employment, and debt far from equilibrium.

Behind this increasing income distribution and employment instability lies cyclically accelerating debt, which, in contrast to the near-equilibrium simulation, falls primarily during the recovery and the boom phases of the cycle and rises during slumps.

The phase diagram of this simulation in Fig. 5.8 makes the system behavior graphically apparent. What is a stable volcano-shaped phase diagram becomes an unstable vortex in which debt overwhelms the other system variables.

The period interactions shown in Fig. 5.9 give some of the dynamics behind this collapse. Whereas in the near-equilibrium dynamics, the debt-to-output ratio began to fall almost as soon as the boom phase was over, here the debt-to-output ratio continues to rise until well into the slump. With year 63 as our starting point, the boom begins at a point when both wages share and the debt-to-output ratio are falling. This increases profit share and leads to a rapid boom financed by renewed borrowing, although the debt-to-output ratio is actually reduced by the more rapid rise in output. However, this eventually results in an acceleration in wages, sharply reduced profits, and an increased debt burden. These events terminate the boom some 2 years later and lead to a long gradual slump, during which time debt continues to accumulate because profits are so heavily diminished. The cycle recurs, with each successive cycle leading to a more extreme hump in the debt-to-output ratio, until the final boom leads to a wages explosion, the debt financing of which (in addition to the preceding debt financing of investment) leads to an unsustainable level of debt that overwhelms the economy.

The behavior of this model thus clearly supports the Fisher–Keynes–Minsky contention that a pure market economy is fundamentally unstable, in that it is prone to fall into a debt-induced depression from which there is no escape, baring "resetting the debt clock" by means of wholesale bankruptcy and debt moratoria. The next extension similarly supports Minsky's claim that the government sector's behavior provides a homeostatic balance that controls and possibly eliminates this tendency to depression.

Adding a government sector

Minsky's contention that countercyclical behavior by government stabilizes the market by constraining its tendency to debt accumulation is explored by the introduction of government spending and taxation as functions of the rate of employment and the profit share of output, respectively. This extension requires a new definition for the net profit share and the rate of change of private debt, and two additional nonlinear functions for the rate of change of government spending with respect to employment and taxation with respect to the gross profit share:

$$\text{net profit share of output } \pi_n = 1 - \omega - t + g - r\,d_k, \tag{5.22}$$

$$\text{rate of change of capitalist debt } \frac{\mathrm{d}}{\mathrm{d}t} D_k = r D_k + I_g - \Pi + T - G, \tag{5.23}$$

$$\text{government spending function } \frac{\mathrm{d}G}{\mathrm{d}t} = g(\lambda)Y, \tag{5.24}$$

$$\text{government taxation function } \frac{\mathrm{d}T}{\mathrm{d}t} = \tau(\pi_n)Y, \tag{5.25}$$

$$\text{rate of change of government debt } \frac{\mathrm{d}}{\mathrm{d}t} D_g = r D_g + G - T \tag{5.26}$$

where $g(\lambda)$ and $\tau(\pi_n)$ are as defined in the glossary of Table 5.1. This extension results in the following six-dimensional model of a mixed-market–state economy:

$$\frac{\mathrm{d}\omega}{\mathrm{d}t} = \omega[w(\lambda) - \alpha],$$

$$\frac{\mathrm{d}\lambda}{\mathrm{d}t} = \lambda\left\{\left[\frac{k(\pi_n/\nu)}{\nu} - \gamma\right] - \alpha - \beta\right\},$$

$$\frac{\mathrm{d}d}{\mathrm{d}t} = d\left\{r - \left[\frac{k(\pi_n/\nu)}{\nu} - \gamma\right]\right\} + k(\pi_n/\nu) - \pi + t - g,$$

Table 5.1. *Glossary*

Term	Definition	Formula
Y	Level of output	
π	Profit rate	
L, λ	Employment, employment rate	$L = Y/a, \lambda = L/N$
Y, a	Output, labor productivity	
α	Productivity growth	$\alpha = \alpha_0 e^{\alpha, t}$
N, β	Population, growth rate	$N = N_0 \, e^{\beta\, t}$
w	Wage rate	$(1/w)(dw/dt) = w(\lambda)$
$P(\lambda)$	Phillips curve	$P(\lambda) = e^{A+B\,\lambda} + C$
π_s	Profit share of output (no finance)	$\pi_s = \Pi/Y$
ω	Wages share of output	$\omega = W/Y = wL/La = w/a$
γ	Depreciation rate	
$k(\pi n)$	Investment function	$k(\pi_n) = e^{D+E\pi_n} + F$
D	Debt	$\frac{dD}{dt} = rD + I - \Pi$
d	Debt-to-output ratio	$d = D/Y$
g_y	Output growth rate	$g_y = (1/Y)(dY/dt)$
π_s	Profit share of output (with finance)	$\pi_s = 1 - \omega - r \cdot d$
$g(\lambda)$	Subsidies function	$g(\lambda) = e^{G+H\lambda} + I$
G, g	Subsidies level, subsidies/output	$g = G/Y$
$t(\pi)$	Taxation function	$\tau(\pi) = e^{J+K\pi} + L$
T, t	Taxes, taxes/output	$t = T/Y$
D_k, d_k	Capitalist debt, debt/output	$d_k = D_k/Y$
D_g, d_g	Government debt, debt/output	$d_g = D_g/Y$
π_s	Gross profit share	$\pi_s = 1 - \omega$
π_n	Net profit share	$\pi_n = 1 - \omega - t + g - rd_k$

$$\frac{dg}{dt} = g(\lambda) - g\left[\frac{k(\pi_n/\nu)}{\nu} - \gamma\right],$$

$$\frac{d}{dt}t = \tau(\pi_n) - t\left[\frac{k(\pi_n/\nu)}{\nu} - \gamma\right],$$

$$\frac{d}{dt}d_g = d_g\left\{r - \left[\frac{k(\pi_n/\nu)}{\nu} - \gamma\right]\right\} + g - t. \tag{5.27}$$

The behavior of this model is consistent with Minsky's hypothesis. The most intriguing aspect, from a complex systems point of view, is that the addition of a government sector transforms a system that was locally stable (about the equilibrium) but globally unstable into a system that is locally unstable but globally stable. At least half the eigenvalues of the linearized version have positive real parts for all values of r, yet, rather than leading to breakdown, the model is constrained by a chaotic limit cycle, as the following simulations indicate.

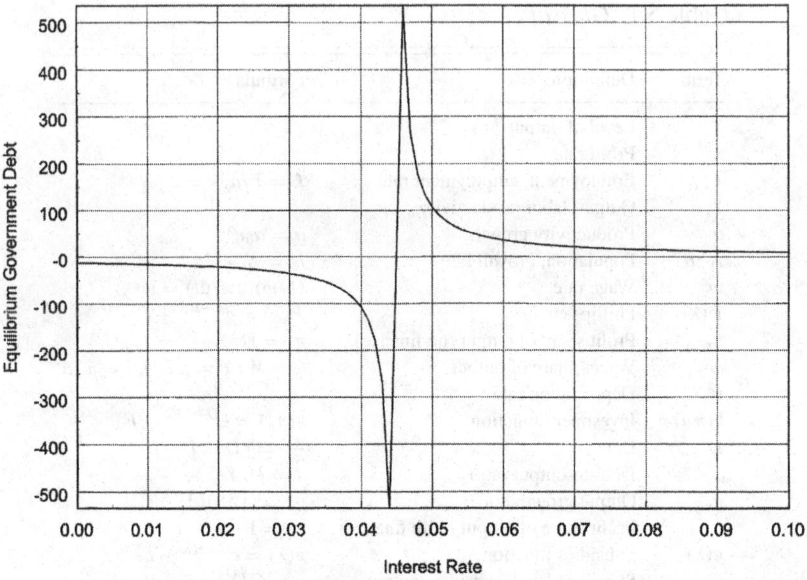

Figure 5.10. Bifurcation in the equilibrium government debt.

The second intriguing feature of this model is the relationship between government debt and the interest rate. As with the preceding model, the equilibrium wages share of output is a negative linear function of the interest rate, but in addition the level of government debt is a rectangular hyperbolic function of the interest rate (see Fig. 5.10):

$$d_g = \frac{t - g}{r - \left[\frac{k(\pi_n/\nu)}{\nu} - \gamma\right]}. \tag{5.28}$$

Thus if the prevailing (real) rate of interest is below the rate of growth of output, then with the equilibrium values for t and g given by the parameter values used in these simulations, the equilibrium value of government debt is negative. Equally, if the rate of interest exceeds the rate of growth, the equilibrium value is positive. Although the actual values differ substantially from equilibrium values because of the system's far-from-equilibrium dynamics, this negative/positive bifurcation remains in any simulation.

Figures 5.11–5.13 show the behavior of the model with an interest rate of 3% and a 0.01 deviation of all system variables from the equilibrium vector.[10]

[10] $(\omega, \lambda, d_k, g, t, d_g) = (0.300604985584, 0.971225057244, 0.070191124862, -0.145020153379, 0.390427727909, -35.696525419245)$.

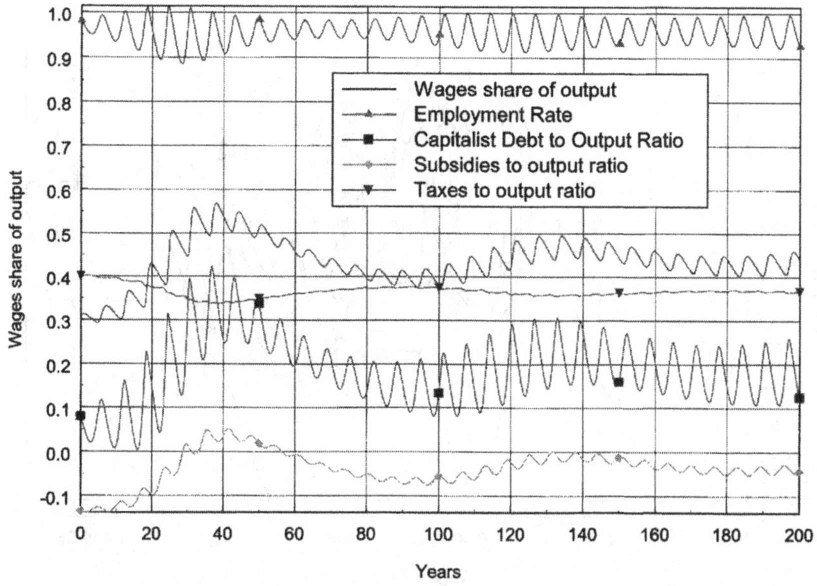

Figure 5.11. Mixed-economy far-from-equilibrium dynamics at low interest.

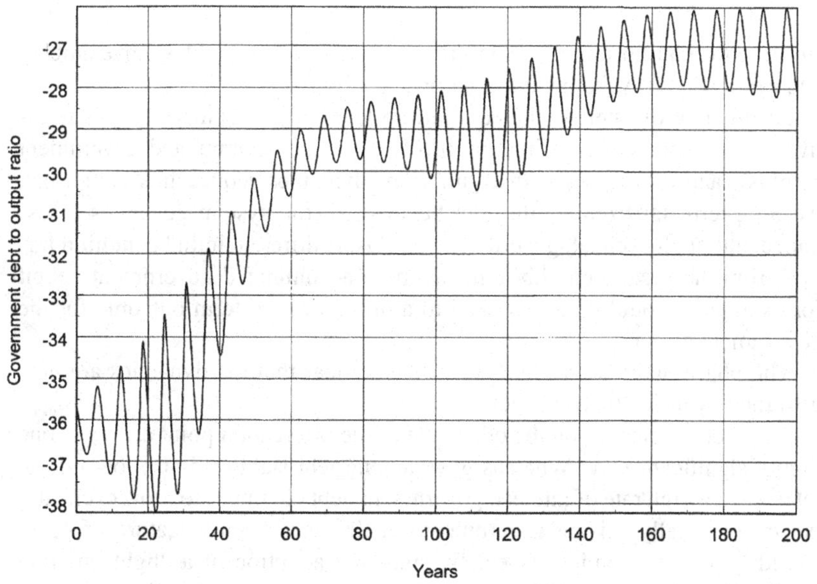

Figure 5.12. Mixed-economy far-from-equilibrium government debt dynamics at low interest.

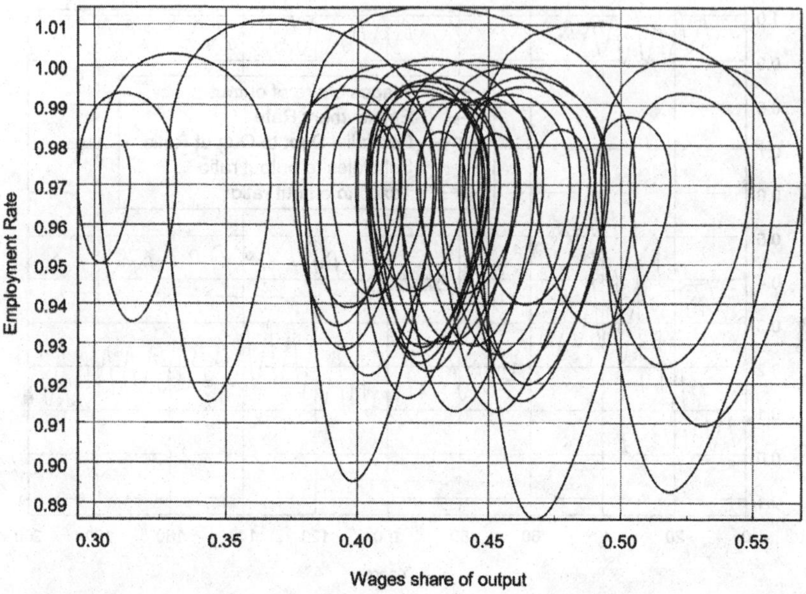

Figure 5.13. Mixed-economy far-from-equilibrium wages share and employment interactions at low interest.

Because the equilibrium vector is a repeller, all system variables move quickly and cyclically away from their equilibrium values.

At this rate of interest, the equilibrium level of government debt is negative (i.e., the equilibrium situation involves a large accumulated government surplus), and although the disequilibrium dynamics reduce this somewhat, the long-term far-from-equilibrium behavior of the system generates a sustained, although cyclical, government surplus. A different initial condition further from the system equilibrium – with an accumulated government deficit for example – could, however, lead to a different long-term outcome for the government sector.

The phase diagram in Fig. 5.13 makes it clear that the dynamics are now governed by a chaotic limit cycle.

The model behavior on the other side of the bifurcation point differs in one highly significant way: Whereas government debt stabilized at a low rate of interest, at a high rate of interest, government debt continues to grow cyclically but exponentially. Rising government deficits have been a feature of post–World War II economies, especially since the adoption of a "fight inflation first" strategy in the mid-1970s in an attempt to control the rate of inflation. The cornerstone of this policy was tight monetary policy – which meant high real

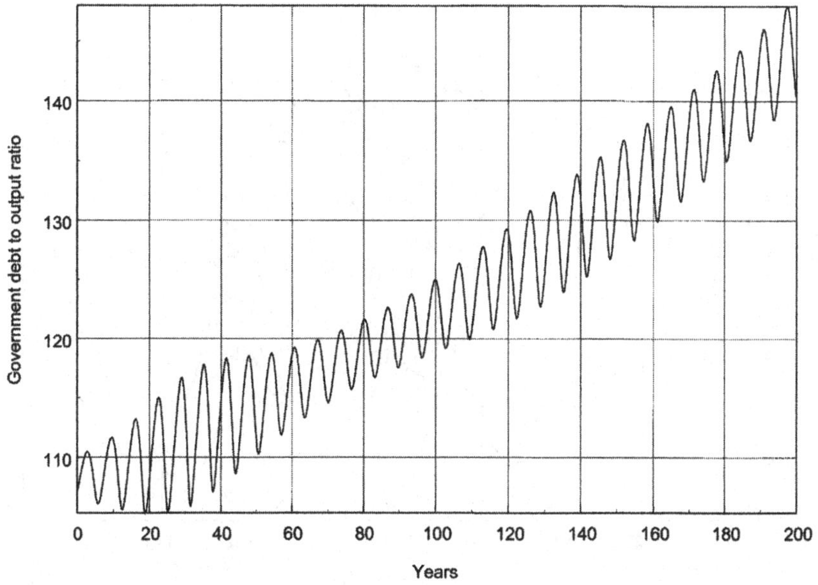

Figure 5.14. Mixed-economy far-from-equilibrium dynamics at high interest.

interest rates. Figures 5.14 and 5.15 demonstrate the behavior of the model with an interest rate of 5% and a 0.01 deviation of all values from the equilibrium vector.

The apparent paradox in Fig. 5.14 of the coincidence of a positive overall government impact on the economy – in that a debt-induced collapse is avoided – and yet a growing accumulated government deficit is explained by the impact of the high rate of interest on the current level of outstanding debt and the already high level of debt implied by starting from the equilibrium position. However, a different initial condition with a low or a negative initial government debt could easily result in a surplus's being accumulated by the government (see Keen 1995), as opposed to the deficit shown here.

As Fig. 5.15 indicates, the qualitative behavior of the model remains the same on either side of the bifurcation in equilibrium government debt.

7 Prices and Fisher's Paradox

Fisher argued that debt accumulation on its own would not be sufficient to cause a depression, but instead would give rise to cycles. However, the model above indicates the accumulation of debt alone can lead to a depression – as the end product of a series of business cycles – as the fundamental asymmetry

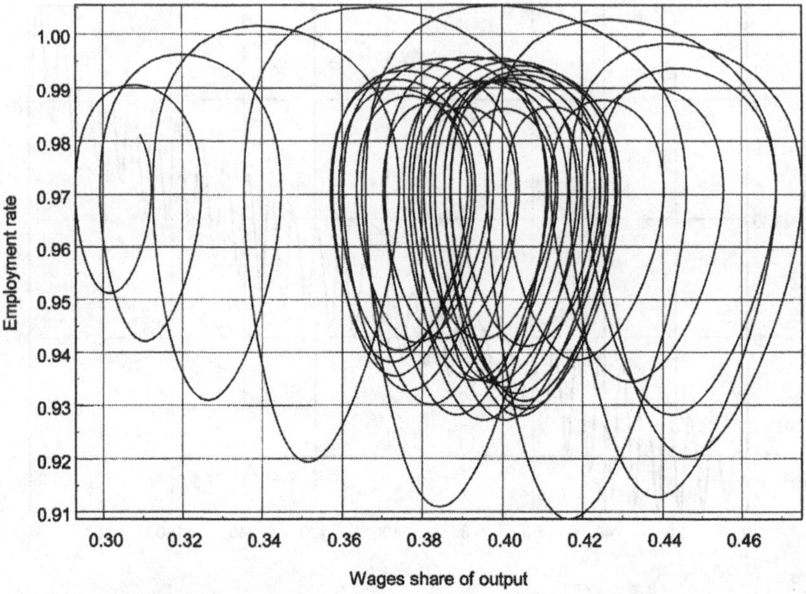

Figure 5.15. Mixed-economy far-from-equilibrium wages share and employment interactions at high interest.

that firms incur debt during booms but have to repay it during slumps asserts itself. Deflation is thus not essential to the occurrence of a depression, but it would accelerate the process and exacerbate its depth by its impact on the rate of bankruptcy. Similarly, Minsky's argument that capital goods prices are expectation driven (Minsky 1982, pp. 64, 80) implies that procyclical movements in capital goods will exacerbate the accumulation of debt, thus hastening the onset of a depression in a market economy.

We can explore these issues by revising the basic system of equations to include consumer prices (P_c) and capital goods prices (P_k). We start with an income shares equation in nominal (money) terms,

$$Y = W + rD + \Pi, \tag{5.29}$$

in which wages can be decomposed into a real wage, a consumer price index, and the level of employment (L):

$$W = wP_cL. \tag{5.30}$$

The wage change relation is now in money terms:

$$\frac{dW}{dt} = \frac{d}{dt}(wP_c) = Ww(\lambda). \tag{5.31}$$

On the other hand, the relations between labor and output and output and capital must now be expressed in real terms:

$$Y_r = \frac{Y}{P_c},\ L = \frac{Y_r}{a} = \frac{Y}{P_c\,a},\ K = \nu Y_r = \nu\frac{Y}{P_c}. \tag{5.32}$$

The introduction of a capital goods price index affects the amount paid by firms for investment goods, but the change in physical productivity continues to depend on the real increment to capital. A distinction is thus required between nominal investment (I_n) that affects bank balances and real gross investment (I_r) that affects the capital stock:

$$I_n = P_k\,k(\pi)Y,\ I_r = k(\pi)Y. \tag{5.33}$$

This results in the following system of equations:

$$\frac{\mathrm{d}\omega}{\mathrm{d}t} = \omega\left[w(\lambda) - \frac{1}{P_c}\frac{\mathrm{d}P_c}{\mathrm{d}t} - \alpha\right],$$

$$\frac{\mathrm{d}\lambda}{\mathrm{d}t} = \lambda\left[\frac{k(\pi)}{\nu} - \gamma - \alpha - \beta\right],$$

$$\frac{\mathrm{d}d}{\mathrm{d}t} = d\left\{r - \frac{1}{P_c}\frac{\mathrm{d}P_c}{\mathrm{d}t} - \left[\frac{k(\pi)}{\nu} - \gamma\right]\right\} + k(\pi)\frac{P_k}{P_c} - \pi. \tag{5.34}$$

Leaving aside the issue of a functional form for the rate of change of the price indices, this set of equations confirms Fisher's and Minsky's insights concerning the impact of commodity price deflation and capital goods prices. As can be seen from the debt relation, a high rate of commodity price inflation reduces the real debt burden, as Minsky emphasizes, whereas conversely price deflation will lead, as Fisher asserts, to an amplification of the real debt burden. The rate of debt accumulation also depends on the ratio of the capital goods price index to the consumer price index, and because the P_k/P_c ratio will rise during a boom, this will accelerate the process of debt accumulation. The price system thus increases the instability of the market economy.

8 Conclusion

The models above and the theories of Fisher and Minsky on which they are based cast a unique light on the economic history of the post-OPEC era. Rather than being a sign of the failure of Keynesian policies, the high inflation of the 1970s may have prevented the 1973 economic crisis from ushering in a depression. Similarly, the eventual success of policies intended to reduce inflation may have unwittingly set the scene for debt deflation to become the most serious economic problem of the late 20th and the early 21st centuries. This prognosis is made all the more likely by the debt crises in East and Northeast Asian developing economies of 1997 (and the subsequent Brazilian crisis of 1998) and Japan's sustained slump since the collapse of its Bubble Economy in the early 1990s.

Indonesia, Malaysia, Thailand, and South Korea have all experienced serious debt-induced crises. None of these countries has developed social security or progressive tax regimes, so that the domestic government sectors cannot significantly temper the deflationary impact of the debt crisis. Although these countries are all likely to suffer significant inflation as a consequence of the currency depreciations, the depreciations may fulfill the same function as price deflation in Fisher and Minsky's theory, as much of the debt involved is unhedged foreign debt. Indeed, the impact of floating exchange rate depreciations may far outweigh anything envisaged by Fisher, with the money market showing a proclivity to heavily devalue a country's currency whenever it believes that the country will not be able to repay its debts. Although it was possible that many of Indonesia's nongovernment borrowers would be unable to repay their debts at an exchange rate of 2500 rupiah to the dollar, it is certain that only the least indebted of them can repay at a rate of over 15,000 rupiah to the dollar. There is no prospect of Indonesia's trading its way out of its private debt crisis at a market-determined exchange rate – and the same quite possibly also applies to South Korea, Thailand, and Malaysia. A debt rescheduling comparable with that of Latin American during the 1970s could, however, be feasible if the precrisis exchange rate were reestablished.

The Japanese economy has been crippled by debts accumulated during the Bubble Economy period of the late 1980s, when real estate speculation resulted in Tokyo's nominal land value exceeding that of Canada. Japan's absence of foreign-denominated debt and substantial financial reserves in the form of foreign bond holdings insulate it from the currency depreciation problems of its Asian nations. Japan's peculiar combination of massive internal debts with its status as the world's leading creditor nation means that any action it takes to avert its domestic crisis will have significant consequences for the global economy.

Although the Japanese government is in a position to give its economy a massive fiscal and monetary boost, the only action that is likely to ameliorate Japan's internal situation and simultaneously ease the problems of its debtors is one that would simultaneously increase the Japanese price level, thus reducing the real debt burden, and cause a devaluation of the yen, thus reducing the burden of debt owed to Japanese nationals by those of other nations. One such action would be an across-the-board increase in Japanese wages, which, unlike failed attempts at monetary and fiscal stimuli during 1997 and 1998, would necessarily lead to inflation by means of the impact of uniformly higher wages on nominal production costs. This action would lead to a devaluation of the yen by the Forex markets, which would thus reduce the burden of yen-denominated debt for Japan's Southeast Asian debtors and lead to an overall approximately neutral impact on Japan's international competitiveness.

It goes without saying that such policies – arbitrated exchange rates, debt rescheduling, and deliberately engineering inflation by means of direct government manipulation of input prices – goes strongly against the dominant grain in both economic theory and policy. There is thus little likelihood of such policies being adopted, at least in the immediate future. There also may be no painless way out of this debt-deflationary process, now that it has begun. The essential policy message of the Financial Instability Hypothesis was that we should avoid such crises in the first place by developing and maintaining institutions and policies that enforce "a 'good financial society' in which the tendency by businesses and bankers to engage in speculative finance is constrained" (Minsky 1977, 1982, p. 69). Because we have manifestly failed to maintain such institutions and policies, we may have to reap the consequences in the form of the second Great Depression of the 20th century. As with the first, it will usher in social upheaval and widespread debt repudiation and conceivably lead to the dismantling of the current international financial system.

In this crisis, as evidenced by the International Monetary Fund's disastrous interventions in Indonesia, conventional economic theory will be one of the most important barriers to understanding what is happening and to working out what can be done to attenuate the damage. Economics has been conditioned by 50 years of moderate to high inflation to regard reflation with suspicion and to be too sanguine about low to negative rates of price change.[11] Yet, as the models in this paper and Fisher and Minsky's theories indicate, reflation and deliberately manufactured inflation may provide the only means by which the debt-deflationary process can be contained. The world may yet pay a high price for the economics profession's choice of the exogenous, linear explanation of cycles some 65 years ago in the depths of the last Great Depression.

REFERENCES

Blatt, J. M. (1980). On the Frisch model of business cycles. *Oxford Econ. Pap.*, **32**, 467–79.

(1983). *Dynamic Economic Systems*, Sharpe, Armonk.

Fisher, I. (1933). *Booms And Depressions: Some First Principles*, Allen and Unwin, London.

(1933a) The debt-deflation theory of great depressions. *Econometrica*, **1**, 337–57.

Frisch, R. (1933). Propagation problems and impulse problems in dynamic economics. In *Economic Essays in Honor of Gustav Cassel*, Allen and Unwin, London, pp. 171–205.

Keen, S. (1995). Finance and economic breakdown: modeling Minsky's Financial Instability Hypothesis. *J. Post Keynesian Econ.*, **17**, 607–35.

[11] Although Alan Greenspan's observation that "deflation can be detrimental for reasons that go beyond those that are also associated with inflation" (see http://www.bog.frb.fed.us/boarddocs/speeches/19980103.htm) gives cause for hope.

Minsky, H. (1977). The Financial Instability Hypothesis: an interpretation of Keynes and an alternative to 'standard' theory. *Nebraska J. Econ. Bus.*, **16**, 5–16, reprinted in Minsky 1982, pp. 59–70.

(1982). *Inflation, Recession and Economic Policy*, Wheatsheaf, Sussex, England.

Pomeau, Y., and Manneville, P. (1980). Intermittent transition to turbulence in dissipative dynamical systems. *Commun. Math. Phys.*, **74**, 189–97.

Samuelson, P. A. (1939). Interactions between the multiplier analysis and the principle of acceleration. *Review of Economics and Statistics*, **20**, 75–78.

Shaw, A., and Desai, M. (1981). Growth cycles with induced technical change. Maastricht University, The Netherlands. *Econ. J.*, **91**, 1006–1010.

CHAPTER 6

The emergence of complex dynamics in a "naturally" nonlinear integrated Keynesian model of monetary growth

Carl Chiarella and Peter Flaschel

We present a fairly general Keynesian disequilibrium model of monetary growth that provides an integration of prototypical models of real growth, inflationary dynamics, and inventory adjustment into a consistent whole.

It makes use of a worker–capitalist example as in Kaldor's growth and distribution theory, an asset market structure as in Sargent's (1987, part I) Keynesian model of monetary growth, a description of the sector of firms that makes use of Malinvaud's (1980) investment theory and of the analysis of Franke and Lux (1993) and Franke (1992) of the Metzlerian process of inventory adjustment, a government sector as in Sargent (1987), a wage–price sector inspired by Rose's (1990) formulation of this sector, and an expectations mechanism with forward- and backward-looking components as in Groth (1988).

The behavior of firms takes into account the fact that firms seldom operate at their desired capacity and with their desired inventories, but deviate in general from these two norms because of unexpected changes in aggregate goods demand.[1]

Our model is complete in the sense that the range of sectors utilized in conventional macrodynamic modeling is integrated here explicitly into a consistent whole, in particular with regard to financing conditions and budget restrictions of households, firms, and the government. There is no model in the traditional

The authors thank G. Winckler, J. Jungeilges, and participants at a Symposium on Nonlinear Dynamics and Econometrics at the Meeting of the Eastern Economic Association for helpful comments on the original version of this chapter. The authors also thank Alexander Khomin for his able programming support. Financial support from Australian Research Council grant A79231467 is also gratefully acknowledged. The usual caveats apply.

[1] The consideration of underutilized or overutilized capital besides an underutilized or overutilized labor force is important, but nevertheless is not a typical feature of the literature on Keynesian dynamics and has indeed been rather neglected by it. See Malinvaud (1980) for an exception in the context of a stationary economy.

Keynesian literature of this generality, although all of its component parts can be considered as known from various sources.

Moreover, Keynesian monetary growth theory is generally not even mentioned in surveys on the literature on monetary growth, as for example in the recent article "Money, inflation and growth" by Orphanides and Solow (1990) in the *Handbook of Monetary Economics*. It appears as if the Keynesian theory of monetary growth (*cum* cycles) is basically nonexistent in the literature. This is an important discontinuity in the development of the literature on monetary growth, which, in our view, prevents a full understanding of the achievements of (traditional) Keynesianism, its scientific possibilities, and the progress that has really been made by the so-called neo- or new- or post-Keynesians.

Our general model gives rise to seven interdependent laws of motion or, by means of a suitable assumption on government expenditures, to a six-dimensional (6D) integrated system of differential equations in which the feedback of the dynamics of the government debt is absent. The general dynamical behavior of our system cannot be studied analytically with currently available techniques, apart from being able to make some very basic statements.

Here it is investigated in three ways:

- Appropriate assumptions allow us to reduce the 6D dynamical system to three two-dimensional (2D) ones that can be investigated analytically from a local as well as a global point of view with respect to their stability properties and their cyclical nature. In this way we isolate the basic cycle-generating mechanisms whose interaction yields the complex dynamical behavior we uncover by numerical simulations in the full model.
- The integrated dynamical behavior of the system is studied numerically by way of Hopf bifurcations and eigenvalue analysis. These studies also illustrate the limited extent to which the results of the 2D investigations carry over to the general 6D case.
- The use of numerical simulation of the trajectories and bifurcation diagrams allows us to show the type of dynamic behavior that is possible in the regions of parameter space that the earlier steps have found to be of interest.

We shall see from these investigations that the full gamut of complex dynamical behavior is possible, from stability of the steady state, to limit cycles, to what appear to be strange attractors. We also investigate the effect on the global dynamics of changes in key parameters such as price-adjustment speeds and fiscal and monetary policy parameters.

In sum, we therefore provide an introduction to Keynesian monetary growth and cycle theory by means of a general prototypic and integrated model. Such a prototype is missing in the literature, which thus lacks a model with which more modern approaches of neo-, new-, or post-Keynesian origin can be usefully compared. It should be noted here that it is not difficult to replace certain modules of the present model with corresponding typical modules of such newer developments. Yet, before doing so, we must understand the structure and the general properties of such a traditional Keynesian model in more detail in order to see properly what has really been accomplished by models with other schemes of rationing (than the Keynesian one), with monopolistic wage and price sectors (as in new-Keynesian models), and with a more advanced description of the working of the asset markets (as in post-Keynesian and other approaches).

The need for research into the dynamic behavior of complete and integrated descriptive models of the Keynesian variety stems from the fact that such models continue to be used in many empirical applications and discussions of policy analysis. Perhaps this is because this class of models provides the most readily applicable theory of business-cycle fluctuations and the impact on these of various government policies. This is so in spite of significant advances over recent years in the development of the microfounded so-called real business-cycle theory. The development of such models has not yet reached the point of being complete from the point of view of the dynamic structure considered here.

It should also be noted that all behavioral and technical relationships in the following model have been chosen to be linear as far as possible. It is not difficult to introduce into the model some well-known nonlinearities that have been used in the literature on real, monetary, and inventory dynamics of Keynesian type. Yet again, before doing so, we should investigate the dynamical properties of this complete Keynesian model in an environment where only unavoidable nonlinearities are present. Such nonlinearities naturally arise from the growth-rate formulation of certain laws of motion, certain unavoidable ratio expressions, and the fact that some state variables of the dynamics have to be multiplied with each other (because of the involvement of value expressions such as total wages). Already on the basis of these most basic types of nonlinearities it can be shown that certain stability problems of dynamic submodels of the general model can be overcome when they are just considered within this broader framework, without any "bending of curves" known to be needed to tame the explosive dynamical behavior of the partial submodels.

The plan of the paper is as follows. In Section 1 we outline the main elements of the model, in particular emphasizing the key linkages and feedbacks among the different sectors and agents of the model that determine its dynamic behavior. In Section 2 we examine the dynamic structure of the model and its naturally occurring nonlinear structure, and we identify the main economic factors that determine this structure. We also examine the steady state of the model and its Jacobian and explore the dynamics of the model numerically by a study of Hopf loci and some simulated trajectories. In Section 3 we study the goods/labor market, money/goods market, and inventory subdynamics that drive the dynamics of the 6D model. In Section 4 we study, by means of numerical simulation, the dynamics of the full seven-dimensional (7D) model and the effect on its complex dynamics of changes in speed of wage and price adjustment as well as key policy parameters. In Section 5 we discuss the effect on the model of one extrinsic nonlinearity that seems to be an institutional reality, namely, downward rigid nominal wages. Section 6 contains conclusions and suggestions for future research.

1 An integrated Keynesian model of monetary growth

The agents in the model consist of households (in their capacity as workers and asset holders), firms (which perform the role of production units and investors), and government (acting as the fiscal and monetary authority). These agents interact on markets for goods, labor, and financial assets. Particular features of the model are that (1) investment is determined by the expected rate of return differential (between expected profit and the expected real rate of interest) and capacity utilization, (2) changes in nominal wages and prices are driven by excess (deficient) capacity in the market for labor and goods, respectively, as well as on each other and the expected rate of inflation, and (3) there is a Metzlerian process of inventory adjustment.

A more detailed discussion of the economic underpinnings of the model as well as its significance in the literature on Keynesian monetary growth models is given in Chiarella and Flaschel (1997).

The equations of this model of IS-LM growth are as follows.[2]

Definitions (remuneration and wealth):

$$\omega = w/p,\ \rho^e = (Y^e - \delta K - \omega L^d)/K, \tag{6.1}$$

$$W = (M + B + p_e E)/p,\ p_b = 1. \tag{6.2}$$

This set of equations introduces variables that are used in the following structural equations of the model, namely, the definition of real wages ω, the expected rate of profit on real capital ρ^e, and the definition of real wealth W. Wealth here is composed of money M, fixed-price bonds B ($p_b = 1$), and equities E, as in Sargent[3] (1987).

Household behavior is described next by the following set of equations.

Households (workers and asset holders):

$$W = (M^d + B^d + p_e E^d)/p,\ M^d = h_1 pY + h_2 pK(r_0 - r), \tag{6.3}$$

$$C = \omega L^d + (1 - s_c)(\rho^e K + rB/p - T), \tag{6.4}$$

[2] See Section 7 for the notation used.

[3] Assuming consols ($p_b = 1/r$) in place of the bonds assumed by Sargent (1987) does not alter the 6D dynamics of the private sector considered below.

$$S_p = s_c(\rho^e K + rB/p - T) = (\dot{M}^d + \dot{B}^d + p_e \dot{E}^d)/p, \tag{6.5}$$

$$\hat{L} = n = \text{const.} \tag{6.6}$$

We here start from Walras's Law of Stocks, which states that real wealth W, in Eq. (6.3), is the constraint for the stock demand for real money balances and real bond and equity holdings at each moment in time. Money demand is specified as a simple linear function of nominal income pY and interest r (r_0 is the steady-state rate of interest) in the usual way.

The form of this function is chosen in this way in order to allow for a simple formula for the rate of interest in the intensive form of the model, i.e., it is chosen for mathematical convenience to some extent and not exclusively for economic reasons.

Nonlinear money demand functions with real wealth in place of the capital stock would be more appropriate and thus should replace this simple function in later extensions.

Consumption C, in Eq. (6.4), is based on classical saving habits with savings out of wages set equal to zero for simplicity. For the time being we assume that real taxes T are paid out of (expected) profit and interest income solely and in a lump-sum fashion. Extending such tax payments to wage income does not make much difference to the model and is here bypassed to make this model comparable with the ones considered in Chiarella and Flaschel (1997). Equation (6.5) provides the definition of real private savings S_p (here of wealth owners) that is then allocated to desired changes in the stock of money, bonds, and equities held.

Finally, in Eq. (6.6), workers are assumed to supply labor L inelastically at each moment in time with a rate of growth $\hat{L}$ given by n, the so-called natural rate of growth.

The behavior of the production sector of the economy is described by the following set of equations.

Firms (production units and investors):

$$Y^p = y^p K, \; y^p = \text{const.}, \; U = Y/Y^p = y/y^p, \; (y = Y/K), \tag{6.7}$$

$$L^d = Y/x, \; x = \text{const.}, \; V = L^d/L = Y/(xL), \tag{6.8}$$

$$I = i_1[\rho^e - (r - \pi)]K + i_2(U - 1)K + nK, \tag{6.9}$$

$$S_f = Y_f = Y - Y^e = \ddot{I}, \tag{6.10}$$

$$\Delta Y^e = Y^e - \delta K - C - I - G = Y^e - Y^d, \tag{6.11}$$

$$p_e \dot{E}/p = I + \Delta Y^e = I + (\dot{N} - \ddot{I}), \tag{6.12}$$

$$I^a = I + \dot{N} = I + \Delta Y^e + \ddot{I} = I^p + \Delta Y^e = p_e \dot{E}/p + \ddot{I}, \tag{6.13}$$

$$\hat{K} = I/K. \tag{6.14}$$

According to Eqs. (6.7) and (6.8), firms produce commodities in amount Y in the technologically simplest way possible by means of a fixed-proportions technology characterized by the potential output–capital ratio $y^p = Y^p/K$ and a fixed ratio x between actual output Y and labor L^d needed to produce this output. This simple concept of technology allows for a straightforward definition of the rate of utilization U, V of capital as well as labor.[4]

In Eq. (6.9), investment per unit of capital I/K is driven by two forces, the rate of return differential between the expected rate of profit ρ^e and the real rate of interest $(r - \pi)$ and the deviation of actual capacity utilization U from the normal or nonaccelerating-inflation rate of capacity utilization $\bar{U} = 1$.

There is also an exogenous trend term in the investment equation that is set equal to the natural rate of growth for reasons of simplicity.

Savings of firms, Eq. (6.10), is equal to the excess of output over expected sales (caused by planned inventory changes), as we assume in this model that expected sales are the basis of firms' dividend payments (after deduction of capital depreciation δK and real wage payments ωL^d).

Equation (6.11) defines the excess of expected demand over actual demand that has to be financed by firms by issuing new equities. We assume here, as in Sargent (1987), that firms issue no bonds and retain no expected earnings. It follows, as expressed in Eq. (6.12), that the total amount of new equities issued by firms must equal in value the sum of intended fixed capital investment and unexpected inventory changes, $\Delta Y^e = \dot{N} - \dot{I}$; compare our later formulation of the inventory adjustment mechanism. Equation (6.13) describes on this basis actual investment I^a from various perspectives and here serves only to add some details about the accounting framework of the type of firms considered. Finally, Eq. (6.14) states that (fixed-business) investment plans of firms are always realized in this Keynesian (demand-oriented) context by way of corresponding inventory changes.

We now turn to a brief description of the government sector.

Government (fiscal and monetary authority):

$$T = \tau(\rho K + rB/p), \tag{6.15}$$

$$G = T - rB/p + \mu_0 M/p + \beta_g(V - 1)K, \tag{6.16}$$

$$S_g = T - rB/p - G[= -(\dot{M} + \dot{B})/p] \text{ (see below)}, \tag{6.17}$$

$$\hat{M} = \mu_0 + \beta_m(\mu_0 - n - \pi), \tag{6.18}$$

$$\dot{B} = pG + rB - pT - \dot{M}[= (\mu_0 - \mu)M]. \tag{6.19}$$

[4] Chiarella and Flaschel (1997, Chap. 5) show that such an approach can be extended to the case of smooth factor substitution without much change in its substance.

The government sector is here described in as simple a way as possible by way of policy rules such that the role of bond financing of government expenditures for the dynamics of the model can be discussed as well as the impact of basic government fiscal and monetary policy rules. In Eq. (6.15), real taxes are assumed to be a fixed proportion of wealth owners' real income.[5] In Eq. (6.16), government expenditures are assumed to be determined by taxes' net of interest and by the steady-state change in the money supply, $\mu_0 M/p$. Furthermore, if there is underemployment of the labor force,[6] in the sense that $V < \bar{V} = 1$ holds, government adds to its expenditures a term $\beta_g(V-1)K$ that is proportional to the disequilibrium on the labor market and that is purely bond financed, whereas – as seen from Eq. (6.16) – the rest of the government deficit is purely money financed. Such a fiscal policy rule may be called a Keynesian one if $\beta_g < 0$ holds, as government then behaves in an anticyclical fashion.

The definition of government savings S_g, Eq. (6.17), is an obvious one. Equation (6.18) states that money supply growth μ is based on a trend term μ_0 plus a term that represents an anti-inflationary policy in the case $\beta_m > 0$.

In view of these various rules for government and central bank behavior, the issue of new bonds by the government is then determined residually by means of Eq. (6.19), which states that money and bond financing must exactly cover the deficit in government expenditure financing.

We now describe the equilibrium conditions of the model:

$$M = M^d = h_1 pY + h_2 pK(r_0 - r)(B = B^d, E = E^d), \tag{6.20}$$

$$p_e E = \rho^e pK/(r - \pi), \tag{6.21}$$

$$\dot{M} = \dot{M}^d, \; \dot{B} = \dot{B}^d, \; (\dot{E} = \dot{E}^d). \tag{6.22}$$

Asset markets are assumed to clear at all times. Equations (6.20) describe this assumption for the money market. Bonds and equities are assumed to be perfect substitutes under static expectations with respect to the price of equities, which is the content of Eq. (6.21). This amounts to assuming, in the light of the assumed Walras's Law of Stocks, that the clearing of the money market implies that the bond and the equity markets are then cleared as well. Finally, in Eqs. (6.22), it is assumed that wealth owners accept the inflows of money and bonds issued by the government for the current period, reallocating them only in the next period by adjusting their portfolios in view of a new situation. It is easy to check by means of the considered saving relationships that the assumed consistency of money and bonds flow supply and flow demand implies the consistency of the flow supply and demand for equities; compare also Eq. (6.23) of the next block of equations.

5 The inclusion of wage taxation is a simple matter; see Chiarella and Flaschel (1997, Chap. 6) for the details.

6 A symmetric situation is assumed in the case of overemployment.

The disequilibrium situation in the goods market is an important component that drives the dynamics of the economy. This situation is described by the following equations.

Disequilibrium situation (goods–market adjustments):

$$S = S_p + S_g + S_f = p_e\dot{E}^d/p + \dot{I} = I + \dot{N} = I^a = p_e\dot{E}/p + \dot{I}, \tag{6.23}$$

$$Y^d = C + I + \delta K + G, \tag{6.24}$$

$$N^d = \beta_{n^d}Y^e,\ \dot{I} = nN^d + \beta_n(N^d - N), \tag{6.25}$$

$$Y = Y^e + \dot{I}, \tag{6.26}$$

$$\dot{Y}^e = nY^e + \beta_{y^e}(Y^d - Y^e), \tag{6.27}$$

$$\dot{N} = Y - Y^d = S - I[S - I^p = Y^e - Y^d]. \tag{6.28}$$

Equation (6.23) of this disequilibrium block of the model describes the various identities that can be related with the ex post identity of savings S and investment I^a for a closed economy. It is added here for accounting purposes solely. Equation (6.24) then defines aggregate demand Y^d, which is never constrained in the present model.

In Eqs. (6.25), desired inventories N^d are assumed to be a constant proportion of expected sales Y^e. Furthermore, intended inventory investment $\dot{I}$ is then determined on this basis by means of adjustment speed β_n multiplied by the current gap between intended and actual inventories $(N^d - N)$ and augmented by a growth term that integrates in the simplest way the fact that this inventory adjustment rule is operating in a growing economy. Output of firms Y in Eq. (6.26) is the sum of expected sales and planned inventory adjustments. Sales expectations are formed here in a purely adaptive way, again augmented by a growth term as shown by Eq. (6.27). Finally, in Eqs. (6.28), actual inventory changes are given by the discrepancy between output Y and actual sales Y^d equal to the difference between total savings S and fixed-business investment I.

We now turn to the last sector of our model, which is the wage–price module or the supply side of the model, as it is often characterized in the literature.

Wage–price sector (adjustment equations):

$$\hat{w} = \beta_w(V - 1) + \kappa_w\hat{p} + (1 - \kappa_w)\pi, \tag{6.29}$$

$$\hat{p} = \beta_p(U - 1) + \kappa_p\hat{w} + (1 - \kappa_p)\pi, \tag{6.30}$$

$$\dot{\pi} = \beta_\pi[\alpha\hat{p} + (1 - \alpha)(\mu_0 - n) - \pi]. \tag{6.31}$$

This supply-side description is based on fairly symmetric assumptions on the causes of wage and price inflation. Wage inflation according to Eq. (6.29) is driven on the one hand by a demand-pull component, given by the deviation of the actual rate of employment V from the nonaccelerating inflation rate of unemployment (NAIRU) rate 1, and on the other hand by a cost-push term measured by a weighted average of the actual rate of price inflation $\hat{p}$ and a medium-run expected rate of inflation π. Similarly, in Eq. (6.30), price inflation is driven by the demand-pull term (given by the deviation of the actual rate of capacity utilization u from the NAIRU rate 1) and the weighted average of the actual rate of wage inflation $\hat{w}$ and a medium-run expected rate of inflation π. This latter expected rate of inflation is in turn determined by a composition of backward-looking (adaptive) and forward-looking (regressive) expectations. This amounts to an inflationary expectations mechanism as in Eq. (6.31), in which expectations are governed in an adaptive way by a weighted average of the actual and the steady-state-rates of inflation. It is also easy to extend this mechanism in a way such that price forecasting rules, as for example those used by the FED (so-called p^* concepts)[7] are explicitly introduced into the forward-looking component of this expectations mechanism.[8]

2 The dynamics of the model with and without government debt

By using as state variables the (ratio) variables $\omega = w/p, l = L/K, m = M/(pK), \pi, y^e = Y^e/K, \nu = N/K$, and $b = B/(pK)$, one can reduce the dynamical system of Section 1 to the following autonomous nonlinear system of seven differential equations:

$$\hat{\omega} = \kappa[(1-\kappa_p)\beta_w(V-1) + (\kappa_w - 1)\beta_p(U-1)], \tag{6.32}$$

$$\hat{l} = -i_1(\rho^e - r + \pi) - i_2(U-1) = n - i(\cdot), \tag{6.33}$$

$$\hat{m} = \mu - \pi - n - \kappa[\beta_p(U-1) + \kappa_p\beta_w(V-1)] + \hat{l}, \tag{6.34}$$

$$\dot{\pi} = \beta_{\pi_1}\kappa[\beta_p(U-1) + \kappa_p\beta_w(V-1)] + \beta_{\pi_2}(\mu_0 - n - \pi), \tag{6.35}$$

$$\dot{y}^e = \beta_{y^e}(y^d - y^e) + \hat{l}y^e, \tag{6.36}$$

$$\dot{\nu} = y - y^d - i(\cdot)\nu, \tag{6.37}$$

$$\begin{aligned} \dot{b} &= (\mu_0 - \mu)m - (\pi + n)b \\ &\quad - \{\kappa[\beta_p(U-1) + \kappa_p\beta w(V-1)] - \hat{l}\}b + \beta_g(V-1). \end{aligned} \tag{6.38}$$

[7] We owe this observation to work of Dimitris Malliaropulos.

[8] We endow our agents with neither the information of the model structure in which they play out their economic roles, nor the computational ability that they would need to form expectations in a way that is currently referred to as "rational" in a large body of literature. Our reasons for adopting this approach are detailed in Chiarella and Flaschel (1997). In essence these reasons revolve around a critique of the so-called jump-variable technique that the adoption of a "rational" expectations approach would necessitate [see Chiarella (1986) and Oxley and George (1994)] as well as a growing body of empirical evidence; see Frankel and Froot (1987, 1990), which suggests that our approach to expectations modeling may be more appropriate. However, here we stress that future research will need to incorporate the effects of heterogeneity of expectations and of learning on the part of the various economic agents of our models.

For output per capital $y = Y/K$ and aggregate demand per capital $y^d = Y^d/K$, we have the following expressions:

$$y = (1 + n\beta_{n^d})y^e + \beta_n(\beta_{n^d} y^e - v), \tag{6.39}$$

$$\begin{aligned} y^d &= \omega y/x + (1 - s_c)(\rho^e - t^n) + i_1(\rho^e - r + \pi) \\ &\quad + i_2(U - 1) + n + \delta + g \\ &= y^e + (i_1 - s_c)\rho^e - i_1(r - \pi) + i_2 U + \text{const.} \end{aligned} \tag{6.40}$$

Here we make use of the following abbreviations:

$$V = l^d/l,\ U = y/y^p,\ l^d = L^d/K = y/x,\ (y, l^d \text{ not const.!}), \tag{6.41}$$

$$\rho^e = y^e - \delta - \omega l^d = y^e - \delta - \omega y/x, \tag{6.42}$$

$$r = r_0 + (h_1 y - m)/h_2, \tag{6.43}$$

$$\mu = \mu_0 + \beta_m(\mu_0 - n - \pi), \tag{6.44}$$

$$t^n = \tau(\rho + rb) - rb,\ g = t^n + \mu_0 m + \beta_g(V - 1). \tag{6.45}$$

In the derivation of this intensive form of the dynamics of the model we have made use of an approach used in Rose (1990). Indeed, the formal structure of our wage and price adjustment equations is the same as that used in Rose (1990), to whom we owe this idea of representing the wage–price module, although its interpretation and application differ considerably from those of Rose. These equations can be conceived as a considerable generalization of many other formulations of wage–price inflation, for example of models that use demand-pull forces with respect to the labor market and cost-push ones in the market for goods.

The above wage and price equations can be reduced to two linear equations in the unknowns $\hat{w} - \pi$ and $\hat{p} - \pi$, which are easily solved, giving rise to the following expressions for the two unknowns:

$$\hat{w} - \pi = \kappa[\beta_w(V - 1) + \kappa_w\beta_p(U - 1)], \tag{6.46}$$

$$\hat{p} - \pi = \kappa[\kappa_p\beta_w(V - 1) + \beta_p(U - 1)]. \tag{6.47}$$

These equations in turn imply that, for the dynamics of the real wage $\omega = w/p$,

$$\hat{\omega} = \hat{w} - \hat{p} = \kappa[(1 - \kappa_p)\beta_w(V - 1) - (1 - \kappa_w)\beta_p(U - 1)], \tag{6.48}$$

which is the first of our above laws of motion. Moreover, the formula for $\hat{p} - \pi$ is repeatedly used in the following laws of motion of the above intensive form of the model. The derivation of these further laws of motion is then a straightforward exercise.

Our dynamic Keynesian model consists of the seven differential equations (6.32)–(6.38), which, together with algebraic equations (6.39)–(6.40), form a nonlinear dynamical system of dimension six. After considerable algebraic manipulation it can be shown that the dynamic structure of this dynamical system has the trilinear form

$$\dot{u} = Au + \text{diag}(u)Bu + \text{diag}(u)C\text{diag}(u)Du + E, \tag{6.49}$$

where $u = (w, 1/l, m, \pi, y^e, \nu, b)^T$, diag$(u)$ is the 7×7 diagonal matrix with elements of u along the diagonal, and the matrices A, B, C, D, and E involve the various coefficients of the model.

We stress again that the model's nonlinear structure equations have come about without the introduction of any nonlinear economic behavioral relationships (e.g., nonlinear investment functions or nonlinear reaction coefficients $\beta_w, \beta_p, \beta_{y^e}, \beta_{\pi_1}$), which are familiar from the literature on nonlinear macroeconomic dynamics.

These natural nonlinearities that are present in the model and that manifest themselves by means of the trilinear in Eq. (6.49) arise from two sources. The first is due to the formulation of some of the dynamic economic laws in terms of growth rates, in particular the money growth rate ($\hat{M} = \mu$), the rate of capital accumulation ($\hat{K} = I$), and the wage and price dynamics in Eqs. (6.46) and (6.47). It might be argued that the use here of growth rates rather than the time derivative itself constitutes the imposition of nonlinear structure. However, the use of growth rates rather than time derivatives here is certainly traditional and seems to be the most natural economic framework supported by many empirical studies. The second source of nonlinearity is the algebraic expression for aggregate demand per unit of capital in Eq. (6.40). This expression contains a number of bilinear terms that arise from the fact that the wage bill that appears in both the aggregate consumption term and in the expression for the profit rate is essentially the product ωy because of the fixed-proportions technology.[9] This system contains the potential for a rich variety of dynamic behavior, given that it is well known from the literature on nonlinear dynamical systems that merely the addition of simple and apparently innocent bilinear terms to linear dynamic models can lead to quite complex dynamical behavior, as evidenced, for example, by the Lorenz equations and the Rössler attractor.

Consider first the steady state of the model about which we can state the following proposition.

Proposition 1.[10] *There is a unique steady-state solution or point of rest of the dynamics of Eqs. (6.32)–(6.37) fulfilling $\omega_0, l_0, m_0 \neq 0$, which is given by the*

[9] Note that use of smooth factor substitution would not eliminate this bilinear nonlinearity but rather replace it with a convex nonlinearity. See Chiarella and Flaschel (1997, Chap. 5).

[10] The proofs of the propositions of this and the next section of the paper are given in Chiarella and Flaschel (1997, Chap. 7) and can be obtained on request from the authors.

following expressions:

$$y_0 = y^p, l_0 = l_0^d = y_0/x, \; y_0^e = y_0^d = y_0/(1 + n\beta_{n^d}), \tag{6.50}$$

$$m_0 = h_1 y_0, \; \pi_0 = \mu_0 - n, \; r_0 = \rho_0^e + \pi_0, \; \nu_0 = \beta_{n^d} y_0^e, \tag{6.51}$$

$$\rho_0^e = \frac{n + \mu_0 m_0 - s_c \pi_0 b_0 (1 - \tau)}{s_c (1 - \tau)(1 + b_0)}, \; \omega_0 = \frac{y_0^e - \delta - \rho_0^e}{l_0^d}, \tag{6.52}$$

$$b_0 = 0. \tag{6.53}$$

We assume that the parameters of the model are chosen such that the steady-state values for ω, l, m, ρ^e, and r are all positive.

Let us assume for the time being that $\beta_g = 0$ and $\beta_m = 0$ hold true and that there is no government debt initially. According to the form of Eq. (6.39) this immediately implies that there will be no government debt as the economy evolves, because of the particularly simple rules we have adopted for government behavior. This allows us to concentrate on the first six laws of motion for the private sector and to arrive at the following conclusion.

Proposition 2. *Consider the Jacobian J of the dynamics of Eqs. (6.32)–(6.37) at the steady state. The determinant of this 6 × 6 matrix,* det J, *is always positive. It follows that the system can lose or gain asymptotic stability only by way of a Hopf bifurcation (if its eigenvalues cross the imaginary axis with positive speed).*

It is tempting to conjecture that the other Routh–Hurwitz conditions for local asymptotic stability might be fulfilled for either generally sluggish or generally fast adjustment speeds. The following numerical investigation of the model, however, shows that nothing of this sort will hold true in general.

Figure 6.1 shows in the top figure on each of the next three pages the Hopf bifurcation locus[11] for the three parameter sets[12] (β_p, β_w), (β_p, β_{π_1}), and (β_{y^e}, β_n), i.e., the locus where a supercritical, subcritical, or degenerate Hopf bifurcation occurs. The vertical lines separate subcritical from supercritical Hopf bifurcations. The data set for these calculations is given in Table 6.1.

Let us consider the (β_w, β_p) space as an example. For any given $d\beta_p$, increasing β_w from 0 to 1 means that the system will reach a point where it will lose its stability in a cyclical fashion (at β_w^H). At a supercritical Hopf bifurcation this will happen by means of the birth of an attracting limit cycle that surrounds the now unstable steady state ($\beta_w > \beta_w^H$). At a subcritical Hopf bifurcation an unstable limit cycle (which exists for $\beta_w < \beta_w^H$, with β_w sufficiently close to β_w^H) will disappear as β_w approaches β_w^H, where the corridor of local asymptotic

[11] These Hopf bifurcation loci have been calculated with the program LOCBIF (see Khibnik et al., 1993).

[12] Denoted by *bp*, etc., in this figure.

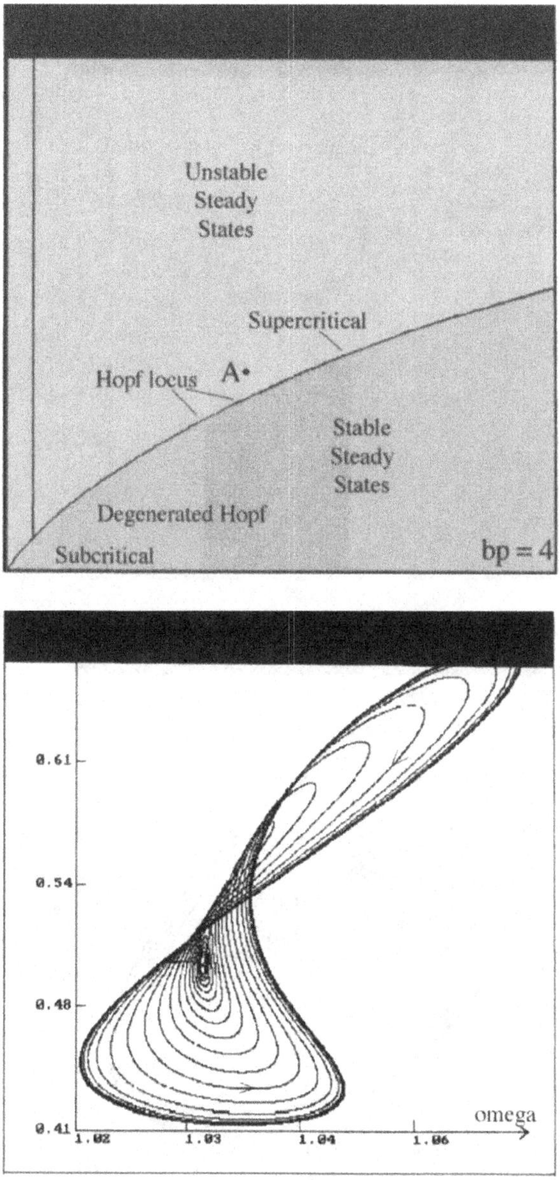

Figure 6.1. Hopf bifurcation curves, stable limit cycles, and stable corridors: real, monetary and inventory cycles (2D projections of the 6D dynamics).

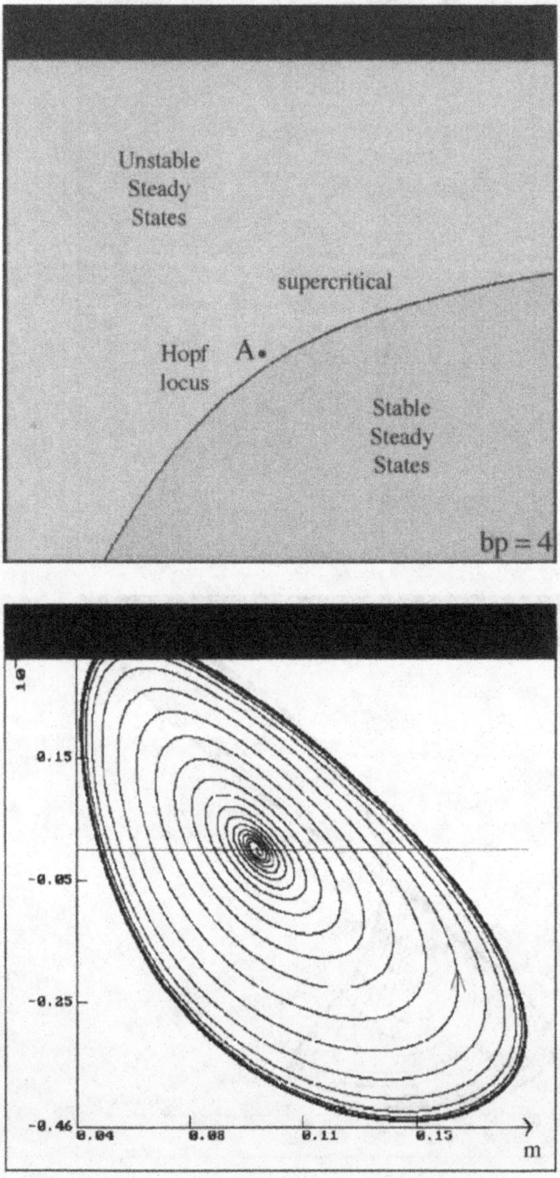

Figure 6.1. (*Continued*)

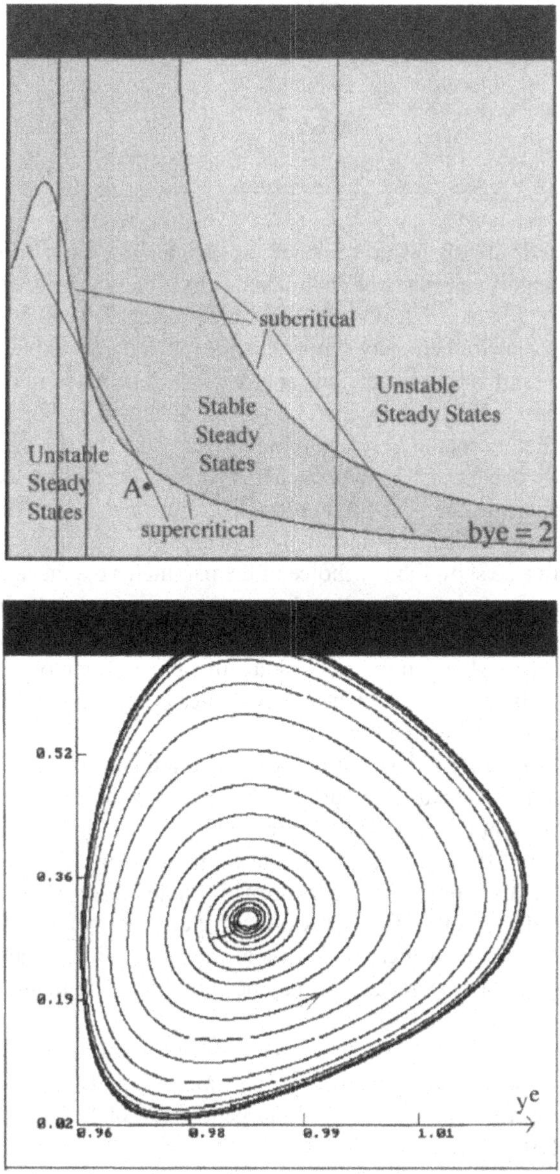

Figure 6.1. (*Continued*)

Table 6.1. *Data set*

$s_c = 0.8$,	$\delta = 0.1$,	$y^p = 1$,	$x = 2$,	$n = \mu_0 = 0.05$
$i_1 = 0.25$,	$i_2 = 0.5$,	$h_1 = 0.1$,	$h_2 = 0.2$	
$t^n = \tau(\rho_0 + r_0 b_0) = 0.3$,	$\beta_m = 0$,	$\beta_g = 0$		
$\beta_{\pi_1} = 0.22$,	$\beta_{\pi_2} = 0.5$			
$\beta_p = 1$,	$\beta_w = 0.21$,	$\kappa_w = \kappa_p = 0.5$		
$\beta_n = 0.2$,	$\beta_{y^e} = 0.75$,	$\beta_{n^d} = 0.3$		

stability that existed beforehand has vanished. At a degenerate Hopf bifurcation, this same loss of stability need not be accompanied by either the birth of a stable limit cycle (above β_w^H) or the death of an unstable limit cycle (below β_w^H), but purely implosive behavior here may simply change into a purely explosive one. These various types of Hopf bifurcations are treated and depicted in detail, for example, in Wiggins (1990, Chap. 3). The (β_p, β_w) diagram in Fig. 6.1 thus basically shows that, except at very small parameter values of β_p, the birth of a stable limit cycle occurs as β_w increases across the depicted Hopf locus.

The same happens in the next bifurcation diagram for β_{π_1}, the adjustment speed of inflationary expectations in the place of β_w, the adjustment speed of wages. This figure also shows that a choice of the parameter β_p, the adjustment speed of prices, sufficiently small will make the 6D dynamics locally unstable.

The two plots considered would suggest that flexible wages, inflationary expectations, and very sluggish prices work against local asymptotic stability. We will return to this question when the 6D dynamics is decomposed into three separate 2D dynamics in Section 3.

The last Hopf bifurcation diagram is for the two adjustment speeds of the Metzlerian inventory mechanism of our 6D dynamical system, i.e., β_{y^e} and β_w, the speed of adjustment of sales expectations and of planned inventory adjustments toward desired inventory stocks. It shows that here there exists a band of stable steady states, limited by a region of unstable steady states for low values of β_{y^e} and β_n as well as for high values of these parameters. Moreover, loss of stability by means of increased β_n is always subcritical, whereas loss of stability by means of a decreased β_n may be subcritical or supercritical (as shown in Fig. 6.1).

The bottom part of the previous three pages of Fig. 6.1 shows an example of a stable limit cycle, generated by means of a supercritical Hopf bifurcation. We emphasize that this stable limit cycle is generated solely by the natural nonlinearities referred to above.

The parameter set in Table 6.1 gives a point just above the Hopf locus in (β_p, β_w) space and (β_p, β_{π_1}) space and just below the lower Hopf curve in (β_{y^e}, β_n) space (point A in Fig. 6.1).

On this basis, the figures on the bottom of Fig. 6.1 show how the limit cycle is approached when the steady state of the model is disturbed by means of a small l shock. We here show the (ω, l), (m, π), and (y^e, ν) projections of this limit cycle. These projections will be compared with the corresponding 2D decompositions of the 6D dynamics in Section 3.

The existence of Hopf bifurcation in conjunction with the dimensionality of the model indicates the possibility of period-doubling behavior and the emergence of complex dynamics. We investigate this issue in Section 4.

3 Prototypical limit cases of the 6D dynamics

It is important to highlight the main economic feedback mechanisms in this model that are interacting with each other to yield the dynamic behavior that we uncover in the full 6D and 7D models by numerical methods.

First, there is a goods–market feedback mechanism whereby the real wage (ω) determines the utilization of capacity (U) and labor (V) that in turn determine the dynamic evolution of nominal wages (w) and prices (p) from which the dynamic evolution of the real wage (ω) flows. This feedback loop has been investigated in isolation by Rose (1967), who demonstrates that it has the potential to generate limit-cycle fluctuations. The interplay of β_w and β_p has an important influence on the generation of such cycles as do the investment coefficients i_1 and i_2.

Second, there are two money/goods–market feedback mechanisms. The first of these operates by means of the effect of expected inflation π on investment, which in turn affects the utilization of labor and capacity, which then drive the dynamics of p and finally π. The relative strengths of β_{π_1} to β_p are important determinants of the stabilizing/destabilizing influence of this feedback loop, which is associated with the Cagan (1956) effect, which when working through the market for goods is nowadays called the Mundell effect. In the second money/goods–market feedback mechanism, the price affects the nominal interest rate (by means of LM equilibrium), which then feeds into investment, which again affects utilization of labor and capacity, which in turn drive the dynamics of p. The interest elasticity of the money demand function h_2 plays an important role in the stability/instability of this loop, which is one of the quintessential elements of conventional Keynesian analysis, based on the so-called Keynes effect.

Third, there is an inventory/goods–market feedback mechanism. Expected aggregate demand and current inventories play a role in determining aggregate demand, actual output, and inventory investment, which in turn determine inventory accumulation and changes in expected aggregate demand. The speed of adjustment of expected aggregate demand β_{y^e} plays a crucial role on the stability/instability of this feedback loop, which is originally due to Metzler (1941).

The various feedback loops referred to above are illustrated in Table 6.2.

In the following subsections we analyze each of these feedback loops by looking at each of the subdynamics in isolation.

Table 6.2. *Main feedback mechanisms and their grouping*

Goods/Labor–Market Dynamics (Rose effects) (state variables ω, l)
$\omega_t \to U_t(\omega_t)$, $V_t(\omega_t) \to \hat{p}(U_t)$, $\hat{w}(V_t) \to \hat{\omega}_t$
Key parameter for stability/instability β_w, β_p
Money/Goods–Market Dynamics (Mundell and Keynes effects) (state variables m, π)
$\pi_t \to I_t(\pi_t) \to U_t(I_t), V_t(I_t) \to \hat{p}(U_t, V_t) \to \dot{\pi}_t$
$p_t \to r_t(p_t) \to I_t(r_t) \to U_t(I_t) \to \hat{p}_t$
Key parameter for stability/instability $\beta_{\pi_1}, \beta_p, h_2$
Inventory Dynamics (Metzler effects) (state variables y^e, z)
Y_t^e, $N_t \to Y_t^d$ $\ddot{I}_t$ $Y_t = Y_t^e + \dot{I}_t \to \dot{N}_t = Y_t - Y_t^d \to \dot{Y}_t^e$
Key parameter for stability/instability β_{y^e}, β_n

The real Rose-type dynamics (Rose 1967)

Freezing the other state variables at their steady-state values through appropriate assumptions on adjustment speed parameters[13] allows us to isolate the real dynamics from the rest of the system; see Chiarella and Flaschel (1997, Chap. 7.3) for details. The resulting 2D dynamics then read as follows:

$$\hat{\omega} = \kappa[(1-\kappa_p)\beta_w(V-1) + (\kappa_w - 1)\beta_p(U-1)], \tag{6.54}$$

$$\hat{l} = -i_1(\rho - r_0 + \pi_0) - i_2(U-1), \tag{6.55}$$

with

$$U = y/y^p,\ V = (y/x)/l,\ \rho = y - \delta - (y/x)\omega.$$

Because of the assumptions made, the value of $y = Y/K$ now has to be calculated from the goods–market equilibrium condition $y = y^d$, which gives

$$y(\omega) = \frac{[(i_1 - s_c)(1 - \omega_0/x) + i_2/y^p]y^p}{(i_1 - s_c)(1 - \omega/x) + i_2/y^p} = \frac{(i_1 - s_c)(1 - \omega_0/x)y^p + i_2}{(i_1 - s_c)(1 - \omega/x)y^p + i_2} y^p. \tag{6.56}$$

The sequence of static and dynamic effects $\omega \to y^d \to y^e \to y$ of the 6D dynamics collapses here into a single-impact effect of wage changes on equilibrium output as described by the preceding function $y(\omega)$. This makes the effect of the real wage on output immediate, but also more complicated.

The function $y(\omega)$ is discussed with respect to its properties in Chiarella and Flaschel (1997, Chap. 4), giving rise there to three different cases. One of these cases will be excluded here from consideration by way of the assumption that $Z = (i_1 - s_c)(1 - \omega_0/x)y^p + i_2 > 0$. This assumption is fulfilled in

[13] $\beta_{y^e} = \beta_n = \infty$, $\beta_{n^d} = 0$, $h_2 = \beta_{\pi_2} = \infty$.

the numerical examples considered here. It restricts the set of admissible parameters i_1, i_2, and s_c such that $\rho'(\omega) < 0$ holds true whenever the function $\rho(\omega) = \{(Z_{y^p})/[(i_1 - s_c)y^p + i_2/(1 - \omega/x)]\} - \delta$ is well defined. The dependence of the rate of profit ρ on the real wage rate ω is therefore the conventional one under this assumption. Nevertheless, the sign of $y'(\omega)$ is still ambiguous, as there then follows sign $y'(\omega) = \text{sign}(i_1 - s_c)$. The real dynamics of Eqs. (6.54) and (6.55) therefore allow for, even under the assumption that $Z > 0$, two very different situations of the dependence of y, U, and V on the real wage ω.

Proposition 3. *The steady state of the dynamics of Eqs. (6.54) and (6.55) is locally asymptotically stable (unstable) in the case $y'(\omega_0) < 0$ if β_w is chosen sufficiently high or β_p sufficiently low (β_w sufficiently low or β_p sufficiently high). The opposite statements apply to the case in which $y'(\omega_0) > 0$.*

Proposition 4. *The Hopf bifurcation locus in (β_p, β_w) space is given by the straight line $\beta_w^H = [(1 - \kappa_w)/(1 - \kappa_p)]\beta_p$.*

The system is thus locally asymptotically stable above this locus if $i_1 < s_c$ and below it in the opposite case. Note that we get Goodwin's (1967) growth-cycle case for $i_1 = s_c$.

With respect to the basic parameter set of Section 6.2 for the 2D dynamics we get $\beta_w^H = \beta_p$ and $y'(\omega) < 0$ ($i_1 = 0.25 < s_c = 0.8$). We thus get the surprising result that wage flexibility destabilizes the 6D system, whereas the opposite is true for the 2D limit case. This striking contrast also holds for price flexibility, now only the other way round.

In this respect, the 2D case gives completely misleading information on the stability properties of the integrated 6D case. An explanation for these occurrences is given by the fact that the dependence of aggregate demand y^d in Eq. (6.40) on ω is opposite to the dependence of the IS-LM equilibrium y on ω, as shown in Eq. (6.56) above.

The monetary Cagan-type dynamics (Cagan 1956)

By means of appropriate assumptions, the following type of monetary subdynamics can be isolated from the rest of the dynamics[14]:

$$\hat{m} = \mu - \pi - \kappa\beta_p(U - 1), \tag{6.57}$$

$$\dot{\pi} = \beta_{\pi_1}\kappa\beta_p(U - 1) + \beta_{\pi_2}(\mu_0 - n - \pi), \tag{6.58}$$

[14] $\beta_{y^e} = \beta_n = \infty,\ \beta_{n^d} = 0,\ \beta_w = 0, \kappa_w = 1, \hat{l} = 0.$

where $U = y/y^p - 1$ and where equilibrium output y is now given by

$$y = \omega_0 y/x + (1 - s_c)(\rho - t^n) + i_1(\rho - r + \pi) + i_2(y/y^p - 1) + \delta + g, \tag{6.59}$$

with

$$\rho = y(1 - \omega_0/x) - \delta, \; r = r_0 + (h_1 y - m)/h_2.$$

Making use of these relationships, we can transform Eq. (6.59) to

$$y = y^p \left[1 + \frac{(i_1/h_2)(m - m_0) + i_1(\pi - \pi_0)}{Q} \right], \tag{6.60}$$

where the expression for Q is given by $Q = h_1 i_1 y^p / h_2 + (s_c - i_1)(1 - \omega_0/x) y^p - i_2$. This shows that the dynamic system is then linear apart from the growth-rate formulation on the left-hand side of the first dynamic law equation (6.57).

Proposition 5. *(a) The dynamical system of Eqs. (6.57) and (6.58) exhibits saddle-point behavior around the steady state if $Q < 0$ holds and exhibits a positive determinant of its Jacobian if $Q > 0$.*

(b) The Hopf locus in (β_p, β_{π_1}) space of the latter case is given by

$$\beta_{\pi_1}^H = \frac{\beta_{\pi_2} y^p}{\beta_p \kappa y_\pi} + \frac{m_0 y_m}{y_n} = \frac{\beta_{\pi_2} Q}{\kappa i_1} \frac{1}{\beta_p} + \frac{h_1 y^p}{h_2}.$$

This locus is therefore a decreasing function of the parameter β_p.

(c) The dynamical system of Eqs. (6.57) and (6.58) is locally asymptotically stable below this locus and unstable above it.

For the basic parameter set of the 6D model of Section 2 (Table 6.1) we have $Q \leq 0$ and thus obtain saddle-path dynamical behavior for this 2D case. Yet, $\det J > 0$ in the 6D case, i.e., these saddle-path dynamics do not show up in the general model in an obvious way. We have calculated in Fig. 6.1 of Section 2 in β_p, β_π space the Hopf locus of the 6D dynamical system.

There is no equivalent to this Hopf locus in the 2D case for the parameter set under consideration.

The Metzler-type inventory dynamics (Metzler 1941)

Again by making appropriate assumptions,[15] we can isolate the following sales expectations and inventory dynamics,

$$\dot{y}^e = \beta_{y^e}(y^d - y^e), \tag{6.61}$$

$$\dot{\nu} = y - y^d, \tag{6.62}$$

[15] $h_2 = \beta_{\pi_2} = \infty, \; \beta_w = 0, \; \kappa_w = 1, \; \hat{l} = 0.$

Table 6.3. *Basic parameter set*

$s_c = 0.8,\ \delta = 0.8,\ y^p = 1,\ x^p = 2,\ n = \mu_0 = 0.05$
$i_1 = 0.25,\ i_2 = 0.5,\ h_1 = 0.1,\ h_2 = 0.2$
$\tau = 0.53,\ \beta_m = 0,\ \beta_g = 0$
$\beta_{\pi_1} = 0.22,\ \beta_{\pi_2} = 1$
$\beta_p = 1.8,\ \beta_w = 0.21,\ \kappa_w = \kappa_p = 0.5$
$\beta_n = 0.1,\ \beta_{y^e} = 0.75,\ \beta_{n^d} = 0.1$

based on the relationships

$$\begin{aligned} y - y^e &= \beta_n(\beta_{n^d} y^e - v), \\ y^d - y^e &= (i_1 - s_c)\rho^e + i_2(y/y^p - 1) - t^n(1 - s_c) - i_1(r_0 - \pi_0) + g \\ &= [(i_1 - s_c)(1 - \omega_0/x) + i_2/y^p]y^e \\ &\quad + [i_2/y^p - (i_1 - s_c)\omega_0/x](y - y^e) + \text{const.} \\ &= (Z/y^p)y^e + Z_1(y - y^e) + \text{const.}, \end{aligned}$$

with $\rho^e = y^e - \delta - \omega_0 y/x$, $Z > 0$, according to the subsection on the real Rose-type dynamics and $Z_1 = i_2/y^p - (i_1 - s_c)\omega_0/x$. This dynamical subsystem is a purely linear one because the natural nonlinearities of the 6D dynamics are not present in it.

Proposition 6. *The steady state of the dynamical system of Eqs. (6.61) and (6.62) is of the saddle-point type in the case $Z > 0$.*

Under the assumptions of the subsection on the real Rose-type dynamics we therefore have that the inventory dynamics (which we have suppressed in this subsection) are unstable for all choices of adjustment speed parameters.

4 Complex dynamics with and without feedbacks from the government budget restraint

In the numerical simulations reported below we use the basic parameter set displayed in Table 6.3 around which we vary some key parameters as discussed in the subsequent sections. The parameter values s_c, n, μ_0, δ, y^p, and x are representative of observed patterns in modern industrial economies. The investment function and money demand parameters are within ranges consistent with some empirical studies. There is much more speculation in the choice of the speed of adjustment parameters and the parameters κ_p and κ_w. The latter we have chosen at 0.5, which represents equal weighting between observed and expected inflation. The relative values of β_{π_1} and β_{π_2} represent greater weight's being given to forward-looking rather than to backward-looking inflationary expectations. The relative values of β_p and β_w represent greater price flexibility compared with wage flexibility. We have chosen the initial value of b as zero, which, together with the assumed values of β_m and β_g ensures that the government budget restraint (GBR) does not feed back into the rest of the system.

For this parameter set the model is stable to the steady state, as seen in Fig. 6.2(a). In Figs. 6.2(b)–6.2(f) we observe[16] the dynamic behavior of the model in the (ω, l) phase plane for decreasing values of β_p, the speed of price adjustment. The model clearly exhibits a period-doubling sequence with a limit cycle appearing because of a Hopf bifurcation at $\beta_p^H \simeq 3.0$ and the period of the cycle doubling toward what appears to be some kind of strange attractor. This type of attractor persists until approximately $\beta_p = 1.8$; for values of β_p much below this value, the model becomes totally unstable. We hesitate to assert definitely that this motion is chaotic as this requires further analysis of Lyapunov exponents.

It is interesting to reflect on the economic significance of the above dynamic behavior. It demonstrates that *ceteris paribus* decreasing price flexibility is locally destabilizing, leading to cyclical behavior. It is important to note that analysis of lower-dimensional subcases (obtained when various speeds of adjustment are set to zero or infinity) commonly considered in the literature indicate the reverse, i.e., that decreasing wage flexibility is locally stabilizing (see, e.g., Chiarella and Flaschel 1997). These observations reinforce the arguments in favor of working with completely specified models.

These calculations also indicate [see Fig. 6.2(f)] that the inventory becomes negative on part of the cycle. This is most likely due to the fact that all nonlinearities that arise from supply-side constraints are neglected in this paper. This may be justified if $\bar{U}$ and $\bar{V}$ are chosen to be sufficiently small[17] and by a suitable form of rationing[18] of government goods demand. In the case in which inventories become exhausted, rationing in government demand implies changes in government bond supply, but this does not feed back into the 6D dynamical system because of the assumptions on $b(0)$, β_m, and β_g. In this way the 6D dynamics can be retained by means of standard non-Walrasian rationing procedures. The addition of nonlinear supply constraints to the model discussed here is considered by Chiarella and Flaschel (1997).

Next we consider the impact of the government fiscal and monetary parameters β_g and β_m, whose role was discussed in the explanation of Eqs. (6.15)–(6.19). The impact of changes in β_g (with β_m held at zero) is shown in Fig. 6.3

[16] All the calculations reported in this and the next section were carried with the computer package SND described in Khomin et al. (1997).

[17] Or – if both are normalized to one as in this chapter – by choosing $V_{\max}$, $U_{\max}$ sufficiently large.

[18] As in non-Walrasian approaches to temporary equilibrium.

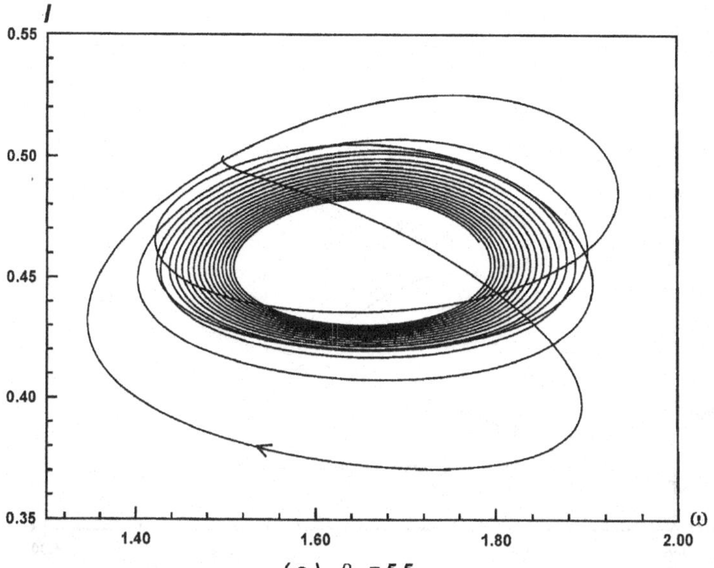

(a) $\beta_p = 5.5$

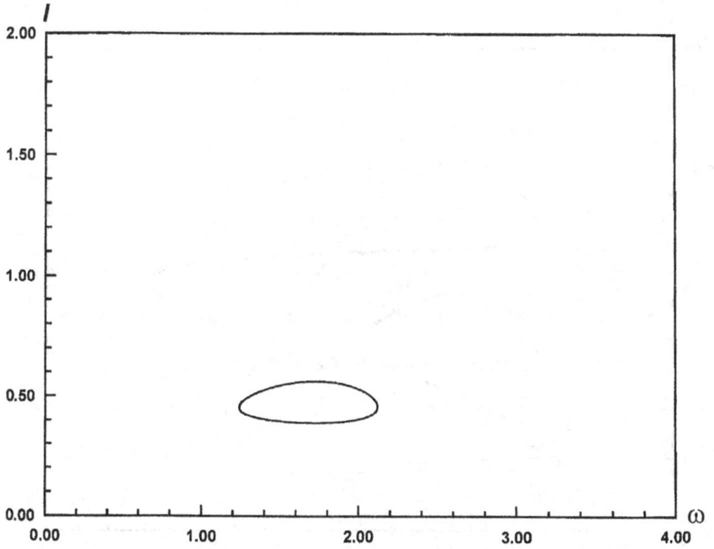

(b) $\beta_p = 4.8$

Figure 6.2. A period-doubling sequence as a function of speed of price adjustment.

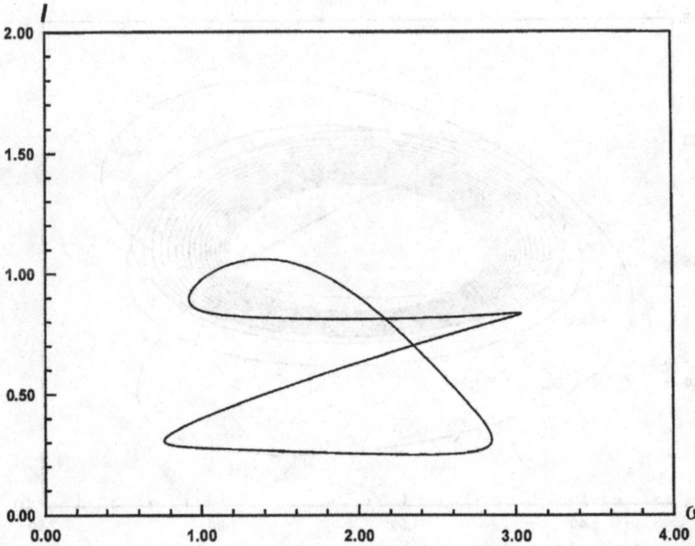

(c) $\beta_p = 4.0$

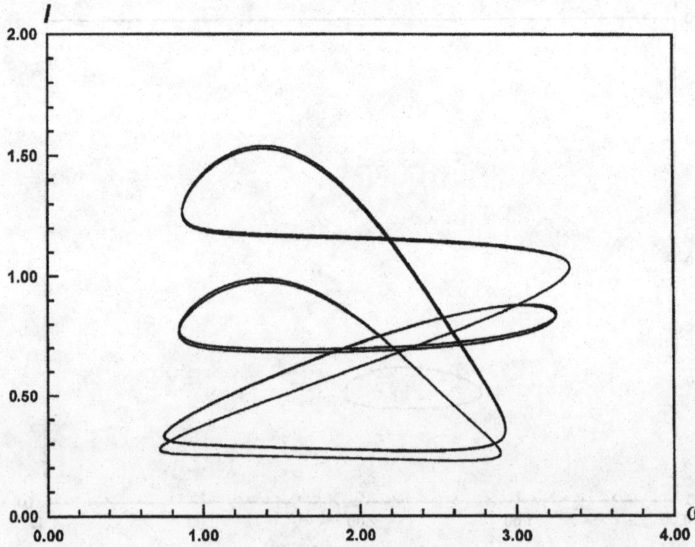

(d) $\beta_p = 3.4$

Figure 6.2. (*Continued*)

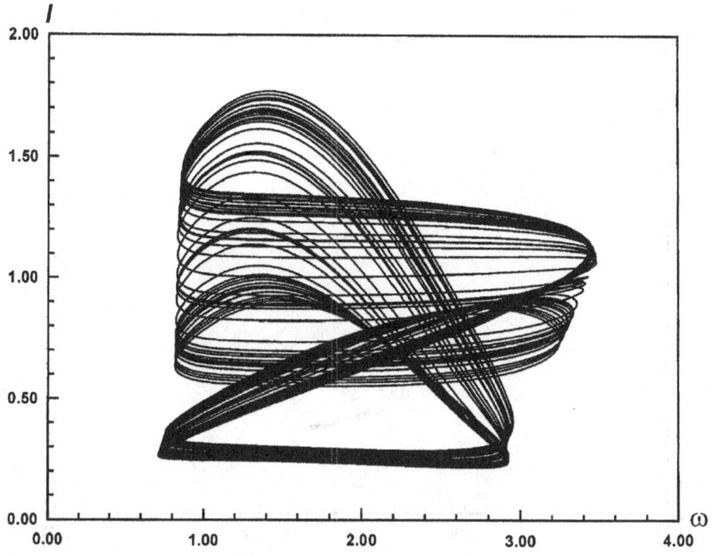

(e) $\beta_p = 3.2$

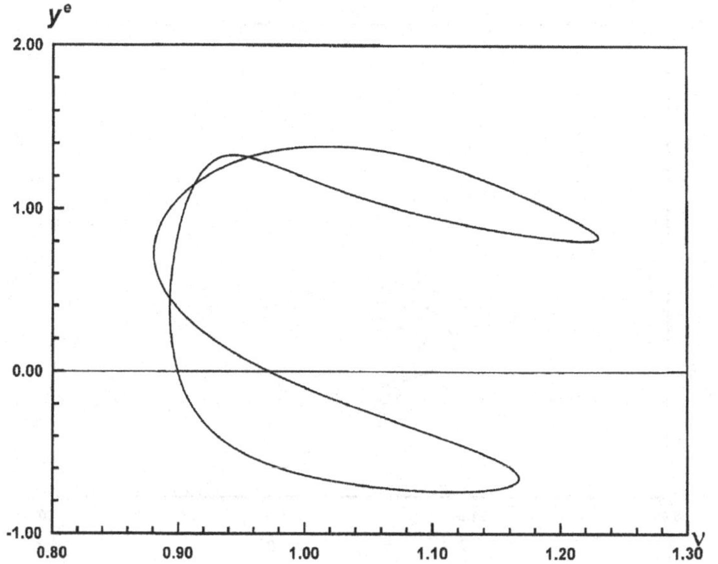

(f) $\beta_p = 4.0$

Figure 6.2. (*Continued*)

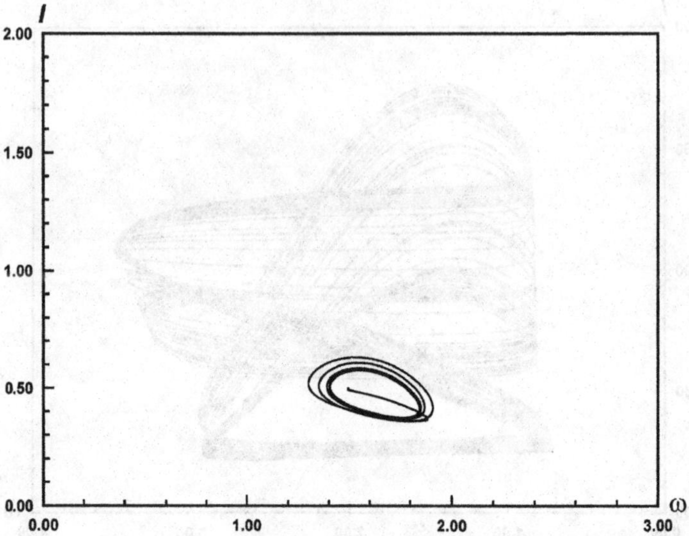

(a) $\beta_p = 3.2$, $\beta_g = -0.05$

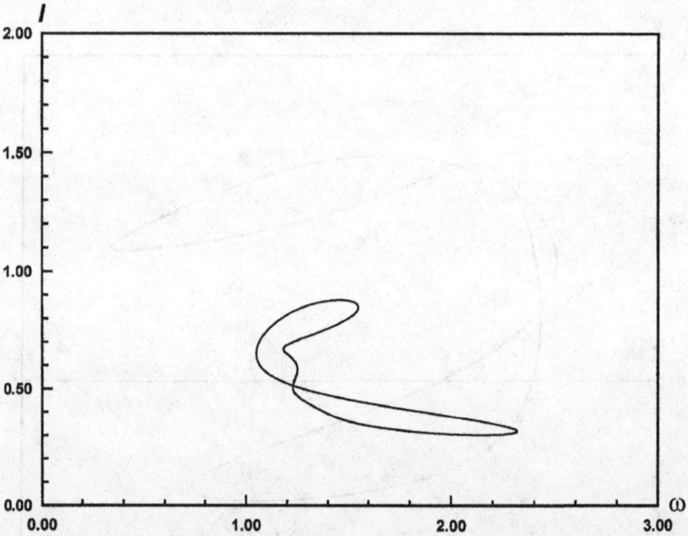

(b) $\beta_p = 3.2$, $\beta_g = -0.2$

Figure 6.3. The impact of fiscal policy by means of variations of the parameter β_g.

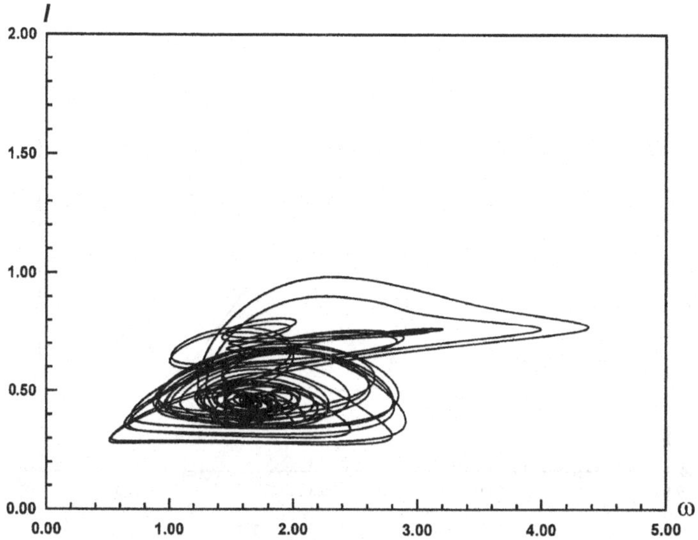

(c) $\beta_p = 3.2, \quad \beta_g = +0.1$

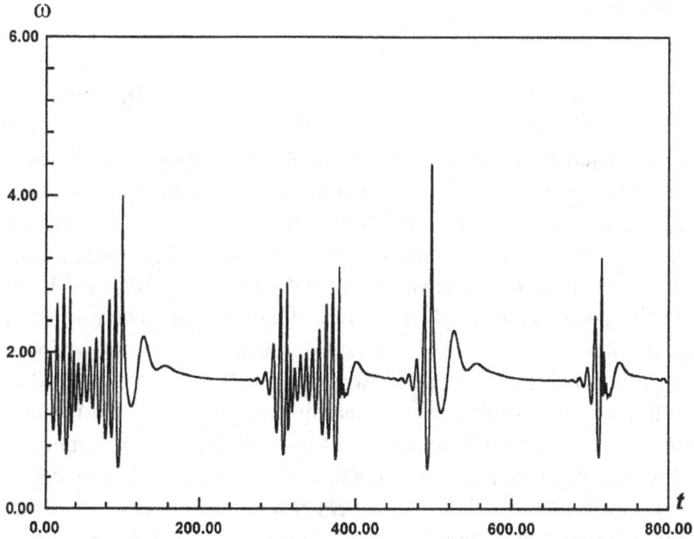

(d) $\beta_p = 3.2, \quad \beta_m = +0.1$

Figure 6.3. (*Continued*)

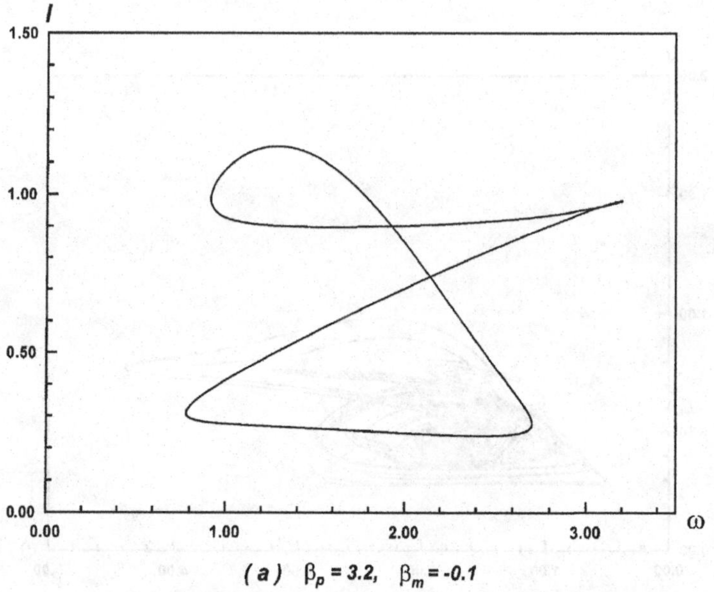

Figure 6.4. The impact of monetary policy by means of variations of the parameter β_m.

for the case $\beta_p = 3.0$ [see Fig. 6.2(e), which has $\beta_g = 0$]. Figures 6.3(a) and 6.3(b) show the effect of increasingly more negative β_g (i.e., stronger traditional Keynesian fiscal policy). We see that a mild Keynesian fiscal policy ($\beta_g = -0.05$) reduces considerably the amplitude of the fluctuations; however, the amplitude increases again as the Keynesian fiscal policy is more strongly applied ($\beta_g = -0.2$) with the amplitude of fluctuations remaining less than that in the $\beta_g = 0$ case. We have also found (results not reported here) that for any of the given values of β_g the period-doubling sequence for decreasing β_p is again observed. We have also found that there is some scope for classical fiscal policy (i.e., $\beta_g > 0$), as shown in Fig. 6.3(c), where $\beta_g = 0.1$. The model in this regime exhibits the interesting phenomenon that a region close to equilibrium is visited for long periods of time. This behavior is more clearly seen in Fig. 6.3(d), which displays ω as a function of time in this case. Very long periods of stable growth are interspersed with short periods of booms and recessions. We have found that values beyond $\beta_g = +0.1$ (for this parameter set) lead the model to be totally unstable.

Next we consider the impact of monetary policy by means of the parameter β_m (but holding $\beta_g = 0$). We recall from the discussion of Section 1 that $\beta_m > 0$ represents an anti-inflationary policy. Figure 6.4 displays the effect of both positive and negative β_m. When β_m is taken to be increasingly negative,

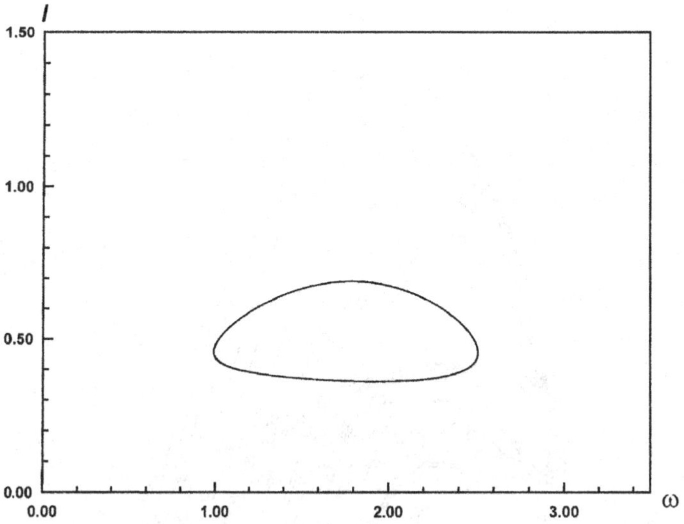

(b) $\beta_p = 3.2, \quad \beta_m = -0.5$

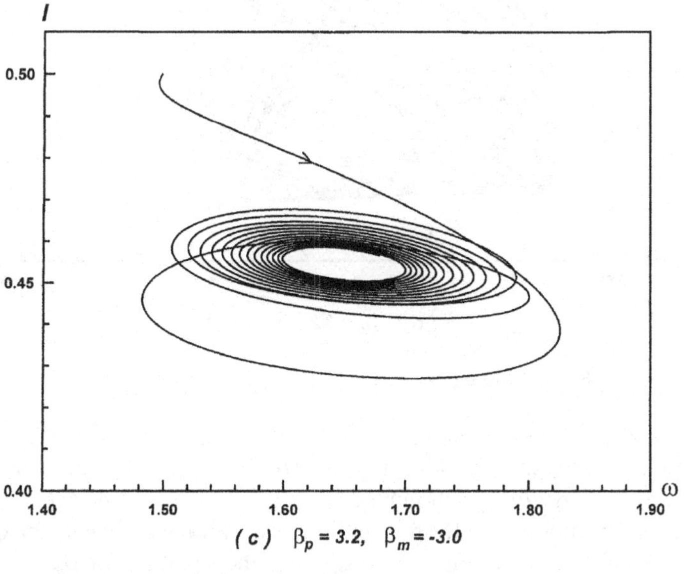

(c) $\beta_p = 3.2, \quad \beta_m = -3.0$

Figure 6.4. (*Continued*)

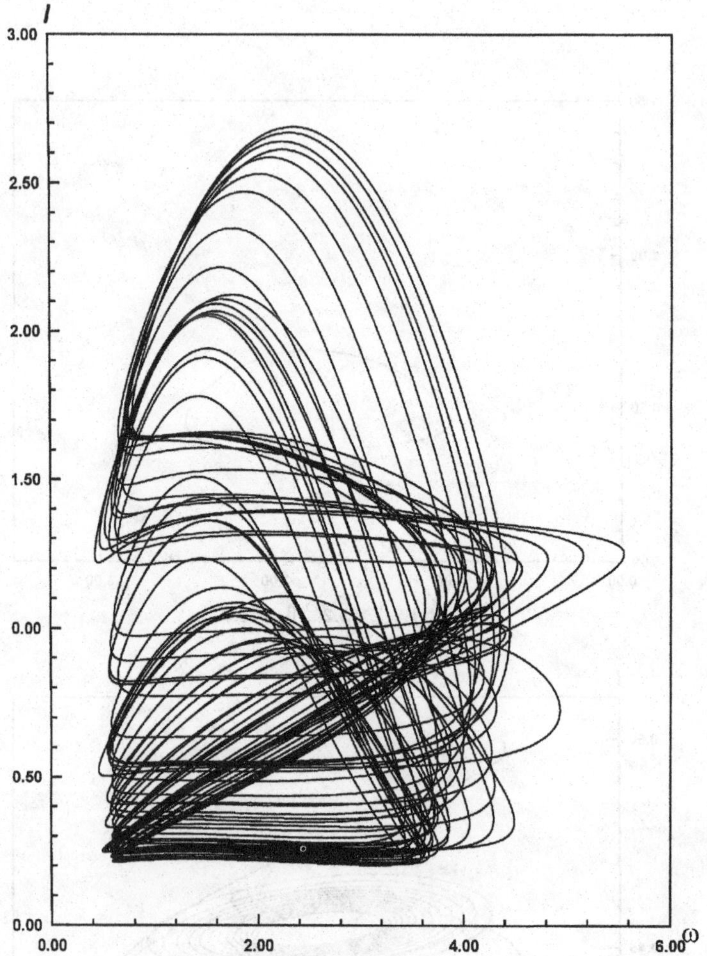

(d) $\beta_p = 3.2$, $\beta_m = +0.1$

Figure 6.4. (*Continued*)

the amplitude of the fluctuations is reduced ($\beta_m = -0.1, -0.5$) and ultimately trajectories converge to equilibrium ($\beta_m = -3.0$); see Figs. 6.4(a)–6.4(c). For positive β_m the amplitude of the fluctuations increases and ultimately the model becomes totally unstable; Fig. 6.4(d) displays the situation for $\beta_m = +0.1$. This behavior of anti-inflationary monetary policy is the opposite of what is normally expected in this class of models. We are not able to offer any intuitive explanation except to suggest that such behavior could be due to the fact that the asset markets are still modeled in a very crude fashion in our model.

5 A kinked Phillips curve and economic feasibility

In this section we discuss a very basic institutional but nevertheless extrinsic nonlinearity as opposed to the natural or intrinsic ones of the main part of this chapter. The purpose of this discussion is to point out that the fluctuations we have considered so far can be very much reduced in amplitude by this additional nonlinearity that is in particular capable of adding economic feasibility to some formerly only mathematically feasible fluctuations of Section 4.

The specific nonlinearity is given by the simple institutional observation that the general level of nominal wages may be more or less flexible upward, but is rigid downward more or less completely. We assume that the money wage Phillips curve is as described above as long as the implied changes in wages are positive, but that it is simply given by 0 in the opposite case. The details of this change in the dynamic structure of the model are spelled out and analyzed numerically in Chiarella and Flaschel (1996) and are not repeated here because of space limitations. Here we point out only that simulations that include this extrinsic nonlinearity indicate that the size of the cycles we investigated beforehand is dramatically reduced and that the model is now economically feasible for speeds of adjustment of the price level whereas it was not even mathematically feasible beforehand.

6 Conclusions

We have analyzed a complete Keynesian model of monetary growth. The model gives rise to a 7D dynamical system; however, by making some additional assumptions about government policy, we are able to reduce the model to a system of six differential equations in which feedback from the GBR is not occurring. The model is nonlinear in a naturally occurring way because of the formulation of some of the economic relationships in terms of growth rates and because of the fact that the wage bill is a product term of two of the dynamically endogenous variables. Thus the model is able to display complex dynamic behavior without the imposition of nonlinear economic behavioral relationships (such as nonlinear investment functions, nonlinear money demand functions, and so forth). The fact that the standard Keynesian model can exhibit complex dynamic behavior in this natural way seems not to have been hitherto appreciated in the literature. Rather, there seems to have been a tacit assumption that nonlinear economic behavioral relationships are necessary for the appearance of complex dynamic behavior. Our analysis reveals that this is not so: The complex dynamic behavior is a result of the interactions of the various markets and sectors that are linked in a high-order dynamical system. However, our model does display some unrealistic features such as negative inventories over certain phases of some cycles that could be eliminated by the kinked Phillips curve discussed in Section 5 or by the introduction of supply constraints. Thus the proper role of nonlinear economic behavioral relationships in this model is to ensure the economic feasibility of the model at extreme points in the cycle. A systematic study of the impact of many standard nonlinear economic behavioral relationships on the model studied here is undertaken in Chiarella and Flaschel (1997).

We have also considered the effect on the dynamics of fiscal and monetary policy by means of simulations. Some of these simulations confirm some widely held perceptions, e.g., Keynesian fiscal policy is stabilizing. However, some simulations indicate unanticipated behavior such as some scope for a stabilizing role for classical fiscal policy and the perverse consequences of an anti-inflationary monetary stance.

Future research needs to extend the framework adopted here in two directions. First, a more complete modeling of the asset markets (particularly with respect to the treatment of bonds and equities) and their impact on the government's dynamic budget constraint is needed. It is interesting to conjecture whether the additional interactions thereby induced eliminate the need for nonlinear economic behavioral relationships to make the cycles economically feasible. Second, a more sophisticated modeling of expectational dynamics (including learning) is called for.

The modeling of expectations consisting of a combination of adaptive and forward-looking expectations may be considered as being too mechanistic in light of recent research into expectational dynamics. A goal of future research would be to incorporate some of the expectation formation schemes of Brock and Hommes (1995). However, the work of these authors suggests that, if anything, this would increase the dynamic complexity of our model.

We have also demonstrated that partial dynamical reasoning can be very misleading, even if based on models that are considered to be of a (proto)typical nature with dynamic implications that can easily understood and explained from such a partial perspective. Such a finding would not be too surprising from an economic point of view if the 6D dynamics had been derived by means of one or more alternative assumptions on economic behavior. Yet, what we have done is but an integration of the partial dynamical views on real wage behavior, inflationary dynamics, and inventory adjustments into a complete model of Keynesian dynamics. This is already sufficient to show, even from a local perspective, that the results that can be obtained for this integrated dynamics cannot be motivated by the insights obtained from the isolated subdynamics as these interact with each other in a nonobvious fashion.

7 Notation

The model of this paper is based on the basically standard macroeconomic notation given in Table 6.4, the parameters used in this paper are given in Table 6.5, and the notation standards used in this paper are given in Table 6.6.

Table 6.4. *Statically or dynamically endogenous variables*

Y	Output
Y^d	Aggregate demand $C + I + \delta K + G$
Y^e	Expected aggregate demand
N	Stock of inventories
N^d	Desired stock of inventories
$\ddot{I}$	Desired inventory investment
L^d	Level of employment
C	Consumption
I	Fixed-business investment
I^p	Planned total investment $I + \ddot{I}$
I^a	Actual total investment $= I + \dot{N}$
r	Nominal rate of interest (price of bonds $p_b = 1$)
p_e	Price of equities
S_p	Private savings
S_f	Savings of firms ($= Y_f$, the income of firms)
S_g	Government savings
$S = S_p + S_f + S_g$	Total savings
T	Real taxes
G	Government expenditure
ρ, ρ^e	Rate of profit (expected rate of profit)
$V = L^d/L$	Rate of employment
Y^p	Potential output
$\Delta Y^e = Y^e - Y^d$	Sales expectations error
$U = Y/Y^p$	Rate of capacity utilization
K	Capital stock
w	Nominal wages
p	Price level
π	Expected rate of inflation (medium run)
M	Money supply (index d: demand)
L	Normal labor supply

Table 6.5. *Parameters*

$\bar{V} = 1$	NAIRU normal labor utilization rate
$\bar{U} = 1$	NAIRU normal capital utilization rate
δ	Depreciation rate
μ_0	Steady growth rate of the money supply
n	Natural growth rate
$i_{1,2} > 0$	Investment parameters
$h_{1,2} > 0$	Money demand parameters
$\beta_w \geq 0$	Wage adjustment parameters
$\beta_p \geq 0$	Price adjustment parameters
$\beta_\pi \geq 0$	Inflationary expectations adjustment parameter
$a \in [0, 1]$	Forward- and backward-looking expectations weights
$\beta_{n^d} > 0$	Desired inventory output ratio

(*Cont.*)

Table 6.5. *(Continued)*

$\beta_n > 0$	Inventory adjustment parameter
$\beta_{y^e} > 0$	Demand expectations adjustment parameter
$\kappa_{w,p} \in [0, 1], \kappa_w \kappa_p \neq 1$	Weights for short- and medium-run inflation
κ	$= (1 - \kappa_w \kappa_p)^{-1}$
$y^p > 0$	Potential output–capital ratio ($\neq y$, the actual ratio)
$x > 0$	Output–labor ratio
τ	Tax rate
β_g	Fiscal policy parameter
β_m	Monetary policy parameter
$s_c \in [0, 1]$	Savings ratio (out of profits and interest)
$s_w \in [0, 1]$	Saving ratio (out of wages, =0 here)

Table 6.6. *Mathematical notation*

$\dot{x}$	Time derivative of variable x
$\hat{x}$	Growth rate of x
l', l_w	Total and partial derivatives
$y_w = y'(l)l_w$	Composite derivatives
r_0, etc.	Steady-state values
$y = Y/K$, etc.	Real variables in intensive form
$m = M/(pK)$, etc.	Nominal variables in intensive form

REFERENCES

Brock, W. A., and Hommes, C. H. (1995). Rational routes to randomness. Working Paper, University of Amsterdam, Amsterdam.

Cagan, P. (1956). The monetary dynamics of hyperinflation. In *Studies in the Quantity Theory of Money*, ed. M. Friedman, University of Chicago Press, Chicago.

Chiarella, C. (1986). Perfect foresight models and the dynamic instability problem from a higher viewpoint. *Econ. Model.*, 283–92.

Chiarella, C., and Flaschel, P. (1996). An integrative approach to 2D-macromodels of growth, price and inventory dynamics. *Chaos, Solitons Fractals*, **7**, 2105–33.

(1997). *Keynesian Monetary Growth Dynamics. Macrofoundations*, Draft Manuscript, School of Finance and Economics, University of Technology Sydney, Sydney.

Franke, R. (1992). *A Metzlerian model of inventory growth cycles*, a nonpublished document.

Franke, R., and Lux, T. (1993). Adaptive expectations and perfect foresight in a nonlinear Metzler model of the inventory cycle. *Scand. J. Econ.* **95**, 355–63.

Frankel, J. A., and Froot, K. A. (1987). Using survey data to test standard propositions regarding exchange rate expectations. *Am. Econ. Rev.*, **77**, 133–53.

(1990). Chartists, fundamentalists and trading in the foreign exchange market. *Am. Econ. Rev.*, **80**, 181–85.

Goodwin, R. M. (1967). A growth cycle. In *Socialism, Capitalism and Economic Growth*, ed. C. H. Feinstein, Cambridge University Press, Cambridge, England, pp. 54–58.

Groth, C. (1988). IS-LM dynamics and the hypothesis of combined adaptive-forward-looking expectations. In *Recent Approaches to Economic Dynamics*, eds. P. Flaschel and M. Krüger, Verlag Peter Lang, New York, pp. 251–65.

Keynes, J. M. (1936). *The General Theory of Employment, Interest and Money*, Macmillan, New York.

Khibnik, A., Kuzenetsov, Y., Levitin, V., and Nikolaev, E. (1993). Continuation techniques and interactive software for bifurcation analysis of ODEs and iterated maps. *Physica D*, **62**, 360–71.

Khomin, A., Flaschel, P., and Chiarella, C. (1997). SND – A computer package for the numerical investigation of Keynesian models of monetary growth. *Research Report No. 3*, School of Finance and Economics, University of Technology Sydney, Sydney.

Malinvaud, E. (1980). *Profitability and Unemployment*, Cambridge University Press, Cambridge, England.

Metzler, L. A. (1941). The nature and stability of inventory cycles. *Rev. Econ. Stat.* **23** 113–29.

Orphanides, A., and Solow, R. M. (1990). Money, inflation and growth. In *Handbook of Monetary Economics*, ed. F. Hahn, North-Holland, Amsterdam, pp. 223–98.

Oxley, L., and George, D. A. R. (1994). Linear saddlepoint dynamics 'on their head'. The scientific content of the new orthodoxy in macrodynamics. *Eur. J. Polit. Econ.*, **10**, 389–400.

Rose, H. (1967). On the nonlinear theory of the employment cycle. *Rev. Econ. Stud.*, **34**, 153–73.

(1990). *Macroeconomic Dynamics. A Marshallian Synthesis*, Blackwell, Oxford, England.

Sargent, T. (1987). *Macroeconomic Theory*, 2nd ed., Academic, New York.

Wiggins, S. (1990). *Introduction to Applied Nonlinear Dynamical Systems and Chaos*, Springer-Verlag, New York.

CHAPTER 7

Stochastic volatility in interest rates and complex dynamics in velocity

William A. Barnett and Haiyang Xu

Some economists continue to insist that linearity is a good assumption for all economic time series, despite the fact that economic theory provides virtually no support for the assumption of linearity; see, e.g., Barnett and Chen (1986, 1988). The controversy is partly due to the fact that the currently available tests do not test for the existence of chaos or nonlinearity produced from within the structure of the economy. As recently pointed out by Day (1992), the tests have no way of determining the sources of the chaos or nonlinearity. In other words, even if the economy is totally linear and stable, the current tests, such as the Brock–Dechert–Scheinkman (Brock 1986), could still catch evidence of nonlinearity or even chaos in economic data if the economy is affected by a chaotic and unstable surrounding weather system. Therefore it is interesting if we can identify some sources of potential nonlinearity and instability within the economic system.

In this chapter we theoretically show that money velocity is nonlinear within a monetary general-equilibrium model and that a traditional money velocity function may be unstable within the economic system. We use the comparison between model simulation and estimation to examine the relevance of our theoretical results. Traditionally money velocity is viewed as a constant or at least a stable function of its few determinants. The unusual behavior of money velocity and the instability of the traditional money demand function since the late 1970s in the United States has called for a reexamination of the traditional views; see, e.g., Stone and Thornton (1987).

Several lines of research have been pursued in recent monetary economic literature. One line of research focuses on the correct measurement of money and challenges the traditional practice of ignoring the aggregation problem in monetary economics research and policy design.[1] Some research focuses on the

[1] For the measurement of money, see Barnett (1980, 1987), Barnett et al. (1991), Belongia (1996), and Serletis and Krause (1995).

effects of institutional change on money velocity; see, e.g., Bordo and Jonung (1981, 1987, and 1989). Another hypothesis, proposed by Friedman (1983), attributes the several substantial declines of M1 velocity in the United States since 1981 to the increased money growth variability following the change of Federal Reserve operating procedures in October 1979. However, empirical tests of this variability hypothesis have not provided uniform evidence.[2] Time-varying coefficient models have been used in econometric modeling of money velocity; see Dueker (1993, 1995).

In this chapter we find that money velocity is nonlinear when there are no uncertainties in nominal interest rates. When interest rates are stochastic and money and income growth are uncertain, we find that money velocity is nonlinear and the coefficients of a traditional money velocity function are stochastic; that is, money velocity has unstable dynamics. More specifically, if the covariances change between interest rates and the consumption growth rate or between interest rates and the real money growth rate, the model shows that in addition to the nonlinearity in money velocity, the coefficients of the money velocity process will shift stochastically. In fact, anything that causes the covariances to change will contribute to a random shift of the coefficients of the money velocity process. These causes could include financial innovations or money growth variability,[3] as previously investigated in the literature. In this sense, our study provides a general and coherent theoretical explanation for the instability of money velocity and nests many earlier explanations as special cases.

We simulate the process of the slope coefficient of a simple traditional money velocity function based on U.S. quarterly data from 1960.1 to 1992.4 and find that the theoretical model generates a volatile slope coefficient when the degree of risk aversion in the model is moderately high, especially during the 1973–1976 and 1979–1982 periods.

The Swamy and Tinsley (1980) random-coefficient model for money velocity is estimated to compare the behavior of the estimated stochastic coefficients with the simulated coefficients from the theoretical model. The estimated stochastic slope coefficient has important similarities with the simulation results. Because the sample size of the data on money velocity is very small for testing nonlinearity, we do not attempt to test for nonlinearity or even chaos in the money velocity data. For recent development in testing nonlinearity and chaos in economics, see Barnett et al. (1995, 1998).

The remainder of this paper is organized as follows. Section 1 develops a monetary general-equilibrium model in which monetary assets provide monetary services as well as interest income. Section 2 derives the theoretical results for money velocity, and it is shown that money velocity is nonlinear. Section 3

[2] See Belongia (1985), Fisher and Serletis (1989), Hall and Noble (1987), and Thornton (1995) for empirical evidence of the variability hypothesis.

[3] For the effect of financial innovation on the economy, see the recent work by Thornton (1994).

generalizes the result when the assumption of certain nominal interest rates is relaxed. The effect of risk aversion and interest rate uncertainty is investigated. It is shown that money velocity may be characterized as a stochastic nonlinear process. Section 4 presents the results from model simulation and from estimation of a random-coefficient model. The last section provides concluding remarks.

1 The Model

In this section we outline an infinite-horizon, representative-agent model with a set of monetary assets that pay interest. Suppose that there exist k monetary assets. Monetary asset i pays nominal return rate R_{it} at the end of time period t. Money supply is assumed to be exogenous and serves as a moving endowment point in the consumer's budget constraint. There exists one nominal bond with holding-period yield R_t, which is also paid at the end of period t. We assume that

$$R_t \geq \max\{R_{it}, i = 1, \ldots, k\}, \quad \forall t.$$

This assumption says that monetary assets are dominated in holding-period returns by the nominal bond, which is assumed to yield no monetary services. The price for the bond in period t is P_{bt}. There exists one equity asset, which is the exogenous endowment asset and yields resource flow $d_t > 0$. The price of one unit of the equity is P_{st}, and dividend d_t per unit is paid before the share is sold. The only consumption good is the resource flow d_t, which is perishable. The price of that consumption good is P_t in period t. There are finitely many identical consumers with utility function $U(c_t, \hat{m}_t)$, which is continuous, increasing, and concave in all of its arguments, where c_t is the demand for consumption goods and $\hat{m}_t = (m_{1t}, m_{2t}, \ldots, m_{kt})$ is a vector of real monetary assets held during period t.

The exogenous supply of monetary asset i in period t is X_{it}; let $\sum_{i=1}^{k} X_{it} = X_t$ be the simple sum aggregate of money supply. The representative consumer is assumed to maximize the infinite lifetime expected utility:

$$E_t \sum_{t=0}^{\infty} \beta^t U(c_t, \hat{m}_t), \tag{7.1}$$

where $\beta \in (0, 1)$ is the subjective rate of time discount and E_t is the expectation operator, conditional on information at time period t. The budget constraint in each period is

$$\begin{aligned} P_t c_t + P_{st} s_t + P_{bt} b_t + P_t \sum_{i=1}^{k} m_{it} & \\ \leq s_{t-1}(d_t P_t + P_{st}) + P_{b,t-1} b_{t-1}(1 + R_{t-1}) & \\ + \sum_{i=1}^{k} m_{i,t-1}(1 + R_{i,t-1}) P_{t-1} + \sum_{i=1}^{k} [X_{it} - (1 + R_{it-1}) X_{i,t-1}], & \end{aligned} \tag{7.2}$$

where s_t is the quantity of equity and b_t is the quantity of bonds held during time period t. The last term of budget constraint (6.2) is different from that in a traditional model. Because we assume that monetary assets pay interest, the supply of money must be adjusted for it.

Money is introduced through the money-in-utility-function approach in this model. In this approach, the utility function must be viewed as the derived utility function that exists if money has positive value in equilibrium.[4] Alternatively, in a cash-in-advance model, it is difficult to justify the existence of a variety of monetary assets that pay different interest rates. In all the cash-in-advance models in the literature, there can exist only one monetary asset in the equilibrium of an economy.

Because monetary assets are dominated or stochastically dominated in returns by the nominal bond, a rational economic agent will not hold monetary assets if monetary assets do not yield monetary services. However, we cannot nest the simple-sum monetary aggregator function in the utility function unless all the monetary assets are perfect substitutes for each other (see Barnett, 1987). To reduce the dimension of the vector of monetary assets to an aggregate index of "money," we need to assume that the utility function $U(c_t, \hat{m}_t)$ is weakly separable in monetary assets and can be written as $\mathbf{F}(c_t, f(\hat{m}_t))$, where $f(\hat{m}_t)$ is a linearly homogenous subutility function.[5] Under this assumption, it can be proved that the Divisia monetary aggregate can track the theoretical function $f(\hat{m}_t)$ exactly in continuous time or up to a third-order remainder term in discrete time, if nominal yields R_t and R_{it} are known at the beginning of the time period.[6] If the agent is risk averse and nominal yields R_t and R_{it} are not known exactly to the agent at the beginning of time interval t, the Divisia aggregate's tracking ability is somewhat compromised. For the purpose of this chapter, we first assume that R_t and R_{it} are known to consumers at the beginning of time interval t, and in Section 3 we will relax this assumption.

Let m_t be the value of the exact monetary aggregate over its components $m_{it}, i = 1, 2, \ldots, k$, so that $m_t = f(\hat{m}_t)$. The utility function $U(c_t, \hat{m}_t)$ consequently can be written as $\mathbf{F}(c_t, m_t)$. To deal with the first-order conditions in terms of the quantity aggregate rather than each individual monetary asset, we have to transform the budget constraint to replace the vector of monetary assets $\hat{m}_t$ with the exact monetary aggregate m_t. To do this, let π_t be the exact money price aggregate (or user cost aggregate) dual to m_t, and let π_{it} be the user cost of monetary asset i, $i = 1, 2, \ldots, k$, in period t. It can be shown that the exact aggregation-theoretic price aggregator function is the unit cost function (Barnett 1987). According to Fisher's factor reversal test, expenditure

[4] Arrow and Hahn (1971) and Feenstra (1986).

[5] For a discussion of macroeconomic dimension reduction, see Barnett (1994).

[6] For the microeconomic theory of monetary aggregation, see Barnett (1987).

on the aggregate must equal expenditure on the components, so that π_t must satisfy

$$\sum_{i=1}^{k} \pi_{it} m_{it} = \pi_t m_t, \tag{7.3}$$

where

$$\pi_{it} = \frac{R_t - R_{it}}{1 + R_t}, \tag{7.4}$$

as derived in Barnett (1978). We define R_{mt} such that

$$\sum_{i=1}^{k} (1 + R_{it}) m_{it} = (1 + R_{mt}) m_t. \tag{7.5}$$

Note that R_{mt} can be interpreted as the aggregate rate of return dual to the exact monetary aggregate. Dividing Eq. (7.5) by $(1 + R_t)$ and adding the resulting equation to Eq. (7.3), we have

$$\sum_{i=1}^{k} m_{it} = \left(\pi_t + \frac{1 + R_{mt}}{1 + R_t} \right) m_t. \tag{7.6}$$

Let M_t^n be the nominal supply-side exact monetary aggregate. We assume that the monetary asset markets are in equilibrium when $M_t^n = m_t P_t$, where $m_t P_t$ is the nominal demand-side exact monetary aggregate.[7]

Under these assumptions, the budget constraint can be written as

$$\begin{aligned} P_t c_t + P_{st} s_t + b_t P_{bt} + P_t m_t \left(\pi_t + \frac{1 + R_{mt}}{1 + R_t} \right) \\ \leq s_{t-1}(d_t P_t + P_{st}) + P_{t-1}(1 + R_{m,t-1}) m_{t-1} + b_{t-1}(1 + R_{t-1}) P_{b,t-1} \\ + M_t^n \left(\pi_t + \frac{1 + R_{mt}}{1 + R_t} \right) - M_{t-1}^n (1 + R_{mt-1}). \end{aligned} \tag{7.7}$$

The representative agent chooses controls $u_t = (c_t, m_t, s_t, b_t)$ for $t \geq 1$ to maximize expected lifetime utility,

$$E_t \sum_{t=0}^{\infty} \beta^t \mathbf{F}(c_t, m_t)$$

[7] Actually there is a possible regulatory wedge between the supply- and the demand-side aggregator functions, when required reserves pay no interest and thereby produce an implicit tax on the supply side. For more discussion on this issue, see Barnett (1987), who provides the formulas for both the demand- and the supply-side exact monetary aggregator functions.

subject to constraint (7.7) with given m_0 and d_0. We have the exact monetary aggregate in both the utility function and the budget constraint, and the macroeconomic dimension reduction is completely consistent with the microeconomic theory of monetary aggregation.

Let

$$z_t = \{m_{t-1}, s_{t-1}, b_{t-1}, c_{t-1}, P_t, P_{st}, P_{bt}, R_t, M_t^n\}$$

be the set of state variables, and let $\mathbf{T}(z_t) = \sum_{t=0}^{\infty} \beta^t \mathbf{F}(c_t, m_t)$. In equilibrium, $\mathbf{T}(z_t)$ must satisfy the following Bellman's equation,

$$\mathbf{T}(z_t) = \max_{u_t} \{\mathbf{F}(c_t, m_t) + \beta E_t T(z_{t+1})\}, \tag{7.8}$$

when the following market-clearing conditions are satisfied:

$$\begin{aligned} c_t &= d_t, \\ s_t &= 1, \\ b_t &= 0, \\ m_t &= M_t^n / P_t. \end{aligned}$$

The equilibrium condition on equities is a normalization, whereas the equilibrium condition on bonds states that bonds are privately issued by some consumers and bought by others, and the net demand for bonds is zero in equilibrium. Recall that the representative agent is aggregated over consumers under Gorman's conditions for the existence of a representative consumer. Hence b_t is net per capita borrowing among consumers, in which lending is negative borrowing. If interest rates are out of equilibrium, net borrowing need not be zero.[8]

2 Money velocity with no nominal risk

In this section we derive the necessary first-order conditions and the equations for money velocity under the assumption that the nominal interest rates are known. The first-order conditions of the maximization problem are

$$\mathbf{F}_{ct} = \lambda_t P_t, \tag{7.9}$$

$$\mathbf{F}_{mt} = \lambda_t P_t \left(\pi_t + \frac{1 + R_{mt}}{1 + R_t} \right) - \beta E_t(\lambda_{t+1})(1 + R_{mt}) P_t, \tag{7.10}$$

$$\lambda_t P_{st} = \beta E_t [\lambda_{t+1}(d_{t+1} P_{t+1} P_{s,t+1})], \tag{7.11}$$

$$\lambda_t = \beta E_t(\lambda_{t+1})(1 + R_t), \tag{7.12}$$

where $\mathbf{F}_{ct}$ and $\mathbf{F}_{mt}$ are the marginal utilities of consumption goods and monetary services, respectively, and λ_t is the Lagrange multiplier of budget constraint

[8] Similarly, see Marshall (1992, p. 1321) and Boyle (1990, p. 1042).

(7.7). Equation (7.10) is the first-order condition for monetary services. Equations (7.11) and (7.12) are standard Euler equations for stocks and bonds.

From Eqs. (7.9), (7.10), and (7.12), we have

$$\pi_t = \frac{\mathbf{F}_{mt}}{\mathbf{F}_{ct}}, \tag{7.13}$$

that is, the marginal rate of substitution between consumption goods and monetary services equals the aggregate user cost of the monetary services.[9] Assume that the utility function takes the constant relative risk-aversion form:

$$\mathbf{F}(c_t, m_t) = \begin{cases} \dfrac{1}{1-\phi}\left(c_t^s m_t^{1-s}\right)^{1-\phi}, & \text{when } \phi \neq 1 \\ \ln\left(c_t^s m_t^{1-s}\right), & \text{when } \phi = 1 \end{cases},$$

where m_t is the real exact monetary aggregate, $s \in (0, 1)$ is a constant, and $\phi \in (0, \infty)$ is the coefficient of relative risk aversion. We get the following relationship:

$$\pi_t = \frac{(1-s)}{s}\frac{c_t}{m_t}. \tag{7.14}$$

When solved for m_t, Eq. (7.14) is the equation of demand for the exact monetary aggregate. Given $c_t = d_t$ and the parameter s, the only determinant of the demand for monetary services in equilibrium is the user cost π_t. Although other factors, such as the inflation rate, are not in this equation directly, they may affect the demand for money through the user cost π_t, which is a function of the nominal interest rates R_t and R_{it}. Given these equilibrium conditions, we can examine the behavior of money velocity.

Traditional money velocity is usually defined as the ratio of nominal income to the simple-sum monetary aggregate:

$$V_t = \frac{P_t d_t}{X_t}.$$

We define the aggregation-theoretic exact money velocity by replacing the simple-sum monetary aggregate with the exact monetary aggregate to get

$$\nu_t = \frac{d_t}{m_t}.$$

Using the definition $\pi_{it} = (R_t - R_{it})/(1 + R_t)$, the identity $\pi_t m_t = \sum_{i=1}^{k} \pi_{it} m_{it}$, and the equilibrium condition $X_{it} = P_t m_{it}$, we have the following

[9] We can get the same result if we start with the maximization problem in terms of the original disaggregated individual monetary assets. See Appendix II.

results from Eq. (7.14):

$$v_t = \frac{s}{1-s}\pi_t, \tag{7.15}$$

$$V_t = \frac{s}{1-s}\Pi_t, \tag{7.16}$$

where

$$\Pi_t = \sum_{i=1}^{k} \frac{\pi_{it} X_{it}}{\sum_{i=1}^{k} X_{it}} = (R_t - R_{smt})(1 + R_t)^{-1},$$

with

$$R_{smt} = \sum_{i=1}^{k} \theta_{it} R_{it},$$

$$\theta_{it} = X_{it} \Bigg/ \sum_{i=1}^{k} X_{it}.$$

Observe that Π_t is a weighted average of the user costs π_{it}, which are the opportunity costs of holding monetary assets instead of the bond. The results of Eqs. (7.15) and (7.16) both say that money velocity is a function of the user costs $\{\pi_{it}, i = 1, 2, \ldots, k\}$. If we define velocity in the traditional way (V_t), then the corresponding determinant should be a weighted average of the user costs π_{it}, with the weights being ratios of the X_{it} to the simple-sum aggregate $X_t = \sum_{i=1}^{k} X_{it}$. If alternatively we define money velocity relative to the theoretic exact monetary aggregate, then the relevant determinant is the user cost aggregate π_t dual to the exact monetary quantity aggregate. Both velocity functions have the same form, with the key elements being the user costs of monetary assets. The equivalence of the forms of the two velocity functions (7.15) and (7.16) depends on our specification of the utility function.

Note that Eq. (7.15) or Eq. (7.16) can be written in a dynamic equation of money velocity. To illustrate this point, let us assume that $R_{it} = 0$ for all i; then $\pi_t = \Pi_t = R_t/(1 + R_t)$. Also from Eqs. (7.9) and (7.10) we have, after substitution of the utility function,

$$\begin{aligned}(1 + R_t)^{-1} &= \beta E_t\left(\frac{\lambda_{t+1}}{\lambda_t}\right)\\ &= \beta E_t\left[\left(\frac{V_{t+1}}{V_t}\right)^{s(1-\phi)-1}\left(\frac{X_{t+1}}{X_t}\right)^{-\phi}\left(\frac{P_{t+1}}{P_t}\right)^{\phi-1}\right].\end{aligned} \tag{7.17}$$

Further, assuming that there is no exogenous uncertainty or letting $(X_{t+1}/X_t) = \eta_x$ and $(d_{t+1}/d_t) = \eta_d$ be constant and using the identity $P_t =$

$(V_t X_t / d_t)$ we have

$$(1+R_t)^{-1} = \beta \left[\left(\frac{V_{t+1}}{V_t} \right)^{s(1-\phi)-1} \eta_x^{-\phi} \left(\frac{V_{t+1}\eta_x}{V_t \eta_d} \right)^{\phi-1} \right]$$

$$= \beta \eta_x^{-1} \eta_d^{1-\phi} \left(\frac{V_{t+1}}{V_t} \right)^{(1-\phi)(s-1)-1}. \tag{7.18}$$

By substituting Eq. (7.18) into Eq. (7.16) we can obtain a dynamic equation of money velocity:

$$V_t = \frac{s}{1-s} - \frac{s}{1-s} \beta \eta_x^{-1} \eta_d^{1-\phi} \left(\frac{V_{t+1}}{V_t} \right)^{(1-\phi)(s-1)-1}. \tag{7.19}$$

If $(1-\phi)(s-1) \neq 1$, Eq. (7.19) shows that money velocity follows a nonlinear dynamic process. The properties of this nonlinear dynamic process depend critically on preference and the growth rate of real income and nominal money aggregate.

The process of velocity in Eq. (7.19) can be rewritten as

$$\nu_{t+1}^e = \gamma \nu_t^e (1 - \nu_t), \tag{7.20}$$

where $\nu_t = (1 - s/s)V_t$, $\gamma = \beta^{-1} \eta_x \eta_d^{\phi-1}$, and $e = (1-\phi)(s-1) - 1$. There exists a steady state in which $V_{t+1} = V_t \neq 0$. It can be seen that, in the steady state,

$$V_t = \frac{s}{1-s} - \frac{s}{1-s} \beta \eta_x^{-1} \eta_d^{1-\phi}. \tag{7.21}$$

The stability of the steady state depends on the parameters γ and e. For example, when $e = 1$ the process in Eq. (7.20) becomes the so-called logistic map, that is,

$$\nu_{t+1} = \gamma \nu_t (1 - \nu_t). \tag{7.22}$$

The properties of the logistic map are now well known. For example, when $\gamma = 3$, the steady state is not stable. When $\gamma = 4$ the Lyapunov characteristic exponent will be positive and therefore the process exhibits sensitive dependence on initial conditions, that is, the limit set of ν_t is chaotic. Note that the conditions $\gamma = 4$ and $e = 1$ in our model are not impossible if agents are very risk averse and s is not very close to 1.

When $e = (1-\phi)(s-1) - 1 \neq 1$, it is not possible in general to determine the values of parameter γ for which the asymptotic motion of ν_t is periodic, aperiodic, or chaotic; see Medio (1992).

In short, money velocity is a variable rather than a constant in the model developed in this section. The taste parameters and the growth rates of money and income determine the dynamic behavior of money velocity. Money velocity follows a complicated nonlinear dynamic process. When exogenous uncertainty is allowed in Section 3, it is shown that the coefficients of the nonlinear dynamic process are stochastic.

3 Money velocity with nominal interest risk

In this section the assumption that nominal interest rates are known is relaxed, and we keep the assumption that the economic agents are risk averse. We focus on the question of whether the model can explain the instability of money velocity reported in the literature through interest rate uncertainty in addition to the nonlinearity analyzed in Section 2.

We start with the monetary aggregation problem. In Section 2, the exact monetary quantity aggregator function $m_t = f(\hat{m}_t)$ can be tracked very accurately by the Divisia monetary aggregate m_t^d because that tracking ability is known under perfect certainty. However, when nominal interest rates are uncertain, the Divisia monetary aggregate's tracking ability is somewhat compromised. That compromise is eliminated by use of the extended Divisia monetary aggregate derived by Barnett and Liu (1994) under risk. Let m_t^G denote the extended Divisia monetary aggregate over the monetary assets. The only difference between m_t^G and m_t^d is the user cost formula used to compute the prices in the Divisia index formula.

Let π_{it}^G denote the generalized user cost of monetary asset i. Barnett and Liu [1994, Eq. (5.6)] prove that

$$\pi_{it}^G = \pi_{it}^e + \psi_{it},$$

where

$$\pi_{it}^e = \frac{E_t(R_t - R_{it})}{E_t(1+R_t)},$$

$$\psi_{it} = \frac{E_t(1+R_{it})}{E_t(1+R_t)} \frac{\operatorname{cov}\left(R_t, \frac{\partial \mathbf{T}}{\partial c_{t+1}}\right)}{\frac{\partial \mathbf{T}}{\partial c_t}} - \frac{\operatorname{cov}\left(R_{it}, \frac{\partial \mathbf{T}}{\partial c_{t+1}}\right)}{\frac{\partial \mathbf{T}}{\partial c_t}},$$

$$\mathbf{T} = E_t \sum_{t=0}^{\infty} \beta^t \mathbf{F}\left(c_t, m_t^G\right).$$

Barnett and Liu (1994) show that the ψ_{it} determine the risk premia in interest rates. Note that π_{it}^G reduces to Eq. (7.4) under perfect certainty.

We define the aggregate generalized user cost π_t^G dual to m_t^G by Fisher's factor reversal test,

$$\sum_{i=1}^{k} \pi_{it}^G m_{it} = \pi_t^G m_t^G,$$

and let

$$\Pi_t^G = \sum_{i=1}^{k} \frac{\pi_{it}^G X_{it}}{\sum_{i=1}^{k} X_{it}}$$

be the weighted average of the individual generalized user costs of monetary assets. We have the following proposition.

Proposition. *When nominal interest rates* (R_t, R_{it}) *are not known with certainty at the beginning of period t, an equation analogous to Eq. (7.13) still holds, and money velocity is a function of the aggregate generalized user cost, which equals the marginal rate of substitution between consumption goods and monetary services, so that*

$$\frac{\mathbf{F}_{mt}}{\mathbf{F}_{ct}} = \pi_t^G, \tag{7.23}$$

$$v_t = \frac{s}{1-s}\pi_t^G, \tag{7.24}$$

$$V_t = \frac{s}{1-s}\Pi_t^G \tag{7.25}$$

Proof: See Appendix I. □

Equation (7.23) can also be proved from the maximization problem without prior aggregation over monetary assets (see Appendix II). Equations (7.24) and (7.25) are analogous to Eqs. (7.15) and (7.16), respectively, although in Eqs. (7.24) and (7.25) the generalized user cost becomes the determinant of money velocity.

We can simplify the generalized user cost π_{it}^G to get a more intuitive equation for money velocity V_t. Dropping the remainder term of a second-order Taylor series approximation to $\mathbf{T}$, we have the approximation

$$\frac{\partial \mathbf{T}}{\partial c_{t+1}} = \left.\frac{\partial \mathbf{T}}{\partial c_{t+1}}\right|_t + (C_{t+1} - C_t)\left(\left.\frac{\partial^2 \mathbf{T}}{\partial c_{t+1}^2}\right|_t\right) + \left(m_{t+1}^G - m_t^G\right)\left(\left.\frac{\partial^2 \mathbf{T}}{\partial c_{t+1}\partial m_{t+1}^e}\right|_t\right),$$

where $|_t$ denotes function values evaluated at the point (c_t, m_t^G). Taking the covariance of the left-hand side with R_t, we get from the right-hand side that

$$\operatorname{cov}\left(R_t, \frac{\partial \mathbf{T}}{\partial c_{t+1}}\right) = \left(\left.\frac{\partial^2 \mathbf{T}}{\partial c_{t+1}^2}\right|_t\right)\operatorname{cov}(R_t, c_{t+1}) + \left(\left.\frac{\partial^2 \mathbf{T}}{\partial c_{t+1}\partial m_{t+1}^G}\right|_t\right)\operatorname{cov}\left(R_t, m_{t+1}^G\right).$$

Let k_1 be defined such that

$$k_1 \equiv \left(-c_t \frac{\partial^2 \mathbf{T}}{\partial c_{t+1}^2}\bigg|_t\right) \bigg/ \left(\frac{\partial \mathbf{T}}{\partial c_t}\right) = \beta(1 - s + s\phi).$$

Then k_1 is the discounted relative risk-aversion parameter, which in our specification is a constant. Similarly, define k_2 such that

$$k_2 \equiv \left(m_t^e \frac{\partial^2 \mathbf{T}}{\partial c_{t+1} \partial m_{t+1}^e}\bigg|_t\right) \bigg/ \left(\frac{\partial \mathbf{T}}{\partial c_t}\right) = \beta(1 - s)(1 - \phi).$$

Now assume that $\sigma_{rc} = \mathrm{cov}(R_t, c_{t+1}/c_t)$ and $\sigma_{rm} = \mathrm{cov}(R_t, m_{t+1}^G/m_t^G)$ are constants. Let $\theta_1 \equiv \{[\mathrm{cov}(R_t, \partial\mathbf{T}/\partial c_{t+1})]/(\partial\mathbf{T}/\partial c_t)\}$ and $\theta_{2i} \equiv \{[\mathrm{cov}(R_{it}, \partial\mathbf{T}/\partial c_{t+1})]/(\partial\mathbf{T}/\partial c_t)\}$. Then it follows that

$$\theta_1 = k_2\sigma_{rm} - k_1\sigma_{rc},$$
$$\theta_{2i} = k_2\sigma_{im} - k_1\sigma_{ic},$$

where

$$\sigma_{im} = \mathrm{cov}\left(R_{it}, m_{t+1}^G/m_t^G\right),$$
$$\sigma_{ic} = \mathrm{cov}(R_{it}, c_{t+1}/c_t)$$

are assumed to be time invariant. It follows that

$$\pi_{it}^G = \pi_{it}^e + \left(1 - \pi_{it}^e\right)\theta_1 - \theta_{2i} = (1 - \theta_1)\pi_{it}^e + (\theta_1 - \theta_{2i}).$$

Let θ_2 be the weighted average of the θ_{2i} such that

$$\theta_2 = \sum_{i=1}^{k} \frac{\theta_{2i} X_{it}}{\sum_{i=1}^{k} X_{it}}.$$

We find that

$$V_t = a_0 + a_1 \Pi_t^e, \tag{7.26}$$

where

$$a_0 = \frac{s}{1-s}(\theta_1 - \theta_2),$$

$$a_1 = \frac{s}{1-s}(1 - \theta_1),$$

$$\Pi_t^e = \sum_{i=1}^{k} \frac{\pi_{it}^e X_{it}}{\sum_{i=1}^{k} X_{it}}.$$

Note that if the covariances $\sigma_{ic}, \sigma_{im}, \sigma_{rc}$, and σ_{rm} are time varying, then a_0 and a_1 are also time varying and Eq. (7.26) is a time-varying or random-coefficient model. Hence, a time-varying coefficient model of money velocity can be justified by the fact that interest rate uncertainty may change over time, as for example from an autoregressive conditional heteroskedasticity (ARCH) process.

It is worthwhile to look at the effect of risk aversion and interest rate uncertainty on money velocity in more detail. Note that under our assumptions about the parameters of the model, we have

$$\begin{aligned} &k_1 > 0, \\ &k_2 > 0, \quad \text{if } \phi < 1 \\ &k_2 < 0, \quad \text{if } \phi > 1. \end{aligned}$$

For expositional purposes, we call $\phi < 1$ low risk aversion and $\phi > 1$ high risk aversion.

In the low-risk-aversion case, if $\sigma_{rm} < 0$, then the larger the value of $|\sigma_{rm}|$, the larger the value of a_1 and the smaller the value of a_0. The net effect of an increase of $|\sigma_{rm}|$ in this case is to reduce the money velocity, as $\Pi_t^e < 1$ and the magnitude of the decrease of the intercept is larger than that of the increase of $a_1 \Pi_t^e$. Therefore, if increased money growth variability raises the value of $|\sigma_{rm}|$ and if the $|\sigma_{im}|$ are not affected, then money velocity will decline. In the high-risk-aversion case, the results are just the opposite. An increase of $|\sigma_{rm}|$ will lead to higher money velocity. It follows that Friedman's (1983) hypothesis that the increased money growth variability causes money velocity to decline can be justified in our model by either (1) $\phi < 1$ and $\sigma_{rm} < 0$ or (2) $\phi > 1$ and $\sigma_{rm} > 0$. Also note that the magnitude of the effect of money growth variability on money velocity depends on other parameters of the model, such as s.

But there remains the effect of uncertainty of the individual monetary asset's own rates of return. Note that the covariances σ_{im} are not important in determining the magnitude of slope a_1, although those covariances are important in determining the value of the velocity function's intercept. Therefore a shift in the values of $|\sigma_{im}|$ will lead to a shift in the intercept of a money velocity function. If increased money growth variability raises both $|\sigma_{rm}|$ and $|\sigma_{im}|$ and if σ_{rm} and σ_{im} have the same sign, then the effect of the money growth variability on money velocity through σ_{rm} will be partially offset. The complicated nature of the effect of money growth variability on money velocity may partially explain the controversies in the empirical literature.

In short, if $\phi \neq 1$, the money growth variability will affect money velocity, but the direction and the magnitude of the effect depend on the degree of risk aversion and the correlation between interest rates and real money growth. If all the covariances are zero, as would be the case under perfect certainty, then Eq. (7.26) reduces to Eq. (7.16), as we would expect.

To further explore the economic interpretation of the coefficients in the money velocity function, note that when the first-order condition on the bond price is used,

$$\lambda_t = \beta E_t[\lambda_{t+1}(1 + R_t)],$$

the parameter θ_1 can be written as

$$\theta_1 = 1 - E_t(1 + R_t)E_t\left[\frac{\mathbf{T}_{c,t+1}}{\mathbf{T}_{ct}}\right],$$

where $E_t[\mathbf{T}_{c,t+1}/\mathbf{T}_{ct}]$ is the expected growth rate of the marginal utility of consumption goods. Therefore the slope coefficient of the money velocity function is

$$a_1 = \frac{s}{1-s}E_t(1 + R_t)E_t\left[\frac{\mathbf{T}_{c,t+1}}{\mathbf{T}_{ct}}\right].$$

If we use $E(R_t - R_{smt})$ as the independent variable in the money velocity function rather than the user cost Π_t^e, we have

$$V_t = a_{0t} + b_t E_t(R_t - R_{smt}), \tag{7.27}$$

where

$$b_t = \frac{s}{1-s}E_t\left[\frac{\mathbf{T}_{c,t+1}}{\mathbf{T}_{ct}}\right].$$

The subscript t in b_t and a_{0t} is used to indicate that the values of b_t and a_{0t} may not be time constant. In our model, given the specification of the utility function, we have

$$b_t = \frac{\beta s}{1-s}E_t\left[\left(\frac{c_{t+1}}{c_t}\right)^{s(1-\phi)-1}\left(\frac{m_{t+1}^G}{m_t^G}\right)^{(1-\phi)(1-s)}\right]. \tag{7.28}$$

From Eq. (7.28) it can be seen that the slope coefficient b_t depends on both the growth rate of consumption and the growth rate of real money stock. If the conditional expectation operator depends on the second or higher moments of the growth-rate processes, the slope process b_t will depend on the variabilities of both the consumption growth rate and the real money growth rate. If $\phi = 1$, the expected growth rate of the real money stock will not affect the coefficient b_t, because in that case, the marginal utility of consumption goods does not depend on the real money stock.

For the property of the dynamics of money velocity, note that, when solved from the equilibrium, the term $E_t(R_t - R_{smt})$ in Eq. (7.27) is a function of (V_{t+1}/V_t), η_{dt}, and η_{xt}, and let it be denoted as $E_t\{h[(V_{t+1}/V_t), \eta_{dt}, \eta_{xt}]\}$. From Eq. (7.28) we have

$$b_t = \frac{\beta s}{1-s}E_t\left[\eta_{dt}\left(\frac{V_{t+1}}{V_t}\right)^{(s-1)(1-\phi)}\right], \tag{7.29}$$

where η_{dt} and η_{xt} are the stochastic growth rates of exogenous income and money. Equation (7.27) can be written as

$$V_t = a_{0t} + \frac{\beta s}{1-s} E_t \left[\eta_{dt} \left(\frac{V_{t+1}}{V_t} \right)^{(s-1)(1-\phi)} \right] E_t \left[h \left(\frac{V_{t+1}}{V_t}, \eta_{dt}, \eta_{xt} \right) \right].$$

If we ignore a_{0t} we can see that, in general, the process of money velocity is stochastic nonlinear in this monetary general-equilibrium model.[10] Therefore we have seen the two sides of a coin. In a structural model [Eq. (7.26)] with Π_t^e as an independent variable, the slope coefficient is stochastic and the function is linear. In a dynamic equation, money velocity can be modeled as a stochastically nonlinear process from the same model. If we find some evidence of stochasticity in the slope coefficient of Eq. (7.26), the possibility of stochastic nonlinearity should be kept in mind when we model the behavior of money velocity.

4 Some empirical results

In this section, we first simulate the slope coefficient b_t by using quarterly data over the period from 1960.1 to 1992.4 for some specifications of parameters to examine the stability of the coefficients in the traditional money velocity function implied by our theoretical model. We then estimate a random-coefficient model of money velocity to examine the stability of the coefficients empirically. The random-coefficient model approach we follow is that of Swamy and Tinsley (1980). The results from both the empirical estimation and the theoretical simulation are compared to see whether the empirical behavior of the money velocity can be explained by the model developed in this chapter.

The data on monetary assets and their corresponding holding-period yields were provided by the Federal Reserve Bank of St. Louis, MO. Output data are Gross National Products (GNPs). The inflation rate is the growth rate of the price deflator for the GNP. The benchmark asset return path is approximated by the upper envelope of the 3-month Treasury bill rate path and the time paths of each individual monetary asset's own rate of return.[11] The growth rate of consumption is replaced with the real GNP growth rate. With M1, which includes no assets that have highly risky rates of return, the regular Divisia monetary aggregate closely tracks the generalized Divisia monetary aggregate. Hence we use ordinary Divisia M1 to measure the theoretical monetary quantity aggregate.

[10] Considering a_{0t} will make the problem more complicated without increasing new intuition.

[11] Even the upper envelope is too low, as the theoretical benchmark asset is completely illiquid and therefore must have a higher expected yield than the upper envelope over any expected yield-curve-adjusted rates of return on monetary assets providing any monetary services.

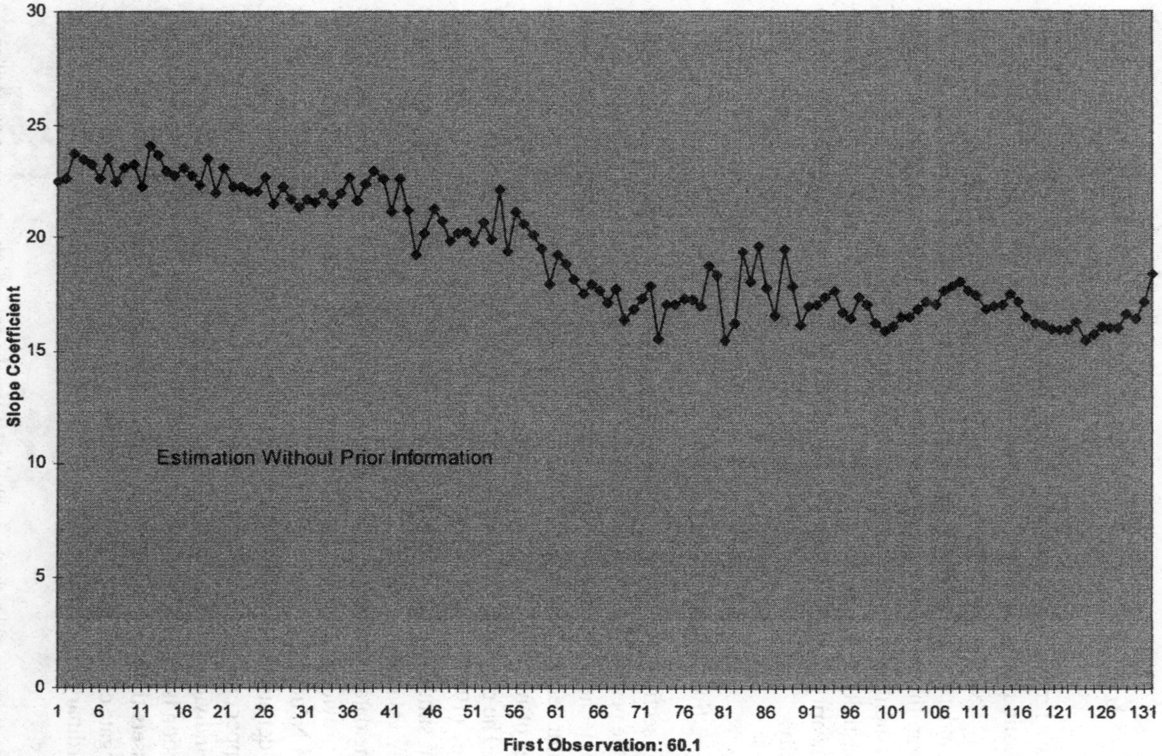

Figure 7.1. Slope coefficient of money velocity function by random-coefficient estimation.

To simulate the process b_t in Eq. (7.27), we first set $\beta = 0.99$, $s = 0.972$, and $\phi \in \{0.5, 2, 5\}$. The three different values of ϕ are chosen to capture the influence of different degrees of risk aversion on the stability of the coefficient b_t. The parameter s affects mainly the sample mean of b_t. We estimate a vector-autoregressive (VAR) model of real money and GNP growth rates by using quarterly data from 1960.1 to 1992.4. The estimated VAR model is then used to estimate the conditional expectation:

$$E_t\left[\left(\frac{c_{t+1}}{c_t}\right)^{s(1-\phi)-1}\left(\frac{m_{t+1}}{m_t}\right)^{(1-\phi)(1-s)}\right].$$

The simulated b_t process is plotted in Fig. 7.1. From Fig. 7.1 it can be seen that when $\phi = 0.5$ (low-risk-aversion case), the simulated slope process b_t is almost constant. When the value of ϕ increases, the variability in b_t also increases. When $\phi = 5$, the process b_t shows a lot of variability. There are two periods during which b_t is extremely volatile. One is from 1972 to 1976 and the other is from 1979 to 1982. The latter period approximately corresponds to the episode of the "monetarist experiment" of the Federal Reserve System. The b_t process also shows some variability in the recent years of 1991–1992. These simulation results confirm the theoretical prediction that if the degree of risk aversion is higher, the traditional money velocity function will be less stable.

These theoretical results from model simulation can be compared with empirical estimation. We estimate Eq. (7.27) with stochastically varying coefficients. We use the asymptotically efficient estimation procedure of Swamy and Tinsley (1980). Letting $a_t = (a_{0t}, b_t)$, we assume that, as in Swamy and Tinsley (1980),

$$a_t = \mathbf{a}^0 + e_t,$$

where $\mathbf{a}^0$ is a vector of constants and

$$e_t = \Phi_1 e_{t-1} + \Phi_2 e_{t-2} + \mathbf{u}_t,$$

where Φ_1 and Φ_2 are matrices of parameters to be estimated and $\mathbf{u}_t$ is a random vector with mean zero and covariance matrix Ω. The estimated b_t process for M1 money velocity is plotted in Fig. 7.2. We estimate the b_t process with both prior information incorporated and with no prior information (i.e., with diffuse prior information) about b_t. The two processes show almost the same movements. From Fig. 7.2 it can be seen that b_t is very volatile during the periods from 1972 to 1974 and from 1979 to 1982. This is approximately coincident with the simulation result with moderate risk aversion.

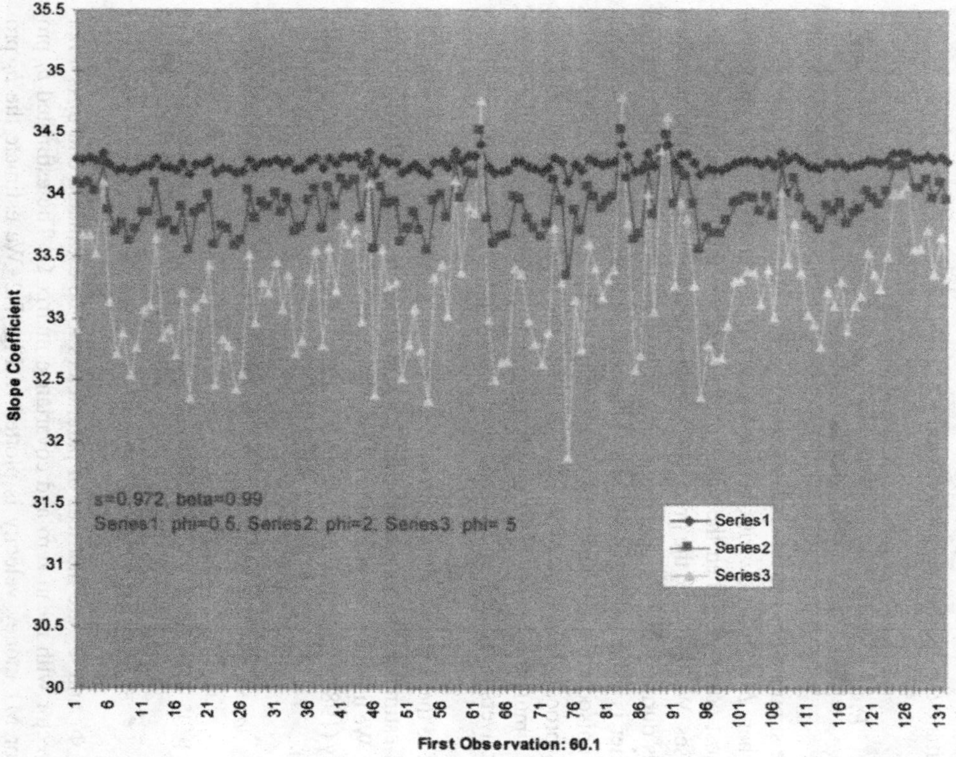

Figure 7.2. Simulated slope coefficient of velocity function.

Overall, the results from model simulation and from model estimation of a random-coefficient model show that our model can capture the main features of the coefficient process b_t in the traditional money velocity equation.

5 Conclusion

We have theoretically explored the dynamics of money velocity. The effects of risk aversion and interest rate uncertainty on money velocity are examined within a monetary general-equilibrium model. This paper indicates that if covariances between interest rates and consumption growth or between interest rates and money growth are generated by an ARCH-type process, the traditional money velocity function will become stochastically unstable and the money velocity process can be characterized as a stochastic nonlinear process. Both model simulation and estimation produce significant variability in the slope of the traditional money velocity function, especially during the 1972–1974 and 1979–1982 periods. This study sheds some new light on the nature of the dynamics of money velocity.

Appendix I

Proof of Proposition: We define Δ_t by setting

$$\sum_{i=1}^{k} (1 - \pi_{it}^G) m_{it} = \Delta_t m_t^G,$$

so that

$$\sum_{i=1}^{k} m_{it} = (\pi_t^G + \Delta_t) m_t^G,$$

and we define R_{mt}^G such that

$$\sum_{i=1}^{k} (1 + R_{it}) m_{it} = (1 + R_{mt}^G) m_t^G.$$

If we write the budget constraint in real terms, first-order conditions (7.9), (7.10), and (7.12) become

$$\mathbf{F}_{ct} = \lambda_t, \tag{7.30}$$

$$\mathbf{F}_{mt} = \lambda_t (\pi_t^G + \Delta_t) - \beta E_t [\lambda_{t+1} (1 + R_{mt}^G)], \tag{7.31}$$

$$\lambda_t = \beta E_t [\lambda_{t+1} (1 + R_t)]. \tag{7.32}$$

From Eq. (7.32) we have

$$E_t\lambda_{t+1} = \frac{\lambda_t/\beta - \mathrm{cov}(\lambda_{t+1}, R_t)}{E_t(1+R_t)}$$

Substituting this equation into Eq. (7.31) we have

$$\mathbf{F}_{mt} = \lambda_t\left(\pi_t^G + \Delta_t\right) - [\lambda_t - \beta_t\,\mathrm{cov}(\lambda_{t+1}, R_t)]\frac{E_t\left(1+R_{mt}^G\right)}{E_t(1+R_t)} - \beta\,\mathrm{cov}\left(\lambda_{t+1}, R_{mt}^G\right).$$

Note that $\lambda_t = \mathbf{F}_{ct} = \mathbf{T}_{ct}$ and $\beta\lambda_{t+1} = \beta\mathbf{F}_{c,t+1} = \mathbf{T}_{c,t+1}$. Therefore

$$\mathbf{F}_{mt} = \mathbf{F}_{ct}\left(\pi_t^G + \Delta_t\right) - \mathbf{F}_{ct}\frac{E_t\left(1+R_{mt}^G\right)}{E_t(1+R_t)} + \frac{E_t\left(1+R_{mt}^G\right)}{E_t(1+R_t)}\mathrm{cov}(\mathbf{T}_{c,t+1}, R_t) - \mathrm{cov}\left(\mathbf{T}_{c,t+1}, R_{mt}^G\right),$$

and hence

$$\frac{\mathbf{F}_{mt}}{\mathbf{F}_{ct}} = \pi_t^G + \Delta_t - \frac{E_t\left(1+R_{mt}^G\right)}{E_t(1+R_t)} + \frac{E_t\left(1+R_{mt}^G\right)}{E_t(1+R_t)}\frac{\mathrm{cov}(\mathbf{T}_{c,t+1}, R_t)}{\mathbf{T}_{ct}} - \frac{\mathrm{cov}\left(\mathbf{T}_{c,t+1}, R_{mt}^G\right)}{\mathbf{T}_{ct}}.$$

Recall that

$$\pi_{it}^G = \frac{E_t(R_t + R_{it})}{E(1+R_t)} + \frac{E_t(1+R_{it})}{E(1+R_t)}\frac{\mathrm{cov}(R_t, \mathbf{T}_{c,t+1})}{\mathbf{T}_{ct}} - \frac{\mathrm{cov}(R_{it}, \mathbf{T}_{c,t+1})}{\mathbf{T}_{ct}},$$

so that

$$\sum_{i=1}^{k}\left(1-\pi_{it}^G\right)m_{it} = \sum_{i=1}^{k}\left\{\frac{E_t(1+R_{it})}{E(1+R_t)}\left[1 - \frac{\mathrm{cov}(R_t, \mathbf{T}_{c,t+1})}{\mathbf{T}_{ct}}\right] + \frac{\mathrm{cov}(R_{it}, \mathbf{T}_{c,t+1})}{\mathbf{T}_{ct}}\right\}m_{it}$$

$$= \left\{\frac{E_t\left(1+R_{mt}^G\right)}{E(1+R_t)}\left[1 - \frac{\mathrm{cov}(R_t, \mathbf{T}_{c,t+1})}{\mathbf{T}_{ct}}\right] + \frac{\mathrm{cov}\left(R_{mt}^G, \mathbf{T}_{c,t+1}\right)}{\mathbf{T}_{ct}}\right\}m_t^G.$$

Therefore

$$\Delta_t = \frac{E_t\left(1+R^G_{mt}\right)}{E_t(1+R_t)} - \frac{E_t\left(1+R^G_{mt}\right)\operatorname{cov}(\mathbf{T}_{c,t+1}, R_t)}{E_t(1+R_t)\quad \mathbf{T}_{ct}} + \frac{\operatorname{cov}\left(\mathbf{T}_{c,t+1}, R^G_{mt}\right)}{\mathbf{T}_{ct}},$$

$$\frac{\mathbf{F}_{mt}}{\mathbf{F}_{ct}} = \pi_t^G. \qquad \square$$

Appendix II

The results in Sections 2 and 3 are in terms of monetary quantity aggregates and their dual user cost price aggregates. In this appendix, we show that if we aggregate over the first-order conditions of each individual disaggregated monetary asset, we can get the same result.

To see this, let us first consider the case of riskless interest rates. The decision problem is to maximize

$$E_t \sum_{t=0}^{\infty} \beta^t U(c_t, \hat{m}_t) \tag{7.33}$$

subject to

$$\begin{aligned} P_t c_t + P_{st} s_t + P_{bt} b_t + P_t \sum_{i=1}^{k} m_{it} \\ \leq s_{t-1}(d_t P_t + P_{st}) + P_{b,t-1} b_{t-1}(1 + R_{t-1}) \\ + \sum_{i=1}^{k} m_{i,t-1}(1 + R_{i,t-1}) P_{t-1} + \sum_{i=1}^{k} [X_{it} - (1 + R_{it-1}) X_{i,t-1}]. \end{aligned} \tag{7.34}$$

The first-order conditions are

$$U_{ct} = \lambda_t P_t, \tag{7.35}$$

$$U_{it} = \lambda_t P_t - \beta E_t(\lambda_{t+1})(1 + R_{it}) P_t, \tag{7.36}$$

$$\lambda P_{st} = \beta E_t[\lambda_{t+1}(d_{t+1} P_{t+1} + P_{s,t+1})], \tag{7.37}$$

$$\lambda_t = \beta E_t(\lambda_{t+1})(1 + R_t), \tag{7.38}$$

where U_{it} is the partial derivative of U with respect to m_{it}.

From Eqs. (7.35), (7.36), and (7.38) we have

$$U_{it} = U_{ct} - \frac{\lambda_t P_t}{1 + R_t}(1 + R_{it}), \tag{7.39}$$

$$= \frac{R_t - R_{it}}{1 + R_t} U_{ct} = \pi_{it} U_{ct}. \tag{7.40}$$

Recall that we have defined $m_t = f(\hat{m}_t)$. The utility function $U(c_t, \hat{m}_t) = \mathbf{F}(c_t, f(\hat{m}_t))$ consequently can be written as $\mathbf{F}(c_t, m_t)$. From Fisher's factor reversal test, we have

$$\sum_{i=1}^{k} \pi_{it} m_{it} = \pi_t m_t,$$

and hence

$$\pi_t \frac{\partial m_t}{\partial m_{it}} = \pi_{it}. \tag{7.41}$$

Taking the summation of Eq. (7.41) over $i = 1, 2, \ldots, k$, we have

$$\sum_{i=1}^{k} U_{it} = U_{ct} \sum_{i=1}^{k} \pi_{it}$$

or

$$\sum_{i=1}^{k} \left(\frac{\partial \mathbf{F}_t}{\partial m_t} \frac{\partial m_t}{\partial m_{it}} \right) = \mathbf{F}_{ct} \sum_{i=1}^{k} \pi_{it},$$

so that

$$\mathbf{F}_{mt} \sum_{i=1}^{k} \frac{\partial m_t}{\partial m_{it}} = \mathbf{F}_{ct} \sum_{i=1}^{k} \pi_{it}.$$

Substituting Eq. (7.41) into the above equation, we have

$$\mathbf{F}_{mt} \frac{1}{\pi_t} \sum_{i=1}^{k} \pi_{it} = \mathbf{F}_{ct} \sum_{i=1}^{k} \pi_{it},$$

so that

$$\frac{\mathbf{F}_{mt}}{\mathbf{F}_{ct}} = \pi_t.$$

We have the same result as that in Section 2.

Now consider uncertain interest rates. In this case Eq. (7.36) becomes

$$U_{it} = \lambda_t P_t - \beta E_t[\lambda_{t+1}(1 + R_{it})] P_t \tag{7.42}$$

and Eq. (7.38) becomes

$$\lambda_t = \beta E_t[\lambda_{t+1}(1 + R_t)], \tag{7.43}$$

whereas Eq. (7.35) remains unchanged.

From Eqs. (7.42) and (7.35) we have

$$U_{it} = U_{ct} - \beta P_t E_t[\lambda_{t+1}(1 + R_{it})]. \tag{7.44}$$

From Eqs. (7.43) and (7.35) we have

$$\begin{aligned} U_{ct} &= \beta E_t[U_{c,t+1}(1+r_t)] \\ &= \beta E_t(U_{c,t+1})E_t(1+r_t) + \beta \operatorname{cov}[U_{c,t+1},(1+r_t)], \end{aligned}$$

where r_t is the real interest rate corresponding to R_t. So we have

$$E_t U_{c,t+1} = \frac{U_{ct} - \beta \operatorname{cov}[U_{c,t+1},(1+r_t)]}{\beta E_t(1+r_t)}. \tag{7.45}$$

Equation (7.44) can be written as

$$U_{it} = U_{ct} - \beta E_t(U_{c,t+1})E_t(1+r_{it}) - \beta \operatorname{cov}(U_{c,t+1}, 1+r_{it}), \tag{7.46}$$

where r_{it} is the real interest rate corresponding to R_{it}.

By substituting Eq. (7.45) into Eq. (7.46) we have

$$U_{it} = U_{ct} - \beta \frac{U_{ct} - \beta \operatorname{cov}(U_{c,t+1}, r_t)}{\beta E_t(1+r_t)} E_t(1+r_{it}) - \beta \operatorname{cov}(U_{c,t+1}, r_{it})$$

or

$$U_{it} = U_{ct}\left[\frac{E_t(r_t - r_{it})}{E_t(1+r_t)} + \frac{\beta \operatorname{cov}(U_{c,t+1}, r_t)}{U_{ct}}\frac{E_t(1+r_{it})}{E_t(1+r_t)} - \frac{\beta \operatorname{cov}(U_{c,t+1}, r_{it})}{U_{ct}}\right].$$

Hence we have

$$U_{it} = U_{ct}\pi_{it}^G, \tag{7.47}$$

where π_{it}^G is the generalized user cost of monetary asset i.

Note that we use π_t^G as the aggregate monetary price index dual to the generalized Divisia quantity aggregate m_t^G. By taking derivatives with respect to m_{it} on both sides of Fisher's factor reversal test condition, $\sum_{i=1}^k \pi_{it}^G m_{it} = \pi_t^G m_t^G$, we have

$$\pi_{it}^G = \pi_t^G \frac{\partial m_t^G}{\partial m_{it}}. \tag{7.48}$$

Taking the summation of Eq. (7.47) over $i = 1, 2, \ldots, k$ and using Eq. (7.48) we have

$$\sum_{i=1}^k U_{it} = U_{ct} \sum_{i=1}^k \pi_{it}^G \tag{7.49}$$

$$= U_{ct}\pi_t^G \sum_{i=1}^k \frac{\partial m_t^G}{\partial m_{it}}. \tag{7.50}$$

Because in this case $U_{it} = [(\partial \mathbf{F}/\partial m_t^G)(\partial m_t^G/\partial m_{it})]$, Eq. (7.49) becomes

$$\frac{\partial \mathbf{F}}{\partial m_t^G} \sum_{i=1}^{k} \frac{\partial m_t^G}{\partial m_{it}} = \mathbf{F}_{ct} \pi_t^G \sum_{i=1}^{k} \frac{\partial m_t^G}{\partial m_{it}}.$$

Therefore

$$\frac{\mathbf{F}_{mt}}{\mathbf{F}_{ct}} = \pi_t^G.$$

This is the same result as that found in Section 3.

REFERENCES

Arrow, K. J., and Hahn, F. (1971). *General Competition Analysis*, Holden-Day, San Francisco.

Barnett, W. A. (1978). The user cost of money. *Econ. Lett.*, **1**, 145–49.

(1980). Economic monetary aggregates: an application of aggregation and index number theory. *J. Econometrics*, **14**, 11–48.

(1987). The microeconomic theory of monetary aggregation. In *New Approaches to Monetary Economics*, eds. W. A. Barnett and K. Singleton, Cambridge University Press, Cambridge, England, pp. 115–68.

(1994). Perspective on the current state of macroeconomic theory. *Int. J. Syst. Sci.*, **25**, 839–48.

Barnett, W. A., and Chen, P. (1986). Economic theory as a generator of measurable attractors. *Mondes Dev.*, **14**, 5–20; reprinted in *Laws of Nature and Human Conduct: Specificities and Unifying Themes*, eds. I. Prigogine and M. Sanglier, G.O.R.D.E.S., Brussels, pp. 209–24.

(1988). The aggregate-theoretic monetary aggregates are chaotic and have strange attractors: an economic application of mathematical chaos. In *Dynamic Econometric Modeling*, eds. W. Barnett, E. Berndt, and H. White, Cambridge University Press, Cambridge, England, pp. 199–246.

Barnett, W. A., and Choi, S. S. (1989). A comparison between the conventional econometric approach to structural inference and the nonparametric chaotic attractor approach. In *Economic Complexity: Chaos, Sunspots, Bubbles and Nonlinearity*, eds. W. Barnett, J. Gewerke, and K. Shell, Cambridge University Press, Cambridge, England, pp. 141–212.

Barnett, W. A., and Liu, Y. (1994). The extended Divisia monetary aggregate with exact tracking under risk. Working Paper, Washington University in St. Louis, St. Louis, MO.

Barnett, W. A., Fisher, D., and Serletis, A. (1991). Consumer theory and the demand for money. *J. Econ. Lit.*, **92**, 2086–2119.

Barnett, W. A., Gallant, A. R., Hinich, M. J., Jungeilges, J. A., Kaplan, D. T., and Jensen, M. J. (1995). Robustness of nonlinearity and chaos tests to measurement error, inference method, and sample size. *J. Econ. Behav. Organ.*, **27**, 301–20.

(1998). A single-blind controlled competition among tests for nonlinearity and chaos. *J. Econometrics*, **82**, 157–92.

Belongia, M. T. (1985). Money growth variability and GNP. *Federal Reserve Bank St. Louis Rev.*, **67** (April), 23–31.

(1996). Measurement matters: recent results from monetary economics re-examined. *J. Polit. Econ.*, **104**, 1065–83.
Bordo, M. D., and Jonung, L. (1981). The long-run behavior of the income velocity of money in five advanced countries, 1870–1975: an institutional approach. *Econ. Inquiry*, **19**, 96–116.
(1987). *The Long-Run Behavior of the Velocity of Circulation*, Cambridge University Press, Cambridge, England.
(1989). The long-run behavior of velocity: the institutional approach revisited. *J. Policy Model.*, **12**, 165–97.
Boyle, G. W. (1990). Money demand and the stock market in a general equilibrium model with variable velocity. *J. Polit. Econ.*, **98**, 1039–53.
Brock, W. A. (1986). Distinguishing random and deterministic systems: Abridged version, *J. Econ. Theory*, **40**, 168–95.
Chrystal, K. A., and MacDonald, R. (1994). Empirical evidence on the recent behavior and usefulness of simple-sum and weighted measures of the money stock. *Federal Reserve Bank St. Louis Rev.*, **76** (March/April), 73–109.
Day, R. H. (1992). Complex economic dynamics: obvious in history, generic in theory, elusive in data. *J. Appl. Econometrics*, **7**, 19–23.
Dueker, M. J. (1993). Can nominal GDP targeting rules stabilize the economy? *Federal Reserve Bank St. Louis Rev.*, **75** (May/June), 15–30.
(1995). Narrow vs. broad measures of money as intermediate targets: some forecast results. *Federal Reserve Bank St. Louis Rev.*, **77** (Jan./Feb.), 41–52.
Feenstra, R. C. (1986). Functional equivalence between liquidity costs and the utility of money. *J. Monet. Econ.*, **17**, 271–91.
Fisher, D., and Serletis, A. (1989). Velocity and the growth of money in the United States, 1970–1985. *J. Macroecon.*, **11**, 323–32.
Friedman, M. (1983). Monetary variability: United States and Japan. *J. Money, Credit, Bank.*, **40**, 339–43.
Hall, T. E., and Noble, N. R. (1987). Velocity and the variability of money growth: evidence from Granger-causality tests. *J. Money, Credit, Bank.*, **44**, 112–116.
Marshall, D. A. (1992). Inflation and asset returns in a monetary economy. *J. Finance*, **47**, 1315–42.
Medio, A. (1992). *Chaotic Dynamics: Theory and Application to Economics*, Cambridge University Press, Cambridge, England.
Serletis, A., and Krause, D. (1995). Nominal stylized facts of U.S. business cycles. Working Paper, University of Calgary, Calgary, Alberta, Canada.
Siklos, P. L. (1993). Income velocity and institutional change: some new time series evidence, 1870–1986. *J. Money, Credit, Bank.*, **25**, 377–92.
Stone, C. C., and Thornton, D. L. (1987). Solving the 1980s' velocity puzzles: a progress report. *Federal Reserve Bank St. Louis Rev.*, **69** (Aug./Sep.), 5–23.
Swamy, P. A. V. B., and Tinsley, P. A. (1980). Linear prediction and estimation methods for regression models with stationary stochastic coefficients. *J. Econometrics*, **12**, 103–42.
Thornton, D. L. (1994). Financial innovation, deregulation and the 'credit view' of monetary policy. *Federal Reserve Bank St. Louis Rev.*, **76** (Jan./Feb.), 31–49.
Thornton, J. (1995). Friedman's money supply volatility hypothesis: some international evidence. *J. Money, Credit, Bank.*, **27**, 288–91.

CHAPTER 8

A genetic-programming-based approach to the generation of foreign-exchange trading models

Andrew Colin

Of all the markets available to the international investor, the global foreign-exchange markets are perhaps the most liquid and heavily traded. The average daily turnover in currencies around the world is estimated to be up to a trillion dollars a day.

Currency markets show myriad different behavior patterns, with quiet periods, intervals of extreme volatility, steady trends, violent reactions to external news events, and positive feedback all seen at various times. Despite the apparent unpredictability of these markets, it is estimated that at least 90% of the turnover in foreign exchange is due to speculative interbank trading by large financial institutions attempting to make short-term returns.

Pressure on capital ratios within the banking sector has led to the investigation of new ways of taking on risk by trading markets in a rigorously controlled manner. As a part of such a strategy, the rest of this chapter describes a class of algorithms to assist in the determination of market direction. However, we stress that directional trading algorithms are only part of a successful investment operation. Equal weight must be given to asset allocation and risk management.

The majority of algorithmic trading systems are those in which a computer program gives directional forecasts for markets, based on recent market activity. Such models are frequently specified in terms of technical indicators or mathematical functions that compress information about an aspect of recent market behavior into a single number. These indicators are then combined into simple rules and used for trading purposes. Sample indicators include moving averages, overbought and oversold indicators, and historical volatilities.

For instance, we might choose to trade the Australian dollar (AUD) against the U.S. dollar (USD). On some days the AUD will appreciate in value with

The author thanks Paul Dentskevitch of Tokai Bank, London, and Frank Brun of the Commonwealth Bank, Sydney, for useful discussions, and the referees to this chapter for their useful and constructive comments.

respect to the USD, and these are the times when we would wish to hold the AUD. On other days, the exchange rate will fall, and in this situation we would wish to convert our AUDs to USDs, which will appreciate in value relative to the AUD. The astute investor can therefore make a profit whether the market rises or falls.

A simple way to signal when one currency is appreciating or depreciating against another is to calculate the average rate over the previous 20 days for yesterday and today, to plot these points on a graph, and to draw a line between the two points. If the gradient of the line is positive, then we interpret this as a signal to hold the AUD and wait for it to appreciate (a long AUD position); if it is negative, we sell the AUD and buy the USD (a short AUD position). This technique can work well in a trending market, but usually loses heavily when the markets are range trading or moving randomly.

Reasons for the increasing growth in popularity of model-driven position taking include the following:

- Computer-based trading offers a complementary risk approach to discretionary risk taking. Frequently a computer model holds a diametrically opposite view to its human counterparts. Given that both the human and the program will generate similar returns over the longer term, having positions cancel each other out in this way will reduce the volatility of returns.
- The sheer number of markets available to trade and the complexity of market activity can overwhelm a human trader.
- Computer models can be tuned, with a combination of risk management and money management techniques, to offer a variety of risk profiles to suit different investors (aggressive, steady growth, etc.).
- A computer-driven approach allows objective testing and (to a certain degree) validation of trading systems.

Unfortunately there are major difficulties in designing effective computer-driven trading systems. Even with easy-to-use software and sophisticated optimization routines, building and validating a model-based trading system is a time- and labor-intensive task, as the search space encompasses indicator types, indicator periods, constants, and all algebraic combinations of these quantities. The size of the search space is thus very large and often defeats conventional optimization techniques. Furthermore, optimization techniques may in fact be inappropriate for many markets because of the relative paucity of data samples. Financial researchers have therefore incorporated ideas from machine learning, statistics, and signal-processing theory to bear on the market forecasting problem, with neural networks, statistics, genetic programming (GP), econometrics, fuzzy logic, and wavelet theory currently prominent.

We describe a GP-based approach to the design of explicit rule-driven trading systems. We refer to Goldberg (1989) for an overview of the subject. Colin (1994) describes several working genetic-algorithm- (GA-) based trading systems and supplies source code in C. A similar study is described in Neely et al. (1997), which also contains excellent references to the literature.

A GA is a technique for using directed random search to solve a complex optimization problem. An initial randomly generated population of chromosomes is constructed, in which the chromosomes are mapped to possible solutions to a problem. In addition, a user-defined fitness function is given, which defines how well a hypothesis matches the terms of the problem.

For instance, in designing the model as described above, the choice of a 20-day average was arbitrary and the period may be seen as a parameter to optimize. The chromosome might thus contain the period of the average, and the fitness function would then evaluate how much profit (or how little loss) a model with this averaging period would make. Other individuals in the population might be models with averaging periods ranging from 2 to 500 days.

A new population is now produced from the previous generation, by means of crossover, mutation, and selection:

- Crossover is the combination of the genetic material from two individuals to produce a third, so that the new expression contains genetic material from both parent individuals.
- Mutation refers to random, low-probability changes to an individual's genetic material.
- Selection is the process of selecting individuals to be passed into the new population. The likelihood of an individual's being chosen is proportional to its fitness, which is calculated from the fitness function.

The process is now repeated many times. As a variety of different solutions is explored in parallel, the system quickly finds the periods that give the highest return.

This technique usually produces excellent solutions to most optimization problems in a fraction of the time required by conventional explicit search techniques. GAs have been used to solve traveling salesman problems, to optimize jet turbine efficiency, in the design of walking machines, and in many other industrial and engineering applications.

A classical GA has a chromosome representation in the form of fixed-length strings of bits or integers. Although efficient to implement, such a data structure has the constraint that the complexity of the solution is always fixed. For instance, a model that looks for the best periods between two moving averages cannot examine a relationship among three or four, even if to do so would improve the characteristics of the model. Furthermore, the relationship between the two moving averages is fixed.

By contrast, the GP approach uses data structures of varying complexity that can grow or shrink as the solution's fitness function requires, by means of appropriately defined crossover and mutation operators. The reader is referred to Koza (1993) for more information on this relatively new field.

A GP system allows us to build as many trading models as required for a given market, without including any a priori assumptions as to the system's complexity. The derived systems may be constrained so that they use complementary indicators, or so that the resulting equity curve will have low cross correlation with previously induced models. A portfolio of models generated by this means may then be expected to generate returns with lower volatility than those from a single model. We examine this idea in more detail below.

1 Genetic-programming implementation

Model representation

We consider a trading model in the following form:

if (**lexpr**) then
  LONG
else
  SHORT,

where LONG means "Take a long position in the instrument against an underlying asset," and SHORT means "Take a short position in the instrument." **lexpr** (short for logical expression) returns a Boolean value. The model may be referred to in the abbreviated form **lexpr**.

Sample models for **lexpr** might be

$$MA[15](c) < c, \tag{8.1}$$

$$MA[15](c) < MA[5](c), \tag{8.2}$$

$$MA[15](c) < MA[5]MA[15](c), \tag{8.3}$$

$$MA[15](c) < MA[5]MA[15](c) + 0.01, \tag{8.4}$$

$$MA[15](c) < c \text{ AND } MA[15](c) < MA[5](c) \tag{8.5}$$

Here, *MA[15](c)* represents the value of the 15-day moving average of the market close. Similarly, *MA[5]MA[15](c)* is shorthand for the value of the 5-day moving average of the 15-day moving average of the market close. The algebraic expressions may use a variety of functions, real numbers, arithmetic operators, and Boolean operators, as long as the expression evaluates to a Boolean.

Data structures

There exists a natural isomorphism between such an expression and a binary tree. For instance, expression (8.1) corresponds to the tree in Fig. 8.1 and the more complex expression (5) to the tree in Fig. 8.2.

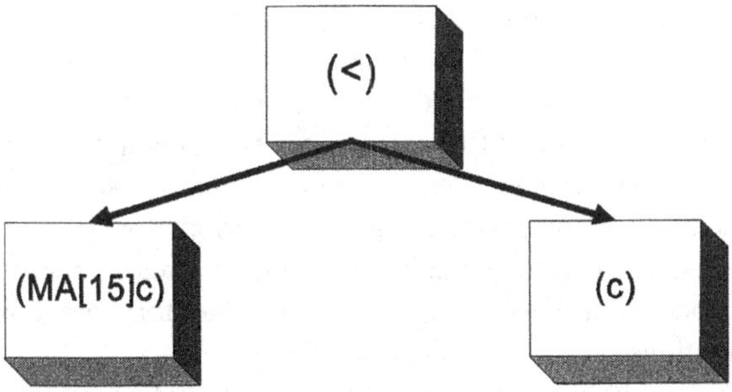

Figure 8.1. Data structure of expression (8.1).

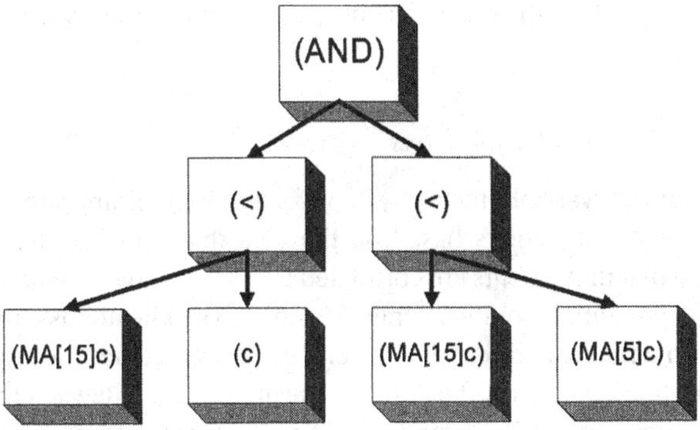

Figure 8.2. Data structure of expression (8.5).

Following earlier work by Forsyth (1982) and Colin (1992), we use a binary tree as the chromosome structure for our system. This data structure suffices for the simple if/then rules we wish to induce, but does not include provision for more complex programming constructs such as looping and recursion.

A binary tree admits a straightforward representation in C in terms of node structures linked by pointers. A node is represented by the structure

```
typedef struct node {
    struct node *parent;
    struct node *left;
    struct node *right;
    unsigned type;
    unsigned ident;
    unsigned args[3];
    unsigned number;
    unsigned *data;
} NODE;
```

The left, right, and parent pointers are links to other nodes. By convention, a terminal node has its left and right sublinks set to point to NULL, as does the parent link of the root node. Fields *type* and *ident* label the type and the subtype, respectively, of a node; for instance, the type might be an arithmetic operator and the subtype the addition operator (see chromosome constraints and operators below). Array *args* contains three periods for use in technical indicator functions, and *number* contains the value of a real number if that is the type of the node. Last, *data* is a pointer to an array for storage results of temporary calculations.

Most operators use only a fraction of this information. For instance, *args* is used only if the node type is a technical indicator. These fields correspond to recessive traits in genes; they are carried about from one generation to another and are expressed only if the environment makes it appropriate for the system to do so.

Technical indicator functions

Functions currently available to the system for model building are shown in Table 8.1. A trend indicator is based on the idea that a market has internal momentum and that movements are correlated in time. A typical trend indicator is a simple or exponential moving average. A sideways indicator assumes that a market trades in a range, and that the nearer a price approaches the edge of the range the more likely is a move back to the mean. Typical sideways indicators include stochastics and WPRs. Both types of indicator, of course, assume that the market is forecastable and would not be expected to work on a random walk. For a more detailed description of the different types of function used by market practitioners, see Murphy (1986).

Other functions, such as volatility indicators, can easily be added to the library if required.

Chromosome constraints

Throughout the setup and subsequent evolution of the population of trading, candidate models must always form grammatical functions. To ensure that all functions conform to the usual rules for well-formed algebraic expressions, we classify each node into one of six types,

{LOGICAL, INEQUAL, ARITHMETIC, REAL, FUNCTION, MARKET}

and apply the following constraints:

(1) The root node of each expression tree always has type *LOGICAL* or *INEQUAL.* This ensures that rules always return a Boolean value, corresponding to a buy/sell signal.

Table 8.1. *Functions available for model building*

Indicator code	Name	Type	Args	Description
ADXR	Raw Welles directional movement index	Trend	3	Part of Welles directional movement index
ADX	Welles average directional movement index	Trend	2	Welles directional movement index
ATR	Average true range	Sideways	1	Welles moving average of true range
CCI	Commodity channel index	Sideways	1	Detects beginning and ending market trends
DETREND	Detrended moving average	Trend	1	Difference of price and moving average of price
DX	Welles directional index	Trend	1	Unsmoothed ADX
FASTD	Lane's stochastic fast D	Sideways	2	Exponential moving average of raw K
OSC	Oscillator	Trend	2	Difference of two moving averages
RAWK	Lane's stochastic K	Sideways	1	Overbought/oversold function
MOM	Momentum	Trend	1	Difference between price now and price (period) days ago
ROC	Rate of change	Trend	1	Rate of change relative to previous intervals
SLOWD	Lane's slow stochastic D	Sideways	3	Double smoothed exponential moving average of raw K
EMA	Exponential moving average	Trend	1	Exponential moving average
SMA	Simple moving average	Trend	1	Simple moving average
RSI	Relative strength indicator	Sideways	1	Welles Wilder's relative strength index
WIAD	Accumulation/ distribution index	Sideways	0	William's accumulation index
WPR	Williams % R	Sideways	1	Location of current price in recent market range
(Identity)	(Identity)	(N/A)	0	Maps price onto itself

(2) The terminal nodes of each tree always have type *MARKET* or *REAL*. Nodes of these types can have no subnodes.
(3) The subnodes of each tree with type *ARITHMETIC* or *INEQUAL* are *ARITHMETIC*, *MARKET*, *FUNCTION*, or *REAL*.
(4) The immediate subnodes of a node with type *LOGICAL* have types *LOGICAL* or *INEQUAL*.
(5) A *FUNCTION* type node represents a unary operator, as a technical indicator can operate on only one market. The left subnode of a node with type *FUNCTION* is therefore of type *FUNCTION*, *ARITHMETIC*, or *MARKET*, and the right subnode is always set to *NULL*. In this way we have included provision for one technical indicator to act on another, so the system allows nested functions (e.g., an overbought/oversold indicator of a moving average of price) or a function acting on the ratio of two prices.

The crossover and mutation operators are defined so that they follow the above rules. The system is therefore unable to generate ungrammatical expressions, no matter how much recombination of genetic material is performed.

Operators

The system defines the following operators for use in trading models:

- $\{+, -, *, /\}$ (arithmetic)
- {AND, OR, AND NOT, OR NOT} (logical)
- $\{>, >=, <<=\}$ (inequal)

The mutation and crossover rules defined above ensure that no operator is ever applied to an inappropriate variable type. In the case of a divide-by-zero error, the expression that generated the offending expression is assigned a high negative fitness so that it will fall to the bottom of the selection pool on subsequent generations. Further evaluation of the expression is then halted.

Real numbers in induced expressions

If required, the system can also incorporate real numbers into its expressions. The range and the resolution are set at the outset of each run (typically, 0 to 1 in increments of 0.01). Sideways indicators typically vary between 0 and 1, which would be an appropriate range for models based on such functions. The user may specify wider ranges when other indicators are under consideration.

Table 8.2. *Part of a typical initial population*

EMA[13]c > ADXR[14,3,18]c and not CCI[3]c >= MOM[5]c and EMA[8]c <= c
1.234 >= ADX[9,18]c
ATR[6]c < CCI[7]c or not WIADc <= DX[12]c
c > ADXR[3,5,11]c and MOM[16]c * OSC[11,11]c < 5.443
ADXR[19,10,4]c >= RAWK[17]DETREND[14]DETREND[10]c and not ADXR[7,8,19]c <= ADXR[13,8,17]c
RAWK[13]CCI[10]c >= FASTD[18,13]c - WPR[18]c – 0.034

Genetic-algorithm setup

After some experimentation, population size was set to 50 individuals with complete population replacement at each generation, representing a compromise between genetic diversity and keeping run times to a reasonable length. Crossover probabilities were 0.5, with each site in a chromosome having the same probability of being the crossover site, and mutation probability was 1%. We performed individual selection by sorting chromosomes into order of performance and then linearly ranking them in fitness from 0.1 (for the least fit) to 0.9 (for the most fit). In this way we avoided the problem of negative fitness, which would have occurred if fitness had simply been set to model returns. Part of a typical initial population is shown in Table 8.2.

Individuals in the system's population are generated through a recursive node allocation routine. A root node is constructed, and a call is made to the system's random-number generator. According to whether the value of the returned number is greater than a predefined quantity σ, branch generation either ends at that point or continues recursively. Small values of σ therefore generate large, bushy rule trees, whereas high values generate small, compact trees.

Constants are defined at run time to set the initial ratios of *MARKET* to *REAL* nodes, the ratios of *LOGICAL* to *ARITHMETIC* nodes, and the ratio of *MARKET* to *FUNCTION* nodes. The user may also set the range of technical indicator periods and the types of technical indicators at the start of each run. In this way the system can generate tailored models that use (for instance) only moving averages or particular types of sideways indicators.

Mutation

The mutation operator can alter any one quantity in a node's set of data fields. Therefore mutation can legally alter a node's *type* (such as changing an arithmetic operator to a technical indicator), its *ident* (converting a + to a − or a moving average to an RSI), or one value from the *args* array (converting a 5-day *MA* to a 25-day *MA*).

Crossover

Two expressions are selected with probability varying as their fitness (see the subsection on selection probabilities) and a crossover site is selected in each, again subject to the rules defined above. A copy of the first parent tree is made, and the subtree consisting of the nodes below the crossover site in the second tree is grafted onto the first tree at the first tree's crossover site, replacing the original subtree.

To illustrate, we apply crossover to the two expressions

$(a < b)$,

$(c < d \text{ AND } e < f)$.

Grammatical descendant expressions might then be

$(c < d)$

$(c < d \text{ AND } a < b)$.

Population stagnation

One drawback of this scheme is that the population is occasionally prone to stagnation, in which all individuals have the same algebraic form and no new forms can arise. This can occur, for instance, when all individuals have the form

$(a \; (\textit{inequality}) \; b)$.

In this case there is no way that two individuals can combine, using the crossover and mutation rules shown above, to produce a new rule with a different topology. To allow new forms to arise, we slightly modified our crossover operator to include new root nodes to arise with low probabilities. The selected subtrees from the parent chromosomes are then grafted onto the subnode sites of this new node.

Fitness function

What defines a good trading model? This could be high returns, but more frequently low volatility or high Sharpe ratio is just as important.

In this study we have examined the following quantities:

- *(return)*
- *(return)/(maximum drawdown)*
- *(return)/(maximum drawdown + transaction costs)*

Because models and returns were substantially the same among these three measures, we used *return* as our fitness measure.

Selection probabilities

A standard roulette wheel scheme was used for selection, in which the likelihood of a rule's being chosen to pass its characteristics onto the next generation is directly proportional to its fitness. For a discussion of selection algorithms, see Goldberg (1989).

2 Model validation

To ensure that the system can indeed form generalizations about the markets of interest, datasets are divided into three equal portions, to which we refer as training data, validation data, and test data. We develop population of models by using the training data. At the conclusion of evolution, we run the models on the validation data, which either can be a continuous sample contiguous with the training data or can intersperse the training data. This provides a useful check against models' overfitting themselves to the training data.

The results presented below are from models generated on training data and run on the separate test dataset.

3 Trading results

We found at an early stage of experimentation that the system found it easier to generate good models if the range of possible technical indicators was restricted at the outset of evolution. This may simply be due to the constraints of computer power available, as cutting down on certain classes of indicators substantially reduces the size of the search space. For the simulations described here, we generated two sets of models for each market: 20 sideways models, by using the functions {*CCI*, *RSI*, *WPR*, *SLOWD*, *FASTD*, *RAWK*, *WIAD*} and 20 trending models, by using the functions {*ADXR*, *ADX*, *MOM*, *OSC*, *DETREND*, *EMA*, *SMA*}.

The graphs in Figs. 8.3–8.6 each represent the cumulative return from trading 40 models together, corresponding to a minimum portfolio increase/decrease of 5% of assigned capital. (If 1 model out of 40 changes its position, so that the number of long models changes from n to $n+1$, then total exposure changes from $\{[n-(40-n)]/40\}$ long to $\{[n+1-(40-n-1)]/40\}$ long, a change of $2/40 = 5\%$. The general result for a portfolio with N models, for which the minimal fractional portfolio increment is $2/N$, follows.)

The models generated were in all cases of a long/short type, simply specifying whether to be long or short the cash market. No neutral positions were taken.

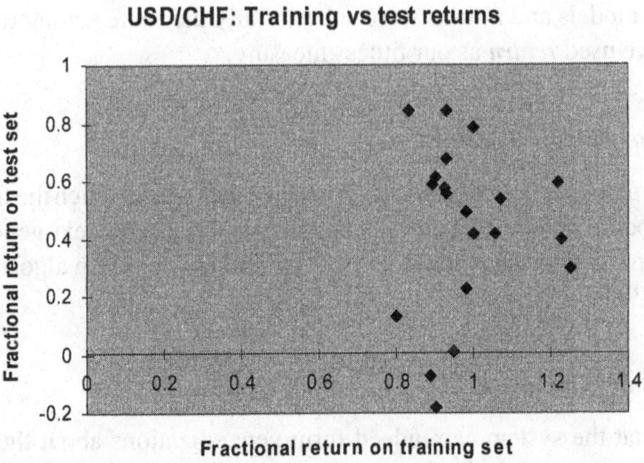

Figure 8.3. USD/Swiss franc: training versus test returns.

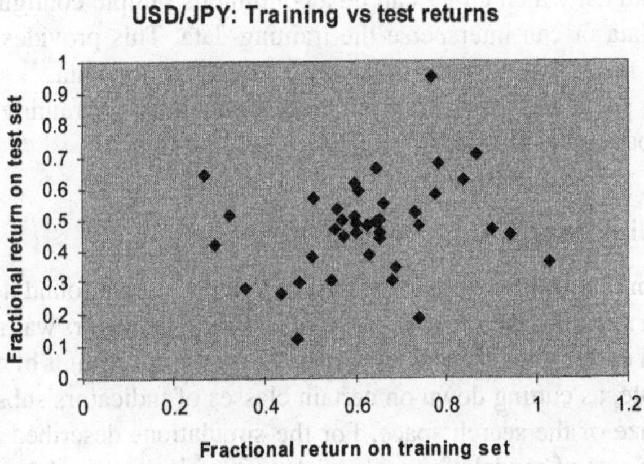

Figure 8.4. USD/Japanese yen: training versus test returns.

Results are shown without leverage, and returns are not compounded. Transaction costs were not taken into account for these results, as our experience in the market suggests that these are likely to be negligible for systems that update their positions on a weekly basis. More importantly, we have also ignored any amounts made or lost from interest rate differentials between currency pairs; however, each model spends approximately equal times long and short the market, so we have assumed that interest gains and losses will approximately cancel out. More work needs to be done in this area to assess systematically the effects of interest rates on returns.

Table 8.3. *Training, validation, and testing data periods*

Market name	Training period	Validation period	Test period
USD/CHF	1974–1981	1981–1988	1988–1995
USD/JPY	1974–1981	1981–1988	1988–1995

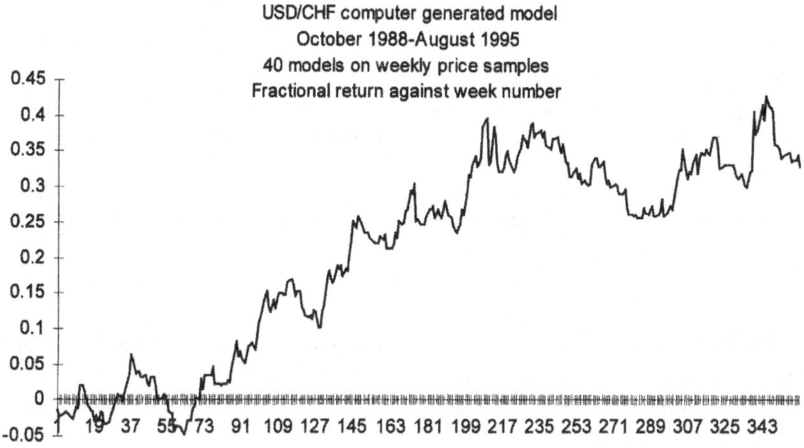

Figure 8.5. USD/Swiss franc computer-generated model October 1988–August 1995 40 models on weekly price samples. Fractional return against week number.

The system was run on the following markets on weekly data over the given time periods. No particular day of the week was selected, as the presence of holidays can lead to missing samples; instead we chose every fifth sample from a daily sample set.

Market data from 1981 to 1988 were used as a validation sample to guard against overfitting (see Table 8.3). However, only three of the 80 models produced negative returns over this period, and so we rejected none of the trading models produced by the program. On the unseen test sample, average returns generated by the system over 7 years of unseen data are ~50%, or ~7% per year on unleveraged capital.

The distributions of cumulative returns for the 40 models built for each market are shown in Figs. 8.3 and 8.4; Figs. 8.5 and 8.6 show the equity curves for the composite systems calculated by averaging returns over all models for that market.

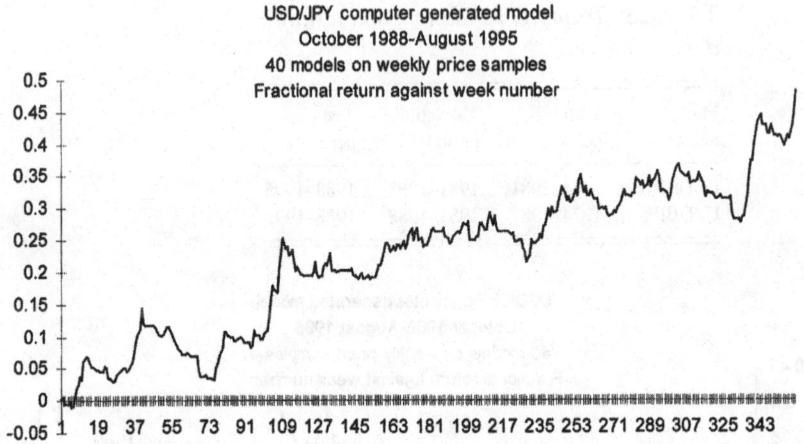

Figure 8.6. USD/Japanese yen computer-generated model October 1988–August 1995 40 models on weekly price samples. Fractional return against week number.

Each trading model used was the one that had the highest fitness from the final generation of a GP run, irrespective of the behavior of this best model on the training set. In all cases training was performed for a fixed number of generations, and then halted (see Section 6).

4 Multiple-model generation

One immediate result of this work is that we can now generate numerous noncorrelated models for the same market. For every market we have examined, the system generates roughly equal numbers of trend-based and overbought/oversold-based models. Trading several such systems on the same market therefore brings a degree of diversification to bear.

For instance, suppose we have generated 20 models for a particular market. At a given time, 15 of these models may be advising a buy and the remaining 5 a sell. Assuming that an equal amount of risk capital has been assigned to each model, then this suggests that $(15 - 5)/20 = 0.5$ of overall risk capital for this market should be assigned to a buy. In this way, we have the desirable features of diversification across numerous views. Furthermore, one or two bad models will not substantially affect the portfolio's return, and overall exposures are likely to be lower for the same net return. When diversification across markets is added to this internal diversification, the effect is to increase portfolio Sharpe ratios.

5 Programming issues

The program was developed in C with Borland Turbo C and run under the 32-bit Watcom C compiler on a Pentium personal computer.

Analysis with a source-code profiler showed that the system spends the majority of processing time calculating the values of the various technical indicators in the model scoring routines. Although it might be possible to reduce these times by precalculating the values of some of the most commonly used functions and periods, the extra complexity and memory requirements were not felt to merit the effort required at this stage. We might also constrain populations so that no identical individuals can arise, but this may lead to the loss of useful subexpressions that are expressed only in later generations.

One problem we anticipated was that there is no predefined level of complexity for models generated. With the crossover operator, the system has the potential to generate very large trees that can grow without bound until the memory of the host computer is exhausted. All memory is explicitly deallocated after use, so no garbage-collection routines are needed.

Fortunately, this turned out to be much less of a problem than expected. It appears that with a suitable amount of training data (>250 points) a sufficient diversity of market behavior has shown that large, complex models are at a disadvantage to small, more compact models in modeling market behavior. Of course, this is precisely the behavior that we would wish to see. The only time we did find very large trees evolving was when the initial population was complex and the training dataset was small, when overfitting would have been expected.

Running the system with a low population (30 individuals or fewer) for many generations (>250) tends to generate highly correlated, overfitted models. We found that better results arose from large populations (>500) over short evolution periods (~5 generations). This ensured a high degree of genetic diversity in the population.

We suggest that the best generalization occurs when a population has sufficient time to learn the macroscopic features of a dataset, which generalize to other datasets, but insufficient time to learn to microscopic features, which do not generalize. We have found similar behavior when applying other machine learning algorithms to financial markets (Colin, 1992).

6 Forecast generation for large portfolios

The primary disadvantage of a multiple-model approach to trading is that some investment in technology has to be made to handle the large numbers of signals generated and to monitor the system's exposures. A portfolio that encompasses 50 markets, each of which is watched by 20 models, must generate and summarize 1000 daily signals. This is probably beyond the inclination of any trader. To automate this process we have integrated a database system with model parsing and forecast generation routines, which are written in C and compiled as dynamic link libraries. The database stores models and market rates and generates a summary of all forecasts and dealing recommendations automatically.

With such a large number of uncorrelated models in play at the same time, the system will also continually make small readjustments to its overall exposure as market conditions change. As long as commission costs are proportional to deal sizes, this should not have an adverse effect on overall profitability.

7 Generation of metamodels

There are several ways in which we can use the GP tool to assist in enhancing model returns. One of the most straightforward is to treat the equity curve generated by a computer-generated model as a market in its own right to which entry and exit rules can be applied. The equity curve can then be run though the GP program to produce a second set of dealing rules. We refer to such a set of expressions as a metamodel, as it describes the interaction of an underlying model with a market.

To illustrate, suppose we have constructed and validated a set of trading rules to apply to the equity curves in Figs. 8.5 and 8.6. These rules will provide a forecast of when profit/loss will rise – suggesting we follow the forecasts of the underlying model – and when it will fall, at which point we may either reduce our exposure, have no exposure at all, or even reverse the underlying position. We have only just begun to work in this area, but our preliminary results suggest that returns can be enhanced by at least 10% per annum when these techniques are applied.

8 Conclusions and future work

This initial study has shown that the GP approach is appropriate for the generation of trading systems and that it is possible to induce models that encompass market behavior with some degree of time invariance. These models are of necessity somewhat crude, but in conjunction with disciplined money management techniques they may be used to enhance portfolio returns.

A straightforward extension to this research would be to extend the model inputs to several markets or to include economic variables. For instance, a system designed to follow movements in the AUD might be given values of interest rates and commodity indices, as well as historical AUD rates. For a very much more sophisticated system, we might look at incorporating techniques from fuzzy logic to induce chains of fuzzy rules. We intend to begin work in these areas in the near future.

REFERENCES

Colin, A. M. (1992). Neural networks and genetic algorithms for financial forecasting. Proc. IJCNN, Beijing.

(1994). Genetic algorithms for financial modeling. In *Trading On The Edge*, ed. G. Deboeck, Wiley, New York.

Forsyth, R. (1982). *Beagle User's Manual*, Warm Boot, Nottingham, England.

(1989). *Machine Learning*, Chapman & Hall, London.

Goldberg, D. E. (1989). *Genetic Algorithms in Search, Optimization and Machine Learning*, Addison-Wesley, Reading, MA.

Koza, J. (1993). *Genetic Programming*, MIT Press, Cambridge, MA.

Murphy, J. J. (1986). *Technical Analysis of the Futures Markets*, New York Institute of Finance, New York.

Neely, C., Weller, P., and Dittmar, R. (1997). *Is Technical Analysis in the Foreign Exchange Market Profitable? A Genetic Programming Approach*, Federal Reserve Bank of St. Louis, St. Louis, MO.

CHAPTER 9

Hybrid option pricing with an optimal weighted implied standard deviation

Paul Lajbcygier, Andrew Flitman, and Marimuthu Palaniswami

This work is concerned with improving option-pricing accuracy. The seminal option-pricing model is the Black–Scholes model (Black and Scholes 1973). Claims that the Black–Scholes valuation model no longer holds are appearing with increasing frequency (Dumas et al. 1996). In fact, Rubinstein (1985) states that, not only is the model failing, it is becoming worse over time.

The failure of the conventional model has motivated a new option-pricing literature, determined to reconcile these pricing anomalies. Those approaches that hold the most promise make minimal assumptions. Some authors assume that the key to improving pricing lies with modeling the underlying standard deviation (Ait-Sahalia and Lo 1998, Dumas et al. 1996, and Ncube 1996). Others use techniques to fit optimal distributions implied by option prices (Rubinstein 1994, Derman and Kani 1994, and White 1995).

This work shows that significant pricing outperformance is possible with a new hybrid approach. The hybrid approach models the differences between the conventional option-pricing model and the actual transaction data.

The conventional pricing model has only one unknown input parameter – the standard deviation. Although the market's optimal forecast for standard deviation is utilized, persistent and systematic biases are found. The biases are a function of the option's moneyness (i.e., ratio of underlying value to option strike price) and time to maturity. These biases are modeled with artificial neural networks (ANNs). ANNs are a form of nonlinear, nonparametric regression. It is found that this modeling enhances out-of-sample option-pricing performance.

This chapter is organized into four sections. The first introduces key concepts and financial terms, the second section describes the method and data used, next the results are presented, and finally conclusions and further work are discussed.

1 Futures and options

A futures contract is an obligation to either buy or sell a specific commodity, known as the underlying, at an agreed price at some time in the future. Futures have an expiry time. At expiry the holder of the future must either buy or sell the underlying at the price specified in the futures contract. The futures market is a no-net-gain market. For each investment there will always be an equal and opposite investment. This implies that for every dollar that one investor makes, another investor, who took the other opposite trade, makes an equal and opposite loss.

Stock market indices are designed to reflect overall movements in a large number of equity (i.e., share) securities. The performance of an equity index is important because it represents the performance of a broadly diversified stock portfolio and gives insights into the broad market risk/return profile.

Index futures are contracts that commit the user to either buy (*go long*) or sell (*go short*) the stocks in the index at the currently determined market price at some point in the future. If the investor believes the index to be going down, the investor should *sell/go short*. If, on the other hand, the investor believe that the index is going up, the investor should *buy/go long*.

Whereas futures are the obligation to buy or sell the underlying at a particular price in the future, options are the right but not the obligation to buy or sell the underlying at a particular price in the future. There are two types of options analogous to long/short futures. The right (but not the obligation) to buy is a *call*. The right (but not the obligation) to sell is a *put*. An investor who uses the right to buy or sell the underlying is said to have *exercised* the option and takes *delivery* of the underlying at the price specified in the option contract. An option, like a future, has a lifetime. However, the holder of the option is not forced to purchase the underlying at the price specified in the option – known as the *strike* – but can choose whether to exercise the option or not. The option has a price or value known as a *premium*. After an option *expires*, its premium is worthless and the option cannot be exercised. An option on a future is the right but not the obligation to purchase the future at the strike price before the expiry.

One final distinction is between American-style and European-style options. American-style options can be exercised at any time before expiration, whereas European-style options can be exercised only at expiry.

The Australian options on futures market

Stock market indices are designed to reflect the overall movement in a broadly diversified equity portfolio. The Australian Stock Exchange (ASX) all ordinaries (AO) share-price index (SPI) is calculated daily and represents a market-value-weighted index of firms that consist of over 95% by value all firms currently listed on the ASX.

A future written on the SPI is traded on the Sydney Futures Exchange (SFE). The SFE is the world's ninth-largest futures market and the largest open outcry market in the Asia–Pacific region. The 1995 average daily volume for SPI futures was 9795 contracts, and the average open interest on futures at month's end was 99,650 contracts.

The SPI futures option is written on the SPI futures contract. Exercise prices are set at intervals of 25 SPI points. Options expire at the close of trading on the last day of trading in the underlying futures and may be exercised on any business day before and including expiration day. Upon exercise, the holder of the option obtains a futures position in the underlying future at a price equal to the exercise price of the option. When the future is marked to market at the close of trading on the exercise day the option holder is able to withdraw any excess. To give an indication of liquidity, in 1995 there were, on average, 3100 SPI options on futures contracts traded daily, with average open interest at month's end being 142,875 contracts.

The SFE is peculiar in that both the option writer and the option buyer must post a margin with the clearing house. The option buyer does not have to pay a full premium to the writer. Instead, a delta-based initial margin from both the buyer and the writer is posted. The option on future is marked to market daily and gains and losses are collected on a daily basis. The writer receives credit for any market move that results in a reduction in premium. The full premium may not be given to the writer until the option is exercised or expires (Martini and Taylor 1995).

The modified-Black model

The Black–Scholes paper is the seminal paper in the option-pricing literature. Black (1976) extended the work of Black and Scholes (1973) to options on futures and provided a solution for European boundary conditions. The Black differential equation is

$$\frac{1}{2}\sigma^2 F^2 \frac{\partial^2 f}{\partial F^2} - rf + \frac{\partial f}{\partial t} = 0, \tag{9.1}$$

where F is the current futures price and f can represent European-style or American-style call or put options on futures.

The SFE uses a system of deposits and margins for both long- and short-option positions that requires a modification in the Black equation. This modification reflects the fact that no interest can be earned on a premium that has not been paid fully up front. Essentially the interest rate r is set to zero in the Black solution.

The modified Black equation is

$$c' = FN(d'1) - XN(d'2), \tag{9.2}$$

where

$$d'1 = \frac{\ln(F/X) + (\sigma^2/2)(T-t)}{\sigma\sqrt{T-t}}, \tag{9.3}$$

$$d'2 = d'1 - \sigma\sqrt{T-t}, \tag{9.4}$$

c' is the premium, F is the underlying price, X is the strike, $T - t$ is the time to maturity (in years), and σ is the standard deviation.

Even though the AO SPI options on futures are American style, Lieu (1990) claims that the early-exercise premium is negligible because of the peculiar margin requirements of the SFE. This is why the European Black formula can be used for American-style options on futures.

Estimating the realized standard deviation

Only one option-pricing parameter is not known with complete certainty at transaction time – the standard deviation. Before the option transaction this cannot be known – an estimate is required.

From a previous option transaction it is possible to work backwards and obtain an implied standard deviation (ISD) as all of the option-pricing parameters are available (except the standard deviation).

There are four possible approaches for estimating the standard deviation:

- by use of weighted ISDs (WISDs)
- modeling ISDs with a time-series approach
- choosing a standard deviation to minimize the root-mean-square error (RMSE) for all prior option transactions by use of an optimization technique
- using a moneyness-adjusted approach

For the dataset under consideration it is argued that the WISD approach is the best. The other methods for standard-deviation estimation have deficiencies. Modeling ISDs with a time-series approach is not possible for various reasons: First, the AO SPI options on futures are reasonably illiquid, so few transactions are available to model; second, strong hourly autocorrelation and mean reversion have been noted on illiquid option markets such as the Spanish IBEX 35 (Refenes and Gonzalez Miranda 1996) and on the Paris stock exchange (Jacquillant et al. 1993); finally, bid–ask bounce can induce negative serial correlation (Roll 1984). Choosing a standard deviation to minimize the RMSE error is also not possible for this dataset because there are not enough valid transactions (Martini and Taylor 1995). A moneyness-adjusted approach is attempted in this work. The empirical option-pricing literature shows that the ISD is a function of moneyness. This is a paradox because, in reality, it is possible to have only a unique realized standard deviation for each future expiry.

Utilizing a moneyness-adjusted WISD can, in theory, mitigate the moneyness effect and hence provide more accurate pricing. In practice, what is found is that moneyness WISDs do not provide more accurate pricing (see below).

Conceptually we can consider the ISD as comprising three components:

- primarily, the market's expectation of true realized standard deviation until expiry; modeled with a WISD.
- a portion that is due to bias (moneyness and maturity bias); modeled with ANNs.
- a portion that is due to noise (bid–ask spread, nonsynchronous data, staleness); not modeled.

WISDs are calculated and used for the standard-deviation estimate in this work because they can mitigate the option-pricing biases, minimize the effect of noise, and therefore obtain the most accurate estimate of the market's standard deviation.

Utilizing the WISD in this way resolves a paradox. The empirical option-pricing literature shows that the ISD is a function of moneyness. This is a paradox because in reality it is possible to have only a unique realized standard deviation for each future expiry. WISDs provide a plausible estimate of the market's realized standard deviation. This does not necessarily imply that the WISD shall be constant over the trading day. As the market incorporates new information, the expected realized standard deviation will change.

Figlewski (1997) has criticized the use of WISD's. He argues that suppressing ISD differences across different options by an averaging process cannot be appropriate when systematic and persistent option-pricing biases exist. Figlewski argues that the biases imply that the market is using a different option-pricing model.

Consistent with Figlewski's argument, a new option-pricing model is estimated in this chapter. Nevertheless, an estimate of standard deviation is required. Although it is argued above that, in general, WISDs provide the optimal standard-deviation estimation approach, it is not clear which WISD is optimal in particular. There are three separate requirements that determine the optimal choice of WISD. The first is that the choice of WISD must be one that minimizes option-pricing error.[1] The second is that the WISD provides an accurate

[1] "...[T]he implied volatility need have little to do with the best possible prediction for the price variability of the underlying asset from the present through option expiration, while it has everything to do with the current and near term supply and demand...." (Figlewski 1997).

predictor of the realized underlying standard deviation.[2] Finally, we desire that the WISD be a plausible predictor of realized standard deviation.

Those WISDs that weigh at-the-money ISDs most heavily fulfill each of the above requirements. Those WISD schemes that give more weight to at-the-money options tend to be the most accurate for price prediction. The reasons for this accuracy are that these options trade with much greater liquidity than others and therefore their ISDs contain more reliable information; also, at-the-money option premiums are most sensitive to changes in the standard deviation (Figlewski 1997). Previous studies show that derivative implied standard deviation (DERISD) is optimal for price prediction (Turvey 1990, Martini and Taylor 1995).

Those WISD schemes that give more weight to at-the-money options tend to be the most accurate for realized standard-deviation prediction too. Corrado and Miller (1996) prove theoretically that at-the-money WISDs are the most efficient (and also "nearly" unbiased) predictors of realized standard deviation. This is verified by various empirical studies (Canina and Figlewski 1993, Chiras and Manaster 1978).

Finally at-the-money WISDs provide plausible realized standard-deviation estimates.

This is not true of WISDs that use ISD estimates from those transactions that have the moneyness most similar to that of the one under consideration. This type of WISD is not a plausible predictor of realized standard deviation.

Neural networks and option pricing

It has been shown that a feedforward neural network is capable of approximating any nonlinear function and was therefore thought to be appropriate in approximating the residuals from the option-pricing function. Recently, many authors have shown that ANNs can be used for option pricing: Hutchinson et al. (1994) and Malliaris and Salchenberger (1993) for the U.S. Standard and Poor (S&P) 500 options on futures, Lajbcygier et al. (1995) and Boek et al. (1995) for the Australian AO SPI options on futures.

The neural-network option-pricing approach has many advantages over conventional option pricing (which includes modified Black). The conventional approach is sensitive to the parametric expression for the underlying's price dynamics – which is constrained by the need for analytical tractability – whereas the neural network determines the underlying's price dynamics and the relationship to the option price inductively.

[2] It is possible to apply arbitrage arguments, which imply that they must be identical. Figlewski (1997) argues that arbitrage arguments do not necessarily hold because option arbitrage strategies are particularly prone to being expensive and risky.

Furthermore, the neural network can adapt to structural changes in the data that a parametric method cannot adapt to. Finally, the neural network is a flexible and powerful tool (albeit data intensive) that is simple to use, whereas the conventional approach requires knowledge of sophisticated mathematics.

The neural-network architecture and training used in this work is standard. The learning rule is backpropagation with momentum equal to 0.5 and learning rate equal to 0.05. The architecture comprises three layers. Each layer has a different number of units – 3 input, 15 hidden, and 1 output unit. The scaling is tanh, logistic, tanh for each layer, respectively.

The aim is to learn the persistent and systematic biases by using the optimal option-pricing model given the optimal standard-deviation estimate. To achieve this aim the entire dataset is divided into 6 monthly periods. By aggregating the data in this way it is hoped that the systematic biases can be modeled by the ANN. For each 6-month period, excluding the first and last, an ANN is trained on the data. The trained ANN is then tested out of sample in the next 6-month period. This is continued for each nonoverlapping 6-month dataset for the entire 3-year dataset. In this way data snooping is minimized.

For each 6-month dataset, 20% of the in-sample training data was extracted randomly and used for a cross-validation set. Training was conducted on the remaining 80% of the in-sample data. Approximately every 200 training epochs[3] the cross-validation dataset performance was measured. Training was halted when training did not improve performance on the cross-validation set (i.e., after 50,000 training calculations).

2 Method

Data

The data for this work consisted of SPI futures data and SPI call options on futures data, both obtained from the SFE. The data used were PIT data, which have been in existence only since 1993 and are accurate to the second. The duration of the data used in this analysis was from January 1993 to December 1995. We considered all options transacted. Not all of the data was used, however, for six reasons. First, there were options listed in the data as expiring in a 10-year period that were erroneous. Second, if for any transaction any one of the WISDs could not be calculated, then the entire transaction was discarded (e.g., for all opening transactions no prior standard deviations were available with the technique described below). Third, to mitigate the nonsynchronous data effect, only those options transacted that had a corresponding future transaction in the minute before the option transaction were used. Fourth, when the

[3] An epoch is an entire sweep of the in-sample training dataset (not including the 20% cross-validation set).

option was trading below intrinsic value, no ISD could be calculated with the method of bisection.[4] Fifth, options with $T - t < 1$ day were omitted. Finally, options deemed to be outliers were omitted.

Three out of the four parameters required for the modified-Black ISD calculation were provided by the SFE in the PIT data: X, C, and $T - t$.[5] The underlying futures price was obtained by an algorithm described below.

As in Hutchinson et al. (1995) the data were separated into continuous 6-month periods to mitigate the nonstationarities and data-snooping bias.

The SFE AO SPI options on futures is a particularly useful market for study because the modified-Black model does not require an interest rate input, the options are on futures and therefore dividend calculations are not required, and finally the usual problems with nontrading of illiquid small-capitalized stock are mitigated because we are not concerned with the physical index but with the future instead.

Data synchronicity

The underlying futures price often used (Hutchinson et al. 1994) is the closing price of the day. It was thought, however, that for the relatively illiquid Australian data, it was important that the data be more synchronous. Hence it was decided to extract the nearest recent SPI futures price that was recorded before the time that the option was transacted. This resulted in underlying values that in most cases were recorded only seconds before the option was transacted. If, however, the underlying future was transacted more than 60 s before the option, the option transaction was discarded.

Outliers

A simple filter rule was used to strip outliers: if an ISD > 30% or if an ISD < 5% then the transaction was deemed to be an outlier and not used in the calculation of any of the WISDs. In this way, 50 outliers were discarded. Sixty percent of the outliers had time to maturities of less than 3 days. Presumably there is a "very short time to maturity" effect or, because of the short time to maturity (and the small time premium), the option value is very sensitive to measurement errors (Dumas et al. 1996, p. 8). There were another 160 "very short time to maturity" options that were not outliers, and these were included in the WISD calculations.

[4] The tolerance is 0.0001 points (see Turvey 1990 and *Financial Analysts Journal*, July–Aug., 1991).

[5] The SFE uses the convention of 365 days in the year, with holidays/weekends included.

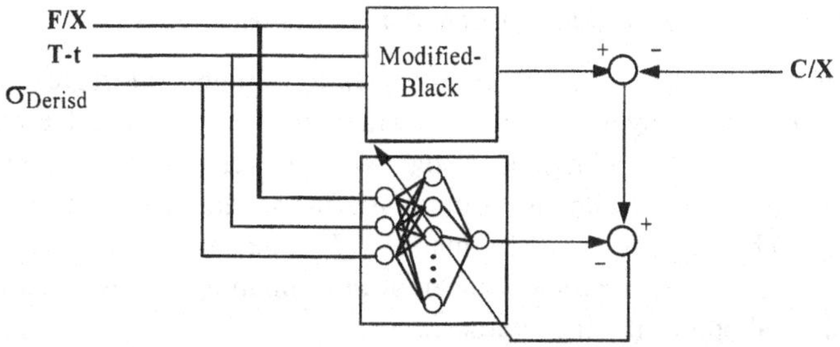

Figure 9.1. Training the neural network on the deviations from the modified-Black equation.

Merton's result

Similar to the theorem of Hutchinson et al. (1994), Merton's theorem (Merton 1973) allows us to use F/X and C/X in place of F, X, and C. Although using this result has been criticized because it assumes that the standard deviation and the underlying price are independent (Ait-Sahalia and Lo 1998) we still use it because it offers the ANN information about strike bias in an explicit manner.

The neural-network, artificial-neural-network hybrid, and linear-hybrid approaches

The different ANN schemes that are used in this work are based on permutations and combinations of different preprocessing.[6] There are two main types of preprocessing steps. The first is to use ratios. We hypothesize that the use of ratios can help the ANN learn moneyness bias. The second is to use the hybrid approach. The basis of the hybrid approach to the problem of option pricing is in using the modified-Black equation as a base and allowing the neural network or linear regression to augment its performance. This can be illustrated as shown in Fig. 9.1.

The values of F, X, $T-t$, standard deviation, and C are obtained or estimated as described above. Essentially, the ANN is presented with targets – the difference between the modified-Black equation and the C/X value taken from the real data:

$$\varepsilon = (C/X)_{\text{Model}} - (C/X)_{\text{Real}}. \tag{9.5}$$

[6] The ANN architecture used was a standard three-layer feedforward ANN with tanh input scaling, logistic hidden-layer activation function, and logistic final-layer activation function. For each ANN there were 3–4 inputs, 15 hidden layers and 1 output neuron. Early stopping was used to prevent overtraining (Bishop 1995, p. 343).

Artificial neural networks and nonparametric regression

Estimating ε from Eq. (9.5) requires regression. In general, regression is the problem of estimating a function of several variables $\varepsilon = \hat{f}(\bar{x}) + \text{error}$. There are many competing techniques for regression. Given a regression problem, it is not known which technique is optimal. This section summarizes the work undertaken by Lajbcygier and Flitman (1997) to determine which technique is best for the regression problem inherent in estimating the residuals from the conventional option-pricing approach.

Only nonparametric regression techniques were considered. Nonparametric regression has the fundamental advantage in that it makes very few assumptions about the unknown function to be estimated. Cherkassky (1992) presents a taxonomy of nonparametric regression techniques. There are three general classes: global-parametric methods assume that the estimating function can be represented as a combination of some basis functions, local-parametric methods approximate the function by fitting simple parametric functions to different subregions of the domain, and adaptive-computation methods adjust their strategy to take into account the behavior of the function to be approximated.

Lajbcygier and Flitman (1997) compare at least one model from each of the above classes. Two global-parametric techniques were used – the linear regression and the nonlinear ANN. The local-parametric technique was represented by kernel regression. Finally, the adaptive technique used was projection-pursuit regression. It was found that ANNs performed marginally better on the whole. Therefore, in this work, the only regression technique considered is the ANN (linear regression is considered also to motivate the nonlinear ANN approach).

Weighted implied standard deviations

The utility of WISDs for finding the most accurate predictor of future standard deviations was discussed in Section 1. In most studies all of the previous day's ISD_{t-1}s are used to calculate a single WISD_t: $\text{WISD}_t = f(\text{ISD}_{t-1})$. This study is rare in that it uses the same-day ISD_ts to calculate the WISD_t, $\text{WISD}_t = f(\text{ISD}_t)$.[7] There are strong intuitive reasons for using the same-day ISD_ts to calculate WISD_ts. First, overnight effects in overseas markets can be quite large, the SFE is not traded overnight (although it has a computerized market, SYCOM, that does trade), and hence opening ISDs can vary by as much as 2% from the previous-day close.[8] Second, it seems sensible to use the most up-to-date ISD estimate rather than to rely on that of the previous day. Finally, $T - t$ will be exactly the same for each option because the options are separated by maturity date (this would not be the case if the previous-day options were used).

[7] Brenner and Galai (1981) also found that additional forecasting power can be achieved by calculating WISD's intraday.

[8] Private correspondence – BZW Melbourne 1997.

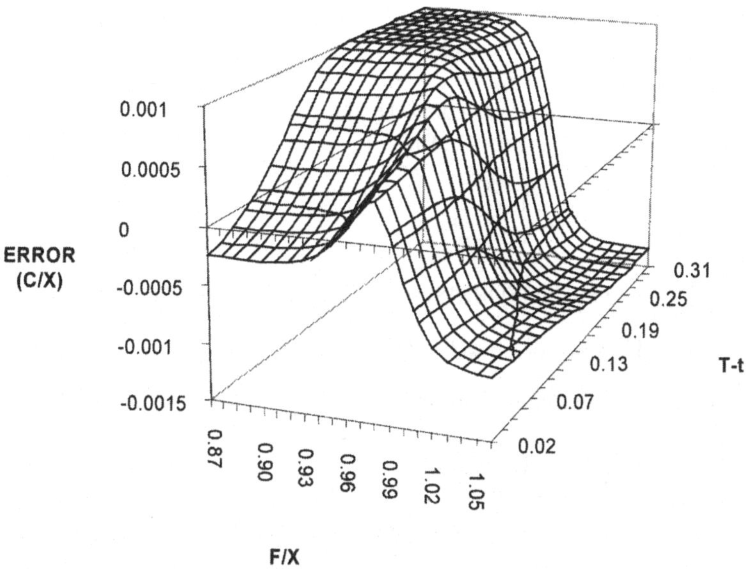

Figure 9.2. Hybrid-ANN output, standard deviation = 0.2.

Finally Lajbcygier (1998) has shown that using the same-day ISD_t provides considerably less error than using previous-day ISD_{t-1}.

Although the next option transaction may be only a few seconds away, the task is to find a WISD that will minimize option-pricing error and realized standard-deviation error, not just pricing error. In fact, the two should be related by arbitrage arguments. If WISD were a biased estimator it would, in theory at least, be able to generate arbitrage profits. The ISD has a small effect on the bias surface of Fig. 9.2; however, the strongest biases exist because of moneyness and maturity, not ISD. These persistent and systematic biases are our main concern in this work, not the short-term forecast of the ISD. It is important to use the least-biased WISD so that spurious biases are not introduced. Furthermore, claims of conventional-model outperformance are not possible with a suboptimal WISD.

There is a subtle problem with using same-day transactions data to calculate WISDs – the "spread-selection bias." The spread-selection bias (Phillips and Smith 1980) occurs if the spread is large[9] (as it is on the SFE) – then what appear as overpriced options really trade on the ask part of the spread and what appear as underpriced options trade on the bid. Although Park and Sears (1985) use only the previous-day transactions to mitigate the spread-selection bias, it is not clear how this approach works. Perhaps, when all the trades over the entire

[9] The market makers at the SFE initially quote a spread on +/− 10 points. In actual fact it has been ascertained through private correspondence with the major brokers in Australia that the spread narrows to +/− 1 point.

day are utilized, the noise that is due to the spread is diminished. Nevertheless, Lajbcygier (1998) has shown that the error in the option price is smaller when same-day ISDs are used.

The first method applies equal weight to all K options in each class and is known as the average ISD (AVEISD):

$$\text{AVEISD} = \frac{1}{K}\sum_{i=1}^{K}\sigma_{\text{imp},i} \tag{9.6}$$

The second method (DERISD) uses a weighting scheme based on vega:

$$\text{VEGA} = \Lambda_{\text{imp},i} = F\sqrt{T-t}N'(d_1'), \tag{9.7}$$

where $N'()$ is the standard normal distribution and d_1' is from Eq. (9.4):

$$\text{DERISD} = \frac{\sqrt{\sum_{i=1}^{K}\sigma_{\text{imp},i}^2\Lambda_{\text{imp},i}^2}}{\sqrt{\sum_{i=1}^{K}\Lambda_{\text{imp},i}^2}}. \tag{9.8}$$

The rationale for DERISD is that it gives more weight to those ISDs (in each class) that are most sensitive to standard deviation.

The third method uses a weighting scheme based on the elasticity of the option-pricing formula (ELISD):

$$\text{ELISD} = \frac{\sum_{i=1}^{K}W_i\sigma_{\text{imp},i}}{\sum_{i=1}^{K}W_i}, \tag{9.9}$$

where

$$W_i = \Lambda_{\text{imp},i}\left(\frac{\sigma_{\text{imp},i}}{C_i}\right). \tag{9.10}$$

The rationale for the ELISD is that investors are more interested in relative percentage change of option price to standard deviation rather than absolute, as in the DERISD.

The next method is LASTISD; this is quite simply the ISD of the last option traded on the day before the one under consideration, in the same time to maturity. The rationale for this approach is that there may be some time structure in the ISDs. A criticism of the approach is that it does not account for the smile.

For comparative purposes, we exploit a priori knowledge of the moneyness bias to choose an appropriate ISD for the modified-Black model. This is ad hoc; we know that the ISDs do not represent the market's ex ante prediction of standard deviation. Nevertheless, by mitigating moneyness bias, these ISD schemes can provide more accurate option pricing. Two moneyness-adjusted ISD schemes are calculated.

The first is Finucane's (1989) high–low linear weighting scheme (HILOISD):

$$\text{HILOISD} = \begin{cases} \dfrac{\sigma_{\text{at}} + (R - R_{\text{at}})(\sigma_{\text{low}} - \sigma_{\text{at}})}{R_{\text{low}} - R_{\text{at}}} & \text{when } R \leqslant R_{\text{at}} \\[2ex] \dfrac{\sigma_{\text{at}} + (R - R_{\text{at}})(\sigma_{\text{low}} - \sigma_{\text{at}})}{R_{\text{high}} - R_{\text{at}}} & \text{when } R > R_{\text{at}} \end{cases}, \tag{9.11}$$

where $R = X/F$, $R_{\text{low}} < R_{\text{at}} < R_{\text{high}}$, and σ_{low} is the ISD calculated at R_{low} and so on. The motivation for the HILOISD is that a piecewise linear weighting function can adjust for moneyness bias.

The next moneyness scheme is FONXISD. FONXISD is the ISD of the previous transacted option whose ratio of the futures price to the option strike price is closest to the current option. A simple algorithm is used that utilizes the ISD from the most similar moneyness option within the same time-to-maturity class of options on the same day.

Only call options were studied in this work. Using both put- and call-option ISDs can be advantageous for options on the physical index. They can mitigate staleness in the physical index that is due to lagged trading of small-capitalized stocks (Fleming et al. 1995). However, this is not necessary for options on futures. Furthermore, it was decided to use only call ISDs and price call options because of evidence of significantly different pricing results presented in Brenner et al. (1985).

Error measures

To reasonably compare the neural-network approach with conventional approaches, more than one measure of closeness of fit was used. In Tables 9.1–9.4 we used the following

$$R^2 = \frac{\left(n\sum xy - \sum x - \sum y\right)^2}{n\sum x^2 - \left(\sum x\right)^2\left[n\sum y^2 - \left(\sum y\right)^2\right]}, \tag{9.12}$$

$$\text{NRMSE} = \sqrt{\frac{\sum(y - x)^2}{\sum(y - \bar{y})^2}}, \tag{9.13}$$

$$\text{MAE} = \frac{1}{n}\sum |y - x|, \tag{9.14}$$

where x is the actual, or target, value and y is the model, or estimated, value. The R^2 value is best when nearest to 1, the normalized RMSE (NRMSE) is best when nearest to 0, and the mean absolute error (MAE) is also best near 0.

Table 9.1. *Pricing errors when WISDs are used for the entire sample with the modified-Black model*

	LASTISD	AVEISD	DERISD	ELISD
RSQ	0.99189	0.99489	0.9953	0.9949
NRMSE	0.09332	0.07722	0.07472	0.08028
MAE	0.00095	0.00084	0.00082	0.00086

Table 9.2. *Pricing errors when moneyness-adjusted WISDs are used for the entire sample with the modified-Black model*

	FONXISD	HILOISD
RSQ	0.99424	0.91064
NRMSE	0.07648	0.29948
MAE	0.00077	0.00112

Table 9.3. *Positive* (+) *value above conventional model, negative* (−) *value below conventional model*

	Short maturity (0–0.15)	Short maturity (0–0.15)
In the money (0.9–1)	+	+
Out of the money (1–1.1)	+/−	−

3 Results

Table 9.1 shows that the DERISD is the best WISD of those considered. It is particularly interesting to note that the worst WISD is the LASTISD. This would suggest that maturity and moneyness biases are more influential in determining trading price than the time evolution of the standard-deviation process.

By using the entire sample, we are biasing the results in favor of the conventional model.

Table 9.2 shows that although the DERISD has the best R_{squared} (RSQ) and NRMSE for the entire sample, the FONXISD has the best MAE. This is not particularly surprising. After all, the DERISD is chosen to be the best forecast

Table 9.4. *Comparison of optimal WISD–DERISD with linear and nonlinear regressions and optimal moneyness ISD–FONX*

	Linear	Hybrid	FONX
	July–December 1993		
RSQ	0.995	0.99517	0.99378
NRMSE	0.07131	0.06985	0.07938
MAE	0.00086	0.00083	0.00087
	January–June 1994		
RSQ	0.99549	0.99569	0.99358
NRMSE	0.07043	0.06841	0.0813
MAE	0.00101	0.00093	0.00098
	July–December 1994		
RSQ	0.99368	0.99371	0.99218
NRMSE	0.08187	0.07958	0.08888
MAE	0.00077	0.00074	0.00077
	January–June 1995		
RSQ	0.99572	0.99563	0.99414
NRMSE	0.06913	0.0704	0.07752
MAE	0.00077	0.0008	0.00074
	July–December 1995		
RSQ	0.9964	0.9967	0.99524
NRMSE	0.06078	0.05759	0.06909
MAE	0.00058	0.00058	0.00064

of ex ante standard deviation whereas FONXISD is chosen to minimize the moneyness bias. It is interesting to note, however, that DERISD is the best on both the other error measures.

HILOISD is a relatively poor predictor of price. Presumably, the assumption that the ISD can be accurately estimated by linear interpolation between the ISDs corresponding to extreme moneyness options does not hold.

DERISD is chosen as the optimal WISD. Table 9.4 compares the out-of-sample results for the DERISD and the FONXISD. For each 6-month period the hybrid DERISD is the best pricing model, except for the first half of 1995. The linear regression results are usually better than the pure FONXISD results; however, they outperform the neural-network results only in the first half of 1995, thus vindicating the nonlinear approach.

The implication of these results is that the deviations around the modified-Black model are not noise but are systematic, possibly because of the breakdown of the assumptions required in the conventional model.

The estimated hybrid option-pricing output estimated on the first 6-month period, January to July 1993, is shown in Fig. 9.2. It plots the output of the modified-Black hybrid ANN as a function of F/X and $T-t$. In general, the surface is complicated, smooth, and implies consistent mispricings in the conventional models of between 2 and -2 points (approximately \$50 and $-$\$50 per option, respectively, if we assume a strike of $X = 2000$).

The most striking feature of the hybrid ANN output is the ridge at $F/X \approx 1$. This divides the options into those that have positive and negative value relative to the conventional option-pricing model.

This is consistent with the studies of both Rubinstein (1994) and Derman and Kani (1994) of the S&P 500 Chicago Boond Options Exchange (CBOE) futures options. Rubinstein (1994) conjectures that this bias is caused by investors' fear of a repeat of the 1987 crash. The shape of the hybrid surface is almost identical to the deviations noted by Corrado and Miller (1996) for the S&P 500. This is quite remarkable, given the different markets.

The results from Table 9.4 indicate that the hybrid-ANN outperformance is marginal.

Is it possible to argue that the goodness of fit can be explained by the greater degrees of freedom for the ANN relative to the conventional model and the linear hybrid? To answer this question let us compare the conventional-model and the hybrid-ANN approach. First, there are sound reasons, based on much empirical option-pricing work, to expect that the conventional model is biased. Second, the statistics presented in are strictly out of sample. The ANN outperformance is real. Finally, when the ANN standard deviations are estimated with bootstrap methods (see Section 4) the hybrid-ANN model is found to be statistically significantly distinguishable from the conventional model.

Consideration of goodness-of-fit arguments leads to the same conclusion when we compare the linear-hybrid and the hybrid-ANN approaches. First, from Fig. 9.2, it is obvious that the relationship among F/X, $T-t$, and the error (or bias) is complicated. A simple linear plane could not adequately describe the surface. Second, the statistics presented in Table 9.4 are strictly out of sample. The ANN outperformance is real. Therefore, after careful consideration, we can conclude that the goodness-of-fit argument cannot explain the hybrid-ANN outperformance.

4 Economic and statistical significance

To determine whether the results are meaningful it is important to consider both economic and statistical significance. There may not be any economic and statistical significance if all methods are good. This is an important consideration, given the extremely good performance of the conventional models.

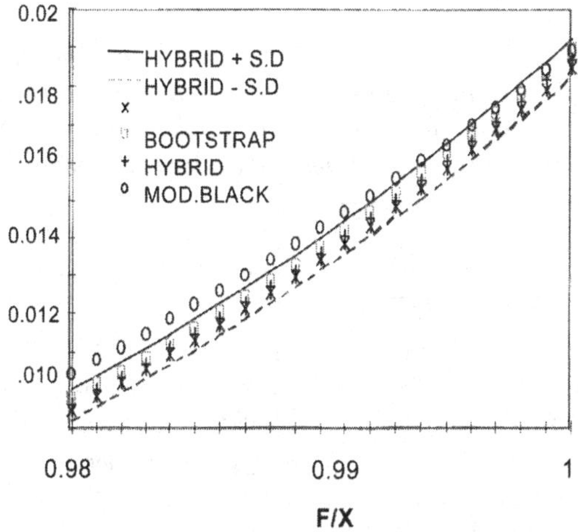

Figure 9.3. At-the-money option-price premium versus F/X. The option-pricing parameters are $T - t = 0.1, s = 0.15, X = 2000$. In the region $0.980 < F/X < 0.995$ the conventional model – the modified-Black model – is statistically significantly distinguishable from the hybrid model. (This is reproduced from Lajbcygier and Connor 1998.)

The issue of trading strategies for the hybrid model have been considered in Lajbcygier (1998), who used the first 6 months of data available (see Fig. 9.3).

The large majority of the research in option pricing involves finding a model that fits the empirical data. Very little research has been done on generating the confidence intervals of the option-pricing model. The confidence intervals will allow both choosing between option-pricing models and deciding when a trade should be executed.

Confidence intervals for option-pricing models are generated by bootstrap methods. For an introduction to bootstrap methods, see Efron and Tibshirani (1993). Bootstrap confidence intervals allow the identification of option prices, which both appear profitable and are outside the range of model uncertainty.

Identification of profitable trades is not the only use for better option-pricing models. The process of limiting exposure of a financial position to changes in underlying assets is known as hedging and is determined by the option-pricing model. One incorporates hedges into the option trading strategy by buying a position in the underlying futures equal to $-\partial f_{\text{hybrid}}(x)/\partial F$, known as the delta of the option position, which allows a small change in the option price to be offset by a change in the future price.

The profitability of various trading strategies is shown in Table 9.5. All trading strategies are based on taking a position on options that are 1 point beyond

Table 9.5. *Trading profitability of the hybrid- and modified-Black-based strategies. Incorporating confidence intervals allows the hybrid model performance to increase by nearly a factor of 10. Note the poor performance of all modified-Black-based strategies. (This is reproduced from Lajbcygier and Connor 1998.)*

Strategy	Number of trades	Equity/number of trades	Variance	Sharpe ratio
Hybrid	449	17.69	382	0.0463
Hybrid + sigma	240	10	289	0.0346
Hybrid + 2 sigma	109	61.17	205	0.2984
Hybrid + 3 sigma	51	48.66	159	0.306
Modified Black	478	−7.24	405	−0.0179
Modified Black + sigma	275	−41.38	275	−0.1289
Modified Black + 2 sigma	142	−3.45	142	−0.0147
Modified Black + 3 sigma	68	−75.63	68	−0.417

the confidence limits of the hybrid model and simultaneously using a one-time hedge. One index point is a reasonable approximation for the costs associated with crossing the bid–ask spread and exchange costs associated with undertaking the option transaction (Gilmore 1997). Because all the options expire on the same date, only a single equity for each model is quoted. The confidence intervals performed as hoped. As one begins to trade outside the region of uncertainty, dramatic improvements in the Sharpe ratio begin and stay.[10] The Sharpe ratio is the standard measure of trading performance; it is the (equity per trade/standard deviation) of returns and is a useful metric because it penalizes risky strategies. This is why a trading strategy based on the hybrid + 3 sigma is comparable with the hybrid + 2 sigma, which makes more equity per trade.

There is an eightfold improvement in Sharpe ratio performance between the hybrid + sigma and hybrid + 2 sigma bands. The two sigma standard-error bands capture most of the trading opportunities associated with the hybrid model, which explains why the Sharpe ratio performance does not improve dramatically for hybrid + 3 sigma.

Note the failure of the standard modified-Black strategy.

5 Further work, discussion, and conclusion

There are natural constraints in the hybrid approach (e.g., when $T - t = 0$, the ANN should be equal to zero also); therefore a new ANN architecture called

[10] It was not necessary to adjust the cash flows when the Sharpe ratio was calculated, as it was assumed that most options expired on the same day and the premium was paid on option expiry.

the constraint hybrid approach will be applied to the pricing of AO SPI options on futures. This work is forthcoming in Lajbcygier (1998).

Hybrid ANN's have been shown to be useful for option pricing in the intraday and ISD domain. The hybrid ANN is proven to be superior for pricing AO SPI options on futures. It is particularly satisfying to outperform the ad hoc FONXISD approach by utilizing an WISD that can estimate both option price and realized standard deviation optimally and that, furthermore is a plausible realized standard-deviation estimate (unlike FONXISD).

The results are interesting primarily because they show that ANNs can increase pricing accuracy when used in conjunction with conventional models and ISDs.

There may be limitations to the accuracy possible from a model motivated by the search for analytical tractability such as the modified-Black model. By augmenting the modified-Black model with the ANN, we were able to learn some of the subtle pricing differences between the analytical model and the market reality. These differences were perhaps due to the limitations of the analytical model and the assumptions on which it rests. Financial distributions are typically leptokurtic, heteroskedastic, and skewed, and therefore models based on the assumption of geometric Brownian motion of the underlying data have been shown to be untrue. The neural network requires no such assumptions.

REFERENCES

Ait-Sahalia, Y., and Lo, A. (1998). Nonparametric estimation of state-price densities implicit in financial asset prices. *J. Finance*, **53**, 499–547.

Bishop, C. (1995). *Neural Networks for Pattern Recognition*, Clarendon, Oxford, England.

Black, F. (1976). The pricing of commodity contracts. *J. Financial Econ.*, **3**, 167–79.

Black, F., and Scholes, M. (1973). The pricing of options and corporate liabilities. *J. Polit. Econ.*, **81**, 637–54.

Boek, C., Lajbcygier, P., Palaniswami, M., and Flitman, A. (1995). A hybrid neural network approach to the pricing of options. In *Proceedings of the International Conference on Neural Networks*, Institute of Electrical and Electronics Engineers, New York.

Brenner, M., and Galai, D. (1981). The properties of the estimated risk of common stocks implied by option prices. Working Paper #112, University of California at Berkeley, Berkeley, CA.

Brenner, M., Courtadon, G., Subrahmanyam, M. (1985). Options on the spot and options on futures, *J. Finance*, **40**, 1303–1317.

Canina, L., and Figlewski, S. (1993). The informational content of implied volatility. *The Review of Financial Studies*, **6**, 659–81.

Cherkassky, V. (1992). Neural networks and nonparametric regression. In *Neural Networks for Signal Processing II*, Institute of Electrical and Electronics Engineers, New York.

Chiras, D., and Manaster, S. (1978). The informational content of option prices and a test of market efficiency. *J. Financial Econ.*, **6**, 213–34.

Corrado, C., and Miller, T. (1996). Efficient option-implied volatility estimators. *J. Futures Markets*, **16**, 247–72.

Derman, E., and Kani, I. (1994). Riding on a smile. *Risk*, **7**(2).

Dumas, B., Fleming, J., and Whaley, R. E. (1996). Implied volatility functions: empirical tests. *J. Finance*, **53**, 2059–2106.

Efron, B., and Tibsharani, R. J. (1993). *An Introduction to Bootstrap*, Chapman and Hall, New York.

Figlewski, S. (1997). Forecasting volatility. *Financial Markets, Inst. Instrum.*, **6**, 1–88.

Fleming, J., Ostediek, B., and Whaley, R. (1995). Predicting stock market volatility: a new measure. *J. Futures Markets*, **15**, 265–302.

Finucane, T. (1989). A simple linear weighting scheme for Black–Scholes implied volatilities. *J. Bank. Finance*, **13**, 321–26.

Gilmore, T. (1997). Correspondence with BZW futures broker, Melbourne, Australia (personal communication).

Hutchinson, J., Lo, A., and Poggio, T. (1994). A non-parametric approach to pricing and hedging derivative securities via learning networks. *J. Finance*, **69**(3), 851–89.

Jacquillant, B., Hamon, J., Handa, P., and Schwartz, R. (1993). The profitability of limit order on the Paris Stock Exchange. Universite Paris Dauphine.

Lajbcygier, P. (1998). Pricing and trading of options with artificial neural networks and bootstrap. Ph.D. Thesis, Department of Business Systems, Monash University, Australia.

Lajbcygier, P., Boek, C., Palaniswami, M., and Flitman, A. (1995). Neural network pricing of all ordinaries options on futures. In *Proceedings NNCM 95*, World Scientific, London.

Lajbcygier, P., and Flitman, A. (1997). A comparison of non-parametric regression techniques for the pricing of options using an optimal implied volatility. In *Proceedings of Neural Networks in the Capital Markets*, eds. A. Weigend, P. Refenes, and A. Mostafa, World Scientific, Caltech.

Lajbcygier, P., and Connor, J. (1998). Improved option pricing using artificial neural networks and bootstrap methods. *Int. J. Neural Syst.*, Special Issue on Data Mining in Finance, **8**, 457–71.

Latane, H., and Rendleman, R. (1976). Standard deviations of stock price ratios implied in option prices. *J. Finance*, **31**, 369–81.

Lieu, D. (1990). Options pricing with futures style margining. *J. Futures Markets*, **10**, 327–38.

Malliaris, M., and Salchenberger, L. (1993). A neural network model for estimating option prices. *Appl. Intell.*, **3**, 193–206.

Martini, C., and Taylor, S. (1995). Test of the modifed-Black formula for options on futures. Working Paper, Department of Accounting and Finance, Melbourne University, Melbourne, Australia.

Merton, R. C. (1973). Theory of rational option pricing. *Bell J. Econ. Manag. Sci.*, **4**, 141–83.

Ncube, M. (1996). Modeling implied volatility with OLS panel data models. *J. Bank. Finance*, **20**, 71–84.

Park, H., and Sears, R. (1985). Estimating stock index futures standard deviation through the price of their options. *J. Futures Markets*, **5**, 223–37.

Phillips, S., and Smith, C. (1980). Trading costs for listed options: The implications for market efficiency. *J. Financial Econ.*, June, 79–120.

Refenes, A. P. N., and Gonzalez Miranda, F. (1996). A principled approach to neural model identification and its application to intraday volatility forecasting. Working Paper, London Business School, London.

Resnick, B., Sheikh, A., and Song, Y. (1993). Time varying volatilities and the calculation of the weighted implied standard deviation. *J. Financial Quant. Anal.*, **28**(3), September; **28**, 417–29.

Roll, R. (1984). A simple implicit measure of the effective bid–ask spread. *J. Finance*, **39**, 1127–39.

Rubinstein, M. (1985). Nonparametric tests of alternative option pricing models using all reported trades and quotes on the 30 most active CBOE option classes from August 23, 1976 through August 31, 1978. *J. Finance*, **40**, 455–80.

(1994). Implied binomial trees, *J. Finance*, **49**, 771–818.

(1995). As simple as one, two, three. *RISK* **8**(1), 42–7.

Turvey, C. (1990). Alternative estimates of weighted implied volatilities from soybean and live cattle options. *J. Futures Markets*, **10**, 353–66.

White, H. (1995). Option pricing in modern finance theory and the relevance of artificial neural networks. *Neural Information Processing Systems Conference Proceedings*, MIT, Cambridge, MA.

Xu, X., and Taylor, S. J. (1995). Conditional volatility and the information efficiency of the PHLX currency options market. *J. Bank. Finance*, **19**, 803–21.

PART III

Market and sectoral dynamics

CHAPTER 10

Evolutionary patterns of multisectoral growth dynamics

Hermann Schnabl

Most studies of economic growth concentrate on aggregate data. However, careful examination of intersectoral growth patterns shows a large divergence among sectors. These are driven as much by intersectoral linkages as they are by the separate characteristics of each sector. Arguing, for example, that a certain sector, e.g., machine tools, has a higher growth potential than, e.g., agriculture certainly is right but does not sufficiently take into account that all sectors are interlaced to each other, but rather to a highly diverging extent that then accounts for a diverging dynamic.

We investigate those interdependencies of sectoral dynamics on an empirical basis by using a time series of German input–output (IO) tables (58 sectors) of more than a decade (1978 to 1990) and derive the growth pattern of the economy in terms of its sectoral growth. Techniques designed to illuminate the impact of one sector's development on others are applied. Thus we proceed in establishing the analytical tools for this purpose in Sections 1 and 2, showing and analyzing the empirical, i.e., factual, observations in Section 3 and deriving a theoretical hypothesis compatible with those findings in Section 4.

The opportunity to analyze those qualitative differences in sectoral interdependencies – with the option also to recognize dynamic differentials – was opened up by the so-called qualitative input–output analysis (QIOA), which was developed by Czayka (1972), Schnabl and Holub (1979), Holub et al. (1985), as well as Holub and Tappeiner, following those just mentioned. In France, some other applications of graph-theoretical methods for structuring production have been brought forward (see Bellet et al. 1989, Torre 1993).

The basic concept of QIOA applies binary transformation of the entries of IO tables according to a defined filter rate. This maps the quantitative transaction matrix T (i.e., quadrant I of a given IO table) into the qualitative so-called adjacency matrix W_0, both with dimension $m \times m$, where m takes values mostly between 25 and 90 sectors. In QIOA the binarization is done by the application of

$$W_{0_{i,j}} = \begin{cases} 1 & \text{if } t_{i,j} \geq \text{filter} \\ 0 & \text{if } t_{i,j} \leq \text{filter} \end{cases}, \qquad (10.1)$$

where filter signifies a given threshold that defines which value of entry t_{ij} is regarded as important and which is not. After binary conversion that defines the so-called adjacency matrix W_0, graph-theoretical methods are applied to the adjacency matrix that automatically trace the given connections between the branches. To obtain the encompassing structure, not only the direct links have to be taken into account, but also the indirect links of the intermediary stages. As proved by Busacker and Saaty (1968, p. 53), those indirect links can be traced by the application of

$$W^k = W_0 \times W^{k-1}, \qquad (10.2)$$

where W_0 denotes the adjacency matrix defined above and W^k denotes the remaining structures at the kth step (see Holub and Schnabl 1985). If the entry w_{il}^k contains a 1, the elements w_{ij} and w_{jl} both must be 1, thus reflecting a two-step connection of sectors i and l by means of sector j, which is exactly produced by the formal process of matrix multiplication. Therefore in graph theory we use matrices and matrix multiplication to represent graphs and to investigate patterns of connectivity.

This method implies the loss of (maybe important) quantitative information and hence is often fervently criticized (e.g., Kleine and Meyer 1981). This critique, however, does not take into account that there is a firm trade-off between a structure and its quantified relations, similar to the expression "you cannot have your cake and eat it too." A structure derived from a bulk of figures (e.g., 3600 entries of a matrix) can be obtained only if one decides which of the 3600 are to be deemed important and therefore kept and which are not. We have to accept the informational loss in order to keep the information of the important ones to form the characteristic structure of the whole.

A possible reaction to this criticism could be to include more quantitative information in the computation steps of structural selection. This could be done in a way that tries to heal some drawbacks that traditional QIOA has: In the process of accounting for intermediary production stages [according to Eq. (10.2)], the quantities of the flows concerned are diminished subsequently until they are completely insignificant. This process is not taken into account at all by the matrix calculations of Eq. (10.2) that, however, are indispensable for the graph-theoretical analysis. Graph-theoretical operations, as used by QIOA, are based on the multiplication of the values 0 and 1. The result of 1×1 is always 1 regardless of how many multiplications have already been carried out in the process, i.e., regardless of the real amount of the quantitative flow remaining at the kth intermediary stage. Hence the term structure should be redefined to adequately incorporate all real delivery flows of all important intermediary stages into the conceptual description of structure. This requires a procedure of analysis that explicitly includes all intermediary stages instead of analyzing intermediary stages only in the starting phase and afterwards treating them as constant, as is done in traditional QIOA. This new method of deriving a structure is called minimal flow analysis (MFA). It can be coarsely understood as a mapping of all those roads of a national road system, broad enough to let pass – let us say a wide load – part of a huge bridge from a given place to any other place.

1 The minimal flow analysis method

A structure that can be determined by the passing of a defined (minimal) filter rate at each production stage from the direct stage to the least-relevant intermediary stage, depicted graphically, is called the minimal flow structure and the analysis achieving this structure is a MFA. This encompasses any given flow to be shown graphically in a structure if (and only if) the condition

$$s_{ij} \geq F \tag{10.3}$$

is met, where F is a filter (or threshold of significance) and s_{ij} represents the quantitative delivery flow from sector i to sector j on any (direct or intermediary) stage. The filter F has to be suitably defined to take the flow into account. For this purpose, layer matrices $T_0, T_1, T_2, \ldots,$ are generated by transformation of the original transaction matrix T as defined above and used also by the QIOA, the sum of which would represent the full matrix T as published by the statistical office. When the input-coefficient matrix A is used, the transaction matrix T can be rewritten as

$$T = A \cdot \langle x \rangle, \tag{10.4}$$

where $\langle x \rangle$ represents the diagonal matrix of production values, given by

$$x = L \cdot y. \tag{10.5}$$

Following the usual statical open-quantity model, the Leontief inverse L in Eq. (10.5) results in the vector of the production values x. If we replace L with its Taylor power series

$$L = I + A + A^2 + A^3 + \cdots + \tag{10.6}$$

the original transaction matrix T can be torn apart by this step into layers corresponding to the Taylor expansion:

$$T = A \cdot \langle (I + A + A^2 + A^3 + \cdots) \cdot y \rangle.$$

Thus we get the individual layers shown in

$$T_0 = A \cdot \langle I \cdot y \rangle, \tag{10.7}$$
$$T_1 = A \cdot \langle A \cdot y \rangle, \tag{10.8}$$
$$T_2 = A \cdot \langle A^{(2)} \cdot y \rangle, \tag{10.9}$$
$$T_3 = A \cdot \langle A^{(3)} \cdot y \rangle, \text{ etc.} \tag{10.10}$$

We then map the resulting quantitative layer tables $T_0, T_1, T_2, T_3, \ldots,$ into the binary adjacency matrices $W_0, W_1, W_2, W_3, \ldots,$ by testing each entry of each layer to find whether its value is higher than or equal to a given filter value F according to condition (10.3). The next graph-theoretical steps that are taken correspond to conventional QIOA (Schnabl and Holub 1979) as shown in Eq. (10.11). The power sequence necessary for the so-called dependency matrix D according to Eq. (10.2) turns into the product

$$W^k = W_k \cdot W^{k-1} \quad \text{or} \quad W^k = \prod_k W_k, \; k = 0, 1, 2, \ldots, \tag{10.11}$$

because – this distinguishes MFA from QIOA – the W_k are different for different k whereas for QIOA $W_k = W_0$ holds for every k. For MFA the stop condition for the W^k is given by $W_k = 0$ because no more connections are left because of vanishing entries in the applied power of the coefficient matrix A^n.

The product sequence of the W^k is then condensed to the Boolean so-called dependency matrix D, analogously to conventional QIOA, by Boolean summation. An entry d_{ij} of D then indicates whether there is a link (of any length) from sector i to j – but as an additional restriction resulting from MFA – of a given minimum-quantity level. The so-called connexity matrix H is obtained analogously to conventional QIOA from the dependency matrix, as shown in[1]

$$h_{ij} = d_{ij} + d_{ji} \tag{10.12}$$

The connexity matrix H resulting from the calculations outlined in Eq. (10.12), in each individual element h_{ij} qualifies the characteristics of linkages between sector i and j. Individual values of h_{ij} are denoted as given in Table 10.1.

The calculation of an H matrix implies a certain given minimum filter value. Which filter value is the right one still remains to be defined. There is, however, yet another advantage of the MFA compared with conventional QIOA that helps in solving this task: a tendency to work out the filter value endogenously. As with

[1] Equation (10.12) is somewhat simpler than the analog of QIOA because MFA focuses only on direct and bilateral links and omits the so-called weak links, which means that no connection could be drawn by pencil if one is following the direction of only the existing arrows.

Table 10.1. *Values of h_{ij}*

h_{ij} value	Meaning
0	Sector i and j are isolated
1	A unidirectional link from sector i to j exists
2	A bilateral link between sector i and j exists, i.e., both delivery flows between sectors i and j have at least the defined minimum

the second approach of QIOA (Holub et al. 1985), MFA scans the range of possible filter values from zero up to a final filter, from which no more bilateral structures can be obtained, in order to increase the dependency of qualitative results on quantitative information. For this purpose all the level-specific H matrices resulting on each single filter level are cumulated to the matrix H_{cum}, which then forms the basis for the further analysis. The individual H matrices stemming from the scanning process and the H_{cum} matrix narrow the range of possible filter values to a small interval of filters or even a single value F_e, as described below. This results from two divergent structural features of the MFA procedure:

- High filter values provide a good structure at the T_0 or W_0 and consequently on the H level, although they reduce scope, i.e., additional intermediary stages or indirect flows are depicted incompletely. This results in a flat structure.
- Low filter values give sufficient scope to include intermediary stages. On the other hand they result in a reduced structural differentiation because they tend to include too many flows in the analysis so that the task of finding a dominant characteristic structure with respect to the significance of flows is not achieved.

An optimum obviously has to be located somewhere in between, i.e., at a filter value that combines sufficient comprehensiveness of structure with reduction to the substantial part of the structure. Both comprehensiveness and reduction to the substantial part are qualitative conditions that need to be put into terms of operationalization. The significance of flows is limited by the acceptable number of depictable flows. The condition of comprehensiveness, though, causes more difficult problems. In this case, it could be thought of as an analogous application of the information measure developed by Shannon and Weaver (1949). Their concept states that information is maximal if the probability of occurrence of a sign is equal for all individual signs. If this is applied to our analogous problem, then the content of information could be maximized if we choose a level for which entropy for qualified sectors with $h_{ij} = 0, 1, 2$ is maximized. Another procedure used was to find the optimum structural similarity between the level-specific H matrix at a certain filter level and the total connexity matrix H_{cum} resulting from filtering with just that specific level. Additional measures were taken from distributions of the resulting H_{cum} matrix entries and by consideration of averages of entries.

The problem of identifying the characteristic production structure encompasses the decomposition or averaging of the cumulated H matrix H_{cum} and the application of the thus-derived endogenized filter F_e described above in the sense of reversing Eq. (10.12).

Let us say that a specific table has been analyzed up to 50 scanning levels; this means that $S_{max} = 50$. Then for all entries i, j of H_{cum} we have $0 < h_{ij} < 100$, where 100 is the entry value of those bilateral links i, j that were resistant to the filter until the end of the scanning process ($2S_{max} = 100$). If we transform the entry values into bars, we would get a mountain range with a pedestal that we can remove without losing much information about relative summit heights of the mountains. If we now remove the pedestal by an amount of $50 \times 1 = 50$, based on the assumption that everywhere we have bilateral sourcing, we are left with entry values that range from 0 to 50. In the resulting matrix H_{res}, high values – e.g., between 35 and 50 – would reflect bilaterally linked sectors whereas values below may be either due to very strong genuinely unidirectional links or asymmetric bilateral links, which turn into their dominant unidirectional part during the drain of the filter-raising scan procedure and thus qualify to be essentially unidirectional. Entries near S_{max} show highly stable bilateral connections, the identification of which is the main goal of MFA, because those connections define a dynamic growth dipole, forming the smallest growth cell of an economy. Because of the coupling of the sectors' input dependency, the raise in the output of one sector would stimulate the deliveries from the other. Bilateral partners thus establish a feedback on themselves. As this bilateral stimulation, in a dynamic sense, is the more intense, the higher the input coefficients a_{ij} and a_{ji} (or the higher their product $a_{ij} \times a_{ji}$), the design of the MFA, by testing their resistance to a rising filter level, will exactly unveil those sectors with the highest growth potential. These growth dipoles could even form growth clusters of an economy. Thus MFA in principle is able to identify the growth centers of an economy by identifying sector dipoles as well as sectoral clusters down to a level at which any further detail would be attainable only at the cost of satisfying clarity.

The revealed structure of an even bigger number of relevant growth sectors always encompasses the structure found for a smaller wanted number to be shown. Thus the structures determined by MFA are monotonically increasing and never imply an unwanted loss if the level of aspiration is altered. This is similar to the water-level picture of a huge iceberg, (which, because of the physical law has an endogenous filter level, namely, its waterline, which always separates 1/7 above from 6/7 of its volume staying beneath the waterline) which we could bias by pumping some tons of lead into its center or – reversing the effect of this measure – by drilling some holes into its center that contain only air instead of ice. The effect in the first instance would be that less would be seen of the iceberg than before, but what still can be seen is identical to the respective part of the iceberg seen before. In the second instance there is to be seen just more, again leaving unchanged the shape of the part already seen before the measure. Although the process of determining the filter level F_e is made to be an automatic procedure, depending only on information given by the tables themselves, there remains a certain possibility of fine tuning this automatic result to a wanted and meaningful range of, let us say, 15–30 relevant links that we can work with and argue on, i.e., putting a bit more plumb or air into the iceberg. The above-described automatic averaging procedures of H_{res} proved to do well for a pretty wide range of sectoral table dimensions from as few as 12 sectors up to ~100 consistently when the same procedure was used.

2 Representation of production structures

There are several ways of graphically representing the results of MFA analysis. A very simple one, which is effective with respect to the identification of sectors (not shown here), is the representation as a chessboard pattern that allows for representing the relevant links as blackened squares in a grid, read as delivery from the row sector to the column sector.

Without a doubt a more important representation is the connection structure shown in Figs. 10.1(a)–10.1(d). Here, the orientation of delivery and the degree of integration or clustering are considered simultaneously. It is depicted by an ellipse that shows the (relevant) connections between the relevant sectors, whereas the irrelevant sectors/flows are omitted. For obtaining the position of an individual sector within the graph, the centrality coefficient z is used (see Table 10.2), which is defined as a ratio of input and output flows, measured as row and column sums of the H_{res} matrix according to

$$z_i = \frac{\text{rowsum}_i - \text{colsum}_i}{\text{rowsum}_i + \text{colsum}_i} + 1 \tag{10.13}$$

in order to transform the domain of z into the interval [0, 2]. Thus a centrality coefficient $z = 1$ would roughly represent as many input relations as it would output relations. This would denote a kind of center of the structure. Practically, z coefficients between 0.7 and 1.3 were marked as central in the graph by a fat circle sector [e.g., sector Chm in Fig. 10.1(a); see Table 10.2 for an explanation of the sector symbols and names].

Consequently those sectors that are not central can be divided into so-called source sectors (in the left part of the ellipse, both on top and bottom) and sink sectors (in the right part of the ellipse). The individual sectors can be identified as belonging to one group or the other in intertemporal comparison.

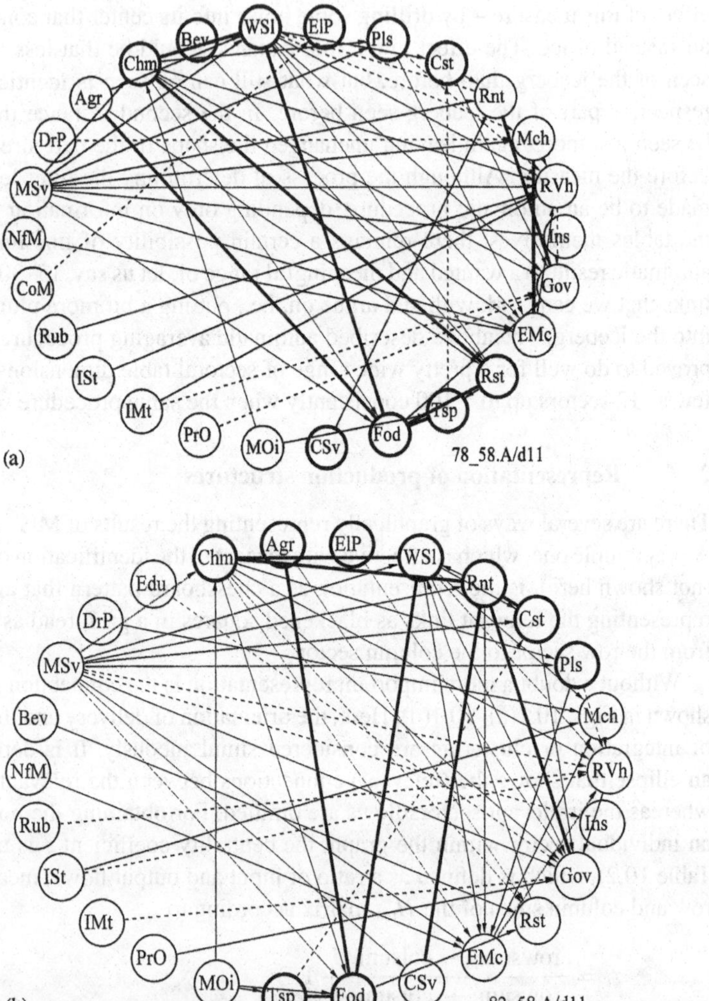

Figure 10.1. Production structures of the years (a) 1978, (b) 1982, (c) 1986, (d) 1990. The notation used is defined in Table 10.2.

Unilateral sourcing is given by solid lines with arrows pointing to the sink sector. Bilateral sourcing is denoted by a fat line without arrows because there is no qualified direction. Dashed lines represent marginal connections, i.e., those on the verge of being shown in the graph (in the analysis carried out here this would be just one filter level below the endogenous threshold F_e). A fat dashed line denotes that on the lowered filter, i.e., F_{e-1}, the connection is bilateral, but is merely unilateral on the proper endogenous filter level F_e.

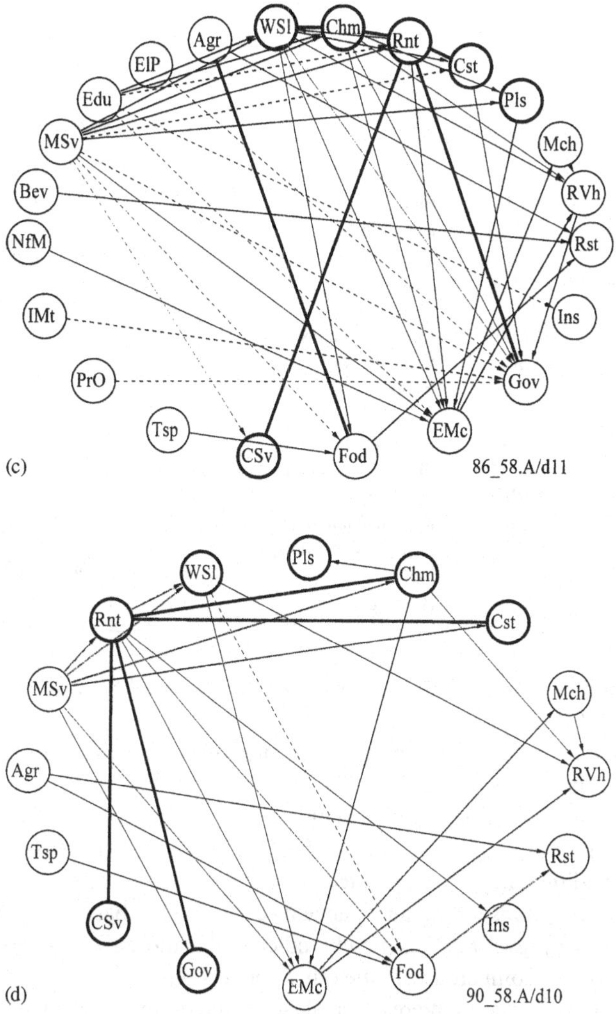

Figure 10.1. *(Continued)*

3 Structural evolution of the German economy 1978–1990

Overall structural change

An overview of the structural evolution in Germany (old Länder) from 1978 to 1990 as given by the graphs for 1978, 1982, 1986, and 1990 is shown in Figs. 10.1(a)–10.1(d), in which each subfigure demonstrates the structure of the year annotated in the corresponding bottom line. A systematic approach regarding the three groups – source, center, and sink – appears to be suitable.

Table 10.2. *IO table*

Number	Symbol	Sector	Coefficients of centrality			
			1978	1982	1986	1990
1	Agr	Agriculture	0.653	0.78	0.456	0
3	ElP	Electrical power	1	0.818	0.416	
6	CoM	Coal mining	0			
9	Chm	Chemistry	0.705	0.772	0.788	0.98
10	MOi	Mineral oil	0.048	0.018		
11	Pls	Plastic products	1.222	1.25	1.152	0.923
12	Rub	Rubber products	0	0		
13	Stn	Stones/clays	0			
16	ISt	Iron/steel	0	0		
17	NfM	Nonferrous metals		0	0	0
19	DrP	Drawing plants		0.529	0.181	
21	Mch	Machinery/equipment	1.505	1.71	1.594	1.472
23	RVh	Road vehicles	1.831	1.841	1.818	2
26	Emc	Electrical machinery	1.316	1.4	1.469	1.365
28	IMt	Iron and metal production		0	0	0
38	Fod	Food	1.047	1.218	1.435	1.476
39	Bev	Beverages	0.8	0	0	

In addition, this approach allows for the identification of moves between the groups and also of episodic events.

The kind of connectivity (unilateral, bilateral) and integration of the sector is shown in the graphs of Figs. 10.1(a)–10.1(d). The dashed lines denote that the respective connection is dying with the progress of time and also that it is being born. Proper interpretation is obtained by a comparison of successive graphs. In addition, it has to be pointed out that the omitted sectors not showing up in the graph represent the unconnected sectors on the basis of the selected endogenous filter level F_e. This merely indicates that those sectors are of minor or no importance compared with the other connections.

It would of course be of interest to analyze the intertemporal changes between 1978 and 1990 in terms of changes between the group of center sectors (fat sectors in the center of the graphs), like chemistry (Chm), wholesale trade (WSl, both upper parts) or food (Fod, lower part of the ellipse), source sectors, i.e., all sectors located left of the center sectors as well as the sink sectors (located right of the center sectors). The latter represent the final destination of all flows respective of their links. Here again it turns out that mostly there is a steady change in position as well as representation as relevant sectors. As we do not have enough space to discuss all those change and their relation to sectoral growth patterns, the interested reader is referred to the more detailed discussion in Schnabl (1994).

Special constellations

There are two special formations that represent an extension of the growth dipole approach: the bilateral triangle (or *n* angle, which is not present in any of the graphs) of Figs. 10.1(a)–10.1(d) and the so-called bilateral star, in which one sector is in the center and others are connected bilaterally (the fat lines) to the same center. This constellation means that a certain sector is functioning as a common relay station within a group of growth dipoles and thus forms a growth core. One bilateral star can be observed in 1978 [Fig. 10.1(a)] with sector food (Fod) in the center and bilateral connections to sectors Agr (agriculture), Rst (restaurants), Tsp (transport), and WSl (wholesale trade). This star denotes the existence of a food-oriented growth paradigm, which still can be observed in the structure of 1982, although the bilateral connection Fod–Rst has changed to a unidirectional delivery path. If we trace this structure through to 1990, we see that it further deteriorates and is totally dissolved with respect to bilaterality in 1990.

On the other hand, the 1978 growth dipole Rnt–Gov (renting–government) is enlarged into a bilateral star, containing CSv (construction services) and Cst (construction) in 1982, further enhanced by Chm (chemistry) in 1986, and showing up as the dominant structure in 1990.

Thus it can be interpreted as the substitution of the "food star" by the "renting star" within 12 years of economic development and change, in which in 1982 both stars coexist and under simplified structural analysis assumptions could coexist in further years as well. As a bilateral star characterizes a special growth center, we also can interpret this observation as a change from an agriculture/food paradigm as a growth source to a renting/housing paradigm and thus as a change in a technology paradigm as well[2] (Dosi 1982).

4 Evolutionary aspects

The analysis set out above shows that the structural graph obviously depicts interbreak twined relations that are plausible with regard to both typical product attributes and the related dynamics of development. This applies to both significance and structural change of these structures. Given an evolutionary perspective, it should be a challenge of its own to identify the determinants of those changes. We could approach this by reconsidering the way MFA displays its results.

As the MFA registers sectors in relation to their volumes of delivery, which are identical to their total revenue and revenue is the product of prices and

[2] As we are in the graph-theoretical sphere, analyzing links and not values, this is the appropriate basis to derive the centrality coefficient, which is a standard procedure in graph theory, in order to have an integration measure. Taking instead the analogon of the T matrix, for example, would mean a break in the logic of the analysis.

quantities, we have to look into the changes that occurred in prices and/or quantities. Regarding the dying star of the food regime, we have a reduction in total revenue in relation to the total revenues of other sectors. This reduction could be due to

- a reduction in prices (as related to prices of other sectors)
- a reduction in quantities sold (as related to the quantities of other sectors)
- a reduction in both quantities and prices.

As a sector can be thought of to be the sole deliverer of the good, the demand function is given by the total demand for this good, i.e., it is a normally sloped market demand function. This context is best described by the so-called Amoroso–Robinson formula:

$$R' = p\left(1 - \frac{1}{\varepsilon}\right), \tag{10.14}$$

where R' denotes the marginal total revenue of the sector, p is the price and, ε is the amount of price elasticity. We reformulate Eq. (10.14) and get

$$R' = p\frac{\varepsilon - 1}{\varepsilon}. \tag{10.15}$$

This can be interpreted as a kind of genetic fitness of the inspected sector, in which R' can be greater than, equal to, or less than zero. This would mean that a sector with elastic demand, i.e., $\varepsilon > 1$, has a tendency to grow, whereas a sector with $\varepsilon < 1$ would of course be a shrinking sector. Unless we have an isoelastic demand (i.e., with $\varepsilon = 1$) that is not supported by empirical observations, the following arguments based on a price elasticity's falling with price might well apply and thus explain our empirical results. Taken as given a linear, negatively sloped demand curve, as shown in Figs. 10.2 and 10.3, research and development (R&D) expenditures leading to (cost-reducing) process innovations tend to shift the offer curve S_1 downward to S_2, thus relocating equilibrium A to B and total revenue on revenue curve R from R_a to R_b, which is much higher than R_a. If we think in stylized terms of a one-product sector, as IO analysis takes it and tries to realize in the IO tables, total revenue R is the mathematical product of quantity x and price p of that good. The ε curve, which on the vertical axes shows the (absolute) price elasticity as depending on quantities x, indicates a reduction in ε, and hence a reduction of further growth potentials as the nonlinear revenue curve R approaches its maximum, where $\varepsilon = 1$ exactly. Thus we can conclude that – as a tendency – the enhancement of process innovation has a positive nonlinear effect on total revenue as long as the price elasticity reduced by this impact stays above 1.

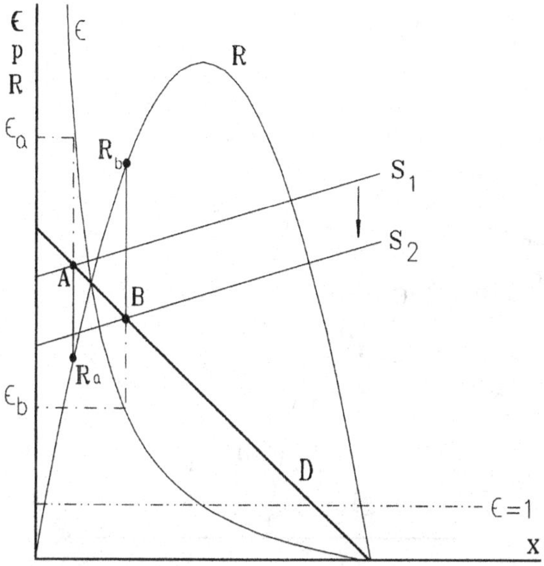

Figure 10.2. Effects of productivity gains.

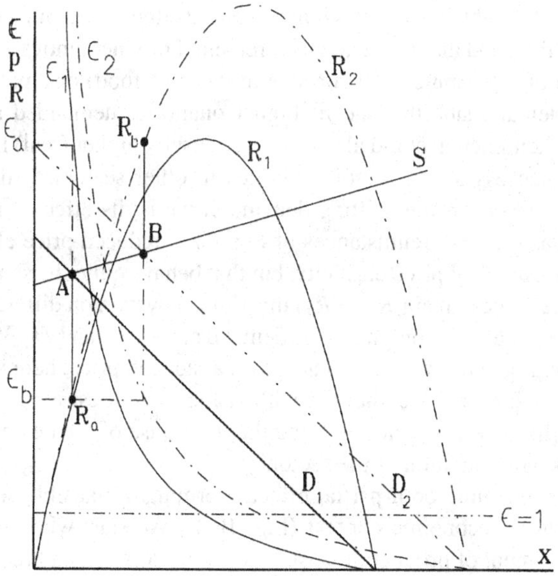

Figure 10.3. Effects of demand shift.

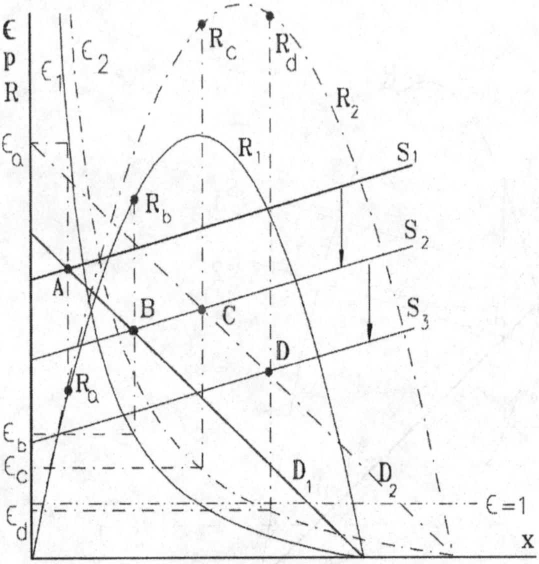

Figure 10.4. Combined effects of growth elements.[3]

Figure 10.3 shows the alternative effect brought about by a shift of the demand curve to the right. This shift might be caused either by an improvement in the quality of the good that is due to an incremental product innovation (e.g., the speeding up of a computer CPU or a better taste of food) or a preference change on the demand side that means higher quantities demanded at same price. This last phenomenon could also be caused just by higher (real) incomes that are due to successful innovation activities in other sectors. It does not matter what the reason for the shifting demand curve is; its effect is roughly the same as it was for the circumstances of Fig. 10.2: reduced price elasticity (on two different curves of price elasticity, but that behave quite the same way) and rising total revenues (again $R_b > R_a$) this time, however, on different total revenue curves R_1 and R_2 belonging to the demand curves D_1 and D_2. Whereas in Fig. 10.2, rising quantity was associated with a reduced price, here we have (as a tendency) rising prices combined with rising quantities, as the supply curve was thought to be constant, implying that the cause of the demand shift did not affect the cost situation of the sector.

In a final step we unite both partial effects, forming a plausible sequence within an observable economic context (Fig. 10.4). We start with an R&D-triggered improvement of production costs, relocating S_1 to S_2 and the market

[3] This is shown in Schnabl and Holub (1979).

equilibrium from A to B. As this was accompanied by a relatively high-price elasticity ε_a, this results in a significant (nonlinear) increase in total revenue, i.e., from R_a to R_b on the revenue curve R_1. We now assume that this might take place in a situation in which the same is happening in other sectors too, so that the rise in income shifts the demand curve to D_2. As a consequence, a further rise in total revenue R_c occurs while still associated with an ongoing reduction of price elasticity ε. As continuing R&D still tends to improve cost, another shift of the supply curve toward S_3 brings about another shift in total revenue (R_d), this time including the effect that the price elasticity has fallen below the magic border of 1 (on the ε_2 curve). This means that further cost improvements (as the result of pure process innovations) will accelerate the process of decay, leading to only a further reduction of the price elasticity, but this time in the range below unity. This means that the sector from the very moment of transgressing the borderline $\varepsilon = 1$ is doomed to shrink. We know this fate from economic history and the concept of old, outdated industries like coal, steel, textiles (in industrialized countries), etc.

As this example is built on stylized facts and moreover depends in its outcome on some subtle relations of – not already identified – parameters of speed and adjustment ratios between supply-side and demand-side elements, which would have to be formulated explicitly (meaning a total research program concerning a multisectoral model with nonlinear reactions including process and product innovations), the above example of course cannot be taken as a kind of proof, but nonetheless it might work as an ex post explanation of our empirical findings, associated with some likelihood also for future development.

Does this scheme of explanation fit with other empirical findings as well as theoretical reasoning? In the first place one is reminded of the so-called Engel law, i.e., the claim made by Engel that the income elasticity of food is less than unity, which was followed by the same claim by Schwabe concerning renting houses. If we take seriously a statement of Pigou that in the very short run the income and price elasticity of a certain good are the same in absolute terms, our findings are confirmed as far as the dying star of the food regime is concerned, but not what regards the rising star, i.e., the renting paradigm. This is easily explained if one realizes that – at least in European countries – the income elasticities for renting are above unity because in developed countries housing is no longer just an existence need but encompasses personal or ego needs such as clothing and vacationing, which also have income elasticities above unity.

On the side of productivity gains there is the well-known argument that process innovation tends to shift supply curves downward or, put in other words, that "prices tend to fall." The analyses put forward in these terms are backed up by recent statistics (IWD 1994) that say that in 1993 the price of bread and potatoes was only 50%, of milk 27%, and eggs 13% of that in 1958, whereas butter figured with a remainder of only 11% – calculated in minutes or hours of work necessary for an average industrial worker to be able to buy those goods in terms of his or her average salary.[4] On the other hand, renting had a reduction to only 70%. Clearly there not only must be competition to transform possible productivity gains into relative price reductions, the good also has to allow for productivity gains, which is hardly the case with the well-known counterexamples of a haircut, theater performances, health care, or similar services, including higher education as given by Fourastié. Of course there seem to be some still unused resources of productivity enhancement within the renting paradigm, e.g., the latest construction robots shown in Japan, but up to now houses are still built as they were in the past hundred years with very little improvement with respect to productivity.

As Appelbaum and Schettkat (1993, 1994) claim – based on arguments of Fourastié and Baumol (Baumol 1967, Schneider and Fourastié 1989) about unbalanced growth potentials – this is even a central cause for contemporary unemployment that is the result of a reversed positive-feedback process, starting the German economic miracle in the 1950s on a broad sectoral basis and continuing until the 1970s. This process, however, has now stopped and is producing high unemployment not only in Germany but also in other European and even other industrialized countries. This is also not very well understood and therefore is again labeled as a miracle (Appelbaum and Schettkat 1994) that by no means can be healed by the average measures taken, especially not by the favored reduction of working time.

Thus the above outline of the nonlinear mechanics of unbalanced sectoral growth could be even more generalized into a theory of miracles for both the sunny side and the shadows that turn up in terms of high and unconfronted unemployment rates and both depending in a nonlinear way on the type and the speed of innovations.

5 Summary and conclusions

The empirical findings given in Section 3 and the theoretical approach outlined in Section 4 make some (hypothetical) suggestions for understanding the nonlinear mechanics of unbalanced sectoral growth. The results show that each measure taken to cure the problem that a sector faces from its point of view either merely shifts the problem or just deepens it. The ubiquitous incremental process innovations of many firms seem to be the appropriate response to competition, but they reduce demand elasticities and thus genetic fitness of the firms respective to the sector lead eventually to their eradication – in terms of the

[4] This is the firm result of analyses by Fourastié and others. See Schneider and Fourastié (1989) in which the so-called real price of many goods, measured in hours or minutes necessary to work to be able to buy them, has an overall reduction by 30% to 50% over 30 years.

observed importance of the sector as measured by MFA. Even an improvement in product quality – which might be the result of process innovations as well as of certain (incremental) product innovations – that regularly would shift the demand curves has the same result in terms of lowering demand elasticities and thus genetic fitness.

Labor productivity, as is due to the said innovations, regularly rises, and therefore the need for labor is reduced to some extent; this also describes the nonlinear development of demand for labor along with this sectoral development. If more sectors start with a young technology at the same time, we get an economic miracle or positive feedback (Appelbaum and Schettkat 1994) among increasing demand, employment, and income. As the used technology becomes worn out, income and price elasticities decrease, until finally the positive feedback turns into a negative one, showing the backside effects of the parables in Fig. 10.2, i.e., nonlinearly decreasing growth down to shrinkage of sector revenues and therefore huge relief rates of labor force with nonlinearly accelerated unemployment rates. This might well be the phase that many European countries are in now.

The analysis showed that either kind of innovation activity tends to set forth this process. There is only one kind of innovation that is able to reverse the above process of downward evolution: generic innovation, as distinct from incremental innovation. Generic or radical innovation in the first place is product innovation that creates new markets and thus new demand. It starts the cycle of growth and decay anew. Examples for those types of innovations are the semiconductor, which led to the construction of modern computers, or the change of energy sources (coal, oil, atomic energy) or other prominent technology paradigms (e.g., materials: iron, plastics, high-tech ceramics) in past history.

The change to a new paradigm brings about the onset of high-price elasticities that then decay along with the exhaustion of the genetic fitness the new good brings about. As a policy implication, this means that we should be able to determine what the average technology age – measured across the sectors – of an economy is and that only an appropriate share in new technologies and products, i.e., a sufficiently high product innovation rate, can provide for the comfortable survival of a national economy, whereas other types of innovation may only delay the seemingly unavoidable economic crash. This is not a new insight, but what may be new to some extent is that this is just a consequence of positive feedback if no provisions are made for it.

Missing or insufficient innovations can at first be recognized by an increasing rate of unemployment because the economy experiences this on the downward track of its evolution and does not show enough power for proper cure, i.e., raising enough product innovations. This seems to be the present state of many European countries, including Germany, as well as other western-type industrialized countries, in which the innovation rate might not be high enough compared with its main Asian competitors but still may be delayed because of still virulent incremental innovating. This is then economic evolution in another sense that might well turn upside down existing economic powers and relations and shake the world economy if nothing is done to overcome the challenges.

As a hope we might state that not only radical innovations like the example given above are required for restarting the cycle and therefore open up employment options; derivatives of generic innovations can suffice if they form new products, like Sony's Walkman. As long as a product is perceived as new, the growth cycle depending on it may restart, as the definition of new is primarily a subjective evaluation from which also demand and elasticity are derived.

REFERENCES

Appelbaum, E., and Schettkat, R. (1993). Employment developments in industrialized economies: explaining common and diverging trends. WZB Discussion Paper FS, Wissenschaftszentrum Berlin, Berlin, pp. 193–313.

(1994). Das Ende der Vollbeschäftigung? Wirtschaftsentwicklung in Industrieländern. *Wirtschaftsdienst*, **4**, 193–202.

Baumol, W. (1967). Macroeconomics of unbalanced growth: the anatomy of urban crisis. *Am. Econ. Rev.*, **57**, 415–26.

Bellet, M., Lallich, S., and Vincent, M. (1989). Clusters, production routes and industrial complexes in the production system. Paper presented at the 9th International Input–Output Conference, Keszthely, Hungary.

Busacker, R. G., and Saaty, T. L. (1968). *Endliche Graphen und Netzwerke*, Oldenbourg, Munich, Vienna.

Czayka, L. (1972). *Qualitative Input–Output Analyze*, Athenäum, Meisenheimam Glan.

Dosi, G. (1982). Technological paradigms and technological trajectories: a suggested interpretation of the determinants and directions of technical change. *Res. Policy*, **2**(3), 147–62.

Holub, H. W., and Schnabl, H. (1985). Qualitative input–output analysis and structural information. *Econ. Model.*, **2**, 67–73.

Holub, H. W., Schnabl, H., and Tappeiner, G. (1985). Qualitative input–output analysis with variable filter. *Z. Gesamte Staatswissenschaft*, **141**, 282–300.

IWD (1994). Informations dienst des Instituts der Deutschen. *Wirtschaft*, **26** (June 30), 2.

Kleine, E., and Meyer, B. (1981). Qualitative oder quantitative Input-Output-Analyze für die Konjunkturpolitik? *Z. Gesamte Staatswissenschaft*, **138**, 129–34.

Schnabl, H. (1994). The evolution of production structures – analyzed by a multilayer procedure. *Econ. Sys. Res.*, **6**(1), 51–68.

Schnabl, H., and Holub, H. W. (1979). Qualitative und quantitative Aspekte der Input–Output Analyze. *Z. Gesamte Staatswissenschaft*, **135**, 657–78.

Schneider, J., and Fourastié, J. (1989). Warum die Preise fallen. NY. (Campus), Frankfurt/M.

Shannon, C. E., and Weaver, W. (1949). *The Mathematical Theory of Communication*, University of Illinois Press, Urbana, IL.

Torre, A. (1993). Filières' and structural change. Anatomy of the alterations of the french productive structure over the period 1970–1986. Paper given at the 10th International Conference on Input–Output Techniques, Seville, Spain.

CHAPTER 11

The detection of evolutionary change in nonlinear economic processes: a new statistical methodology

John Foster and Phillip Wild

Over the past decade, there has been a dramatic increase in interest in evolutionary approaches to economic analysis. New journals, such as the *Journal of Evolutionary Economics*, have appeared, and new research networks, such as the *European Association for Evolutionary Political Economy*, have recorded rapidly growing memberships. A large literature now exists concerning evolutionary change in economic processes (Hodgson 1993, Andersen 1994, and Nelson 1995). From an economic-modeling perspective, evolutionary economic processes can be defined in terms of three fundamental, but interconnected, characteristics that they possess: First, they are, in some degree, time irreversible; second, as a consequence, adaptation must involve structural change; and third, such change must involve true uncertainty. Despite the rise in interest in evolutionary change in economics, there have been comparatively few contributions that consider the impact of this new perspective on econometric modeling by use of time-series data. Furthermore, even fewer contributors have considered ways in which such data could be used both to identify and to understand evolutionary processes.

There is little doubt that widespread acceptance of the evolutionary perspective in the broader community of economists will depend, to a significant extent, on the success that evolutionary economists have in offering a coherent approach to econometric modeling. In the largely nonexperimental science of economics, the bulk of the information at our disposal is in the form of time-series data. These data offer a rich source of quantitative economic history. However, at present, econometric modeling is dominated by cointegration testing and error-correction models (ECMs) that are designed to search for nonevolutionary explanations of why time series are related to each other. History is viewed as a

We are grateful to the Australian Research Council for their large grant support of the research from which this chapter is derived. We are also grateful to Brian Lovell (UQ Electrical Engineering) for introducing us to state-of-the-art methods for computing time-varying spectra. However, all responsibility for errors and omissions remains with the authors.

state of short-run disequilibrium with asymptotic tendencies toward long-run equilibrium positions, determined by timeless economic logic. Implausible as this pragmatic methodology may appear to some, it offers a union between theoretical abstraction and econometric practice that holds attractions for those interested in economic forecasting. Only by the presentation of a coherent alternative approach to econometric estimation will the evolutionary perspective on economics gain widespread acceptance.

Foster (1992, 1994a, 1994b) and Foster and Wild (1995) attempted to model, econometrically, evolutionary processes, embodied in time-series data, by using a nonlinear logistic diffusion approach. Inspired by the empirical literature to be found in industrial economics and in the business strategy literature, as well as the more theoretical literature on self-organization, the models estimated were taken to reflect underlying, endogenously driven evolutionary processes. However, it became apparent in this program of research that identification of a logistic diffusion model of a variable is necessary, but not sufficient, for the existence of an evolutionary process. A significant literature exists in which the logistic equation is viewed as a device for modeling disequilibrium adjustment in an equilibrium context (see Dixon 1994). Thus the evidence produced can be viewed as a particular case of an ECM. The question then arises as to ways in which this particular form of observational equivalence can be overcome. This is the subject of this chapter.

An important distinction between the conventional equilibrium/disequilibrium view of a process and the evolutionary view is that a logistic trajectory should be nonequilibrium in the latter with increasing potential for instability, rather than stability, as the capacity limit is approached and saturation increases. This is not a trivial distinction as instability and discontinuity preclude forecasting of the conventional fixed-parameter type. Instead, the problem becomes one of assessing the likelihood of discontinuity occurring and devising policies to cope with such circumstances. Such concerns are regarded as of fundamental importance in business strategy (see Foster 1986 for an optimistic assessment of the possibilities and Hannan and Freeman 1989 for a more pessimistic view). Typically, business strategists seek to identify logistic trajectories and argue that a process that moves increasingly beyond the point of inflexion into the saturation phase is increasingly likely to experience a discontinuity. However, the fact that, in economic systems, logistic diffusion curves tend to be continually moving upward, along with capacity limits, means that it is not straightforward to eyeball logistic curves and neither is it easy to quantify instability and to assess the potential for a nonlinear discontinuity.

In physics, mathematical and statistical representations of structural transformation have been developed in the field of synergetics, which is a subfield of self-organization. Foster and Wild (1996) examined the possibility of using synergetics in the style of Weidlich and Haag (1982) to assess the likelihood of discontinuity in economic processes. It was concluded that methods used successfully in physics, in the context of controlled experiments, are unworkable in the presence of nonexperimental time-series data. It was not thought that the proposals of, for example, Weidlich and Braun (1991) and Zhang (1991), concerning the application of synergetics in economics, could be made operational with such data, given their historical character. It was further argued that the "historicalness" of economic data offered the possibility of a different, statistically based approach to detecting structural transition.

In this chapter, we offer an alternative that is grounded firmly in the statistical properties of time-series data and that builds on econometric models of diffusion processes with logistic trajectories. We explain how the residual variances of such models can be decomposed, by using spectral methods, in a manner that can establish whether or not time irreversibility exists, whether the process can be viewed as nonequilibrium in character – providing evidence of structural change – and whether the process is unstable in the saturation phase of logistic diffusion – providing evidence of true uncertainty. We explain how fixed- and moving-window spectral methods can be used, with the help of computer graphics, to discover whether an identified logistic diffusion model depicts an evolutionary process.

The chapter is organized as follows. In Section 1 we present the general case in which spectral methods can be of assistance in establishing whether an economic process, embodied in time-series data, is evolutionary in character. In Section 2, we explain the notion of time-dependent spectra. In Section 3 we introduce the short-time Fourier transform (STFT) method of making operational the idea of a time-varying spectrum. In Section 4 we briefly discuss some statistical considerations of applying the STFT. In Section 5, we discuss the application of the STFT in the context of an economic process, which has already been identified as a logistic diffusion one, by using econometric methods. Section 6 contains some conclusions and recommendations for further research.

1 Spectral interpretation of an evolutionary process

It is apparent from the literature on evolutionary processes, arising in both the natural and the social sciences, that such processes display some similar behavioral properties. A crucial property is the existence of a system hierarchy that is connected through the existence of flows of activating phenomena in the form of energy and information. Each subsystem in a hierarchy faces a set of boundary constraints on development determined, in part, by its environment and, in part, by its place in the hierarchy. For example, the growth of a financial institution is affected by the regulatory structure within which it has to operate and a range of factors emanating from the economic and business environment. Over time, a subsystem will undergo an endogenous process of self-organization, whereby increases in organization and complexity enable it to gain access to an evolutionary niche until it is, ultimately, constrained by a capacity limit. The interaction among these endogenous dynamics, exogenous shocks, and boundary constraints will typically result in a nonlinear transformation from a mildly nonlinear growth step to a strongly nonlinear discontinuity. This latter occurrence can range from a gear change, whereby a new evolutionary niche is acquired, through to the extinction of the subsystem, along with the process under investigation.

When structural transition occurs, short-term factors will be of crucial importance in determining the future path of the evolutionary process. The effect of random influences can therefore be significant. If a new evolutionary niche arises, the effect of randomness on the system's path will tend to decrease, even though random fluctuations typically increase in the early stage of a logistic diffusion process. Empirical studies of innovation (see Foster 1986) indicate that a high degree of robustness to random disturbances is displayed as the middle (inflexion) stage is approached. The emergent stage is typically accompanied by cooperative interactions (see Wollin 1995) and an intensive generation of new structures that are well fitted to stimulate future growth.

As the end of the evolutionary step is approached, we enter the saturation stage that is characterized by a decrease in the rate of growth. At this stage, some structures that were built for the purpose of growth are no longer necessary and the subsystem may begin to decompose as the transition stage is entered. In biological systems, this will often mean that the existing structures will be destroyed and recycled as inputs into new structures. In the economic context, this may or may not result in destruction, perhaps depending on whether the subsystem is located at the core or periphery of the economic system's hierarchical arrangement. However, all transitions will involve some degree of rearrangement of resources.

When an observed process is entering the saturation phase, it should begin to exhibit some type of critical behavior. If an estimated model of a logistic diffusion process can be constructed, as in Foster and Wild (1995), then the onset of critical behavior should be detectable in the residual variance structure, as described in, for example, its power-spectrum representation. The onset of criticality is likely to be reflected in a power-spectrum decomposition that is characterized by dominant high-frequency components. Moreover, the different stages of a logistic diffusion process should be associated with different spectral decompositions.

The possibility of a changing spectral decomposition is closely linked to the fact that evolutionary processes are nonautonomous in character and governed by time-dependent laws and tendencies. Therefore any attempt to investigate the asymptotic (i.e., equilibrium) properties of such systems constitutes a misspecification of an (nonequilibrium) evolutionary process, yielding misleading information concerning the stability of the process. This follows because asymptotic conceptions of system dynamics are based on the transformation of a time-dependent (nonautonomous) system into an autonomous (time-independent) system. Furthermore, a key property of autonomous systems is that the structural characteristics are held fixed (see Azariadis 1993, p. 9), a circumstance hardly conducive, by definition, to the modeling of evolutionary processes.

If the conventional definition of a power spectrum (based on linear moments) is adopted, a changing spectral decomposition can provide direct evidence of time irreversibility in the process in question (Subba Rao and Gabr 1984, p. 10). Because time irreversibility is a necessary, but not sufficient, condition for an evolutionary process to exist, then such evidence constitutes a first test as to whether a process is evolutionary. Furthermore, a process that has a shifting spectral decomposition, which gives greater prominence to higher-frequency components over time along a logistic diffusion path, can be viewed as one that is undergoing structural change, as such evidence offers both necessary and sufficient conditions for the existence of a nonequilibrium evolutionary process. The observation of increasing prominence of high-frequency components in the saturation stage would indicate that the process is increasingly vulnerable to structural transition.

In the emergent stage of logistic diffusion we would expect to observe Granger's (1966) so-called typical spectral shape, in which low-frequency components dominate in terms of power (Granger and Hatanka 1964, pp. 55–57; Granger and Engle 1983, p. 95). It is well known that this stage of a logistic diffusion path approximates exponential growth and we would expect to see patterns in the residuals that show an asymptotic tendency toward a long-run, steady-state growth rate. As we have pointed out, the evidence from innovation studies confirms considerable robustness to exogenous shocks, which induce stable disequilibrium fluctuations, in this stage of the diffusion process. In the saturation stage of the logistic diffusion process, we would expect high-frequency components to dominate because growth is highly constrained and therefore determined by short-run transitory factors. In such circumstances, the effects of exogenous shocks are likely to be more readily propagated through the system, given the prominence of shorter cycles, with the potential to initiate changes in both amplitude and phase – factors capable of instigating structural transition.

Transition in structure will tend to be highly nonlinear. Furthermore, the existence of explosive behavior (i.e., existence of unstable roots), associated with the logistic diffusion process, is likely to not only induce nonstationarity, in terms of trends in mean and variance, but also nonlinear (non-Gaussian) behavior as the capacity limit is approached. Indeed, it is difficult to envisage the complex dynamics conventionally associated with structural transition without the accompanying existence of nonlinear, non-Gaussian behavior. Thus there are strong a priori reasons for expecting that conventional spectral techniques, based on the linear moments of the process, will not be sufficient to describe adequately the process during structural transition. Instead, nonlinear (higher-order) moments would have to be included in any valid assessment of the process during transition. It would be necessary to use techniques based on the concept of the polyspectrum (higher-order spectra).

Therefore we would expect structural transition to exhibit both departures from stationarity (especially in the form of shifts in spectral decomposition and total variance) and from Gaussian properties (departures from linearity). Much of the literature on nonlinear dynamics stresses only the importance of nonlinearity, whereas time-series investigations tend to focus on only the question of nonstationarity. In an evolutionary setting it is clear that both are important to consider. In the emergent phase of the logistic diffusion process, nonstationarity considerations can be expected to dominate. In the saturation phase, nonlinearity considerations should become increasingly important as the process in question is forced toward a capacity limit. In this chapter, we limit discussion to the issue of nonstationarity.

2 The notion of time-dependent spectra

The notion of a power spectrum has been associated with wide-sense (covariance) stationary processes. These processes have the property that their joint (linear) moments – mean and (auto)covariance – exist and are identical, that is, they are independent of time (Priestley 1988, p. 5). Fourier analysis permits a series to be decomposed into individual frequency components and allows the relative intensity of each component to be determined. This approach is particularly useful when there is a long observation horizon. However, it is often the short-term variation in a time series that contains the information of particular interest. In this case, conventional methods of estimating spectra do not give an indication of when frequencies became important or when changes in the structure of the time series occurred (Cohen 1989, p. 941; Lovell 1991, p. 1).

One of the key properties of the conventional spectral representation of stationary processes is that it possesses a physical interpretation as a power–frequency distribution. However, one of the most controversial issues arising in the literature concerns our ability to extend the conventional framework to nonstationary processes while maintaining this particular physical interpretation (Lovell 1991, pp. 140–141; Loynes 1968; Priestley 1965, 1988, pp. 142–145). Specifically, the extension to nonstationary processes will mean that the physical interpretation of the spectrum must be a time-varying (or time-dependent) construct (Priestley 1988, p. 141). As such, we are concerned with the time–frequency representation (TFR) of a random process (Hammond et al. 1993, p. 355).

Historically, two parallel developments have occurred. First, estimation of time-varying spectra has been widely implemented with the so-called STFT (Cohen 1989, p. 963; Lovell 1991, pp. 1–2). It should be noted that the methodology underpinning the STFT is consistent conceptually with the way spectral analysis has been conventionally applied to economic time series. Second, time–frequency distributions (TFDs) have been developed as a joint function of time and frequency. These have been viewed as capable of describing the energy (power) density of a time series simultaneously in both time and frequency.[1] Conceptually, TFDs describe time–frequency distributions in a manner analogous to the way in which a joint probability density function describes the behavior of two random variables (Cohen 1989, p. 941; Lovell 1991, p. 2). Frequency estimation occurs through the identification of the first moments of TFDs (Lovell 1991, pp. 13, 16, 105).

However, the applicability of TFDs as a practical means of determining time-varying spectra in economic contexts is limited. In particular, the underlying theory and concepts, which are drawn from signal theory, do not necessarily fit with comparable theory and generation processes associated with economic time series.[2] Generally it is argued that, in determining the spectral properties of an economic time series, we cannot proceed on the basis that a time series will consist of a finite number of periodic components. The process will, necessarily, have a continuous spectrum.[3] Furthermore, most economic time series are modeled as real stationary processes. This means that we must consider, in principle, all frequency values w in the interval $[0, \pi]$. This contrasts with analytic expressions for the power spectrum that are often based on complex stationary processes because of mathematical convenience.[4] These approaches contrast with the conventional treatment of TFDs.

Specifically, most TFDs are represented as amplitude-modulated processes, and corresponding specifications would have little meaning intuitively in most

[1] Some of the more well-known TFDs include the Wigner–Ville distribution, Page distribution, Rihaczek distribution, and synthesis work initiated by Mark and Classen and Mecklenbrauker. A comprehensive survey can be found in Cohen (1989, pp. 943–944).

[2] In fact, the practical applicability of TFDs in signal processing is also seen as being very limited, especially when the signal is a multicomponent signal (Lovell 1991, p. 13). Therefore the main worth of TFDs is seen primarily in terms of their use as analytic (theoretical) devices.

[3] This type of spectrum is associated with the nondeterministic (absolutely continuous) component of the power-spectral distribution $F(w)$. Consult Granger and Hatanata (1964, p. 30), Koopmans (1974, pp. 49–50), Koopmans (1983, p. 175), Nerlove (1964, p. 247), and Priestley (1981, p. 229).

[4] Useful expositions on the theory underlying spectral analysis can be found in Burley (1969), Granger and Hatanaka (1964), Granger and Engle (1983), Koopmans (1974), Nerlove (1964), and Priestley (1981).

economic applications.[5] The actual frequency component being estimated is, furthermore, a single frequency – the so-called instantaneous frequency (IF). Serious problems can arise in the estimation and interpretation of the IF for a multicomponent signal.[6] In particular, the existence of cross terms generated by the interaction among frequency components can induce major interpretation problems (Lovell 1991, p. 5). A further complicating factor is that economic series are real and not analytic. This means that it is very difficult to separate phase and slowly varying amplitude from knowledge of the economic time series itself (Lovell 1991, p. 13).

Heuristically, extension to general types of nonstationary processes leads to an associated notion of a continuously changing spectrum, displaying the general property of time dependence. Some examples might assist in conveying the meaning of this important concept. We adopt an example used previously by Priestley (1988, pp. 141–142) and assume a simple nonstationary process that takes the form

$$X_t = \begin{cases} X_{t(1)}, & t \leqslant t_0 \\ X_{t(2)}, & t > t_0 \end{cases},$$

where $\{X_{t(1)}, X_{t(2)}\}$ are each stationary processes, but with different covariance structures. Assume further that the structural change point t_0 is known. Then a natural way of describing the power–frequency properties of the process $\{X_t\}$ would be to introduce two spectra, one for the interval $t \leqslant t_0$ and another for the interval $t > t_0$. This framework can be extended to the more general model, $X_t = X_{t(i)}, t_i \leqslant t < t_{i+1}$, where $\{X_{t(i)}\}$ are different stationary processes. The different properties of $\{X_t\}$ can be described by a different spectrum for each interval $[t_i, t_{i+1}]$.[7]

Another useful example is outlined by Cohen (1989, p. 941). Suppose that the objective is to examine light from sunrise to sunset by use of Fourier analysis. It is evident that the energy-density spectrum we would obtain would be different from what it would be in parts of the day. In particular, it could not tell us what the energy spectrum was during a dramatic sunset, for example, taken over a 15-min period during the sunset. Rather, in this circumstance, and provided changes are relatively slow, we could Fourier analyze 5-min samples of the

[5] In economic applications, spectral methods have been mainly used to decompose time series into permanent, seasonal, and transitory component, which requires the use of a frequency-modulated approach.

[6] In fact, time-domain methods might generate a more efficient estimation method for estimating the instantaneous frequency by effectively extracting it from a time-varying parameter process (Lovell 1991, p. 13).

[7] Each $\{X_{t(i)}\}$ can be termed a semistationary process, with the interval (t_i, t_{i+1}) constituting the interval of time over which the process is approximately stationary (Priestley 1965, 1988, pp. 149–151).

signal and get a reasonably good idea of how the spectrum during sunset differed from the spectrum for an average 5-min period near noon. We can refine this even further by sliding the 5-min window along the period of investigation, i.e., from sunrise to sunset. This would mean that we take the spectrum with a 5-min observation window at each instant of time, deriving an energy spectrum as a continuous function of time. This is acceptable, provided that the 5-min time windows do not themselves contain any rapid changes. This procedure would give an indication of how the spectral composition of light changed through the course of the day. However, if some significant changes occurred within some 5-min windows, we would have to shorten the window length appropriately.

Of course, the estimation of a time-dependent (or dynamic; Brillinger 1993, p. 335) spectrum cannot be accomplished for a particular instant of time. However, if we assume that the spectrum changes smoothly over time, we can, by using local functions of the data, estimate some form of average spectrum of the process in any neighborhood of a particular time instant (Cohen 1989, p. 964). Therefore the concept of an evolutionary (or time-dependent) spectrum is applicable to a class of nonstationary processes whose statistical properties are changing smoothly through time (Priestley 1988, p. 142).

Another problem with the extension of the notion of spectrum to nonstationary processes relates to the notion of frequency, which is regarded as being crucial to the physical interpretation of the spectrum as a power–frequency distribution. Considerable debate has centered on whether the conventional meaning of frequency can be maintained, but no consensus appears to exist (consult Lovell 1991, pp. 140–141; Loynes 1968; and Priestley 1965, 1988, pp. 142–145).

The main reason why it is possible to interpret the spectrum of a wide-sense stationary process as a power–frequency distribution is that the spectral representation is a sum of sine and cosine waves with varying frequencies and random amplitudes and phases (Priestley 1981, pp. 15–17, 1988, pp. 5–6). It follows that the component in the process $X(t)$ that has frequency w can be identified, and it is meaningful to discuss the contribution of this component to the total power of the process. In contrast, it has been argued that, for nonstationary processes, the spectral representation cannot be represented as a sum of sine and cosine waves (with orthogonal coefficients) because these constructs are themselves stationary. Rather, the spectral representation will have to be viewed as a sum of some other kinds of functions that allow for the time-varying character of the nonstationary process under investigation.

Two main methods for computing time-varying spectra have been identified in the literature. The first is the so-called frequency-modulated approach commonly used in engineering applications and underpinning the moving-window method of spectral analysis – commonly termed the spectrogram. When this approach is used, the amplitude of the process is viewed as unchanging. In terms of estimation, this method entails the use of the Fourier transform of a time-varying (local) autocorrelation function (Hammond et al. 1993, p. 359). We obtain an estimate of the spectrum in the vicinity of time period t by performing Fourier analysis on the time series within a short-time observation window centered about period t. We can then obtain a short-time spectral estimate as a function of time by sliding the observation window along the time series and centering it consecutively on each time period in the observation horizon (Lovell 1991, p. 2).

The second main method is Priestley's amplitude-modulation approach.[8] Priestley argues that for the term frequency to be meaningful, the function $X(t)$ (which explains $\{X_t\}$) must have an oscillatory form. Functions $X(t)$ can then be characterized as having a Fourier transform that is concentrated around a particular point w_0 ($\pm w_0$ in the real case). It is argued that

"...if we have a non-periodic function $X(t)$ whose Fourier transform has an absolute maximum at the point w_0, we may define w_0 as the frequency of this function, the argument being that locally $X(t)$ behaves like a sine wave with (conventional) frequency w_0, modulated by a 'smoothly varying' amplitude function" (Priestley 1988, p. 144).

It is evident that the concept of an oscillatory function is quite general, encompassing both amplitude- and frequency-modulated processes. Specifically, two different Fourier representations of oscillatory functions are valid: We may think of $X(t)$ as consisting of either an infinite number of frequency components with constant amplitudes (a frequency-modulated approach) or as just two frequency components with time-varying amplitudes (an amplitude-modulated approach; Priestley 1988, p. 144). In this respect, one could apply the STFT approach that encompasses a frequency-modulated form of oscillatory function – an approach adopted, for example, by Rao and Shapiro (1970) and subsequently cited by Priestley as an application of the concept of evolutionary spectrum (Priestley 1988, pp. 173–174).

However, in Priestley's exposition of evolutionary spectra, the key building block is the replacement of the conventional sine and cosine representation e^{jwt} with an amplitude-modulated form $A_t(w)e^{jwt}$. The term oscillatory, in this respect, refers to the term $A_t(w)$ that must vary slowly through time compared with e^{jwt} (Hammond et al., 1993, p. 358). This approach gives preference to an oscillatory function that has an amplitude-modulated form. However, the applicability of this approach to nonparametric economic applications appears to be limited, especially if no frequency-modulated methods have been used beforehand to identify frequency or cyclic components of potential interest.

[8] Priestley's seminal contributions can be found in Priestley (1965, 1966) with interesting discussion in Loynes (1968), Hammond (1983), Martin (1981), Priestley (1988, Chap. 6).

3 The short-time spectral representation of time series

The Fourier transform has played a key role in the analysis of signals and linear time-invariant systems in the natural sciences. The effectiveness of the Fourier transform is a result of the fact that it provides a unique representation for signals in terms of the eigenfunctions of linear time-invariant systems (the systems' complex exponentials). There is a unique correspondence between the Fourier integral and the Fourier transform of a signal, with either one being equally valid representations of a signal (Portnoff 1980, p. 55). However, conventional representations of the Fourier transform have certain practical and conceptual limitations, reflecting the fact that they represent, for each frequency w, the global (in time) characteristics of the signal. One practical limitation is that, in principle, the entire signal (time series) must be known if one is to obtain from its transform a complete characterization of its (in time) properties (Flanagan 1972, p. 142; Portnoff 1980, p. 55).

An additional complicating issue is the fact that all joint functions of time and frequency will not necessarily be valid STFT representations. This is particularly likely when the signal being investigated contains time-varying amplitude and frequency patterns. This basic difficulty reflects the fact that no unique law exists that relates frequency and time.[9] However, if the structure of the process is varying slowly through time, then the application of the STFT should be valid. In practice, the STFT has been used for two particular purposes. First, it has been used as an intermediate representation of a signal within the context of linear systems theory. In this context, a crucial requirement is that the original signal must be able to be recovered from the STFT. This is generally possible because of the mathematical structure that is imposed on the short-time Fourier transform. Specifically, the structure ensures that the original signal can be synthesized from its Fourier transform by taking the inverse Fourier transform with respect to the frequency w.[10]

The second type of application corresponds to a nonstationary representation of the signal (time series). It should be noted, in this latter context, that the above-mentioned synthesis is not required when the STFT is being used to provide a nonstationary representation of the time series (Allen and Rabiner 1977, p. 1559; Portnoff 1980, p. 58; Schafer and Rabiner 1973). We are of the view that the spectral representation of a logistic diffusion process corresponds to this particular type of application. Specifically, we are interested in identifying

[9] Consult Kodera et al. (1978, p. 65), for a discussion of this issue. Another related issue is that many TFDs can behave dramatically differently while each satisfies the conditions imposed on marginal distributions, thereby yielding acceptable definitions and distributions for energy density and instantaneous power (Cohen 1989, p. 943).

[10] A detailed discussion about the structure of Fourier transforms and the issue of synthesis is contained in Portnoff (1980, pp. 58–62).

and assessing whether the emerging pattern of nonstationarity of the residual properties of such a process displays any indication of instability and time irreversibility in accordance with the spectral theory outlined above.

To apply the Fourier transform in practice, the signal (time series) must be modified so that the transform exists for integration over known (past) values. We obtain this by deriving a so-called running spectrum, which has real time as an independent variable and with the spectral computation being based on weighted past values of the signal. As such, a portion of the time series will be analyzed as seen through a specified time window or weighting function. The window (weighting) function is, in turn, chosen to ensure that the product of signal and window is Fourier transformable.

With regard to economic applications of the STFT, the key building block is the notion of the short-time autocorrelation[11] (or equivalent autocovariance function). The choice of the autocorrelation functions is straightforward, given the ease with which they can be used as a basis for estimating periodicities in time series (Rabiner and Schafer 1978, p. 141). Specifically, if a signal $X(t)$ is an ongoing stationary random series, then its autocorrelation functions and its power-density (distribution) spectrum are linked by Fourier transforms. Moreover, when the symmetry of these two functions is taken into account, the power spectrum is typically computed by means of a cosine transform.[12] The method based on the autocovariance function is outlined below.

In the natural sciences, power spectra for discrete random processes are based on the use of the discrete-time Fourier transform (DFT). The major advantage of this method is that it can handle very large data sets efficiently. In economic applications, data series are usually relatively modest, and the advantage of using the DFT is not so obvious. The application of algorithms, based on the STFT, can be viewed as applying a moving observation window to conventional Fourier transform algorithms. As such, the spectral properties for a given short-time observation window are viewed as being equivalent to those derived from conventional formulas – except that the process is now regarded as being semistationary, being derived from local functions of data. In economic applications, the computation of the power spectrum proceeds on the basis that we have a realization from a stochastic process.[13] Conventionally,

[11] Flanagan (1972, p. 155) and Rabiner and Schafer (1978, pp. 141–149, 162–164). A general theoretical discussion about the link between the autocorrelation/autocovariance function and spectral density function can be found in Priestley (1981, pp. 210–215).

[12] Specifically, the covariance function will be a real and even function of the delay parameter m, and the spectra are real and even (symmetrical). The Fourier transform can then be expressed as a cosine transformation (Flanagan, 1977, p. 156).

[13] A stochastic process is an ordered set of random variables $X(t)$ with a sample space that is doubly infinite – that is, extending from $-\infty$ to ∞ at each point in time and with time itself extending from $-\infty$ to ∞.

it is also assumed that the stochastic process is wide-sense stationary. The computation of the power spectrum is based on taking the Fourier transform of the autocovariance function of the stochastic process.

It is possible to estimate the autocovariance function by

$$C(s) = \frac{1}{n}\sum_{t=1}^{n-s}(x_t - x^m)(x_{t+s} - x^m), \tag{11.1}$$

where x^m is the estimated mean of the process and is given by

$$x^m = \frac{1}{n}\sum_{t=1}^{n} x_t. \tag{11.2}$$

In general, only a finite number of observations will be available, say, n observations.[14] Then $(n-1)$ will be the largest lag for which the autocovariance function can be determined. The estimated spectrum will take the form

$$g^e(w) = \frac{1}{2\pi}\left[C(0) + 2\sum_{s=1}^{n-1} C(s)\cos(ws)\right]. \tag{11.3}$$

The power spectrum $g(w)$ gives a measure of the average contribution that the frequency components within the frequency band $(w, w + dw)$ make to the overall variance of the univariate process X_t (Granger and Hatanaka 1964, p. 30; Koopmans 1974, pp. 11–12; Nerlove 1964, p. 248; Priestley 1981, pp. 206–210). This particular estimator is asymptotically unbiased but is not consistent.[15]

In the literature, the conventional method used to overcome this problem (and obtain a consistent estimator) is through the use of lag windows.[16] Using lag windows can be shown to be equivalent to the use of an estimator of the form

$$g^e(w) = \frac{1}{2\pi}\left[C(0) + 2\sum_{s=1}^{m-1} \alpha(s)C(s)\cos(ws)\right], \tag{11.4}$$

where $\alpha(s) = 1 - s/m$, m is the number of lags used in the computation of the covariance function $C(s)$, and $\alpha(s)$ is termed a lag window (Granger and

[14] One implication of this is that only a finite number of frequency bands will be able to be estimated. Therefore, the analyst is seeking to estimate the average value of the power spectrum over a finite set of frequency bands (Granger and Hatanaka 1964, pp. 44, 54).

[15] Specifically, as the number of observations increase, more terms will be subsequently added to the series. However, instead of obtaining better estimates of the spectrum at each frequency in a given set of frequencies, we will actually end up estimating the spectrum for a greater number of frequencies (Nerlove 1964, p. 252; Priestley 1981, p. 432).

[16] A detailed discussion of spectral estimation is contained in Kay (1988, Chap. 5), Priestley (1981, Chap. 7), and Subba Rao and Gabr (1984, Chap. 2).

Hatanaka 1964, pp. 59–60; Jenkins and Watts 1968, pp. 258–260; Priestley 1981, 433–434). In the context of short-time analysis, $g^e(w)$ will be taken to represent the STFT of the autocovariance function $C(s)$ that is, in turn, calculated from a fixed partition (portion) of the original time series $X(t)$ (Allen and Rabiner 1977, p. 1558; Flanagan 1972, pp. 142–144; Portnoff 1980, pp. 57–58). The lag window $\alpha(s)$ effectively introduces the smoothing required for obtaining a consistent estimate of the power spectrum. In general, $g^e(w)$ will become a function of time as the fixed partition of $X(t)$ is translated through time. In this latter context, $g^e(w)$ will represent the local behavior of $X(t)$ as effectively viewed through a sliding window.

The lag window $\alpha(s)$ indicated above is the so-called Bartlett window. Two common and widely used lag windows are the Tukey and the Parzen windows (Priestley 1981, pp. 443–444). These are given respectively by

$$\alpha_T(s) = \frac{1}{2}\left[1 + \cos\left(\frac{\pi s}{m}\right)\right], \tag{11.5}$$

$$\alpha_P(s) = \begin{cases} 1 - 6e^2(1-e) & \text{for } 0 < s \leqslant \dfrac{m}{2} \\ 2(1-e)^3 & \text{for } \dfrac{m}{2} \leqslant s < m \end{cases}, \tag{11.6}$$

where $e = s/m$.

At the outset, it is important to define a window consistent with the desired time–frequency resolution of the short-time transform (Allen and Rabiner 1977, p. 1558). The window function controls the relative weight that is imposed on the different parts of the signal. Moreover, if the length of the time windows is reduced, the STFT can then be used to estimate local quantities. However, a trade-off exists between time and frequency resolution in the spectrogram for a particular window (Cohen 1989, pp. 941, 963; Flanagan 1972, p. 160).

4 Empirical methods that use time-varying spectra

Two methods of applying time-varying spectral methods have been used to investigate patterns of nonstationarity and related issues, such as time irreversibility.

The first method is based on the use of confidence bounds to establish the statistical bona fides of observed varying spectral patterns. We implement this by taking, for example, the first and the last 100 (nonoverlapping) observations of the process and by using confidence intervals to establish whether the observed spectral patterns are robust. If this can be established then, to the extent that observed spectral patterns are different, evidence of time irreversibility will immediately follow.

In general, it is possible to compute confidence intervals for the power spectrum, provided nonoverlapping data segments are used, with the details dependent on the particular lag window adopted in the estimation of the spectrum. Specifically, the quantity $g^e(w)/g(w)$ is approximately distributed as a chi-squared distribution with σ degrees of freedom and with $\sigma = 3.71\, n/m$ for the Parzen window (Jenkins and Watts 1968, pp. 252, 255; Priestley 1981, pp. 467–468). It is possible to derive the $100(1-\beta)\%$ confidence interval for $g(w)$, which can be activated as

$$\log g^e(w) + \log\left(\frac{\alpha}{\text{Chi} - 2_{(a)}\left(1 - \frac{\beta}{2}\right)}\right),$$
$$\log g^e(w) + \log\left(\frac{\alpha}{\text{Chi} - 2_{(a)}\left(\frac{\beta}{2}\right)}\right). \tag{11.7}$$

The second method often follows application of the first and involves a systematic reduction in the size of data partitions in order to estimate nonstationary patterns more rigorously. This entails the use of overlapping data partitions, so the use of confidence intervals is not strictly valid. However, some indication of the qualitative validity of the resulting spectral pattern, often plotted as a function of time, is discernible from the first method. The lowest permissible bound for the size of the data partitions is also crucially dependent on whether high- or low-frequency components are prominent. If high-frequency components are prominent, then smaller data partition sizes can be used. However, in general, there are no generic rules or an established distribution theory associated with this latter method. Thus it should be viewed as a descriptive method, based on a much experimentation and the experience of the analyst.

5 The estimation of time-varying spectra in evolutionary economic contexts

It was established in Section 4 that, in terms of power-spectrum estimation, the short-time method entails the (implicit) use of the Fourier transform of a time-varying (local) autocovariance function [see Eq. (11.4)]. The use of short-time methodology generates average estimates in the vicinity of a specific time period through the use of a short-time observation window centered about period t. Furthermore, by use of a sliding (fixed-length) observation window, centered consecutively on each time period in the observation horizon, it is possible to obtain a short-time spectral estimate as a function of time.

The above methodology was adopted by Rao and Shapiro (1970). Given their actual power and cross-spectrum formulas, they used the concept of evolutionary spectra that was determined by computing "…successive spectra of overlapping portions of the time series" (Rao and Shapiro 1970, p. 210). This process was likened to "...viewing the series through a moving time window of fixed length" (Rao and Shapiro 1970, p. 210).

As such, this method clearly corresponds to that outlined in the previous paragraph.

We have not been able to find any other economic applications of the moving-window (STFT) approach.[17] In general, the application of the moving-window technique involves two broad operations. First, the total number of observations must be partitioned into overlapping segments of fixed length. For example, if the total number of observations N is 300, the fixed length of the basic data partition n can be set at 100 observations. The initial partition will then comprise observations 1–100. The next data partition will involve observations 2–101, etc. The second step is to set the autocovariance lag (number of frequencies to be estimated) that corresponds to the variable m in Section 4. A rule of thumb that is often used is that m should be chosen so that it is $n/4$. However, this rule is not universally accepted, and the most appropriate choice should be made on the basis of evidence obtained from the particular context of investigation.

The actual choice of variables n and m will affect the degree of frequency resolution and stability obtained from the estimation procedure. Specifically, the size of n will determine the effective upper bound that m can have – the larger the n, the larger m can be. The choice of large m will increase frequency resolution, however, at the expense of reduced smoothness (stability) of the estimated spectra.

The degree of overlap will also determine the temporal pattern of spectral decomposition. Two issues are relevant here. The first relates to the degree of overlap. For example, assuming monthly data, does the investigator move the data partition ahead 1 month, a quarter, or a year? The larger the extent of overlap (for example, moving the data partition ahead by a month instead of 12 months), the less likely it is that the assumption of a smoothly varying structure will be violated. The second issue relates to the extent of consecutive averaging that is undertaken. Consecutive averaging involves the determination of a number of consecutive power spectra with a moving observation window containing a high degree of overlap. The averaging for each frequency will then be obtained by computation of the mean value from the consecutive power spectrums that were estimated. If a large amount of consecutive averaging is permitted, this assists stability by smoothing the spectral estimates, but at the expense of frequency resolution. For example, a major structural change might be lost in the process of averaging.

A situation in which consecutive averaging might be worthwhile is that in which the stages of a logistic diffusion process have been estimated (identified)

[17] A recent economic application that uses Priestley's amplitude-modulated approach can be found in Artis et al. (1992).

in the time domain and can be assigned to particular (consecutive) expanses of time within the observation horizon. In this case, consecutive averaging could be used to obtain an average spectral decomposition for the distinct stages of the observed process.

It should also be stressed that, in interpreting spectrogram plots, emphasis should be placed on observing and interpreting frequency components in a very broad way. For example, in attempting to establish that a process has dominant long-run properties, we require only that low-frequency components should dominate high-frequency components within a short-time context. This means that one can say something about changes in spectral decomposition between low- and high-frequency components in a comparative sense. However, if windows of short length are used, there will not be enough observations to estimate robustly low-frequency components in such a way that allows a rigorous assessment of the long-run properties of the system. In fact, in the context of short-time analysis, most long-run cyclical properties will be grouped together with components conventionally associated with trend. However, the problem of rigorously estimating low-frequency components is not crucial, provided that low-frequency components can dominate high-frequency components in some comparative or relative sense.

Various indicators relevant to the investigation of a critical phenomenon will be discernible from the use of time-varying spectra. First, the total variance of the process can change with application of short-time spectral techniques as well as the resulting spectral decomposition. These measures can be examined by use of computer graphics. For instance, shifts in spectral decomposition will be discernible from changes in the shape of the resulting plot through time. Moreover, summary statistics such as total variance and percentage change in power at each frequency can be computed and examined.

6 Conclusions

It has been argued that the presence of evolutionary change in time-series data, in the form of a logistic diffusion process, should give rise to a residual variance structure that changes in fundamental ways as developmental structural change proceeds from the emergent to the saturation stage. Specifically, in the emergent growth-intensive stage, the spectral decomposition should show dominant low-frequency components. The middle stage – around the point of inflection – should have a relative concentration of power at middle-frequency components. Third, and most importantly, the saturation stage should have a spectral decomposition that has most power concentrated at high-frequency components. The observation of such a change in residual variance structure can be interpreted as reflecting the shifting roles that deterministic and stochastic forces play in an evolutionary process, identifiable in time-series data.

Fitting a logistic equation to time-series data does not, in itself, provide conclusive evidence that a nonequilibrium evolutionary process exists. Indeed, in the bulk of empirical studies, which have used the logistic equation, it has been viewed as a specification of a disequilibrium process between points of equilibrium. The use of time-varying spectra can establish whether time irreversibility exists and whether a nonequilibrium process exists because of the presence of structural change. If we define an evolutionary process as one that exhibits time irreversibility, structural change, and true uncertainty, then the application of time-varying spectra can offer a test of the first two of these features. The existence of true uncertainty can also be confirmed if the process in question can be shown to be in an unstable state, with only high-frequency components dominating. The absence of dominating low-frequency components means that long-run equilibrium interpretations cannot be made, and therefore no probabilistic information concerning the future course of events is available. Of course, if a sharp nonlinear discontinuity in the saturation phase is observed, this also confirms ex post that true uncertainty must have been present in the process under investigation. However, when a process shifts relatively smoothly from one logistic diffusion path to another, the presence of true uncertainty is less obvious, except through the careful examination of spectral decompositions.

The main method of spectral analysis we have focused on, in relation to the investigation of time-dependent spectral properties, is the frequency-modulated approach underpinning the moving-window method of computing time-varying spectra. This approach involves the estimation of a range of frequencies in order to investigate the relative importance of low- and high-frequency components in accordance with the spectral theory of evolutionary processes. In terms of estimation, this method entails the use of the Fourier transform of a time-varying (local) autocorrelation (or autocovariance) function. In this chapter, we have limited attention to issues relating to nonstationarity in evolutionary processes. However, criticality and structural transformation involve issues concerning nonlinearity that cannot be examined in any formal manner with the methods we have discussed. Higher-order moments must be included in any spectral assessment of the role of nonlinearity in structural transition. This would involve the use of the polyspectrum and the design of a method of application appropriate to economic contexts. This remains an area of further development of the methodology that we have proposed.

REFERENCES

Allen, J. B., and Rabiner, L. R. (1977). A unified approach to short-time Fourier analysis and synthesis. *Proc. IEEE*, **65**, 1558–64.

Andersen, E. S. (1994). *Evolutionary Economics: Post-Schumpeterian Contributions*, Pinter, London.

Artis, M. J., Bladen-Hovell, R., and Nachane, D. M. (1992). Instability of the velocity of money: a new approach based on the evolutionary spectrum. CEPR Discussion Paper 735, Centre for Economic Policy Research, London.

Azariadis, C. (1993). *Intertemporal Macroeconomics*, Blackwell, Cambridge, England.

Brillinger, D. R. (1993). An application of statistics to seismology: dispersion and modes. In *Developments in Time Series Analysis, In Honor of Maurice B. Priestley*, ed. T. Subba Rao, Chapman & Hall, London, pp. 331–41.

Burley, S. P. (1969). A spectral analysis of the Australian business cycle. *Austral. Econ. Pap.*, **8**(13), 193–218.

Cohen, L. (1989). Time–frequency distributions – a review. *Proc. IEEE*, **77**, 941–81.

Dixon, R. (1994). The logistic family of discrete dynamic models. In *Chaos and Non-Linear Models in Economics: Theory and Applications*, eds. J. Creedy and V. Martin, Elgar, Aldershot, England.

Flanagan, J. L. (1972). *Speech Analysis Synthesis and Perception*, 2nd ed., Springer-Verlag, New York.

Foster, J. (1992). The determination of Sterling M3, 1963–88: an evolutionary macroeconomic approach. *Econ. J.*, **102**, 481–96.

(1994a). The evolutionary macroeconomic approach to econometric modeling: a comparison of Sterling and Australian dollar M3 determination. In *The Political Economy of Complexity: Evolutionary Approaches to Economic Order and Disorder*, eds. R. Delorme and K. Dopfer, Elgar, Aldershot, England, pp. 282–301.

(1994b). An evolutionary macroeconomic model of Australian dollar M3 determination: 1967–93. *Appl. Econ.*, **26**, 1109–20.

Foster, J., and Wild, P. (1995). The logistic diffusion approach to econometric modeling in the presence of evolutionary change. Economics Discussion Paper 182 (September), University of Queensland, Brisbane, Queensland, Australia.

(1996). Economic evolution and the science of synergetics. *J. Evol. Econ.*, **6**, 239–60.

Foster, R. (1986). *Innovation*, Macmillan, London.

Granger, C. W. J. (1966). The typical spectral shape of an economic variable. *Econometrica*, **34**, 150–61.

Granger, C. W. J., and Engle, R. (1983). Applications of spectral analysis in econometrics. In *Handbook of Statistics*, eds. D. Brillinger and R. Krishnaiah, North-Holland, Amsterdam, **3**, 93–109.

Granger, C. W. J., and Hatanaka, M. (1964). *Spectral Analysis of Economic Time Series*, Princeton University Press, Princeton, New Jersey.

Hammond, J. K. (1983). Evolutionary spectra in random vibrations. *J. R. Stat. Soc. Ser. B*, **35**, 167–88.

Hammond, J. K., Harrison, R. F., Tsao, Y. H., and Lee, J. S. (1993). The prediction of time-frequency spectra using covariance-equivalent models. In *Developments in Time Series Analysis, In Honor of Maurice B. Priestley*, ed. T. Subba Rao, Chapman & Hall, London, pp. 355–73.

Hannan, M. T., and Freeman, J. (1989). *Organizational Ecology*, Harvard University Press, Cambridge, MA.

Hodgson, J. (1993). *Economics and Evolution*, Polity, Cambridge, England.

Jenkins, G. M., and Watts, D. G. (1968). *Spectral Analysis and Its Applications*, Holden-Day, San Francisco.

Kay, S. M. (1988). *Modern Spectral Estimation*, Prentice-Hall, Englewood Cliffs, NJ.

Kodera, K., Gendrin, R., and de Villedary, C. (1978). Analysis of time-varying signals with small BT values. *IEEE Trans. Acoust. Speech Signal Process.*, **ASSP-26**(1), 64–76.

Koopmans, L. H. (1974). *The Spectral Analysis of Time Series*, Academic, New York.
(1983). A spectral analysis primer. In *Handbook of Statistics*, eds. D. Brillinger and R. Krishnaiah, North-Holland, Amsterdam, **3**, 169–83.
Lovell, B. C. (1991). Techniques for non-stationary spectral analysis. Ph.D. Thesis, Department of Electrical Engineering, University of Queensland, Brisbane, Queensland, Australia.
Loynes, R. M. (1968). On the concept of spectrum for non-stationary processes. *J. R. Stat. Soc. Ser. B*, **30**, 1–30.
Martin, W. (1981). Line tracking in non-stationary processes. *Signal Process.*, **3**, 147–55.
Nelson, R. (1995). Recent evolutionary theorizing about economic change. *J. Econ. Lit.*, **33**, 48–90.
Nerlove, M. (1964). Spectral analysis of seasonal adjustment procedures. *Econometrica*, **32**, 241–85.
Peschel, M., and Mende, W. (1986). *The Predator–Prey Model: Do We Live in a Volterra World?*, Springer-Verlag, New York.
Portnoff, M. R. (1980). Time–frequency representation of digital signals and systems based on short-time Fourier analysis. *IEEE Trans. Acoust. Speech Signal Process.*, **ASSP-28**(1), 55–69.
Priestley, M. B. (1965). Evolutionary spectra and non-stationary processes. *J. R. Stat. Soc. Ser. B*, **27**, 204–37.
(1966). Design relations for non-stationary processes. *J. R. Stat. Soc. Ser. B*, **28**, 228–40.
(1981). *Spectral Analysis and Time Series*, Academic, London.
(1988). *Non-Linear and Non-Stationary Time Series Analysis*, Academic, London.
Rabiner, L. R., and Schafer, R. W. (1978). *Digital Processing of Speech Signals*, Prentice-Hall, Englewood Cliffs, NJ.
Rao, A. G., and Shapiro, A. (1970). Adaptive smoothing using evolutionary spectra. *Manage. Sci.*, **17**, 208–218.
Schafer, R. W., and Rabiner, L. R. (1973). Design and simulation of a speech analysis-synthesis system based on short-time Fourier analysis. *IEEE Trans. Audio Electroacoust.*, **AU-21**(3), 165–74.
Subba Rao, T., and Gabr, M. M. (1984). *An Introduction to Bispectral Analysis and Bilinear Time Series Models*, Springer-Verlag, Berlin.
Weidlich, M., and Braun, M. (1991). The master equation approach to nonlinear economic processes. *Pap. Econ. Evol.*, No. 9101.
Weidlich, W., Haag, G. (1982). *Concepts and Models of a Quantitative Sociology: The Dynamics of Interacting Populations*, Springer-Verlag, Berlin.
Wollin, A. S. (1995). A hierarchy-based punctuated equilibrium model of the processes of emergence and change of new rural industries. Ph.D. Thesis, Griffith University, Brisbane, Queensland, Australia.
Zhang, W. (1991). *Synergetic Economics: Time and Change in Nonlinear Economics*. Springer, Berlin.

CHAPTER 12

Ergodic chaos in a piecewise linear cobweb model

Akio Matsumoto

The emergence of complex dynamics in a cobweb model augmented with upper and lower bounds for output variations is demonstrated. The purpose is to consider the implications of the output constraints on the dynamic behavior of an agricultural economy.

The traditional cobweb model, which has monotonic specifications of demand and supply and naive or adaptive expectations formation, can produce only three types of dynamics: convergence to an equilibrium, convergence to period-2 cycles, or divergence. None of these types, however, is satisfactory to explain the irregular and asymmetric fluctuations of agricultural goods markets.

To overcome those limitations, the literature on nonlinear cobweb dynamics has been expanding with the help of new developments in nonlinear dynamics.[1] Several stability results have been established that show the existence of chaotic fluctuations as well as the convergence to stable periodic cycles. The literature fall into two groups. In the first, we have endogenous nonlinear cobweb models in which the supply-and/or-demand curves are nonlinear (see Jensen and Urban 1984, Chiarella 1988, Finkenstädt and Kuhbier 1992, and Hommes 1994). By nonlinear behavioral assumptions, transition maps in the first group are more or less similar to the logistic map that is able to give rise to complex dynamics involving chaos. In the second, we find a linear cobweb model with a upper bound for variations of output. Owing to the upper-quantity constraint, the transition map in the second ground is also nonlinear (or, more precisely, piecewise linear) in spite of the linear behavioral specifications. In particular, it is similar to the tent map that is able to generate complex dynamics. The upper bound not only prevents the price (or quantity) dynamics from explosive oscillations but also works to generate persistent irregular fluctuations (see Cugno and Montrucchio 1980, Nusse and Hommes 1990, and Huang 1995). However,

[1] The traditional cobweb model has been extended in other directions in which the effects of several production time lags or the effects of exogenous stochastic factors are analyzed.

the piecewise linear model with the upper bound has a possibility of almost all trajectories escaping from the domain of the transition map for some parameter constellations. In such a case, trajectories are negatively unbounded and thus the model is unable to track the price–quantity evolution in an economically meaningful region. Not much has yet been revealed with respect to a device that makes output trajectories remain nonnegative. The purpose of this chapter is to demonstrate the possibility of economically meaningful complex dynamics for the case in which a linear cobweb model augments the lower bound for variations of output in addition to the upper bound. It is intuitively clear that unstable trajectories bounce back to a bounded region and keep fluctuating within it. However, it has not yet been investigated whether complex dynamics may appear in the case in which output variations are bounded from above and below. This chapter demonstrates, through numerical examples, that the linear cobweb model augmented with the upper and the lower bounds can generate a wide spectrum of dynamic behavior ranging from stable periodic cycles to ergodic chaos.

This chapter is organized as follows. In Section 1 the linear cobweb model is set up with upper and lower bounds for output variations. In Section 2 the model is simulated to explore the relations between the output constraints and the output dynamics. Concluding remarks are made in Section 4.

1 Piecewise linear cobweb model

The simplest version of the traditional cobweb model is made up of the following four equations in discrete time:

$$\begin{aligned} q_t^d &= D(p_t), \text{ demand,} \\ q_t^s &= S(p_t^e), \text{ supply,} \\ q_t &= q_t^d = q_t^s, \text{ temporary equilibrium,} \\ p_t^e &= p_{t-1}, \text{ naive expectation.} \end{aligned} \tag{12.1}$$

This model can be reduced to a one-dimensional difference equation of output or price:

$$q_{t+1} = S[D^{-1}(q_t)] \quad \text{or} \quad p_{t+1} = D^{-1}[S(p_t)]. \tag{12.2}$$

In the simple version, the demand function as well as the supply function is assumed to be monotonic and thus the composite map, $S[D^{-1}(q_t)]$ or $D^{-1}[S(p_t)]$, is also monotonic. Its slope evaluated at the equilibrium point characterizes dynamics, as it equals an eigenvalue of the dynamic equation. As long as the slope lies between 0° and −45°, the equilibrium point is stable. The stable trajectories of price or quantity converge to a stationary state, which does not go with persistent fluctuations observed in the real world. As the slope steepens beyond $-45°$, the equilibrium point is unstable. The unstable trajectories explosively oscillate, which also contradicts the actual dynamic behavior. When the slope is equal to $-45°$, period-2 cycles can appear. However, the nature of regular cycles is unlike the irregular nature of the actual cycles. Thus such a simple cobweb model has difficulties in explaining cyclical and erratic movements observed in statistical data of the agricultural good (e.g., see the data provided by Finkenstädt and Kuhbier 1992).

By using linear supply-and-demand functions, Cugno and Montrucchio (1984) modified the traditional cobweb model by introducing an upper bound a imposed on the positive growth rate of q_t:

$$\begin{aligned} &S(p_{t-1}) = -a + bp_{t-1}, \quad a > 0, b > 0, \\ &D^{-1}(q_t) = c - dq_t, \quad c > 0, d > 0, \\ &q_{t+1} \leq q_{t+1}^U = (1+\alpha)q_t, \quad \alpha > 0, \end{aligned} \tag{12.3}$$

where the last device is found in Day[2] (1980, 1994). Substituting the second equation of Eqs. (12.3) into the first and taking account of the third equation yield the following piecewise linear transition map:

$$q_{t+1} = \max[(1+a)q_t, bc - a - bdq_t]. \tag{12.4}$$

It is a tent map in which a maximizer is

$$Q_M = \frac{bc - a}{1 + a + bd}. \tag{12.5}$$

Constructing this piecewise linear model, Cugno and Montrucchio (1984) clarify the following conditions under which the transition map can give rise to chaotic dynamics:

$$\frac{1+a}{a} \geq bd \geq \frac{2+a}{1+a}. \tag{12.6}$$

In condition (12.6), the first condition guarantees trajectories to be nonnegative and the second condition with equality guarantees Q_M to be a period-3 point. By the Li–Yorke chaos theorem, the period-3 point implies that transition map (12.4) satisfying condition (12.6) generates the persistent and irregular (i.e., chaotic) motions of output. Furthermore, recognizing the fact that transition map (12.4) is expansive (i.e., the slope in the absolute value is greater than 1) and unimodal in an unstable economy where $bd > 1$, Nusse and Hommes (1990) replace condition (12.6) with a weaker condition,

$$\frac{1+a}{a} \geq bd > 1, \tag{12.7}$$

[2] Day (1980, p. 197) considers the symmetric upper and lower constraints.

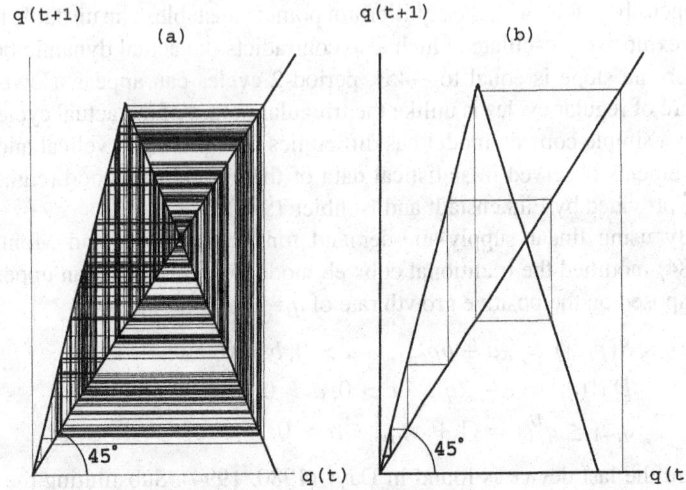

Figure 12.1. Examples of chaotic trajectory and escaping trajectory.

and demonstrate that transition map (12.4) generates the Li–Yorke chaos as well as the "sensitive dependence on initial values" chaos.

There is a possibility that a set of parameters may violate the first inequality condition of condition (12.6) or (12.7). In such a case, almost all trajectories (with respect to the Lebesgue measure) eventually escape from a economically meaningful interval between 0 and $[(bc - a)/(bd)]$ and fall to zero if a nonnegative constraint is implicitly assumed or go to negative infinity if not. Figures 12.1(a) and 12.1(b) are graphical representations of output trajectories generated by transition map (12.4). In those simulations, we start with the same initial value of q_t and set it to be 0.05. We take a and $bc - a$ to be 1.5 and 5, respectively. The simulations are performed under two different values of bd: bd is taken to be $20/13 \simeq 1.54$ in Fig. 12.1(a) and to be 2 in Fig. 12.1(b). Because $[(1 + a)/a] = 5/3 \simeq 1.67$, it can be checked that the former value of bd satisfies condition (7) but the latter violates it. In consequence, as those figures suggested, the trajectory in Fig. 12.1(a) is chaotically oscillating within the bounded interval and that in Fig. 12.1(b) escapes from the domain of the transition map.

To get rid of such economically meaningless dynamics, we modify the Cugno–Montrucchio version of the cobweb model by introducing the lower bound for variations of output. If we observe the real economic world, it is not surprising that a competitive firm prevents output tomorrow from changing drastically from output today, taking into account various constraints such as capacity constraints, financial constraints, and cautious response to demand uncertainty.[3] Having recognized this fact, we impose a lower bound β on the negative growth rate of output,

$$q_{t+1} \geq q_t^L = (1 - \beta)q_{t-1}, \quad 1 > \beta > 0, \tag{12.8}$$

to the Cugno–Montrucchio model given by Eqs. (12.3). The lower-bound constraint, analogous to the upper-bound constraint, has the effect of preventing output in period t from decreasing by more than $100\beta\%$ from the output of period $t - 1$.

The lower bound and the upper bound work to compress trajectories into a cone spanned by $q_{t+1}^U = (1+\alpha)q_t$ and $q_t^L = (1-\beta)q_{t-1}$ in the phase space. In consequence, the transition map becomes a map with three line segments and two kinked points,

$$f(q_t) = \begin{cases} (1+\alpha)q_t & \text{for } q_t \leq Q_M \\ bc - a - bdq_t & \text{for } Q_M \leq q_t \leq Q_m, \\ (1-\beta)q_t & \text{for } q_t \geq Q_m \end{cases} \tag{12.9}$$

where a minimizer Q_m is calculated as

$$Q_m = \frac{bc - a}{1 - \beta + bd}. \tag{12.10}$$

In a compact form, transition map (12.9) is

$$f(q_t) = \min\{(1-\beta)q_t, \max[(1+\alpha)q_t, bc - a - bdq_t]\}.$$

Under the assumptions of positive parameters, $bd > 0$, $bc - a > 0$, $\alpha > 0$, and $\beta > 0$, transition map (12.9) has the tilted-z profile and its nonlinearity becomes more pronounced when bd gets larger. Let q^* be a stationary state satisfying $q^* = f(q^*)$ {i.e., $q^* = [(bc-a)/(1+bd)]$}. If $bd > 1$, it is oscillatory unstable but fluctuations are bounded by the upper and the lower constraints of output. Three cases can be distinguished, depending on the relative magnitudes between α and β: (1) $(1+\alpha)(1-\beta) = 1$; (2) $(1+\alpha)(1-\beta) < 1$; and (3) $(1+\alpha)(1-\beta) > 1$. The typical profiles of the transition map under conditions (1), (2), and (3) are depicted in Figs. 12.2(a), 12.2(b), and 12.2(c), respectively, where the horizontal axis is q_t and the vertical axis is q_{t+1}. We call condition (1) the symmetric condition as the upper-bound locus and the lower-bound locus deviated from the 45° line by the same degree – the former positively and the latter negatively. We call condition (2) the upper asymmetric condition as the upper-bound locus is deviated from the 45° less than the lower-bound locus, and we call condition (3) the lower asymmetric condition as the lower-bound locus is deviated less than the upper-bound locus. By simulating the model

[3] Huang (1995) presumes that those constraints limit the positive growth rate of output. We assume that those constraints also can work in the opposite direction to limit the negative growth rate.

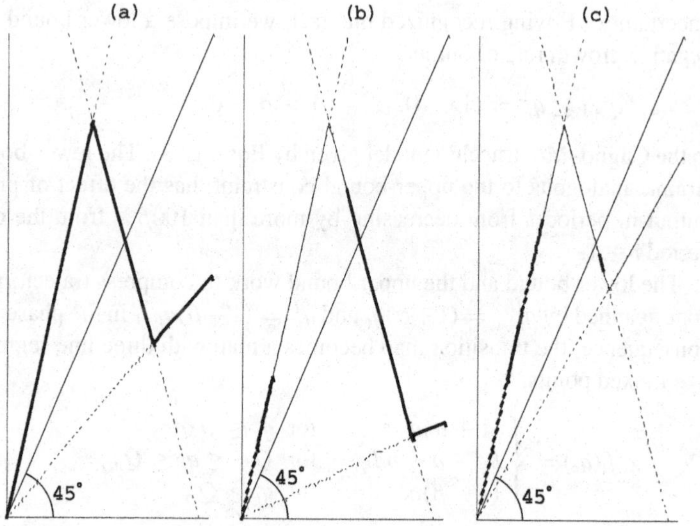

Figure 12.2. Three profiles of the transition map $f(q_t) = \min\{(1-\beta)q_t, \max[(1+a)q_t, bc - a - bdq_t]\}$.

under the different values of $bd(>1)$, we demonstrate that piecewise linear cobweb model (12.9) can generate various dynamics under each of these three parameter constellations for α and β.

2 Simulation of the model

To explore the dynamic behavior of output q, we simulate the model under the different values of bd, in which b and $1/d$ reflect the slopes of supply and demand curves, respectively. In bifurcation diagrams below, bd is taken to be a bifurcation parameter and the calculations are done under different values of α and β.

Symmetric case

The first simulation is shown in Fig. 12.3. It is performed with $\alpha = 1$ and $\beta = 0.5$, which, as verified, satisfy the symmetric-constraint condition, $(1+\alpha)(1-\beta) = 1$. The inverse of the bifurcation parameter, $1/bd$, is varied in decrements of 0.02 from 1 to 0. For each value of $1/bd, f(q_t)$ is iterated 400 times. Although the last 300 iterates are plotted on the vertical axis, only two points are shown in the bifurcation diagram. Thus Fig. 12.3 suggests that the symmetric-constrained cobweb model can give rise to period-2 cycles. These results are verified as follows. In Fig. 12.4, the dashed line is a graph of $f(q)$,

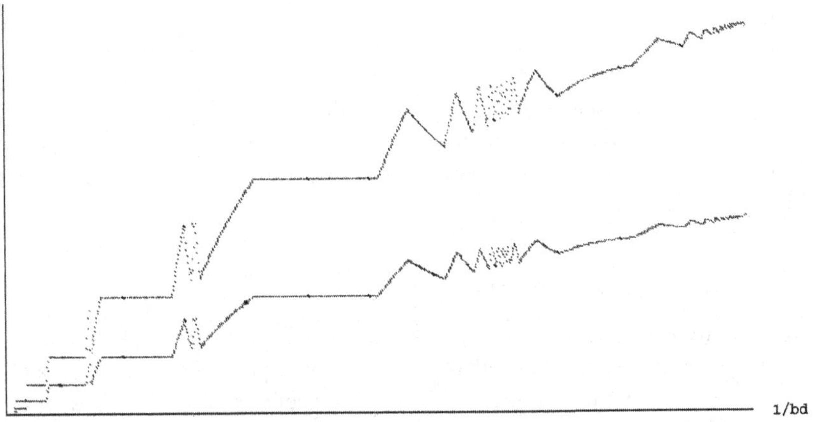

Figure 12.3. Bifurcation diagram in the symmetric case $(1+\alpha)(1-\beta)=1$.

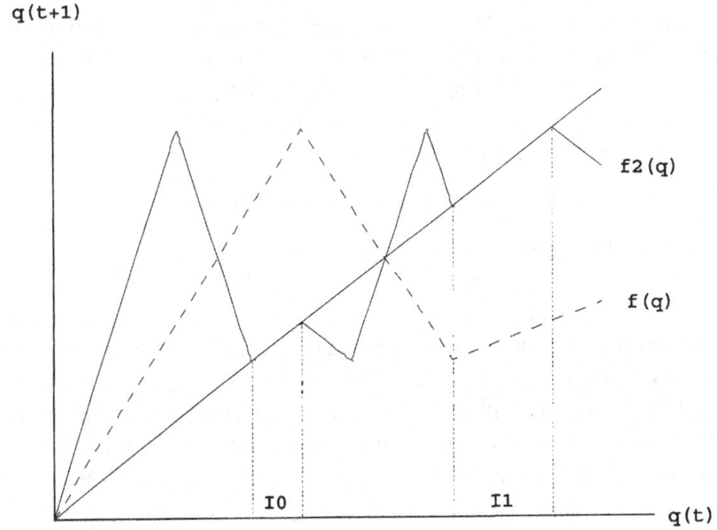

Figure 12.4. Graphs of $f(q)$ and $f^2(q) := f[f(q)]$.

and the solid straight line is a graph of $f^2(q) := f[f(q)]$, the second iteration of $f(q)$. We denote a local minimum by $Q_{\min} := f(Q_m)$ and a local maximum by $Q_{\max} := f(Q_M)$. Because $Q_{\min} < Q_M < Q_m < Q_{\max}$ holds in the symmetric case, an interval $I := [Q_{\min}, Q_{\max}]$ is the trapping interval, that is, any output trajectories starting outside the interval enter it within finite iterations and one starting inside remains there. As can be seen, the graph of $f^2(q)$ has two parts that are identical to the 45° line. This means that the corresponding two subintervals of I, $I_0 := [Q_{\min}, Q_M]$ and $I_1 := [Q_m, Q_{\max}]$ are sets of fixed points of $f^2(q)$ or sets of periodic points with period 2 of $f(q)$ [i.e., $f(I_0) = I_1, f(I_1) = I_0$.] Every trajectory emanating from an interval $\overline{I_0 \cup I_1 \cup \{q^*\}}$ enters into $I_0 \cup I_1$ after finite iterations. Thus we have stable period-2 cycles in the symmetric case.

Upper asymmetric case

Because the transition map, $f(q)$, has the upper and the lower bounds, it induces any trajectories, which are repelled by the unstable equilibrium, to bounce back to a vicinity of the equilibrium point. Thus we can define a trapping interval by an interval that eventually traps all trajectories. A restriction of $f(q)$ to the trapping interval governs the asymptotic behavior of q. Two distinct trapping intervals can be identified, which depends on the relation between the maximum $Q_{\max}$ and the minimizer Q_m: one interval is defined when $Q_{\max} \leq Q_m$, and the other is defined when $Q_{\max} > Q_m$. Rewriting the upper asymmetric condition as $[\alpha/(1+\alpha)] < \beta$, we can define $(bd)^U$ by $(bd)^U := \beta[(1+\alpha)/\alpha] > 1$. It can be checked that $Q_{\max} \leq Q_m$ holds for $1 < bd \leq (bd)^U$ and $Q_{\max} > Q_m$ for $bd > (bd)^U$.

Let $V_1 := [f(Q_{\max}), Q_{\max}]$; It is the trapping interval for $1 < bd \leq (bd)^U$. Consequently the restriction of $f(q_t)$ to V_1,

$$f|_{V_1}(q_t) = \min[(1+\alpha)q_t, bc - a - bdq_t], \tag{12.11}$$

generates trajectories that are eventually confined in V_1. It is an asymmetric tent map that is essentially the same as (12.2). Because it is expansive and unimodal, the restricted map $f|_{V_1}(q_t)$ can generate ergodic chaos.[4] Furthermore, we can obtain a complete characterization of transition map (12.9) by applying the results of Ito et al. (1979) and Day and Shafer (1987). A trajectory generated by $f|_{V_1}(q_t)$ is depicted in Fig. 12.5(a) in which bd is taken to be 1.2 and the bold line on the $q(t)$ axis is the trapping interval V_1. It can be seen that a trajectory keeps aperiodically oscillating around the equilibrium point within the trapping interval. Let $V_2 := [Q_{\min}, Q_{\max}]$, which is the trapping interval for $bd > (bd)^U$. Because V_2 contains two kinked points, Q_M and Q_m, a restriction of $f(q_t)$ to V_2,

$$f|_{V_2}(q_t) = \max\{(1-\beta)q_t, \min[(1+\alpha)q_t, bc - a - bdq_t]\} \tag{12.12}$$

takes on a tilted-z shape. Day and Schafer (1987) also make some characterizations for such a map with three line segments and two turning points.

[4] See Eq. (3) in property 5 of Nusse and Hommes (1990, p. 13). Also see theorem 3 of Day and Schafer (1987, pp. 352–53).

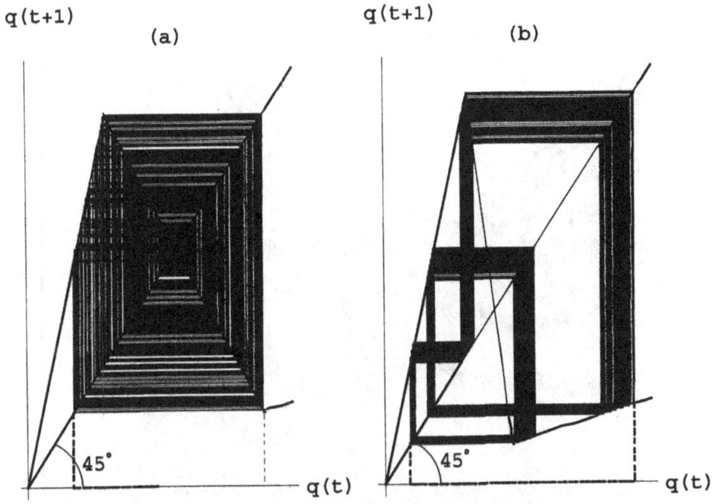

Figure 12.5. Two time paths of chaotic trajectory generated by $f|_{V_1}(q)$ and of noisy chaos with period 5 by $f|_{V_2}(q)$.

Figure 12.5(b) depicts trajectories generated by $f|_{V_2}(q_t)$ in which bd is taken to be 5 and the bold line on the $q(t)$ axis is the trapping interval V_2. It can be seen that trajectories periodically visit from one interval to another but aperiodically oscillate within the interval, it is called noisy chaos with period 5.

A bifurcation diagram in the upper asymmetric case is shown in Fig. 12.6, which has been calculated by fixing $\alpha = 2$ and $\beta = 0.8$ and decreasing $1/bd$ from 1 to 0. The switching of the transition map from $f|_{V_1}(q_t)$ to $f|_{V_2}(q_t)$ takes place at $1/(bd)^U$. Chaotic dynamics in Fig. 12.5(a) emerges along a vertical dashed line aa, passing through $1/1.2 \simeq 0.83$ whereas noisy chaos with period 5 in Fig. 12.5(b) emerges along a vertical dashed line bb, passing through a point $1/5 = 0.2$.

Lower asymmetric case

Analysis in the lower asymmetric case is similar to that in the upper asymmetric case. In Fig. 12.7 the bifurcation diagram in the lower asymmetric case is shown. The simulation is done with $\alpha = 3.2$ and $\beta = 4/9$, which satisfy the lower asymmetric condition $(1 + \alpha)(1 - \beta) > 1$. Once the bifurcation parameter $1/bd$ is less than unity, the stable-quantity equilibrium becomes unstable and bifurcates to asymptotically stable period-2 cycles, noisy chaos with period 2^2, noisy chaos with period 2^1, and noisy chaos with period 2^0 (i.e., chaos). As $1/bd$ is decreased further, the asymptotically stable period-3 cycle emerges

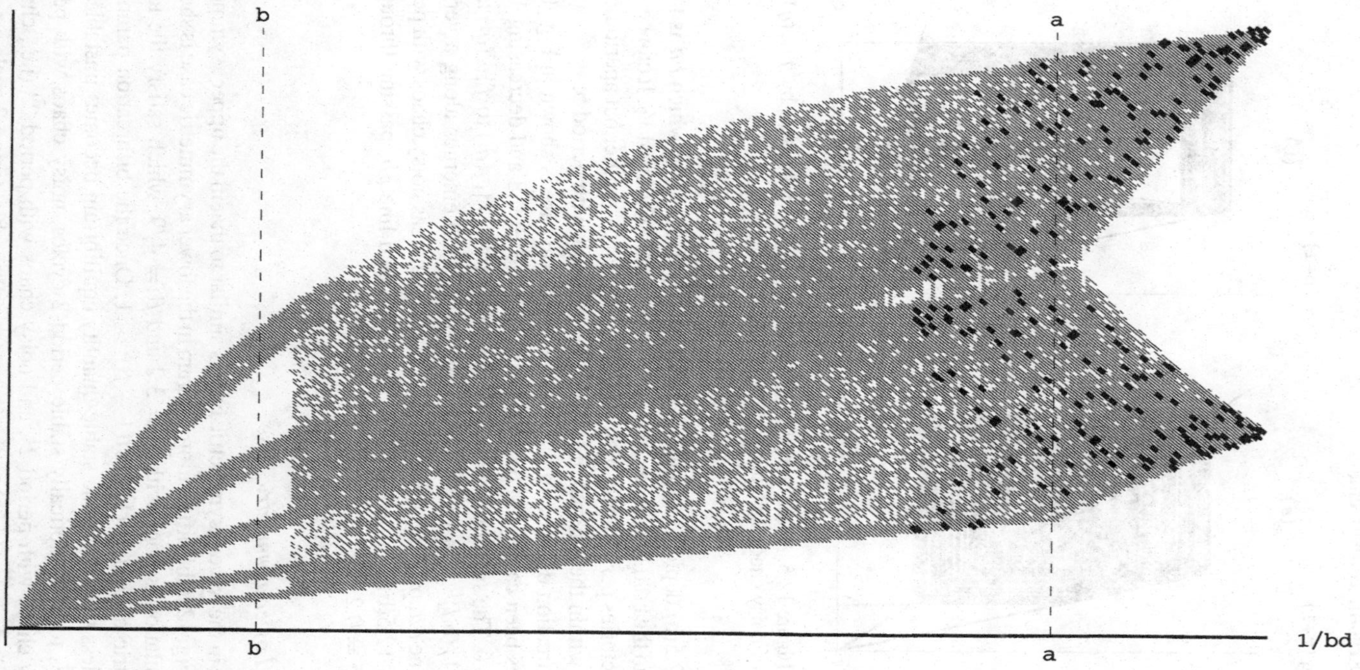

Figure 12.6. Bifurcation diagram in the upper asymmetric case $(1 + a)(1 - \beta) < 1$.

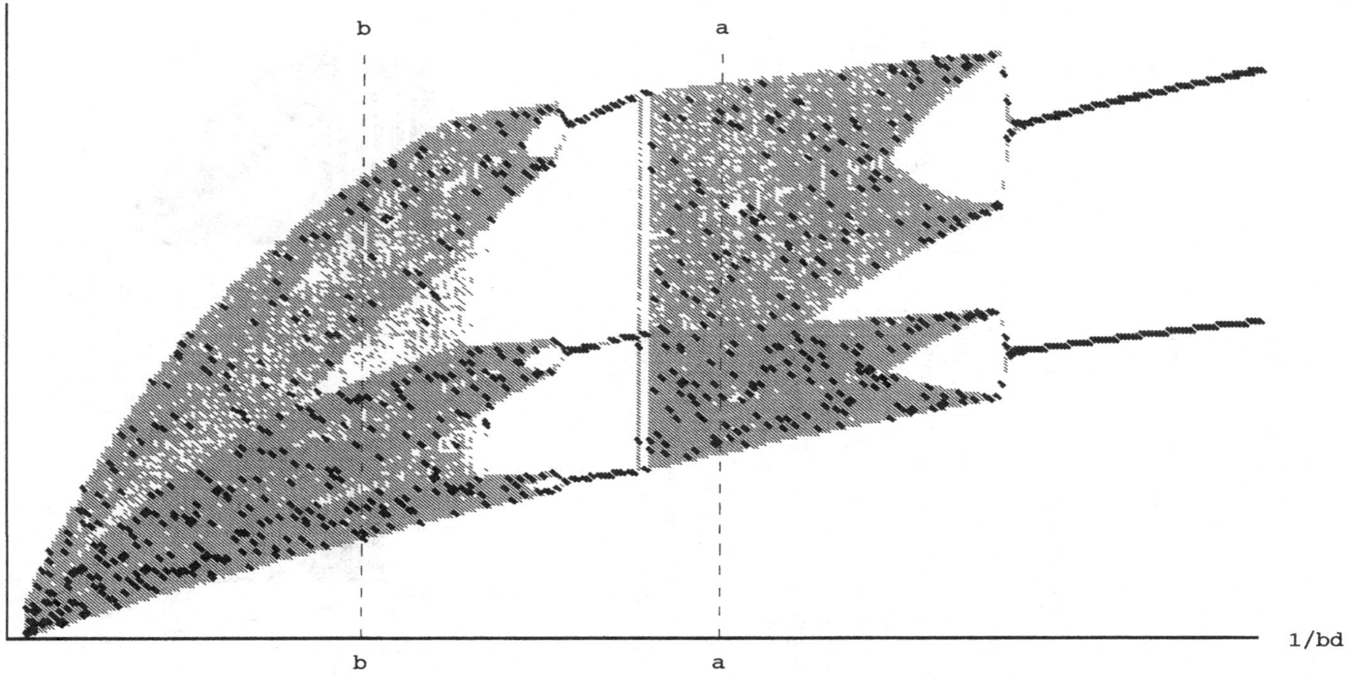

Figure 12.7. Bifurcation diagram in the lower asymmetric case $(1 + a)(1 - \beta) > 1$.

(i.e., window phenomenon occurs). When $1/bd$ is decreased further, the period-3 cycle bifurcates to the noisy chaos with period 3×2^1, one with period 3×2^0, and then to chaos. As in the upper asymmetric case, the switching of a transition map takes place. In order to see this, let $(bd)^L := \{a[(1-\beta)/\beta]\} > 1$, where the last inequality is due to the lower asymmetric condition. For $1 < bd \leq (bd)^L$, we have $Q_M < Q_{\min}$ so that $U_1 := [Q_{\min}, f(Q_{\min})]$ can be a trapping interval. A restriction of $f(q)$ to U_1,

$$f|_{U_1}(q) = \max[bc - a - bdq_t, (1 - \beta)q_t], \tag{12.13}$$

has an asymmetric tent-shaped profile. $f|_{U_1}(q)$ is, however, not expansive because it has a slope less than unity (i.e., $\{[\partial f|_{U_1}(q)]/\partial q\} = 1-\beta < 1$) on an interval $[Q_{\min}, Q_M)$ and one greater than unity (i.e., $|\{[\partial f|_{U_1}(q)]/\partial q\}| = bd > 1$) on $[Q_M, f(Q_{\min})]$. Although the results of Day and Schafer (1987) cannot be applied to a nonexpansive map, some results of Ito et al. (1979) are useful to characterize it. For $bd > (bd)^L$, we have $Q_{\min} < Q_M$ so that $U_2 := [Q_{\min}, Q_{\max}]$ can be a trapping interval that has two kinked points, Q_M and Q_m.

The restriction of the transition map to U_2, denoted by $f|_{U_2}(q)$, is linearly conjugate to Eq. (12) and possesses a tilted-z-shaped profile. Figure 12.8 shows two numerical examples of chaotic trajectories; Fig. 12.8(a) is a trajectory generated by $f|_{U_1}(q)$ that emerges along the vertical dashed line *aa* in Fig. 12.7, and Fig. 12.8(b) is a trajectory generated by $f|_{U_2}(q)$ that emerges along the vertical dashed line *bb*.

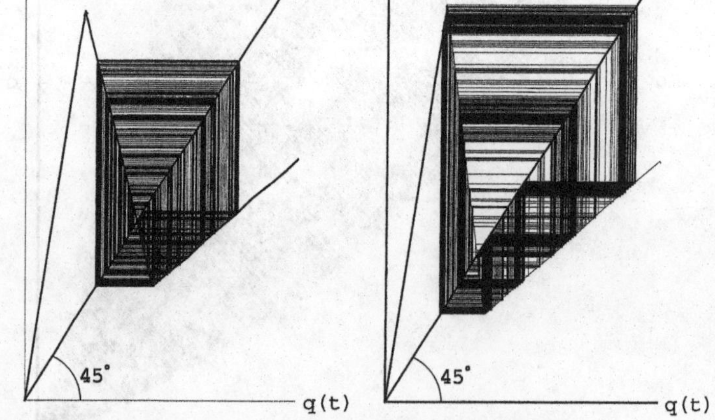

Figure 12.8. Two chaotic time paths generated by $f|_{U_1}(q)$ and $f|_{U_2}(q)$.

3 Concluding remarks

This chapter investigates the dynamic structure of the linear cobweb model with upper and lower bounds for variations on output. By the exogenous bounds, the transition map becomes nonlinear (i.e., piecewise linear) even though the behavioral specifications of supply and demand are linear. Simulating the model under different values of bd, it was demonstrated that the piecewise linear cobweb model may generate chaotic behavior if the output constraints are asymmetric and that it can generate stable period-2 cycles whose amplitudes depend on the prevailing parameter constellations (i.e., choice of initial point, values of bd, etc.) if the output constraints are symmetric. Although the bifurcation diagrams in asymmetric cases imply the emergence of chaotic behavior, the bifurcation example of chaos is different according to whether the output constraints are upper or lower asymmetric. In the upper symmetric case, the transition map generates persistent and aperiodic cycles for any values of bd greater than unity. The control system (i.e., the restriction of the transition map to the trapping interval) switches from the expansive map to the tilted-z-shaped map as bd is increased. In consequence, noisy chaos with period 2 and then true chaos appear as bd exceeds unity. Noisy chaos with period 5 appears if bd is further increased. On the other hand, in the lower asymmetric case, the control system switches from a nonexpansive tent map to the tilted-z-shaped map. As bd is increased from unity, the stable-output equilibrium is unstable and bifurcates to stable period-2 cycles, to noisy chaos with period 2^2, to chaos with period 2, and then to true chaos (i.e., noisy chaos with period 1), the last of which shrinks to zero as bd goes to infinity.

The fact that this model can justify the persistent and aperiodic fluctuations in a disequilibrium agricultural economy is itself worth note. What implications do the simulations have for a linear cobweb model augmented with the upper and lower bounds? The emergence of complex dynamics involving ergodic chaos depends on a combination of parameters, bd, α, and β. $bd > 1$ is necessary for generations of chaos in the asymmetric cases. Here b measures the steepness of the supply curve, α is the upper bound imposed on the positive growth rate of output, and β is the lower bound on the negative growth rate. These are decision variables of a producer. d measures the steepness of the inverse demand curve and is a decision variable of a consumer. Thus it can be stated that one source of such complex dynamics is an interaction between agents in the disequilibrium market. Although those parameters' values are exogenously given within our framework, it is of interest to investigate how each agent determines values of his or her decision variables.

REFERENCES

Chiarella, C. (1988). The cobweb model. Its instability and the onset of chaos. *Econ. Model.*, **5**, 377–84.

Cugno, F., and Montrucchio, L. (1980). Some new techniques for modeling nonlinear economic fluctuations: a brief survey. In *Nonlinear Models of Fluctuating Growth*, eds. R. M. Goodwin, M. Krüger, and A. Vercelli LNEM 228, Springer-Verlag, Berlin, pp. 146–65.

(1984). Cobweb theorem, adaptive expectations and chaotic dynamics, Rivista Internazionale di Scienze Economiche e Commerciali, **31**, 713–24.

Day, R. (1980). Cobweb models with explicit suboptimization. In *Modeling Economic Change: the Recursive Programming Approach*, eds. R. Day and A. Cigno, North-Holland, Amsterdam, pp. 191–215.

(1994). *Complex Economic Dynamics, Volume 1. An Introduction to Dynamical Systems and Market Mechanisms*, MIT Press, London.

Day, R., and Schafer, W. (1987). Ergodic fluctuations in deterministic economic model. *J. Econ. Behav. Organiz.*, **8**, 339–61.

Finkenstädt, B., and Kuhbier, P. (1992). Chaotic dynamics in agricultural markets. *Ann. Oper. Res.*, **37**, 73–96.

Hommes, C. (1994). Dynamic of the cobweb model with adaptive expectations and nonlinear supply and demand, *J. Econ. Behav. Organiz.*, **24**, 315–35.

Huang, W. (1995). Caution implies profit. *J. Econ. Behaviour and Organisation*, **7**, 257–77.

Ito, S., Tanaka, S., and Nakada, H. (1979). On unimodal linear transformation and chaos II. *Tokyo J. Math.*, **2**, 241–59.

Jensen, R., and Urban, R. (1984). Chaotic price behavior in a non-linear cobweb model. *Econ. Lett.*, **15**, 235–40.

Matsumoto, A. (1996). Ergodic chaos in inventory oscillations; an example. *Chaos, Solitons Fractals*, **7**, 2175–88.

Nusse, H., and Hommes, C. (1990). Resolution of chaos with application to a modified Samuelson model. *J. Econ. Dyn. Control*, **14**, 1–19.

CHAPTER 13

The cobweb model and a modified genetic algorithm

Janice Gaffney, Krystyna Parrott, Charles Pearce, and Franz Salzborn

An important characteristic of markets for certain goods is the significant time lag between the time at which the economic agents (producers) make their decisions to supply the good and the time of the market at which the good is actually sold. Agricultural markets typically have this feature. The simplest models describing the behavior of these markets are the cobweb models of price and quantity adjustment in a single market. A huge literature on these has developed. Chiarella (1990) has given a comprehensive review of these from their inception with Leontief (1934; see Leontief 1966 for a more accessible text) up to 1990.

The range of behavior with different versions of the cobweb model is appreciable and under suitable assumptions even chaotic behavior is possible (see, for example, Jenson and Urban 1984 and Chiarella 1988). However, data from real markets do not support the conclusions about market instability (see, for example, Meadows 1970). Furthermore, these conclusions are also not supported by the data from experimental markets (Carlson 1967, Holt and Williamil 1986). Struck by the stability he had observed in the experimental market, Carlson (1968) showed that for normally sloped demand-and-supply curves, if economic agents base their price forecasts on an arithmetic average of all previous prices, the cobweb model is always stable.

The evidence of experimental markets provided an inspiration for a study of a cobweb model by Arifovic (1994), who used a genetic algorithm (GA). Her paper broke fresh ground in several ways and is discussed in a number of places in the book of Dawid (1996) on the modeling of adaptive learning by GAs. The form of cobweb model she used and the parameter settings she adopted for the simulations were chosen so that direct comparisons could be made with an actual set of laboratory experiments by Wellford (1989).

An early account of the principles involved in the construction of GAs is that of Holland (1975). The description of the GA on which Arifovic (1994) largely based her versions of the GA is found in Goldberg (1989). Part one of the two-part survey article of Beasley et al. (1993a) provides a good summary of GAs from a modern perspective. See also the recent text of Dawid (1996).

Arifovic treated two GA models. Our starting point is her single-population model. In Section 3.5 of his book, Dawid suggested that there may be interpretational difficulties with Arifovic's second, multipopulation, GA model in the cobweb context. This is allied to the important question of the extent to which GAs constitute only a technical algorithm inspired by biological evolution, rather than a natural model for learning within society.

This chapter was motivated by this concern within the context of the single-population GA. We make modifications to the first Arifovic GA model guided by economic concerns. In Section 1 we describe the equations of the basic cobweb model and show how the specification of the cobweb model used for the simulations is obtained. Section 2 is a detailed account of the GA that was constructed for our simulations. The results of our simulations are presented in Section 3, and some concluding remarks are given in Section 4.

1 The cobweb model and experimental markets

The basic cobweb model is described by the following three equations:

$$\text{Demand:} \quad D_t = a + bp_t. \tag{13.1}$$

$$\text{Supply:} \quad Q_t = c + dp_{t-1}. \tag{13.2}$$

$$\text{Market clearing:} \quad D_t = Q_t. \tag{13.3}$$

The model is discrete with $t = 0, 1, 2 \ldots$. The quantity demanded at time t is D_t, the quantity supplied is Q_t, the market price is p_t, and a, b, c, and d are constants. The model is clearly linear. The substitution of Eqs. (13.1) and (13.2) into Eq. (13.3) yields a first-order difference equation for p_t, and the analysis of this equation then gives the condition for the asymptotic stability of the solution as $|d| < |b|$.

To understand how market experiments are used to investigate the cobweb model, it is useful first to consider some of the assumptions that are implicit in the above formulation of the cobweb model. Equation (13.1) is a statement of the assumption that the demand at the time of the market under consideration is given by a linear demand curve. Equation (13.2) involves the assumption that the producers must make decisions about the quantity they supply ahead of the market, i.e., there is a supply-response lag, the assumption that the producers have a linear supply function that is a function of the market price, and the assumption that the producers expect the market price to be the price they observe in the current market. Furthermore, if it is assumed that the producers construct a supply function by solving an optimization problem in a competitive environment, because the supply function is linear the cost of production function of the producers must be a quadratic function of quantity. Equation (13.3) closes the model and is a statement of the assumption that the market price adjusts so that all of the good supplied to the market is sold.

In market experiments, the experimental design ensures that Eqs. (13.1) and (13.3) are satisfied so that the behavior of the producers that is modeled in the cobweb model by Eq. (13.2) can be studied.

In the experiments, n subjects playing the role of n producers in a competitive environment each make a production decision. These individual decisions are added up to give the total quantity of the good supplied to each market. Thus, for market,

$$Q_t = \sum_{i=1}^{n} q_{i,t}, \tag{13.4}$$

where Q_t is the aggregate quantity supplied and $q_{i,t}$ is the quantity supplied by the ith producer (subject). Although the subjects make their decisions as they see fit, they do so in the same economic circumstances. Each is given identical cost of production functions and instructed to make production decisions to maximize profit.

Experiments typically simulate the dynamical behavior of a market for up to 30 market periods in the following fashion. The experiment begins with each subject making a production decision. These decisions are collected, and the aggregate production is determined. The market clearing price p_t is calculated next with the demand schedule relevant to the particular experiment. In the market experiment simulations of the cobweb model, Eqs. (13.1) and (13.3) [and also (13.4)] are thus combined to give

$$p_t = A - B\sum_{i=1}^{n} q_{i,t}, \tag{13.5}$$

where the parameters A and B are derived from a demand schedule. Once the market-clearing price has been calculated, it is communicated to the subjects so they can determine their profit from the sale of the quantity of good they have supplied to the market. The subjects then make their production decisions for the next market and so on. As the market evolves, the subjects have more information on which to base their decisions, i.e., the price information from previous markets; however, a competitive environment is maintained because they do not know the production decisions of the other subjects. Also there is nothing in the experimental design to directly force the subjects to use the cost of production schedule or the price information generated by the market in the fashion suggested by Eq. (13.2), apart from forcing them to make a decision ahead of the market.

However, if all of the subjects did indeed structure their production decisions by first using the cost of production information provided to solve an optimization problem (marginal cost information is given to help with this calculation), then the experiment would simulate the behavior of n profit-maximizing producers in a competitive market. Thus if the cost of production for the ith producer, $C_{i,t}$ is given by

$$C_{i,t} = xq_{i,t} + \tfrac{1}{2}yn(q_{i,t})^2,$$

then the expected profit for each firm, $\pi^e_{i,t}$, is

$$\pi^e_{i,t} = p^e_t q_{i,t} - xq_{i,t} - \tfrac{1}{2}yn(q_{i,t})^2,$$

where p^e_t is the expected price of the good at t. The first-order condition gives the profit-maximizing quantity $q_{i,t}$. This quantity is

$$q_{i,t} = \frac{1}{yn}(p^e_t - x).$$

For the market to be in equilibrium, the price expectations of all the producers must be realized. Thus all of the producers must produce the quantity $q_t = q^*$ and expect price $p^e_t = p*$, where

$$q^* = \frac{1}{yn}(p^* - x),$$

$$p^* = A - B\sum_{i=1}^{n} q^*.$$

Hence

$$q^* = \frac{A - x}{n(B + y)}, \quad p^* = \frac{Bx + Ay}{B + y}, \tag{13.6}$$

and the corresponding equilibrium aggregate supply $Q^* = nq^*$ is

$$Q^* = \frac{A - x}{B + y}.$$

The parameterization of the functions for the above derivation is given in Arifovic (1994) and has been adopted because it is useful in the design of the experiments and simulations.

The purpose of this derivation is to obtain the equilibrium aggregate quantity and price and to show how the market experiments and supply function (13.2) can be connected.

2 The genetic algorithm

The starting point of GAs is a population of possible solutions to a search or optimization problem. For this application we consider the population at time t to be the collection of production decisions $q_{i,t}$, $i = 1, \ldots, n$ made by the n producers. The specification of the population of solutions that we used is the same as that used by Arifovic for the single-population GA except we did not use a binary representation. This is commented on below.

Once the solutions have been identified they are represented by chromosomes, i.e., a suitable coding of the solution as a string of values. This string has traditionally been a sequence of binary digits. Thus for Arifovic's GA each $q_{i,t}$ is approximated by a binary string of length l ($q_{i,t} \in [0, \bar{q}]$ where $\bar{q}$ is the maximum quantity that can be produced and is chosen so that the profits are nonnegative).

The next step in setting up a GA is to define a suitable fitness function. This function assigns a single value of fitness to a given chromosome. In applications of GAs to optimization problems involving a function, it is usual to identify the fitness function with the function being optimized so that the fitness of a chromosome is simply the value of the solution corresponding to the chromosome.

In our application (and also Arifovic's) the fitness $\mu_{i,t}$ of a chromosome corresponding to $q_{i,t}$ is determined by the value of the profit this decision earns in market t. Thus,

$$\mu_{i,t} = p_t q_{i,t} - C_{i,t}. \tag{13.7}$$

(The fitness of two chromosomes $q_{i,t}$ and $q_{i',t'}$ that are identical can therefore be different because p_t and $p_{t'}$ may not be equal.)

In running a standard GA, three operators are applied to the population of chromosomes. Parents are selected for reproduction, and crossover and mutation are used to generate offspring. Our basic GA includes these operators. Following Arifovic, we also consider an augmented GA that includes these three operators and an election operator.

Parents are selected from the current population for reproduction by a random process that favors the most fit. We used the most basic method, stochastic sampling. This method uses the ratio of the fitness of each chromosome to the total fitness of all the chromosomes to define its probability of selection. Thus the probability $P(q_{i,t})$ that a chromosome $q_{i,t}$ is chosen is given by

$$P(q_{i,t}) = \mu_{i,t} \Big/ \sum_{i=1}^{n} \mu_{i,t}, \quad i = 1, \ldots, n. \tag{13.8}$$

We randomly sample from the distribution given by Eq. (13.8) by using roulette selection (see, for example, Davis 1991 for a description of how this can be implemented). Roulette selection involves giving each chromosome a sector of a biased roulette wheel in which the size of sector allocated is in proportion to its fitness. The wheel is then, in effect, spun to choose a parent.

Once a set of parents have been selected (the mating pool), pairs of parents are randomly selected from the pool and their chromosomes are recombined by crossover. In a conventional GA in which chromosomes are binary strings, a single-point crossover involves cutting the strings at a randomly chosen position and exchanging the segments to the right of the crossover position to produce two new chromosomes.

Suppose that two chromosomes are of the forms

$$x = , \ldots, 01, \ldots, y = , \ldots, 10, \ldots.$$

A crossover at the specified loci given would result in new chromosomes $u = , \ldots, 00 \ldots, v = , \ldots, 11 \ldots.$

It may be noted that if these are treated as real binary numbers then $u < x$ and $v > y$. In fact it is easily verified that the situation can arise in which u is less than both x and y and v is greater than both x and y. This contrasts sharply with the phenomenon of averaging alluded to in the context of real and experimental market data and invites the question of how appropriate the crossover mechanism is for modeling in an economic rather than a biological context.

Accordingly we propose, instead of using crossover as a basic mechanism for producing offspring from x and y, to use instead an averaging procedure. For reasons of simplicity and symmetry, in this short exploratory work we make use of the arithmetic average $(x + y)/2$. More general averaging procedures are allowed in the companion chapter by Pearce (Chap. 14). From a GA point of view, our procedure results in some restriction of the production of new genetic material that, one may wonder, could negatively affect the convergence of the algorithm. By contrast, from an economic viewpoint, averaging may be expected to have a stabilizing influence.

The GA does not depend on strings' being binary (see the discussion of Beasley et al. 1993b). As no special reason has been put forward for the use of binary strings in an economic context, we use for computational convenience decimal strings, i.e., floating-point numbers.

A standard GA has mutation that applies through the changing of a randomly located locus on a chromosome. When a mutation occurs the various possible chromosomes that can be produced are all at the same genetic distance from the unmutated chromosome.

With the use of binary or other strings to represent floating-point numbers, an altogether different result arises from mutation. Mutation will make a small change to a number unless the bit mutated lies near the beginning of a string. The underlying genetic idea is therefore better translated into an economic context when the chromosome is replaced with a randomly generated one. Again this might perhaps be expected to have a destabilizing influence on the convergence of the algorithm.

The election operator that we use for the augmented GA is similar to the election operator used by Arifovic. In our basic GA, the whole population of chromosomes, (i.e., the decisions of the producers) is replaced in each generation. However, with election, children are tested for potential fitness before they are accepted. The set of chromosomes of the children created by the GA represents the set of potential new decisions of the producers. It seems reasonable to assume that before the producers replace their current decisions with new decisions they compare any potential new decisions with their current decisions. So, in line with the assumptions of the basic cobweb model that producers expect the current market price to prevail in the next market, we assume that they compare their decisions by using the current market price to calculate the profit they would make from each decision and take to the next market the decision that returns the higher profit.

Thus in our augmented GA, the election operator uses the current fitness function to compare the new and current decision of each producer and replaces the current decision with the new decision only if it is better. Arifovic's election operator is implemented in the same way: The election operator first uses the current fitness function to compare the fitness of parents and their children and then chooses the two most fit from the four individuals (two parents and two children).

For an application of a GA to the cobweb model with n producers, in which the individuals in the population represent the decisions of the producers and the tth generation of the population represents their decisions for market period t, the number of individuals in each generation of the population must always be n. Thus, in implementing the GAs, the application of the genetic operators, selection, crossover, and mutation yields n children that, for the basic GA, comprise the next generation. For the augmented GA a further operator, election, is applied to these children to give the next generation.

The GAs begin with an initial population that is generated randomly, and the algorithms are then applied iteratively for T generations. To accommodate the cobweb model, after the members of the generation labeled by t have been determined, their production decisions are aggregated and the market price p_t is calculated with Eq. (13.5). This value of p_t is inserted in the fitness function

Table 13.1. *Parameter values of the cobweb model used in GA simulations*

Parameters	A	B	x	y
Stable	2.184	0.0152	0	0.016
Unstable	2.296	0.016	0	0.016

Table 13.2. *Crossover and mutation rates used in GA simulations*

Set	1	2	3	4	5	6	7	8
p_{cross}	0.6	0.6	0.75	0.7	0.9	0.9	0.3	0.3
p_{mut}	0.0033	0.033	0.0033	0.033	0.0033	0.033	0.0033	0.033

given by Eq. (13.7), which is then used in the algorithm to determine the members in the generation $t + 1$.

3 Results of the simulations

The simulations reported here were conducted for the two sets of parameter values for the cobweb model given in Table 13.1, with our basic and augmented GAs. The equilibrium prices and quantities for these values are easily calculated from Eqs. (13.6). In each case $p^* = 1.12$ and $Q^* = 70$.

These particular values were chosen because they are the values used by Arifovic in her simulations that originated from the experiments of Wellford. One set is stable in the sense described in Section 1 and the other is unstable. The eight different sets of crossover and mutation rates are given in Table 13.2. These crossover and mutation rates are those used by Arifovic.

Arifovic conducted simulations by using her GAs and obtained results that were essentially the same for both the single-population and multipopulation designs. She found that the simulations with the basic GA did not converge to the equilibrium values in any simulation, in contrast to the augmented GA for which every simulation converged to the equilibrium values.

In line with the simulations of Arifovic, each of our simulations was conducted for 200 periods. Our results, which are given in Table 13.3, broadly confirm her findings but are, however, much smoother. We also have found that our augmented GA always converges to the equilibrium values but that with the basic GA this result is not guaranteed.

The price patterns resulting from a simulation of the cobweb model made with the parameter values given in Table 13.1 for the unstable case and for the first set of genetic operator rates ($p_{\text{cross}} = 0.6$ and $p_{\text{mut}} = 0.0033$) are illustrated in Fig. 13.1.

Table 13.3. *Results of the simulations*

GA set		1	2	3	4	5	6	7	8
Basic	$\bar{P}$	1.1559	1.236	1.1863	1.2587	1.1823	1.2713	1.1642	1.1785
stable	δ	0.0301	0.0608	0.0321	0.059	0.0358	0.0586	0.0254	0.0525
	δ_R	0.0631	0.1324	0.079	0.1515	0.0744	0.1629	0.0616	0.0806
Basic	$\bar{P}$	1.1619	1.2552	1.196	1.2801	1.1948	1.2972	1.1701	1.198
unstable	δ	0.034	0.0669	0.0361	0.064	0.0412	0.0659	0.0278	0.0601
	δ_R	0.0712	0.1526	0.0899	0.1731	0.0884	0.1898	0.0689	0.1006
Augment	$\bar{P}$	1.1201	1.1201	1.1201	1.1201	1.1201	1.1201	1.1201	1.1201
stable	δ	0.0029	0.0029	0.0029	0.0029	0.0025	0.0025	0.0028	0.0029
	δ_R	0.0029	0.0029	0.0029	0.0029	0.0025	0.0025	0.0028	0.0029
Augment	$\bar{P}$	1.1201	1.1201	1.1201	1.12	1.1201	1.1201	1.1201	1.1201
unstable	δ	0.0033	0.0034	0.0032	0.0031	0.0028	0.0028	0.0033	0.0033
	δ_R	0.0033	0.0034	0.0032	0.0031	0.0028	0.0028	0.0033	0.0033

Note: $\bar{P}$ = average price of a simulation (200 periods), δ = standard deviation about the average price of the simulation, δ_R = standard deviation about the equilibrium price.

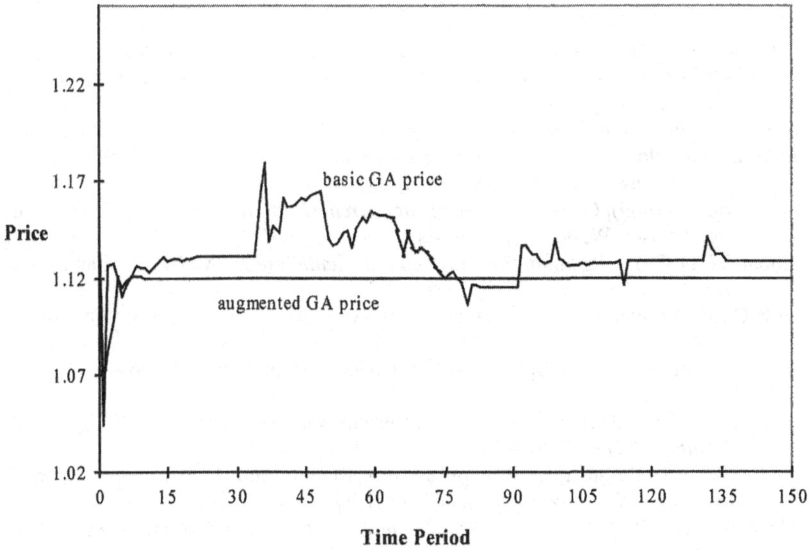

Figure 13.1. Basic and augmented GA price patterns – 7th set of the cobweb model parameter values, 1st set of genetic operator rates.

4 Conclusions

In advance it was an open possibility that the substantial changes to crossover and mutation we have introduced might produce very different looking results from those of Arifovic. In fact, in a broad aspect the results of our simulations are similar. Although the level of the plots is similar to that arising from the simulations of Arifovic, the plots are much less jagged. This fits with our remarks on averaging and is also, we believe, more appropriate in an economic context. This suggests that the GA is very robust indeed. It also shows that the results of Arifovic persist when the underlying genetic ideas are more closely translated into economic equivalents.

REFERENCES

Arifovic, A. (1994). Genetic algorithm learning and the cobweb model. *J. Econ. Dyn. and Control*, **18**, 3–27.

Beasley, D., Bull, D., and Martin, R. (1993a). An overview of genetic algorithms: part 1, fundamentals. *Univ. Comput.*, **15**, 58–69.

(1993b). An overview of genetic algorithms: part 2, research topic. *Univ. Comput.*, **15**, 170–81.

Carlson, J. A. (1967). The stability of an experimental market with a supply-response lag. *South. Econ. J.*, **33**, 305–21.

(1968). An invariably stable cobweb model. *Rev. Econ. Stud.*, **35**, 360–62.

Chiarella, C. (1988). The cobweb model: its instability and the onset of chaos. *Econ. Model.*, **5**, 377–84.

(1990). *The Elements of a Nonlinear Theory of Economic Dynamics*, Vol. 343 of Springer-Verlag Lecture Notes in Economics and Mathematical Systems Series, Springer-Verlag, New York.

Davis, L. (1991). *Handbook of Genetic Algorithms*, Van Nostrand Reinhold, New York.

Dawid, H. (1996). *Adaptive Learning by Genetic Algorithms: Analytic Results and Applications to Economic Models*, Springer-Verlag, New York.

Goldberg, D. (1989). *Genetic Algorithms in Search, Optimization and Machine Learning*, Addison-Wesley, Reading, Mass.

Holland, J. (1975). *Adaptation in Natural and Artificial Systems*, MIT Press, Cambridge, MA.

Holt, C., and Williamil, A. (1986). A laboratory experiment with a single-person cobweb. *Atlantic Econ. J.*, **219**, 51–54.

Jenson, R., and Urban, R. (1984). Chaotic behavior in a non-linear cobweb model. *Econ. Lett.*, **15**, 235–40.

Leontief, W. W. (1934). Verzögerte Angebotsanpassing und partielles Gleichgewicht. *Z. Nationalökon.*, **5**, 670–76.

(1966). Delayed adjustment of supply and partial equilibrium. In *Essays in Economics: Theories and Theorizing*, Oxford University Press, London.

Meadows, D. (1970). *Dynamics of Commodity Production Cycles*, Wright-Allen, Cambridge, MA.

Wellford, C. (1989). A laboratory analysis of price dynamics and expectations in the cobweb model, *Discussion paper 89-15*, University of Arizona, Tuscon, AZ.

CHAPTER 14

The convergence of genetic learning algorithms, with particular reference to recent cobweb models

C. E. M. Pearce

Since the publication of the seminal monograph of Holland (1975), genetic algorithms (GAs) have been used extensively to study the evolution of complex systems that embody learning behavior. The modeling power of GAs is very great, and the bibliography of Dawid's recent book (1996) mentions several other books and many research articles in this area and the closely allied field of simulated annealing. However, as Dawid commented, economists tend to use rather simple mathematical models to describe the learning behavior of rational agents so as to keep to situations that are analytically tractable.

A complication for applications in economics is that the payoff to an agent in even a single-commodity market depends on the actions of the rest of that market, that is, the fitness function in the GA is state dependent. Dawid appears to have been the first to have carried out a mathematical analysis of a GA with a state-dependent fitness function, which he does by using a modification of a Markov chain model of Nix and Vose (1992).

Dawid's primary result is that as the mutation probability in a GA tends to zero, its stationary distribution converges to one in which the probability is concentrated on states that are uniform, that is, all strings in the population have equal bit values. He argues further that uniform states are the appropriate ones to exhibit a natural economic equilibrium.

This result may be viewed as a refinement of a theorem of Rudolph (1994), who shows that a GA with strictly positive mutation probability does not converge to any uniform state.

The aim in this chapter is to indicate how some of the basic results relating to nonconvergence in GAs hold in a much more general setting than has been subject previously to mathematical analysis. For a focused discussion, particular reference is made to the use of GAs in connection with cobweb models, for

The author thanks an anonymous referee for helpful comments made on an earlier draft of this article.

which some interesting generalizations have been made recently. A heuristic discussion is given of the convergence results obtained numerically by Gaffney et al. (2000).

1 Cobweb models

Cobweb models have been used for over half a century to describe the evolution of the market price and the volume of production for a single commodity for which there is a significant supply-response lag. Economic agents make production decisions for the next market with the intention of maximizing profit. The actual price depends on the quantity of the commodity produced, which in turn depends on a prediction as to what price will apply. For a comprehensive review of the literature on cobweb models up to 1990 see Chiarella (1990).

Recently a GA and a related augmented genetic algorithm (AGA) have been used by Arifovic (1994) in single-population and multipopulation models for the learning process involved in making successive price predictions. This important paper receives a number of references in Dawid's book. The key ideas involved in the single-population model are discussed in this volume in a companion chapter by Gaffney et al. and accordingly is given in outline only. Arifovic provided motivation for the use of GAs in this context and noted some earlier applications in economics. She found that a GA could capture several features of the experimental behavior of human subjects better than three other learning algorithms. The parameter values she took were chosen in accordance with experimental values that had been obtained by Wellford (1989). With these, prices and quantities converged to the rational-expectation equilibrium values for all parameter choices when the AGA was used, but failed to converge for the basic GA.

Gaffney et al. replace the operation of crossover with simple arithmetic averaging of the two quantities selected at random from the population at time t as potential parents for an individual at time $t+1$. A value is chosen at random in accordance with a uniform distribution to effect the phenomenon of mutation. It is argued that this somewhat dramatic substitution better translates the underlying genetic ideas into an economic context. The work breaks further fresh ground in that predicted prices may depend on the past history of the market and in that the state space used has infinitely many states. Despite these differences, the convergence results obtained are the same as those of Arifovic, although the plots are much smoother. These results are beyond the scope of extant theory in the literature.

This raises the question of the generality of these results. For what ranges of parameter values do they hold? And what other variants of the GA procedure give the same or similar results? These questions are of interest in a general economic setting because of the growing use of GAs.

It turns out that some of the observed behavior stems from quite general structural considerations for which much of the specific detail of the papers cited above is irrelevant. In Section 2 the single-population GA of Arifovic and Gaffney et al. is recapitulated, the key ingredients are isolated, and generalized versions of their models are presented. In Section 3 two theorems for the basic GA are established. These show that, under conditions of some generality, convergence to rational-expectation equilibrium values will not occur. In the rather special case of a state-independent fitness function (which does not cover the models of Arifovic or Gaffney et al.), it is possible to give a simple treatment of the convergence of the AGA under fairly general conditions. This is done in Section 4. The considerably richer and more interesting example of state-dependent fitness functions considered by Gaffney et al. is discussed heuristically in Section 5. Section 6 concludes with a review of the results.

2 GA models

Existing models

We consider first some existing GAs and dress them with an interpretation appropriate for use as cobweb models.

In a GA model, there is for each time $t = 0, 1, \ldots,$ a population of n quantities $\{q_{i,t};\ 1 \leq i \leq n\}$. In Arifovic and Gaffney et al., it is supposed that there is a fixed number n of economic agents who supply a commodity to the market at times $t = 0, 1, \ldots,$ and $q_{i,t}$ represents the quantity offered to the market by agent i at time t.

Customarily in a GA, $q_{i,t}$ is represented as a string $(a^1_{i,t}, a^2_{i,t}, \ldots, a^l_{i,t})$ of binary bits $a^r_{i,t} \in \{0, 1\}$. However, as noted by Beasley et al. (1993), it is more convenient for some applications to use strings of floating-point numbers. Gaffney et al. bypass the string representation completely and take the values $q_{i,t}$ as real numbers on an interval $[0, \bar{q}]$, where $\bar{q}$ denotes the maximum quantity that can be produced and is chosen so that profits are nonnegative.

The quantities $q_{i,t} (i = 1, \ldots, n)$ are regarded as a population of "parents" or "chromosomes" at time t. The determination of the population at time $t+1$ is determined by three operations: selection, mutation, and crossover. In an AGA, as adopted by Arifovic and Gaffney et al., there is a further operation: election. We consider each of these operations in turn. Election is further addressed in Section 5.

Each individual at time $t+1$ arises from two parents chosen from the population at time t. Selection of parents from the current population for reproduction is done by probabilistic sampling. In Arifovic and Gaffney et al., each parent at time t is chosen independently from $\{q_{1,t}, \ldots, q_{n,t}\}$ in accordance with its genetic fitness. The choice $q_{i,t}$ is made with a probability $P(q_{i,t}; Q_t)$, where $Q_t = \sum_{i=1}^{n} q_{i,t}$.

The relative values of the probabilities reflect the relative profits these quantities earn in the market at time t. Arifovic and Gaffney et al. use a specific form for the (continuous) function, giving the cost of production in terms of $q_{i,t}$ and the prevailing price at time t. This is used in defining $P(q_{i,t}; Q_t)$.

In traditional GA models, if the parents of $q_{i,t+1}$ are $q_{j,t}$ and $q_{k,t}$, then crossover gives two offspring of the form $(a^1_{i,t+1}, a^2_{i,t+1}, \ldots, a^l_{i,t+1})$, where each $a^r_{i,t+1}$ is $a^r_{j,t+1}$ or $a^r_{k,t+1}$. The number of crossovers or alternations $a^r_{j,t+1}a^{r+1}_{k,t+1}$ or $a^r_{k,t+1}a^{r+1}_{j,t+1}$ in the offspring is determined randomly. By contrast, Gaffney et al. determine $q_{i,t+1}$ as $q_{i,t+1} = \frac{1}{2}[q_{j,t} + q_{k,t}]$.

A single offspring is produced from each averaging. Mutation in a conventional GA alters the chromosome of a child (or parent) by changing the values of one or more randomly chosen bits in the binary string. Mutations are rare. Beasley et al. suggest a typical mutation probability of 0.001 at a given position. Gaffney et al. replace a chromosome with one that is randomly generated in accordance with a uniform distribution on $[0, \bar{q}]$. Thus their model allows an infinite variety of possible values $q_{i,t}$ as opposed to a maximal number of 2^l in a binary chromosomic model.

Arifovic and Gaffney et al. assume a specific form for the cost of production to the ith producer that is quadratic in the quantity $q_{i,t}$ produced at time t. They show that when this applies, there is a unique quantity q^* in the interval $[0, \bar{q}]$ that is optimal in the sense that when each agent produces q^*, profits are maximized. This optimal quantity is central to the final operation, election, which applies in the AGA. In this, the effects of mutation for agent i operate only if they result in the making of a higher profit.

3 A general model

We now formulate a general, flexible GA model that allows for a variety of economically realistic models. We distinguish a discrete version, based on strings, and a continuous version in which individual values can take arbitrary values on an interval $[0, \bar{q}]$. To begin, we assume quite generally that an individual $q_{i,t+1}$ in the population at time $t+1$ derives from m parents $(1 \le m \le n)$ selected from the population at time t. We order the parents and denote the jth parent by $q_{i,j,t} (1 \le j \le m)$.

With random selection for the parents of the ith individual at time t, as in existing models, all individuals at a given time are probabilistically equivalent. It is natural in the context of the cobweb model to posit some sort of continuing identity to the ith agent. Invoking an ordered parentage enables us to achieve such a continuing identity, say by making $q_{i,t}$ the first parent of $q_{i,t+1}$ and treating it specially under the various operations. In commercial transactions it is also natural to envisage each agent as being influenced by the actions of a number of other agents with whom he or she is in geographical contiguity or other relevant association. The notion of more than two parents is thus appropriate in an economic context just as two are appropriate in a strictly biological context.

We remark parenthetically that our model allows more flexibility even in the standard case $m = 2$ of two parents. The usual choice of two parents randomly selected in accordance with genetic fitness actually allows those parents to coincide. Our present choice allows us to preclude this if we wish and also to introduce an asymmetry in respect to the selection of the two parents. This is useful in connection with modeling sex-linked characteristics by use of GAs.

We may associate a general selection procedure with multiparentage. Suppose that $\omega_{i,t+1} := [\omega_{i,t+1}(1), \ldots, \omega_{i,t+1}(m)]$ denotes an ordered m-tuple of elements chosen from $\{1, 2, \ldots, n\}$, possibly with repetitions. We assume that the parents of $q_{i,t+1}$ are given by $\omega_{i,t+1}$ with probability $\nu(i, \omega_{i,t+1})$. This probability can depend on both i and on any of the quantities produced and prices holding up to time t. General mechanisms may be used for regulating how the child is produced once the parents have been selected. With the discrete version, we may specify crossover rules that involve both stochastic and deterministic ingredients. With the continuous version, it is natural to work in terms of general weighted arithmetic averages. In this case we take

$$q_{i,t+1} = \sum_{j=1}^{m} \lambda_{i,j,t}(\omega_{i,t+1}) q_{i,j,t},$$

where $\lambda_{i,j,t} \geq 0$ and $\sum_j \lambda_{i,j,t} = 1$.

Here the value of $\lambda_{i,j,t}(\omega_{i,t+1})$ may depend in a quite complicated way on the entire past history of the evolution of the market.

For mutation, we proceed differently in the discrete and the continuous models. With the discrete model, we assume the following.

Condition 1. *There is at least one string q_1^* and a positive number ρ such that every string (other than q_1^*) has a probability of at least ρ of mutating to q_1^*.*

For the continuous model, we use an analogous assumption.

Condition 2. *There is a value $q_1^* \leq \bar{q}$ and a function $\gamma(\cdot)$ taking positive values for real, positive arguments with the following property. If $I \subset [0, \bar{q}]$ is an interval of length δ that contains q_1^*, then the probability of mutation to a value in I is at least $\gamma(\delta)$ for every $\gamma(\delta)$ for every $q_{i,t} \neq q_1^*$.*

These conditions permit the mutation rates to depend on both time and on the history of the market process up to time t.

We remark that in Arifovic, Condition 1 holds for every string, whereas in Gaffney et al., Condition 2 holds for every $q_1^* \in [0, \bar{q}]$.

Finally, we address election, which applies to the AGA. For each i, this depends on a fitness function, which is a scalar function $f_i(q) = f_i(q; q_{1,t}, q_{2,t}, \ldots, q_{n,t})$. In Section 4, we consider the special case in which $f_i = f$ and introduce Conditions 3 and 4 below. In Section 5 we treat the state-dependent model of Gaffney et al. The next condition relates to the discrete AGA.

Condition 3. *The function f has a unique maximum, which is achieved only when $q_{i,t} = q^*$ for $1 \le i \le n$, for a unique value q^*.*

A slightly stronger assumption is made for the continuous AGA.

Condition 4. *Condition 3 applies. In addition, for all $\varepsilon > 0$ sufficiently small, the ordered sequences of values $(q_{1,t}, q_{2,t}, \ldots, q_{n,t})$ for which $|f(q^*, q^*, \ldots, q^*) - f(q_{1,t}, q_{2,t}, \ldots, q_{n,t})| < \varepsilon$ form a convex set B_ε that is symmetric in its coordinates and the diameter of which tends to zero as $\varepsilon \to 0$.*

4 GA results

The method of proof in our first result involves a modification of the second Borel–Cantelli lemma (see Feller 1950, Chap. 3). The variant we produce does not require the usual assumption of independence.

Theorem 1. *Suppose that Condition 2 holds in the continuous GA and choose $\varepsilon > 0$. Then with probability one, $|q_{i,t} - q_1^*| < \varepsilon$ for all $i = 1, \ldots, n$ occurs for infinitely many values of t.*

Proof: Any individual at time $t + 1$ suffers a mutation to cause $q_{i,t+1} \in [q_1^* - \varepsilon, q_1^* + \varepsilon]$ to occur with probability at least $\gamma(2\varepsilon)$. Hence the event $A_t \equiv \{q_{i,t+1} \in [q^* - \varepsilon, q^* + \varepsilon]\}$ for $\{i = 1 \ldots, n\}$ occurs with probability at least $[\gamma(2\varepsilon)]^n$. This occurs regardless of what mutations occur at other time points. □

The events A_t are not independent, but if B_t is the sigma algebra generated by the history of the process up to time t, then the conditional probability $P(A_t|B_t)$ satisfies $P(A_t|B_t) = E[I(A_t)|B_t] \ge [\rho\gamma(2\varepsilon)]^n = p_\varepsilon$, say. In particular $P[A_t|(\bigcup_{s=1}^{t-1} A_s)^c] \ge p_\varepsilon$. Thus

$$\begin{aligned} P\left(\bigcup_{s=1}^{t} A_s\right) &= P\left(\bigcup_{s=1}^{t-1} A_s\right) + P\left(A_t \Big\backslash \bigcup_{s=1}^{t-1} A_s\right) \\ &= P\left(\bigcup_{s=1}^{t-1} A_s\right) + P\left[A_t \,\Bigg|\, \left(\bigcup_{s=1}^{t-1} A_s\right)^c\right] P\left[\left(\bigcup_{s=1}^{t-1} A_s\right)^c\right] \\ &\ge P\left(\bigcup_{s=1}^{t-1} A_s\right) + p_\varepsilon \left[1 - P\left(\bigcup_{s=1}^{t-1} A_s\right)\right]. \end{aligned}$$

Let $P(\bigcup_{s=1}^{\infty} A_s) = x > 0$. Take $0 < \delta < x$. Then we may choose t sufficiently large that $x - \delta < P(\bigcup_{s=1}^{t-1} A_s) \leq x$. Hence, by Theorem 1, $x \geq p_\varepsilon + (1-p_\varepsilon)(x-\delta)$ or $x \geq 1 - [(1-p_\varepsilon)/p_\varepsilon]\delta$. As this is true for $\delta > 0$ arbitrarily small, we must have $x = 1$.

Thus with probability one at least one of the events A_t occurs. Suppose A_T occurs. An exactly similar argument shows that with probability one, A_t occurs for at least one $t > T$. We deduce that with probability one A_t occurs for denumerably many values of t.

Corollary 1. *If Condition 2 is satisfied in a continuous GA for two distinct values q_1^*, q_2^*, then it cannot happen that $\{q_{i,t}\}$ converges almost surely to any value q^* as $t \to \infty$.*

Proof: By Theorem 1, the sequence $\{q_{i,t}\}$ has two distinct points of accumulation q_1^*, q_2^*, which contradicts its almost sure convergence to any point value.

Similar results hold for the discrete version of the GA, with the difference that we may take ε as zero throughout. □

Theorem 2. *Suppose Condition 1 holds in the discrete GA. Then with probability one the event $q_{i,t} = q_1^*$ for all $i = 1, \ldots, n$ occurs for infinitely many values of t.*

Proof: The proof is that of Theorem 1, mutatis mutandis. □

As with Corollary 1, we may deduce the following.

Corollary 2. *If Condition 1 is satisfied in the discrete GA for two distinct values q_1^*, q_2^*, then it cannot happen that $\{q_{i,t}\}$ converges almost surely to any value q^* as $t \to \infty$.*

5 AGA results: the state-independent case

We now address some restricted situations involving a state-independent fitness function, in which almost sure convergence to point values does occur.

Theorem 3. *Suppose Condition 4 holds in the continuous AGA. Then $q_{i,t} \to q^*$ $(i = 1, \ldots, n)$ with probability one as $t \to \infty$.*

Proof: Choose $\varepsilon > 0$ sufficiently small that Condition 4 applies. Arguing as in Theorem 1, we have with probability one that there exists a time t for which $(q_{1,t}, q_{2,t}, \ldots, q_{n,t}) \in B_\varepsilon$. In the absence of mutations, offspring are produced by arithmetic averaging and so the population at time $t+1$ will also lie in B_ε.

On the other hand, if mutation produces a value outside B_ε, then the election operation suppresses that mutation. Hence $(q_{1,s}, q_{2,s}, \ldots, q_{n,s}) \in B_\varepsilon$ for all times $s \geq t$. This holds for each $\varepsilon > 0$, and by its meaning $B_\eta \subset B_\varepsilon$ if $0 < \eta < \varepsilon$. Also, it is implicit in Condition 4 that $B_\varepsilon \to \{(q^*, q^*, \ldots, q^*)\}$ as $\varepsilon \to 0$. The result follows. □

A slightly strengthened conclusion is available for the discrete AGA.

Theorem 4. *Suppose that Condition 3 holds in the discrete AGA. Then with probability one $q_{i,t} = q^*$ $(i = 1, \ldots, n)$ for all t sufficiently large.*

Proof: As in Section 4, with probability one $(q_{1,t}, q_{2,t}, \ldots, q_{n,t}) = (q^*, \ldots, q^*)$ occurs for some t. In the absence of mutation, the population at time $t+1$ is also $(q^*, \ldots, q^*)$. By Condition 3, any mutation produces a value that is suppressed by the election operation. The result follows. □

6 AGA convergence: an heuristic

We now consider the augmented algorithm adopted by Gaffney et al. Here the market price p_t obtaining at time $t = 0, 1, 2, \ldots,$ is given in terms of the total amount Q_t produced for the market at time t by a linear relation $p_t = A - BQ_t$. For $i = 1, \ldots, n$, agent i produces an amount $q_{i,t}$ for the market at time t, so that $Q_t = \sum_{i=1}^n q_{i,t}$. The net profit realized by the ith agent in the tth market takes a functional form

$$\begin{aligned}\mu_t(q_{i,t}) &= p_t q_{i,t} - x q_{i,t} - \frac{1}{2} y n q_{i,t}^2 \\ &= \left(A - x - BQ_t - \frac{1}{2} y n q_{i,t}\right) q_{i,t},\end{aligned}$$

which is called the fitness of $q_{i,t}$ at time t. In the above, A, B, x, and y are all positive and it is implicit that the quantities $q_{i,t}$ take nonnegative values such that p_t and $\mu_t(q_{i,t})$ are positive, with each value $q_{i,t}$ lying on an interval $(0, \bar{q})$. For convenience the notation is slightly compressed, as, in fact, $\mu_t(q_{i,t}) = \mu(q_{i,t}; Q_t)$.

The quantities $q_{i,t+1} (i = 1, \ldots, n)$ produced for the market at time $t+1$ are determined from the quantities $q_{i,t} (i = 1, \ldots, n)$ as follows.

First, for each i, a pair of potential parents is chosen by random selection (with replacement) in accordance with the respective probabilities $\phi_t(q_{i,t}) = \mu_t(q_{i,t}) / \sum_{j=1}^n \mu_t(q_{j,t})$. This pair of parents, $q_{k,t}$ and $q_{l,t}$, say, gives rise to an offspring value $(q_{k,t} + q_{l,t})/2$. With a small mutation probability p_m, this quantity is further replaced with a value chosen at random in accordance with the uniform distribution on $(0, \bar{q})$.

Finally, the device of election is applied. The offspring q produced by the procedure outlined in the preceding paragraph would, if it had occurred in place of $q_{i,t}$ in the previous market, have had a potential fitness $\mu_{i,t}(q) = [A - x - B(Q_t - q_{i,t} + q) - \frac{1}{2}ynq]q$ that varies from one choice of $q_{i,t}$ to another. Again $\mu_{i,t}(q)$ is actually $\mu(q; q_{i,t}; Q_t)$. The election operator applies by choosing

$$q_{i,t+1} = \begin{cases} q & \text{if } \mu_{i,t}(q) > \mu_{i,t} \\ q_{i,t} & \text{otherwise} \end{cases}.$$

A proper study of the dynamical system prescribing the probabilistic evolution of the vector sequence $(q_{1,t}, \ldots, q_{n,t})_{t \geq 0}$ is beyond the space limitations of this chapter. We confine ourselves to a heuristic account of it.

The fitness $\mu_{i,t}(q)$ is a strictly convex function of q with a unique maximum at the value $q^*_{i,t+1}$ given by $\mathrm{d}/\mathrm{d}q\,\mu_{i,t}(q) = 0$, that is, $A - x - B(Q_t - q_{i,t}) - (2B + yn)q^*_{i,t+1} = 0$ or $q^*_{i,t+1} = \{[A - x - B(Q_t - q_{i,t})]/(2B + yn)\}$.

The inequality $\mu_{i,t}(q) > \mu_t(q_{i,t})$ obtains if and only if q lies between the roots of the quadratic equation $\mu_{i,t}(q) - \mu_t(q_{i,t}) = 0$, that is, between $q = q_{i,t}$ and

$$q = \frac{A - x - B(Q_t - q_{i,t})}{B + \frac{1}{2}yn} - q_{i,t} = 2q^*_{i,t+1} - q_{i,t}.$$

Thus those values q potentially fitter than $q_{i,t}$ at time t are precisely those values making up the open interval with midpoint $q^*_{i,t+1}$ and having $q_{i,t}$ as one end point. The fitness function has its maximum at the midpoint and decreases symmetrically as one moves toward the end points.

Put

$$\lambda_t = \frac{A - x - BQ_t}{B + yn}. \tag{14.1}$$

A simple calculation gives

$$2q^*_{i,t+1} - q_{i,t} = a(\lambda_t - q_{i,t}), \tag{14.2}$$

where $a = (B + yn)/(2B + yn)$. It follows that $q^*_{i,t+1} > q_{i,t}$ if $q_{i,t} < \lambda_t$ and $q^*_{i,t+1} < q_{i,t}$ if $q_{i,t} > \lambda_t$. Further, the whole interval of values potentially fitter than $q_{i,t}$ at time t lie on the same side of λ_t as does $q_{i,t}$, and the interval is shorter the closer $q_{i,t}$ is to λ_t.

Suppose that at time t

$$\min_i q_{i,t} < \lambda_t, \quad \max_i q_{i,t} > \lambda_t. \tag{14.3}$$

If $q_{i,t} = \lambda_t$, then $q_{i,t+1} = \lambda_t$. If $q_{i,t} < \lambda_t$, then $q_{i,t} < q_{i,t+1}$ occurs with positive probability and $q_{i,t+1} < \lambda_t$, whereas if $q_{i,t} > \lambda_t$, then $q_{i,t} > q_{i,t+1}$ occurs with positive probability and $q_{i,t+1} > \lambda_t$.

Define $C_t = \{q_{1,t}, \ldots, q_{n,t}\}$ and $\mathrm{diam}(C_t) = \max_i q_{i,t} - \min_i q_{i,t}$. Then, conditional on inequalities (14.3), $\mathrm{diam}(C_{t+1}) \leq \mathrm{diam}(C_t)$ and $E[\mathrm{diam}(C_{t+1}| C_t)$ satisfies inequalities (14.3)] $< \mathrm{diam}(C_t)$.

If inequalities (14.3) are not satisfied, then either

$$q_{i,t} \leq q_{i,t+1} \leq \lambda_t, \quad \forall i = 1, \ldots, n, \tag{14.4}$$

or

$$q_{i,t} \geq q_{i,t+1} \geq \lambda_t, \quad \forall i = 1, \ldots, n. \tag{14.5}$$

In the former case it can happen that $\mathrm{diam}(C_{t+1}) > \mathrm{diam}(C_t)$. However, this is not what tends to happen. If there are at least two distinct values $q_{i,t}$, then the width of the interval that election permits for $q_{i,t+1}$ is strictly greater for any $q_{i,t}$ satisfying $q_{i,t} = \min_j q_{j,t}$ than for any $q_{i,t}$ that does not. Further, any $q_{i,t}$ with $q_{i,t} = \max_j q_{j,t}$ can increase only by mutation (and not even that if $q_{i,t} = \lambda_t$) whereas the former may also be able to increase by averaging. Hence, unless C_t involves only one distinct point, we are led to anticipate that the expectation of $\mathrm{diam}(C_{t+1})$ conditional on C_t will be strictly less than $\mathrm{diam}(C_t)$ with probability one. A similar argument applies when relation (14.5) holds.

Thus setting aside for the moment the possibility of C_t consisting of a single distinct point, we expect $\mathrm{diam}(C_t)$ to keep decreasing on averaging. The wording about conditional expectations suggests a supermartingale argument to demonstrate that the sequence $[\mathrm{diam}(C_t)]_{t\geq 0}$ converges to a limiting value as $t \to 0$ with probability one.

When C_t lies entirely below λ_t, then $q_{i,t} \leq q_{i,t+1}$ so that $Q_{t+1} \geq Q_t$ and consequently $\lambda_{t+1} \leq \lambda_t$. This may bring about the situation in which C_{t+1} spans both sides of λ_{t+1} and so there is no possibility that $\mathrm{diam}(C_{t+2}) > \mathrm{diam}(C_{t+1})$. A similar remark applies when C_t lies entirely above λ_t.

Somewhat delicate estimates are required if we are to establish rigorously that in fact $\mathrm{diam}(C_t) \to 0$ with probability one as $t \to \infty$. We do not dwell further on this point here but instead pursue the implications of this line of inference. At this point we allow again the suspended possibility that C_t contains just a single distinct value, which we now recognize as just a particular instance of the situation with $\mathrm{diam}(C_t) \to 0$ with probability one as $t \to \infty$.

As averaging and election can only leave the values $q_{i,t}$ unaffected or bring them closer together, the process will spend very long periods in almost uniform states with which for each succeeding t the set C_t assumes a close cluster of values of, on average, nonincreasing diameter. Such periods are interrupted by rare mutations that provide the possibility of fresh genetic material and have the effect of disrupting the cluster, allowing it to reform about a center that moves closer to λ_t.

It might be thought that the effect of mutation would be to reduce continually the separation between the cluster center Q_t/n at time t and λ_t to zero as $t \to \infty$. However, this cannot be the case, as the discussion in Section 7 shows. Foreshadowing this, suppose, if possible, that $\lambda_t - Q_t/n \to 0$ with probability one as $t \to \infty$.

A consequence of Eq. (14.2) is that $q^*_{i,t+1} - q_{i,t} \to 0$ with probability one as $q_{i,t} - \lambda \to 0$ and so the probability of a mutation allowed by election tends to zero as $t \to \infty$. Asymptotically, with increasing time t, we then approach a stable situation with each $q_{i,t} \approx \lambda_t$. By Eq. (14.1) we then have $\lambda_t \approx [(A - x - Bn\lambda_t)/(+yn)]$ and so $q_{i,t} \approx \lambda_t \approx \{(A - x)/[B + n(B + y)]\} = q^\dagger$, say.

7 Discussion

In Theorems 1 and 2, no explicit consideration has been given to the usual detail of cobweb models: criteria for stability and instability, linearity or nonlinearity of the supply-and-demand functions, market clearing, and the form of price prediction. Indeed, we have not had occasion to consider prices explicitly at all! From a GA point of view, we have not needed to enter into particularities of the fitness function and the question of optimization until we reached Theorems 3 and 4. Further, the paucity of independence requirements means that our model embraces a wide spectrum of highly complicated special cases.

Although we have not discussed the point, some of the probabilities can themselves involve further processes. These features indicate that the results of Theorems 1 and 2 and their corollaries are very general ones. Theorems 1 and 2 indicate incidentally that in simulation work a naive stopping rule $|q_{i,t} - q'| < \varepsilon$ for $i = 1, \ldots, n$ would give misleading indications about convergence.

The dynamics discussed in Section 6 are reminiscent of the description by Dawid of a conventional GA. The process first moves toward a uniform state. It spends a lot of time near this, with occasional mutations providing a transfer from a regime near one uniform state to a regime near another.

The probability of mutation decreases as $t \to \infty$. However, this occurs only by virtue of changes of state with time; the mutation rate is actually a function of state. In this respect the AGA is not unlike simulated annealing. In simulated annealing, however, the rate of mutation proceeds to zero at a rate that is a suitable function of t.

Finally, we note that our limit $Q^\dagger$ is different from the rational expectations equilibrium $q^* = \{(A - x)/[n(B + y)]\}$ presented by Gaffney et al. by means of a deterministic analysis.

The parameters of Table 1 of Gaffney et al. give $q^* = 7/3$, $Q^* = 70$, $p^* = 1.120$ (all exactly) with $n = 30$ in both the Wellman stable and unstable parameter cases. This is in excellent agreement with the results of their simulations.

If it were the case that $q_{i,t} - \lambda_t \to 0\,(i = 1, \ldots, n)$ with probability one for $t \to \infty$, then we would have from the concluding discussion of Section 6 that $q_{i,t} \to q^\dagger$ with probability one as $t \to \infty$. Some calculations then give $q^\dagger = 2.296$, with limiting values $Q^\dagger = 68.88$ and $p^\dagger = 1.137$ in the Wellford stable case and $q^\dagger = 2.294$, $Q^\dagger = 68.82$, and $p^\dagger = 1.140$ in the Wellford unstable case. These values are quite at variance with the results of simulation.

We are thus given to expect the result $q_{i,t} \to \{(A - x)/[n(B + y)]\}$ $(i = 1, \ldots, n)$ with probability one as $t \to \infty$, which leads to $\lambda_t \to [(A - x)/(B + yn)][y/(B + y)]$ with probability one as $t \to \infty$.

REFERENCES

Arifovic, J. (1994). Genetic algorithm learning and the cobweb model. *J. Econ. Dyn. Control*, **18**, 3–27.

Beasley, D., Bull, D., and Martin, R. (1993). An overview of genetic algorithms: part 2, research topics. *Univ. Comput.*, **15**, 170–81.

Chiarella, C. (1990). *The Elements of a Nonlinear Theory of Economic Dynamics*, Vol. 343 of Springer-Verlag Lecture Notes in Economics and Mathematical Systems Series, Springer-Verlag, New York.

Dawid, H. (1996). *Adaptive Learning by Genetic Algorithms*, Springer, Berlin.

Feller, W. (1950). *An Introduction to Probability Theory and its Applications*, Wiley, New York, Vol. I.

Gaffney, J. M., Parrott, K., Pearce, C. E. M., and Salzborn, F. J. M. (2000). The cobweb model and a modified genetic algorithm. Chapter 13 of this volume.

Holland, J. H. (1975). *Adaptation in Natural and Artificial Systems: An Introductory Analysis with Applications to Biology, Control, and Artificial Intelligence*, MIT Press, Cambridge, MA.

Nix, A. E., and Vose, M. D. (1992). Modeling genetic algorithms with Markov chains. *Ann. Math. Artif. Intell.*, **5**, 79–88.

Rudolph, G. (1994). Convergence results of canonical genetic algorithms. IEEE *Trans. Neural Networks*, **5**, 96–101.

Wellford, C. P. (1989). A laboratory analysis of price dynamics and expectations in the cobweb model. Discussion Paper 89-15, University of Arizona, Tucson, AZ.

PART IV

Marketing and interdependent behavior

CHAPTER 15

A complex-systems simulation approach to evaluating plan-based and reactive trading strategies

Robert B. Johnston and John M. Betts

Should we plan for the future or should we react to the situation in which we find ourselves? Over the past decade this question has been increasingly asked in a number of academic disciplines and practitioner fields. It has arisen in the context of the design of autonomous systems, such as robots and software agents, in which the notion that systems based on reaction can achieve complex and robust behaviors has been argued forcefully by a group of workers (Brooks 1986, Agre and Chapman 1987, Agre 1988, Brooks 1991b) challenging the established planning-based paradigm (Fikes and Nilson 1971, Raphael 1976) that has proved to be computationally expensive and brittle (Brooks 1991a).

It has also arisen in the area of design of management systems (Johnston and Brennan 1996), particularly manufacturing operations systems (Johnston 1995), in which the influence of Japanese just-in-time reactive, or so-called pull, methods (Schonberger 1982, Monden 1983) have produced a strong challenge to western plan-based, or push, systems such as material requirements planning (MRP) (Orlicky 1975, Wight 1981) and optimized production technology, (Jacobs 1983, Goldratt 1988). Again the issue arises in inventory control (Jacobs and Whybark 1992) and in warehousing and physical distribution (Hummel and Stenger 1988). Even in strategic management the efficacy of planning has recently been challenged (Mintzberg 1994). The question is one of importance for management because planning systems generally require high levels of information technology investment and non-value-adding processes such as data collection.

The authors acknowledge financial assistance for this work from the Monash Research Fund, the Faculty of Information and Computer Technology, the Department of Business Systems, and the Institute for Research and Advancement in Public Services, (IRAP), Norwalk, CT, and we particularly thank Bernard Zimmern, President of IRAP, and Anthony Kitchener for their ongoing keen interest in, and generous support of, this project. We also thank an anonymous reviewer for helpful suggestions.

Plans hold out the prospect of a good or even optimal performance in a predictable world but, being information intensive, are costly to implement. They may also not fail gracefully if the present is not exactly as it was predicted in the past. In contrast, reactive systems promise to be simpler, able to take advantage of opportunities as they arise, and, although they are unlikely to achieve optimal results, they are likely to be more robust in a changing and complex world.

This chapter describes an attempt to answer the opening question within the context of trading and inventory replenishment by use of a multiagent complex-systems simulation. In this context, plan-based and reactive systems have been investigated with a number of methodologies. These include comparison of success cases (Aggarwal and Aggarwal 1985), conceptual analysis (Van Der Linden and Grunwald 1980, Schonberger 1983, Schmitt et al. 1985, DeToni et al. 1988, Grunwald et al. 1989), control theory (Walbank 1988), survey of industry adoption (Newman and Sridharan 1992), analytical modeling (Ettienne 1983), and simulation (Krajewski et al. 1987, Striekwold 1990, Jacobs and Whybark 1992). However, in most of these studies the issue at stake is not simply planning versus reacting but the comparison of production and inventory management philosophies that include other elements and techniques. This study is motivated by the desire to model the simplest inventory replenishment situation in which the planning and the reacting can be defined in order to gain insight into the trade-off that is involved in a choice between the two.

1 Modeling methodology

Traditional analytical and simulation approaches tend to make rather unrealistic, limited assumptions about the environment in which a firm acts and about the measures that are to be used to judge the policies. The standard approach is to model a single instance of a company's acting in a synthetically specified environment. The environment is either completely predictable (Ettienne 1983, Rees et al. 1989) or uncertainty is introduced stochastically by some distributional assumption (Fortuin 1981, Krajewski et al. 1987, Striekwold 1990, Jacobs and Whybark 1992). The environment is not influenced by the actions of the company, and it presents a limited range of situations to the company – uncertainty is not the same as variability. The usual objective of these studies is to find policy settings that achieve good, or preferably optimal, values of some utility variable.

In reality, the separation of agent and environment is not so clear cut – the environment of a given agent consists of the actions of other agents, similar or different in behavior. The consequent feedback results in complex and unpredictable interactions. A given agent may be presented with an environment that is not just uncertain but wildly changing over its lifetime so that survival, bringing with it issues of risk and robustness, becomes as important an issue as optimal performance. Resources are limited, introducing nonlinear effects that are difficult to model in the traditional approach. Finally, there is a population of agents of a given type that may show considerable dispersion in the effectiveness of a given strategy. All these effects are difficult to study in the traditional single-agent/synthetic-environment approach with the result that these studies tend to focus on the rather narrow criterion of optimizing some utility variable. Because we suspect that the planning/reacting issue is related to the relative importance that one places on optimality and robustness when dealing with a complex world, these studies may be biased toward a positive evaluation of planning because it would not be surprising if planning were generally a more optimal strategy.

Motivated by these shortcomings in the existing literature, the simulation study described here has two important novel features. First, it is a multiagent simulation in which a group of highly idealized trading agents interact directly by using planning or reactive strategies to trade a single generic product. Their own actions create a dynamic and complex environment in which they act, and measures other than optimality can be used to assess their relative performance. For instance, agent lifetime can be examined as a measure of the robustness of the agent's policy. The proportion of agents with a given policy in the population is a measure of the niche size for that policy. Variation in performance across a population by use of a policy can be examined as a measure of the risk of a policy.

Second, the study uses a parsimonious modeling approach. An attempt has been made to create the simplest model of interacting agents that includes all the features needed to create the phenomena under study and no more. These features include a population of agents, a simple activity – trading – that can be evaluated, simple policies to dictate the actions of the agents, feedback among the actions of different agents and among populations, an environment of tunable harshness generated self-referentially by the actions of the agents, competition, and the need to survive. The things that have been left out include production of the traded goods (see Bak et al. 1993), value adding, separate classes of producers and end consumers (see Vriend 1994), bargaining, price setting, and money, none of which seem to be central to the issue of planning and reacting.

Because the resulting model has a small number of free parameters, we have been able to vary each parameter, allowing confident statements to be made about the range of behavior exhibited by the model. The model may not bear a close resemblance to the real world but it is not our intention to make recommendations about what real companies should do in real situations. Rather, it allows us to make a thorough study of a model of the essential features of a real-world problem, so what is sacrificed in detail is made up for in generality.

2 Concepts and terminology of the simulation

The model consists of a collection of uniquely numbered agents who interact directly with each other through ordering and trading (rather than indirectly through a pricing mechanism). Each agent is both a vendor and a customer, trading in a single generic product. There is no value adding to the product and no separate class of raw-material producers or end consumers, the objective of the interaction being simply to trade with other agents as a vendor, necessitating the acquisition of product from other agents as a customer. Consequently, the amount of the product in the simulation is held fixed, with the product simply moving about among the agents. Agents also carry integer-valued buffer stocks of the product as a hedge against uncertainty. Note that the terms trading, vendor, and customer are being used in a rather nonstandard way in this paper owing to the absence of the notion of value.

Progress of the simulation through time is recorded by the current period number, and the product can be received by a customer only a certain lead time (specified globally as a number of periods) after the period in which ordering takes place. Agents make commitments to supply the product by means of a publicly accessible order file, the records of which store the vendor agent number, the customer agent number, the period for supply (determined by the lead time and the current period), and a sequential order number. Each order is for a single unit of the product. An order begins as a customer request for supply, with a filled customer number and blank vendor number. It becomes a firm commitment when an agent places his or her number on the order as a vendor. Some orders are never committed to and are eventually deleted.

The agents have no intelligence or learning – their ordering behavior is completely determined by certain agent-level policy settings and some global simulation parameters. The policy settings consist of a Boolean agent type (planner or reactor) and a safety-stock setting. The essential difference between the agent types is that planners enter into orders as customers for the future supply of product from other agents and also as vendors for the future supply of product to other agents when product arrives. Reactors, on the other hand, only commit to orders from other agents for supply of the product to maintain their safety-stock setting one lead time into the future and they can trade to only immediate demand. Planners uses a global setting of orders per period as the forecast demands and plan out to the first period in which the product can be supplied within the lead time. Reactors are not just planners with a short planning horizon: There is an essential difference in their approach to the future. Planner activity is based on a representation of complete future transactions contained in the order file. Reactor activity is directed to maintaining preparedness, and commitments to customers are made at the last moment.

At each new period, orders that fall due result in trades taking place. The trading process is exhaustive in the sense that chains of dependence in which an agent, because of lack of stock, requires the receipt of goods from a vendor order to supply another commitment are chased to a vendor who can supply, and then enacted. However, cyclic trading arrangements in which no agent has stock are not considered to result in valid trades. The number of successful trades that an agent conducts as a vendor is recorded on an agent file, as is the closing-period stock. Planned trades can fail to eventuate for two reasons: The vendor cannot supply because he or she has no current or expected stock, or the vendor no longer exists in the simulation (see below). In either case the agent can seek to obtain the stock that fails to arrive, because of a vendor default, from a reactor agent through an opportunistic trade. Thus reactors can trade goods as vendors only through the opportunistic trading mechanism.

An instantaneous turn rate is calculated each period and used as a measure of the ongoing performance of the agent. This turn rate is the number of trades per period divided by the period-end stock level. Turn rate appears to be an appropriate measure of trading performance because it measures the efficiency with which an agent uses his or her resources (stock) to create activity (trades). It is also a surrogate measure of return on investment, so judging policies by turn rate can be thought of as judging them by whether an investor would choose that policy.

Exponentially smoothed values for number of trades and period-end stock were experimented with in earlier versions of the simulation. However, this introduces the smoothing factor as an extra adjustable parameter for which there is no principled way to determine a value. It also necessitates a honeymoon period during which a new agent cannot be deleted so that the smoothing can pass the start-up transient. Smoothing also affects the turn-rate distribution, particularly its dispersion. The approach of using raw turn-rate values is simplest, and, in order to reduce the lumpiness of the turn-rate distribution, the largest practical values of the stock and the order parameters were used in these simulations.

Agents are terminated if their turn rate falls below a preset cutoff turn rate. Defaulting because of termination of agents who have commitments as vendors and customers into future periods and lack of available stock for all agents to fulfill the commitments made according to policy create the unpredictability of the planned future in the model. Accordingly, the global stock level, the cutoff turn rate, and the product lead time can be all used to tune the unpredictability, or harshness, of the trading environment. Because of their effect on connectivity of the web of commitments, the number of orders per period and the number of agents in the simulation are also found to influence harshness. The default rate, defined as the ratio of defaulting commitments to all trades, is found to be a good measure of environmental harshness and measures the dissimilarity between the present and that predicted when committing to orders.

3 Details of the algorithms

Following the choice of initial global parameters and policy settings of the initial population, at each period four major procedures are performed: trading, attrition, ordering, and committing, as shown in Fig. 15.1.

Trading procedure

A pass is made of the current period group in the order file. The stock situation and existence of the vendor is checked. If the vendor cannot supply the order because of lack of stock, or the vendor has been deleted earlier, the order is given a holding status that sorts it to the end of the current period group. If the order can be supplied, then the stock is moved and the vendor's statistics are updated. The customer now certainly has stock so a chain of order processing consequent on the supply of this stock is performed until an agent with no further commitments is reached. This chain includes orders that were formerly placed on hold because of lack of stock. Then main order pass is resumed. The process continues until only hold status orders remain in the current period group. The only orders that remain are those that cannot be supplied by the vendor, even allowing for further receipts by the vendor, which includes cyclic trading arrangements in which no vendor has any stock.

The customers of these orders can now be supplied by a reactor agent, rather than the original planned vendor, through an opportunistic trade. The agent file is searched for a reactor with stock, the trade is made, and the reactor's trade data are updated. The sequence in which the agents are checked is random and randomized between searches.

The trading algorithm is the most complex and processing-intensive part of the simulation. However, it is believed that this exhaustive approach to trading is desirable because it allows lean trading through a chain of commitments with little buffer stock to be rewarded.

Attrition procedure

Any agent whose instantaneous turn rate is below a globally set cutoff turn rate is deleted from the simulation. This results in any commitments made by that agent as a vendor or a customer not being honored. A new agent is created with a policy randomly chosen from the saved initial population, given a new agent number and the old agent's stock (to conserve stock) and introduced into the simulation population. The new agent is protected from deletion for a period equal to the product lead time as the agent cannot receive product as a customer in this period.

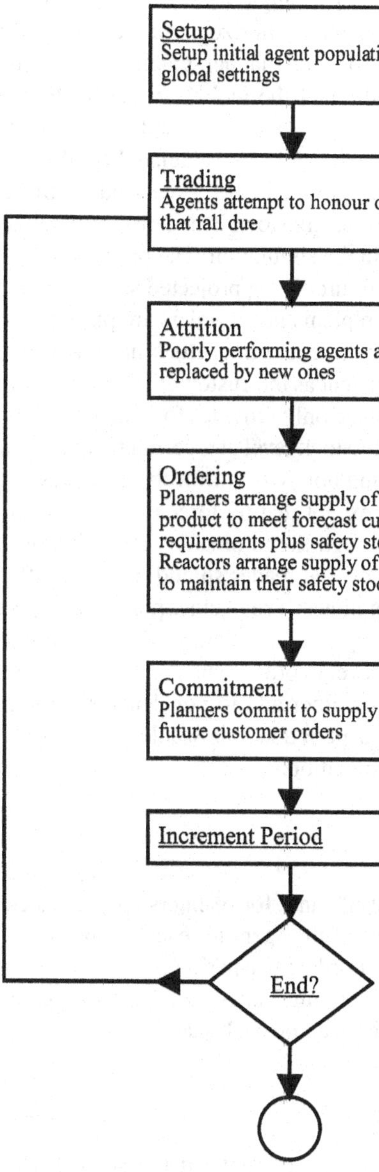

Figure 15.1. Schematic of the simulation program.

Ordering procedure

The ordering algorithm for planners is a single-level MRP calculation (Jacobs and Whybark 1992), based on a planning horizon equal to the lead time for the product, and the forecast that, for each planner, the number of orders filled as a customer in each period will equal the global setting of the number of orders per period. Starting from the actual stock on hand in the current period, a projected starting stock in the next period is calculated by the addition of expected receipts of goods and the subtraction of forecasted or firm customer orders for goods. If the projected starting stock is negative, it is replaced with zero, as there is no backordering in the simulation. The process is repeated out to the period a lead time into the future. If the projected stock in this period is less than the safety-stock setting, replenishment orders are placed on the order file in sufficient numbers to make projected final stock up to the safety-stock setting. These are orders with the agent as the customer and no vendor number.

For the reactors, the ordering stage only provides for placing orders to bring the projected stock up to the safety-stock level at a period that is one lead time into the future. The reactor ordering policy is thus of the base-stock type. The algorithm is as that for planners, except that no forecast of customer requirements is taken into account. Although the term safety stock is used for both reactor and planner ordering policy, the reader should note the different role that safety stock plays in the two policies: The planner policy attempts to maintain this level of stock as a hedge against uncertainty whereas the reactors are attempting to maintain this stock level in order to be prepared for opportunistic trades. Planners and reactors can neither add to nor delete orders in periods within the lead time of the current period as this would essentially eliminate the lead-time concept from the simulation.

Committing procedure

A pass is made through the agent file and, for planners only, a check is made on the current actual commitments of the agent for each period out to the lead time. If this is less than the global orders-per-period parameter, the order file is searched for orders to which to commit. This search is performed in random agent number sequence and randomized on each search.

4 Results and discussion

The results of 27 trials with the model are presented in this section. The purpose of these trials was to explore the parameter space of the model thoroughly by varying each free parameter of the simulation separately. To get sensible results for the distribution of the turn rate, which is a ratio of whole numbers, it is necessary to use rather large settings for orders per period and total stock. This affects the simulation time dramatically. Consequently a full factorial variation of all free parameters is out of the question. Instead, a standard parameter setting was chosen (trial 1) on the basis of previous trials that represented an environment of medium harshness, and each free parameter was varied, one at a time, through at least two settings, one each side of its standard setting.

The planner safety stock was not varied, as previous trials indicated that the ratio of average stock to safety stock, which controls the scarcity of stock, was the pertinent variable. Reactor safety stock has been varied from the planner value in some trials because, as noted in Section 3, safety stock has a different role for planners and reactors. In the starting population, each agent was given an equal stock. In keeping with the intention to vary one parameter at a time, the cutoff turn rates were adjusted in each trial to maintain a fixed proportion of the expected overall turn rate for the simulation, except in the trails in which the turn rate was the parameter being varied. The definition of expected turn rate used was orders per period divided by average stock per agent. The parameter settings used in the 27 trials are shown in Table 15.1 and derived statistics are given in Table 15.2. Apart from agent proportions used in Fig. 15.2, the data were not recorded until the 100th period to avoid the start-up transient. Only agents entering the simulation after that period were included in statistics. An instantaneous turn rate was recorded for every agent in every period between periods 200 and 400, and lifetime and lifetime turn-rate statistics were recorded as the agents were deleted.

Three characterizations of the relative fortunes of planners and reactors are now discussed. They are the proportion of reactors in the population, agent lifetimes, and agent turn rates. For each statistic, the results of six of the trials (18, 3, 1, 2, 14, 17) that represent a series of increasing environmental harshness controlled by the average stock available per agent in the simulation (10, 9, 7, 5, 3, 2 units, respectively) are discussed first. Another such series is available in the dataset with lead time as the harshness variable, and the results are very similar to those of the set presented. Then the conclusions drawn are checked against the full set of 27 trials in which harshness is altered when other parameters are varied.

Figure 15.2 shows the time-series data for the number of reactors in each simulation (there are 50 agents in the 6 trials). When there is sufficient stock for all agents to fulfill their policy (stock = 10 units), after a brief transient there are no order defaults and thus there are no reactors in the population. This is a predictable world, and the planners are all able to achieve their desired performance. As the available stock is decreased (stock = 9 units) not all planned orders can be fulfilled, which leads to increased defaulting and an opportunity for reactors to survive, initially in small numbers. Through the dynamics of the interaction, the proportion of reactors and planners is adjusted

Table 15.1. *Parameter settings for all trials*

Trial number	Stock per agent	Lead time	Orders per period	Number of agents	Cutoff proportional	Cutoff actual	Planner safety stock	Reactor safety stock
1	7	2	15	50	0.2	0.4286	10	10
2	5	2	15	50	0.2	0.6000	10	10
3	9	2	15	50	0.2	0.3333	10	10
4	7	1	15	50	0.2	0.4286	10	10
5	7	3	15	50	0.2	0.4286	10	10
6	7	4	15	50	0.2	0.4286	10	10
7	7	2	10	50	0.2	0.2857	10	10
8	7	2	20	50	0.2	0.5714	10	10
9	7	2	15	50	0.1	0.2143	10	10
10	7	2	15	50	0.3	0.6429	10	10
11	7	2	15	24	0.2	0.4286	10	10
12	7	2	15	100	0.2	0.4286	10	10
13	7	5	15	50	0.2	0.4286	10	10
14	3	2	15	50	0.2	1.0000	10	10
15	7	6	15	50	0.2	0.4286	10	10
16	7	7	15	50	0.2	0.4286	10	10
17	2	2	15	50	0.2	1.5000	10	10
18	10	2	15	50	0.2	0.3	10	10
19	7	2	15	50	0.2	0.4286	10	15
20	7	2	15	50	0.2	0.4286	10	5
21	7	2	15	50	0.2	0.4286	10	3
22	7	3	15	50	0.2	0.4286	10	5
23	7	3	15	50	0.2	0.4286	10	15
24	7	5	15	50	0.2	0.4286	10	5
25	7	5	15	50	0.2	0.4286	10	15
26	7	3	15	50	0.2	0.4286	10	3
27	7	5	15	50	0.2	0.4286	10	3

under the influence of a number of conflicting forces. The defaulting of planners increases the opportunity for reactors to do well. However, the presence of reactors also tends to repair the planner's policy by providing last-minute stock replenishment. The planner subpopulation needs to be small if the planners are all to fulfill their safety-stock requirement in the face of stock shortage. However, they can compete with the volatile reactors with less than perfect performance. The proportion of reactors increases steadily as the proportion of order defaults increases because of stock scarcity and reaches a maximum of 56% when stock is 3 units per agent. If stock is further reduced, eventually defaulting is so severe that neither planners nor reactors are able to replenish stock, and trading breaks down completely. The agent proportion then becomes identical to the replacement proportion of 50%. The results indicate that the

Table 15.2. *Derived statistics for all trials*

	Normalized lifetime turn rate				Lifetime						
	Planner		Reactor		Planner		Reactor		Proportions		
Run	med	iqr	med	iqr	med	iqr	med	iqr	Reactors	Defaults	Opportunity
1	0.81	0.21	0.37	0.47	31	58	3	6	0.12	0.12	0.04
2	0.26	0.23	0.29	0.52	1	2	1	3	0.4	0.4	0.16
3	0.98	0.09	0.45	0.42	186	199	1	4	0.01	0.02	0.01
4	0.86	0.09	0.28	0.33	20	37	2	6	0.14	0.1	0.05
5	0.14	0.18	0.31	0.7	1	1	1	3	0.51	0.58	0.27
6	0.06	0.14	0.42	2.1	1	1	0	2	0.56	0.76	0.35
7	0.81	0.18	0.27	0.37	19	43	2	4	0.11	0.12	0.04
8	0.81	0.15	0.74	1.33	38	83	5	8	0.1	0.11	0.03
9	0.77	0.19	0.26	0.29	26	47	4	9	0.15	0.13	0.05
10	0.29	0.24	0.26	0.31	1	0	1	2	0.41	0.39	0.17
11	0.78	0.20	0.45	0.54	28	71	2	8	0.08	0.11	0.03
12	0.79	0.19	0.42	0.75	28	49	4	7	0.13	0.13	0.04
13	0.02	0.11	0.79	186.67	0	1	0	2	0.53	0.83	0.34
14	0.13	0.20	0.3	1.69	1	1	0	2	0.56	0.63	0.28
15	0.01	0.09	0.84	233.33	0	1	0	1	0.52	0.88	0.31
16	0.01	0.09	1.17	326.67	0	1	0	2	0.49	0.9	0.25
17	0.09	0.15	0.53	93.33	0	1	0	1	0.53	0.67	0.23
18	1.00	0.00	N/A	N/A	∞	0	0	0	0	0	N/A
19	0.80	0.21	0.31	0.32	28	48	2	5	0.12	0.16	0.06
20	0.81	0.10	1.68	5.69	50	102	4	8	0.09	0.08	0.02
21	0.72	0.49	4.67	232.63	28	79	2	7	0.09	0.1	0.01
22	0.17	0.13	1.21	186.48	1	0	1	3	0.4	0.39	0.15
23	0.13	0.21	0.22	0.51	1	1	1	3	0.52	0.63	0.3
24	0.04	0.14	2.15	280	0	1	0	2	0.54	0.82	0.29
25	0.02	0.10	0.47	4.2	0	1	0	2	0.53	0.85	0.35
26	0.17	0.13	3.03	279.67	1	1	1	4	0.38	0.33	0.11
27	0.06	0.16	4.81	233.33	1	1	0	2	0.51	0.81	0.27

niche for reactor agents increases as the future becomes less predictable and peaks close to the complete breakdown of order.

Figure 15.3 shows the proportion of reactors in all 27 trials plotted against the proportion of defaulting trades. The results all lie close to a single curve, indicating quite clearly that the order default rate is the major explanatory variable. To a good approximation, each of the variables that affects environment harshness does so in the same way – by reducing the degree to which planned commitments are actually realized.

Figure 15.4 shows box plots of agent lifetimes for planners and reactors against the stock available per agent for the six trials. The lifetime plus one

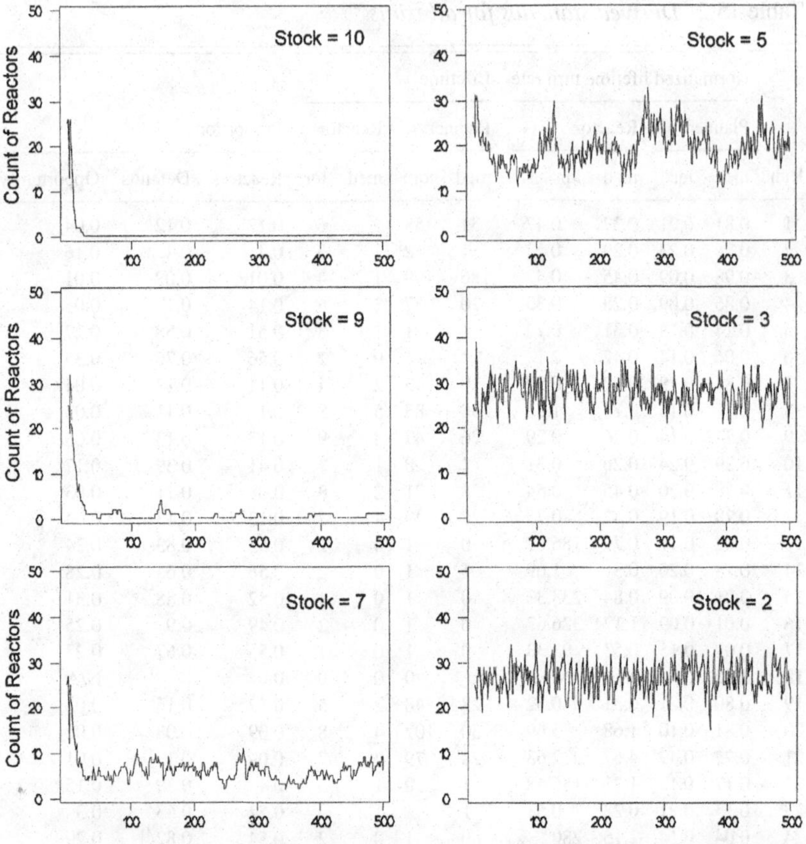

Figure 15.2. Time series of number of reactors for 500 periods for 6 values of stock per agent (trials 18, 3, 1, 2, 14, 17).

period is plotted on a logarithmic scale, and the box plots show lower quartile, median, upper quartile, and outliers. Agent lifetime is expected to be a good measure of policy robustness because it measures the ability of the policy to withstand the variety of situations that the environment presents to the agent. It is found that the lifetime of planner agents, which is infinite when stock is adequate, is strongly affected by the defaulting caused by stock scarcity. The robustness of the planning policy decreases rapidly as the world becomes less predictable. Reactors share their niche with other reactors in an essentially probabilistic manner so that uncertainty affects the number of reactors much more than their lifetime, which is rather short anyway.

Figure 15.5 shows the median lifetimes for planners and reactors against default rate, for all 27 trials. Again, within the limits of the discreteness of the

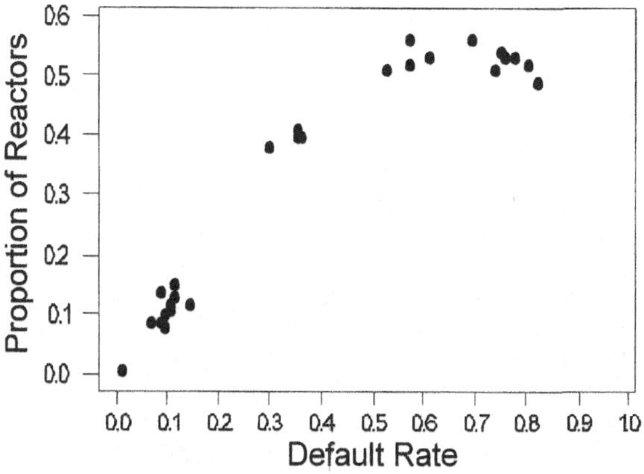

Figure 15.3. Proportion of reactors against default rate for all trials.

data, the points nearly fall on a single curve for each case. Therefore again it appears that policy type and default rate explain the data.

Now consider the turn rate achieved by agents who are using different policies. As with lifetime, a population of each variety of agent must be considered, with consequent spread in the turn rates achieved. Taking the turn rate to be a surrogate measure for the rate of return achieved by an investor's backing a randomly chosen agent from one of the two populations, then the central tendency of each population measures the expected rate of return and the dispersion of the population measures the risk of the investment. The tools of investment and portfolio analysis (Peirson et al. 1995) become appropriate to the choice between reacting and planning.

Figure 15.6 shows box plots of median lifetime turn rates for planners and reactors against average stock per agent. Turn rates are given as a ratio to the expected turn rate defined as number of orders per period divided by average stock per agent. When the lifetime turn rate is used, all dispersion is due to differences across the agent population whereas an instantaneous turn rate combines the variability across the population and along the lifetime of agents. Because the turn rate is a ratio, the data are skewed with a long upper tail. Turn rates tend asymptotically to infinity for agents who trade with little or no stock held between periods, i.e., just-in-time trading. Hence median and interquartile ranges have been used as the measures of central tendency and spread.

Consider first the median turn rate. For planners, the expected return in the early trials is close to that expected from the global parameter settings but as the environment becomes harsher and the future becomes less predictable, it falls off considerably. For the reactors, it remains approximately constant at just less than half the best planner rate for early trials and even appears to increase in the

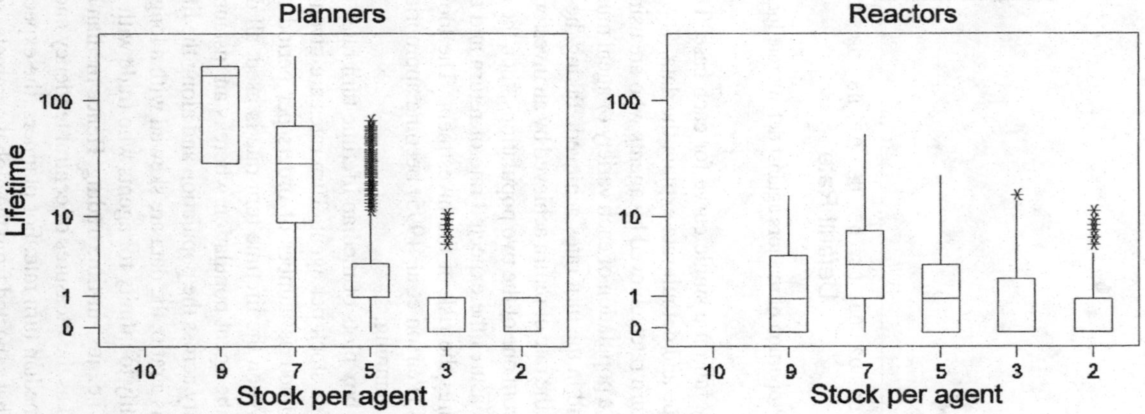

Figure 15.4. Lifetime against stock per agent (trials 18, 3, 1, 2, 14, 17).

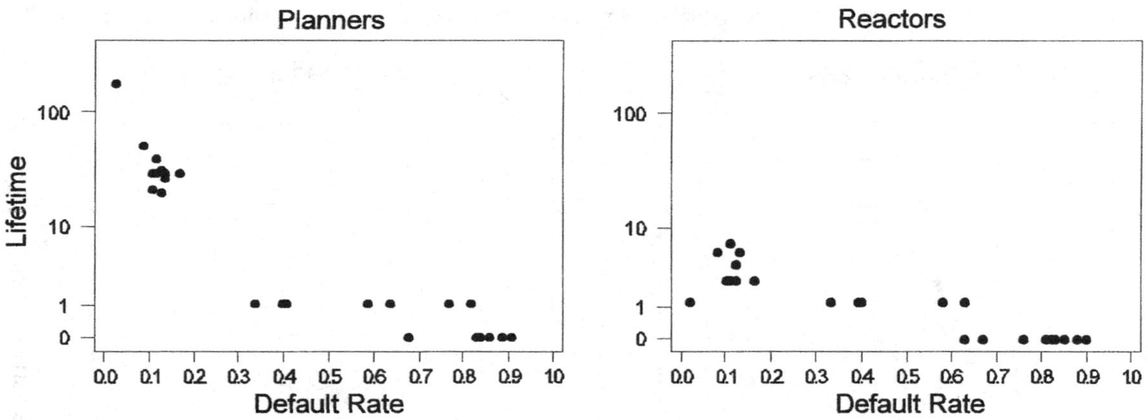

Figure 15.5. Lifetime against default rate for all trials.

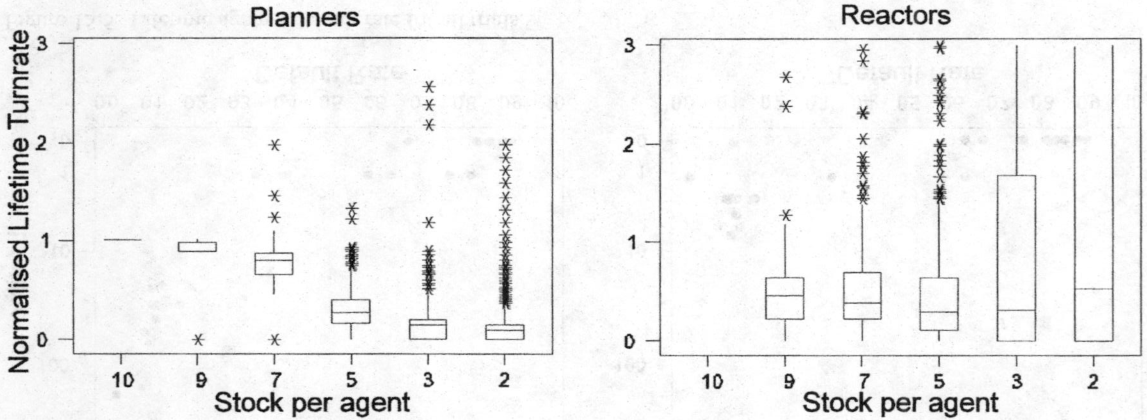

Figure 15.6. Median normalized lifetime turn rate against stock per agent (trials 18, 3, 1, 2, 14, 17).

harsher trials. Once again, reactors are less coupled to uncertainty than planners. Thus a risk-indifferent investor, who considers only expected return and not risk, would favor planning in the early trials and reactors in the harsher trials. However, it is normally assumed that the commercial investor is risk averting and the dispersion in returns, i.e., risk, must be considered as well. The planning policy is exceptionally risk free in the early trials in which the majority of agents achieve nearly all predicted trades, but the risk increases somewhat as the world get less predictable, as indicated by increased dispersion. For reacting the turn-rate spread is larger even in the early trials and gets very large as harshness increases. Although reacting maintains or improves its median performance as harshness is increased, it is an inherently risky policy and gets more so as predictability is lost. The risk-averse investor would be suspicious of the spread in outcomes of reacting in the early trials and would not be particularly enticed by the long tail of high returns because this investor assigns diminishing utility to high returns. However, as the expected return from planning decreases and its risk increases, the risk-averse investor would be less concerned with the risk of the reacting policy and more concerned with the diminishing returns of planning. It is not possible to say from the present data if there is a point at which reacting would be favored by a risk-averse investor, and this would depend on the precise indifference curves for the investor and the turn-rate distributions. On the other hand, the risk-seeking investor, or gambler, would be seduced by the long tail of the reactor distribution and would choose reacting in the harsher environments because large gains are assigned higher utility proportionally than small gains.

Figure 15.7 shows the median normalized turn rates for all 27 trials. In the preceding discussions the behavior of the model was largely explained by agent type and default rate with no apparent systematic effect of other parameter changes. Provided that the reactor safety stock is greater or equal to that of the planners, and apart from a certain spread in the reactor data, which appear to have no systematic relation to the parameters varied, once again for lifetime median turn rate the variables of policy type and default rate appear to explain most of the variation. This observation is not true unless the turn rates are normalized with respect to the overall expected turn rate, as defined above. These results also support the conclusion that there is a degree of harshness beyond which reacting is a more attractive policy, at least to a risk-neutral or risk-seeking investor.

However, the model behaves somewhat differently when the reactors have a very low safety-stock setting. When the reactor safety stock is small compared with the planner safety stock, the reactors achieve very large turn rates at all harshness settings. A smaller and opposite effect is seen in planner turn rate. However, when the reactor safety stock is comparable with or greater than the planner safety stock, the reactor turn rates converge with those for other trials at

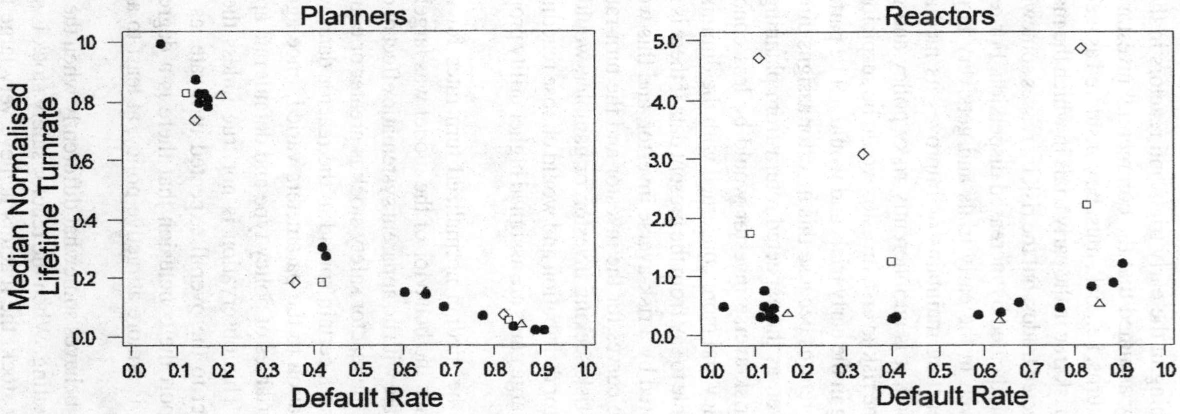

Figure 15.7. Median normalized lifetime turn rate against default rate for all trials. Different values for the reactor safety stock setting are indicated by the symbol used ◇, 3; □, 5; •, 10; △, 15. Planner safety stock is 10 in all trials.

the same default rate. Under these conditions changes in the reactor safety stock, relative to that of planners, result in a shift along only the agent proportion/default rate curve (compare trials 5 and 23, for example). In other words, the population adapts to this variation in the same way as it does to changes in other harshness-related variables and the data are once again explained almost entirely by just agent type and default rate. At the low reactor safety-stock settings, the reactor safety stock limits the number of trades a reactor can achieve per period, whereas for the planners this is limited by the global trades per period setting. It appears that if the reactors are attempting a very modest level of activity, the availability of opportunistic trades is so reliable that they operate with near-zero stock, so that despite a low trade rate they achieve very high turn rates.

5 Conclusion

The results of a multiagent simulation of planners and reactors competing in an environment of their own making has been presented. Because of the parsimonious nature of the model, it has been possible to investigate its behavior over a wide range of free parameter settings, giving confidence in the conclusions drawn. Although planning is a clearly superior policy in predictable environments, its performance is degraded severely and rapidly with increasing unpredictability and reacting becomes increasingly attractive as judged by several measures. The model is found to be robust in the sense that various ways of varying the harshness of the model world yield similar results. It appears that, in the main, the results are a function of just two variables – agent type and order default rate. The main contribution of the work is not to make specific recommendations about planning and reacting, however, but to show that when agents are modeled as interacting in something approaching a complex system, judgment of the merits of the two strategies becomes rather more problematic than in studies in which the agent environment interaction is specified more synthetically.

A possible weakness of the work may be seen in the distinctly bounded rationality of the planners who do not learn from past performance. However, it must be noted that the population as a whole does adapt to the past performance of both reactors and planners. So, although the planners may be rather rigid, because their environment is specified self-referentially in this simulation approach, an interesting and arguably realistic accommodation is achieved between the agents and an environment that is at least partially determined by their own actions. Uncertainty arises in a natural way from the bounded rationality of the agents. Computational difficulty aside, it is hard to see how one could, in keeping with the aim of the simulation, model a closed system of fully rational agents with simple deterministic rules and have uncertainty arise in a natural way. One would be forced to introduce uncertainty by hand, by using some distributional assumptions, an approach that was criticized in Section 1.

It remains to test the sensitivity of the model to changes in the order in which agents are processed at certain points in the algorithm. These were all random order in this chapter. It would also be interesting to see if chaotic interactions occur at any parameter setting. This would not seem unlikely, given the nonlinearities in the model.

REFERENCES

Aggarwal, S. C., and Aggarwal, S. 1985. The management of manufacturing operations: an appraisal of recent developments. *Int. J. Oper. Prod. Manage.*, **5**(3), 21–38.

Agre, P. E. (1988). *The Dynamic Structure of Every Day Life.* Technical Report 1085, MIT Artificial Intelligence Laboratory, Cambridge, MA.

Agre, P. E., and Chapman, D. 1987. Pengi: an implementation of a theory of activity. In *Proceedings of AAAI-87. The Sixth National Conference on Artificial Intelligence*, Morgan Kaufmann, Los Altos, CA, pp. 268–72.

Bak, P., Chen, K., Scheinkman, J., and Woodford, M. (1993). Aggregate fluctuations from independent sectorial shocks: self-organized criticality in a model of production and inventory dynamics. Working Paper 93-01-004, Sante Fe Institute, Sante Fe, NM.

Brooks, R. A. (1986). A robust layered control system for a mobile robot. *IEEE Trans. Rob. Autom.*, **2**(1), 14–23.

(1991a). Intelligence without reason. A.I. Memo 1293, MIT Artificial Intelligence Laboratory, Cambridge, MA.

(1991b). Intelligence without representation. *Artif. Intell.* **47**, 139–59.

DeToni, A., Caputo, M., and Vinelli, A. (1988). Production management techniques: push–pull classification and application conditions. *Int. J. Oper. Prod. Manage.*, **8**(2), 35–51.

Ettienne, E. C. (1983). Comparative behavior of statistical inventory control and materials requirements planning under varying industrial conditions: presentation and evaluation of a model. *Int. J. Oper. Prod. Manage.*, **3**(2), 3–17.

Fikes, R. E., and Nilson, N. J. (1971). STRIPS: a new approach to the application of theorem proving to problem solving. *Artif. Intell.* **2**, 189–208.

Fortuin, L. (1981). A comparison of SIC and MRP, two methods for material procurement in industry. *Eur. J. Oper. Res.*, **6**, 386–92.

Goldratt, E. M. (1988). Computerized shop floor scheduling. *Int. J. Prod. Res.*, **26**, 443–55.

Grunwald, H., Striekwold, P. E. T., and Weeda, P. J. (1989). A framework for quantitative comparison of production control concepts. *Int. J. Prod. Res.*, **27**, 281–92.

Hummel, J. W., and Stenger, A. J. (1988). An evaluation of proactive vs. reactive replenishment systems. *Int. J. Phys. Distrib. Mater. Manage.*, **18**(4), 3–13.

Jacobs, F. R. (1983). The OPT scheduling system: a review of a new production scheduling system. *Prod. Invent. Manage.*, **24**(3), 47–51.

Jacobs, F. R., and Whybark, D. C. (1992). A comparison of reorder point and material requirements planning inventory control logic. *Decision Sci.*, **23**, 332–42.

Johnston, R. B. (1995). Making manufacturing practices tacit: a case study of computer aided production management and lean production. *J. Oper. Res. Soc.*, **46**, 1174–83.

Johnston, R. B., and Brennan, M. (1996). Planning or organizing: the significance of theories of activity for the management of operations. *OMEGA, Int. J. Manage. Sci.*, **24**, 367–84.

Krajewski, L. J., King, B. E., Ritzman, L. P., and Wong, D. S. (1987). Kanban, MRP, and shaping the manufacturing environment. *Manage. Sci.*, **33**, 39–57.
Mintzberg, H. (1994). *The Fall and Rise of Strategic Planning*, Free Press, New York.
Monden, Y. (1983). *Toyota Production System*, Institute of Industrial Engineers, Norcross.
Newman, W., and Sridharan, V. (1992). Manufacturing planning and control: is there one definitive answer? *Prod. Invent. Manage. J.*, **33**, 50–53.
Orlicky, J. (1975). *Material Requirements Planning*, McGraw-Hill, New York.
Peirson, G., Bird, R., and Brown, R. (1995). *Business Finance*, McGraw-Hill, Sydney.
Raphael, B. (1976). The robot 'Shakey' and 'his' successors. *Comput. People*, **25**(10), 7.
Rees, L. P., Huang, P. Y., and Taylor III, B. W. (1989). A comparative analysis of an MRP lot-for-lot system and a Kanban system for a multistage production system. *Int. J. Prod. Res.*, **27**, 1427–43.
Schmitt, T. G., Klastorin, T., and Shtub, A. (1985). Production classification system: concepts, models and strategies. *Int. J. Prod. Res.*, **23**, 563–78.
Schonberger, R. J. (1982). *Japanese Manufacturing Techniques: Nine Hidden Lessons in Simplicity*, Free Press, New York.
(1983). Selecting the right manufacturing inventory system: western and Japanese approaches. *Prod. Invent. Manage.*, **24**(2), 33–44.
Striekwold, P. E. T. (1990). A quantitative comparison of production and inventory control concepts. *Int. J. Prod. Res.*, **28**, 1921–37.
Van Der Linden, P. M. J., and Grunwald, H. (1980). On the choice of production control system. *Int. J. Prod. Res.*, **18**, 273–79.
Vriend, N. J. (1994). Self-organized markets in a decentralized economy. Working Paper 94-03-013, Sante Fe Institute, Sante Fe, NM.
Walbank, M. (1988). Information flows – the foundation of manufacturing and stock management. *Eng. Costs Prod. Econ.*, **15**, 245–60.
Wight, O. W. (1981). *Manufacturing Resource Planning: MRP II*, Oliver Wight, Essex Junction, England.

CHAPTER 16

Genetic algorithms and evolutionary games

Xin Yao and Paul Darwen

The 2-player iterated prisoner's dilemma (2IPD) game is a 2×2 non-zero-sum noncooperative game, in which non-zero sum indicates that the benefits obtained by a player are not necessarily the same as the penalties received by another player, and noncooperative indicates that no preplay communication is permitted between the players (Colman 1982, Rapoport 1966). It has been widely studied in such diverse fields as economics, mathematical game theory, political science, and artificial intelligence.

In the prisoner's dilemma, each player has a choice of two operations: either cooperate with the other player, or defect. Payoff to both players is calculated according to Table 16.1.[1] In the iterated prisoner's dilemma (IPD), this step is repeated many times and each player can remember previous steps.

Although the 2IPD has been studied extensively for more than three decades, there are many real-world problems, especially many social and economic ones, that cannot be modeled by the 2IPD. Hardin (1968) described some examples of such problems. More examples can be found in Colman's book (1982, pp. 156–159). The N-player iterated prisoner's dilemma (NIPD) is a more realistic and general game that can model those problems. In comparing the NIPD with the 2IPD, Davis et al. (1976, p. 520) commented that

> "[t]he N-player case (NPD) has greater generality and applicability to real-life situations. In addition to the problems of energy conservation, ecology, and overpopulation, many other real-life problems can be represented by the NPD paradigm."

Colman (1982, p. 142) and Glance and Huberman (1993, 1994) have also indicated that the NIPD is "qualitatively different" from the 2IPD and that "... certain strategies that work well for individuals in the Prisoner's Dilemma fail in large groups."

[1] The values S, P, R, and T must satisfy $T > R > P > S$ and $R > (S+T)/2$. In the 2IPD game, the above interaction is repeated many times, and both players can remember previous outcomes.

Table 16.1. *The payoff matrix for the 2IPD game*[1]

	Cooperate		Defect	
Cooperate		R		T
	R		S	
Defect		S		P
	P		P	

Table 16.2. *The payoff matrix of the NIPD game*

Player A	C	C_0	C_1	C_2	$\cdots$	C_{n-1}
	D	D_0	D_1	D_2	$\cdots$	D_{n-1}

The NIPD game can be defined by the following three properties (Colman 1982, p. 159):

(1) Each player faces two choices between cooperation (C) and defection (D).
(2) The D option is dominant for each player, i.e., each is better off choosing D than C, no matter how many of the other players choose C.
(3) The dominant D strategies intersect in a deficient equilibrium. In particular, the outcome if all players choose their nondominant C strategies is preferable from every player's point of view to the one in which everyone chooses D, but no one is motivated to deviate unilaterally from D.

Table 16.2 shows the payoff matrix of the N-player game, for which the following conditions must be satisfied:

(1) $D_i > C_i$ for $0 \leq i \leq n-1$,
(2) $D_{i+1} > D_i$ and $C_{i+1} > C_i$ for $0 \leq i < n-1$,
(3) $C_i > (D_i + C_{i-1})/2$ for $0 < i \leq n-1$.

The payoff matrix is symmetric for each player.

A large number of values satisfy the requirements of Table 16.2. We choose values so that, if n_c is the number of cooperators in the N-player game, then the payoff for cooperation is $(2n_c - 2)$ and the payoff for defection is $(2n_c + 1)$. Table 16.3 shows an example of the N-player game.

With this choice, simple algebra reveals that if m_c cooperative moves are made out of m moves of an N-player game, then the average per-round payoff

Table 16.3. *An example of the N-player game*

		0	1	2		$n-1$
Player A	C	0	2	4	…	$2(n-1)$
	D	1	3	5	…	$2(n-1)+1$

(a) is given by

$$a = 1 + \frac{m_c}{m}(2N - 3). \qquad (16.1)$$

This lets us measure how common cooperation was just by looking at the average per-round payoff.

There has been a lot of research on the evolution of cooperation in the 2IPD by use of genetic algorithms (GAs) and evolutionary programming in recent years (Axelrod 1987, Chess 1988, Lindgren 1991, Fogel 1991 and 1993, Marks 1992, Darwen and Yao 1995). Axelrod (1987) used GAs to evolve a population of strategies in which each strategy plays the 2IPD game with every other strategy in the population. In other words, the performance or fitness of a strategy is evaluated when the 2IPD game is played with every other strategy in the population. The environment in which a strategy evolves consists of all the remaining strategies in the population. Because strategies in the population are constantly changing as a result of evolution, a strategy will be evaluated by a different environment in every generation. All the strategies in the population are coevolving in their dynamic environments. Axelrod found that such dynamic environments produced strategies that performed very well against their population. Fogel (1991) described similar experiments, but used finite-state machines to represent strategies and evolutionary programming to evolve them. One of the advantages of using finite-state machines is the avoidance of a user-specified history length, which is necessary in order to encode a strategy in chromosomes.

Experimental studies on the NIPD have been relatively few in spite of its importance and its qualitative difference from the 2IPD. Marks (1992) investigated a 3IPD. Cheung et al. (1997) described an application of the 4IPD to the Australian petroleum industry. In this chapter we concentrate on the more complex and rich NIPD, in which N can be as large as 16. Three major issues are investigated: (1) Can cooperation emerge from a population of random strategies? In other words, can cooperation be learned through simulated evolution? (2) What is the impact of the group size N, i.e., the number of players, on the evolution of cooperation? (3) How stable are the evolved strategies? A related issue from the point of view of machine learning is the generalization ability of evolved strategies. We investigate this issue through a series of empirical studies.

The rest of this paper is organized as follows. Section 1 describes how to evolve 2IPD and NIPD by using a GA and the setup of our experiments. Section 2 presents our experimental results on the evolution of cooperation for the 2-or-more-player IPD. Section 3 investigates the impact of NIPD's group size on the evolution of cooperation. Section 4 discusses evolutionarily stable strategies in the NIPD. Section 5 studies the generalization ability of evolved strategies. Finally, Section 6 concludes with a short summary of this chapter and a few remarks.

1 An evolutionary approach to the prisoner's dilemma game

In this section we describe the evolutionary approach to the NIPD, introduce a new representation (encoding) scheme for NIPD strategies in addition to generalizing Axelrod's scheme (1987), and give other implementation details for our experiments.

Genotypical representation of strategies

We use a GA to evolve strategies for the NIPD. The most important issue here is the representation of strategies. We use two different representations, both of which are lookup tables that give an action for every possible contingency.

One way of representing strategies for the NIPD is to generalize the representation scheme used by Axelrod (1987). In this scheme, each genotype is a lookup table that covers every possible history of the last few steps. A history in such a game is represented as a binary string of ln bits, where the first l bits represent the player's own previous l actions (most recent to the left, oldest to the right), and the other $n-1$ groups of l bits represent the previous actions of the other players. For example, during a game of 3IPD with a remembered history of two steps, $n = 3, l = 2$, one player might see this history:

$$n = 3, l = 2\text{: example history } 11 \;\; 00 \;\; 01.$$

The first l bits, 11, means this player has defected (a 1) for both of the previous $l = 2$ steps. The previous steps of the other players are then listed in order: 00 means the first of the other players cooperated (a 0) on the previous l steps, and the last of the other players cooperated (0) on the most recent step and defected (1) on the step before, as represented by 01.

For the NIPD remembering l previous steps, there are 2^{ln} possible histories. The lookup-table genotype therefore contains an action (cooperate 0 or defect 1) for each of these possible histories. So we need at least 2^{ln} bits to represent a strategy. At the beginning of each game, there are no previous l steps of play from which to look up the next action, so each genotype should also contain its own extra bits that define the presumed pregame moves. The total genotype length is therefore $2^{ln} + ln$ bits. We use this genotype for the first set of results below, Figs. 16.1–16.4.

This Axelrod-style representation scheme, however, suffers from two drawbacks. First, it does not scale well as the number of players increases. Second, it provides more information than is necessary by telling which of the other players cooperated or defected, when the only information needed is how many of the other players cooperated or defected. Such redundant information reduced the efficiency of the evolution greatly in our experiments with this representation scheme. To improve on this, we propose a new representation scheme that is more compact and efficient.

In our new representation scheme, each individual is regarded as a set of rules stored in a lookup table that covers every possible history. A history of length l is represented by

(1) l bits for the player's own previous l moves, in which a 1 indicates defection and a 0 cooperation, and
(2) another $l \log_2 n$ bits for the number of cooperators among the other $n - 1$ players, where n is the number of the players in the game. This requires that n be a power of 2.

For example, if we are looking at eight players who can remember the three most recent rounds, then one of the players would see the history as

History for 8 players, 3 steps: 001 111 110 101 (12 bits).

Here, the 001 indicates the player's own actions: The most recent action (on the left) was a 0, indicating cooperation, and the action three steps ago (on the right), was a 1, i.e., defection. The 111 gives the number of cooperators among the other seven players in the most recent round, i.e., there were $111_2 = 7$ cooperators. The 101 gives the number of cooperators among the other seven players three steps ago, i.e., there were $101_2 = 5$ cooperators. The most recent events are always on the left; previous events are on the right.

In the above example, there are $2^{12} = 2048$ possible histories. So 2048 bits are needed to represent all possible strategies. In the general case of an N-player game with history length l, each history needs $l + l \log_2 n$ bits to represent a strategy and there are $2^{l+l \log_2 n}$ such histories. A strategy is represented by a binary string that gives an action for each of those possible histories. In the above example, the history 001 111 110 101 would cause the strategy to do whatever is listed in bit 1013, the decimal number for the binary 001 111 110 101.

Because there are no previous l rounds at the beginning of a game, we have to specify them with another $l(1 + \log_2 n)$ bit. Hence each strategy is finally represented by a binary string of length $2^{l+l \log_2 n} + l(1 + \log_2 n)$, which

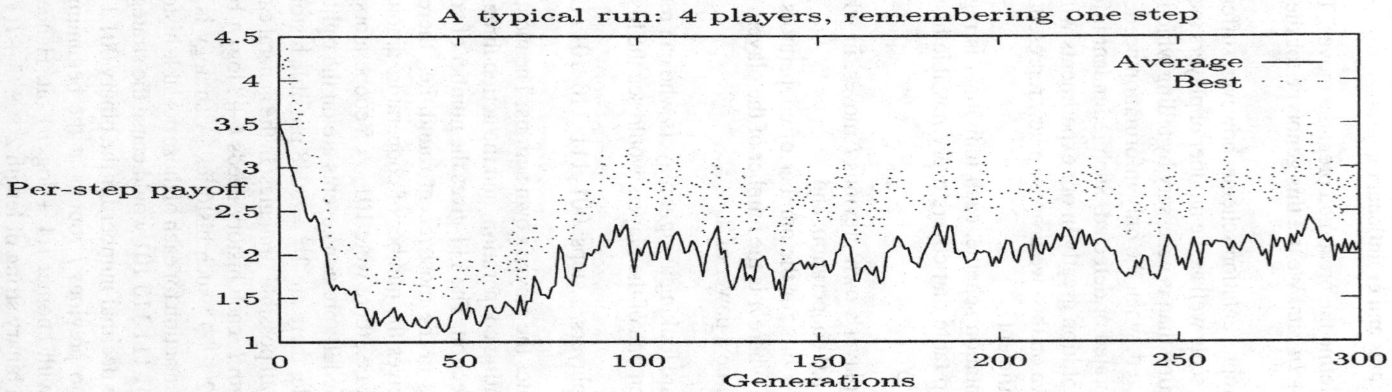

Figure 16.1. A typical run.

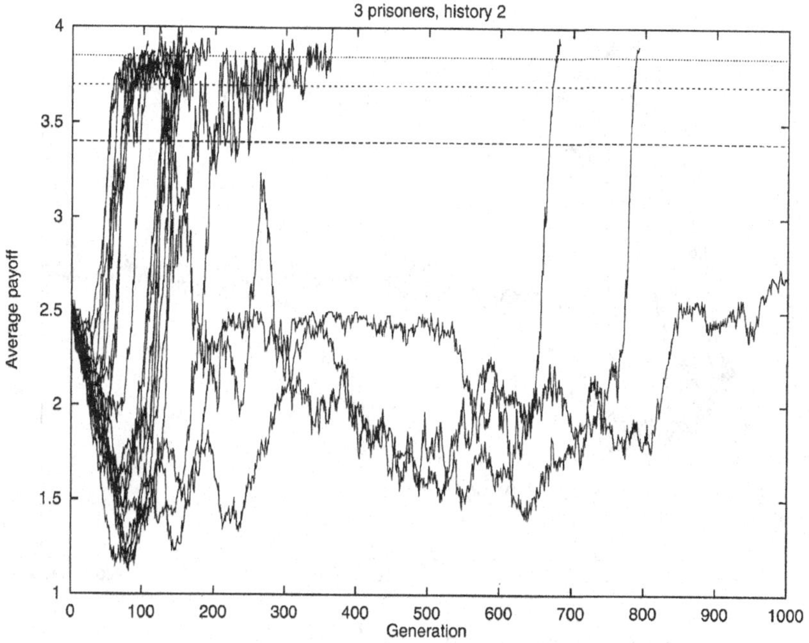

Figure 16.2. 3 players, history 2, old genotype. Results of 20 runs for the 3IPD with history 2. Cooperation almost always emerges. Only 1 out of 20 runs fails to reach 95% cooperation using Axelrod's representation scheme.

is significantly shorter than the length of the Axelrod-style representation scheme.

Genetic algorithm parameters

For all the experiments presented in this chapter, the population size is 100, the mutation rate is 0.001, and the crossover rate is 0.6. Rank-based selection was used, with the worst performer assigned an average of 0.75 offspring and the best assigned 1.25 offspring.

A typical run

A typical run with four players with a history 1 ($n = 4, l = 1$) is shown in Fig. 16.1. At each generation, 1000 games of the 4IPD are played, with each group of four players selected randomly with replacement from the population. Each of these 1000 games lasts for 100 rounds. Starting from a random population, defection is usually the better strategy, and the average payoff plummets initially. As time passes, some cooperation becomes more profitable.

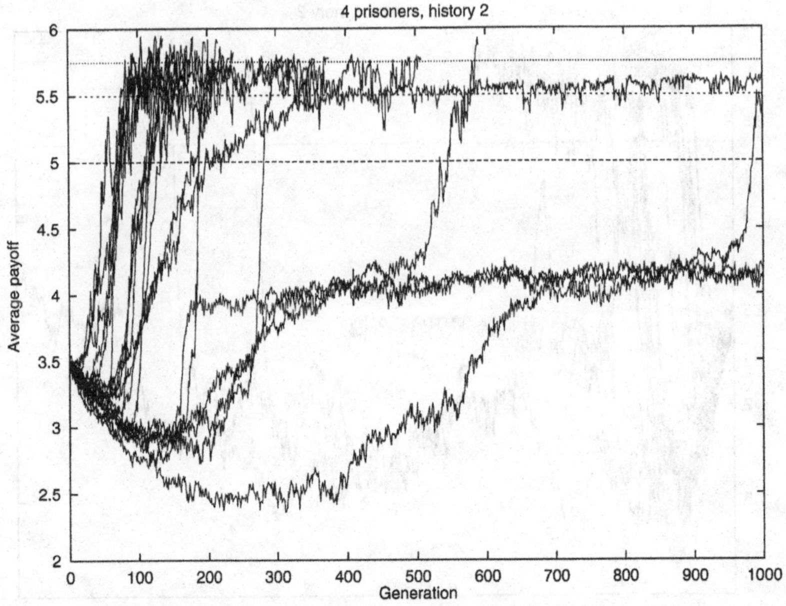

Figure 16.3. 4 players, history 2, old genotype.[2]

This shows the average and best payoff at each generation for a population of 100 individuals. Each individual is a strategy. At each generation, 1000 games of 4IPD are played, with each group of four players selected randomly with replacement from the population. Each of these 1000 games lasts for 100 rounds. Starting from a random population, defection is the better strategy, and the average payoff initially plummets. As time passes, some cooperation becomes more profitable.

2 The evolution of cooperation in the NIPD

To investigate whether cooperation can emerge from a population of random strategies in the NIPD, we carried out a number of experiments by using Axelrod's representation scheme of strategies. Figures 16.2–16.5 show the results of our experiments. Twenty runs were conducted for each experiment. In each of the runs, the program stopped when more than five generations passed, with the average payoff above the 95% cooperation level. Figure 16.2 shows the results of 20 runs of the 3IPD with history 2: out of 20 runs, there is only

[2] Results of 20 runs for the 4IPD with history 2. Cooperation emerges from most of the runs. Only 4 out of 20 runs fail to reach 95% cooperation when Axelrod's representation scheme is used.

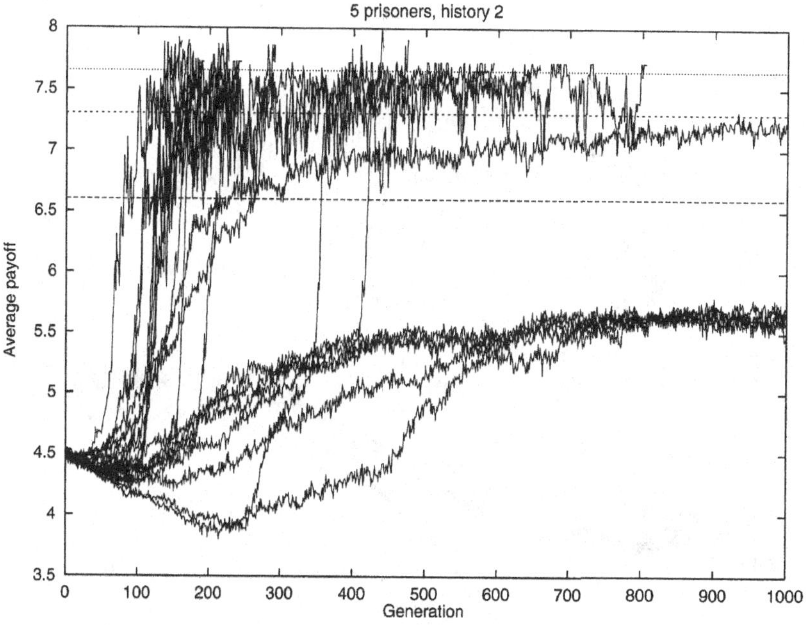

Figure 16.4. 5 players, history 2, old genotype.[3]

1 that fails to reach 95% cooperation. Figure 16.3 shows the results of 20 runs of the 4IPD with history 2: 4 out of 20 runs fail to reach the 95% cooperation level, but only 1 of those fails to reach 80% cooperation. Figure 16.4 shows the results of 20 runs of the 5IPD with history 2: 6 out of 20 runs do not reach the 80% cooperation level. Figure 16.5 shows the results of 20 runs of the 6IPD with history 2: 9 out of 20 runs stay below the 80% cooperation level.

It is quite clear from Figs. 16.2–16.5 that cooperation can emerge from a population of random strategies. Cooperation can be learned through evolution. There is no teacher in this learning process. Learning is achieved through interactions among all strategies in the population. All the strategies in the population are coevolving because the fitness of any strategy depends on the fitness of other strategies in the population.

It is also obvious from Figs. 16.2–16.5 that there is no guarantee that cooperation always emerges within a specific number of generations. As the number of players increases, the evolution of cooperation seems to be more difficult. To look at this issue further, we need to investigate the NIPD with more than six players. As pointed out above, Axelrod's representation scheme of strategies

[3] Results of 20 runs for the 5IPD with history 2. Cooperation emerges from most of the runs. Only 6 out of 20 runs fail to reach 80% cooperation when Axelrod's representation scheme is used.

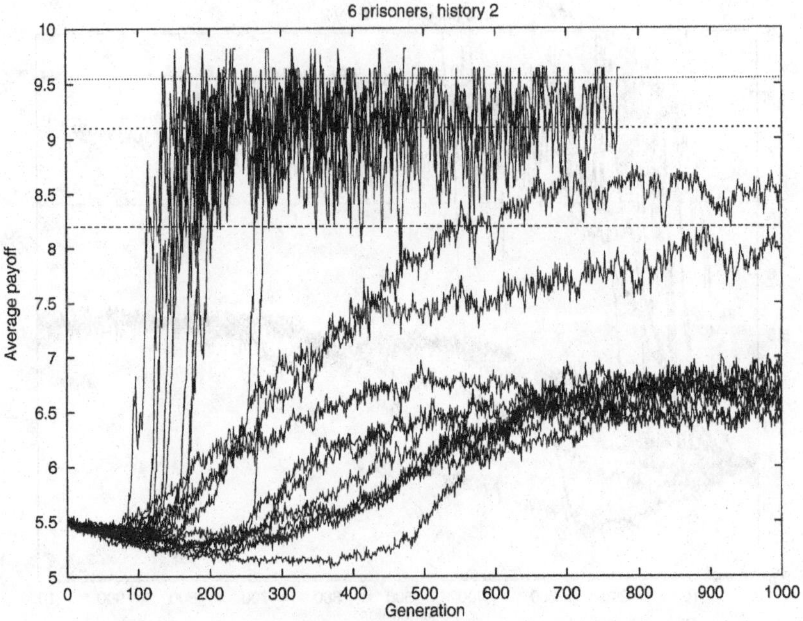

Figure 16.5. 6 players, history 2, old genotype.[4]

has poor scalability. We use our new representation scheme in Section 3 to study further the impact of the group size on the evolution of cooperation.

3 Impact of the group size on the evolution of cooperation

We carried out a series of experiments with the 2IPD, 4IPD, 8IPD, and 16IPD by using our representation scheme of strategies. Figure 16.6 shows the results of 10 runs of the 2IPD with history 3. Out of 10 runs, there are only 3 that fail to reach 90% cooperation and only 1 that goes to almost all defection. Figure 16.7 shows the results of 10 runs of the 4IPD with history 3, in which some of the runs reach cooperation but more than half of the 10 runs fail to evolve cooperation. Figure 16.8 shows the results of 10 runs of the 8IPD game with history length 2, in which none of the runs reaches cooperation. Figure 16.9 shows 10 runs of the 16IPD, in which no sign of cooperation can be seen.

For the 2IPD with history 3, cooperation emerges most of the time. Only 3 out of 10 runs fail to reach 90% cooperation, and only 1 run goes to almost all

[4] Results of 20 runs for the 6IPD with history 2. Cooperation emerges from over 50% of the runs. 9 out of 20 runs fail to reach 80% cooperation when Axelrod's representation scheme is used.

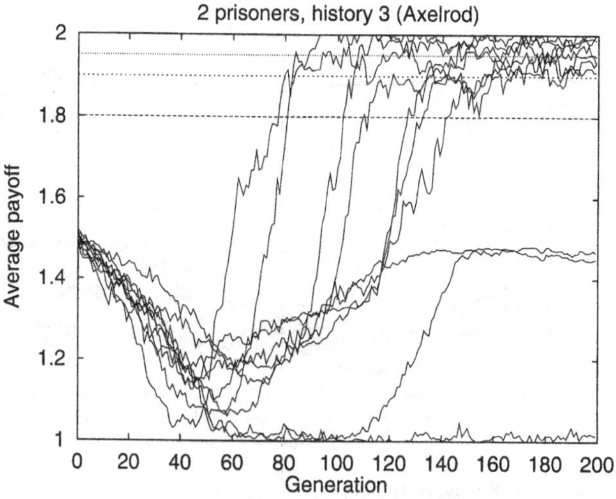

Figure 16.6. 2 players, history 3.

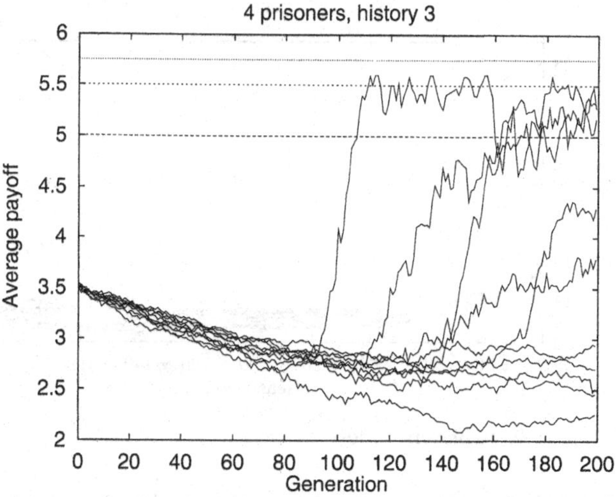

Figure 16.7. 4 players, history 3.[5]

defection. The horizontal lines at the top show the 95%, 90%, and 80% levels of cooperation.

These results confirm that cooperation can still be evolved in larger groups, but it is more difficult to evolve cooperation as the group size increases. Glance

[5] For the 4IPD with history 3, cooperation breaks out some of the time.

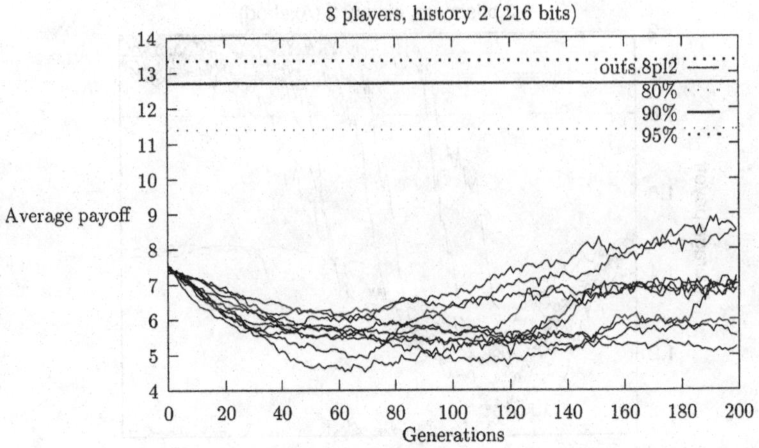

Figure 16.8. 8 players, history 2.

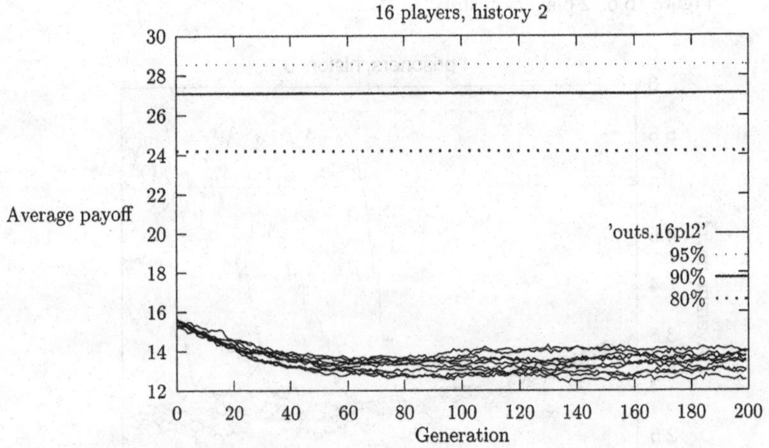

Figure 16.9. 16 players, history 2.

and Huberman (1993, 1994) arrived at a similar conclusion by using a model based on many-particle systems. We first suspected that the failure to evolve cooperation in larger groups was caused by larger search spaces and insufficient running time as more players were involved in 8IPD and 16IPD games. This is, however, not the case. The search space of the 8IPD game with history length 2 is actually smaller than that of the 4IPD game with history length 3. To confirm that the failure to evolve cooperation is not caused by insufficient running time, we examined the convergence of the 8IPD game. Figure 16.10 shows that at generation 200 the population has mostly converged for all 10 runs.

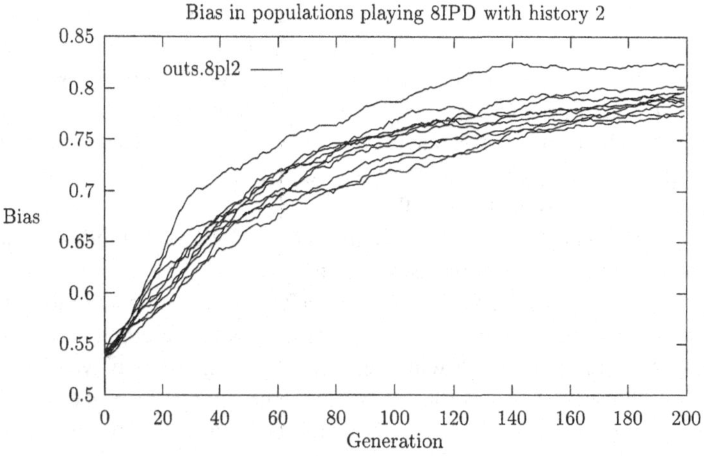

Figure 16.10. Bias for 8 players, history 2.[6]

For the 8IPD with history 2, cooperation never emerges. The horizontal lines at the top show the 95%, 90%, and 80% levels of cooperation. To demonstrate that these runs have converged, Fig. 16.10 shows the bias of the populations.

For the 16IPD with history 2, cooperation never emerges. The horizontal lines at the top show the 95%, 90%, and 80% levels of cooperation.

It is worth mentioning that the evolution of cooperation by use of simulations does depend on some implementation details, such as the genotypical representation of strategies and the values used in the payoff matrix. So cooperation may be evolved in the 8IPD game if a different representation scheme and different payoff values are used. Although we cannot prove it rigorously, we think that for any representation scheme and payoff values there will always be an upper limit on the group size over which cooperation cannot be evolved.

4 Evolutionary stability in the NIPD

We know from our previous empirical studies (Yao 1996) that cooperation can be evolved from a population of random strategies. In this section we investigate how stable a strategy (or a group of strategies) is. The concept of evolutionary stability provides a useful tool to analyze strategies for playing the game. Evolutionary stability has been proposed by Smith (1974, 1982) to analyze stable strategies. An evolutionarily stable strategy is one that cannot be

[6] In 10 runs of the 8IPD with history 2, from which cooperation never emerges, the bias demonstrates that the populations have converged. Bias is the average proportion of the most prominent value in each position. A bias of 0.75 means that, on average, each bit position has converged to either 75% 0 or 75% 1.

invaded by other strategies or combinations of strategies (Smith 1974, 1982). It has been shown that no finite mixture of pure strategies can be evolutionarily stable in the 2IPD (Boyd and Lorberbaum 1987, Farrell and Ware 1989), in which a pure strategy is a complete plan of action, specifying in advance what moves (choices) a particular player will make in all possible situations that might arise during the course of the game (Colman 1982, p. 7). This section extends these results to the NIPD.

To facilitate our theoretical analysis of evolutionary stability in the NIPD, we need to introduce some assumptions.

The NIPD considered in this section has an infinite population of players. There are a finite number of distinct strategies in the population. Strategy S_i occurs in the population with frequency f_i. A game is played by n players randomly selected from the population. The payoff from one round of play is determined by Table 16.3. The game continues to play the second round with probability w, the third round with w^2, etc. In general, the game plays for t $(t \geq 1)$ rounds with probability w^{t-1}. The only information available to each player at round t is his or her complete history of previous $t-1$ interactions with other $n-1$ players in the game.

Evolutionary stability in the N-player game is more complex than that in the 2-player case. We provide a general definition based on the idea of uninvadability.[7] Let $E(S_i \mid S_{j_1}, S_{j_2}, \ldots, S_{j_{N-1}})$ be the expected payoff of strategy S_i playing with $(S_{j_1}, S_{j_2}, \ldots, S_{j_{N-1}})$ and f_k be the frequency of S_k in a population P. We can define $[V(S_i \mid P) = \sum_{j_1, j_2, \ldots, j_{N-1}} f_{j_1} f_{j_2} \cdots f_{j_{N-1}} E(S_i \mid S_{j_1}, S_{j_2}, \ldots, S_{j_{N-1}})$, where the summation goes over all the different combinations of $N-1$ strategies. Then we define S_i as an S if the following inequality can be satisfied: i.e., for all $S_j (S_j \neq S_i)$ in P,

$$V(S_i \mid P) > V(S_j \mid P). \qquad (16.2)$$

It is clear from our definition that an S cannot be invaded by any other strategy or combination of strategies because of the strict inequality in inequality (16.2).

Theorem 1. *In the infinite NIPD in which the probability of further interaction is sufficiently high, every finite history of interactions among the N players occurs with positive probability in any evolutionarily stable mixture of pure strategies (Yao 1996).*

Corollary 1. *No finite mixture of pure strategies in the infinite NIPD can be evolutionarily stable if the probability of further interaction w is sufficiently high (Yao 1996).*

[7] Although there might be other similar definitions of the ESS in N-player games, our definition reflects the essence of the ESS and is sufficient to show our main results.

The above results appear to be rather negative. They imply that even though cooperative strategies can be evolved, they can never be evolutionarily stable. They will eventually change to noncooperative strategies. However, the above NIPD model assumes that no one will make mistakes, that is, everyone who intends to cooperate (or defect) cooperates (or defects). This is, however, not the case in the real world. People do make mistakes in the real world. Someone who intends to cooperate may end up with defection and vice versa because of noise, etc. It can be shown that evolutionarily stable strategies do exist when there is a positive probability of both types of mistakes (C for D or D for C) on every step of the game tree and the probability is independent of players (Yao 1996).

5 Coevolutionary learning and generalization

The idea of having a computer algorithm learn from its own experience and thus create expertise without being exposed to a human teacher has been around for a long time. For GAs, both Hillis (1991) and Axelrod (1987) have attempted coevolution, in which a GA population is evaluated by how well it performs against itself or another GA population, starting from a random population. Expertise is thus bootstrapped from nothing, without an expert teacher. This is certainly a promising idea, but does it work? So far, no one has investigated whether the results of coevolutionary learning are robust, that is, whether they generalize well. If a strategy is produced by a coevolving population, will that strategy perform well against opponents never seen by that population? To investigate this issue, we need to pick the best strategies produced by the coevolutionary learning system and let them play against a set of test strategies that has not been seen by the coevolutionary system. In this section we describe some experiments that test the generalization ability of coevolved strategies for the 8IPD game with history length 1.

Test strategies

The unseen test strategies used in our study should be reasonably standard and representative, that is, they are neither very poor (or else they will be exploited by their evolved opponents) nor very good (or else they will exploit their evolved opponent). We need unseen strategies that are adequate against a large range of opponents, but not *the* best.

To obtain such strategies, we did a limited enumerative search to find the strategies that performed best against a large number of random opponents. As most random opponents perform poorly, beating many random opponents provides a mediocre standard of play against a wide range of opponents. We limited this search to manageable proportions by fixing certain bits in a strategy's genotype that seemed to be sensible, such as always defecting after every other

Table 16.4. *Enumerative search results*

Mean	Standard deviation	Decimal	Binary genotype
8.1	0.083	1026040	1111 1010 0111 1111 1000
8.093	0.083	1022965	1111 1001 1011 1111 0101
8.091	0.083	1018871	1111 1000 1011 1111 0111
8.088	0.083	1032181	1111 1011 1111 1111 0101
8.088	0.083	1020921	1111 1001 0011 1111 1001
8.082	0.083	1028087	1111 1010 1111 1111 0111
8.077	0.083	1023990	1111 1001 1111 1111 0110
8.076	0.083	1037305	1111 1101 0011 1111 1001
8.076	0.083	1017846	1111 1000 0111 1111 0110

strategy defects. The top few strategies found from such a limited enumerative search are listed in Table 16.4.[8]

Learning and testing

We compared three different methods for implementing the coevolutionary learning system. The three methods differ in the way in which each individual is evaluated, i.e., which opponents are chosen to evaluate an individual's fitness. The three methods are

(1) choosing from among the individuals in the GA population, i.e., normal coevolution of a single population as in Axelrod's implementation (Axelrod 1987);
(2) choosing from a pool made of the evolving GA population and the best 25 strategies from the enumerative search, which remain fixed;
(3) choosing from a pool made of the evolving GA population and the best 25 strategies from the enumerative search, but the probability of choosing one of the 25 is four times higher.

For each of these, we obtained the best 25 strategies from the last generation of the GA and tested it against a pool made up of both the seen and the unseen enumerative search strategies, 50 in all.

We compared the performance by rotating the 3 groups, i.e., we tested the seen 25 against a pool of the 25 unseen plus the 25 GA strategies, then we tested the unseen 25 against the 25 seen plus the 25 GA strategies.

[8] Top few strategies from a partial enumerative search for strategies that play well against a large number of random opponents. This provides unseen test opponents to test the generalization of strategies produced by coevolution. The first 4 bits were fixed to 1, as were the 11th–16th bits. Virtually all of the best 50 strategies started by cooperating.

Table 16.5. *Normal coevolution, no extra strategies in evaluation. GA strategies play against themselves 8pl1 (35% cooperative) against itself*

		Mean	Standard deviation	Standard deviation of mean	Mean of opponents
0	11100001111011000000	7.240	3.980	0.130	6.300
1	11000001111011000000	7.290	3.980	0.130	6.390
2	11100000111111100000	7.340	3.050	0.090	8.430
3	1100010111111010000	7.260	3.200	0.100	7.890
4	11100101111111100000	7.180	4.160	0.130	5.880
5	1100000111111010000	7.000	3.090	0.090	8.110
6	11100101111111000000	7.170	4.130	0.130	6.130
7	1100001111111010000	7.240	4.030	0.130	6.290
8	100000111111010000	7.170	3.120	0.090	8.340
9	1100100111111110000	7.710	3.520	0.110	7.950
10	10100000111111100000	7.27	3.08	0.09	8.39

Table 16.6. *GA strategies play against unseen strategies from enumerative search*[9]

		Mean	Standard deviation	Standard deviation of mean	Mean of opponents
0	11100001111011000000	5.525	2.330	0.074	5.340
1	11000001111011000000	5.627	2.421	0.077	5.502
2	11100000111111100000	5.605	2.568	0.081	5.027
3	1100010111111010000	5.087	2.064	0.065	5.419
4	11100101111111100000	5.283	2.210	0.070	4.532
5	1100000111111010000	5.477	2.547	0.081	6.337
6	11100101111111000000	5.116	1.877	0.059	4.473
7	1100001111111010000	5.392	2.370	0.075	5.378
8	100000111111010000	5.385	2.531	0.080	6.530
9	10100000111111100000	5.461	2.383	0.075	4.900
10	1100100111111110000	5.146	2.271	0.072	5.237

[9] Results of ordinary coevolution, with no extra strategies during the GA evaluation. The GA strategies manage some cooperation among themselves and hold their own against strategies they have not seen before. Coevolution, with addition of 25 fixed strategies from enumerative search. GA strategies play against themselves.

Table 16.7. *Coevolution, with addition of 25 fixed strategies from enumerative search. GA strategies playing against themselves*

		Mean	Standard deviation	Standard deviation of mean	Mean of opponents
0	11111000011111100000	11.678	1.715	0.054	11.965
1	11111000011111100000	11.706	1.553	0.049	11.994
2	11111000011111100000	11.440	1.603	0.051	11.922
3	11111000011111100000	11.721	1.581	0.050	12.027
4	11111000111111100000	13.264	2.521	0.080	10.636
5	11111000011111100000	11.714	1.584	0.050	12.025
6	11111000011111100000	11.420	1.669	0.053	11.895
7	11111000011111100000	11.678	1.705	0.054	11.985
8	11011000001111100000	11.618	1.781	0.056	11.958
9	11111000011111100000	11.670	1.688	0.053	11.974
10	11111000011111100000	11.649	1.697	0.054	11.973

Table 16.8. *GA strategies play against pool of 25 seen and 25 unseen strategies from enumerative search*[10]

		Mean	Standard deviation	Standard deviation of mean	Mean of opponents
0	11111000011111100000	5.209	3.212	0.102	5.634
1	11111000011111100000	5.494	3.451	0.109	5.828
2	11111000011111100000	5.152	2.771	0.088	5.934
3	11111000011111100000	5.600	3.561	0.113	5.907
4	11111000111111100000	5.619	2.929	0.093	4.629
5	11111000011111100000	5.336	3.369	0.107	5.724
6	11111000011111100000	4.971	2.541	0.080	5.741
7	11111000011111100000	5.447	3.481	0.110	5.791
8	11011000001111100000	5.591	3.276	0.104	5.923
9	11111000011111100000	5.245	3.200	0.101	5.673
10	11111000011111100000	5.392	3.341	0.106	5.771

Experimental results

For each of the three evaluation methods, Tables 16.5–16.10 show the performance of the best strategies from the GA's last generation against opponents from (1) themselves, and (2) a pool made up of both the seen and unseen strategies from the enumerative search.

[10] Adding 25 fixed strategies to the evaluation procedure, along with the 100 coevolving GA individuals, causes the GA to produce strategies that can cooperate more with each other, but are not exploited by the more noncooperative strategies from the enumerative search.

Table 16.9. *Coevolution, with the addition of 25 fixed strategies, which are 4 times as likely to be selected into the group of 8 players for 8IPD. GA strategies play against themselves*[11]

		Mean	Standard deviation	Standard deviation of mean	Mean of opponents
0	11111000011111100000	12.575	1.737	0.055	12.740
1	11111000011111100000	12.468	1.939	0.061	12.641
2	10111000011111000000	12.400	2.130	0.067	12.593
3	11111000011111100000	12.557	1.864	0.059	12.709
4	11111000011111100000	12.556	1.488	0.047	12.820
5	11111000011111000000	12.490	1.454	0.046	12.772
6	10111000011111100000	12.392	2.087	0.066	12.568
7	11111001011111100000	13.204	2.457	0.078	10.713
8	11111000011111100000	12.551	1.852	0.059	12.700
9	11111000011111100000	12.560	1.904	0.060	12.718
10	11111000011111100000	12.494	1.835	0.058	12.669

Table 16.10. *GA strategies play against pool of 25 seen and 25 unseen strategies from enumerative search*[12]

		Mean	Standard deviation	Standard deviation of mean	Mean of opponents
0	11111000011111100000	5.209	3.212	0.102	5.634
1	11111000011111100000	5.494	3.451	0.109	5.828
2	10111000011111000000	5.635	3.12	0.099	6.217
3	11111000011111100000	5.6	3.561	0.113	5.907
4	11111000011111100000	5.187	2.835	0.09	5.966
5	11111000011111000000	5.132	2.762	0.087	5.91
6	10111000011111100000	5.375	3.159	0.1	5.753
7	11111001011111100000	5.447	3.481	0.11	5.788
8	11111000011111100000	5.422	3.34	0.116	5.765
9	11111000011111100000	5.245	3.2	0.101	5.673
10	11111000011111100000	5.392	3.341	0.106	5.771

[11] Best 25 strategies from GA search play against a pool of (1) 25 best from enumerative search, and (2) 25 unseen strategies from enumerative search. Note there is little diversity in the GA population.

[12] Increasing the importance of the extra 25 fixed strategies causes the coevolutionary GA to produce strategies that are even more cooperative among themselves, but are still not exploited by the unseen strategies of the enumerative search.

Discussion

Tables 16.5 and 16.6 demonstrate that the coevolution with the 8IPD produces strategies that are not very cooperative, as also demonstrated in Fig. 16.8 in Section 3. Because the 8IPD is a game in which it is easy to get exploited, coevolution will first create strategies that can deal with noncooperative strategies. The evolved strategies in Tables 16.5 and 16.6 are cautious with each other and are not exploited by the unseen strategies from the enumerative search.

Adding fixed but not very cooperative strategies to the GA's evaluation procedure has a surprising effect. The evolved strategies in Tables 16.8 and 16.10 can cooperate well with other cooperators without being exploited by the strategies from the enumerative search, half of which it has never seen before, that is, normal coevolution produces strategies that do not cooperate well with each other and are not exploited by unseen noncooperative strategies. Coevolution with the addition of extra noncooperative strategies gives more general strategies that do cooperate well with each other, but are still not exploited by unseen noncooperative strategies. The experimental results also seem to indicate that the evolved strategies learn to cooperate with other cooperators better while maintaining their ability in dealing with noncooperative strategies when the evolutionary environment contains a higher proportion of extra fixed strategies.

6 Conclusions

In this chapter we investigate three important issues in evolving NIPD strategies. It shows experimentally that cooperation can emerge from a population of random strategies. As the group size of the NIPD increases, the evolution of cooperation becomes more difficult. We also show analytically that no finite mixture of pure strategies in the infinite NIPD can be evolutionarily stable if the probability of further interaction is sufficiently high. However, evolutionary stability can be achieved if mistakes are allowed in the NIPD. Generalization is a key issue in machine learning. Evolutionary learning is no exception. We study the issue through a set of experiments, which shed lights on how well the evolved strategies generalize. It is observed that Axelrod's evolutionary learning method tends to evolve strategies that overspecialize to their evolving population. Adding some fixed expert strategies in the environment can alleviate the problem, but cannot solve the problem entirely. More work needs to be done to evolve strategies that generalize well without external fixed expert strategies.

The NIPD is a very complex and rich game that can model numerous economic and social phenomena. There are many variants of the game. These variants can also be studied with the same approach described in this chapter.

REFERENCES

Axelrod, R. (1987). The evolution of strategies in the iterated prisoner's dilemma. In *Genetic Algorithms and Simulated Annealing*, ed. L. Davis, Morgan Kaufmann, San Mateo, CA, pp. 32–41.

Boyd, R., and Lorberbaum, J. P. (1987). No pure strategy is evolutionarily stable in the repeated prisoner's dilemma game. *Nature (London)*, **327**(7 May), 58–9.

Chess, D. M. (1988). Simulating the evolution of behaviors: the iterated prisoners' dilemma problem. *Complex Sys.*, **2**, 663–70.

Cheung, Y., Bedingfield, S., and Huxford, S. (1997). Oligopolistic behavior for the Australian petroleum industry. In *Proceedings of the International Conference on Computational Intelligence and Multimedia Applications (ICCIMA'97)*, eds. B. Verma and X. Yao, The University of Griffith, Gold Coast, Queensland, Australia.

Colman, A. M. (1982). *Game Theory and Experimental Games*, Pergamon, Oxford, England.

Darwen, P. J., and Yao, X. (1995). On evolving robust strategies for iterated prisoner's dilemma. In *Progress in Evolutionary Computation*, ed. X. Lao, Vol. 956 of Springer-Verlag Lecture Notes in Artificial Intelligence Series, Springer-Verlag, Heidelberg, pp. 276–92.

Davis, J. H., Laughlin, P. R., and Komorita, S. S. (1976). The social psychology of small groups. *Annu. Rev. Psychol.*, **27**, 501–42.

Farrell, J., and Ware, R. (1989). Evolutionary stability in the repeated prisoner's dilemma. *Theor. Popul. Biol.*, **36**, 161–66.

Fogel, D. B. (1991). The evolution of intelligent decision making in gaming. *Cybernet. Sys. Int. J.*, **22**, 223–36.

(1993). Evolving behaviors in the iterated prisoner's dilemma. *Evol. Comput.*, **1**, 77–97.

Glance, N. S., and Huberman, B. A. (1993). The outbreak of cooperation. *J. Math. Sociol.*, **17**, 281–302.

(1994). The dynamics of social dilemmas. *Sci. Am.*, **270**(3), 58–63.

Hardin, G. (1968). The tragedy of the commons. *Science*, **162**, 1243–48.

Hillis, W. D. (1991). Co-evolving parasites improve simulated evolution as an optimization procedure. In *Santa Fe Institute Studies in the Sciences of Complexity*, Addison-Wesley, Reading, MA, **10**, 313–23.

Lindgren, K. (1991). Evolutionary phenomena in simple dynamics. In *Artificial Life II: Santa Fe Institute Studies in the Sciences of Complexity*, eds. C. G. Langton, C. Taylor, J. D. Farmer, and S. Rasmussen, Addison-Wesley, Reading, MA, **10**, 295–312.

Marks, R. E. (1992). Breeding optimal strategies: optimal behavior foroligopolists. *J. Evol. Econ.*, 17–38.

Rapoport, A. (1966). Optimal policies for the prisoner's dilemma. Technical Report 50, The Psychometric Laboratory, University of North Carolina, Chapel Hill, NC.

Smith, J. M. (1974). The theory of games and the evolution of animal conflict. *J. Theor. Biol.*, **47**, 209–21.

(1982). *Evolution and The Theory of Games*, Cambridge University Press, Cambridge, England.

Yao, X. (1996). Evolutionary stability in the *N*-person prisoner's dilemma. *BioSystems*, **37**, 189–97.

CHAPTER 17

Evolved perception and the validation of simulation models

Robert Marks

Economics has been a predominantly analytical discipline in its search for necessity – reducing the complex phenomena of interacting agents to interactions of one or two causes, holding all else unchanging (*ceteris paribus*) and then attempting to reintroduce the complexity through additivity, making the assumption of linearity. But sometimes all the king's horses and all the king's men... and nonlinearities and other complexities have stymied the search for necessity through additivity. This has led to two sorts of solutions: nonlinear dynamics, in which second-order interactions are specifically modeled, and simulations, in which the search for necessary conditions is abandoned and, rather, sufficiency is the goal. What are the consequences in the aggregate of individual agents behaving just so – what assumptions at the microlevel are sufficient for the emergence of a specific pattern of economic phenomena? There are many instances of the search for sufficient conditions elsewhere in this volume, but one aspect of this research approach has been relatively neglected: the issue of validation from historical data. In the standard analytical approach, linear regression has been used to derive coefficients in the linear relationships among a dependent variable and a set of independent (causative) variables. In general, there has been no shortage of data. With the recent approach of simulation for sufficiency, there has been little use of historical data: Data series for complex economic repeated interactions are uncommon, and anyway the nature of sufficiency – "these coefficients in this model may result in this emergent behavior" – may not be generalizable. But there is a need for greater use of historical data, both to aid in the derivation of coefficients and to help validate the models. This latter function is important in helping convince, first, the profession and, later, skeptical policymakers that the simulation models are something more than toy stories of how the economy just might work.

I thank Hermann Schnabl, David Midgley, Robert Wood, and Robert Kohn for valuable suggestions. Research support was provided by the Australian Graduate School of Management, the Australian Research Council, and the Max–Planck–Institute, Jena, Germany.

A general characteristic of simulation models, however, results in difficulties when one attempts to fit them to historical data: In general, the historical agents will have had many degrees of freedom in which to act, and have used them. [Indeed, had they not done so, the models would have been very simple and the level of potential surprise (Lave and March 1975) much less and the value of the modeling exercise much reduced.]

With continuous models, this is not an issue, but with discrete models there is a trade-off: More degrees of freedom are more realistic, but more degrees of freedom result in the phenomenon dubbed by Bellman as the "curse of dimensionality" (Rust 1997, footnote 6). What is meant is that with many degrees of freedom, the number of potential states grows quickly, as is demonstrated below.

Surely the answer is to use continuous models and to avoid discrete models? Well, if the phenomena being modeled are such that continuity holds, so that functional relationships are continuous, then, of course, avoid discrete models. For relationships in which the variables can be classified or measured with interval or ratio scales, continuity holds, but for nominal scales it does not, and for ordinal scales it may not.

1 An example: the rivalrous dance

Two gas stations face each other across an intersection. They sell different brands of gas, regarded as perfect substitutes by almost all motorists. As a consequence, almost all sales go to the station selling cheaper gas at any time. Prices are not stable, but move up and down, often in an asymmetric pattern of gradual falls followed by sharp rises (Slade 1992 describes such situations in the Vancouver market.) Sometimes, a move as small as 0.1c per gallon by one seller will elicit a responding price change by its rival; at other times there will be no response. How can we model this interaction while paying attention to the observations that both sellers are interested in maximizing their profits over time and that both sellers are economizing on their use of information? To generalize, information of one's rival's strategic behavior is costly to obtain and to process, so profit maximization includes cost-minimizing behavior on the perception and the use of information.

In a competitive market, that is, when there are many rivals selling perfect substitutes to a large number of buyers, this is not an issue, as firms will be selling at the going price. But when the products are not homogeneous and when the number of sellers is small – the case, for instance, of branded goods sold in oligopolies – there will be a range of prices (and other marketing instruments' levels) at any instant, and there will be a jockeying through time as firms move along their sales-profits trade-offs: sometimes going for sales and market share at the expense of profits (at lower prices) and at other times the opposite. This rivalrous dance has been analyzed within the framework of strategic game theory (Midgley et al. 1997, Marks et al. 1995, Marks 1998).

Historical data of actual responses by sellers competing through time has been used to endogenize three aspects of a stimulus-response model of a seller in such a market: first, the way in which each seller partitions the signals he or she receives of the actions of others; second, the way in which each seller decides on a set of possible responses; third, the best mapping from perceived signal to best action. The metric used is average profits over many periods, in which we use established market models to map from the players' actions, taken together, and each player's period profit. When completed, this research program will allow use of historical data to estimate each seller's endogenous decisions of perception, response, and action.

In a static setting, it is relatively easy to determine whether a small price change by a rival should be responded to. In a dynamic interaction, however, the response is not obvious, as any single change may be part of a longer-term pattern or may be the start of an attempt to signal the end of a price war (if upward, after a period of low prices) or to steal rivals' sales (if downward, after a period of high prices). Just which it might be is not always clear, especially with costly observing, processing, and recalling of prices, present and past.

For our stimulus-response agent, the stimulus is the state of the market and the response is the combination of price and other marketing actions chosen in the next period – we confine ourselves to discrete time, as our data show only once-weekly changes in actions: an iterated oligopoly. The state of the market includes the actions of all players in previous periods, and the number of weeks remembered is endogenous. This seems to be a simple model, but when there are more than two players, or more than a handful of possible prices, or more than one period's memory of past prices, the number of possible states grows quickly. In Midgley et al. (1997), it is shown that if there are p players, a possible actions per period, and m periods of memory, then the number of states is given by a^{mp}. With four players, eight possible actions, and two-period memory, the number of possible states is thus almost 17 million. This "curse of dimensionality" poses a severe problem for estimation of such models.

Although agents may choose their actions from a continuous set, I believe that partitioning to reduce the number of states is appropriate for two reasons: first, on grounds of tractability, and, second, because partitioning seems a good description of actual behavior.[1] Agents apparently partition the space of possible actions and respond only when a rival's action changes the state, suitably defined by use of the partitioning. This behavior is consistent with the observation that information gathering and processing is a costly activity, to be economized: Small changes in a rival's price may not be worth responding to, which brings us back to the observation above: Only when a rival's price change is sufficiently large to change the state will the seller (the economic actor) respond.

[1] Think of the large number of words the Inuit have to describe snow as a measure of the fineness of their perception partition for kinds of snow.

On the face of it, the best partitioning should be that which loses the least information. This has been made operational in Marks (1998), by a search for the partitioning that minimizes the entropy, as is discussed below. But information is not an end in itself, as we have implicitly assumed. Rather, information is a means to an end – to maximize net return in the repeated interaction among the players.[2]

The next stage of our ongoing research program is to search for the best combination of information partitioning and the consequent mapping from state to action, by using exogenous actions, as we have done previously. The last stage of the program must be to endogenize the choice of actions too, so that we are searching for the best combination of perceived states (partitions), action mappings, and final actions in the repeated interactions.

Such a model is discrete: Because the numbers of the states of the model are arbitrary and because we have no wish to constrain our machine-learning algorithm, the model scales are nominal: A change in input from a state, say number 24, to another, say number 25, will not necessarily result in a change of action from number 3, say, to number 4. We must use discrete formulations instead of continuous functions.

This causes no difficulty for digital computing; indeed, it is the continuous models that in principle are ill-suited to digital computing. The problems with discrete models arise when we consider the number of possible states – the curse of dimensionality – as discussed above.

2 Coffee sellers

In the course of earlier work on the U.S. retail ground coffee market, in which we modeled players as responding simply to the past prices and other marketing actions of their strategic rivals (Marks et al. 1995, Midgley et al. 1997), we became aware of the importance of modeling not just the patterns of response of the strategic players, but also their perceptions, both in looking back and in discerning whether small price movements of their rivals' are strategically significant. How might such perceptions be endogenized? A firm answer to the question of how players partition[3] their perceptions of others' actions, both through time and across the price space, will also provide information on how much or how little information they choose to use: in short, how boundedly rational players are (Rubinstein 1998).

[2] As Radner (1972, p. 8) puts it, "One information function [or partitioning] is better than another if the maximum expected utility achievable with the first is greater than the maximum expected utility achievable with the second." Here, this corresponds to the maximum average profit of a brand in repeated interaction with others.

[3] The concept of partitioning in order to use the coarsest (or minimal) partition that is as informative as the nonpartitioned space was introduced by Blackwell and Girshick (1954).

In the coffee market we observed the price to vary from approximately \$1.50 per pound to approximately \$3 per pound. Because cluster analysis shows that some prices and marketing actions are used more frequently than are others for each brand, the earlier studies used four of these by each brand as the actions in its simulation. But even with this severe partitioning of action space, we found that the historical profit performances could be improved by our simple four-action, one-round-memory artificial agents.

But cluster analysis is a crude technique. We wish to use the data to examine the price partitions that the players actually used. Such partitions will generally be in terms of price (and marketing action) levels, but the boundaries introduced mean that (away from the boundary) a one-cent-a-pound change in price is not a signal responded to by the other players, whereas (at the boundary) such a small price change will be seen as strategically significant by the rival players. It may be that we should partition the first differences of prices, so that a small change in price will not be perceived as a strategically significant shift (no matter where the price was before the shift); only a price change (positive or negative, symmetrically?) will be seen as such.

3 Formalities

We first formalize the process that each player uses in deciding his or her action in the market from one week to the next by using a framework outlined by Lipman (1995). Each week, faced with the actual external state (or E state), the player perceives an internal state (or P state), which will update his or her beliefs, on which is conditioned his or her action for the week, which together with the actions of his or her strategic rivals determines his or her profit that week.

There is a finite set of external states (or E states). The E states are defined by the prices (and marketing actions) that each of the players determined for its brand for a large number of weeks into the past. $\Omega = A_1 \times A_2 \times A_3 \times A_4$, where A_i is the vector of brand i's prices (or actions) for all weeks into the past. Figure 17.1 illustrates the model from the external E state to final payoffs.

But it is unlikely that players perceive the information partition at its objective fineness, as defined in the E state. Nor is it likely that players remember more than a few weeks past in determining the internal state θ. There is a function $\zeta : \Omega \rightarrow \Theta$ that tells which perceived P state θ the player observes as a function of the E state, where ζ is the perception function: in E state ω, the player observes P state $\theta = \zeta(\omega)$.

As a consequence, the true information content of the P state θ is that ω is one of the E states generating this P state: the true E state ω is some element $\zeta^{-1}(\theta)$. If the P state is optimally determined, then the lost information is valueless to the player – the player is no worse off with the coarser partition

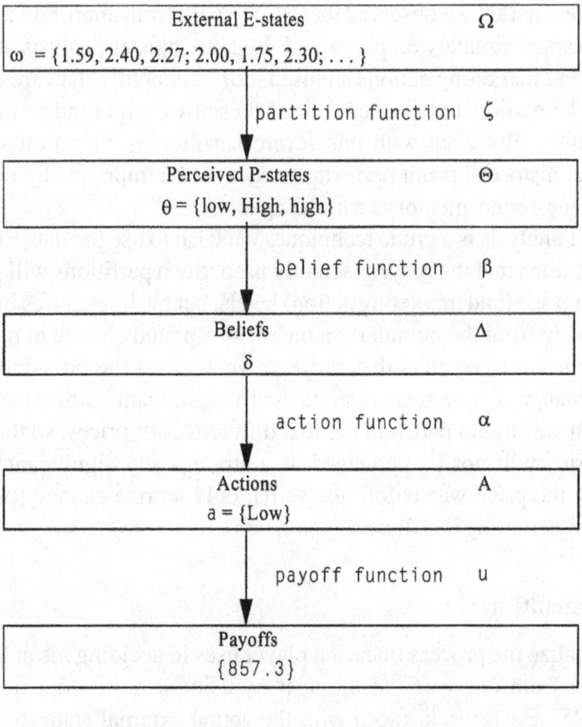

Figure 17.1. From external state to payoff: the player modeled.

of the P state than with the finer partition of the E state. But if the P state is suboptimal, then the lost information is valuable, in that its use would result in a perception of the rivals' behavior that would on average result in a higher profit for the player.

There will be a set of actions the player can choose from, denoted by A, with at least two elements. How or whether these actions are related to the perceived P states is an empirical issue. Note that because such perceptions are subjective, there is no guarantee that different players will perceive the same sets of P states.

There will also be a profit function (usually in the form of a payoff matrix) $u : A \times \Omega \rightarrow R$, which describes how the state affects the value of the different actions available to any player. Note that the profit function includes the true E state of the market during the present week (including all players' current actions), which will not be available to the players until after they have each chosen their actions. Note, too, that players will know only their perceived states, not the true external states, even later. In general, one can assume a prior probability distribution q on Ω, although in this model the probability distribution over external states is determined endogenously by the choices of the players in the market.

How does the P state θ determine beliefs about the external state? Let Δ denote the set of probability distributions on Ω. Then $\beta : \Theta \rightarrow \Delta$ is the belief function. Beliefs matter because actions are contingent on them. The mapping from belief to action $a : \Delta \rightarrow A$ is the action function.

Following Lipman, we can check the internal consistency of the belief function β. No processing: $\delta = \beta(\theta) \forall \theta$, which suggests $\delta = q$, the prior distribution. Full processing: $\theta \neq \theta' \Rightarrow \beta(\theta) \neq \beta(\theta')$. We expect $\beta(\theta)$ to put probability 1 on the set $\zeta^{-1}(\theta)$. As Lipman puts it, the player should be able to say to himself or herself, "My beliefs are δ, but I know I'd have these beliefs if and only if $\omega \in W$. So I shouldn't be putting any probability on states outside W."

Lipman distinguishes between interim optimality and ex ante optimality. For the former, an action function $a : a(\delta)$ that maximizes the following function for all δ must be derived:

$$\sum_{\omega \in W} u(a, \omega)\delta. \tag{17.1}$$

Then a behavior rule must be constructed by letting $f(\omega)$ equal the action $a(\delta)$ in which P state $\zeta(\omega)$ results in action δ, that is, for each $\omega : \beta[\zeta(\omega)] = \delta$, let $f(\omega) = a(\delta)$. This describes how the player will behave in searching for any given solution.

If $\beta[\zeta(\omega)] = \beta[\zeta(\omega')]$, then $f(\omega) = f(\omega')$. If the player has the same beliefs in two E states, then the player's behavior is the same in those E states; that is, f is measurable with respect to $\beta(\zeta)$.

In the earlier studies of Marks et al., we derived Eq. (17.1) and we used firms' profits to proxy for u. Our action function was $a(\delta)$, where δ is the player's belief of the E state: We explicitly separated the determination of δ and the determination of a.

Lipman raises the following question: Is it odd to model bounded rationality by assuming optimal information processing? Why not just choose optimally a given ω? Well, we assume general knowledge, that is, how to solve, not the specific solution. The model shows how to choose β and f contingent on ω. Moreover, if players do not achieve optimal β and f, then the model of the world as the player sees it is not completely specified.

4 Radner's framework

Radner (1972, pp. 3–8) presents a nonstrategic antecedent of the model of Marks et al. An act is a function from the set S of states of the world to the set C of consequences. For any act a and any state s, let $a(s)$ denote the corresponding consequence that follows from a choice of a and the occurrence of s. A function

u on the set of consequences C is the utility function. A function ϕ on the set of states of the world S is the subjective probability function, such that the expected utility function U, defined on acts by

$$U(a) = \sum_s u[a(s)]\phi(s),$$

represents the ordering. (The state of the world could include others' actions, but Radner is not interested explicitly in strategic interactions.)

Let Y denote the set of alternative signals that the decision maker can receive. (These are our partitions of P states.) The information function η associates to each state s a signal $y = \eta(s)$. (This is our partition function.) Let D be the set of alternative decisions available. Let $\rho(s, d)$ be the consequence of decision d if state s obtains. The decision is chosen according to a decision function δ, so that, if state s obtains, then the signal will be $\eta(s)$, and the decision taken will be $\delta[\eta(s)]$, and the consequence will be $\rho\{s, \delta[\eta(s)]\}$. Therefore to each information function η and each decision function δ there corresponds an act $a(s) = \rho\{s, \delta[\eta(s)]\}$. The set of acts available depends on the set of available information and the decision functions, which are mappings from P state to actions, in our terms.

For a given information (or partition) function η, therefore, the problem is to choose an optimal decision function δ from the set of all possible decision functions from the set Y of signals to the set D of signals. For each signal, an optimal decision maximizes the conditional expected utility of the consequence, given the signal, which is Radner's principle of maximum expected utility.

For any state s and decision d, he defines the payoff $w(s, d)$ as

$$w(s, d) = u[\rho(s, d)]$$

where w is the payoff function. The expected utility of an information function η and a decision function δ can be expressed as

$$U(\eta, \delta) = \sum_s \phi(s)w\{s, \delta[\eta(s)]\}.$$

For the given information function, to each signal η is associated the set S_y of all states that give rise to the signal y, that is, the set of states s such that $\eta(s) = y$. For any decision function δ that uses the information function η, all states in the same set S_y must lead to the same decision.

∴ The expected utility of (η, δ) is

$$\begin{aligned} U(\eta, \delta) &= \sum_s \phi(s)w\{s, \delta[\eta(s)]\} \\ &= \sum_y P(y) \sum_{s \in S_y}^{s} P(S|y)w[s, \delta(y)], \end{aligned}$$

where $P(y)$ is the probability of the signal y and $P(s|y)$ is the conditional probability of the state s, given the signal y, that is,

$$P(y) = \sum_{s \in S_y} \phi(s),$$

$$P(s|y) = \phi(s)/P(y),$$

for s in S_y. We assume that $P(y) \neq 0$ for every signal y in Y.

So maximizing $U(y, \delta)$ is equivalent to choosing for each signal (of a partition) y a decision d that maximizes the conditional expectation $\sum_{s \in S_y} P(s|y)w(s, d)$. If two decision functions use the same information (or partition) function, then we can say that the first is better than the second if (with the given information function) it gives a higher expected utility than the second. But the comparison of information functions is not as simple: We must compare the expected utility of information functions when used with their corresponding optimal decision functions.

5 Comparisons of information structures

McGuire (1972) presents a version of Blackwell's theorem and discusses its importance for deriving measures of informativeness.

Blackwell's Theorem. *An information structure P is regarded as "generally more informative" than information structure Q ($P \supseteq Q$) if for all payoff matrices U the set u(Q,U) is contained in the set u(P,U).*

Let partitions or information structures P and Q possess a common (finite) state-of-the-world set S and finite signal sets Y and Z, respectively. Then the following is true:

$$P \supseteq Q,$$

which imposes a very incomplete ordering on the set of all information structures or partitions.

Any search for a one-dimensional measure of informativeness is a vain one: There exists no real-valued function f on the set of information structures or partitions such that

$$f(P) \geq f(Q) \text{ iff } P \supseteq Q.$$

In particular, entropy cannot individually serve as an indicator of informativeness.

6 Partition models

Information processing can be summarized by a partition Π of the set of E states Ω. A partition Π of a set Ω is a collection of subsets of Ω with the property that

$\omega \in \Omega$ is in exactly one of these subsets. The elements of the partition Π are often referred to as events. Intuitively, a partition Π is said to be finer than a partition Π' when learning which event of Π contains a given ω conveys more information than learning only which event of Ω' contains ω; the converse is a coarser partition.

The partition Π is easily interpreted in terms of information processing: If Π has only one event (the entire set Ω), then the player is not processing his or her input P states at all, which corresponds to the case in which $\beta(\theta) = q$ for every P state θ. By contrast, a partition that has a different event for each different E state ω involves complete processing: The player processes the information so thoroughly that he or she recognizes every possible distinction between inputs. His or her partition could not be finer.

Because Π summarizes information processing, write $V(\Pi)$ instead of $V(\beta)$ for the expected profit associated with information processing according to the belief function β, which is identical to the expected profit associated with the information partition Π. If we further assume that the cost of a given information processing function β depends on only the partition that β generates, then we can work with $c(\Pi)$ instead of $c(\beta)$ for the expected information processing costs.

7 Players as stimulus-response machines

One reason for studying game-playing machines is that they can be used to give a formal description of the concept of "bounded rationality" (Simon 1972, Rubinstein 1998), as finite machines must by definition be bounded. An automaton consists of a number of internal states, one of which is designated the initial state; a transition function, which specifies how the automaton changes states in response to the other players' actions; and an output function, which maps state to action. See Marks (1992) for a fuller treatment. In Marks et al. (1995) and Midgley et al. (1997) we used the genetic algorithm to determine the initial state and the mapping from state to action.

Let I denote the set of possible histories of play (of actions). Then with three players $I = A_1 \times A_2 \times A_3$, where A_i is the history of player i's actions in the game. A strategy in the game is a function σ that specifies an action as a function of the state of the game, which in turn is a function of the history of the game. If the game has an unlimited number of rounds, then after any history h the remaining game is still infinite. Hence a strategy for the overall game σ specifies a continuation strategy following h for the game. Kalai and Stanford (1988) call this the induced strategy $\sigma|h$. We can say that two histories, h and h', are equivalent under σ if they lead to the same induced strategy; $\sigma|h = \sigma|h'$.

Lipman argues that it is easy to show that this is an equivalence relation, so that it generates a partition of the history set I, which can be denoted by $I(\sigma)$.

If the player knows which event of this partition a history lies in, then the player knows enough about the history to determine the strategy it induces. Kalai and Stanford show that the number of internal states of the smallest automaton that plays a given strategy is equal to the number of sets in this partition when the "Moore machine" representation is used.

In the earlier studies of Marks et al., the set of external states Ω is the set of histories $I = A_1 \times A_2 \times A_3$, in which we model the strategic interaction of three brand managers as players. We arbitrarily chose a time partition of one-round memory, so that no actions of more than a week ago were directly perceived by the players (although indirect influences through others' actions last week were not, of course, excluded). To partition the large number of possible prices, we used cluster analysis on historical data of the oligopoly in order to partition the price space into four bands, again an arbitrarily chosen number. The partitions varied with brand.

These techniques allowed us to map the E state of brands' prices (and other marketing actions) for many weeks into a much coarser P state of one week's data, suitably partitioned: an exogenous perception function $\zeta : \Omega \to \Theta$. As described, we then used machine learning to search for better mappings from P state to action, or $a[\beta(\theta)]$. Note that, by using machine representations, we did not explicitly model beliefs δ, or a belief function $(\beta : \Theta \to \Delta)$, or how actions are mapped from $(a : \Delta \to A)$. Instead, we defined our response function as a mapping from P state to action: $\gamma : \Theta \to A$.

The set of actions A is the set of strategies for the repeated game. Hence, following Lipman, any strategy σ can be described as a behavior rule f from $I(\sigma)$ into A, where $f(h) = \sigma|h$. Thus we can separate the choice of a strategy σ into the choice, first, of a partition on the set of histories Π, and, second, of a function from Π to the set of strategies or actions. If used, the cost function c is usually taken as an increasing function of the number of events of the partition only, $c(\Pi)$, although other functions are possible.

8 Optimal partitioning

Lipman (1995) discusses a class of models in which, although the E state is observed directly, it is classified according to which of two sets it falls: whether or not it is above a certain real-valued threshold.[4] There seems no reason why the concept should not be generalized to multiple thresholds. The exogenous partitioning of the earlier studies of Marks et al. was into four regions, requiring three thresholds, but we have considered finer partitions, although the programming effort increases in the fineness.

[4] If the E state is not already expressed as a real number, it must first be translated into a real number. In our case, however, prices are real numbers, up to the integers.

A first cut

We start by considering the simplest partition of the price space, into two regions, a dichotomous partition between low and high prices. The question is where best to draw the boundary between the two regions. To explore this issue, we set up a model in which the choice of where to divide the region between the lowest price and the highest price is one of eight points, dividing the price space into nine equal regions. See Marks (1998) for an operationalization of these techniques.

From above, the set of external states Ω of the market with three strategic players is the set of histories $I = A_1 \times A_2 \times A_3$, but we wish to define a new set of market states based on the perceived states Θ. Instead of the set of E-state histories I, define a set of histories $\hat{I}_i = \hat{A}_{1i} \times \hat{A}_{3i} \times \hat{A}_{3i}$, where $\hat{A}_{ji}$ is the history of actions of player j as perceived by player i. As soon as we introduce subjective perceptions into the game, we introduce the possibility of subjective histories too, but, so long as the partitioning that gives rise to the perceived actions of self and others is endogenous, no player could improve his or her payoffs by changing his or her partitioning of the price space, at least in equilibrium. From a learning or evolutionary viewpoint, players will adjust their perceptions (their partitioning) so as to end up close to their notional equilibrium partitioning.

Measures of optimality

Which partitioning is best? To attempt to answer this question, consider the simplest nontrivial partition: high or low.

A dichotomous partition divides the price line into two regions only: low (below some partition point λ) and high (above it); there remains the empirical issue of the optimal location of the dichotomous partition point. Because there is only 1 degree of freedom in its choice, we can plot any measure against its location. Two measures are

(1) the number of perceived states
(2) the closely related measure of sample alog entropy across all perceived states, from Eq. (17.3).

The two measures are brand or player independent, as they do not require consideration of the actions that result from the perceived states, by player.

Consider the partition that loses the least amount of information.[5] One candidate is the partition (or partitions) that results in the highest number of perceived states, but there is a more informative measure: Theil (1981), in discussing the

[5] Later we shall heed McGuire and Radner (1972) and consider a metric not of information but of profit, as a function of partitioning.

general issue of information measures associated with events, suggests entropy.[6] Entropy H is given by

$$H \equiv -\sum_{i=0}^{N-1} p_i \log_b p_i, \tag{17.2}$$

where there are N perceived states and the probability (or observed frequency) of state i is p_i. Theil argues on axiomatic grounds that entropy is justified.

The maximum number of perceived states is equivalent to entropy as an information measure only when each state is equally likely or frequent, as is readily seen in Eq. (17.2) with $p_i = 1/N, \forall i$. With nonuniform distribution of states, the measure of the maximum number of states N throws away information about each state's frequency. Nonetheless, the two measures are empirically close in determining the optimal partition point with dichotomous partitioning. To better compare the two measures, we use the antilogarithm of entropy, or alog entropy (AE), which is given by the expression

$$\text{AE} \equiv \text{antilog}_b\, H \equiv b^H = \frac{1}{\prod_{i=0}^{N-1} p_i^{p_i}} \tag{17.3}$$

where b is the base of the logarithm used in Eq. (17.2). This measure, unlike entropy, has the additional benefit of being independent of the base b. The units of the measure of alog entropy are equivalent states.

Marks (1998) reports empirical studies of these two measures by using a data set of historical interactions in a mature, iterated oligopoly.

A player-specific measure

There is the possibility of a third brand- or player-specific measure, as there is no constraint on players to respond identically to the same observed state, and they do not.

With 1-week memory, three players, and dichotomous partitioning, there are $2^3 = 8$ possible states of the market, as defined by the partition point between low and high. Modeling the players as stimulus-response automata, capable of perceiving eight market states for the previous week's prices, we classify each player's prices into eight possible regions, equally spread between that brand's minimum and maximum prices.

[6] Of course, information is merely the means to an end: the player's profits or expected profits in a stochastic game. But, as McGuire (1972) argues, the search for a one-dimensional measure of "informativeness" – the value of a "information structure" or partition – is in vain; entropy included. See Section 3. See also Radner (1987, p. 300): "... there is no numerical measure of quantity of information that can rank all information structures [partitions] in order of value, independent of the decision problem in which the information is used."

If we have specified the model correctly and if the partition point is optimally chosen, we might expect that there is a one-to-one mapping of perceived state to action. (With, say, four price regions, we might expect a two-to-one mapping, in which perceived information is abandoned in the choice of action.)

The brand- or player-specific measure of the mean number of action mappings per observed state given the maximum number of observed states could result in three thresholds or points of partitioning per player, Π_{ij}, player i's point of partitioning player j's price actions into low and high regions. This allows subjective partitioning across players, and also allows each player to customize his or her perceptions of each of his or her rivals and himself or herself.

The measure of best used with this measure means that the definition of states that follows from the partitioning is better when, in the limit, each action is supported by a unique state. If, in the limit, we find that we cannot reduce the number of actions per state to one across all states, then this may be thought of as one or more of several possibilities: a misspecification of the model (it may be, for instance, that players respond to the first differences in prices – price changes – rather than where in price space a rival player has chosen to act), or that the assumption of a deterministic state to action behavior for each player is wrong, with some mixed-strategy element instead. Another possibility is that players did not have the data that we are using when they made their choice; and a further possibility is that weekly marketing actions (prices etc.) were decided not on a weekly basis, but beforehand over a block of weeks:

(1) For a given partition point and for a given brand, determine into which region of eight equally spaced regions between the minimum and maximum prices for that brand the next week's price falls.
(2) With the discrete states for a given partition point and the price regions for a given brand as determined above, now calculate an 8×8 matrix whose elements indicate the number of times state i resulted in a price for a given brand in range j after 1 week, across all weeks of data. With 1-week memory, 8 price regions provide the coarse, dichotomous partitioning of the price space with something to support: with fewer than 8 price ranges there is unnecessary information, which will in general be costly to obtain. The matrix is brand or player specific. Because the row dimension of the matrix is equal to the number of possible states, a different definition of state may result in a different number of rows for this matrix.
(3) This matrix allows easy counting of the number of distinct action mappings from state to price region for the brand or player under examination and for the given partition point. (Some states may not appear in the data.)
(4) Use a lexicographic ranking: If the number of states is less than all, then ignore this partition. If the number of states is equal to the maximum,

then the best partition is that that minimizes the mean number of mappings from state to price region. A (minimum) single mapping for each state would correspond to an ideal fit between partition (and states) and the brand's pricing behavior (as segmented into price regions). Call this measure the state-mapping brand-specific measure.

We have not derived comparative empirical results for this third measure.

9 Conclusion

As the power of computers has grown and numerical techniques have improved, there has been a growing demand for simulation techniques in economics. This has been reflected by the emergence of new journals and conferences that specialize in the theory, development, and application of simulation techniques in economics. A relatively undeveloped area of application has been the use of simulation with historical data, and it has been argued that there are particular issues and problems associated with the validation of these models, in particular the issue of the need to partition the historical data. From a learning or evolutionary viewpoint, we assume that players will have adjusted their perceptions (their partitioning) so as to end up close to their notional equilibrium partitioning.

Partitioning enables validation to occur by reducing the large number of states that the unpartitioned historical data would demand, but partitioning does not come without a cost: the loss of some information. Whether the lost information is important can be answered only by examination of lost opportunities for profit making on the part of the simulated firms, because, first, information is not an end in itself, but only a means to performing better in the oligopoly markets such as those discussed here, and, second, despite the attractiveness of entropy as a measure of information, there can be no one-dimensional measure of informativeness.

Nonetheless, three measures have been discussed that might be used in a first cut at examining almost optimal partitioning: the number of perceived states, a player-specific measure, and, of course, entropy. Ideally, we should consider the impact on the firm's profitability of changes in the partitioning scheme. But this must await further research.

REFERENCES

Blackwell, D., and Girshick, M. A. (1954). *Theory of Games and Statistical Decisions*, Wiley, New York.

Kalai, E., and Stanford, W. (1988). Finite rationality and interpersonal complexity in repeated games. *Econometrica*, **65**, 397–410.

Lave, C. P., and March, J. G. (1975). *An Introduction to Models in the Social Sciences*, Harper & Row, New York.

Lipman, B. L. (1995). Information processing and bounded rationality: a survey. *Can. J. Econ.*, **28**(1), 42–67.

Marks, R. E. (1992). Repeated games and finite automata. In *Recent Developments in Game Theory*, eds. J. Creedy, J. Eichberger, and J. Borland, Elgar, London, pp. 43–64.

1998. Evolved perception and behavior in oligopolies. *J. Econ. Dyn. Control*, **22**, 1209–33.

Marks, R. E., Midgley, D. F., and Cooper, L. (1995). Adaptive behavior in an oligopoly. In *Evolutionary Algorithms in Management Applications*, eds. J. Biethahn and V. Nissen, Springer-Verlag, Berlin, pp. 225–39.

McGuire, C. B. (1972). Comparisons of information structures. In *Decision and Organization: A Volume in Honor of Jacob Marschak*, eds. C. B. McGuire and R. Radner, North-Holland, Amsterdam, Chap. 5, pp. 101–50.

McGuire, C. B., and Radner, R. eds. (1972). *Decision and Organization: A Volume in Honor of Jacob Marschak*, North-Holland, Amsterdam.

Midgley, D. F., Marks, R. E., and Cooper, L. G. (1997). Breeding competitive strategies. *Manage. Sci.*, **43**, 257–75.

Radner, R. (1972). Normative theory of individual decision: an introduction. In *Decision and Organization: A Volume in Honor of Jacob Marschak*, eds. C. B. McGuire and R. Radner, North-Holland, Amsterdam, Chap. 1, pp. 1–18.

Radner, R. (1987). Teams. In *Allocation, Information, and Markets*, eds. J. Eatwell, M. Milgate, and P. Newman, Norton, New York, pp. 295–304; first published in *The New Palgrave*, Norton, New York.

Rubinstein, A. (1998). *Modeling Bounded Rationality*, MIT Press, Cambridge, MA.

Rust, J. (1997). Using randomization to break the curse of dimensionality. *Econometrica*, **65**, 487–516.

Simon, H. A. (1972). Theories of bounded rationality. In *Decision and Organization: A Volume in Honor of Jacob Marschak*, eds. C.B. McGuire and R. Radner, North-Holland, Amsterdam, Chap. 8, pp. 161–88.

Slade, M. E. (1992). Vancouver's gasoline-price wars: an empirical exercise in uncovering supergame strategies. *Rev. Econ. Stud.*, **95**, 257–74.

Theil, H. (1981). The maximum entropy distribution: second progress report, and appendix. Reports 8119 and 8120, Department of Economics and Graduate School of Business, Center for Mathematical Studies in Business and Economics, University of Chicago, Chicago, IL.

CHAPTER 18

The application of cellular-automata and agent models to network externalities in consumers' theory: a generalization-of-life game

Sobei H. Oda, Ken Miura, Kanji Ueda, and Yasunori Baba

It is usually assumed in economic theories that a consumer's utility depends only on his or her own consumption: A person's preference is not affected by other people's behavior. However, this is not always the case; to buy a suit, an antique, or a computer, one may consider how many other people have the same product. If a person's optimal decision depends on the number of those who make the same decision, it is said that there are behavioral dependencies resulting from network externalities. In this chapter we develop a cellular-automata (CA) model to describe the dynamics of markets with network externalities.

Behavioral dependence resulting from network externalities is not a new subject in economics. Not a few theoretical and empirical studies have been done about it among consumers since Liebenstein (1948) introduced the concept of bandwagon and snob effects; among recent related studies are those of Choi (1994), Church and King (1993), Curien and Gensollen (1990), Ducan (1990), Kesteloot (1992), and Liebowitz and Margolis (1994). Unfortunately, the conventional equilibrium analysis of markets with network externalities (Pyndyck and Rubinfeld 1990) seems to inappropriately express the dynamic process of such markets. Recent studies of Bikhchandani et al. (1992), Arthur and Lane (1993), Narduzzio and Warglien (1996), and Lane and Vescovini (1996) are more dynamical and clarify some interesting patterns of diffusion processes.

Nevertheless these mathematical models presume that behavioral dependence is sequential: They assume that the kth person observes all or some of his or her $k-1$ preceding persons but not in reverse.

The CA model is a more advantageous formulation of a market with network externalities, because it can express a market in which people affect and are affected by their neighbors. In fact, since Schelling (1978) applied CA to examine how a society evolves if people prefer that at least some fractions of their neighbors be of their own color, a number of CA models have been applied to economics and other social sciences; see the references of Epstein and Axtell (1996), whose sugar space model is one of the most recent applications of CA to economics. We present a CA model along this line of study.

Our basic idea regards cells as those who may or may not buy a product according to its price and the number of their neighbors who purchased the product last time. By doing so, in contrast to the equilibrium approach, we can describe how a market with network externalities evolves if people repeatedly gather local information, do a small calculation to make a decision, and put it into practice.

A distinctive feature of our mode is the parametric treatment of the neighborhood size. It is usually assumed that the neighborhood of each cell, or the set of cells that may affect it, consists of the adjoining four or nine cells. The variety of CA lies in the birth and death rules: An example is that a living cell will survive only if two or three of its eight neighbors are alive whereas a dying cell will come back to life only if three of its neighbors are alive (Poundstone 1984) . To the contrary, our birth and death rules are always very simple: that a conformist (snob) will buy a product if and only if more (less) than a certain number of his or her neighbors purchase it, but we examine cases in which each person has more neighbors, say 8, 24, 48, ... As the number of neighbors increases, we can expect that the dynamics of the number of purchasers becomes nearer to the dynamics expected by the aggregate model that presumes all consumers observe all consumers. Our main purpose is to use simulations to clarify both the validity and the limit of the aggregate model and the well-known S-shaped diffusion curve (Rogers 1995).

This chapter is organized in the following way. In Section 1 we review the conventional equilibrium analysis of a market with network externalities, mentioning why it can only inappropriately express the dynamics of such markets. In Section 2 we present our CA model. In Section 3 we explain some results from the simulations of our model. The first half of the section is assigned to the cases in which all are identical conformists, whereas the second half is allotted to the cases in which there are conformists and snobs. Being cautious about deriving general statements only from simulations, we could say that in both analyses the long-run equilibrium – if there exists such a situation – can differ from the one defined in Section 1. Last, in Section 4, we mention some aspects of our analysis as a CA model and an economic/marketing theory.

1 Equilibrium analysis

The simplest equilibrium analysis of the market with network externalities is summarized in the following way (Pyndyck and Rubinfeld 1990). Suppose that consumer k buys a commodity if and only if its price P does not exceed his or her reservation price P_k:

$$X_k = \begin{cases} 1, & P \leq P_k \\ 0, & \text{otherwise} \end{cases}, \tag{18.1}$$

where X_k stands for consumer k's demand for the commodity (it is assumed that no consumer purchases more than one unit of the commodity even if it is very cheap). If there is a network externality,

$$P_k = f_k(N_k), \tag{18.2}$$

where N_k stands for the number of purchasers of the commodity that consumer k expects. Consumer k is called a conformist (snob) if f_k is an increasing (decreasing) function of N_k. Under the circumstances, X_k is a function of P and N_k:

$$X_k = F_k(P, N_k). \tag{18.3}$$

Let $X = S(P)$ be the market supply function. Equilibrium is defined by

$$S(P) = X = \sum_k F_k(P, X). \tag{18.4}$$

Then, because market demand equals market supply while every buyer correctly expects market demand, $N_k = X$, neither sellers (producers) nor purchasers (consumers) have reason for changing their decision.

Under some conditions Eq. (18.4) defines a unique equilibrium set of price and quantity. Yet how it can be realized? It is often assumed that commodities are neither sold nor bought till all sellers and buyers fix their decisions: First the equilibrium set of price and quantity (P^*, X^*) is discovered by auction and then X^* units of the commodity are produced to be sold at the price of P^*. This is the dichotomy of information processing (communication and calculation) and economic activities (selling and buying).

Rarely is it the case in the real world. As an example, consumers may find a type of suit that is in fashion when they see someone wearing it on the street. In the circumstances a person's economic activity (to buy and put on a suit) generates information (which suit is in fashion) and affects other persons' economic activity (which suit they purchase). Information processing and physical activities interact with each other in the real economy.

Bikhchandani et al. (1992), Arthur and Lane (1993), Narduzzio and Warglien (1996), and Lane and Vescovini (1996) have developed such models in which consumers' decision making may depend on their preceding consumers' behavior: The kth person can observe all or some of the $(k-1)$th persons' activities (to buy a product or not or to buy a commodity or the other one) and then determine his or her behavior.

In the circumstances, the dichotomy is not presumed, but network externalities are one dimensional and one directional: The kth person is not seen by the preceding $k - 1$ persons. We should, however, like to examine cases in which network externalities are two dimensional and interactive: cases in which a person's behavior affects and is affected by his or her neighbors' behavior. Such externalities may be too complicated to be analyzed mathematically, but they can readily formulated in terms of CA.

2 Cellular-automata model

Let us imagine a peaceful village in which people go for a walk every weekend. The only concern of the villagers during weekdays is whether they will go out with a rose on the coming weekend. Apart from the price of a rose and one's own preference (some may like roses more than others), one may consider whether those who may be seen during the walk put on a rose; a person may be delighted by seeing a neighbor wearing a rose, whereas another person may be disappointed by it.

Let us suppose that the village which is divided into B^2 squares like a chessboard and that a person lives in each square. We designate the villager living in the (i, j) square as V_{ij} and define his or her neighbors as

$$N_{ij}(R_{ij}) = \left\{ V_{mn} \left| \begin{array}{l} \max(1, i - R_{ij}) \leq m \leq \min(B, i + R_{ij}) \\ \max(1, j - R_{ij}) \leq n \leq \min(B, j + R_{ij}) \\ V_{mn} \neq V_{ij} \end{array} \right. \right\} \tag{18.5}$$

Let us also assume that to wear a rose on the Saturday of the tth week $(1 \leq t)$, one must buy a rose at the price of P on the previous day and that if V_{ij} purchases and wears a rose, his or her utility increases by

$$\bar{P}_{ij}[1 + a_{ij}\sigma_{ij}(t)] - P, \tag{18.6}$$

where $\bar{P}_{ij}$ is a positive constant, a_{ij} is a constant that is positive or negative according to whether V_{ij} is a conformist or a snob, and $\sigma_{ij}(t)$ represents the local ratio of rose wearers whom V_{ij} observes on the Saturday of the tth week:

$$a_{ij}(t) = \frac{\sum_{V_{mn} \in N_{ij}} X_{mn}(t)}{E_{ij}(i)E_{ij}(j) - 1}, \tag{18.7}$$

where the numerator of the right-hand side stands for the number of the V_{ij}'s neighbors who put on a rose on the weekend and the denominator represents the number of the V_{ij}'s neighbors:

$$X_{mn}(t) = \begin{cases} 1, & \text{if } V_{mn} \text{ puts on a rose on the Saturday of the } t\text{th week} \\ 0, & \text{otherwise} \end{cases}, \tag{18.8}$$

$$E_{ij}(k) = \begin{cases} B & \text{if } B \leq 1 + 2R_{ij} \\ 1 + R_{ij} + k & \text{if } k - R_{ij} < 1 \text{ and } k + R_{ij} \leq B \\ 1 + R_{ij} + B - k & \text{if } 1 \leq k - R_{ij} \text{ and } B < k + R_{ij} \\ 1 + 2R_{ij} & \text{otherwise} \end{cases}. \tag{18.9}$$

The difficulty that villagers may feel on every Friday is that they must decide whether they buy a rose or not without knowing how many of their neighbors will wear a rose on the next day. Under the circumstances V_{ij} could not but determine $X_{ij}(t)$ according to his or her expectation on $\sigma_{ij}(t)$:

$$X_{ij}(t) = F_{ij}[P, \hat{\sigma}_{ij}(t)], \tag{18.10}$$

where $\hat{\sigma}_{ij}$ stands for the V_{ij}'s expectation on $\sigma_{ij}(t)$ and

$$F_{ij}(P, \hat{\sigma}) = \begin{cases} 1, & \text{if } P \leq \bar{P}_{ij}(1 + a_{ij}\hat{\sigma}) \\ 0, & \text{otherwise} \end{cases}. \tag{18.11}$$

As to the determination of $\hat{\sigma}_{ij}(t)$, we assume the following simple rule:

$$\hat{\sigma}_{ij}(t) = \sigma_{ij}(t-1). \tag{18.12}$$

As to the initial condition, we define the central part of the village as the C^2 square at the center of the B^2 square village ($0 < C \leq B$). We assume that at the initial point in time ($t = 0$), no one wears a rose outside the central part whereas everyone living in the central part may put on a rose independently at the probability of s ($0 < s \leq 1$); consequently, approximately $100s\%$ of the central inhabitants put on a rose in the 0th week: $s \approx \sigma(0)$.

From all the above-mentioned assumptions and conditions, the overall ratio of rose-wearing people,

$$\sigma(t) = \frac{\sum_{j=1}^{B}\sum_{i=1}^{B} X_{ij}(t)}{B^2}, \tag{18.13}$$

is uniquely determined.

Following the definition in Section 1, we can define an equilibrium as a situation in which no one has regrets. On the Saturday of the tth week V_{ij} does not regret the previous day's decision if he or she sees $\sigma_{ij}(t)$ is such that

$X_{ij}(t) = F_{ij}[P, \sigma_{ij}(t)]$. Hence the set of X^*_{ij} defines an equilibrium if the following is satisfied for all i and j:

$$X^*_{ij} = F_{ij}\left(P, \frac{\sum_{V_{mn}\in N_{ij}} X^*_{mn}}{E_{ij}(i)E_{ij}(j) - 1}\right). \tag{18.14}$$

Checking this for all the 2^{B^2} possible combinations of X^*_{ij}, we can either say that there is no equilibrium or obtain every equilibrium set of X^*_{ij}. The equilibrium ratio of rose-wearing people is

$$\sigma^* = \frac{\sum_{j=1}^{B}\sum_{i=1}^{B} X^*_{ij}}{B^2}. \tag{18.15}$$

However, because finding the equilibrium set of X^*_{ij} may require a very large computational quantity for large B, we regard such $\sigma^\#$ that satisfies

$$\frac{\sum_{j=1}^{B}\sum_{i=1}^{B} F_{ij}(P, \sigma^\#)}{B^2} - \sigma^\# = 0 \tag{18.16}$$

as the approximation of σ^*. In fact $\sigma^\#$ represents the precise value of σ^* if everyone's neighborhood is the whole village (then everyone is a neighbor of everyone else): $\sigma^\# = \sigma^*$ if $B \leq 1 + 2R_{ij}$ for all i and j. Because Eq. (18.16) is essentially the same as Eq. (18.3), this is presumed in the analysis of Section 1.

We make a few simulations in Section 3. Because we use some variations of the above-mentioned basic model, we conclude this section by mentioning some variations.

First, we may assume that no villager can be original enough to recognize the habit of rose wearing without seeing someone wearing a rose:

$$X_{ij}(t) = 0 \quad \text{if } \sigma_{ij}(u) = 0 \quad \text{for all } 0 \leq u \leq \iota - 1. \tag{18.17}$$

As we see in Section 3, this additional assumption can be significant if C is small.

Second, we may replace Eq. (18.7) with

$$\sigma_{ij}(t) = \frac{X_{ij}(t) + \sum_{V_{mn}\in N_{ij}} X_{mn}(t)}{E_{ij}(i)E_{ij}(j)} \tag{18.18}$$

and modify Eq. (18.13) accordingly. This replacement implies that villagers take their previous decision into the calculation of the local ratio of rose-wearing people. Scarcely does this modification affect the qualitative properties of the model. As we see in Section 3, however, if R_{ij} is small, the difference between Eqs. (11.7) and (18.18) may be large enough to affect the dynamics considerably in quantitative terms.

Third, we can suppose that the village lies on the surface of a torus by combining opposite edges of the square village. On this periodic boundary condition, the village has no periphery; for example V_{1j}'s northern neighbor is V_{Bj} whereas V_{i1}'s western neighbor of is V_{iB}. Hence the number of V_{ij}'s neighbors is always $\min[(1+2R_{ij})^2, B^2] - \frac{1}{2} \pm \frac{1}{2}$; for example if $R_{11} = 1$, V_{ij} has in all eight or nine neighbors: V_{BB}, V_{B1}, V_{B2}, V_{1B}, V_{2B}, V_{12}, V_{21}, V_{22} [and V_{11} if $\sigma_{ij}(t)$ is of Eq. (18.18) type]. Because this is useful to see how the dynamics develop in a hypothetical market that has no central point, we often use this variant in Section 3.

3 Simulations

Cases in which consumers are homogeneous

Let us start with the cases in which all villagers are conformists of the same type while the price of a rose is fixed between the minimum and the maximum reservation price of villagers:

$$R_{ij} = R, \quad P_{ij} = \bar{P}, \quad a_{ij} = a, \quad \bar{P} < P < \bar{P}(1+a) \quad \text{for all } i \text{ and } j, \tag{18.19}$$

that is, any consumer will buy a rose at time $t+1$ if and only if more than $100[(P-\bar{P})/\bar{P}]$ percent of his or her neighbors purchase it at time t. An equilibrium value of $\sigma(t)$ is defined as a fixed point of the return map:

$$s(t) = \frac{\sum_{j=1}^{B} \sum_{i=1}^{B} F_{ij}[P, s(t-1)]}{B^2}. \tag{18.20}$$

As is readily checked, there are three equilibrium values:

$$\sigma_1^{\#} = 0, \quad \sigma_2^{\#} = \frac{1}{a}\frac{P-\bar{P}}{\bar{P}}, \quad \text{and} \quad \sigma_3^{\#} = 1. \tag{18.21}$$

The return map of the model of this subsection is shown in Fig. 18.1; the equilibrium values are given at the intersections of the map and the 45° line.[1]

If $B \leq 1 + 2R$, everyone's neighborhood is the whole village. Then $\sigma_{ij}(t-1)$ is common to all villagers so that the return map perfectly describes the dynamics of $\sigma(t)$: $\sigma(t) = s(t)$ for all $t \geq 1$. As is readily checked, $\sigma(t) = 0$ for all $t \geq 1$ if $\sigma(0) < \sigma_2^{\#}$, whereas $\sigma(t) = 1$ for all $t \geq 1$ if $\sigma(0) > \sigma_2^{\#}$, that is, the dynamics of $\sigma(t)$ in the aggregate model in which all villagers observe all villagers is quite simple: Rose-wearing behavior will have spread all over the

[1] Strictly speaking, $\sigma_2^{\#}$ does not satisfy Eq. (18.16), because if $\hat{\sigma}_{ij}(t) = \sigma_2^{\#}$ for all i and j, Eq. (18.10) implies that $X_{ij}(t) = 1$ for all i and j so that $\sigma(t) = 1 \neq \sigma_2^{\#}$. The fact is that $\sigma_2^{\#}$ is an equilibrium only if villagers may or may not buy a rose whose price equals their reservation price. However, having checked that no simulation in the text is affected if the first condition of Eq. (18.11) is replaced with $P < \bar{P}_{ij}(1 + a_{ij}\hat{\sigma})$, we ignore this throughout the analysis.

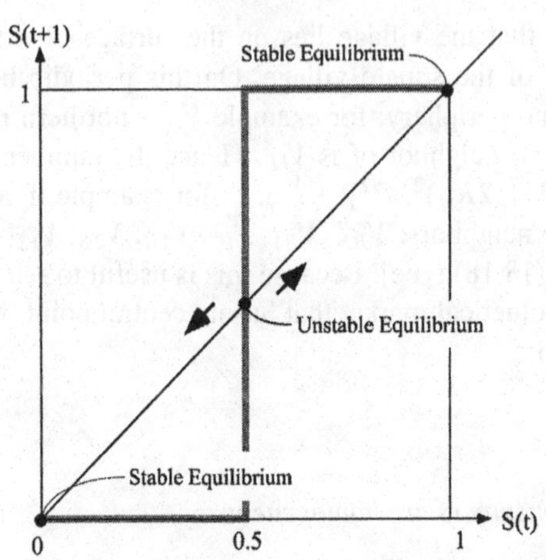

Figure 18.1. Return map. Where all villagers are identical conformists.

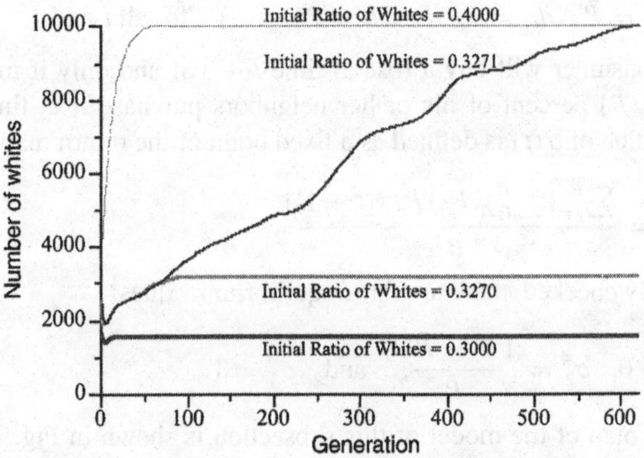

Figure 18.2. Dynamics of identical conformists for different mutual values, where $1 + 2R \leq B$.

village or died out in a week according to whether the number of the initial rose wearers exceeds a certain critical value or not; the situation will be maintained from the second week onward.

How does the dynamics of $\sigma(t)$ change if $1 + 2R \leq B$? As an example, let us examine the CA model with the minimum R (i.e., $R = 1$) or the cases in which villagers observe only their eight next-door neighbors. See Fig. 18.2, in which the curve of $\sigma(t)$ is drawn for various initial values. Here the initial rose wearers are distributed randomly with coupling: For example, initial rose wearers for $\sigma(t) = 0.2$ are randomly chosen and they are all initial rose wearers for $\sigma(t) = 0.3$. From the figure we can see both similarity and difference between the dynamics of $\sigma(t)$ in the aggregate model and its dynamics in the CA model. The long-run dynamics of $\sigma(t)$ in the aggregate model is basically maintained: From any initial value, $\sigma(t)$ virtually converges at a certain long-run equilibrium value; $\sigma(t)$ ceases to change completely or it continues to fluctuate with very small amplitude (less than 10, or 0.1% of the total population). Yet it takes more than 1 week for $\sigma(t)$ to reach the equilibrium value, which may not be zero or one: $0 < \lim_{t\to\infty} < 1$ if $0.1532 \leq \sigma(t) \leq 3422$.

Let us examine such a long-run equilibrium in which $0 < \sigma(t) < 1$ more closely. In fact, not only the total population of rose wearers but also their distribution are virtually fixed in the long run. See Fig. 18.3, where three final distribution patterns are shown (in this and the following maps of the village, white points represent rose wearers and black points stand for non-rose wearers). The final black–white patterns, which are something like a cow's skin, are

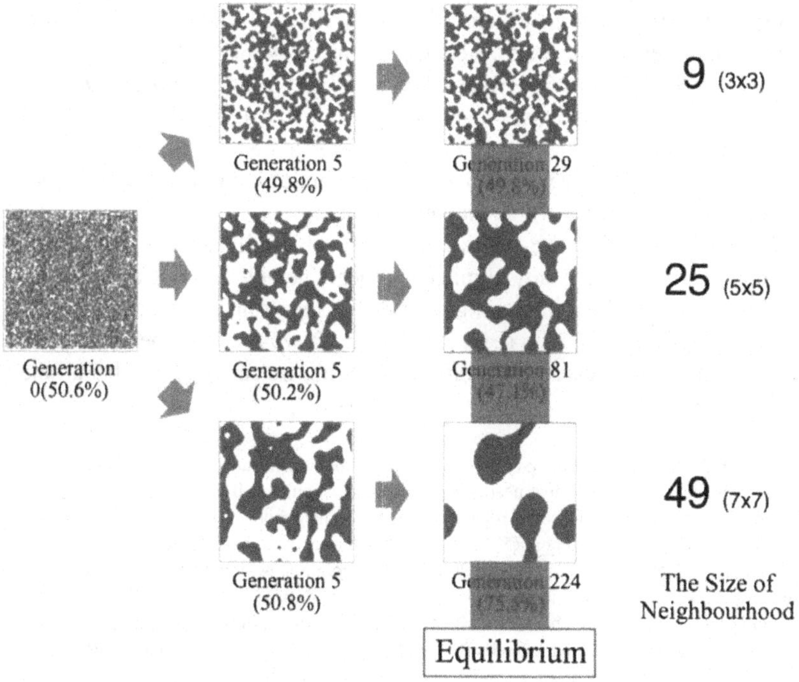

Figure 18.3. Final states where $1 + 2R \leq B$.

always obtainable: For large enough t, no points change color or only some points on the black–white border repeat to change color.[2]

In other words all or almost all X_{ij} remain to be zero or one for large enough t and consequently $\sigma(t)$ ceases to change in the long run; in such cases $\sigma(t)$ keeps a constant value whereas many X_{ij} repeatedly change the value.

However, although the long-run equilibrium is always obtainable not only at the aggregate level but also at the microlevel, each equilibrium is quite sensitive to the initial distribution of rose wearers. Actually, we can find a butterfly effect. Figure 18.4 illustrates how different limit values of 0.4973 and 1 are obtained from very similar initial values: 0.3422 and 0.3424. In fact, the two initial conditions are also similar on the disaggregate level: Out of 10,000 cells, only 1 is not common. As a result, the development of the black–white patterns is apparently indistinguishable until the pattern ceases to change in most areas of the village. However, the initial small difference survives so that the lower large white area connects with the middle area in this case whereas they remain separate in the other case. Although all the other areas are identical and remain unchanged in both cases, the connected white area grows to cover all over the village so that the value reaches unity in the former case.

Of course, the range in which $0 < \lim_{t\to\infty} \sigma(t) < 1$ becomes short as the number of neighbors increases. Actually in our simulations, the range, which is nearly 20% of the possible value of σ, $0.1532 \leq \sigma(0) \leq 0.3422$ if $R = 1$, becomes short as R increases and vanishes at $R = 4$. In addition, it takes fewer weeks for $\sigma(t)$ to reach one or zero. This is quite natural, but we should remember that $\sigma(t)$ may not follow such a dynamics the return map suggests if people observe not the whole market but only their neighborhood.

We can now conclude the analysis of cases in which villagers are all identical conformists who observe only a limited number of neighbors. First, all or almost all villagers are divided into two groups in the long run: those who continue to buy a rose and those who never purchase it. If we see only the final stable distribution of rose wearers and non-rose wearers, we can only say that all the

[2] In Fig. 18.3 we can see that the greater R is, the larger the patterns are. The reason is intuitively understandable: Those who live nearby have common neighbors. If R increases, the number of common neighbors increases in relation to that of all neighbors; V_{ij} and V_{ij+1} share 4 persons among each of 8 neighbors (50%) if $R = 1$, whereas they share 18 persons out of each 24 neighbors (75%) if $R = 2$. The greater the ratio of common neighbors, the more likely they are to have a closer local ratio of rose-wearing people and thus make the same decision. We should make a few remarks here. First, if R increases, as shown in the figure, it usually takes longer until the final black–white patterns appear. [Yet it is not a general rule that the final value of $\sigma(t)$ is larger for a greater R; completely opposite cases are also observed in our simulation.] Second, although what is stated in this note applies to almost all cases, it is not always so. The initial condition and parameters are the same as the ones for the first (3 × 3) case of Fig. 18.3 except that $\sigma_{ij}(t)$ is defined not by Eq. (18.7) but by Eq. (18.18).

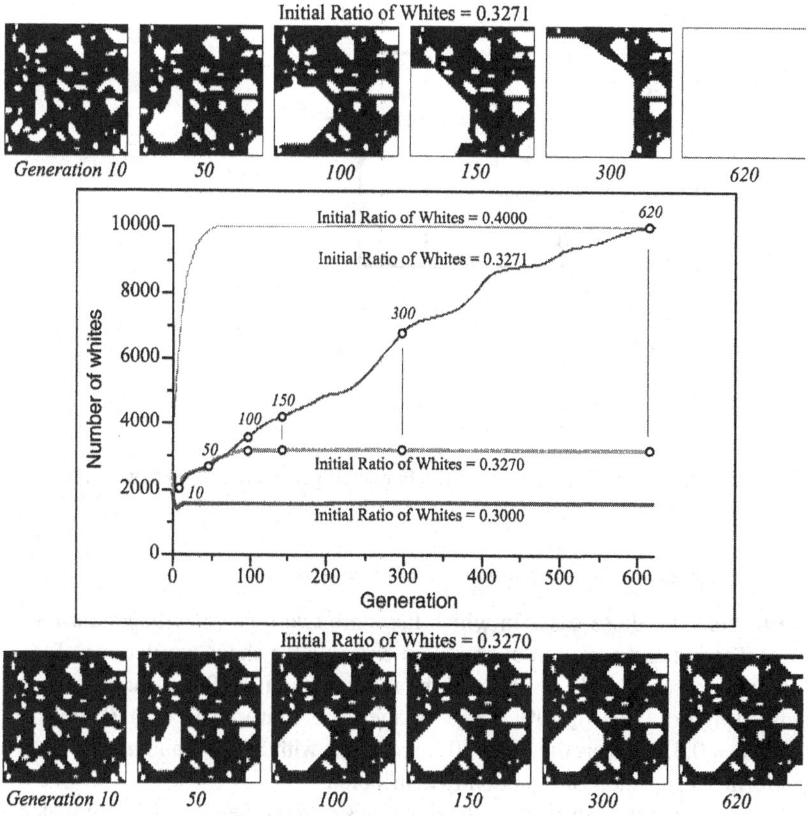

Figure 18.4. Sensitive dependence on initial conditions for $1 + 2R \leq B$.

villagers are perfectly divided into two groups of consumers: those who have a reservation price higher than the market price and those who have a reservation price lower than it. Nevertheless they do not make the same decision because they have different demand functions. They behave differently because they have the same demand function $F_{ij}(P, \hat{\sigma})$, where $\hat{\sigma}$ is different from person to person. This could not be realized without considering the history or by experiment (e.g., changing the addresses of villagers).

Second, it is virtually impossible to predict the final number of rose wearers (not to mention their final distribution) from their initial distribution; the former depends on the latter in a complicated manner. It is practically by chance that a person becomes a rose wearer (remember Fig. 18.4). The final lasting behavior of 5027 persons (more than half the population) is influenced by the initial accidental behavior of a person who may live far from where they live.

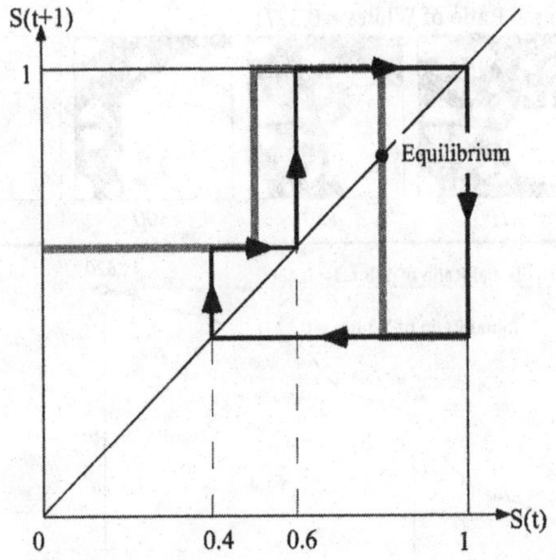

Figure 18.5. Return map of $S(t)$. For heterogeneous consumers with a unique but unstable equilibrium.

Cases in which consumers are heterogeneous

Let us consider those cases in which there are two types of villagers: a type of conformist and a type of snob. As an example we show simulations of the following case: $B = C = 100$ with boundary condition $P = 1$ and $\sigma_{ij}(t)$ is defined by Eq. (18.18); 40% of the villagers are conformists with $\bar{P}_{ij} = 1.1$ and $a_{ij} = 0.3$, whereas the other 60% are snobs with $\bar{P}_{ij} = 1$ and $a_{ij} = -0.3$; conformists and snobs are randomly distributed.

Let us start our analysis with the dynamics of $\sigma(t)$. See Fig. 18.5, in which the return map is shown. As stated in the preceding subsection, it determines $\sigma(t)$ completely if $B \leq 1 + 2R$. Although $\sigma^{\#} = 0.8$ is the unique equilibrium, it does not attract $\sigma(t)$. Except for the special case in which $\sigma(0) = \sigma^{\#}$, $\sigma(t)$ immediately follows the three-period limit cycle: $0.6 \to 1.0 \to 0.4 \to 0.6$. Again as in the preceding subsection, the return map governs the dynamics of $\sigma(t)$ in the long run if R is not so large. In fact, in our simulations $\sigma(t)$ soon falls into the limit cycle without exception if $R \geq 5$ or if the number of neighbors is ~12% of the population.

Let us examine the dynamics of $\sigma(t)$ in the aggregate. Figure 18.5 is the return map of $S(t)$, in which there is a unique equilibrium value: $\sigma^{\#} = 0.8$. As in the preceding case, however, it is an unstable equilibrium, which does not seem to attract $\sigma(t)$. The three-period limit cycle, $0.6 \to 1.0 \to 0.4 \to 0.6\ldots$, seems much more relevant to the dynamics of $\sigma(t)$. Again as in the preceding case, the limit cycle completely determines the dynamics of $\sigma(t)$ if $B \leq 1 + 2R$ and governs it even if R is much smaller: In our simulations $\sigma(t)$ soon falls into the cycle without exception if $R \geq 5$ (or if the number of each villager's neighbors is 121/10,000 of the population); see Fig. 18.6 (the case in which $R = 4$ is on

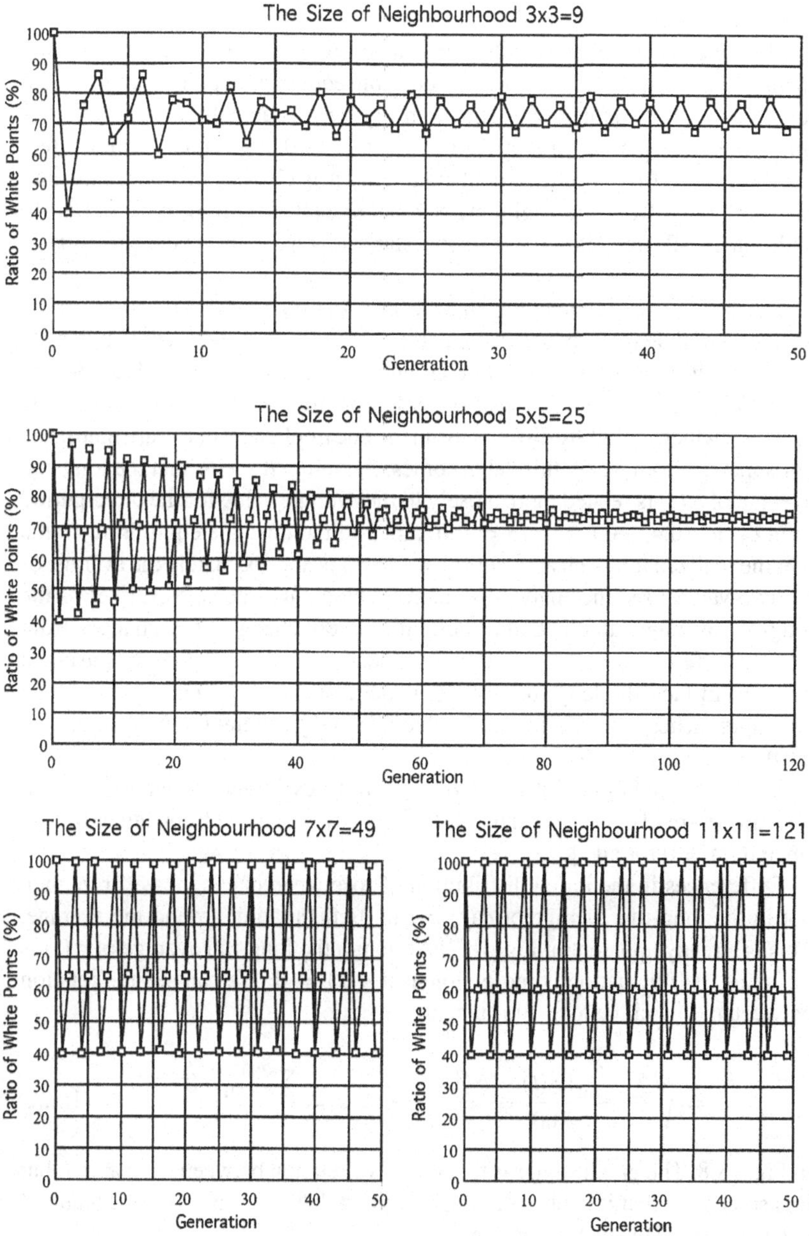

Figure 18.6. Limit cycles for heterogeneous consumers where $B \leq 1 + 2R$.

the border; then a three-period limit cycle survives, but it is slightly different from one the return map implies).

Here we see a unique equilibrium value: $\sigma = 0.8$. For the same reason mentioned in Fig. 18.2, however, this unstable equilibrium point does not seem to attract $\sigma(t)$; the situation as shown in Fig. 18.6 is actually the case. If anything, the three-period limit cycle, $0.6 \to 1.0 \to 0.4 \to 0.6, \ldots$, may affect the dynamics of $\sigma(t)$. In fact, mathematically it is obvious that $\sigma(t)$ falls into the limit cycle from the beginning if $\sigma(t) = s(t)$ (i.e., if $B \leq 1 + 2R$). In addition in all simulations $\sigma(t)$ soon starts to repeat the cycle precisely if $R \geq 5$.

If $R \leq 3$, however, something like the three-period limit cycle is not observed at all or is visible for only first some periods. As Fig. 18.6 shows, the limit cycle gradually disappears so that $\sigma(t)$ continues to fluctuate with small amplitude near 0.72 in the long run (the case is borderline; then a three-period limit cycle survives, which is slightly different from the one implied by the return map). It is not apparent from where this value comes: Although it seems that the long-run average of $\sigma(t)$ is related more closely to the average value for the three-period limit cycle, $(0.4 + 0.6 + 1)/3 = 0.67$, than to the unstable equilibrium value 0.8, the realized long-run average value of $\sigma(t)$ is approximately the average of the two values; see the analysis in the following paragraphs. Nevertheless the long-run average value is quite stable: it scarcely changes if R changes from 1 to 3. Differences in $\sigma(0)$ and/or R do not survive in the long-run average of $\sigma(0)$. In fact, the long-run average is quite stable. See Fig. 18.7, in which $\sigma(t)$ approaches the virtually same value from very different initial conditions: $\sigma(0) = 0.0001$ and $\sigma(0) = 1$.

In all our simulations for $R \leq 3, \sigma(t)$ approaches the above-mentioned value with a very small error (less than 0.5%) from any initial condition but $\sigma(0) = 0$ [then $\sigma(t) = 0$ for all t].

Differences in the initial distribution of rose wearers can, however, remain not in the long-run average of $\sigma(t)$ but in its fluctuation around the average. This is already apparent in Fig. 18.7: Although the long-run average of $\sigma(t)$ is the same, its fluctuation is more violent if $\sigma(t) = 0$. We can see the relation between $\sigma(t)$ and the long-run standard deviation,

$$s = \sqrt{\frac{\sum_{t=201}^{300}[\sigma(t) - \bar{\sigma}]^2}{100}} \quad \text{where } \bar{\sigma} = \frac{\sum_{t=201}^{300}\sigma(t)}{100}, \tag{18.22}$$

in Fig. 18.8. The graph suggests that there is a relation between $\sigma(0)$ and S, but it is so chaotic that it is virtually impossible to define S a priori if the value of $\sigma(0)$ is given. This may concern marketers.

Having seen the dynamics of the aggregate value $\sigma(t)$, we conclude this section by mentioning the dynamics of each $X_{ij}(t)$. As it is obvious whether a

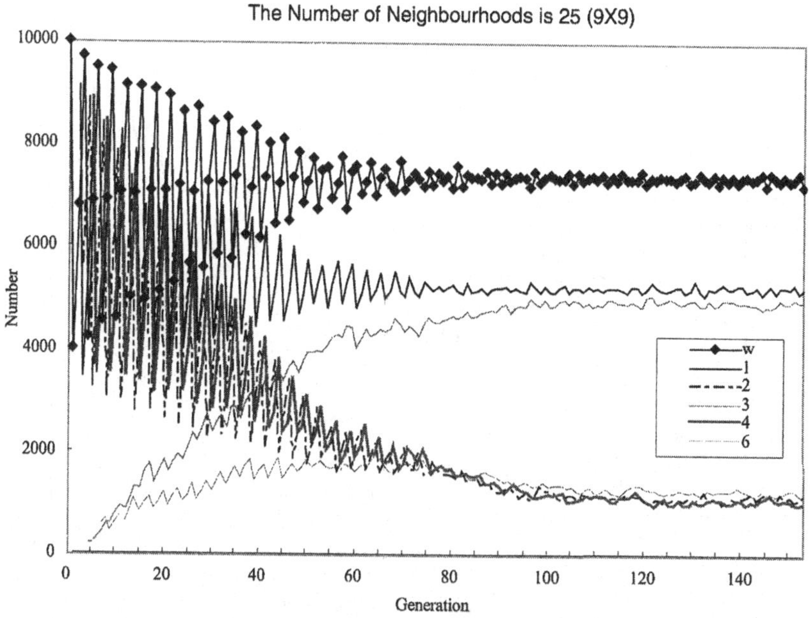

Figure 18.7. Stable long run averages despite different initial conditions.

limit cycle governs all the points, let us consider only cases in which $R \leq 3$. See Fig. 18.10, in which the value of line k represents $Y_k(t)$ or the number of points at which $X_{ij}(t) \neq X_{ij}(t-k)$. Obviously $Y_k(t) = 0$ if the black–white patterns at time t are identical to the patterns at time $t-k$. If $Y_k(t) = 0$ for all t, the same patterns appear every k times. The maximum value of $Y_K(t)$ is the total population, or 10,000 in the example. If $Y_k(t)$ =10,000 for all t, all the black–white patterns are reversed every k time; consequently the same patterns appear every $2k$ times. If $Y_k(t) = 5000$, just 50% of the points have the same value at time t as they had at time $t-k$; as a result the distribution of white points at time t may be completely different from the one at time $t-k$.

If $R \leq 3$, the three-period cycle mentioned by the return map is completely lost in the long run. As the three-period limit cycle suggested by the return map disappears, $Y_3(t)$ gradually increases to a level near 5000 and fluctuates around it with small amplitude. This suggests that the following interpretation is not correct: The global three-period limit cycle from $\sigma(0)$ [as rose wearers are distributed randomly at time 0, $\sigma_{ij}(0)$ is significantly different from $\sigma(0)$ at few points] is gradually divided into many local three-period different phased cycles so that the sequence of $X_{ij}(t)$, $X_{ij}(t+1)$, and $X_{ij}(t+2)$ is (0, 1, 1) at

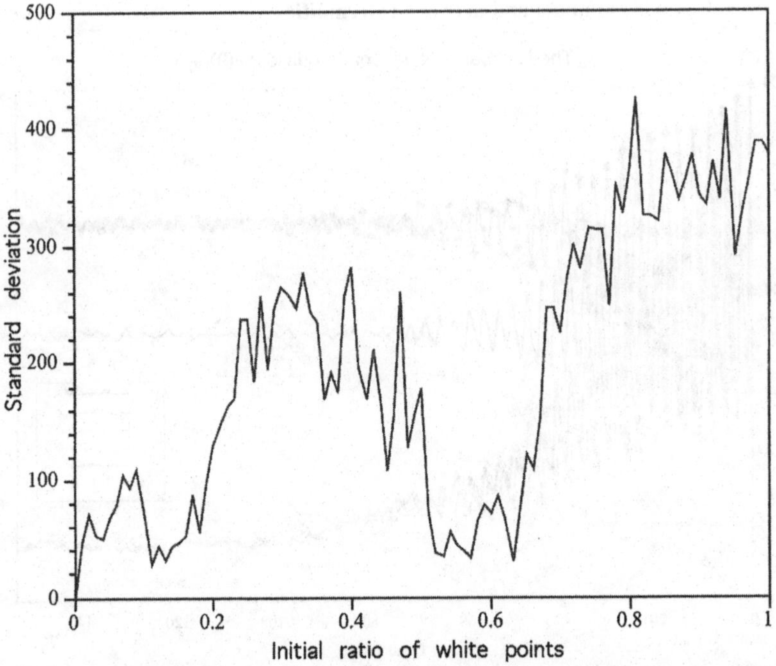

Figure 18.8. Volatile relation between initial distribution and standard deviation.

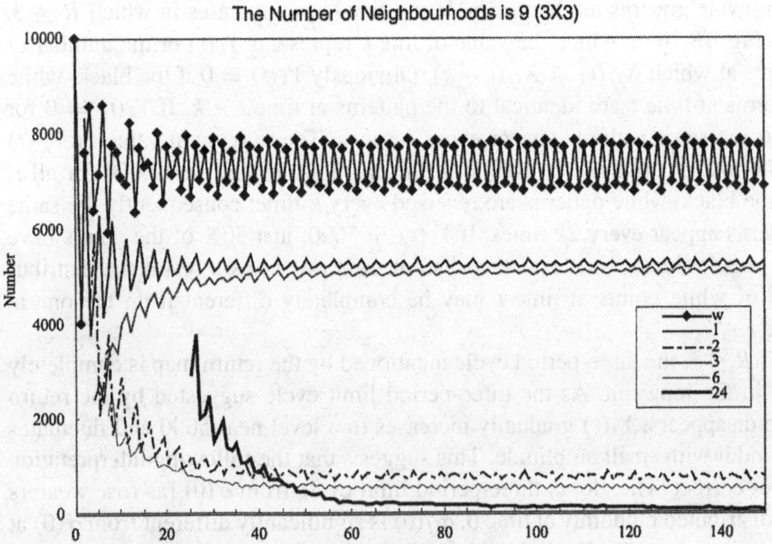

Figure 18.9. Dynamics of $X_{ij}(t)$ over time.

one third of the points, $(1, 0, 1)$ at another third, and $(1, 1, 0)$ at the other third in the long run. If so, $\sigma(t) = 2/3$ and $Y_3(t) = 0$ for all large enough t. The three-period cycle disappears even locally in the long-run equilibrium in which $\sigma(t)$ is stable (this is our definition of the long-run equilibrium).

Nevertheless $X_{ij}(t)$ does not change value randomly in the long-run equilibrium. In fact $Y_1(t)$ is ~5000 and $Y_2(t)$ is ~1000 for large enough t. If $Y_1(t) = 5000$ and $Y_2(t) = 0$, $X_{ij}(t-2) = X_{ij}(t-1) = X_{ij}(t)$ at 5000 points whereas $X_{ij}(t-2) \neq X_{ij}(t-1) \neq X_{ij}(t)$ at the other 5000 points. In other words, every point keeps the same color or changes color twice from time $t-2$ to t; no point changes color only once during the period, which cannot be observed if every point changes color randomly. Of course, because $Y_2(t)$ is not zero but ~1000, you cannot assert that a white pattern will be white the next time if $Y_2(t)$ is not zero. Yet this prediction comes true at the probability of 90%; probabilistic short-run prediction is possible in the long-run equilibrium.

In the long run, the completely same black-white patterns repeatedly appear at the same interval. This results from the fact that the distribution of white points at time t is uniquely determined by their distribution at the previous time whereas the possible number of the distribution of white points is finite (2^{10000} in our example). In other words, there exists a certain finite number K such that for large enough t for all i and j, $X_{ij}(t) = X_{ij}(t+K)$.

Nevertheless K may be extremely great. In fact we have checked that $Y_k(t) \neq 0$ if $k < 100$. As mentioned in relation to Fig. 18.9, $Y_{24}(t)$ is lower than 100 (1% of population) for all large enough t. This implies that more than 9900 points will have the same color at time t and for all large enough t. Hence the black–white pattern at $t = t_0$ is quite similar to the pattern at time $t = t_0 + 24$, which will be similar to the pattern at time $t = t_0 + 48$, which will be similar to the pattern at time $t = t_0 + 72$.... Nevertheless the black–white pattern at $t = t_0 + 2400$ may be quite different from the pattern at $t = t_0$. In fact, although the difference is so small (less than 1%) that it cannot be shown in Fig. 18.7, we have checked that $Y_{24}(t) < Y_{48}(t) < Y_{72}(t)$.

Let us conclude the cases in which consumers are heterogeneous. Unlike the cases in which consumers are homogeneous, we can predict the final value of $\sigma(t)$, which is independent of initial conditions. Nevertheless stable $\sigma(t)$ does not necessarily imply stable $X_{ij}(t)$. In fact, in our simulations for $R \leq 3$, each person continues to change behavior in such a very complicated (but not random) manner that we can virtually say nothing about the behavior of individual consumers. In other words, the stability of the aggregate value is one thing, but that of individuals' behavior is another. In the first subsection of this section the distribution of rose wearers is stacked in the long run, but the final distribution may change completely if initial conditions change slightly, whereas in the second subsection the distribution never ceases to

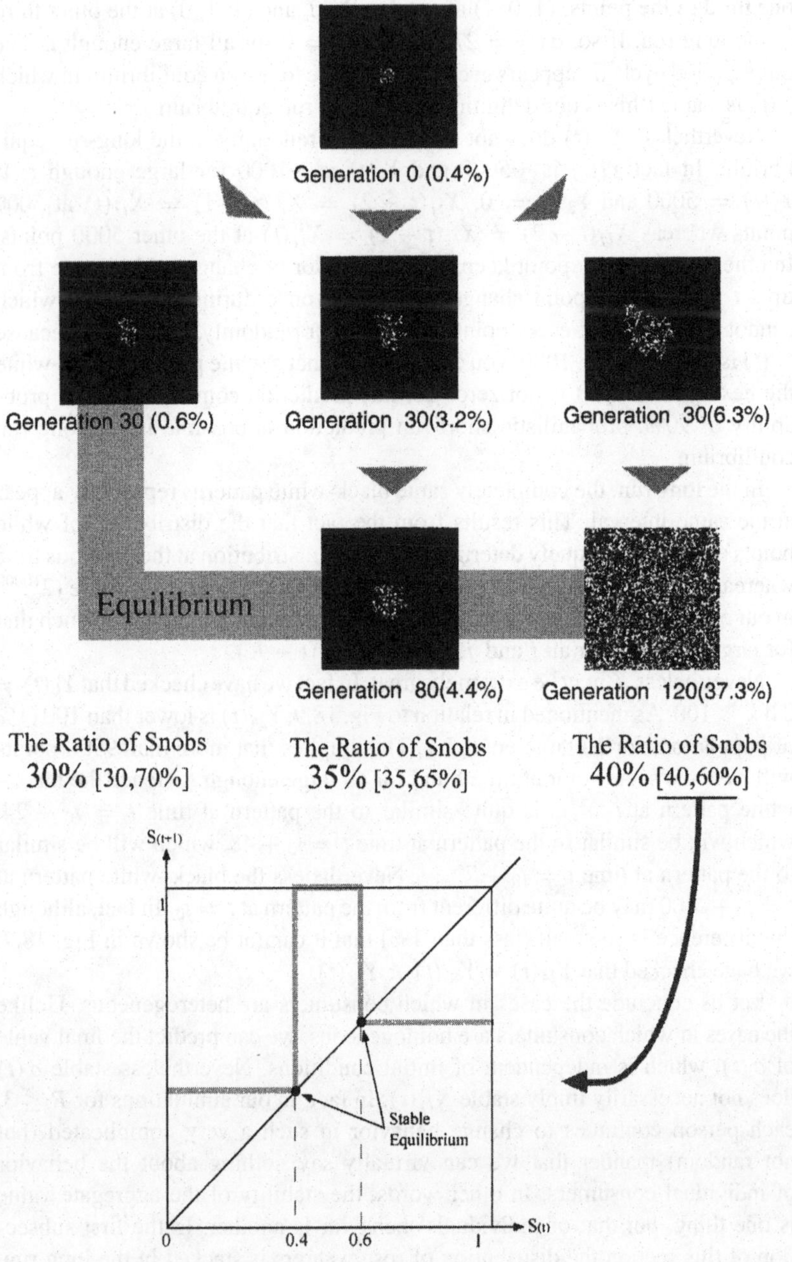

Figure 18.10. Predictable aggregate outcomes with heterogeneous consumers but unpredictable individual behaviors.

change, but the final percentage of rose wearers is virtually independent of initial conditions.[3]

We may compare our simulations in this section with marketing theories. Rogers (1995) and other marketing theorists claim that consumers can be classified according to when they purchase a new product; for example, Rogers and Shoemaker (1971) classify them as innovators (2.5%), early adopters (13.5%), early majority (34%), late majority (34%), and laggards (16%) according to the timing of purchasing a new product. From our viewpoint, however, the timing of purchasing does not correspond to the type of consumer; two consumers of the same type may make a different decision if their local condition is different. In addition, why the diffusion curve, or the curve to show the current or cumulative sales or quantity of a new product, is like a logistic curve is explained by the heterogeneity of consumers: Different types of consumers buy a new product at different points in the diffusion process. As Fig. 18.3 suggests, however, an S-shaped diffusion curve is obtainable if consumers are all homogeneous, but locally available information may differ from person to person. From our viewpoint, the heterogeneity of consumers is necessary not for the existence of an S-shaped diffusion curve but for its stability. If all consumers are homogeneous, our CA model becomes a CA model in which the birth and the death rules are not locally different. Once a pattern from which white points spread boundlessly is formed in a small neighborhood – even if white points can grow nowhere else – it can spread all over the world. However, if heterogeneous consumers are seeded randomly, whether the number of white points (rose wearers) grows or not is locally different. In other words, whether white points spread or not cannot be determined by local initial conditions. They spread only if it is possible globally, and as a result the diffusion process becomes robust.

4 Concluding remarks

Our CA model can be regarded as the generalization of the aggregate model in which all consumers observe the whole market. If everyone observes everyone, the local condition that may affect one's behavior is common to all consumers so that the evolution of the market is perfectly explained in aggregate terms; in our model, if all villagers observe all villagers, the percentage of rose wearers among neighbors $\sigma_{ij}(t-1)$ is common to all villagers so that the dynamics of the percentage of rose wearers in the village $\sigma(t)$ is perfectly explained by its return map. Yet if people observe only their neighbors, such an aggregate approach may fail to explain the market dynamics; in our simulations for $100 \leq B \leq 300$, such

[3] Macroscopic stability and microscopic stability are not always contractive. If there are conformists and snobs and the former are the majority, the return map defines a unique equilibrium, which is stable. Then, even for the smallest R, it is often observed that all conformists continue to buy while all snobs never buy in the long run.

long-run dynamics that is not suggested by the return map (e.g., convergence to an unstable equilibrium) can be observed for some initial conditions if N is smaller than 4 or 5. Because the total population is B^2 and the number of neighbors is $(1 + 2N)^2$, this implies that the return map analysis may not hold true even in the long run if each villager observes less than ~5% of the whole village. We should not stress this percentage only by simulations without mathematical proof, although, having done a number simulations, we have not examined every case for $100 \leq B \leq 300$, and the critical percentage may not be neutral to proportional changes in B^2 and $(1 + 2N)^2$. We could, however, conclude that the number of neighbors whose behavior has directly affected a consumer's behavior should be considered in the analysis of the behavioral dependence generated by network externalities.

We now conclude this chapter with a few more general remarks. Our model can be seen from three different points: as an economic theory, a marketing theory, and a model of CA. Let us reconsider our analysis in the reverse order.

As a model of CA our model is a generalization of the conventional life game (Poundstone 1984). Our birth and death rules (to live or die if the number of neighbors is more or less than a certain number) is simpler and less interesting than the standard ones (to be able to live only if the number of neighbors is neither too large nor too small). However, the introduction of locally different rules will be able to create a number of applications of CA in various fields, complicating the return map of $s(t)$ and consequently the dynamics of $\sigma(t)$.

As a marketing theory, this may give a microeconomic foundation to the theory of the diffusion process of new products. Rogers (1995) and other marketing theorists claim, based on numerous empirical studies, that because the valuation of new products and the locally available information differ from person to person, consumers adopt in such different time lags that the quantity of a new product grows along with a S-shaped curve (something like a logistic curve). As far as we know, however, the relation among heterogeneity of purchasers, difference in locally accessible information, and the shape of the diffusion curve has not been examined explicitly in terms of mathematics or simulation. Our model and analysis could have some meaning in the circumstances; simulations suggest that the diffusion curve is unstable if purchasers are homogeneous conformists whereas it is stable if purchasers consist of conformists and snobs.

As an economic theory, the analysis shows how the actual market process can be distorted by the dichotomy of information process and physical activities. This tradition, which describes economic activities on the supposition that no physical transactions are put into practice until all necessary communication and calculation for optimization are done completely, has permeated into economic theories so widely and deeply that it is rarely mentioned – to say nothing of being criticized – explicitly; two important exceptions are the books of Hicks (1939) and Kornai (1971). Apart from such assumptions as differentiability and convexity of functions, which ensure the existence of an equilibrium (hopefully with its uniqueness and stability), the dichotomy that presumes that the real world can be predicted or simulated perfectly before actual transactions cannot be maintained from the viewpoint of computational quantity and the complexity of the real world. Even if the benefit of decentralized decision making in the market economy may be basically explained by the present equilibrium theories, the merit and the robustness of interactive information process and economic transactions in ever-changing economies have yet to be analyzed. We hope our model can make some contribution toward developing economic theories in this direction.

REFERENCES

Arthur, W. B., and Lane, D. A. (1993). Information contagion. *Econ. Dyn. Struc. Change*, **4**, 81–104.

Bikhchandani, S., Hirshleifer, D., and Welch, I. (1992). A theory of fads, fashion, custom, and cultural change as informational cascades. *J. Polit. Econ.*, **100**, 993–1026.

Choi, J. P. (1994). Competitive choice and planned obsolescence. *J. Ind. Econ.*, **42**, 167–82.

Church, J., and King, I. (1993). Bilingualism and network externalities. *Can. J. Econ.*, **26**, 337–45.

Curien, N., and Gensollen, M. (1990). Network externality: its impact on growth and pricing of the telephone service. In *Essays in Honor of Edmond Malinvaud*, eds. P. Champsaur and E. Malinvaud, MIT Press, Cambridge, MA.

Ducan, G. M. (1990). The effect of probabilistic demands on the structure of cost functions. *J. Risk Uncertainty*, **3**, 211–20.

Epstein, M. E., and Axtell, R. (1996). *Growing Artificial Societies*, MIT Press, Cambridge, MA.

Hicks, J. R. (1939). *Value and Capital: An Inquiry into some Fundamental Principles of Economic Theory*, Oxford University Press, Oxford, England.

Kesteloot, K. (1992). Multimarket cooperation with scope effects in demand. *J. Econ.*, **55**, 245–64.

Kornai, J. (1971). *Anti-Equilibrium: On Economic Systems Theory and the Task of Research*, North-Holland, Amsterdam.

Lane, D., and Vescovini, R. (1996). Decision rules and market share: aggregation in information contagion model. *Ind. Cooper. Change*, **5**, 127–47.

Liebenstein, H. (1948). Bandwagon, snob, and Veblen effects in the theory of consumers' demand. *Q. J. Econ.*, **62**, 165–201.

Liebowitz, S. J., and Margolis, S. E. (1994). Network externality: an uncommon tragedy. *J. Econ. Perspect.*, **8**, 133–50.

Narduzzio, A., and Warglien, M. (1996). Learning from the experiences of others: an experiment on information contagion. *Ind. Cooper. Change*, **5**, 113–25.

Poundstone, W. (1984). *The Recursive Universe: Cosmic Complexity and the Limits of Scientific Knowledge*, William Morrow, New York.

Pyndyck, R. S., and Rubinfeld, D. L. (1990). *Microeconomics*, Macmillan, New York, pp. 113–117.

Rogers, E. M. (1995). *Diffusion of Innovation*, Free Press, New York.

Rogers, E. M., and Shoemaker, F. F. (1971). *Communication of Innovations*, Free Press, New York.

Schelling T. C. (1978). *Micromotives and Macrobehavior*, Norton, New York.

[illegible] (1992) Multiproduct competition with some specific [illegible], 56, 215–34.

CHAPTER 19

Engendering change

Joshua S. Gans

When the decentralized decisions of individual agents in the economy lead to two or more equilibria that can be Pareto ranked, the problem of coordination failure is possible. The economy could be trapped at a low-efficiency equilibrium requiring the government, or some other external party, to intervene in an attempt to coordinate the actions of agents to reach a more efficient equilibrium.[1] Recently, such situations have been given renewed interest in formal economic theory (see Cooper and John 1988, Gans 1991). Although this literature has been able to characterize the economic conditions that lead to coordination failure and hence the need for intervention, virtually no attention has been given to what this need entails theoretically. It is my goal in this chapter to make a start at addressing theoretically the particulars of facilitating transition between equilibria.

To restate: In its coordinating role, a government needs to convince individuals to change their behavior in order to facilitate an escape from a low equilibrium trap. A low-efficiency equilibrium is a problem because it is stable, but unlike, for example, the equilibrium in a pure public goods problem, it is not globally stable. This means that if individuals can be persuaded to change their behavior by a sufficient amount, the conditions for a successful escape can be met and a virtuous cycle can begin. But changing individuals' behavior to provide the basis necessary for escape involves changing their expectations and beliefs. These very beliefs have accommodated to the lower equilibrium, leading individuals to take actions to reinforce those beliefs. Thus the goal of

[1] The problem of coordination failure is related to the more familiar public goods problem. In those situations, the equilibrium outcome of interactions of agents may not coincide with the Pareto optimal resource allocation. In such a situation, it is the role of government to establish an equilibrium that yields the Pareto optimal allocation. In contrast, the role of government in the presence of coordination failure is to facilitate a movement from one equilibrium to another that is Pareto superior. Both types of problem share in common the notion that payoffs and decisions of self-interested agents are affected by the actions of other agents through nonmarket interaction.

government policy is to break the hold of accommodation by enough to form the basis for an escape.[2]

Although escape, once begun, involves no additional role for the government, breaking the hold of accommodation of individuals involves substantial cost. These costs rise with the number of individuals who need to be targeted for change and with the degree to which they have to change their behavior. Thus the optimal policy choice (i.e., the one that minimizes transition costs) often involves choosing between attacking on a wide front or storming the hill. The choice depends on how far one has to push on the front and how significant the hill is. And, in the context of game-theoretic models with multiple Pareto-rankable equilibria, it is seen that the nature of accommodating beliefs can be the critical variable in the decision equation.

To motivate my analysis, in Section 1 I describe the problem of discrimination in the labor market that possesses many of the characteristics of coordination failure problems. In Section 2 I then discuss the dynamics of escape and what precisely needs to be done to generate upward momentum. In Section 3 I consider the alternative (balanced and unbalanced) mechanisms for achieving individual change and some of the difficulties involved in the context of statistical discrimination. The economic characteristics that can drive the government's choice of mechanism are analyzed and discussed in Section 4. In Section 5 I conclude by addressing unresolved issues and directions for future research.

1 Specific example: discrimination in the labor market

To analyze the policy choices facing governments in their coordinating role, it helps to have a specific context in mind. As a motivating context, I choose the situation of statistical discrimination in the labor market. Models of such situations have the quality that there can exist both discriminatory and nondiscriminatory equilibria. Thus the overall policy goal for the government would be to facilitate a transition away from discrimination. As such, the class of models I am examining are in the spirit of Arrow (1972a, 1972b, 1973) and Phelps (1972). According to these theories, discrimination is the result of self-fulfilling prophecies on the part of employers and potential workers, rather than being embedded in tastes per se (see Becker 1957). Looking to this type of statistical discrimination allows us to focus on some of the economic trade-offs we would expect to confront a government in its coordinating role.

Although more complete analyses are present in the literature, in this chapter I highlight only the important qualitative properties of statistical discrimination models. As such, it is convenient here to focus attention on the discriminated-against group that I assume is small relative to the labor market. This means that

[2] The terminology of "accommodation" and "escape" I borrow from Myrdal (1957) and Galbraith (1979).

the labor-market equilibrium for other groups need not be considered explicitly. In addition, for analytical and notational convenience, I assume that workers in the discriminated-against group are drawn from a set $\Lambda \equiv [0, 1]$, a continuum.

Worker i receives a wage w_i and has marginal product q_i. However, the worker can improve this marginal product by investing in education or other personal factors, for example, "the habits of action and thought that favor good performance in skilled jobs, steadiness, punctuality, responsiveness, and initiative" (Arrow 1972a, p. 105) Each worker chooses a single-dimensional investment level x_i from a compact strategy space $X_i \subset \Re$ (as in Kremer 1993). The payoff to worker i is assumed to be $\vartheta_i = \vartheta_i(w_i, x_i)$, with $\vartheta_{i1} > 0$ and $\vartheta_{i2} < 0$, so that although additional investment is costly to workers, they do benefit if this results in a greater wage.

The insight of models of statistical discrimination is that if the marginal product of an individual worker is observed imperfectly, then it is possible that information concerning the productivity of other members of the group they belong to may influence the wage they receive.[3] Thus the returns workers receive on their personal investments are dependent on the investments other workers from their group make. For example, often the labor market and the final product market are assumed to be competitive with workers receiving their expected marginal product, leading to the wage schedule $w_i = E[q_i | \Im_i]$.[4] In such models, the expectation of a worker's marginal product is based on the beliefs of employers who use information ($\Im_i$), a composition of two types: (1) a test of the worker's ability, and (2) the knowledge of the societal group the worker belongs to and a point estimate of the general investment level of a worker in that group, $\bar{x}$. Here it is supposed that $\bar{x} = f(\{x_i\}_{i \in \Lambda})$, where f is some aggregator function that is nondecreasing in each worker's investment. Its value influences the wage a worker from that group receives. As long as the test of a worker's ability is an imperfect indicator of marginal product, it can be shown that it will be optimal for employers to rely on their knowledge of $\bar{x}$ in addition to the test (Phelps 1972, Kremer 1993). However, if the test provides some information to employers as to workers' individual productivities, the workers' wages will be influenced, albeit imperfectly, by the workers' own personal investments.

By undertaking personal investment, workers can be viewed as contributing to a public good $\bar{x}$ that improves everyone's payoffs. This is because a higher $\bar{x}$ results in higher wages for everyone in the group. What distinguishes this

[3] As Arrow (1972a, 1972b) notes, the force of the imperfect information argument relies on employers' making some specific investment in workers before the employers can observe the workers' true productivity.

[4] See, for example, Arrow (1973), Lundberg and Startz (1983), and Kremer (1993). An alternative way of describing the problem of discrimination would be to assume that a worker's observed ability affected his or her job placement. Thus the returns to personal investment would take the form of the quality of the position a worker received. Models along this line include those of Milgrom and Oster (1987), Coate and Loury (1993), and Athey et al. (1994).

from a pure public good problem is that workers also receive a private benefit from their own personal investment as a result of the use of an individual test by employers. Thus a worker's payoff becomes $\vartheta_i = \vartheta_i[w(x_i, \bar{x}), x_i]$, where w is nondecreasing in both its arguments. Under certain conditions, however, the wage function can have the quality that the marginal impact of individual personal investment on wages is nondecreasing in the aggregate investment, $\bar{x}$ (Arrow 1973 and Kremer 1993). In such situations,

$$\frac{\frac{\partial \vartheta_i}{\partial w}\frac{\partial w}{\partial x_i}}{\frac{\partial \vartheta_i}{\partial x_i}}$$

is nondecreasing in $\bar{x}$.

This condition implies the definition of strategic complementarity as used by Milgrom and Shannon (1994).[5] For what follows I assume this condition on payoffs.

Strategic complementarity present in workers' payoffs means that their best response correspondences are monotone nondecreasing in $\bar{x}$ (Milgrom and Shannon 1994). In notation, let $B_i(\bar{x}) \equiv \{x_i \in X | \pi_i(x_i, \bar{x}) \geq \pi_i(x_i', \bar{x}), \forall x_i' \neq x_i\}$ denote the best response set for worker i when $\bar{x}$ is produced. If B_i is single valued for worker i, this monotonicity is depicted in Fig. 19.1. Thus, as other workers raise their personal investments, this raises $\bar{x}$, which in turn raises the optimal personal investment for an individual worker.

What are the possible equilibria of this type of game? To simplify matters, I assume for the rest of the chapter that all workers have the same underlying economic characteristics (although their observed characteristics may ultimately differ in equilibrium) and focus my attention on pure strategy symmetric Nash equilibria (SNE). As such, I suppress the worker subscript in what follows. $\hat{x}$ is therefore a SNE strategy profile for the discrimination game if (1) $\hat{x} \in B(\bar{x})$, $\forall i$, and (2) $\bar{x} = f(\{\hat{x}\}; \theta)$. Thus, in equilibrium, workers choose levels of investment that maximize their payoffs, and the aggregate level of education used by employers is consistent with these maximal choices, capturing the notion of a self-fulfilling prophecy.

[5] In actuality, this game should probably be referred to as a game with aggregate strategic complementarities. This is because the strategies of other workers are embodied in the point-estimate employer belief regarding the average level of worker education. This, in turn, is an aggregate of worker investments. Thus it shares a common link with many applications of games with strategic complementarities (e.g., Cooper and John 1988, Murphy et al. 1989), but it is distinguished slightly from the game-theoretic literature on the subject (e.g., Milgrom and Roberts 1990). In a technical appendix note reproduced here (Gans, 1994) I find that the conditions under which games with aggregate strategic complementarities are a special case of games with strategic complementarities. The most important condition to note here is that the aggregator function be nondecreasing in each x_i.

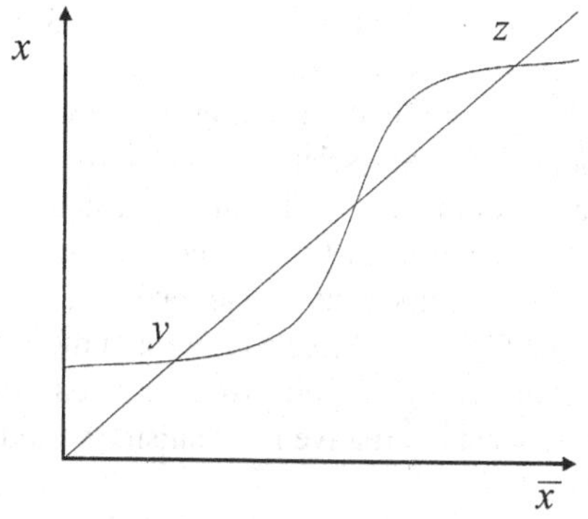

Figure 19.1. Multiple equilibria.

Strategic complementarities mean that there is the possibility of multiple equilibria (see Fig. 19.1). There could be a low investment equilibrium with associated strategy profile y, in which workers invest little reinforcing low employer expectations regarding the level of productivity of a worker from the group. In addition, there could also be a high equilibrium, with strategy profile $z > y$, in which workers invest high amounts in their productivity, generating high employer expectations of the marginal product of individual workers from the group. And because $\pi(x, \bar{x})$ is nondecreasing in $\bar{x}$, the highest equilibrium will always be preferred by workers (Milgrom and Roberts 1990, Theorem 6). To focus discussion on transition issues, in what follows I will assume that there are only two stable SNE corresponding to strategy choices, $y < z$. Equilibria with higher outcomes are preferred by workers and because they are paid their marginal products, employers presumably prefer higher outcomes as well. Thus it is a desirable policy goal for the government to facilitate a transition to the high equilibrium.

Much attention has been given to modeling how multiple equilibria can arise in a model of statistical discrimination[6] than what the general trade-offs are that a government faces in coordinating economic change. This is not to

[6] There have been numerous models within economics similar to the one sketched here. Myrdal (1944) clearly had some notion that a positive feedback and complementarity between worker action and employer expectations lay at the heart of the discrimination problem. But it was not until the work of Arrow (1972a, 1972b, 1973) and Phelps (1972) that the idea of modeling discrimination as a statistical phenomenon with multiple potential equilibria in the labor market was developed. Both of those theories emphasized imperfect information as lying at the heart of the problem, in that employers would find it advantageous to use group information in employer evaluations and that this could generate self-fulfilling prophecies and negative stereotypes. More recently, there has been a revival in such models focusing on discrimination within organizations that leave the observed wage schedule unaltered (Milgrom and Oster 1987, Coate and Loury 1993, Athey, et al. 1994).

say that policy matters have not received attention. Indeed, the opposite is certainly true. Questions of differing policy goals and instruments under a taste-embedded versus a statistical discrimination setting have received much attention. In addition, throughout the social sciences there have been many empirical studies into the successes or otherwise of affirmative action policies and the like (e.g., Sowell 1983). However, in formal economics, there have been little synthesis and focus on the important considerations entering into government decision making in the face of multiple equilibria of the kind faced here. So although these models have, in the past, pointed out the need for change, there has been little discussion of what alternative mechanisms would be best for actually engendering change.

2 Dynamics of escape

Myrdal was the first economist to recognize the possibility that a virtuous circle could break the equilibrium of discrimination. After outlining the feedbacks generating the problem, Myrdal continued,

> "[w]hite prejudice and low Negro standards thus mutually "cause" each other. If at a point of time things tend to remain about as they are, this means that the two forces balance each other: white prejudice and the consequent discrimination against the Negroes block their efforts to raise their low plane of living; this, on the other hand, forms part of the causation of the prejudice on the side of whites which leads them to discriminatory behavior.
>
> Such a static "accommodation" is, however, entirely fortuitous and by no means a stable equilibrium position. If either of the two factors should change, this is bound to bring a change in the other factor, too, and start a cumulative process of mutual interaction in which the change in one factor would continuously be supported by the reaction of the other factor and so on in a circular way. The whole system would move in the direction of the primary change, but much further. Even if the original push or pull were to cease after a time, both factors would be permanently changed, or the process of interacting changes would even continue without any neutralization in sight" (Myrdal 1957, pp. 16–17).

Myrdal seems here to be implying that a virtuous circle could arise quite easily. However, as Swan (1962) points out, the notion of complementarity between the beliefs of employers and minority workers could also lead to vicious circles as well. It is my goal in this section to formalize and make precise such notions of circular and cumulative causation and in the process examine the requirements for a successful escape.

The hold of accommodation will be broken if the workers can be persuaded that it is worth their while to undertake personal investments in their productivity. In the situation described in Section 1, the greater the observed expectations of employers regarding the investment level of a given worker from the group, the larger an individual worker's investment. Nonetheless, the danger is that if these observed employer beliefs are not high enough, the resulting investment will not justify even those beliefs and they will fall back to their low equilibrium levels. As it turns out, however, under certain dynamic assumptions, there does exist a critical level of aggregate employer beliefs such that, if those beliefs are generated, the process will not unravel and the hold of accommodation will be broken.

In showing how this is so, the first order of business is to make some assumptions about how beliefs evolve over time. It has already been assumed that employer beliefs about a worker's investment are some nondecreasing function of the current actual education investments of the group, i.e., $\bar{x} = f(\{x_i\}_{i \in \Lambda})$. What is crucial, however, is that workers be persuaded to change their behavior. This will depend on their expectations regarding what the future level of employer beliefs will be. To see this, observe that at time t, each worker solves $\max_{x_{i,t} \in X} \pi(x_{i,t}, \bar{x}_t)$. Here, each worker maximizes his or her payoff contingent on his or her expectation regarding the aggregate employer beliefs in that period. The dynamic sequence of observation and action is depicted in Fig. 19.2. For simplicity, it is assumed that when there are multiple best responses to a set of beliefs, then the highest strategy is chosen. Note, however, that is possible that sophisticated agents forming rational expectations could, even at strategies close to the high equilibrium, form expectations that drive them back to the low equilibrium. Thus some restrictions on how workers use past observations of the aggregate to form their expectations are required for ensuring that an escape, once begun, will continue.

Given this, how might workers adjust their expectations over time? $\bar{x}_t$ is considered to be the state variable in the analysis that follows. Consider the following very weak definition of adaptive expectations.

Definition. *Suppose that a worker's conditional probability density function of current employer beliefs is $g(\bar{x}_t|\bar{x}_{t-1})$. Expectations are adaptive if $g(\bar{x}_t|\bar{x}_{t-1})$*

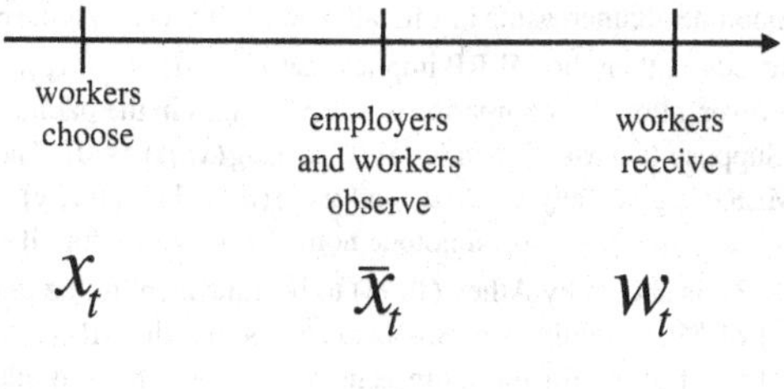

Figure 19.2. Time line.

satisfies the (generalized) monotone likelihood ratio property in $\bar{x}_{t-1}$, for any history $\{\bar{x}_{t-2}, \bar{x}_{t-3}, \ldots\}$.[7]

The (generalized) monotone likelihood ratio property used in this way means that if the past aggregate estimate of worker education is higher, then the probability that this period's education aggregate exceeds any given level is greater. This merely says that if the previous period's personal investments for all workers improve, then so will their expectations regarding what this period's personal investment will be. If workers use only the immediate past observation of employer beliefs to form their expectations, i.e., setting $\pi(x_{i,t}, \bar{x}_t) = \pi(x_{i,t}, \bar{x}_{t-1})$ and maximizing that function, then the resulting dynamics are Marshallian or best-reply dynamics. Thus it can be seen that this often-used adjustment dynamic is a special case of the definition of adaptive expectations given here.

Theorem 1 (Momentum). *Consider any game with aggregate strategic complementarities. Suppose that players adjust their strategies optimally (i.e., play highest best responses) by using adaptive expectations. Then if $x_t \geq x_{t-1}$ for some t, $x_s \leq x_{s+1} \leq \cdots$ for all $s > t$. And if $x_t \leq x_{t-1}$ for some t, then $x_s \geq x_{s+1} \geq \cdots$ for all $s > t$.*

This definition allows a variant of a theorem from Milgrom et al. (1991) to be stated for multiperson decision contexts and games – their momentum theorem deals with adjustment processes in certain contracting problems.

Proof: Because this is a game with strategic complementarities, p satisfies the single-crossing property in $(x_t; \bar{x}_t)$. Moreover, by Theorem 5.1 of Athey (1994), because $g(\bar{x}_t|\bar{x}_{t-1})$ satisfies the (generalized) monotone likelihood ratio property (MLRP) in $\bar{x}_{t-1}$, $E[p]$ satisfies the single-crossing property in $(x_t; \bar{x}_{t-1})$. Consequently, workers' best response correspondences are monotone nondecreasing in $\bar{x}_{t-1}$ at each t (Milgrom and Shannon 1994). Suppose that $x_t \geq x_{t-1}$;

[7] A probability density function, $g(x; \mu)$ satisfies the monotone likelihood ratio property (MLRP) in a parameter μ if $\frac{g(x;\mu)}{g(x;\mu')}$ is monotone nonincreasing in x for all $\mu < \mu'$. If $G(x; \mu)$ is the probability that the random variable exceeds x, then the MLRP implies that $G(x; \mu) \leq G(x; \mu')$ for all x. This definition does not, however, allow for comparisons when changes in the parameter μ alter the support of the density. Suppose that $x \in \Re$, and let $S(\mu) \equiv \{x|g(x; \mu) > 0\}$. Then $g(x; \mu)$ satisfies the (generalized) MLRP if given any $x \in S(\mu)$ and $y \in S(\mu')$, (1) $\min[x, y] \in S(\mu)$ and $\max[x, y] \in S(\mu')$; (2) for all $\mu < \mu'$, $\frac{g(x;\mu)}{g(x;\mu')}$ is monotone nonincreasing in x for all $x \in S(\mu) \cap S(\mu')$. The (generalized) MLRP is shown by Athey (1994) to be equivalent to the definition by Ormiston and Schlee (1993) of MLR dominance. She also shows that the MLRP is a special case of the (generalized) MLRP. I allow for the more general definition here to allow for the possibility that agents' expectations per unit one mass on a single level of x, something essential in game-theoretic contexts. This definition is also applied in Gans (1995).

we can conclude that $\bar{x}_t \geq \bar{x}_{t-1}$, as f is monotone in each worker's strategy. Then each player's best response at time $t+1$, is nondecreasing in $\bar{x}_t$, $x_{t+1} \geq x_t$. The theorem then follows by induction. The proof of the second part is analogous to the first.

Theorem 1 captures Myrdal's intuition that a virtuous cycle or escape, once begun, will have a momentum of its own. If ever there is a time such that workers wish to adjust their optimal investment upward, that will feed back on itself to generate employer beliefs that continue to be justified by further upward movements in education for all workers. Note, however, that the theorem relies on expectations' being adaptive. If expectations were not so, then, in this general formulation, it could not be guaranteed that an upward cycle, once begun, would sustain its upward momentum.[8]

The above results show that there exists some critical level of employer beliefs such that if, by intervention, a government can generate those beliefs, upward momentum will be generated and an escape from the trap of the low equilibrium will have been achieved. This critical level is defined, in the myopic best-reply dynamic case, by,

$$f^* = \arg\min_{\bar{x}}\{f(\{B(\bar{x})\}) \geq \bar{x}\}. \tag{19.1}$$

If this critical level is generated, in the absence of any other shock, the state of play will not return to the discriminating equilibrium. What it does not say, however, is how far the escape will go. Under best-reply dynamics, the outcome of play of the game will converge to the high static equilibrium. In other cases, the conditions of the theorem do not place enough restrictions to allow us to predict to where play might converge. For instance, the outcome of the path could be a Nash equilibrium or indeed, the state played could keep rising indefinitely, past the level of the high equilibrium. Continued momentum, is, of course, desirable from a welfare point of view because the state $\bar{x}$ enters positively into all worker's payoffs.

For the government to intervene and generate a level of the aggregate that escapes the basin of attraction of the low equilibrium, the adjustment process must be, in some sense, path dependent, that is, the adjustment path taken depends more on the history of past play than other factors (e.g., future expectations). Adaptive expectations have this property, although convergence could be to an outcome other than the high static equilibrium. Best-reply dynamics possesses

[8] Note also, that if agents were forward looking and maximized the present value of payoffs this period, i.e., solved $\max_{\{x_{i,t}\}} \sum_{s \geq t} \delta^{s-t}\pi(x_{i,s}, \bar{x}_s)$, $0 < \delta < 1$, Theorem 1 would continue to hold. In addition, allowing for heterogeneous payoffs does not alter the momentum result if the player set is assumed to be finite. In that case, the result would state that if ever there was a time that a single worker adjusted optimal investment upwards, systemic momentum would follow.

both an adaptive quality and predict convergence to some equilibrium.[9] Other dynamic adjustment processes that would also converge to some Nash equilibrium rely on more sophisticated expectations formation, but lose the path dependence that would prevent adjustment after intervention from returning play to the low equilibrium – e.g., rational expectations. If, however, one were to suppose that there were costs to the upward adjustment of strategies then it is possible that even under sophisticated expectation formation some separation of the basins of attraction of the high and the low equilibria is possible.

There have been two general approaches to incorporating adjustment costs to analyze the transition between equilibria in games. In a series of papers, Matsuyama (1991, 1992) has analyzed dynamics in models with multiple equilibria in which agents are able to adjust their strategies only intermittently. In addition, he assumes perfect foresight on the part of agents as to the future paths of states. What prevents dynamic paths from potentially returning to the low equilibrium is that, if the probability that agents would be able to alter their strategy in any given period is low enough, the possible future paths for the state are constrained. Thus, if agents' discount rates are sufficiently high and if the initial condition of the system is above a critical state, then even if all other agents who were able to change used low strategies, it would still be optimal for any agent to play a high strategy. The intermittent adjustment process puts some lower bound on feasible paths for the state, which in turn constrains even paths of rational expectation.

It would be beyond the scope of this chapter to explore such adjustment dynamics in detail. In all other applications with this method to date, the strategy choice of agents is binary and the aggregate of concern is additively separable in each individuals strategy, for instance, some average. Nonetheless, if we were to view the government as intervening to change initial conditions, then the Matsuyama dynamic seems to imply that there will exist some critical level of the aggregate such that if this is generated all future paths will converge to the high equilibrium.[10]

The other method by which one could incorporate more sophisticated expectations formation assumptions into adjustment dynamics and still guarantee convergence to the high equilibrium is if the use of government policy actually eliminated the low equilibrium. Milgrom and Roberts (1991) have analyzed learning and adjustment processes in games. They define a class of learning processes that includes best-reply dynamics and more sophisticated types of dynamics – such processes are consistent with adaptive learning. If educational changes were irreversible to some degree, then intervention may remove the low equilibrium. Then, as Milgrom and Roberts (1991) have shown, play will converge

[9] Indeed, support for this type of adjustment behavior is part of the experimental literature (see Meyer et al. 1992 and Van Huyck et al. 1997).

[10] For an excellent discussion of the roles of history and expectations along these lines see Krugman (1991).

to the unique higher equilibrium regardless of the dynamic process assumed – whether sophisticated or merely adaptive. Gans (1994) demonstrates this process in more detail and the circumstances under which it might be relevant.

In summary then, a necessary element of any successful government policy to engender change is to ensure a sustained escape. Indeed, it could be argued that when one is considering policy in the face of coordination failure, it is critical that the details of the situation at hand imply some dynamic adjustment behavior that is path dependent for the government to intervene successfully. However, in situations in which the dynamic permits a significant role for history, the goal of the government is to lift the aggregate of employer beliefs above some critical level f^*. Beyond that level, transition will be completed by the adjustment behavior of individual workers. But generating that critical level depends on changing individual behavior already in the grip of accommodation. To avoid adding complicating conditions to the following analysis, I assume that the expectations of workers depend on only the immediate past level of aggregate employer beliefs. This removes any additional difficulties in generating the critical aggregate caused by long-standing low expectations as expectations will evolve in a manner similar to best-reply dynamics. If this were not the case then, regardless of the dynamics adjustment behavior assumed, a government would have to intervene for longer periods of time in order to convince workers to improve their education in the face of greater employer beliefs. The other issues involved in achieving the critical aggregate are the subject of Section 3.

3 Changing individual behavior

Given the discussion in Section 2, the transitional subgoal of the government is clear: to generate the critical level of employer beliefs. One way to do this would be to intervene and change the beliefs of employers. But changing beliefs requires evidence, and this is a scarce commodity in a world of self-fulfilling prophecies. Alternatively, one could legislate directly to avoid discrimination through an affirmative action policy, that is, one could move to equalize (observable) outcomes between groups. But recent theoretical discussions cast doubt on the effectiveness of outcome-based affirmative action policies because of enforcement difficulties (Lundberg 1991) and the potential for patronization of minority workers (Coate and Loury 1993).[11] Empirical doubts along similar lines are given by Sowell (1983) and Steele (1992).

Thus the likely candidates for agents of change are the discriminated-against workers themselves. Because all workers contribute to generating employer beliefs, changing their incentives to invest in their productivity possesses the same qualities as getting individuals to contribute to the provision of a public good.

[11] Schelling's (1978) discussion of the losses incurred by groups in transition also provide another set of arguments that diminish the desirability of outcome based affirmative action policies.

The problem is that each worker perceives losses as a result of greater educational investment, although others making investments would enhance their own expected payoff. Given that we are currently at the low equilibrium, this means that changing an individual worker's behavior is bound to be costly. For instance, one possible mechanism for individual change would be to subsidize all workers for their expected ex ante losses on their educational return. But regardless of the actual mechanism, changing individual i's investment from its low equilibrium value y to another value x entails a cost that I write as $c_i(y, x)$. This is the individual transition cost. So if the government were to push on a wide front in a balanced way, then it needs to incur the individual transition costs of ensuring that all workers invest an amount x^*, where x^* satisfies $f^* = f(\{x^*\}_{i \in \Lambda})$. Thus the total cost of this transition mechanism would be

$$\mathrm{TC}_b = \int_0^1 c_i(y, x^*)\mathrm{d}i = c(y, x^*). \tag{19.2}$$

This is the sum of all the individual transition costs.

But a balanced mechanism targeting all workers equally for change is not the only way a government could generate the critical level of employer beliefs. A myriad of unbalanced mechanisms could be imagined in which only a subset of workers is targeted. For simplicity, suppose that when the government targets some workers, it tries to induce them to change their strategy choices by the same amount. The balanced mechanism is a special case of this type of mechanism, with all workers being targeted to change their strategy to x^*. Because f is nondecreasing, any mechanism that targets some subset of workers must necessarily induce those workers to change their strategy choice to some $\tilde{x} > x^*$. Thus, for any given target choice of strategy $\tilde{x}$, some critical mass of workers would need to be targeted for change to $\tilde{x}$ in order to generate the critical aggregate. The critical mass when workers are induced to invest $\tilde{x}$, $k^*(\tilde{x})$, is determined by $k^*(\tilde{x}) \in \{k \subseteq \Lambda \mid f^* = f((\{y\}_{i \notin k}, \{\tilde{x}\}_{i \in k}))\}$. All mechanisms targeting some subset of workers, i.e., $k^*(\tilde{x}) < 1$, are called unbalanced transition mechanisms, with mechanisms with a lower $k^*(\tilde{x})$ being described as more unbalanced.

Of course, inducing individual workers to change to some $\tilde{x} > x^*$ is a harder task than getting them to change to x^* and therefore more costly. Thus, I suppose, quite naturally, that $c(y, x)$ is increasing in x. The total transition cost for any given unbalanced mechanism is

$$\mathrm{TC}_u(\tilde{x}) = \int_0^{k^*(\tilde{x})} c_i(y, \tilde{x})\mathrm{d}i = k^*(\tilde{x})c(y, \tilde{x}). \tag{19.3}$$

Note that the definition of an unbalanced mechanism makes some implicit assumptions about the nature of the interaction between the government and employers. When the government intervenes to change the beliefs of employers by altering the investments of a group of workers, it is assumed that employers cannot distinguish among those workers who were targeted for change and those who were not. If they were able to make such a distinction then this might mean that employers separate their beliefs about targeted and nontargeted workers. In this case, the positive benefits of intervention will not spill over to the workers not targeted, harming the possibility of an escape. Therefore, given the large set of workers, for analytical convenience this possibility is assumed away.

Therefore, as remarked on above, the choice for the government is between moving a small amount on a wide front versus large pushes on limited fronts. To be sure, all mechanisms, balanced or unbalanced, will be sufficient to achieve a successful escape. Each breaks the hold of accommodation to the low equilibrium trap. But each mechanism may entail very different costs on the part of the government. As such, this will be its crucial dimension in the choice of alternative mechanisms. Having identified the important decision element for a government interested in engendering change, the rest of this chapter is directed toward identifying characteristics that will guide that choice.

4 Characterizing the optimal policy choice

In choosing the scope of its policy, i.e., the number of workers it targets, the government faces a trade-off between the costs of targeting an additional worker and the costs of greater individual transition costs to change behavior by a greater amount. This trade-off exists because, in order to ensure escape, any policy choice pair $(\tilde{x}, k^*)$ is constrained to lie within the set $G \equiv \{(x \in X, k \subset \Lambda) | f(\{y\}_{i \notin k}, \{x\}_{i \in k}) \geq f^*\}$. Thus the policy choice of the government in its coordinating role is determined by the optimization problem $\min_{(x,k)} kc(y, x)$ subject to $(x, k) \in G$. In general, however, there is no guarantee that the functions and sets involved in this minimization problem are convex or even continuous. Thus, in order to say something more about what determines the optimal choice of the government, we need to adopt some parameterization of the relevant aggregate and of the transition costs.

Let me begin with the aggregate. Returning to the discrimination context, the relevant aggregate was employer beliefs regarding the average level of personal investment of the group of workers. Thus far, I have assumed that employer beliefs could be represented only by some function $\bar{x} = f(\{x_i\}_{i \in \Lambda})$ that is nondecreasing in each worker's actual investment. It has not been necessary to ascribe a functional form for f for any of the results presented in the sections above. When it comes to analyzing the relative costs of balanced and unbalanced transition mechanisms, however, assuming specific functional forms becomes crucial.

Here I introduce a simple functional form as a description of how employers form their beliefs on the basis of observed educational levels of workers from the group. Employer beliefs regarding $\bar{x}$ are determined by

$$\bar{x} = f(\{x_i\}) = \left(\int_0^1 x_i^{\alpha} \mathrm{d}i\right)^{\frac{1}{\alpha}}, \quad \alpha > 0. \tag{19.4}$$

This is the commonly used constant elasticity of substitution (CES) aggregator (see Cornes 1993).[12] To see its properties, observe that if $\alpha = 1$, we have the ordinary mean of the investment levels, $\int_0^1 x_i di$. In this case, by investing more, each worker contributes precisely that amount to the generation of improved employer beliefs. On the other hand, as α approaches 0, employer beliefs become a geometric average, $\exp \int_0^1 \ln x_i di$. Here, an investment by a worker contributes a lower amount to employer beliefs if the worker's investment is greater than that of other workers, but a greater amount if it is smaller than others' investments – so bad apples tend to spoil the bunch. Finally, observe that as α approaches infinity, $\bar{x}$ approaches $\max[\{x_i\}]$. In this case, the worker with the greatest education level determines employer beliefs.

The parameter α is, in this model, a measure of the flexibility of employer beliefs. If α is high, employer beliefs adjust relatively easily to improvements in a number of workers' education levels. On the other hand, if α is low, employer beliefs are relatively harder to change and improvements rely increasingly on the simultaneous improvement of many workers' education.

What considerations justify this parameterization of employer beliefs? One possible justification is that inflexibility (low α) describes a situation (i.e., type of labor market) in which employers are more inherently prejudiced. This would result in a model that combines aspects of taste-generated and statistical discrimination, although here inherent prejudice is embedded in the determinants of beliefs rather than in utility functions. Nonetheless, such an explanation might beg the question of why competition does not eradicate those employers who hold such beliefs. This was the original motivation behind developing models of statistical discrimination in the first place (see Arrow 1972a).

That beliefs are rigid might originate in optimizing behavior. For example, as Kremer (1993) argues, employers may be using a production technology in which the marginal product of workers of a given ability is raised by having co-workers of greater ability – the so-called O-ring production function. In that case, employers would find it optimal to match workers of equal ability. The CES aggregate therefore represents what employers care about. Indeed, it is often a stated element of statistical discrimination that there are gains to the division of labor, i.e., complementarities, that preclude discriminated against workers

[12] This function form is a symmetric CES production function or the generalized mean of Hardy et al. (1952). It has been used in various forms in economics, recently, by Dixit and Stiglitz (1977), Romer (1987), and Cornes (1993).

from forming their own firms to compete with discriminating employers (see Arrow 1972b).[13]

Regardless of the explanation underlying it, with this specification for employer beliefs, one can see how flexibility α will be critical in determining the relative costliness of balanced and unbalanced mechanisms. As above, suppose there are two Pareto-rankable equilibria, with all workers investing y and z, respectively, with $y < z$. There exists a critical level of the aggregate f^* that is the policy maker's goal. The critical strategy for the balanced mechanism x^* is determined by,

$$f^* = \left(\int_0^1 x^{*\alpha} \mathrm{d}i\right)^{\frac{1}{\alpha}} \Rightarrow x^* = f^*. \tag{19.5}$$

Note that x^* does not depend on α because of the (assumed) homogeneity of the employer belief function. The critical mass for any unbalanced mechanism with target worker investment $\tilde{x}$ is determined by,

$$f^* = \left[\int_0^{k^*(\tilde{x})} \tilde{x}^\alpha \mathrm{d}i + \int_{k^*(\tilde{x})}^1 y^\alpha \mathrm{d}i\right]^{\frac{1}{\alpha}} \Leftrightarrow k^*(\tilde{x}) = \frac{f^{*\alpha} - y^\alpha}{\tilde{x}^\alpha - y^\alpha}. \tag{19.6}$$

Under this parameterization therefore, $k^*(\tilde{x})$ is a continuously differentiable function from X into [0,1].

If $c(y, x)$ is also smooth we can represent the government's transition minimization problem as in Fig. 19.3. The curve g represents the function $c(y, \tilde{x}(k^*))$, where $\tilde{x}(k^*)$ is the inverse of $k^*(\tilde{x})$. This inverse exists because k^* is monotonically decreasing in $\tilde{x}$. A simple check also verifies that as long as $c(y, x)$ is not too concave in x, g is convex. The curve TC represents the total transition cost function:

$$c(y, \tilde{x}) = \frac{\mathrm{TC}}{k^*(\tilde{x})}. \tag{19.7}$$

Figure 19.3 shows the types of optimal policies that are possible. In Fig. 19.3(a), the balanced mechanism minimizes transition costs, whereas in Fig. 19.3(b), an interior solution is depicted. In Fig. 19.3(c), targeting a small number of workers to use a high strategy is optimal.

What is of interest, however, is how different levels of a change the optimal policy choice of the government. In general, $c(y, x)$ will not be smooth and may

[13] An alternative explanation, based on an observation of Meg Meyer, is that the information employers receive about the group's aggregate ability comes from information sources that are unreliable and that alternative information sources that are more reliable are prohibitively costly for employers to acquire. The expected gains from having a reliable source of information do not outweigh the additional costs associated with sampling from that source. Of course, it would be beyond the scope of this paper to explore in detail this alternative explanation for statistical discrimination.

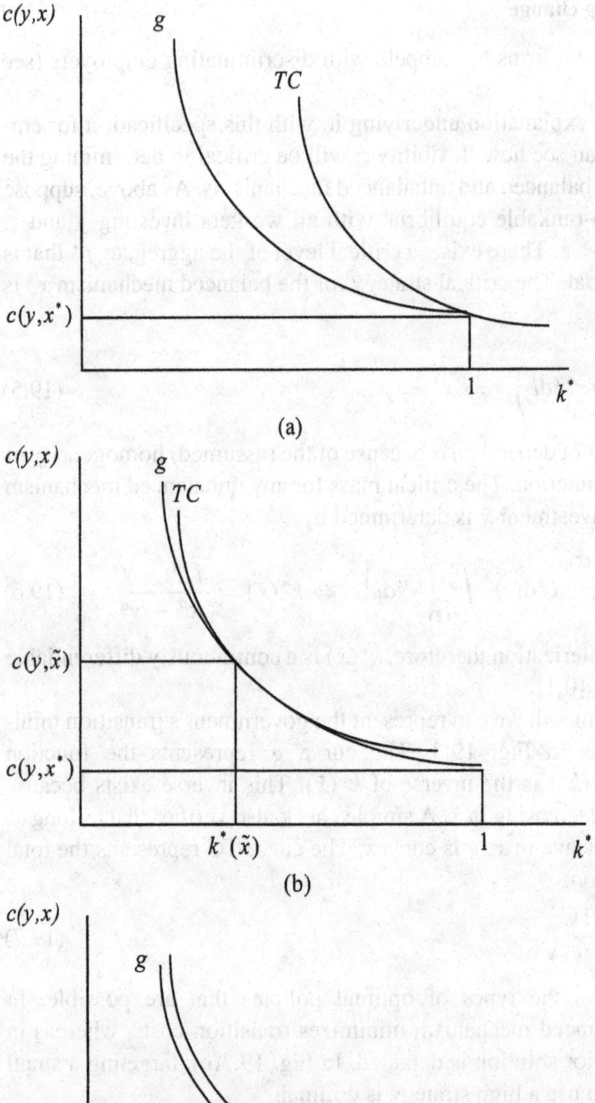

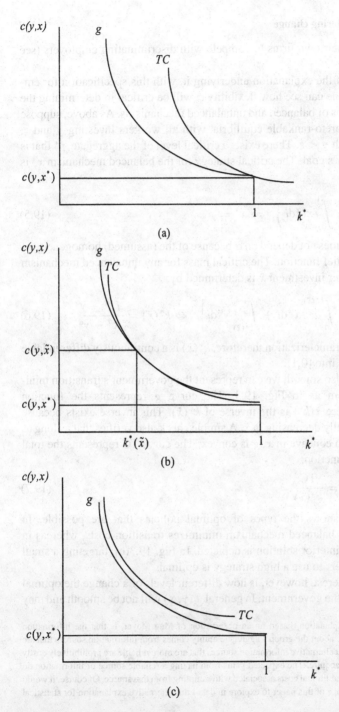

Figure 19.3. Optimal policy choices.

be concave or convex. Nonetheless, even without such restrictive assumptions, the following comparative statics result is still available.[14]

Theorem 2. *In symmetric games with aggregate strategic complementarities and a CES aggregator, the degree of unbalance in the cost minimizing transition policy is nondecreasing in α.*

Proof: First, observe that k^* is decreasing in α and that it is submodular in $(\tilde{x}, \alpha)$. We need to show that $\{[\partial k^*(\tilde{x})]/\partial\alpha\}c(y, \tilde{x})$ is decreasing in $\tilde{x}$. That this is so follows from the submodularity of k^* and the assumption that c is increasing in x. Thus, total transition costs are submodular in $(\tilde{x}, \alpha)$. By Topkis' monotonicity theorem (Milgrom and Shannon 1994), the optimal choice of $\tilde{x}$ is increasing in α. The theorem follows from the fact that k^* is decreasing in $\tilde{x}$.

Theorem 2 identifies the characteristics of employer beliefs as a significant determinant of the government's cost-minimizing choice of transition mechanisms. In situations in which beliefs are relatively inflexible, in order to generate the critical aggregate in a cost-effective manner, resources have to be spread thinner with the mechanism being more balanced. Thus the particular transition policy may differ across different labor markets and even different regions. For example, in some markets (e.g., popular music performers), beliefs may be fairly flexible, whereas in others (e.g., CEO positions for women), beliefs could well be extremely rigid. But the overriding conclusion is that, regardless of other potential characteristics of payoff functions, the more inflexible beliefs are, the wider the front one has to push to generate the critical aggregate and break the hold of accommodation.

Parameterizations of the aggregate aside, there are other characteristics of economic significance that could influence the nature of the transition mechanism chosen by the government. For example, the actual level of the critical aggregate, although the target of all transition mechanisms, could influence the relative costs of mechanisms. Indeed, it is simple to check that the cost-minimizing target strategy is nondecreasing in f^* and hence a higher critical aggregate implies a more unbalanced mechanism.

What factors might cause the critical aggregate to be greater? The Matsuyama adjustment process discussed in Section 2 and the analysis of Krugman (1991) are suggestive of the notion that as agents become more far-sighted or as the ability to adjust strategy choices becomes greater, the basin of attraction of the high equilibrium shrinks. This means that the critical aggregate

[14] The homogeneity of the aggregator is not critical for this result, and the theorem would still hold if $\bar{x} = \int_0^1 x_i^\alpha \, di$.

that ensures convergence a successful escape is greater and hence a more unbalanced mechanism will be preferred.

Another potential influence on the choice of mechanism is the level of individual increasing returns. If the total costs associated with raising personal investment rise at a slower rate, then the marginal increase in individual transition costs associated with a higher target strategy could be lower. This could be the case because of initial start-up costs in improving human capital. Thus we could imagine individual transition costs to be some function $c(y, x; b)$, where b parameterizes the marginal cost increase of a higher x. It is straightforward to show that lower levels of b imply a greater target strategy and hence a more unbalanced mechanism. Thus greater individual returns to scale of investment will tend to cause the government to favor a more unbalanced mechanism.

In summary, in this section, it has been shown that the government will find a more unbalanced mechanism to be cost minimizing the more flexible are employer beliefs, the higher the critical aggregate is, and the more personal investment is characterized by individual increasing returns to scale. Indeed, for a resource-starved policy maker, paying attention to these economic characteristics may determine what type of successful escape is feasible at all.

5 Conclusions and extensions

The particular policy choices facing a government in its coordination role have been neglected by economists until now. This chapter has highlighted, within the context of a model of statistical discrimination in the labor market, some of the issues confronting governments attempting to change an economy or game from one equilibrium to another. In so doing, the possibility of escape (under adaptive expectations) was identified. Moreover, the notion that individual agents need to be convinced to change their behavior by a sufficient amount to break the hold of accommodation was emphasized. In such situations, the policy choices facing a government involve how best to change individual behavior to move them out of the basin of attraction of the low equilibrium. Note, though, that these considerations apply to many models with public good elements that exhibit strategic complementarities beyond the application discussed here.

Given these findings, this chapter has turned to focus on whether a government should target a small number of individuals for change or adopt a wider coverage. In the context of discrimination in the labor market, the flexibility of employer beliefs and individual returns to scale were singled out as critical determinants of whether a balanced or an unbalanced mechanism was cost minimizing. But the assumptions of the game presented abstract from other factors that might affect the choice of balanced or unbalanced change.

First, the worker's strategy choice is currently assumed to be unidimensional. One could imagine that it is more complex than this. Indeed, it may be multidimensional, taking into account differing aspects of education and other investments that improve productivity. Much of the analysis will continue to hold if vectors of strategy variables available to an agent were in turn complementary with one another (Milgrom and Roberts 1990). If this is the case, one could then expand the range of mechanisms available for change. For instance, one might have unbalanced mechanisms that attempt to change an individual's behavior on all dimensions or perhaps target some variables by a large amount, leaving the rest to adjust by later momentum.

Second, the game as presented is symmetric in that all workers possess the same payoff functions, face the same aggregate, and have the same impact on the aggregate. Introducing heterogeneity complicates matters by making the definitions of balanced and unbalanced mechanisms less clean. Suppose, however, that agents differed in only their costs of investment, that is, $\pi_i = w(t, \tilde{x}) - \gamma_i x$, where γ_i is the individual investment cost. In that case, because all agents make the same contribution to aggregate employer beliefs, it is clear that the definition of a balanced mechanism remains the same, whereas the least cost unbalanced mechanism would have those with the lowest investment costs being targeted first. This would continue to be the case if those with the lowest costs also had the greatest impact on the aggregate. However, if this were not the case, then a trade-off between low costs and greater contributions to the aggregate exists. Nonetheless, a complete analysis of the issues of the optimal composition of a critical mass lies beyond the scope of this chapter.

Throughout the chapter the government was assumed to be a purely external facilitator of change and to possess an external source of resources. Government intervention did not permanently change the best-response correspondences of agents, or, if it did, it did so positively. But it is well documented from social psychology that social interventions can have unintended negative feedback effects. In the 1930s, what has become known as the Cambridge–Somerville experiments were conducted in impoverished neighborhoods near Boston. The idea was to take a selection of children from these neighborhoods and devote (virtually) unlimited social work and other resources to helping them escape poverty traps. Thus education and health care were provided. Regular visits, monitoring, and counseling were provided by social workers, basically all the ingredients that one could hope for. Nonetheless, years later, the basic social statistics for measuring an enhanced socioeconomic condition showed little improvement and, on some dimensions, a worsening of children's situations. A suggested reason for the failure of the intervention was an unintended effect: Children receiving aid suffered from isolation from their peers. The negative effects of this were enough to cancel the positive benefits of the intervention.[15]

[15] For a discussion of this experiment see Ross and Nisbett (1991).

Such considerations, also documented in the case of discrimination by Steele (1992), were not part of the above analysis. In the analysis of this chapter, all costs of achieving individual change were subsumed in the function $c(y, x)$. Negative feedbacks would enter into these costs and their identification can be of considerable importance for achieving a successful transition. In addition, the discussion in this chapter assumes individual transition costs to be independent of the actions of other agents. Fruitful extensions would include relaxing this assumption.

Finally then, the government is currently assumed to know with certainty the critical aggregate, strategies, and masses to provide the basis of escape and the real individual transition costs. As is indicated by the preceding paragraphs, an interesting and important extension would be to explore more completely relaxations of this assumption, and this might change the choice between balanced and unbalanced mechanisms.

By examining the flexibility of employer beliefs, this chapter has highlighted the degree of substitutability of individual worker's investments in altering employer beliefs as determining how widespread a government's policy to eliminate discrimination ought to be. This is because once employer beliefs, regardless of how they are achieved, reach some critical level, the discrimination will be removed by a momentum of attrition of stereotypes and of improvements in workers' incentives to take investments that improve their own marginal productivity. Therefore the costs and the trade-offs associated with changing the behavior of workers to raise employer beliefs to this critical level are the appropriate focuses of the government. Such issues are also present in other situations of coordination failure and the choices facing policy makers in facilitating transition are, in that respect, similar. Nonetheless, this chapter represents only a first step in understanding policy in the face of multiple equilibria and in other economic contexts; the critical variables that drive choices may well be different and more complex.

REFERENCES

Arrow, K. J. (1972a). Models of job discrimination. In *Racial Discrimination in Economic Life*, ed. A. H. Pascal, Heath, Lexington, MA.

(1972b). Some mathematical models of race discrimination in the labor market. In *Racial Discrimination in Economic Life*, ed. A. H. Pascal, Heath, Lexington, MA.

(1973). The theory of discrimination. In *Discrimination in Labor Markets*, eds. O. Ashenfelter and A. Rees, Princeton University Press, Princeton, NJ.

Athey, S. (1994). Monotone comparative statics in stochastic optimization problems. Mimeo, Stanford University, Stanford, CA.

Athey, S., Avery, C., and Zemsky, P. (1994). Mentoring and discrimination in organizations. Research Paper 1321, Graduate School of Business, Stanford University, Stanford, CA.

Becker, G. S. (1957). *The Economics of Discrimination*, University of Chicago Press, Chicago.

Coate, S., and Loury, G. C. (1993). Will affirmative action policies eliminate negative stereotypes? *Am. Econ. Rev.*, **83**, 1220–40.

Cooper, R., and John, A. (1988). Coordinating coordination failures in Keynesian models. *Q. J. Econ.*, **103**, 441–63.

Cornes, R. (1993). Dyke maintenance and other stories: some neglected types of public goods. *Q. J. Econ.*, **108**, 259–72.

Dixit, A., and Stiglitz, J. E. (1978). Monopolistic competition and optimal product diversity. *American Economic Review*, **68**, 297–308.

Galbraith, J. K. (1979). *The Nature of Mass Poverty*, Penguin, Harmondsworth, England.

Gans, J. S. (1991). Chaos theory, nonlinearities, and economics: a speculative note. *Econ. Pap.*, **10**, 40–53.

(1994). *Essays on Economic Growth and Change*, Ph.D. dissertation, Stanford University, Stanford, CA.

(1995). Best replies and adaptive learning. *Math. Social Sci.*, **30**, 221–34.

(1997). Industrialization policy and the big push. In *Increasing Returns and Economic Analysis*, eds. K. J. Arrow, McMillan, London.

Hardy, G. H., Littlewood, J. E., and Polya, G. (1952). *Inequalities*, Cambridge University Press, Cambridge.

Hirschman, A. O. (1958). *The Strategy of Economic Development*, Yale University Press, New Haven, CT.

Kremer, M. (1993). The O-ring theory of economic development. *Q. J. Econ.*, **108**, 551–76.

Krugman, P. R. (1991). History versus expectations. *Q. J. Econ.*, **106**, 651–67.

Lundberg, S. J. (1991). The enforcement of equal opportunity laws under imperfect information: affirmative action and alternatives. *Q. J. Econ.*, **106**, 309–26.

Lundberg, S. J., and Startz, R. (1983). Private discrimination and social intervention in competitive labor markets. *Am. Econ. Rev.*, **73**, 340–47.

Matsuyama, K. (1991). Increasing returns, industrialization and indeterminacy of equilibria. *Q. J. Econ.*, **106**, 617–50.

(1992). The market size, entrepreneurship, and the big push. *J. Jpn. Int. Econ.*, **6**, 347–64.

Meyer, D. J., Van Huyck, J. B., Battalio, R. C., and Saving, T. R. (1992). History's role in coordinating decentralized allocation decisions. *J. Polit. Econ.*, **100**, 292–316.

Milgrom, P., and Oster, S. (1987). Job discrimination, market forces and the invisibility hypothesis. *Q. J. Econ.*, **102**, 453–76.

Milgrom, P., and Roberts, J. (1990). Rationalizability, learning, and equilibrium in games with strategic complementarities. *Econometrica*, **58**, 1255–77.

(1991). Adaptive and sophisticated learning in normal form games. *Games Econ. Behav.*, **3**, 82–100.

Milgrom, P., and Shannon, C. (1994). Monotone comparative statics. *Econometrica*, **62**, 157–80.

Milgrom, P., Qian, Y., and Roberts, J. (1991). Complementarities, momentum and the evolution of modern manufacturing. *Am. Econ. Rev.*, **81**(2), 85–89.

Murphy, K. M., Shleifer, A., and Vishny, R. W. (1989). Industrialization and the big push. *J. Polit. Econ.*, **97**, 1003–26.

Myrdal, G. (1944). *An American Dilemma: The Negro Problem and Modern Democracy*, Harper, New York.

(1957). *Economic Theory and Underdeveloped Regions*, Duckworth, London.

Ormiston, M. B., and Schlee, E. E. (1993). Comparative statics under uncertainty for a class of economic agents. *J. Econ. Theo.*, **61**, 412–22.

Phelps, E. (1972). The statistical theory of racism and sexism. *Am. Econ. Rev.*, **62**, 659–61.

Romer, P. M. (1987). Growth based on increasing returns due to specialisation. *American Economic Review*, **77**(2), 56–62.

Ross, L., and Nisbett, R. E. (1991). *The Person and the Situation: Perspectives in Social Psychology*, McGraw-Hill, New York.

Shelling, T. C. (1978). *Micromotives and Macrobehaviour*, Norton, New York.

Sowell, T. (1983). *The Economics and Politics of Race*, Morrow, New York.

Steele, C. (1992). Race and the schooling of black Americans. *Atlantic Monthly*, April, 68–78.

Swan, T. (1962). Cumulative causation. *Econ. Rec.*, December, **38**, 421–26.

Van Huyck, J. B., Cook, J. P., and Battalio, R. C. (1997). Adaptive behavior and coordination failure. *J. Economic Behavior and Organization*, **32**, 483–503.